# GROVER CLEVELAND
## THE MAN AND THE STATESMAN

### VOLUME ONE

GROVER CLEVELAND
1903

# GROVER CLEVELAND

## THE MAN AND THE STATESMAN

*An Authorized Biography*

BY

ROBERT McELROY, Ph.D., LL.D., F.R.H.S.

EDWARDS PROFESSOR OF AMERICAN HISTORY
PRINCETON UNIVERSITY

*With an introduction by*

ELIHU ROOT

TWO VOLUMES IN ONE

HARPER & BROTHERS PUBLISHERS
NEW YORK AND LONDON

GROVER CLEVELAND

THE MAN AND THE STATESMAN

Copyright, 1923
By Harper & Brothers
Printed in the U. S. A.

G-Z

To

My Wife
whose vermilion pencil deprived
the world of my noblest sentences

# CONTENTS

## VOLUME I

CHAPTER                                                                     PAGE

I    HEREDITY AND ENVIRONMENT . . . . . . . .   1

II    THE VETO MAYOR . . . . . . . . . . .   24

III    THE REFORM GOVERNOR . . . . . . . . .   37

IV    THE MUGWUMP CAMPAIGN OF 1884 . . . . .   72

V    ALONE IN THE WHITE HOUSE . . . . . . .   100

VI    FACING THE POLITICAL BREAD-LINE . . . . . .   117

VII    THE INDEPENDENCE OF THE EXECUTIVE . . . .   166

VIII    CLEVELAND AND THE VETERANS OF THE CIVIL WAR .   189

IX    CLEVELAND AND THE WARDS OF THE NATION, THE AMERICAN INDIANS . . . . . . . . .   218

X    CLEVELAND, BISMARCK, AND SAMOA . . . . . .   240

XI    THROWING AWAY THE PRESIDENCY . . . . . .   264

XII    RETIRES TO NEW YORK . . . . . . . . .   302

XIII    AN UNPRECEDENTED RESTORATION . . . . . .   324

# INTRODUCTION

We have been told recently that there are too many biographies. The complaint indicates a sense of compulsion to read them. This can come only from a belief that they probably contain something which ought not to be overlooked. The real ground of the condemnation, therefore, is not that biographies are not worth reading, but that they ought to be read and that they therefore impose additional obligations upon men who may perhaps feel overburdened. The condemnation thus becomes a justification.

The most obvious appeal of a biography to the generations which have direct or close knowledge of the man written about; which have knowledge of the things he has done, of the affairs in which he has played part, of the men with or against whom he has worked—is really a very narrow and minor function of biography. The more important function is as an effective mode of presenting history for the benefit of the future, which has to get its knowledge entirely from books or traditions. Biography makes a period interesting by throwing a high light on a central figure and establishing a relation between all the conditions and incidents of the time with that figure. If only one of the significant figures of a period were made the subject of biography there would be an effect of disproportion due to overemphasis. But that is seldom if ever the case. Men worth writing about are naturally grouped in periods. Their biographies reproduce the same background with different emphasis. On looking at the period from all these different points of view taken together, we see life in the round standing out from the canvas, with a quality of human interest which it seems quite impossible for any impartial historian to create. Of course there must be balance. If you read Morley's Gladstone you must read Moneypenny's Disraeli and the rest of the great Victorian biographies. If you read the life of Jefferson you must also read the lives of Hamilton, and of Marshall and of Adams. If you read Cavour you must also read Garibaldi and Mazzini. The important question is not whether there are too many or too few biographies, but whether the biography of an important period in the world's life is well balanced, whether all the personal points of view, from which enlightenment and correction may come, are adequately represented, so that the aggregate biographies of a period as a whole will convey a correct as well as an interesting conception.

The biography of Grover Cleveland, which Professor McElroy has now completed with great labor and sympathy, is of special importance to the understanding of a very critical period in American history—the period of readjustment to the new conditions created by the Civil War. The readjustment involved, not merely a recovery from the enormous losses of the war which included the entire abolition of property in slaves, but also the great reconciliation between the peoples of the two sections, who, after four years of fighting, of killing and wounding each other, were to try the experiment of living together again as parts of the same people sharing in the conduct of the same government. It was a reconciliation which had to be effected by the same generation which fought the war, because if that generation died unreconciled, bequeathing its resentments and hatreds to a younger generation, the undertaking would have been almost hope-less. Inherited hatreds are almost ineradicable. That the reconciliation was effected within the life of that gen-eration and that survivors of the Union and Confederate Armies came to work together with harmony and mutual confidence in the government at Washington, is one of the greatest of American achievements. It was not an easy process but it was aided by two reactions in the sober sense of the North. One, the reaction against the grave error of reconstruction legislation which went upon the theory that by merely giving a vote to the negro he would be made competent to govern. The North became rather ashamed of the exercise of power which inflicted real in-justice upon the people of the South by the application of this false theory. The other reaction, also in the dominant North, was against the undue use made by political managers for personal and organization pur-poses, of the old spirit and memories and shibboleths of the war. For the first twenty years after the war these feelings served to control in the selection of the members of government at Washington. But as the dominant political organization during this long lease of power be-came more compact and autocratic great numbers of people in the North who sympathized with the war feel-ing became quite unwilling that it should be utilized for the benefit of a political organization in which they had no practical voice. Under these circumstances the Demo-cratic party, which could not hope to secure control in the nation except by Southern votes, was fortunate enough to find in Mr. Cleveland a man of such a strong person-ality and such clearly demonstrated capacity upon lines quite outside of the old Civil War contest, that his nomi-nation for the Presidency would divide the Northern vote. As we look back forty years we can see that it was time for new motives to assert themselves in American politics. There could not be a real reunion of States in patriotic sympathy without moral as well as legal amnesty, without really letting bygones be bygones. So long as the control of government turned upon the sympathies and resentments of the Civil War it was inevitable that there should be a sense of proscription by the defeated party which revived bitter feelings upon both sides in every election. The only way in which a change could come was by making the control of government turn upon the new issues which the developing life of the country was bringing on and which did not depend at all upon the old Civil War divisions. There is a certain satisfaction in considering how perfectly Mr. Cleveland was adapted to the requirements of that situation. He was a Northerner and a Democrat, and so available. He was a party man without answering to the ordinary conception of a politician. He belonged to a party as a natural incident to the business of citizenship. He inherited traditions from the earlier days, not so very far remote, when it was considered every man's business to do his part towards maintaining the peace and order of the community. He accepted that as a part of a normal American life; but he never was a political leader in a personal sense and he never tried to be. He never tried to collect about himself any group of followers who would promote his fortunes in the expectation that he would promote theirs. As an incident in the career of a young lawyer he came to be appointed Assistant District Attorney in Buffalo and in that subordinate office he exhibited qualities which led after a time to his being made sheriff, and then mayor of Buffalo, and then governor of the State of New York. He had strong common sense, simplicity and directness without subtlety, instinctive and immovable integrity, perfect courage, a kindly nature with great capacity for friendship and with great capacity also for wrath which made him a dangerous man to trifle with. There was nothing visionary or fanatical about him, but he had a natural hatred for fraud and false pretense, and a strong instinct for detecting the essential quality of conduct by the application of old and simple tests of morality. There was no self-seeking about him. In all his public employments he thought about his job and not about himself. His official judgment was never disturbed by any question as to the effect upon his personal fortunes. He had an exceptionally good mind; a still more exceptionally rugged strength of character; altogether a powerful and attractive personality. When the Presidential nominations of 1884 came to be made Grover Cleveland in his various offices had done more of the honest and courageous things which good government requires and which decent people like to have done, than any other Democrat. That made him the available candidate to change the current of American politics. His election upon that record practically closed the old era of politics dominated by the past and began the new era of politics looking to the future. The strength and courage of his administrations as President confirmed the new departure. No thoughtful and patriotic American, to whatever party he may belong, and however much his opinions may differ from those of Mr. Cleveland, can read the story of those administrations without admiration and sympathy, or without a sense of satisfaction that his country can on occasion produce and honor such a man as Grover Cleveland.

ELIHU ROOT.

# GROVER CLEVELAND
## THE MAN AND THE STATESMAN

# GROVER CLEVELAND

## CHAPTER I

### HEREDITY AND ENVIRONMENT

*"If a man were permitted to make all the homes, he need not care who should make the laws of a nation."*
—GROVER CLEVELAND.

THE task of the historian is to separate truth from the propaganda of the past, and in the case of a biography this task is often rendered most difficult by the attempts of the subject to prepare his biographer's way before him. But Grover Cleveland made no such attempt. His mind was occupied with present duties, not future fame, and he was content to allow the muse of history to write her verdict without his personal aid. As a result we have neither autobiography nor personal memoir to guide or to misguide us. What we know of Grover Cleveland, the man, has been gathered almost wholly from his contemporaries, and from casual references in letters and speeches written with no thought of the verdict of history. What we know of Grover Cleveland, the statesman, has been culled from documents equally guiltless of propaganda. For, although in later life he published a number of monographs dealing with important incidents in his presidential career, they are, one and all, as impersonal as a presidential message or an executive order; and this is the more remarkable in a man who passed into history before he passed into silence.

I

According to certain genealogical tables which Dr. David Starr Jordan has examined and accepted, Grover Cleveland, George Washington, King Henry V of England, Theodore Roosevelt, Robert E. Lee, Henry Adams, Jonathan Edwards, Ulysses S. Grant, Benjamin Harrison, Patrick Henry, Thomas Jefferson, J. Pierpont Morgan, and John D. Rockefeller were descended from a common ancestry, "each showing one of the many 'direct lines' leading down from Isabel de Vermandois," who died in 1131.

Although interesting, this appears of little real significance, since, as the same authority points out, every person now living would find, should he count back, that, allowing three generations to a century, he has had more than one hundred and thirty-four million ancestors since the year 1100, and more than twice that number if he counted "intervening forbears."

But genealogical studies had little interest for Mr. Cleveland. His indifference to his personal history was equaled by his lack of interest in his family history; and it is due solely to the efforts of others that in England we can trace his family line to the Norman conquest and beyond, while in this country we follow it through all the generations which make up the history of the American people since 1635, when Moses Cleveland landed in Massachusetts, an indented apprentice from Ipswich.

The name Cleveland is of Saxon origin. The estate or the district Cleveland, near the historic town of Whitby, was so called "because of the clefts or cleaves which abounded there." In early days the name was spelled Cliveland, Clyveland, Clievland, Cleivland, Cleaveland, Clevland, Cleveland, Cleffland, Clifland, or in other ways, if others be possible, according to the fancy of the writer. Such liberties were taken with all names in those happy days of phonetic freedom. But Cleveland or Clyveland, Cliveland or Clifland, every line of the family runs back to England. The genealogical tree is a veritable English oak, with no branch grafted from the Continent.

Starting with Moses, born in 1624, the American branch very properly passes to Aaron, and for four consecutive generations the oldest son bears the latter name. In 1770, however, William Cleveland appeared to break the succession, and his son, Richard Falley Cleveland, was Grover Cleveland's father.

Richard Falley Cleveland was born at Norwich, Connecticut, June 19, 1804. He received his college training at Yale, where he took high honors as of the class of 1824. Soon after graduation, his aim being the Presbyterian ministry, he accepted a post as tutor in Baltimore, where he began his theological studies and at the same time earned enough money to make possible a few months in the Princeton Theological Seminary. In 1828, he was ordained, and accepted the pastorate of the First Congregational Church at Windham, Connecticut. He had, however, left his heart in Baltimore, and in 1829 he returned to recover it, and with it her in whose keeping he had left it, the gentle Ann Neal.

Ann Neal, the mother of Cleveland, has left few traces to aid the biographer eager to do her justice. We know that she was of Irish and French descent, that her father was a publisher of law books in Baltimore, and that she was born in that city on February 4, 1806; but beyond that we know little except that love came early into her life in the handsome person of Richard Cleveland, and that her devotion stood the test of time, changing conditions, and an always scanty income. A country clergyman's life in those days meant constant sacrifice, and Ann Neal's sacrifice began when as a bride she returned with her husband to Windham where, in conformity to prevailing local standards, she willingly gave up many innocent enjoyments that the minister's influence might not be jeopardized, or the cause they both loved weakened.

When Ann left her father's house, her colored maid, who had cared for her from infancy, begged to be allowed to accompany her. Thus attended, and rejoicing in many bright articles of personal adornment, she entered the New England manse only to find that colored maids were regarded as unnecessary luxuries, and objectionable, as savoring of slavery. She soon understood also that jewelry was unbecoming a minister's wife. So the faithful servant was cheerfully returned to her Southern home, the treasured little ornaments were laid aside without a sigh, and the bright heart of Ann Neal Cleveland beat under costumes suitable to the wife of a village minister of New England. But the young couple were poor only in goods. They had education, culture, congeniality, and spiritual wealth—resources sufficient to encourage hope of a happy future.

The young wife was not long called upon to walk in the ways of the Puritan. In 1833 the field of their joint labors was transferred to the more familiar atmosphere of Portsmouth, Virginia; and two years later they settled down to the seven years of Richard Cleveland's pastorate at Caldwell, New Jersey.

The Cleveland family had grown since the days in Windham. Two children, Anna, and William Neal, had been born in Connecticut, Mary Allen during the brief pastorate at Portsmouth, and Richard Cecil almost as soon as the trunks were unpacked in the little manse at Caldwell. Less than two years later, on March 18, 1837, the fifth child was born, and they called him Stephen Grover in honor of the late pastor, whose service at Caldwell had lasted almost half a century, and whose name was there greatly beloved.

In 1841 Reverend Richard Cleveland accepted a call as pastor of a church in Fayetteville, New York, and to Fayetteville, with the others, went the young Grover, traveling the way of the patient, on an Erie Canal boat, which in those days was a method so slow that the Clevelands were weeks on the journey. Fayetteville, in 1841, was a quiet village, with a good academy, which served the older Cleveland children both as educational and social center. But there were no kindergartens in those days and the education of Grover, the four-year-old, had to wait. His training, however, did not wait. Filial reverence, strict obedience, unquestioning belief in parental wisdom, and ready compliance with parental commands were the presuppositions of life, according to the Puritan creed which dominated the family. "Often and often as a boy," he declared in later years, "I was compelled to get out of my warm bed at night, to hang up a hat or other garment which I had left on the floor."

The commands of the Bible, the memorizing of the Westminster Catechism, the strictest observance of Sunday as the Puritan had understood it, were the elements upon which the character of Grover Cleveland were built. Father, mother, and nine children were all supported by the minister's salary, which seldom exceeded six hundred dollars a year.

Under such conditions, simple, cultivated, religious, Grover Cleveland passed the most formative years of his life. With the help of the academy and of his intelligent and well-trained father, he acquired a reasonable proficiency in Latin and mathematics, and an interest in religious questions which lasted throughout his life.

In the home of his childhood vexed questions such as Sabbath observance were not debated. Each child understood that six days were made for work and play, and one for worship. When the long shadows began to fall on Sabbath eve, playthings were put away, clothes carefully arranged for use on the morrow, an early supper was prepared, in order that there might be ample time for the weekly bath, at which the elder sisters assisted with conscientious thoroughness. For clean hands as well as a pure heart were considered appropriate accompaniments of the day of rest.

While the steaming tubs were playing their part on one side of the kitchen, the one servant, a self-respecting Canadian woman, was preparing the material for Sunday dinner on the other. A peck of potatoes, the roast, the rice pudding with its spices and raisins, all had to be got ready on Saturday.

When the little Clevelands, with ears shining and at times with hearts resentful at the memory of too vigorous gouging, had been tucked into bed, the elder members of the family retired to the church to practice hymns for the service of the morrow. Sunday was itself a discipline —two sermons a day, with Sunday school between, and a prayer meeting in the evening which, on the first Sunday of each month, took the form of a missionary lecture and always closed with the singing of the hymn, "From Greenland's Icy Mountains."

With the end of afternoon service, the strain of piety was a little lightened, and the family assembled for a substantial meal at three-thirty. A walk in the garden or in the orchard beyond the house followed, and at twilight the pastor met his family for an hour of private worship. Then the little ones were sent to bed, while their elders returned to the church for an evening meeting.

Such was the atmosphere in which Grover Cleveland passed his childhood. It inevitably tended to produce a keen sense of personal responsibility, to make trustworthy character; for its ethical basis was absolute. It taught that there is a right which is eternally right, and a wrong which must remain forever wrong.

To one of Mr. Cleveland's sisters we are indebted for the following memory which shows how early the sense of responsibility was developed in the boy: "It was a very busy day and the last baby was more than usually troublesome. Grover was pressed into service as baby-tender, and encouraged to believe that sleep would soon end his task. The vision of a little round-faced, blue-eyed boy rocking a cradle, with a far-away look out of the window where the 'fellers' were sliding down the hill, is very clear in my memory. His heart was with the boys, but his hand steadily kept the cradle in motion.

"The wide-open eyes of the infant were met by Grover with an hypnotic stare, as he monotonously droned out the refrain, ' 'T is a sin to steal a pin, and how much more a greater thing.' He tried all keys and all modulations; but the baby smile persisted, and the baby eyes watched every motion with a sleepless interest.

"Convinced at last that the combined concert and pantomime were too exciting, Grover changed his tactics. He suddenly disappeared beneath the cradle, hushed his lullaby, and moved the rockers, slowly and quietly, back and forth, from his unseen position. After a few moments, he rose stealthily, and peered cautiously over the side of the cradle, only to be greeted by that same baby smile, and those wide-open baby eyes. Then, with a despairing glance out of the window toward the hill where the 'fellers' slid, and with tears in his blue eyes, Grover Cleveland dropped resignedly to the floor again, and resumed his monotonous rocking. There he lay, listening, sobbing and doing his duty, until relieved by an older sister who came to the rescue."

Alvah Woodworth, once proprietor of the iron foundry at Manlius, New York, has left us the story of how Grover Cleveland and the Bangs boys prepared to hail a certain glorious fourth of July. They had gathered a little wagon-load of old iron and brought it to Woodworth to be melted and molded into a cannon.

"Puffing and perspiring," he says, "they toiled along, one boy between the shafts, pulling, and the other two back of the wagon, pushing. When they had arrived opposite the village foundry, they halted. One of the boys— he was the youngest and shortest of the trio—then made it known . . . that they desired to exchange their load of old iron in return for a small cannon, which the proprietor was to make for them in time to use in their fourth of July celebration.

"The foundryman weighed up the iron and found that there was not a sufficient quantity to pay for the job. This rather staggered the boys for a moment, but their spokesman [Grover Cleveland], who seemed to be a lad of resources, soon found a way out of the difficulty. His proposition was that the foundryman should go ahead and make the cannon, and after the arduous work of the fourth was disposed of he and his fellow patriots would drag up another load of iron to square up accounts. The proprietor of the foundry looked the boys over keenly and decided he could trust them. So the cannon was made and used and, true to their word, the boys delivered to the foundryman a second load of old iron as payment for the balance they owed him."

That this was done promptly we can infer from Grover's appreciation of the value of time, as shown by an essay which he wrote at the age of nine:

Fayetteville Academy *Sept. 5, 1846.*
*Time.*

Time is divided into seconds—minutes, hours, days, weeks month years and centurys. If we expect to become great and good men and be respected and esteemed by our friends we must inprove our time when we are young. George Washington inproved his time when he was a boy and he was not sorry when he was at the head of a large army fighting for his country. A great meny of our great men wer poor and had smal means of obtaining an education but by improving their time when they were young and in school they obtained their high standing Jackson was a poor boy but he was placed in school and by improving his time he found himself a president of the United States guiding and directing a powerful nation. If we wish to become great and usful in the world we must improve our time in school.

S. G. CLEVELAND.

That the atmosphere of Fayetteville did not always breed progressive and enlightened citizens is abundantly demonstrated by a letter which President Cleveland received, two years after he entered the White House:

*March 22, 1887.*

Grover Cleveland
Washington
D C
DEAR GROVER

Hank Stebbins told me the other day that you was elected president I just couldnt believe it—I often won-

derd whare you was—I haint herd of you for years . . .
I have got a good job . . . here but I would like to live in
Washington—Can you give me a job there for the sake
of old times—Sallie Hornakers is dead had a rising.
Please rite to your old friend and schoolmate.

For nine years Richard Cleveland served the people
of Fayetteville as pastor. Then his health began to fail,
and the strain of sustaining so large a family upon so
meager a salary was heavy. When, therefore, the American Home Missionary Society offered him an agency
with a salary of $1000 a year, he accepted the appoint-
ment, which involved a change of residence to Clinton,
N. Y. The move was made in 1851, when Stephen Grover
was fourteen years of age, but he always remembered
with pleasure those youthful days at Fayetteville. In
after years, as President of the United States, he returned
for a flying visit, and his brief speech is one of the few
autobiographical touches that he left among his papers.

"As I find myself once more in this pretty village,"
he said, "the sports and pastimes of my youth come back
to my mind. I take warm interest in being with you once
more. Some of you more than forty years ago were
my schoolfellows and playmates. I can recall the faces
of some that are now no more.

"I have been reminded to-day by an old resident of
the many deaths which occurred among those I knew
since I took my departure from you, and I was astonished
to find that I could remember so many of the old names
in driving from the foot of the street to the parsonage
and the academy. There were Cobb, Parker, Gillett,
McVicker, Worden, Palmer, Horner, Edwards, Noble,
Deacon Flint, and many others. I recall old Green Lake
and the fish I tried to catch and never did, and the tra-

ditional panther on its shores which used to shorten my excursions thitherward. I've heard so much howling in the past two years that I don't think I should be frightened by the panther now.

"If some of the old householders were here I could tell them who it was that used to take off their front gates. I mention this because I have been accused of so many worse crimes since I have been in Washington that I consider taking off gates something of a virtue.

"I would be sadly at fault if I failed to recall the many inestimable benefits I received at your hands—my early education, the training of the Sunday school, the religious advantages, the advantages of your social life. These are things which have gone with me in every step in life. And so, when in short intervals of freedom from the cares and duties of my office, my mind revels in retrospection, these early recollections are the truest, pleasantest, and brightest spots on which my memory lights.

"And so, you see, I have taken you and your village with me, and whether you are willing or not, I have made you a part of this administration. I have been a sad truant, but, now that you have seen me, keep your eyes ever upon me as I strive to do my duty in behalf of the people of this country. And it shall be my desire so to act that I may receive the approbation of these, my oldest and best friends."

At Clinton the Cleveland children enjoyed educational advantages far superior to those of Fayetteville, and the atmosphere of Hamilton College fostered in Grover the ambition already created by the influence of a scholarly father and a mother wise enough to understand the supreme advantages of a thorough intellectual training. But his brief sojourn here failed to develop in him any unusual scholarly gifts. As a student he did not shine.

The wonderful powers of application and concentration which later distinguished him were not yet apparent. He made friends more effectively than grades, and his friendships lasted.

He has himself left us an account of his Clinton days:

"It was here, in the school at the foot of College Hill, that I began my preparation for college life and enjoyed the anticipation of a collegiate education. We had two teachers in our school. One became afterward a judge in Chicago, and the other passed through the legal profession to the ministry, and within the last two years was living farther West.

"I read a little Latin with two other boys in the class. I think I floundered through four books of the Æneid. The other boys had nice large modern editions of Virgil, with big print and plenty of notes to help one over the hard places. Mine was a little old-fashioned copy which my father used before me, with no notes, and which was only translated by hard knocks. I believe I have forgiven those other boys for their persistent refusal to allow me the use of the notes in their books. At any rate, they do not seem to have been overtaken by any dire retribution, for one of them is now a rich and prosperous lawyer in Buffalo, and the other is a professor in your college and the orator of to-day's celebration. The struggles with ten lines of Virgil, which at first made up my daily task, are amusing as remembered now; but with them I am also forced to remember, that, instead of being the beginning of the higher education for which I honestly longed, they occurred near the end of my school advantages. This suggests a disappointment which no lapse of time can alleviate, and a deprivation I have sadly felt with every passing year. . . .

"I don't know that I should indulge further recollections that must seem very little like centennial history; but I want to establish as well as I can my right to be here. I might speak of the college faculty, who cast such a pleasing though sober shade of dignity over the place, and who, with other educated and substantial citizens, made up the best of social life. I was a boy then, and slightly felt the atmosphere of this condition; but, notwithstanding, I believe I absorbed a lasting appreciation of the intelligence and refinement which made this a delightful home.

"I know that you will bear with me, my friends, if I yield to the impulse which the mention of home creates, and speak of my own home here, and how through the memories which cluster about it I may claim a tender relationship to your village. Here it was that our family circle entire, parents and children, lived day after day in loving and affectionate converse; and here, for the last time, we met around the family altar and thanked God that our household was unbroken by death or separation. We never met together in any other home after leaving this, and Death followed closely our departure.

"And thus it is that, as with advancing years I survey the havoc Death has made, and as the thoughts of my early home become more sacred, the remembrance of this pleasant spot, so related, is revived and chastened."

Hamilton College was the Mecca of his dreams. His brother, William, was already nearing the end of his course, and Grover's turn was soon to come. But necessity is a stern master, and at this point it took control. The imperative need of relief for the hard-pressed family treasury sent Grover back to Fayetteville to work in a village store. Here he made himself useful in various ways, receiving in return a salary of fifty dollars for the first year, and one hundred for the second, with board and lodging furnished without charge.

Life in a western New York village in those days partook somewhat of the conditions of the frontier. Comforts were few, and of these still fewer fell to the lot of John McVicar's clerks. But the boys gave little thought to their physical surroundings. From the pen of his fellow clerk, F. G. Tibbitts, we have this picture of their daily life:

"It was our duty to wait on customers, sweep and clean up, open and close the place, run errands, and do a turn for neighbors at odd times. . . . Our room was . . . a large, unfurnished room. The bed was a plain, pine one, with cords upon which to lay the tick. . . . In that room, without carpet, without wall paper, without pictures, bare, drear, and desolate, we two lived together one whole year. In the winter we fairly froze sometimes. There was no stove in the room, heat coming up from a pipe leading from the store below. . . . Grover used to rise, in those days, at about five o'clock in the summer and half-past five in the winter. He would go out to an old green pump that then stood in the square, used for watering horses, and make his morning toilet in the trough; then back to the store; open up; sweep out; build the fire; dust up; lay out the goods. By and by, about seven o'clock, along would come Mr. McVicar."

At the end of two years Grover returned to Clinton to continue his preparation for entering college; but his plans were soon again swept aside by the ruthless hand of fate. His father, whose health was still failing, shortly resigned his too arduous post at Clinton to accept a rural pastorate at Holland Patent, near Utica.

The move was made in the autumn of 1853, the last earthly autumn for that devoted servant of God. Three

Sundays he preached to his new congregation, and then death came suddenly. He was only forty-nine, poor in the goods of this world, but rich in a record of noble and unselfish service.

The tidings reached Grover through the voice of a newsboy crying papers in the street. He had driven to Utica with his sister, Mary, who was preparing for her wedding to Mr. M. E. Hoyt, and wished to make some purchases. As he sat in the carriage waiting, the cry reached him. His father had died only a few moments after his departure from Holland Patent.

This sudden and untimely death changed Grover's entire outlook. He was now sixteen years old, and abundantly supplied with brothers and sisters. Otherwise, he had inherited only the world to live in, and immediate self-support was imperative. He therefore sought a position and soon found one in the New York Institute for the Blind. But a single year having convinced him that such a life was not for him, he returned to Holland Patent, and patiently canvassed the neighborhood for employment with a future.

Disappointment followed. There seemed no satisfactory opening in that general region, and reluctantly he was forced to consider some other locality. In those days the trade winds blew steadily in one direction for young men of ambition and scant means, and Grover at last decided to go West. His earnings had been generously placed in the family sinking fund, which had sunk so low that he was compelled to borrow twenty-five dollars to pay the expense of his intended journey. For this he gave a personal note, promising to pay when convenient. Twelve years later he sent to his benefactor the following letter:

My dear Mr. Townsend:

I am now in condition to pay my note which you hold given for money borrowed some years ago. I suppose I might have paid it long before, but I have never thought you were in need of it, and I had other purposes for my money. I have forgotten the date of the note. If you will send me it I will mail you the principal and interest. The loan you made me was my start in life, and I shall always preserve the note as an interesting reminder of your kindness. Let me hear from you soon. With many kind wishes to Mrs. Townsend and your family, I am yours, very respectfully,

GROVER CLEVELAND.

The town of Cleveland, Ohio, was his intended destination, the name, given in honor of his kinsman, General Moses Cleveland, seeming to him a good omen. But at Buffalo fate again intervened, this time in the person of his uncle, Lewis Allen, a well-known shorthorn cattle breeder, whose home was at Black Rock, on the outskirts of the city. Having stopped here for a brief visit, the traveler was persuaded to accept an offer of work on Mr. Allen's herd book, which netted him sixty dollars in cash, and deprived Ohio of another President of the United States; for Buffalo became henceforth his home.

His life in the Allen household was pleasant, even luxurious, and his earnings sufficient for his personal needs. But, although circumstances had forced him to abandon all idea of a college training, he was still resolved, with a resolution singularly like the law of the Medes and Persians "which altereth not," to study law. Mr. Allen easily secured for him a clerkship in the firm of Rogers, Bowen and Rogers, whose senior member had a very simple theory of education: "If a boy has brains he will find out for himself without any telling." Grover Cleveland was accordingly given a table, a shelf of law books, and permission to study law, in so far as that occupation did not interfere with his clerical duties.

His own account of his persistent struggle for education is characteristically direct and impersonal:

"I know a young man who, when quite young, determined to acquire a college education and enter the legal profession.

"The door to a college education was inexorably closed against him.

"He at once set his heart on studying law without collegiate training. When it soon appeared that even this must be postponed, he quite cheerfully set about finding any kind of honest work.

"After an unsuccessful quest for employment near home, he started for the West. He had adversity in abundance.

"He had plenty of willingness to work, plenty of faith and a fair stock of perseverance in reserve. He had no misgivings.

"After securing a temporary job, he was handed Blackstone's Commentaries and turned loose to browse in the library of a law office.

"When, on the first day of his study, all the partners and clerks forgot he was in a corner of the library and locked him in during the dinner hour he merely said to himself, 'Some day I will be better remembered.'

"He actually enjoyed his adversities.

"Even then he was called stubborn. After he had become President of the United States he was still called stubborn, and he is accused of stubbornness to this very day."

His independence of character, to use a somewhat

milder term, was conspicuously displayed in 1856, in connection with the first Presidential candidate upon the ticket called Republican by its friends, and black Republican by its enemies. Grover's host and relative, who had been a Whig, became Chairman of the Republican County Committee; but his young kinsman chose the Democratic party because, as he later explained, it seemed to him to represent greater solidarity and conservatism. He was repelled by the Frémont candidacy, which struck him as "having a good deal of fuss and feathers about it."

Being only nineteen years of age, he could not vote, but he could work. And so began the record of party service which characterized him throughout life, save when, as President, he turned aside from party to become the representative of all the people.

Four years of study prepared him for admission to the New York bar and four years more he remained with the firm of Rogers, Bowen, and Rogers as managing clerk. This congenial post he vacated in 1863, to accept a call to public service, his colleagues of the Buffalo bar having without his solicitation fixed upon him as the best available man for Assistant District Attorney of Erie County. The District Attorney and Cleveland's chief, C. C. Torrance, was in failing health, and more and more the burdens of the office fell to the young assistant. These he bore without shrinking, and by them proved his capacity for hard work, his legal skill, and his strength of character.

He won the confidence of judge and juries alike by his open, fair-minded approach to all questions, by his painstaking mastery of the facts in each case, and by his sturdy common sense. He allowed no case to come to trial until he had made conscientious preparation, and frequently he spent the whole night writing out his argument, and committing it to memory. His power of endurance was phenomenal, his memory no less so.

This office gave him valuable experience and at the same time enabled him to continue to meet the obligation, which he rejoiced to acknowledge, of giving financial aid to his mother. It was this obligation which caused him to remain out of service when Lincoln's call for troops went forth, and to avail himself of the legal right to hire a substitute when he was drafted, a course which later caused him no little embarrassment during excited political campaigns.

To those who watched his work as Assistant District Attorney Cleveland's devotion to duty was fully apparent. He met his obligations so fully and effectively that, when the elections of 1865 approached, he was the natural and inevitable choice of the Democrats for the office of District Attorney. Again the nomination was made without his solicitation, and apparently even without his knowledge. He was defeated by the Republican candidate, his intimate friend, Lyman K. Bass, and at once resumed his law practice, not as clerk now, but as partner of former State Treasurer Major Isaac K. Vanderpoel. In 1869, Vanderpoel resigned and the firm became Laning, Cleveland, and Folsom.

Grover Cleveland was now twenty-eight years of age, with a variety of experiences to his credit. He had missed the college education which he had coveted, but in its place he had learned the lessons of that more exacting taskmaster, human experience. The returns from the firm were not large, but his tastes were simple, and wealth, "a superfluity of the things one does not want," as Lincoln defined it, was never his goal.

His attitude toward life was fairly represented by a quaint illuminated motto which hung over his bed in his

sleeping room above his law office. It represented the
allegorical figures of Life, Duty, and Death, underneath
which was inscribed the motto: "As thy days are, so shall
thy strength be." "If I have any coat of arms and em-
blem," he once remarked to a friend, "it is that. It is a
motto I chose years ago and I devised that form to keep
it with me."

He was content with his simple apartment, his group
of intimates at "Dutchman's," or some other favorite
resort, and he dreamed of a future of law practice, with a
possible judgeship at the end of a long vista. With this
goal in mind, he declined the flattering offer of the
Assistant District Attorneyship for the Northern District
of New York, with its prestige and promise of quick
advancement, feeling that he had already spent too much
time on side issues, if he was to grow into a real jurist.

But a crisis was approaching. In 1870 the Democrats
of Erie County faced an important local election, with a
normally large Republican majority to be overcome.
Cleveland was popular, and had recently made a strong
race for District Attorney. On the day before the convention, therefore, he was offered the nomination for the
lucrative office of Sheriff. Such a suggestion had never
entered his mind, and at first it made no strong appeal
to him. He therefore declined it. But the Democratic
leaders were persistent, his sense of party obligation was
strong, and the financial rewards in the event of victory
were enticingly large. He therefore consented to
reconsider.

"I know," he said to William Dorsheimer, whose
advice he was asking, "that it is not usual for lawyers to
be sheriffs. . . . But there are some reasons why I should
consider the matter carefully. I have been compelled
to earn my living since I was seventeen. I have never

had time for reading, nor for thorough professional study. The sheriff's office would take me out of practice, but it would keep me about the courts, and in professional relations. It would give me considerable leisure, which I could devote to self-improvement. Besides, it would enable me to save a modest competency, and give me the pecuniary independence which otherwise I may never have. I have come for your advice. What would you do in my place?"

Dorsheimer's counsel confirmed his own deliberate judgment, and he accepted the nomination. His county, normally Republican, gave him a majority of a hundred votes, and at once he became the hope, and soon the despair, of the hungry pack of Democratic politicians bent on gain. For years they had watched the Republicans fatten on the spoils which went with this office. Their day had come at last. A Democrat was Sheriff of Erie County.

But it was not long before the politicians began to understand just what they had accomplished in persuading Grover Cleveland to enter politics. To their consternation, they found that only one type of contractor could win the favor of the new Sheriff, namely, he whose bid was lowest. Generous as he was with his own money, he was exasperatingly careful with the money of the people whose faith had elevated him to office. He believed in business methods for public offices, and ruthlessly applied the principle to the one under his charge.

He soon discovered, by the use of his own tape line, that the contractor who furnished wood for the county jail was giving short measure, and at once a new contractor was found, and the activities of the former one limited to the task of making good his deficiencies. A crooked miller shortly received similar attentions, and other dishonest contractors in turn faced an unexpected reckoning.

When, at the end of his term, he retired, he went out of office with a very large augmentation of the reputation for honesty and fearlessness which had secured his nomination. He had held an office of unsavory traditions and supremely unpleasant duties, and had held it against the grafters of his own party.

The next eight years saw Grover Cleveland again at the practice of the law. To the miscellaneous business which came to his firm, Bass, Cleveland, and Bissell (later Cleveland and Bissell), he devoted all of his vast energy, as of old working time and again all night over a case.

John G. Milburn, one of his lifelong friends, gives an attractive picture of Mr. Cleveland at this time:

"He was an outstanding lawyer at the Buffalo bar, but with a distinctly local reputation and acquaintance. . . . He was a prominent citizen, deeply respected for his independence, force of character, and inbred integrity. He was genial and companionable, with his intimacies mainly among men. . . . He was more inclined to circumscribe his professional work than to extend it; but he did his work with an extraordinary thoroughness. That thoroughness was a specific characteristic. He gave his best to everything he did. I have known him, when engaged in the trial of an important case, to work on it all through the night and resume the trial the next morning, after a cold bath and breakfast, as fresh as if he had had a long night's sleep. His physical endurance was extraordinary, beyond anything I have ever known. He would subject himself to enormous strains of work and I never heard him complain of fatigue. . . . His commanding qualities were those of judgment, earnestness, and moral force, lightened by a keen sense of humor. At the bar and among men they gave him a marked and powerful position and influence. He was recognized on all sides as a power in the community, which would be more and more visible as some emergency arose bringing it into full play. That is the man as I saw him in 1881."

It was during this period that Mr. Chauncey M. Depew, then President of the New York Central Railroad, offered him the attorneyship of the company in western New York, which would have brought him in a salary of some fifteen thousand dollars, while permitting him to retain his personal practice. Mr. Cleveland answered that he had set the limit to the work he could do satisfactorily to himself, that he was making ten thousand a year, which, with the income from what he had saved, was ample for his needs, and that no addition to that income could induce him to change his plans or assume new personal obligations.

He loved to do his work at his own convenience, and was satisfied with existing conditions. But his reputation as a fearless and able public servant had already spread to the camp of the reformers, and the hour was approaching when he would again be called to leave his private pursuits and take up the duties of a still more important office in the service of the people. Although far from suspecting it, he was upon the threshold of a great career, reached with unprecedented suddenness: for within four years he was to be, in quick succession, Mayor of Buffalo, Governor of New York, and President of the United States.

# CHAPTER II

## THE VETO MAYOR

*"Unswerving loyalty to duty, constant devotion to truth, and a clear conscience will overcome every discouragement and surely lead the way to usefulness and high achievement."*
—GROVER CLEVELAND.

IN 1881, a ring composed of members of both political parties was in control of the Board of Aldermen of Buffalo, and their works of corruption were a scandal to honest men. Leading members of both parties, determined upon reform, therefore consulted together. It was evident that to form a third party was to court certain defeat, and that to attempt to break into the Republican Convention and force the nomination of a reform candidate was equally futile. The Republicans being entrenched, the only hope of dislodging the bi-party ring which was working through them was to force the nomination of a reform mayor upon the Democratic Convention. And so they turned to the office of Cleveland and Bissell and offered to Grover Cleveland the Democratic nomination for Mayor of Buffalo.

Pointing to his paper-laden table and asking his visitors to look at the interests he represented, the trusts that had been reposed in him, Mr. Cleveland declined the offer. Balked for the moment, but not wholly discouraged, the reformers faced the convention, which proceeded to make its nominations. Through their effort, the head of the ticket was left undetermined, in the hope that Mr. Cleveland might be prevailed upon to reconsider. When the ticket, in this incomplete form, was shown to him with the suggestion that the vacant line was for his name, he scanned it critically and announced that he would accept if the name of John C. Sheehan, for Comptroller, were removed.

This was an astounding proposition, for Sheehan was the political boss of the convention. It was, however, an ultimatum, and Cleveland's name was an essential factor in the plans of the reformers. The ring-rule sympathizers, too, were not averse to his nomination, which they felt would soothe the reform element and, by a defeat, convince them of their helplessness. So Sheehan retired, Grover Cleveland was nominated by acclamation, and the Independents, who had formed a temporary political organization of their own, at once endorsed him.

The nomination settled, Mr. Cleveland astonished both friend and foe by declaring that he knew the politicians had consented to his nomination because they counted confidently upon his defeat, but that he intended to be elected. If elected, he further assured them, with the memory of Samuel J. Tilden and the presidential election of 1876 in mind, he would not be counted out.

His formal letter of acceptance was in the frank and simple style with which America and the world later became so familiar. He did not seek for new and striking phrases, nor did he pretend that he could bring to the problems of the office an unexampled wisdom, or an inspiration denied to other men. He frankly spoke old truths, and pledged his honor to them. The letter is not, and was not intended to be thought, a pathfinder, but it is a reliable introduction to the mind of an honest man, seeking to serve the people.

The keynote of this letter lies in the phrase, "Public officials are the trustees of the people." From it the political genius of William C. Hudson later created the famous slogan, "Public office is a public trust." But though the form was Hudson's, the sentiment was Cleveland's, and by it he ever regulated the conduct of his official life, whether as Sheriff, as Mayor, as Governor, or as President.

To the confusion of the bi-party ring, Grover Cleveland was elected Mayor of Buffalo by the largest majority ever given to a candidate for that office. Although frankly proclaiming himself a Democrat, he drew from the best element of both parties, and that his victory was largely personal is shown by the fact that, at the same election, the Republican state ticket was successful in Buffalo. Without effort, and almost against his will, he secured a majority of 3,530 in a city which, two years before, had given a plurality of over three thousand to the Republican candidate for Governor, Alonzo B. Cornell.

On January 1, 1882, the new Mayor entered upon the duties of his office. He was not yet forty-five but, save for a brief period of four years between his two terms as President of the United States, his career as a lawyer was over. Henceforth he belonged to the people.

Mr. Cleveland's tasks as Mayor of Buffalo were grim tasks, made harder by the fact that the enthusiasm for reform had not been strong enough to give him a sympathetic council. To present his inaugural message to a body whom he had been chosen to chasten was a task requiring courage not only, but also a certain discretion which, with a dominant opposition, is the better part of valor. He prepared this document with extreme care, but with no desire to mask his intentions. He had been chosen in the interest of civic reform, and he frankly declared his purpose of instituting civic reform. With the certain touch of the man who knows his facts, he pointed out specific abuses, assuring his unappreciative hearers that:

"We hold the money of the people in our hands, to be used for their purposes and to further their interests as members of the municipality, and it is quite apparent that, when any part of the funds which the taxpayers have thus intrusted to us are diverted to other purposes, or when, by design or neglect, we allow a greater sum to be applied to any municipal purpose than is necessary, we have, to that extent, violated our duty. There surely is no difference in his duties and obligations, whether a person is intrusted with the money of one man or many. . . ."

And Mayor Cleveland was not content to express his convictions by words alone. His commission from the people was not to change the ethical standards of his colleagues in the government, but to alter their practices. From theory, therefore, he turned to action.

Concerning the street department, he reported to the council, most of whom needed no information upon the subject: "Investigation . . . has developed the most shameful neglect of duty. . . . The mismanagement of affairs of this department has led directly to the wasting (to use no stronger term) of the people's money." And he followed the general statement by a shocking bill of particulars.

So clear was his meaning, so certain to catch the ear and arouse the enthusiasm of a machine-ridden people, that his opponents, at this point, attempted to prevent the reading of the message. But he could neither be checked nor diverted by discourtesy from the course which seemed to him plain duty: to state his views and purposes to the men upon whom rested, conjointly with himself, the responsibility for legislation, the duty of reform. The message was the challenge, and the reply came soon.

The charter of the city of Buffalo made provision that the Common Council should select one daily newspaper as the official organ, and pay it a subsidy for publishing the proceedings of the Council; and the action of the Council, in this matter, was expressly exempted from the operation of the Mayor's veto. In his message, Mayor Cleveland had specifically referred to this fact, but had suggested that this printing, which involved the expenditure of thousands of dollars, be given to the lowest bidder. In view of the publicity which the press gave to the message, the Council had been compelled to accept the suggestion and advertise for bids. The fact then became apparent to all, that, under the old system, the city had been paying two prices for its work, only one of which had gone to the printer. With sighs for lost spoils, the ring accepted the lowest bid, and at once devised new methods for securing new spoils.

They drew a bill providing that certain German papers should be paid for printing official digests of the proceedings of the Council. This was a plan of graft indicative of a paucity of imagination, and Mayor Cleveland, in vetoing it, exposed its too obvious fallacy. The German papers, from their desire to serve their public, he explained, "will publish a synopsis much more satisfactory to their subscribers than any which the city clerk will be apt to prepare . . . and without any compensation from the city. . . . The effect of the resolution . . . is (therefore) to give these newspapers eight hundred dollars each for doing no more than they will . . . be obliged to do without it. This comes very near being a most objectionable subsidy." This made the issue so clear that it would have been politically unsafe to push the resolution farther, and the matter was dropped.

Mr. Cleveland's courage and the sincerity of his demands for reform were shortly again put to the test by his enemies in the Council; for the dreamers of unjust subsidies and unearned gains now knew themselves to be his enemies. He had informed the Council that "of the total deaths reported . . . thirty-six per cent . . . have been from zymotic diseases, dependent, in some degree at least, upon surrounding conditions, . . . and preventable." The Board of Health, having been commissioned to report upon the situation, declared that insufficient sewerage was the chief cause of the condition, and that it could be easily remedied by the building of an adequate system of sewers and by introducing Niagara water into every house and closing up every well. To hasten the completion of this enormous undertaking, and to make it more difficult for the ring to pass it over to favored contractors and thus rob the public treasury by needless expenditures, Mr. Cleveland suggested to the Council that as they and the city engineers were already fully occupied with their regular routine duties, the construction of the sewer should be put in the hands of a commission of citizens.

This suggestion, if adopted, meant that the finest opportunity for "graft" ever offered a Buffalo City Council would be snatched from them, and the opposition promptly opened an attack through the city engineer, who argued "in the interest of the public," that such a work, if handed over to a commission, would result in "permanent loss and injury to the records of this department." Though large, he declared, the work could be carried out quite easily, though it would be an advantage to have

added to his office "a consulting engineer of acknowledged ability in this specialty."

Here was a challenge which the Mayor met promptly
and definitely. "I am utterly amazed to learn," he declared, ". . . that the job . . . is such an easy one. Every
member of your honorable body knows very well that
for many years the problem of . . . how the Main and
Hamburg Streets canal nuisance should be abated has
occupied . . . the attention of our city officials. I find in
the Council proceedings of eleven years ago that this canal
was declared a great nuisance. . . . The actual result of
all their endeavors to master this easy subject has been
the establishment of a wheel in the water adjoining the
canal." He further showed that the very city engineer
who was insisting upon his right to do this large and
important work had allowed four months to pass without
so much as a report of progress concerning a similar
though smaller problem which had recently been referred
to him. Upon which task, he scornfully declared, "not
a stroke of real work has yet been done, and yet there
seems to have been considerable skillful engineering
talent employed, at quite an expense. . . . Either the
work has not been easy or considerable money has been
wasted."

Having presented these facts, and confident in the
strength of public support, Cleveland was ready for a
trial of strength; but the Council, while still determined
to keep the work within its own control, preferred the
safer methods of indirection. They prepared a bill providing for a commission, but one so shorn of power as to
leave the way open to the control which they desired.
Mayor Cleveland promptly recognized the strategy and
blocked it. The Council was forced to yield and a commission was formed, on the lines desired by the Mayor.

Mr. Cleveland next presented his nominations for the commission. The Council rejected them, but the determination of the honest Mayor was even stronger than that of the would-be grafters. Moreover, Mr. Cleveland had recently held them up to the scorn and contempt of the city and they feared to push him to such lengths so soon again. Having discovered a shameful scheme to assign the street-cleaning contract to one George Talbot at figures calculated to throw a small fortune into his hands, the Mayor had intervened and forced the Council to award it to the lowest bidder. He thus, at one stroke, saved the city over one hundred thousand dollars and attracted national attention by a veto message describing the intended deal as "a most barefaced, impudent, and shameless scheme to betray the interests of the people." When, therefore, he resubmitted the names for his commission with the comment that "their rejection . . . was the result of haste and confusion," the Council, having found their master, instantly confirmed them.

It is a matter of little permanent importance that the new commission did the work promptly and upon reasonable terms. But it is of wide significance that, as Mayor of Buffalo, Grover Cleveland accomplished, in the face of entrenched selfishness, the reforms for which the people had been vainly calling, and that before the end of his strenuous term of office, he was beginning to be thought of as the type of man for a reform governor of New York. It is also of general significance that these experiences, multiplied many times over, made of him a reformer in root and branch. They caused him fully to realize the insidious dangers which ever beset popular government, and to set his face still more uncompromisingly toward reform.

Each bill presented to him received his patient study

and not one veto was ever issued unadvisedly. His carefully written arguments were constructive rather than
destructive, aiming at the creation of a system which
would stop the abuses which he saw so clearly and pointed
out so fearlessly. Over and over again they contain
fundamental discussions of public morality. He spoke
not as a mayor dealing with the comparatively insignificant interests of a small city, but as a statesman enunciating the great principles upon which free government
rests. And so his vetoes, while gaining for him each day
a more bitter enmity from the political boss and the
would-be grafter, steadily raised him in the respect of
honest men.

In spite of his firmness, however, in spite of the consuming heat of his wrath when once aroused, he was in
general considerate in his dealings with his Council, and
often, in the more difficult problems which came before
him, he showed the depth of his human sympathy. Those
unfortunate little ones, the children of the streets, were
his especial care, and found in him a watchful and resourceful friend. He also insisted that the poorer quarters of the city should have every possible protection and
advantage.

In the summer of 1882, he received a resolution of
the Council directing the street commissioner to replace
a pump which, in the interest of public health, had been
removed. His veto message breathes scorn and contempt
for the authors of the measure. "The particular well,"
he declared, ". . . stands third in the list as to the extent
of contamination. . . . If there is in the mind of anyone
the idea that it is not necessary to supply the poor and
laboring people in the vicinity of this well with water
as pure and healthful as that furnished to their richer
and more pretentious fellow citizens, I desire to say that

I have no sympathy with such a notion. On the contrary, I believe that the poor who toil should of all others have access to what nature intended for their refreshment— wholesome and pure water."

In all these conflicts the Mayor, while almost uniformly victorious, never developed the executive bacillus of personal egotism, or the pretense of phenomenal wisdom. His messages continued to be simple, straightforward statements of facts verified by careful study, and citations of laws quoted with meticulous exactness. When found in error, he willingly admitted the fact, but he never allowed such admissions to cause him to distrust his own judgment in matters concerning which he had not been shown to be wrong.

The telling title of "Veto Mayor" was won by his policy of pinning the crime upon the criminal. Deliberate dishonesty, according to his practical philosophy, is not to be regarded in the abstract. Wherever it exists, it is distinctly personal, and public duty requires that it be dealt with in terms of individuals. His strong and fearless pronouncements were like blasts of a trumpet of the age of heroes, and were the more effective because it was a matter of record that his words were but the precursors of actions even more fearless.

It is said of Napoleon that at the bridge of Lodi he suddenly saw himself for the first time a possible world figure. In Albany, in the once locally famous Flanagan murder case, according to the interpretation of Buffalo contemporaries, Mayor Cleveland first realized that there might be for him a larger career than that of provincial mayor or district lawyer. The case itself is of no more importance than thousands of cases which crowd the books of our criminal courts.

In 1880 Martin Flanagan killed John Kairns, fore-

man in a grain elevator in which Flanagan was employed.
The case was tried and Flanagan was sentenced to death
for murder in the first degree. Appeals to the Superior
Court of Buffalo, and later to the Court of Appeals, confirmed the verdict. As the date set for the execution
approached, the case became the subject of conversation
at the corner table in the Tifft House, where Mr. Cleveland ordinarily lunched with a body of close friends. In
his absence, the company decided that Flanagan had not
had a fair trial and agreed to wait upon Mayor Cleveland
and ask him to procure from Governor Cornell a stay of
execution, in order that the facts in the case might be
again examined. The stay was granted, and Mayor
Cleveland reviewed the case himself, discovering evidence which convinced him that Flanagan ought not to
be executed.

He found, according to F. D. Locke, who was associated with the reopening of the case, that "one of Flanagan's counsel, the one who could plead, had been so drunk
during the trial that the other, who could not plead, had
been compelled to sum up without notice." It appeared
also that Flanagan "had killed his man with a short-
bladed barlow knife which no one would have supposed
a deadly weapon. He stabbed, furthermore, in the right
side, ignorant of the fact that his antagonist had a displaced heart, which was thus pierced." These facts
established, Mr. Cleveland's duty was plain. He must
go to Albany, appear before the Governor, and plead for
the life of the doomed man.

The trip was planned in consultation with the men
who had first approached him in the matter. Mr. John
Allen, a director of the New York Central Railroad, and
a frequenter of the corner table at the Tifft House, arranged for a special car into which were bundled most

of the jurymen who had convicted Flanagan, a body of witnesses, packages of affidavits, the District Attorney, and a number of citizens who had aided the Mayor in preparing his case. Mr. Cleveland's methods were always thorough, and in this case they had been particularly so, for a human life depended upon his efforts.

The Governor received them in the Executive Chamber, with the unencouraging courtesy of a man whose boast it was that he seldom used his power of pardon. Mr. Cleveland opened the hearing with a carefully prepared statement of the facts and circumstances of the crime, together with a review of the trial, pointing out his reasons for questioning the justice of the verdict. The Governor appeared little impressed. Affidavits, letters, papers, recommendations from the jurors followed. Still the Governor remained unresponsive. The District Attorney, Mr. Edward W. Hatch, was then called upon by the Governor for a summary of the facts of the case as revealed by the evidence at the trial. Mr. Hatch declared that the evidence had justified the verdict, and that the appeals which had been taken had revealed no errors.

At this point, Governor Cornell considered that enough had been said, and declined to listen to an additional plea of Mr. Box of Buffalo. His refusal was so peremptory that Box dared not further insist upon his right to speak, but Mayor Cleveland sprang to his feet and faced the Governor with the words: "We come to you as to a king, pleading for mercy. It is your duty to hear us to the end." And Governor Cornell did hear him to the end, and the end was a commutation of the sentence of the doomed man.

In conversation with a friend, some months later, the Governor remarked: "There is a remarkable man in Buffalo. . . . His name is Cleveland, and although he is Mayor of the city, he recently came to see me in a legal capacity on behalf of a convicted murderer, under sentence of death. His appeal to me for executive clemency was totally unlike any I heretofore have received. It was without sentiment. It was a cold, dispassionate presentation of the unfortunate circumstances under which the killing was done, the provocation, and the shadow of presumptive justification for the act. . . . I was so impressed with the sincerity and the legal cocksureness of the man that I commuted the sentence."

Grover Cleveland who, as Sheriff of Erie County, had with his own hands hanged a malefactor rather than put upon the shoulders of another a responsibility which belonged to his office, thus saved another unfortunate from the same fate, because he believed the sentence to be unjust. In his effort to secure the ends of justice, he matched his will, his brain, and his legal skill against a man of great power and reputed ability, and carried his point. He had come to the bridge of Lodi, and the days of his greatness were not far off. The next time he entered that Executive Chamber, it was as Governor of New York.

# CHAPTER III

## THE REFORM GOVERNOR

*"Let us look for guidance to the principles of true Democracy, which are enduring because they are right, and invincible because they are just."*

—GROVER CLEVELAND.

AS Mayor of Buffalo, Grover Cleveland had accomplished definite results. He had fought a winning battle for the people against entrenched crookedness, against a "gang" which a Republican daily, the *Express,* described as "the most corrupt combination ever formed in the Council." And so successfully had he fought that, at the end of his strenuous term, he was in the minds of local reform leaders as a candidate for Governor of New York.

Among his fellows he was reckoned "a good fellow," which meant that he lived as they lived, a life by no means saintly, but irreproachably honest, and in general commendable. He drank a little, but not to excess. He played poker, but only for sums so small as to involve no hardship either to winner or to loser. His profession was always his chief interest and he was known in the Buffalo district as a man of parts, who could be trusted to serve the people tirelessly and fearlessly, and without raising, even in his own mind, the question, "Will it pay *me?*"

Outside the Buffalo district, the public as yet knew little of him, save as the ringing words of his more important vetoes had gained a wider currency, by their

37

appeal to virile, courageous, fighting manhood. To those familiar with the politics of New York State at that period it was evident that there at least the great Republican experiment needed a leader built on the lines of a man of war, and on September 20, 1882, that need was emphasized anew by the nomination of Charles J. Folger as Republican candidate for Governor of New York. The announcement of this nomination was received with an outburst of indignation by the reform element of both parties. Henry Ward Beecher, in words which reached every corner of the land, declared that it had been achieved by bribery and forgery, and added the opinion that the machine "should be rebuked in a manner it cannot fail to understand."

Folger himself was regarded as a gentleman of high character and exemplary life, but it was felt that he had been chosen for the Republicans and not by them. Only a few months before the nomination, President Arthur had taken him from the bench of the New York Court of Appeals and had made him Secretary of the Treasury with the purpose, so his enemies believed, of using him to prevent the renomination of Governor Cornell. At the psychological moment, a telegram from Washington had made him the Administration candidate. In his interest, delegates had been coerced, efficient public servants had been removed to be replaced by the President's partisans, and about the patronage-packed convention had hovered the agents of Jay Gould, laying plans for special privileges. By such methods, as one of the New York City Republican journals complained, "the wishes of 450,000 Republicans were overridden by the will of Chester A. Arthur, accidental President by the grace of Guiteau's bullet."

In view of these facts, the followers of the uncertain

presidential dreams of James G. Blaine saw in Folger's nomination a plan to defeat their "peerless leader" in the next presidential campaign, and watched with eager expectancy the preparations for the Democratic State Convention which should select Folger's antagonist.

Early in the summer of 1882, Mr. Cleveland received news of the illness of his mother, and departed at once for Holland Patent. During his prolonged absence his friends in Buffalo quietly launched a movement for his nomination as Democratic candidate for Governor. In his own district the suggestion met with instant favor, and from the first it was evident that the sixty delegates of his judicial district could be counted on to support him in the convention. Reports were sent to him from time to time, but he gave them little attention. His mother was dying, and all his thought was for her.

"During those last sad days of waiting," writes one who spent them with him, "no one would have supposed that any political ambitions were in his mind. Never once, during the last two weeks of her illness, did he leave the home town; and when the many letters and telegrams arrived, he answered them with no apparent concern, so that even the family group were not aware of the possibilities that lay so definitely before him."

On July 19th his mother died, with her seven surviving children about her. She was buried beside her husband, and Grover Cleveland returned to his official duties with a remark about "the desolation of a life without a mother's prayers."

Arrived in Buffalo, he found the movement for his nomination well advanced and superbly organized. At first he took little interest, though he did not discourage the movement, as he was a candidate for a place on the Supreme Bench of his district, and the prominent mention of his name in connection with the governorship would further this ambition. He was, therefore, content that his friends should continue their work.

As he watched their progress, he slowly became more interested. "I am not actively seeking the nomination for Governor," . . . he wrote to Edgar K. Apgar, who had urged him to visit Dan Manning, master of the well-oiled Democratic machine at Albany, and heir to the methods of the Albany Regency. "I know that neither my acquaintance in political circles throughout the state, nor my standing in the state Democracy, would for a moment suggest my name . . . and if it were not for my abiding faith in the success of an honest effort to perform public duty, I should at times distrust my ability to properly bear the responsibilities of the place in case of election.

"I am entirely certain, that if there is anything of my candidacy, it rests upon the fact that my location, and an entire freedom from the influence of all and any kind of factional disturbance, might make me an available candidate. If my name is presented to the Convention, I should think it would be presented upon that theory. And I am sure, if I were nominated, and could be the instrument of bringing about the united action of the party at the polls, I should feel that I had been of great value to the people and to the party.

"When an interview with Mr. Manning was first suggested, some time ago, my impulse was at once to find my way to him by way of showing my respect for his position in the party, and the regard I have learned to entertain for him as a gentleman. Upon reflection, however, it has occurred to me that if we meet by appointment, it will of course be known that we have been together, and it will not the less surely be falsely *alleged,* that an understanding has been arrived at between us, and pledges made which make me his man. Would not this lying interpretation be used in answer to the claim that I am free from any alliances? Might not the friends of other candidates claim that one who was proclaimed as a free candidate, and yet had an understanding with Mr. Manning or his friends, ought not to be nominated? What would be the effect of such an appeal, on the Convention, or afterwards on the election? . . .

"I ask you then . . . whether . . . the chances of an election will not be better if this visit is not made as you suggest. May I not in this way avoid even the appearance of being anything except what I really am; and may I not, thus, absolutely preclude the pretense that I am not a sound, plain, uncomplaining Democrat and an absolutely free man?"

Meanwhile his political promoters, Democrats, Republicans, and Independents alike, were actively seeking his nomination. In the spacious gardens of Mr. George Urban, a Republican of Buffalo, they built a log cabin, in the midst of a grove of hickories. Beside the cabin stood a concrete base for the keg of beer which in Buffalo was the inevitable concomitant of every political conference. Around this base three benches formed a triangle abutting upon a hickory, which shaded the "throne chair." On these benches beneath the emblematic trees his friends met with their chosen leader, Grover Cleveland, and with his at first reluctant co-operation, secretly planned their pre-convention campaign.

Cleveland's leadership had not come by chance. From his earliest days in Buffalo he had been active in politics, not with a view to winning office, but as a civic duty. Urban, although a Republican leader, had often employed Cleveland's talent for peacemaking, realizing that the latter was in close touch with the masses before he began much contact with the classes, and that he easily maintained sympathetic relations with both without offense to either. When political troubles arose in the people's section, they would send for Cleveland, who "would sit down among the brothers of discontent, play with them, drink with them a while, and then peacefully settle their controversy."

By September, mysterious hints of a "dark horse" in Erie County were causing political prophets to wonder, and expectant officials, accustomed to fatten upon party spoils, to come perilously near to prayer. Grover Cleveland, enemy of the faithful spoilsmen of Buffalo, the man who had refused to pay his personal followers out of the public treasury, lived in Erie County. Could these rumors refer to him?

As the date of the convention approached, Mr. Cleveland saw clearly that his nomination was within the range of possibilities, and threw his tremendous energies into the scale. Now, for the first time, he appeared in the character of a politician seeking office; a keen, resourceful, courageous leader, cautious in counsel, a field marshal in action. Three days before the convention, he sent to Wilson S. Bissell the following orders regarding Daniel Manning.

*Sept. 19, '82,*
1 o'c. A.M.

DEAR BISSELL:

John B. Manning has been in to see me to-night and has much to say about treachery, &c. I listened to all.

He talks Congressman at large.

I still listened.

Now do just as I tell you without asking any questions. When Dan and Scheu get there, have them go the first thing to Dan'l Manning and urge with the *utmost vehemence* my nomination.

Never mind what he says—have them pound away.

I am quite sure he thinks these two good friends are cool and jealous and don't want to see me nominated. And I am sure he has in his head the idea of Congressman at large and I think it is based upon what he thinks as to the real feelings of some of my friends—or that we think are friends.

Of course I know how it is, but I want Manning to be convinced that he is wrong in his premises.

I heard the same old song—if I had come to see him my nomination would have been assured, &c., Flower has much money, &c. . . .

G. C.

The situation which appeared when the Democratic State Convention met at Syracuse was one requiring both skill and courage. Delegates from Tammany Hall were clamoring for seats, and their astute leader, Kelly, was looking for help. Kings County presented her candidate, General Henry W. Slocum, the choice of Tilden; Jefferson County presented hers, Roswell P. Flower, ex-Congressman and ex-Chairman of the Executive State Committee. Each claimed 156 votes out of a total of 384, thus leaving a possible 72 for the third candidate, should one venture to emerge. Between Slocum and Flower, however, there was fierce conflict, and this fact offered hope to the Cleveland minority.

In the eagerness of battle both Slocum and Flower had made what they considered satisfactory terms with Manning, whose major aim was to prevent the seating of the Tammany Hall delegates. Kelly knew this and, with the to-be-expected wisdom of the serpent, set himself the task of outwitting them both. He contrived to convince the managers of each that the nomination of their respective candidates would be assured if only the Tammany delegates could be seated. Thus the followers of Flower and Slocum united and forced the seating of Kelly's delegation.

But when the thing was done, when the Tammany men were secure in their seats, and three ballots had failed to decide between the candidates, Kelly suddenly demanded that the Tammany delegation be called again, and upon that signal every brave voted for Grover Cleveland, amid a scene of almost unprecedented excitement. When the third ballot was finally officially registered, Grover Cleveland's nomination was beyond question. He had two hundred and eleven votes as against one hundred and fifty-six for Slocum and fifteen for Flower; and, upon motion of the leader of the Slocum men, Cleveland was generously voted to be the unanimous choice of the convention.

When the clans departed, the Flower men, the Slocum men, and the Tammany Hall braves all thought they understood what had happened. Tammany Hall had given recalcitrant Democrats a lesson in New York politics, the lesson that the Big Chief hears all, sees all, knows all. Flower and Slocum had walked with Daniel Manning, and Tammany had punished them, giving the prize to the man who, as was supposed, had not so walked.

The sequel, however, proves that even a Tammany leader in a New York State Convention, in what is considered good tiger weather, may meet his match. Grover Cleveland had made his political reputation as a reformer, but he was wise enough to know that one must reform a tiger by methods quite different from those needed for men. And so, having reconsidered the cautious program outlined in his August letter to Apgar, he had come to the convention city of Syracuse itself—not openly, but in the quiet of a late evening, when even tigers were asleep. For a few brief hours he had been closeted with Manning, and had departed as unostentatiously as he had come. His work, however, had been done before his departure. Manning had not captured Grover Cleveland. Grover Cleveland had captured Manning, who remained ever after an active, consistent Cleveland man. And of this visit Tammany had no inkling.

Kelly left the Syracuse Convention serene in the thought that he had named the candidate. Manning felt confident that *he* had named him, while the knights of the hickory grove did not need to debate the question. Their task was to plan the election of an unowned candidate for Governor, the Honorable Grover Cleveland.

Cleveland's nomination was thus neither an accident nor the result of a blind partisan conflict, but a victory by intention. Manning had nominated him, but was not entitled to consider him in any sense his man. Kelly had nominated him, but with the blinders on, and could claim no proprietorship; for Grover Cleveland had kept himself free, if elected, to serve the people and to act in their interests alone, an achievement of political skill of which Thomas Jefferson might have been justly proud. He deserved, and he received, the support of the intelligent reformers who understood how profoundly reform movements need political brains in leadership and political skill in management.

The day after the ticket was chosen Mr. Cleveland wrote to David B. Hill, Mayor of Elmira, who had been nominated Lieutenant Governor: "Accept my hearty congratulations on your nomination. . . . Now let us go to work and show the people of the state what two bachelor mayors can do."

Cleveland's letter accepting the nomination was a frank declaration of war upon such politicians as pervert to private ends the machinery designed to serve the people. It was downright, specific, Clevelandesque. It made promises which could neither be misunderstood by others nor repudiated through ingenious interpretations by himself, and it caused the 'braves' of both parties to get out their war paint and their tomahawks. They knew by his past record what his future policy was likely to prove. With Cleveland as Governor, no party affiliation would serve to shield a scoundrel.

He did not write as a man seeking the support of hungry partisans, but as one calling honest men to battle for reform. He placed himself squarely on the side of those who, throughout the nation, were working for civil service reform, and as squarely on the side of honest elections. "The expenditure of money to influence the action of people at the polls, . . ." he said, "is calculated to excite the gravest concern. When this pernicious agency is successfully employed, a representative form of government becomes a sham, and laws passed under its baleful influence cease to protect, but are made the means by which the rights of the people are sacrificed and the public treasury despoiled."

Had Grover Cleveland been a politician, with the record of a spoilsman behind him, his promises would have meant little. They might have deceived a few of the simple, disgusted a few of the honest, caused mirth to a few other spoilsmen, and thus fulfilled their intended mission; for Americans had long since learned that, as the devil can quote Scripture, so the most dangerous type of demagogue can sing of ideals in false notes not easily distinguishable from true. But Mr. Cleveland had already put into practice the ideals which he announced, and Republicans bent on reform rallied to his support with an enthusiasm equal to that of his Democratic followers.

On the day of the election, as he sat in his office thinking of the responsibilities soon to be his, he wrote to his brother, the Rev. William N. Cleveland, a letter which reveals at once his simplicity, his modesty, and his essentially religious point of view:

> Mayor's Office, Buffalo, N. Y.
> *November 7, 1882.*

MY DEAR BROTHER:

I have just voted. I sit here in the Mayor's office alone, with the exception of an artist from Frank Leslie's newspaper, who is sketching the office. If mother were here I should be writing to her, and I feel as if it were time to write to someone who will believe what I write.

I have been for some time in the atmosphere of certain success, so that I have been sure that I should assume the duties of the high office for which I have been named. I have tried hard in the light of this fact to properly appreciate the responsibilities that will rest upon me, and they are much—too much to be underestimated. But the thought that has troubled me is: Can I well perform my duties, and in such a manner as to do some good to the people of the State? I know there is room for it, and I know that I am honest and sincere in that desire to do well, but the question is whether I know enough to accomplish what I desire. . . .

I will tell you, first of all others, the policy I intend to adopt, and that is to make the matter a business engagement between the people of the State and myself, in

which the obligation on my side is to perform the duties
assigned me with an eye single to the interests of my
employers.   I shall have no idea of re-election or any
higher political preferment in my head, but be very
thankful and happy if I can well serve one term as the
people's Governor.   Do you know that if mother were
alive I should feel so much safer?   I have always thought
her prayers had much to do with my success.   I shall
expect you to help me in that way. . . .

> Your affectionate brother,
> GROVER CLEVELAND.

When the vote was counted it was found that Grover
Cleveland had received 535,318 out of a total of 915,539,
a majority too large for a mere party victory.   It represented the voice of New York's better self, speaking in
terms of reform.   But it also represented the determination of Blaine's followers that President Arthur's candidate should not be chosen.   By the thousands they had
absented themselves from the polls, and so helped to give
prominence to a personality far more dangerous to the
ambition of their brilliant leader than Arthur could ever
have been.

As Governor of New York, Grover Cleveland transferred to his larger sphere of activity the habits of plain
living, incessant labor, and courageous action which had
characterized him during his brief period as Mayor
of Buffalo.   With a spacious residence at his disposal—
spacious as compared with the simple bachelor apartments which he had occupied during his Buffalo days—
he developed no taste for society.   At times, as custom
required, he threw open the doors of the Executive Mansion.   But he viewed these functions as a species of penance, rather than as a diversion—a penance which, with

his colored steward, William Sinclair, in control, usually extended beyond the evening concerned. "William," he wrote to Bissell, the day after one of these functions, "has been making me eat up the remains of the reception."

| He began to study the records before he began to draw his salary; and as soon as the ceremony of inauguration was over, withdrew to his office and settled down to work, leaving with the astonished attendants an order to "admit at once anyone who asks to see the Governor." This in itself was a revolution. It was the opening of "the forbidden city," for the Governors of New York had long been accustomed to surround themselves with formalities which rendered them difficult of access. But Grover Cleveland liked to meet his adversaries face to face, to fight his battles in the open. Life in a country store, at Fayetteville, and later amid the intimate surroundings of Buffalo, had done for him what the intimacies of the country store did for Patrick Henry, Henry Clay, Abraham Lincoln, and numerous other American statesmen who used this "frontier clubhouse" as their social center. It taught him to understand humanity. In the Buffalo hotel, bar, or restaurant, he had met upon terms of intimacy, farmers, cattlemen, commercial travelers, politicians, and the rest of the varied assortment of Americans who congregated there. He had learned how they think, scheme, plan, and fight, and he trusted his ability to deal with them, without taking advantage of the shelter which high executive office offers. /

To the eager spoilsman, as to all others, he was easily accessible, and he did not speak in Delphic phrase. To the oft-repeated question, "Is it not due me on account of my work during the campaign?" his reply was: "I don't know that I fully understand you." But when the explanation was made, and the spoilsman's motto in any of its myriad forms was displayed, he made it abundantly clear that the new Governor acknowledged no allegiance to a tradition which sanctioned payment for partisan services out of the people's treasury.

Rendered suspicious by his previous official experiences, he took nothing on faith, but studied with extreme care each bill sent up for his signature. Those which he considered in the public interest he signed. Those which he regarded as unwise, inexpedient, or worse (and there were many of the latter class) he vetoed. Those which were susceptible of alterations which would make them good laws, he laboriously altered, and returned with the suggestion that he could sign them if changed. He had not learned—indeed he never learned—to conserve his own strength by delegating the labor of such investigations to others. As a result, he expended his vast energies upon details usually left in the hands of subordinates. Applications for pardons added enormously to his labors, for he reviewed each case himself and worked out his decisions according to the laws of evidence, being unwilling either to deny or to grant appeals upon the basis of any but his own mental processes.

It is easy for those wedded to modern methods of executive efficiency to scorn such apparent wastefulness; but it gave to Governor Cleveland's public documents a ring of certitude which left his less laborious antagonists at a disadvantage. They soon understood that when the Governor stated a fact, it was useless to attempt to prove it fiction; when he referred to a statute, it was wasted energy to check up his reference. And the public came to realize that when he cried "Wolf! wolf!" they must not allow themselves to be deceived by sheep's clothing, for in the end the wolf was certain to appear, and the Governor's warnings to be justified.

When a public man wins a reputation for unimpeachable honesty, he takes hold upon public confidence; but until he can show in addition that he has wisdom, his hold is easily loosened. Grover Cleveland, in the two years of his governorship, impressed the people with both his honesty and his wisdom, and to these he added the quality of courage which gave a touch of the dramatic so essential to political success. He dared to defend the rights of small holders, and of the State, against the unjust demands of corporations; but he was equally ready to face the less popular duty of defending the rights of corporations when the public, misled by demagogues or by the no less dangerous valor of ignorance, clamored for their destruction.

When the First National Bank of Buffalo failed, he refused to sign a bill authorizing the Comptroller to lighten its liabilities. "The bank has failed," he said in his veto message, "and is unable to refund the State's deposits. The securities in the bond have thus become liable . . . and I can see no reason why they should be relieved. I am willing to do what I can to check the growing impression that contracts with the State will not be insisted upon or may be evaded. The money deposited with the bank was public money . . . and I regard it the duty of all having the care of state affairs to see to it that no part is lost. . . ."

Public officials, according to his philosophy, are not advocates seeking to gain something for their client, the Government, but guardians of that right and justice whose preservation is essential both to Government and individual. A severe test of this principle came in the spring of 1883, in the form of the Five-Cent Fare Bill. This bill was what the politician calls "vote-getting legislation," being designed to reduce the cost of living and to give the citizen more for his money. It enabled him to ride for five cents to places which it had previously cost him ten cents to reach. The facts were as follows:

The elevated railroads of New York City were allowed by their charters to charge a ten cent fare for any distance between the Battery and Harlem River, except at the rush hours, when they must carry passengers at five cents each. The New York Legislature, yielding to a strong popular sentiment, passed Assembly Bill Number 58 prohibiting the collection of more than five cents for any distance between these points at any hour.

Mr. Cleveland studied the bill and found that it arbitrarily deprived the Manhattan Railway Company of a right granted by charter. Promptly, and with characteristic disregard of "good politics," he prepared an elaborately reasoned veto message insisting that the bill should not become a law. "I am not unmindful, . . ." he said, "that this bill originated in response to the demand of a large portion of the people of New York for cheaper rates . . . [but] there exists a contract in favor of this company, which is protected by that clause of the Constitution of the United States which prohibits the passage of a law by any state impairing the obligation of contracts."

After a detailed examination of the origin and specific nature of this contract, with the considerations which might be thought to have rendered it inoperative, or to have justified its violation, he added: "While the charters of corporations may be altered or repealed, it must be done in subordination to the Constitution of the United States, which is the supreme law of the land. This leads to the conclusion that the alteration of a charter cannot be made the pretext for the passage of a law which impairs the obligation of a contract." He argued that the companies had fulfilled their obligations, had paid into the public treasury over $120,000, and had met a public need which previous projectors had failed to meet. "I am not aware," he said, "that the corporations have, by any default, forfeited any of their rights; and if they have, the remedy is at hand under existing laws. . . . The State should be not only strictly just, but scrupulously fair, and in its relation to the citizen every legal and moral obligation should be recognized. This can only be done by legislating without vindictiveness or prejudice, and with a firm determination to deal justly and fairly with those from whom we exact obedience."

This argument should be read in its entirety by that increasing body of Americans who to-day are inclined to denounce property rights and to demand that the State disregard them. In it, Grover Cleveland took his stand squarely upon the solid foundation of the rights of property, and the people of New York sustained him. His clear-cut decision, wrote Andrew D. White, was "that, whatever his sympathies for the working people might be, he could not, as an honest man, allow such a bill to pass, and come what might, he would not. . . . Glad was I to see that the Governor rose above all the noise and claptrap which was raised about the question, went to the fundamental point of the matter, and vetoed the bill. I think his course at that time gained him the respect of every thinking man in the State."

Theodore Roosevelt, then a New York Assemblyman of twenty-three, was conspicuous among those who had rallied to the "noise and claptrap" and had driven the bill through the New York Legislature. In the clear light of the Governor's veto message, however, he saw his error and, with the frank, generous courage which always characterized him, acknowledged it. "I have to say with

shame," he announced in an astonishing confession before the Legislature, "that when I voted for this bill I
did not act as I think I ought to have acted and as I generally have acted on the floor of this House. I have to
confess that I weakly yielded, partly in a vindictive spirit
toward the infernal thieves and conscienceless swindlers
who have had the elevated railroad in charge, and partly
to the popular voice of New York. I realize that they
[managers of the railway] have done the most incalculable wrong to this community with their hired newspaper,
with their corruption of the judiciary, with their corruption of past legislatures. It is not a question of doing
right to them. They are merely common thieves. It is
not a question of doing justice to them. It is a question
of doing justice to ourselves. It is a question of standing
by what we honestly believe to be right, even if in so doing we antagonize the feelings of our constituents."

The mind of the elder reformer had touched and
illuminated with its clear reasoning the mind of the
younger reformer, who at once altered his course and
followed the Governor. "I believed," Roosevelt wrote
in his autobiography, many years later, "the veto was
proper, and those who felt as I did supported the veto,
for although it was entirely right that the fare should be
reduced to five cents, which was soon afterwards done,
the method was unwise, and would have set a mischievous
precedent."

The night after the veto message, while Mr. Cleveland was preparing for bed, he said to himself, as he
afterwards confessed to Richard Watson Gilder, "By
to-morrow at this time I will be the most unpopular man
in the state of New York.

"As I got into bed that night," he later declared to
Joseph Bucklin Bishop, "I said to myself, 'Grover Cleve-

land, you have done the business for yourself to-night.'
The next morning I went down to the Executive Office
feeling pretty blue, but putting a smiling face on it. I
didn't look at the morning papers; I didn't think they had
anything to say that I cared to see. I went through my
morning mail with my secretary, Dan Lamont, pretending
all the time that I didn't care about the papers, but thinking of them all the time, just the same. When we had
finished I said as indifferently as I could, 'Seen the morning papers, Dan?' He said, 'Yes.' 'What have they got
to say about me, anything?' 'Why, yes, they are all praising you.' 'They are? Well, here, let me see them.' I
tell you, I grabbed them pretty quickly, and felt a good
deal better."

There were, however, many who were little inclined
to join in the applause. A few nights after the appearance of the veto, Governor Cleveland appeared in a
theatre and the audience rose and hissed him. They did
not know that at the very time of the veto he was using
his influence to get the elevated railway to try the five-
cent fare, of which he heartily approved. His veto was
aimed, not at the measure, but at the method, which he
felt to be a clear breach of public faith. Therefore, in
utter disregard of the political penalties which he believed such a course would entail, he defied the people
for the people's good, not as an autocrat, but as a representative who considered it his duty to give the public
the benefit of his judgment as well as of his energy.

Before the mingled sounds of approval and denunciation regarding the veto had died away, the Governor
found himself compelled to take action which brought
him into open and bitter conflict with John Kelly and
Tammany Hall, whose influence had been so potent a
factor in securing for him the post of Governor of New

York.  State Senator Thomas F. Grady, one of Tammany's favorite sons, had been a thorn in the side of the Cleveland administration from the day of the assembling of the legislature.  But now, as the end of the last session approached, he became unbearable, boldly standing, in combination with the two other Tammany senators and the Republicans, in the way of the Cleveland program, even after it had received legislative sanction.

On the last day of the session two of the Governor's most cherished reform measures—a bill regulating the duties of harbor masters, and a bill for reducing the expenses of the Immigration Commission and placing it under a single Commissioner—were passed, and the Governor at once made the nominations necessary for their immediate operation.  These nominations the Grady-Republican combine managed to "hang up," thus postponing the reforms at least until the convening of a new legislature.  Mr. Cleveland's indignant protest was answered by a bitter personal attack from Grady, and the stolid refusal of the combination to allow action on the nominations.

When the session ended, with the reforms inoperative, Kelly assured the Governor's angry followers that Grady's course had been without the advice of Tammany, and that his attack upon the Governor was disapproved and would be properly rebuked.  He even declared himself in full accord with Mr. Cleveland's policies, and anxious to make the administration a success.  Ten days later, however, he sent Grady with his proxy into a meeting of the State Committee, and announced his intention of renominating him for the Senate.  In view of these facts, Mr. Cleveland drafted and sent to Kelly the following specific note:

Executive Chamber, Albany.

*October 20, 1883.*

HON. JOHN KELLY

MY DEAR SIR:

It is not without hesitation that I write this. I have determined to do so, however, because I see no reason why I should not be entirely frank with you.

I am anxious that Mr. Grady should not be returned to the next Senate. I do not wish to conceal the fact that my personal comfort and satisfaction are involved in the matter. But I know that good legislation, based upon a pure desire to promote the interests of the people and the improvement of legislative methods, are also deeply involved.

I forbear to write in detail of the other considerations having relation to the welfare of the party and the approval to be secured by a change for the better in the character of its representatives. These things will occur to you without suggestion from me.

Yours very truly,

GROVER CLEVELAND.

Kelly put this letter in his pocket and proceeded with his plans for returning Senator Grady to Albany. The Governor gave out no copy, and made no public comment, being content to allow the Tammany leader to meet the suggestion in his own way. The move for Democratic unity, for a union of Tammany Democrats, Irving Hall Democrats, and County Democrats, in the face of the coming election, seemed the only hope of electing Democratic state senators, and Governor Cleveland did not feel it necessary to endanger that unity by a too open insistence upon Grady's elimination.

But what Cleveland felt it unnecessary to do, local organizations promptly accomplished. The Sixth District defied Kelly and nominated ex-Justice Timothy J. Campbell for the State Senate. Kelly next attempted to have Grady nominated in the Fifth District; but the leaders there would tolerate no such suggestion, insisting that Colonel M. C. Murphy was, and would remain, their candidate. At this point, Grady wisely declared that he would not run in any district, and the matter was settled, without the Governor's letter being called into use. The indignant Tammanyites, however, played into the hands of the grateful Republicans, by abandoning the union idea and making straight Tammany nominations for the Senate in all senatorial districts.

In order to lend color to the story that the Governor had interfered in New York City politics, Kelly gave the Grady letter to the New York *World,* which published it on November 2d, suppressing the name of the recipient. In the same column appeared a statement from Kelly that "All the disaffection existing in the Democratic party to-day in this country has its root and center in the brain of the Executive. He has allowed his personal spite towards Senator Grady to get the better of his judgment, and yet Grady has done nothing to merit such a spirit of revenge on the part of the Governor. Senator Grady's reply to the Governor's message bringing the Senate to task for failing to confirm his nominations for harbor masters, port wardens, and Commissioner of Immigration just before the adjournment of the last session was dignified and his grounds for the statements uttered at the time were, to my mind, well taken." With the exception of a brief acknowledgment of the authenticity of the Grady letter, and the statement that it had been written to Kelly, the Governor held his peace; and in this divided condition, the New York Democracy faced the elections.

The Republican factions, the Stalwarts and the Half-Breeds, on the other hand, had for the time buried the hatchet, and the result was Republican unity and victory over a divided Democracy. Democratic majorities in both houses were changed to minorities, and even the New York *World,* which for three days insisted that the Democrats had won, was forced to admit, on November 9th, that "The Senate will stand nineteen Republicans, thirteen Democrats. . . . The new Assembly will be composed of seventy-three Republicans and fifty-five Democrats." Thus Assemblyman Theodore Roosevelt came back to his seat, with the comfortable feeling that he was leading a dominant party, though ready to co-operate with the Governor in all measures of sound and progressive reform.

Four days after the election, Grady, in a fiery speech in Tammany Hall, bitterly attacked the Governor; and Kelly sustained the attack by again publishing the Grady letter, this time in facsimile beneath the headlines: "How Harmony Fell Through in New York." He editorially interpreted the letter as an attempted interference of the Executive with the action of the people in choosing their representatives. The Tammany papers throughout the state, taking the cue, raised the cry of executive interference, and the Republican press gladly followed suit.

Until almost the end of November, Mr. Cleveland made no further statement concerning the Grady incident. But, on the twenty-third, the New York *Herald* sent a special correspondent to Albany to get the Governor's views regarding the matter. He found Mr. Cleveland, for once, not only ready but eager to talk through

the press, and not disposed to measure his words too carefully.

"Mr. Cleveland sat in his large revolving chair, alone.
He looked vigorous and buoyant, the Hancock standard
of two hundred and fifty pounds having evidently been
long since reached.

" 'This letter of yours to Kelly,' said the correspondent, 'has caused a great deal of talk.'

"The heavy chair of the Governor moved a little
nearer as he replied :

" 'Indeed? Well, I suppose so. Why?'

" 'That is for you to say,' the reporter responded.

" 'I hold,' said the Governor, 'that it was the proper
thing, under the circumstances, to send that letter.'

" 'You think Grady was not a proper representative
to send back to the Senate?' queried the visitor.

" 'I do, most assuredly,' Mr. Cleveland answered.
'His action in the Senate has been against the interests
of the people and of good government, and his ready
tongue gave him power to be of great aid to bad men. I
believed that the Democratic party could not afford to endorse such a course, and that his rejection would be a great
benefit to the party and to the people. What's the use
of striving for the Senate, County Democrats argue, and
have Grady holding the balance of power to sell us out
to the Republicans?'

" 'But about the letter, Governor?' asked the reporter.

"The big armchair again moved closer, and the Governor said : 'I sat down without the knowledge of any person and wrote to Kelly—this man who had been assuring
me of his anxiety to give me aid in my work. I suggested, not for my personal comfort, which I did not deny
would be subserved, but for the good of the public service,
that he who had the power to say "Go" or "Come" should

not force the nomination of Grady upon the Democrats of the State. No man ever acted with a more positive desire to serve the State than I did when I wrote that letter to a man claiming to be my friend. I suggested that he who had the power should favor some better man for the Senate.'

" 'Did Kelly ever answer your letter?' asked the interviewer.

" 'No,' replied the Governor. 'If he had been what I took him to be, and believed in Grady's nomination, he would have so written frankly in reply. He put the letter in his pocket, and, I understand, called in his district leaders in Grady's district and stated his purpose to nominate him. The responses understood to be from these leaders were that Grady could not be elected in his home district. Then Mr. Kelly went to the Fifth District, where Colonel M. C. Murphy had been nominated in pursuance of an understanding between all the organizations in the district. In violation of this understanding he sought to renominate Grady there. Then and not till then did Mr. Grady announce his retirement, a retirement which was forced by the fact that he could not be elected. All this time my letter had been in Kelly's pocket.

" 'What then? Mr. Kelly—whom many who opposed him in politics believed to be a gentleman—took this private, personal letter, written, as he knew, for his own eyes only, to the New York *World,* and requested its publication, together with a story that that letter prevented union nominations in New York and would make the Senate Republican. At the same time Mr. Kelly's newspaper was openly attacking and seeking the defeat of four Democratic Senators outside of New York—Henry C.

Nelson, James Mackin, John C. Jacobs, and John J. Kiernan, and one or more Democratic Assemblymen.'

"When asked whether he still believed that the Grady letter should have been sent to Kelly, Mr. Cleveland replied: 'Most undoubtedly. The letter was . . . written in the interest of the people, to better the representation in the Senate of this State. Its reception proved to me that the man who had been assuring me of his friendship was my enemy, and that of the cause which I had espoused. It gave an opportunity for this enemy to openly and coarsely insult me as Governor of the State. To say that this letter should not have been written from one gentleman to another—the one anxious to better the public service, and the other having it in his power to do it—is nonsense. To say that a man should go three hundred miles to say what he should not put on paper is the rankest kind of hypocrisy. This criticism can only be based upon the assumption that a man might say in conversation with another what he might afterward find it convenient to deny when there was no positive corroborative evidence to be brought forward as to the facts. It is unfortunate for the Democratic party that this "boss" system exists. While it does exist it became a necessity—a disagreeable necessity, I assure you—for me to recognize it, and consequently to address that letter to Kelly. However, the time is fast approaching when this odious system will be swept away and the voice of the people alone be recognized as potent in determining nominations to public offices.'

"After a brief pause, the Governor added: 'The will of the people had, I suppose, nothing to do with the nomination of Mr. Grady. It began and ended with the will of Mr. Kelly, and his election after nomination depended upon the same power, bounded only by the trades and dickers that could be made with the so-called leaders, and the freedom of the field from other candidates. This is not a condition consistent with true democracy, and it is not a condition most favorable to good government; but I had nothing to do with creating it. I merely conceded it as I found it and wrote to the man who had the whole matter in his keeping. . . . If this be treason I can't see how I can escape its consequences. I have supposed that Mr. Grady was not put in his old field because Mr. Campbell insisted on running in opposition to him. Campbell's majority indicates that the people were quite willing to vote for somebody besides Grady.' "

The sequel showed that from that date Tammany Hall was ever "quite willing to vote for somebody besides" Grover Cleveland. The Governor had incurred for his whole future the bitter enmity of the most powerful of all Democratic clubs, Tammany Hall, and that with the presidential year only a few weeks ahead.

Mr. Cleveland watched the old year out with the satisfying belief that his first year as Governor was successfully completed. As he thought of the assembling of the Legislature on the following day, he checked up certain tangible proofs of definite achievement. Before him lay the manuscripts of forty-four executive vetoes, some consisting of elaborate arguments, some containing but a dozen lines, but each representing much patient labor, for, in each case he had himself investigated both the facts and the law involved. He counted, with equal pride, the number of appeals for executive clemency which he had examined and determined. Of the four hundred and forty-nine, thirty-nine were marked "Pardoned"; seventeen sentences had been commuted; one respite had been granted, and one hundred and eighty-one prayers denied. The rest remained to be studied and disposed of in the months to come.

His message for the new Legislature was ready, and dated January 1, 1884. It was devoted wholly to state affairs, and remarkable in its frankness. In his inaugural message he had spoken with the modesty which becomes a man new to office. Now, however, with a year of intensive study behind him, he wrote with singular directness, bluntly denouncing specific abuses, in utter disregard of the feelings and of the votes of those responsible for them. His enumeration of his own achievements as Governor he presented without mock modesty, indeed, with conscious pride:

"The most practical and thorough civil service reform has gained a place in the policy of the State," he declared. "Political assessments upon employes in the public departments have been prohibited. The rights of all citizens at primary elections have been protected by law. A bureau has been established to collect information and statistics touching the relations between labor and capital. The sale of forest lands at the source of our important streams has been prohibited, thereby checking threatened disaster to the commerce on our waterways. Debts and obligations for the payment of money owned though not actually held within the State, have been made subject to taxation, thus preventing an unfair evasion of liability for the support of the Government. Business principles have been introduced in the construction and care of the new capitol, and other public buildings, and waste and extravagance thereby prevented. A law has been passed for the better administration of the immigration bureau and the prevention of its abuses. The people have been protected by placing co-operative insurance companies under the control and supervision of the Insurance Department. The fees of receivers have been reduced and regulated in the interests of creditors of investment companies. A court of claims has been established where the demands of a citizen against the State may be properly determined. These legislative accomplishments, and others of less importance and prominence, may be cited in proof of the fact that the substantial interests of the people of the State have not been neglected."

His successes had been of varied character, his conflicts numerous, and his victories of gratifying frequency. But in his frank avowal of success, there is no sign of the dangerous complacency which considers the work done as soon as the blue prints are complete. He saw clearly the evils which still held firm footing in the commonwealth, and pointed them out with perfect frankness. He told the Legislature that it was accused of recessing too often, and for inadequate reasons, clearly intimating his own sympathy with the critics.

His comments upon the problem of corporations and their regulation anticipated the views later advanced by President Roosevelt. But Cleveland's plan called for state regulation, while Roosevelt's later solution was through Federal action. "It is a grave question," declared Governor Cleveland's message, "whether the formation of these artificial bodies ought not to be checked or better regulated and in some way supervised. At any rate, they should always be kept well in hand, and the funds . . . protected by the State which has invited their investment. While the stockholders are the owners of the corporate property, notoriously they are oftentimes completely in the power of the directors and managers, who acquire a majority of the stock, and by this means perpetuate their control, using the corporate property and franchise for their benefit and profit, regardless of the interests and rights of the minority stockholders. Immense salaries are paid to officers; transactions are consummated by which the directors make money, while the rank and file among the stockholders lose it; the honest investor waits for dividends, and the directors grow rich. It is suspected, too, that large sums are spent under various disguises in efforts to influence legislation."

The oft-repeated suggestion that redress is always open to small holders before the courts, he scornfully dismissed with the words: "It is a hollow mockery. . . . Under existing statutes, the law's delay, perplexity, and uncertainty lead to despair." Pitiless publicity was the remedy which he urged as a protection against dishonest tendencies. "The State," he declared, "should either refuse to allow these corporations to exist under its authority and patronage, or acknowledging their paternity and its responsibility, should provide a simple, easy way for its people . . . to discover how the funds . . . are spent, and how their affairs are conducted. . . . This might well be accomplished by requiring corporations to frequently file reports, made out with the utmost detail, and which would not allow lobby expenses to be hidden under the pretext of legal services and counsel fees. . . . Such requirements might not be favorable to stock speculation, but they would protect the innocent investors. . . . The honestly conducted and strong corporations would have nothing to fear; the badly managed and weak ought to be exposed."

During his second year as Governor a bill was sent up to him which served admirably as the occasion for a frank expression of his views upon representative government and executive authority, views which should delight the soul of every advocate of the short ballot. It provided that, after January 1, 1885, "all appointments to office in the city of New York now made by the Mayor and confirmed by the Board of Aldermen, shall be made by the Mayor without such confirmation," and thus involved enormous concentration of power in the hands of the Mayor of New York.

In approving it the Governor declared: "I cannot see that any principle of democratic rule is more violated in the one case than in the other. . . . Nor are the rights of the people to self-government, in theory and principle, better protected when the power of appointment is vested in twenty-five men . . . than when this power is put in the hands of one man. . . . If the chief executive of the city is to be held responsible for its order and good government, he should not be hampered by any interference with his selection of subordinate administrative officers; nor should he be permitted to find in a divided responsibility an excuse for any neglect of the best interests of the people. . . . No instance has been cited in which a bad appointment has been prevented by the refusal of the Board of Aldermen . . . to confirm a nomination [and] an absolute and undivided responsibility . . . accords with correct business principles."

The reply to such theories has generally been, "Despotism, danger to republican government!" But Governor Cleveland recognized no such danger. "I can hardly realize the unprincipled boldness of the man who would accept at the hands of his neighbors this sacred trust, and, standing alone in the full light of public observation . . . willfully prostitute his powers and defy the will of the people. To say that such a man could by such means perpetuate his wicked rule, concedes either that the people are vile, or that self-government is a deplorable failure."

In republics there is a law of natural selection, not

invariably operative, but generally so. Few men reach the heights of power unless, in some important respects at least, they are gifted above their fellows. Grover Cleveland had the homely gift of common sense, the heroic gift of unflinching courage, the rare gift of long patience, and the divine gift of unimpeachable honesty. For such a man the times were calling. But the call did not fall upon too willing ears. Less than four months before the meeting of the Democratic National Convention, he wrote to Mr. Charles S. Fairchild:

"It is absolutely true that I have always regarded any suggestion of my candidacy for a place higher than the one I now occupy, as a serious mistake on every ground except merely personal ones; and on such latter grounds as *entirely inadmissible*. . . . I should not feel perhaps that I ought to refuse to do what the sentiment of my party should require of me—but I believe that there is no such sentiment that will embarrass me; and if there is it can be guided in the proper direction and enlightened.

"I have but one ambition, and that is to make a good Governor and do something for the people of the State and by such means, benefit the party to which I belong. I feel now that I shall desire to retire from public life at the close of my present term; and, making every allowance for a change of sentiment, it is absolutely certain, that an endorsement by the offer of a second term will satisfy every wish I can possibly entertain, at all related to political life. You see I tell you frankly not only what I don't want, but what possibly I may want. My expectation is, however, that I shall be able to somewhat prepare the way for better things, and that then I shall be relieved as one who has performed his purpose in political affairs. With this I shall be content."

William C. Hudson, in his *Random Recollections of*

*an Old Political Reporter,* says that when Mr. Cleveland's associates at Albany gathered around him, in the summer of 1884, predicting his nomination by the Democratic National Convention, he replied: "Go away, boys, and let me do my work as Governor. You're always trying to get me into a scrape." And Frank W. Mack has left us an account of a visit to Governor Cleveland, just three days before the State Convention, called to choose delegates-at-large to Chicago:

"He was alone and his greeting was that of a man . . . who welcomed other comradeship than that of his own thoughts."

" 'Well, you come from the outside world?' he half questioned.

" 'Yes, Governor, and things seem to be coming your way.'

"He turned a look, half quizzical, half apprehensive. There was no glint of pleased ambition in the face that averted itself . . . and when he sighed heavily, it was more than half a groan.

" 'It looks that way to you, too, does it?'

" 'I certainly can see no other outcome—who, by the way, has the distinction of sharing my views?'

"Mr. Cleveland turned a tired face toward the great, sun-lighted window. Somewhere in the big features was an expression as of one harried.

" 'Dorsheimer was just up here,' he spoke, 'and he used exactly the same words that you did.'

" 'You seem not highly gleeful, Mr. Governor, as to the outlook,' I ventured. The spectacle of a man saddened by the prospect of a presidential nomination was new to me, and rather disconcerting. . . . I looked on, silent.

" 'Yes,' he muttered to himself at length; 'yes, I believe things are coming this way . . . and I feel certain now that I cannot escape it.'

"'Escape the nomination?' I blurted.

"'Yes, the nomination—escape the nomination, I say. Tell me this. Can you understand me—might anybody understand me—when I say that, if I were to indulge my personal impulse at this moment, I would go away into some forest, hide in some fastness where no man could reach and where this awful burden might never find me?'"

In the State Convention itself, however, there appeared among the Governor's followers no trace of their chief's aversion. They went to Syracuse determined to secure a delegation committed to his nomination, and every device was employed to that end. Circumstances, however, made success impossible. From the very beginning appeared the perennial conflict between the regular state organization and Tammany Hall, the former under the skillful leadership of Daniel Manning, working for Cleveland; the latter, led by the no less astute John Kelly, bitterly opposing him. Both factions knew that the question of Cleveland's nomination would probably depend upon whether the Manning forces or the Kelly forces could secure control of the New York delegation to be selected at Saratoga. Besides this great division in the New York Democracy, there were many minor divisions, causing numerous and delicate cases of contesting state delegates and locally supported would-be delegates to the National Convention. These Manning and D-Cady Herrick, Chairman of the Committee on Contested Seats, and a staunch Cleveland man, adjusted upon the basis of the general policy of avoiding an open conflict with Kelly or any of his allies.

Mr. Cleveland's administration as Governor was approved by resolution, the invariable courtesy extended by the New York Democracy to Democratic governors of New York, and understood to be merely a form. But when the Cleveland men urged upon Manning the passage of a resolution instructing the delegation to vote for the Governor at Chicago, the leader wisely declined to allow the resolution to be presented, explaining that in his opinion it could not be carried. Instead, instructions were adopted directing the New York delegates to the Democratic National Convention to vote, on the first ballot, for the man favored by the majority of those delegates. More than this he did not dare to attempt. Thus the initial vote of New York was left undetermined, to be settled in caucus by the delegates themselves after reaching Chicago.

# CHAPTER IV

## THE MUGWUMP CAMPAIGN OF 1884

*"Let us be steadfast in our beliefs, unmoved by clamor, and untempted by an inordinate desire for success at any cost of principle and consistency. Thus will we serve our country best; thus shall we know the joy that mere success can never know."*

—GROVER CLEVELAND.

THE Republican party faced the presidential year 1884 with an accumulation of burdens due in part to long power, in part to the fact that the Civil War had rendered the opposition too long helpless. A strong opposition is as essential to government as is the party in power, a fact which the British recognize in the phrases: "His Majesty's Government" and "His Majesty's Opposition," and when the opposition is silenced, careless administration, ill-considered legislation, and the attendant evils of graft in high places result.

Upon the Democrats, popular judgment had placed the responsibility for rebellion, and the Republican leaders of reconstruction days had not allowed them to escape the full contumely of the verdict, pointing the finger of scorn at them, as a mere faction born for failure and defeat. Thus had the opposition been silenced, and the fact that at no time since reconstruction had the Republicans won at the same time the Presidency, the Senate, and the House had not checked their pride, or curbed their increasing heedlessness. Intent on party gains, which at times they dangerously confused with questions of private interests, they had continued to capitalize error, by proclaiming that it was the Republican party which alone had saved the Union, freed the slave, crushed the menacing head of secession, and preserved a republic which they were therefore entitled to rule. In their plausible and complacent clamorings they forgot how many noble Democrats lay in their narrow graves in North and South, having given their lives for the cause of human freedom and a united republic. They forgot that Sherman and McClellan, Meade and Sheridan, Stanton and Chase, all staunch defenders of the nation, all heroes of the cause, were Democrats. Their party literature and their political speeches failed to recall the fact that even Abraham Lincoln had received his second nomination, not from the Republican party alone, but from a Union convention representing loyal Democrats and Republicans alike. Nor did they recall the fact that even during the dark days of the war Democrats had cast never less than forty-six per cent of the popular vote in the non-seceding states.

When the opposition had again become vocal, it pointed at disgraceful deeds and unprecedented official scandals wrought under the banner of the Republicans. The list is too long to recount in full, but it was not too long for the use of Democratic partisans and reformers of all parties in the campaign of 1884: One Secretary of War had resigned in order to avoid impeachment for bribery. The Navy Department had been a house of refuge for the type of jobber which Mr. Cleveland had faced and conquered as Mayor of Buffalo and as Governor of New York. The Whisky Ring had walked as purchaser in the very colonnades of the Capitol. A Speaker of the House of Representatives, with associates from both halls of Congress, was soiled by connection with the famous Crédit Mobilier.

The cries of the distressed and humiliated apostles of reforms that never came are concentrated in the speech of Senator Hoar of Massachusetts, delivered in connection with the proposed impeachment of Secretary of War Belknap in May, 1876: "My own public life has been a very brief and insignificant one, extending little beyond the duration of a single term of senatorial office. But in this brief period, I have seen five judges of a high court of the United States driven from office by threats of impeachment for corruption or maladministration. . . . I have seen the chairman of the Committee on Military Affairs in the House rise in his place and demand the expulsion of four of his associates for making sale of their official privilege of selecting the youths to be educated at our great military school. When the greatest railroad of the world, binding together the continent and uniting the two great seas which wash our shores, was finished, I have seen our national triumph and exultation turned to bitterness and shame by the unanimous reports of three committees of Congress—two of the House and one here, —that every step of that mighty enterprise had been taken in fraud. I have heard in the highest places the shameless doctrine avowed, by men grown old in public office, that the true way by which power should be gained in the Republic is to bribe the people with the offices created for their service, and the true end for which it should be used when gained is the promotion of selfish ambition and the gratification of personal revenge. I have heard that suspicion haunts the footsteps of the trusted companions of the President."

It was this burden which must fall upon the Republican candidate of 1884, a burden which only giant moral strength, in the shape of a candidate of spotless reputation, could hope to bear. When the Republican National Convention assembled at Chicago, on June 3, 1884, it had many candidates, but one dominant leader, James G. Blaine, a man of brilliant powers and magnetic personality, yet one whose past touched, more or less intimately, the dark spots in the party's recent history. The unsavory memories left by the great railroad frauds still clung to him, although it had been his voice which had demanded investigation. The committee appointed had not managed to connect him with crime, but in the minds of many men his acquittal was the Scotch verdict, "not proven."

In 1876, Blaine had been the strongest leader in the Republican Convention, receiving 351 votes even on the seventh and final ballot, and would almost certainly have been nominated, had not the memory of shocking incidents insisted upon associating themselves with his name. Again, in the convention of 1880, these past scandals had risen in men's minds and he had once more been rejected as a candidate. With such a record behind him, Blaine was quite as vulnerable as he was masterful. But despite his obvious disadvantage, despite the mutterings of revolt among Independents and liberal Republicans bent on reform, the magic of the magnetic statesman, the "white plumed knight" as his adoring followers called him, now at last triumphed and Blaine was nominated.

In placing his name before the convention, Judge William H. West of Ohio employed high language and brilliant epigram: "Four and twenty years of the grandest history in the annals of recorded time have distinguished the ascendency of the Republican party. Skies have lowered, and reverses have threatened. Our flag is still there, waving above the mansion of the Presidency; not a stain on its folds, not a cloud on its glory." At this the advocates of reform doubtless saw a vision of Oakes

Ames, John D. Sanborn, William A. Richardson, Schuyler Colfax, William W. Belknap, and a host of associates, and wondered at the speaker's calm assurance.

"To it," continued Judge West, "are stretched the imploring hands of ten million of political bondmen of the South; while, above, from the portals of light, is looking down the spirit of the immortal martyr who first bore it to victory, bidding us hail and Godspeed. In six campaigns has that symbol of union, of freedom, of humanity, and of progress, been borne in triumph. . . . Shall that banner triumph again?"

As soon as Blaine's nomination was assured, the question began to be whispered about, "What will George William Curtis and his followers do?" Curtis and Carl Schurz were the recognized leaders of the reform movement in the Republican party, and it was not difficult to foresee their open revolt from the leadership proposed for them. To their minds it was no longer a question of Democratic or Republican victory. "Republicans!" cried Schurz, "do you not see that the best Republican principles have already been defeated by that Republican nomination? Do you not see that those principles, which were the great soul of the Republican party, command you to maintain good government at any cost, be it even the timely sacrifice of party ascendency?"

The final decision regarding the attitude of the Independents lay, of course, with the Democrats. Should they name a real reformer, strong Mugwump support was assured by the character of the Republican candidate. Two weeks after the adjournment of the Republican National Convention, Daniel Manning dispatched William C. Hudson to Chicago, to open the Cleveland headquarters at the Palmer House and prepare to receive the delegations as they should arrive. Manning and Lamont had provided him with a list of the New York delegates, arranged in three sections. The first contained the names of those certain to support the Governor; the second, those believed to be opposed to his nomination; and the third, with six or eight names, was labeled "doubtful or undeclared." "If we cannot win these doubtful men," he said to Hudson, "we cannot hope to make a successful presentation of the Governor's name. Now, I want you to devote yourself to these doubtful men. Find out the conditions surrounding them, the influences, political, commercial and moral, . . . and if they are inclined to be against us, find out why. . . . We must subject them to pressure . . . but first we must learn the sort of pressure that should be applied."

Upon reaching Chicago, Hudson found that Tammany Hall had anticipated his methods, for Thomas F. Grady was already at work there "fixing" the local press, but fixing it against the New York Governor, and laying plans to induce the convention to absolve the New York delegation from its instructions. Blaine engines were also at work, seeking to eliminate Cleveland, whom they counted as their leader's most formidable opponent. Skillfully both forces were tampering with the Irish, seeking to make it appear that Grover Cleveland was the irreconcilable enemy of their race, a bigoted Presbyterian, trained to consider the Church of Rome "the Scarlet Woman" of Holy Writ.

The work of counteracting these sinister forces was far from complete when, on July 8th, the Democrats swarmed into the city for their convention. Most conspicuous among these was the Tammany Hall delegation, six hundred strong, headed by John Kelly, the most famous professional politician in America, and known to be there for the express purpose of defeating the dreams of the Cleveland men who had ventured to push a New York Democrat without the advice and consent of the organization. Crowds had met the "Tigers" at the station, and had wondered at their numbers as they defiled from their two special trains. Only a few wore delegates' badges, but all were there to intimidate the convention and defeat Cleveland.

Although generally recognized as the leading candidate, Cleveland was to these Tammany men only an enemy of the order, a Democrat who had refused to divide the spoils and must be made to pay the penalty of his insurgency. They had watched his career, and were determined to have a candidate of less downright methods. Nor had they forgotten the Grady letter and the Governor's denunciation of boss rule and Tammany methods in his interview with the New York *Herald,* reported shortly after the state elections of 1883.

In addition to the traditional two-thirds rule which Martin Van Buren and Andrew Jackson had created for the Democratic party in 1832, this particular convention declared that no state delegation should alter its vote until the completion of the roll call. The New York Convention had instructed its delegation to cast its seventy-two votes for the candidate favored by a majority of its members, but it was by no means certain whom that majority favored. The work of putting pressure upon the doubtful New York delegates had not yet succeeded to the point of making Cleveland sure of the support of his own state on the first ballot. Even on the morning fixed for the decision Manning was in doubt, for two New York delegates had mysteriously disappeared, and the most careful search had failed to discover them. When at last they were found and led into the meeting of the state delegation, confesses Hudson, "one of them bore the promise of . . . a state office. . . . The two made the majority by which Cleveland was named in that caucus, on the last day before the meeting of the convention. . . . 'By what small chances do we live in history.' "

Thus, when the convention opened, Cleveland was sure of the entire New York vote on the first ballot, unless the Tammany delegates could devise some method of breaking down the unit rule. Accordingly, on the first day of the convention, Mr. Thomas F. Grady moved that the National Convention absolve the New York delegation from its obligation to obey the instructions of the State Convention. This bold move failed, and, in failing, strengthened Mr. Cleveland's chances, as 463 of the 792 delegates who voted refused to sanction this movement to rob him of his delegates. Their refusal was due not so much to superior virtue as to the attitude of the Independent Republicans, the so-called "Mugwumps," whose many votes were waiting for the Democratic ballot box, should a candidate be nominated who could be trusted to carry out reform. Blaine's nomination had resulted in the formation of independent committees in Boston and New York, which had opened correspondence with anti-Blaine factions throughout the nation; and these had intimated their purpose to vote the Democratic ticket, should a suitable candidate be named by the Chicago convention.

On the second day the real struggle began. The venerable Samuel J. Tilden, in a letter to Daniel Manning, Chairman of the Democratic State Committee of New York, had definitely declared his desire that his name should not be considered. "I ought not," he said, "to assume a task which I have not the physical strength to carry through. . . . To reform the administration of the Federal Government, to realize my own ideal, and to fulfill the just expectations of the people, would indeed warrant . . . the sacrifices which the undertaking would involve. But in my condition of advancing years and declining strength, I feel no assurance of my ability to accomplish these objects. I am, therefore, constrained to say, definitely, that I cannot assume the labors of an administration or of a canvass."

The field was, therefore, open for younger men, and the first name presented was that of Senator Thomas F. Bayard, whom Governor Cleveland considered the most desirable of the candidates. Thomas A. Hendricks was next recognized by the chair, and presented the name of Joseph E. McDonald as the unanimous choice of the State of Indiana. Allen G. Thurman and John G. Carlisle were then proposed; and Daniel N. Lockwood mounted the platform to present the name of Grover Cleveland. His words were effective, for they were the recital of achievement, and of recent achievement.

"A little more than three years ago," he said, "I had the honor at the city of Buffalo to present the name of this same gentleman for the office of mayor of that city. It was presented then for the same reason, and from the same causes, that we present it now. It was because the government of that city had become corrupt, had become debauched, and political integrity sat not in high places. The people looked for a man who would represent honest government, and without any hesitation they named Grover Cleveland.

"The result of that election and of his holding that office was, that in less than nine months the State of New York found herself in a position to want just such a candidate and for just such a purpose. At the State Convention of 1882 his name was placed in nomination for the office of Governor of the State of New York. The same people, the same class of people, knew that that meant honest government, it meant pure government, it meant Democratic government, and it was ratified; and, gentlemen, now, after eighteen months of service there the Democracy of the State of New York come to you and ask you to go to the country, to go to the independent and Democratic voters of the country, to go to the young men of the country, the new blood of the country, and present the name of Grover Cleveland as your standard bearer."

Instantly Mr. Grady presented the objections of the Tammany group, and in reply Mr. E. K. Apgar pointed to the reform element and warned the convention of impending defeat should the counsels of the Tammany delegates prevail.

"There are," he said, "a hundred thousand men in the State of New York who do not care a snap of their finger whether the Republican party or the Democratic party, as such, shall carry the election. They vote in every election according to the issues and the candidates presented. These men absolutely hold the control of the politics of New York in their hands. They are the balance of power. You must have their vote or you cannot win. . . . These men unitedly, to a man, implore you to nominate . . . Governor Tilden's successor, elected Governor for the same causes. They ask you to place him in nomination in order that all elements opposed to the longer continuance of the Republican party in power may be united and make its defeat certain."

Other nominations and other speeches followed, but the name of Grover Cleveland continued to be the center of enthusiasm, an enthusiasm which was raised to a clamor by the brilliant eulogium of Governor Edward S. Bragg of Wisconsin, who, voicing the sentiment of the young

men of the West, declared, "They love him most for the
enemies he has made." In these words he gave a campaign cry, certain to echo and re-echo throughout a nation
grown weary of machine rule, and ever responsive to attacks upon Tammany Hall.

At midnight of the third day the first ballot was taken,
and Kelly was forced by the still unrepealed unit rule
to cast Tammany's vote for the Governor of New York
whom he so ardently desired to defeat. Grover Cleveland
received more than twice as many votes as any other candidate, but still lacked the necessary two-thirds majority.

### FIRST BALLOT

Total number of votes ................. 820

Votes necessary to nomination .......... 547

| | | | |
|---|---|---|---|
| Cleveland .... | 392 | Carlisle ...... | 27 |
| Bayard ...... | 170 | Flower ...... | 4 |
| Thurman .... | 88 | Hoadley .... | 3 |
| Randall ..... | 78 | Hendricks ... | 1 |
| McDonald ... | 56 | Tilden ...... | 1 |

A careful study of the details of this ballot greatly encouraged the Cleveland men. His 392 votes came from
thirty-eight of the forty-seven states and territories represented in the convention. This indicated a national enthusiasm, and meant that he would soon fall heir to many
votes which had been given, on the first ballot, to favorite
sons. At this point, to the consternation of many Cleveland men, Manning effected an adjournment. He had
noticed that many of the older delegates had left the hall,
and feared that a second ballot might show fewer votes
for Cleveland.

John Kelly, Benjamin F. Butler, and other foes of the
Governor of New York spent the small hours of the night

staging a stampede for Thomas A. Hendricks. In connivance with the sergeant-at-arms, they packed the galleries with men pledged to raise the cry of "Hendricks for
President," as soon as the well-known Indiana delegate
should appear at the morning session. These plans
Manning discovered, and skillfully nullified by sending
a messenger to each member of the convention, warning
him of the plot. When at the appointed hour, therefore,
Hendricks made his appearance before the convention,
the galleries rang with shouts and applause; but the delegations sat unmoved. Only the little knot of Tammany
delegates joined in the cry for "Hendricks! Hendricks!"

As the second ballot proceeded, it became more and
more evident that the intrigues of the past night had not
weakened the Cleveland forces. Randall's friends withdrew his name. McDonald's Indiana delegation was
transferred to the column of Governor Hendricks.
Illinois announced thirty-eight votes for Grover Cleveland, and New York gave him seventy-two, despite the
objections of Tammany Hall. As state after state was
called, Cleveland's column steadily increased, and Thomas
A. Hendricks's total also mounted, though less rapidly.
When the roll call was ended, it was evident that Cleveland's strength was irresistible, although he was still
seventy-two votes short of a two-thirds majority. At once
delegation after delegation eagerly clamored for recognition by the chair, in order that it might change its votes
to the winning candidate; and, at one o'clock, when the
revised ballot was read, Cleveland showed a total of 683
votes, 136 more than the number required for nomination.
Tammany was beaten again by Grover Cleveland, and
the hall resounded with the cry: "We love him for the
enemies he has made."

The following table shows the final result:

Cleveland ..................... 683
Bayard ........................ 81½
Hendricks ..................... 45½
Randall ....................... 4
Thurman ...................... 4
McDonald ..................... 2

Governor Hendricks was then nominated as the vice-presidential candidate, and the convention, after singing "Praise God from Whom All Blessings Flow," adjourned, to face a fiercer fight upon a wider stage.

During the meeting of the Chicago convention, Governor Cleveland remained at his post in Albany, disposing of his executive work in his usual methodical manner. The *World's* Albany dispatch tells the story of how he received the news of his nomination:

"It was 1:45 p. m. when General Farnsworth heard what he supposed to be a cannon shot. He held up his hand, exclaiming, 'Listen!' The wind was westerly, but the next and succeeding shots were distinctly heard, and it was known that Cleveland was nominated, the first dispatch to the Governor being received a few moments later.

"General Farnsworth, after hearing the second shot, jumped up and exclaimed: 'They are firing a salute, Governor, over your nomination.'

" 'That's what it means,' added Colonel Lamont.

" 'Do you think so?' said the Governor, quietly. 'Well,' he continued, 'anyhow, we'll finish up this work.'

"The work was resumed, and General Farnsworth began reading again from his proof.

"In a couple of minutes the telephone rang, and a

voice said: 'Tell the Governor he has been nominated on the second ballot.' Lamont repeated the words.

" 'Is that so, Dan?' said the Governor, as his face brightened up for the first time. 'By jove, that is something, isn't it?'

"All present at once tendered their congratulations and Colonel Lamont grew enthusiastic. Suddenly the Governor said:

" 'Dan, I wish you would telephone the news to the Mansion. Sister will want to hear it. . . .'

"Telegrams now began pouring in, and during the day and evening some 1,500 were received."

That evening Albany was illuminated and the nominee reviewed a parade in which 5000 of his fellow citizens marched, after which he delivered his first message as a national figure:

"Fellow-Citizens: . . . The American people are about to exercise, in its highest sense, their power of right and sovereignty. They are to call in review before them their public servants and the representatives of political parties, and demand of them an account of their stewardship.

"Parties may be so long in power, and may become so arrogant and careless of the interests of the people, as to grow heedless of their responsibility to their masters. But the time comes, as certainly as death, when the people weigh them in the balance.

"The issues to be adjudicated by the nation's great assize are made up and are about to be submitted. We believe that the people are not receiving at the hands of the party which for nearly twenty-four years has directed the affairs of the nation, the full benefits to which they are entitled, of a pure, just and economical rule; and we believe that the ascendency of genuine Democratic principles will insure a better government, and greater happiness and prosperity to all the people.

"To reach the sober thought of the nation, and to dislodge an enemy intrenched behind spoils and patronage involve a struggle, which, if we underestimate, we invite defeat. I am profoundly impressed with the responsibility of the part assigned to me in this contest. My heart, I know, is in the cause, and I pledge you that no effort of mine shall be wanting to secure the victory which I believe to be within the achievement of the Democratic hosts.

"Let us, then, enter upon the campaign now fairly opened, each one appreciating well the part he has to perform, ready, with solid front, to do battle for better government, confidently, courageously, always honorably, and with a firm reliance upon the intelligence and patriotism of the American people."

Among the Democrats who had witnessed the nomination at Chicago, the first to reach Albany was the well-known reporter, William C. Hudson. He at once called upon the Governor, and was told that the first move would be the preparation of a campaign document, to embody the outstanding achievements of the candidate's past political career. This Hudson was asked to write, and he at once began the work of studying Mr. Cleveland's state papers and public addresses in search of material.

Daniel Lamont, Francis Lynde Stetson, and other Cleveland leaders were consulted, and when the manuscript was complete, Hudson, with the newspaper man's habit of headlines, searched for a phrase to head the appeal. He recalled the fact that in the Democratic national platform of 1876 had appeared these words: "Presidents, vice-presidents, judges, senators, representatives, cabinet officers—these and all others in authority are the people's servants. Their offices are not a private perquisite; they are a public trust."

In studying Mr. Cleveland's own speeches and messages, he discovered that the same idea of trusteeship was again and again repeated. In accepting the nomination for Mayor of Buffalo in 1881, Mr. Cleveland had said: "Public officials are the trustees of the people, and hold their places and exercise their powers for the benefit of the people." In his first annual message as Mayor of Buffalo, he had declared: "We are the trustees and agents of our fellow citizens, holding their funds in sacred trust." In accepting the nomination as Governor of New York, he had phrased the idea even more clumsily: "Public officers are the servants and agents of the people, to execute laws which the people have made and within the limits of a constitution which they have established."

Clearly none of these sentences could serve as a head-line. Therefore, writes Hudson, "I went at the making of one. . . . Public Office is a Public Trust was the result. . . . It was the dogmatic form of what he had expressed with greater elucidation. . . . I took it to the Governor for his inspection. His eye at once went to the top line and, pointing to it, he asked:

" 'Where the deuce did I say that?'

" 'You've said it a dozen times publicly, but not in those few words,' I replied.

" 'That's so,' he said. 'That's what I believe. That's what I've said a little better because more fully.'

" 'But this has the merit of brevity,' I persisted, 'and that is what is required here. The question is, Will you stand for this form?'

" 'Oh, yes,' replied the Governor. 'That's what I believe. I'll stand for it and make it my own.' "

Within a few hours the country was ringing with

"Grover Cleveland's greatest phrase: 'Public Office is a Public Trust.'" But throughout the campaign, and throughout the remainder of his life, Grover Cleveland continued to express this, his most cherished conviction, not in the words of Hudson's brilliant slogan, but in ponderous phrases of his own which he persisted in considering better because longer.

Mr. Cleveland's nomination aroused again in the hearts of the advocates of reform those hopes which campaign promises had so often deceived. "The Democratic party," declared Carl Schurz, speaking for the reform group called "Mugwumps," "has never presented a candidate whom any friend of good government, Democratic or Republican, could see step into the presidential chair with a greater feeling of security." From the first it was evident that Mr. Cleveland would receive a very large percentage of the votes of reformers of whatever party, although Theodore Roosevelt expressed the opinion, "Civil service is not safer in Mr. Cleveland's hands than in Mr. Blaine's," an opinion which he dramatically defended in an article in the *North American Review* a year later, but subsequently repudiated.

A careful survey of Mr. Cleveland's political career soon convinced the Republican campaign leaders that nothing could be gained by turning public attention in that direction. His record was above criticism. He had administered his public trusts with admirable efficiency. He had never shown a trace of the spirit of the demagogue, nor had he permitted the dictation of party machines, having frankly defied the authority of Tammany Hall and its masterful chief boss. He had, in the most literal sense, administered public office as a public trust, and even their ingenuity could not make a case against him.

For a time they turned to the old sectional issue, the dangers which would follow a too-controlling voice of the solid South. The negroes were warned that the election of a Democrat to the Presidency would be speedily followed by a restoration of slavery. Sectional hostilities which had begun to fade by reason of lapse of time and wise methods of conciliation were eagerly revived. But a new generation had come upon the scene, which could not be greatly moved by the "waving of the bloody shirt."

The tariff issue was then attempted, and special interests summoned to the fight. They responded eagerly, but tariff could not be made to appeal to the mass of voters, as the Democrats had reassured their minds by the platform declaration: "The Democratic party is pledged to revise the tariff in a spirit of fairness to all interests. But in making reductions in taxes, it is not proposed to injure any domestic industries, but rather to promote their healthy growth." They had also been cautious enough to assure voters of their determination to protect the higher rate of wages then prevailing.

In New York, the Tammany organization worked in harmony with the special interests to the advantage of Blaine, until Mr. Hendricks, a good machine Democrat of the old school, was sent to deal with Kelly, when the Tammany machine consented to give a grudging support to the candidate of its own party. That no concession by way of party graft would be made to them by Mr. Cleveland they well knew. During the entire campaign he insisted that there should be no trafficking in offices, no yielding to pressure from machine men. "I had rather be beaten . . ." he wrote to Lamont, "than to truckle to Butler or Kelly. I don't want any pledge made for me that will violate my professions or betray and deceive the good people that believe in me."

The white light of legitimate political criticism having failed, the unprincipled element had recourse to the red light of personal defamation, and the campaign became, as Andrew D. White expressed it, "the vilest political campaign ever waged." When we recall the days of 1800, when Aaron Burr and Thomas Jefferson faced one another in a conflict which threatened civil war; the election of 1824, when Andrew Jackson and his ruthless partisans were fixing upon Clay the false charge of "bargain and corruption"; and the election of 1876, when the nation was on the verge of war over the question whether Tilden or Hayes had been elected, this statement seems extreme. But no one even casually familiar with the details of Mr. Cleveland's first race for the Presidency can doubt that there were excellent reasons for this opinion.

From the first, the Mugwump attacks upon Mr. Blaine were violent and offensively personal. "The Republican National Convention," Carl Schurz declared, soon after the nomination, "has with brutal directness . . . forced upon the country . . . a man whose unclean record it cannot deny and dare not face," words which, re-echoed by many Mugwump speakers, left no doubt as to the answer to the oft-repeated question, "What will George William Curtis and his followers do?" Obviously they intended to parade the shades of old associates whom Mr. Blaine desired forgotten, and to interpret Scotch verdicts as though they had been convictions.

Neither could there be any doubt what the Blaine men would do, in the face of such attacks upon their leader. Under the conditions, the retort courteous could hardly have been expected from politicians intent upon winning for their party the greatest elective office in the world. Unable, however, to point to corresponding questionable incidents in the public life of the Democratic nominee, they flooded the country with personal slanders concerning his private life, interpreting vague rumor as demonstrated truth, and incidental truth as typical of a life the general rectitude of which was beyond question.

Mr. Cleveland generously attempted to shield his opponent from attacks of a similar character. Upon one occasion, his friends purchased papers to be used as the basis of an attack upon Mr. Blaine's private life. When they were placed in the Governor's hands he tore them into tiny bits, and threw the pieces into the fire, with the remark, "The other side can have a monopoly of all the dirt in this campaign."

But despite Mr. Cleveland's desires to the contrary, scandalous stories were circulated concerning Mr. Blaine's private life, which even the generous efforts of his opponent could not recall. "I am glad you wrote as you did in regard to the Blaine scandal," Mr. Cleveland said to Lamont on August 14th. "I am very sorry it was printed, and I hope it will die out at once." It did not die out, however, and James G. Blaine, whose private life is now admitted to have been above reproach, was paraded in cartoon and story as "the tattooed man"; while Grover Cleveland became, in the hands of unscrupulous slanderers, a man without honor, moral sensibility, or sense of shame.

Unskilled in sophistry and new to the darker ways of national politics, Grover Cleveland faced his accusers, his slanderers, and his judges, the sovereign people, conscious of the general rectitude of his life, and courageously determined to bear the burdens of his sins in so far as guilt was his. When his friend, Charles W. Goodyear, reported that a particularly violent attack was to be made upon him by the enemy press the following day, regarding an incident in his earlier life, and asked what to say in reply, Cleveland telegraphed: "Whatever you say, tell the truth." And his friends told the truth, echoing his confession from platform, press, and pulpit. They properly denied, however, the inferences which his enemies drew from his confession, insisting and establishing by incontrovertible evidence that in general Grover Cleveland's private life was as creditable as even his enemies admitted his public life to have been.

His opponents next turned their energies to the idea of weakening his hold upon the northern wing of the Democratic party, who resented the unjust accusation, so frequently made, that, by virtue of membership in their party, they had favored disunion. To make it appear that the Democratic candidate, though sound of health and of military age, had been unwilling to respond to Lincoln's call to arms in 1861 seemed certain to bring about the desertion of this element, which was essential to Mr. Cleveland's success. They therefore industriously circulated the story that he had dishonorably escaped service during the Civil War by sending a convict to fight in his place. The effect of this form of attack was soon apparent, especially in Grand Army circles, and every effort was made to get the real circumstances of his exemption from service before the country. The facts were as follows: His two brothers, Richard Cecil and Louis Frederick, had enlisted in the Union Army, having elected Grover to remain at home. According to Mr. George F. Parker, Mr. Cleveland gave him the following account of how the decision was reached:

"When the war came there were three men of fighting age in our family. We were poor, and mother and sisters depended on us for support. We held a family council and decided that two of us should enlist in the United States Army and the third stay at home for the support of the family. We decided it by drawing cuts. The two long and one short pieces of paper were put by mother in the leaves of the old family Bible. She held it while we drew. My brothers drew the long slips, and at once enlisted, and I abided by my duty to the helpless women."

Later he was drafted, and for the same reason exercised his legal right provided in the Enrollment Act of March 3, 1863, to hire a substitute. The hiring of the substitute instead of asking for exemption was to his credit, as the Enrollment Act contained a clause under which he might reasonably have claimed exemption. But he made no such claim, preferring to answer the call of his country by the payment of money which the law declared the honest equivalent of the personal service which he was unable to give.

In view of these facts, it was not difficult for Mr. Cleveland to justify his conduct to anyone willing to examine a rather complicated set of circumstances. But this could not be expected of the great voting public in the midst of a presidential campaign. The charge was easy to circulate, the refutation extremely difficult. In October, 1884, the junior vice-commandant of the Koltes Post, New York City, sent the Governor a copy of a circular letter, bearing the signatures of two war veterans, and making the charge that Grover Cleveland's substitute was a convict. In response to the vice-commandant's friendly request for a denial, to be circulated over the candidate's own signature, the following answer was promptly returned:

Executive Mansion, Albany, *Oct. 24, 1884.*
MR. GEORGE F. DOGE:
My dear Sir:
Your letter of the 23rd, inclosing copy of a circular issued at Buffalo for distribution to the veteran soldiers

of the State, is received, and I thank you for calling my attention to this new development of political mendacity.

So far as this circular has any reference to me it is in all respects calculated to deceive, and in all prejudicial statements it is absolutely false.

I was drafted the first day the draft was put in operation. Being then assistant district attorney, I had plenty of opportunity to secure a convict substitute with no expense, and, in fact, was urged to do so. I refused, however, and hired a man to go who was a sailor on the lakes, and who had just arrived in port and been paid off. I don't know that he was ever arrested, and I am sure he was not a convict. I borrowed the money to pay him for going as my substitute, and I think before I paid him he had more money than I had. I often heard from him while he was in the service, and I saw him quite frequently after he returned.

If he is alive yet I don't think either of the noble veterans who signed this circular would care to meet him after he had read it.

I know Mr. Lyth and Mr. Oatman, whose names are appended to the circular, and I am astonished to find them in such business.

Yours very truly,
GROVER CLEVELAND.

This seemed to some of Mr. Cleveland's eager supporters a poor method of playing the game. Allowing their candidate to go his own way, they proceeded to hunt up, or make up, a substitute for Mr. Blaine, whose heart, they scornfully declared, "prompted him to rush to the front and dye his hands in the blood of rebels, but whose legs wouldn't move a peg."

The Irish vote in 1884 was, as now, of great importance, especially in the State of New York, and Mr. Blaine was in an advantageous position with reference to it, as his mother was a Roman Catholic. Toward the end of October, after a strenuous speech-making tour in the Middle West, Blaine arrived in New York, where he received, at his quarters in the Fifth Avenue Hotel, a delegation of clergymen, ardent reformers who had refused to follow their Mugwump brethren into the Cleveland ranks. Unfortunately for the candidate whom they sought to serve, their leader, Dr. Samuel Burchard, was primed with an epoch-making address—how epoch-making he little suspected. Blaine seemed to listen, but his mind apparently wandered; for otherwise his trained political judgment would surely have suppressed the orator's finest phrase: "We are Republicans, and don't propose to leave our party and identify ourselves with the party whose antecedents have been Rum, Romanism, and Rebellion."

It was one of those alliterative sentences which should never be allowed to pass without careful inspection. To his sorrow, Blaine failed to inspect it, and it charged the ranks of his Irish Catholic friends and scattered them like "the chaff which the wind driveth away."

"The Burchard accident," writes John Devoy in his pamphlet, 'Cleveland and the Irish,' "occurring at the last moment, turned back just enough of the Irish seceders to give New York by a miserably meager majority to the Mugwumps." "From Rum, Romanism and Rebellion," said the New York *World,* ". . . Mr. Blaine proceeded to a merry banquet of the millionaires at Delmonico's, where champagne frothed and brandy sparkled in glasses that glittered like jewels. The clergymen would have been proud of Mr. Blaine, no doubt, if they had seen him in the midst of the mighty winebibbers. It was Mr. Blaine's black Wednesday."

Of these incidents the Cleveland press, of course, made the freest possible use, interpreting them in the manner most likely to aid the cause of their candidate; and in New York there was added the wrath of Roscoe Conkling, who cherished a bitter personal hatred of Mr. Blaine, on account of a speech delivered eighteen years before, in which the powerful Senator from New York had been paraded as "a grandiloquent swell" with a "turkey-gobbler strut."

Blaine suffered also by virtue of a labor conflict then raging between the New York *Tribune* and Typographical Union Number Six, the "Big Six," as it called itself. It was a vicarious atonement; for neither Blaine nor his party was directly concerned in the conflict, which had been in progress for many months. The *Tribune* had discharged certain union workmen, and had failed to carry out certain contracts made with the union. As Blaine was the Republican candidate, and as the Republican National Convention of 1884 had refused to repudiate the *Tribune,* its official organ, the "Big Six" declared against Blaine, and worked for Grover Cleveland, influencing, perhaps, enough votes to tip the scale in the close contest in New York State.

When the polls opened the tension of uncertainty pervaded the nation; Democrats and Republicans alike, while openly professing full confidence of victory, secretly entertained forebodings of defeat. And when the polls were closed, and the returns began to be circulated, the uncertainty increased, and with it whisperings of possible things worse even than defeat.

It was soon evident that Cleveland had carried Connecticut, Indiana, New Jersey, and the solid South; but

New York was essential to victory, and her choice remained uncertain. The *Sun,* then a greenbacker, and therefore no friend to Mr. Cleveland, conceded his election; but the Associated Press, which received returns, not by counties but by election districts, insisted that it was a Republican victory. Mr. Cleveland wisely kept his own counsel, and waited for a definite verdict.

Three days later the leading New York City dailies, with the exception of the *Tribune,* agreed that Cleveland had been chosen. Republican politicians, however, accepted the view of the *Tribune,* that Blaine was elected; and the Democrats became alarmed, recalling the election of 1876, when their opponents had snatched victory from their hands by counting out Samuel J. Tilden, the choice of the nation. "Perhaps," they whispered, "that game is to be tried again." When the Republican National Committee, in spite of the inconclusive returns, boldly declared, "There is no ground for doubt that the honest vote of this State has been given to the Republican candidate," hot-headed Democrats talked of violence. The streets of New York took on a dangerously tense atmosphere as the eager crowds, waiting for further returns, called for the hanging of Jay Gould, and manifested other tendencies disconcerting to Blaine's supporters.

Still Mr. Cleveland gave no expression of opinion, and worked at his tasks as Governor as though conditions were normal, allowing no detail of official duty to escape him. On the tenth day after the election, the Republicans were forced to concede the choice of Cleveland. And upon receiving the news, he remarked: "I am glad of it; very glad. There will now be no trouble. If they had not, I should have felt it my duty to take my seat anyhow." His victory at the polls, when all the figures were in, proved scant indeed. He had carried New York by only 1047 votes, though his supporters insisted that, but for the influence of Blaine's money, this majority would have been at least 50,000.

It is quite evident, however, that the Blaine money was not the only money used in the campaign. The Democrats liberally financed their leaders, as a memorandum preserved among the papers of Colonel Lamont clearly proves. It is dated February 5, 1885, and presents a list of "Contributors to the Campaign Fund of the National Democratic Committee, 1884." The largest single item is: "William H. Barnum, $27,500." William L. Scott, of Erie, Pennsylvania, is credited with a gift of $24,000, Cooper-Hewitt $20,000, Oswald Ottendorfer $18,000, R. P. Flower and D. Willis James $16,000 each, William C. Whitney $15,250, A. P. Gorman $14,908.25, Daniel Manning, Albany, $13,675. The memorandum totals $453,126.61, a large sum for the year 1884; but the list includes no contributions from Grover Cleveland, although a letter to Bissell shows that he contributed at one time $5,000. "I send you . . . my check on Albany for $3,500," he wrote on September 11th, "and on Buffalo for $1,500, making up my subscription to the National Committee." It is, therefore, fair to assume that even the grand total of almost half a million dollars does not tell the whole story of the campaign funds of the Democrats.

Mr. Cleveland's letters, from the date of the first mention of his name in connection with the Presidency, show how fully he realized the burden of responsibility which goes with that office; and after his election, he spoke at times like a doomed man. "I look upon the four years next to come," he wrote to Bissell, in acknowledging his victory, "as a dreadful, self-inflicted penance for the good of my country. I can see no pleasure in it, and no satisfaction, only a hope that I may be of service to my people."

The first mad rush of triumphant Democrats seeking office appalled him. "I am sick at heart and perplexed in brain during the most of my working hours," he wrote to Bissell, on December 25th. "I almost think the professions of most of my pretended friends are but the means they employ to accomplish personal and selfish ends. It's so hard to discover their springs of action, and it seems so forlorn to feel that on the question as to who shall be trusted, I should be so much at sea. I wonder if I must for the third time face the difficulties of a new official life almost *alone*."

# CHAPTER V

## ALONE IN THE WHITE HOUSE

*"The President, and the President alone, represents the
American citizen, no matter how humble or in how remote a
corner of the globe."*

—GROVER CLEVELAND.

A FEW days after his election to the Presidency,
while walking with an intimate friend in the outskirts of Buffalo, Mr. Cleveland exclaimed, "Henceforth
I must have no friends." From that moment, in his apparently simple personality, men discovered two per-
sonalities—the one, as of old, genial and approachable,
with a capacity for delightful intimacies; the other, an
official self, austere, forbidding. He loved his friends,
but when conscious of an attempt to capitalize friendship, to gain executive favors by virtue of personal connections with the President of the United States, the
kindly, often humorous, lines of his face hardened into
bronze, and he became cold and unapproachable. He
would, in such humor, lose a friend or make an enemy
without apparent emotion, for his attitude toward appointments was unchangeable: "A personal use of a
trusteeship is at war with its spirit, and gratifying myself and my friends by the use of public offices, simply
because I have the power to do so, would be malfeasance
in fact, though I was accused of it nowhere except in my
own conscience."

But though no pressure, however strong, could make
him recede from this determination, he gladly paid

tribute to friendship wherever it could be done without sacrifice of these standards. During the winter preceding the inauguration, a distinguished lawyer who had ardently supported his campaign was recommended for the post of Attorney General. He had the backing of many of the new President's intimate associates, and the plea was advanced that one of his near relatives, now dead, had been a law partner of the President in the Buffalo days. But the appeal fell on deaf ears. The President-elect did not consider the candidate the best choice for the high office which he sought, and declined to appoint him. The cry of ingratitude, so often heard by Mr. Cleveland during his troubled days at Washington, was of course raised, but he calmly went his way, to all intents and purposes unmoved by the attacks which in truth deeply grieved him.

Some time later, a friend of the dead partner sought out the latter's grave in a cemetery three hundred miles from Buffalo and found that a handsome monument had been erected over the grave which bore every evidence of regular care and attention. He inquired of a gardener as to who was responsible, and learned that three years before Grover Cleveland had ordered the monument and had set aside a stated sum for the care of the grave. Grover Cleveland, the man, had paid this loving tribute to his dead friend, out of his own purse; but Grover Cleveland, the President, declined to honor a draft upon the people's offices made in his name. And under the stinging charge of ingratitude he did not reveal the secret of that dead friend's grave.

It has been said that a President is known by the appointments he makes. And this is partly true. A small President is likely to choose small men to surround him, unwilling to invite the co-operation of great minds, lest his own be dwarfed by comparison. As an appointing agent Mr. Cleveland was not inerrant, but his mistakes came from no such petty jealousies. The average of his appointments is high as compared with any executive of his time, nor did he in his choice of men make secret concessions to standards which he was unwilling to profess openly.

He began selecting a Cabinet as soon as the November elections were over, his plan being to allow the names of contemplated appointees to reach the public early, in order that there might be the fullest criticism before they were sent to the Senate for confirmation. Like Lincoln, he had directed his friends to make no bargains which would bind him if elected. Like Lincoln, when elected, he found that bargains had been made which he now felt in honor bound to recognize, even against his own desires.

Bayard, for example, if we may accept the testimony of St. Clair McKelway, he wished to appoint as Secretary of the Treasury; but, these covenants preventing, Bayard was instead made Secretary of State, in which great office he interpreted the best traditions and the loftiest ideals of the nation. After the turmoil of office was over, after Mr. Bayard was dead, his Chief thus recorded his mature estimate of the man whom he had chosen to lead in his first Cabinet: "Nothing good said of Mr. Bayard could be beyond the truth, and his life furnishes the best possible example of patriotic devotion to country and duty." And the American people have very generally accepted that verdict.

William F. Vilas of Wisconsin was among the first to be recommended for a cabinet position. As Chairman of the National Democratic Convention, and Chairman of the Notification Committee sent officially to inform Mr. Cleveland of his selection as the party candidate in

1884, he was distinctly a national figure; and in addition his strength lay chiefly in the great Northwest, where the Democrats were eager to hold the ground already gained. Mr. Cleveland therefore appointed him Postmaster General.

William C. Endicott, whom he chose for Secretary of War, was backed by the Massachusetts Independents. He had been the Democratic candidate for Governor in 1884, and, as a Judge on the Supreme Bench of the state, he had proved his ability, his soundness, and his breadth of view.

For Secretary of the Navy, Mr. Cleveland selected William C. Whitney, who had shown such consummate skill during the campaign in New York that he had come to be looked upon as a Democratic machine politician, in spite of the fact that he had given effective aid to Tilden in destroying the Tweed Ring. He was a man of independent means, excellent education, and high social position, widely known in many and varied circles, including that of the sportsman.

In 1882, while in Syracuse as a delegate to the New York State Democratic Convention, Mr. Whitney had run in to advise with "Dan" Manning as to the best means of defeating Flower for the governorship. As he entered Manning's office, he noticed a large, portly gentleman comfortably seated, and evidently waiting for an interview. Bowing politely, Whitney passed on to Manning's chair, where he urged the latter to unite with the county Democracy of New York and nominate "that man Cleveland from Buffalo." He later learned to his surprise that, at the interview, "that man Cleveland from Buffalo" had himself been present, in the person of the portly gentleman in the chair.

Through the influence of Mr. Tilden, Whitney had

been appointed Corporation Counsel of New York City, in which post he had made a brilliant record. His private fortune, supplemented by his marriage with a daughter of the Standard Oil magnate, Henry B. Payne, enabled him to play politics with a liberal hand, and in 1884 he had been an important member of the inner group which had engineered the Cleveland nomination. His wealth, his connections, and his effective partisan services were, of course, pleaded as reasons against his nomination. But Mr. Cleveland, after carefully examining the situation, felt that Mr. Whitney's appointment was for the best interests of the country, and his name remained on the list despite protests.

For two of the three remaining cabinet posts, the Department of the Interior and the office of Attorney General, Mr. Cleveland turned to the ranks of the late Confederate Government, thereby emphasizing his determination that, so far as his Administration was concerned, there should no longer be a North and a South. Lucius Q. C. Lamar, his choice for Secretary of the Interior, had drafted the Mississippi Ordinance of Secession in 1861, and had served for two years in the Confederate Army. But he had been wise enough to recognize the end when it came, and in his services to his reunited country had won a position which entitled him to recognition as a representative of the new South. The announcement that his name was considered for such a post was a signal for a flood of protests. "As a Union soldier," wrote one protestant, ". . . I beg to remind the President-elect that the Pension Bureau, with its three hundred thousand pension claims of Union soldiers still unsettled, is in this department, and I can imagine what will be said all through the North and at every Grand Army Post over such a selection." The President-elect was himself quite able to imagine what would be said, but he was not thinking in terms of Grand Army posts, but of a nation reunited after civil war. Lamar remained on the slate, and, as Cabinet officer and later as a Supreme Court Judge, he fully justified the courageous independence which had given him his chance. Of him, Chief Justice Fuller declared: "His was the most suggestive mind that I ever knew."

In the selection of Augustus H. Garland as Attorney General, President Cleveland did even greater violence to the opinions of such men as could not forget, such victors as thought it wise to be ungenerous. Garland, once Governor of Arkansas and now a United States Senator, had been a member of the Confederate Congress. But, like Lamar, he had accepted the verdict of trial by combat, and had worked wisely and effectively toward a reunion of hearts, North and South. "To him," wrote fifty members of the Arkansas Legislature, "we are most indebted for our restoration to an equal place in the Union, and equal representation in the national councils." And Samuel J. Tilden emphasized his fitness for office by expressing the opinion that he ought not to be taken out of the Senate at the beginning of a Democratic administration.

Daniel Manning was selected as Secretary of the Treasury, partly in fulfillment of campaign promises made contrary to Mr. Cleveland's orders, but not entirely so. During the winter and spring following the election, letters urging his appointment had come from many men, representing varied interests and shades of political opinion—bank presidents, lawyers, politicians, journalists. In addition, Mr. Cleveland knew, from personal contact, that Manning was both able and honest, a type of leader whom he delighted to honor. When, therefore, at the very end of the process of cabinet making, Mr. Cleveland, for the first time, asked Mr. Tilden's opinion, he was quite ready to concede what the latter asked—and Manning, to quote from a letter of Tilden to Watterson, "was coerced into the Treasury." In a letter to McKelway, Manning thus avowed his distaste for the position: "I came here unwillingly in the performance of a duty that carried with it, so far as I am concerned, no tinge of ambition. I shall go on, doing that duty . . . at a very considerable sacrifice, only for the sake of the party, whose principles I inherited and came to love as I grew to the years of manhood. I would very gladly return home, any day, to private life. . . . I shall eagerly welcome the opportunity for such a return whenever it occurs, the sooner the better." Through his close personal relations with Mr. Manning, Mr. Tilden exerted a strong influence upon the financial policies of the Cleveland Administration, and these all looked toward the preservation of the gold standard.

In these cabinet selections, which were complete before Inauguration Day, the President-elect, while showing respect for the varied elements which composed his party, made it quite clear that he sought a truly national body of counselors, men able to think for all sections; for Mr. Cleveland was determined to be no mere party President. It was also a significant fact that among them was not a single man with whom he had been upon terms of personal intimacy.

His choice was satisfactory to the country at large, in spite of the interpretation of a lady who wrote, a few weeks later: "Mr. President Cleveland, I would love to have something from the White House. Please send me scraps of your cravats and your cabinet to make a block in my crazy quilt." Of the many tempting offers of help which he was obliged to decline, the following is an example, somewhat ambiguous, but undoubtedly sincere: "If you could see your way clear and the right material in a colored man for your Cabinet, you would thereby clinch the lip-service of the Democrats as scouted by the Republicans, and attach the race to the party which would be to the advantage of both."

As Inauguration Day approached, Gold Democrats, especially the old Democratic leader, Samuel J. Tilden, brought pressure to bear to induce Mr. Cleveland to state publicly his determination to maintain the gold standard. To him such a declaration seemed unnecessary, as he was already fully committed to the cause which they had at heart. At length, however, only eight days before his inauguration, at the earnest solicitation of Tilden and other sound money leaders, he consented to sign a letter prepared for him by Manton Marble. He knew, of course, that Presidents often delegate the task of drafting important papers, but it was a practice quite foreign to his own methods, and, although the letter accurately expressed his views, he consented with reluctance:

To the Hon. A. J. Warner and others, Members of
      the Forty-eighth Congress:
Gentlemen:
      The letter which I have had the honor to receive from you invites, and indeed obliges, me to give expression to some grave public necessities, although in advance of the moment when they would become the objects of my official care and partial responsibility. Your solicitude that my judgment shall have been carefully and deliberately formed is entirely just, and I accept the suggestion in the same friendly spirit in which it has been made. It is also fully justified by the nature of the financial crisis

which, under the operation of the act of Congress of February 28, 1878, is now close at hand.

By a compliance with the requirements of that law all the vaults of the Federal Treasury have been and are heaped full of silver coins, which are now worth less than eighty-five per cent of the gold dollar prescribed as the unit of value in section 16 of the act of February 12, 1873, and which, with the silver certificates representing such coin, are receivable for all public dues. Being thus receivable, while also constantly increasing in quantity at the rate of $28,000,000 a year, it has followed of necessity that the flow of gold into the Treasury has steadily diminished. Silver and silver certificates have displaced and are now displacing the gold in the Federal Treasury now available for the gold obligations of the United States and for redemption of the United States notes called "greenbacks." If not already encroached upon, it is perilously near such encroachment.

These are facts which, as they do not admit of difference of opinion, call for no argument. They have been forewarned to us in the official reports of every Secretary of the Treasury, from 1878 till now. They are plainly affirmed in the last December report of the present Secretary of the Treasury to the Speaker of the present House of Representatives. They appear in the official documents of this Congress, and in the records of the New York Clearing House, of which the Treasury is a member, and through which the bulk of the receipts and payments of the Federal Government and country pass.

These being the facts of our present condition, our danger, and our duty to avert that danger, would seem to be plain. I hope that you concur with me and with the great majority of our fellow citizens, in deeming it most desirable at the present juncture to maintain and continue in use the mass of our gold coin, as well as the mass of silver already coined. This is possible by a present suspension of the purchase and coinage of silver. I am not aware that by any other method it is possible. It is of momentous importance to prevent the two metals from parting company; to prevent the increasing displacement of gold by the increasing coinage of silver; to prevent the disuse of gold in the customhouses of the United States in the daily business of the people; to prevent the ultimate expulsion of gold by silver.

Such a financial crisis as these events would certainly precipitate, were it now to follow upon so long a period of commercial depression, would involve the people of every city and every state in the Union in a prolonged and disastrous trouble. The revival of business enterprise and prosperity so ardently desired, and apparently so near, would be hopelessly postponed. Gold would be withdrawn to its hoarding places, and an unprecedented contraction in the actual volume of our currency would speedily take place.

Saddest of all, in every workshop, mill, factory, store, and on every railroad and farm the wages of labor, already depressed, would suffer still further depression by a scaling down of the purchasing power of every so-called dollar paid into the hands of toil. From these impending calamities, it is surely a most patriotic and grateful duty of the representatives of the people to deliver them.

I am, gentlemen, with sincere respect, your fellow-citizen,

GROVER CLEVELAND.

Albany, February 24, 1885.

A few days after this letter appeared, Mr. Tilden wrote with complacent brevity:

*Confidential*

Graystone, Yonkers, N. Y.
*February 28, 1885.*

DEAR MR. CLEVELAND:

Your silver letter is absolutely perfect. It is the only silver thing I know of that transmutes itself into gold.

Very truly yours,

S. J. TILDEN.

But it was the last time Tilden was ever able to hold the reins. From this time, while treating the famous ex-party chief with all due courtesy, Mr. Cleveland made it quite evident that he would tolerate no dictation, no controlling influence, a course which caused Tilden to describe him as "the kind of man who would rather do something badly himself than have somebody else do it well." Years later, in a conversation with George F. Parker, Mr. Cleveland referred to the incident and added: "Whether as Mayor, Governor, or President, that was the first and last time I ever signed anything, either enunciating or advocating a policy, which was not written wholly by myself."

In his inaugural address, Mr. Cleveland promised fidelity to sound finance and to civil service reform, justice to the Indian, fair play to the American laborer, and an efficient and honest administration in the interest of all the people.

The oath of office was administered by Chief Justice Waite, who used for the ceremony the little Bible which Mr. Cleveland kept always at hand, and upon the fly-leaf of which appear the words: "My son, Stephen Grover Cleveland, from his loving Mother." Colonel Lamont once said that he had first seen this Bible in Mr. Cleveland's law office in Buffalo. Later it was kept on the bureau in his bedroom; but while he was President it occupied the upper left-hand drawer of the desk that was presented to the President of the United States by the Queen of England as a memento of the Sir John Franklin expedition to the Arctic regions. Before returning this precious book to the President, the Clerk of the Supreme Court entered this record on the flyleaf: "It was used to administer the oath of office to Grover Cleveland, President of the United States, on the fourth of March, 1885."

The inauguration formalities finished, the Cabinet confirmed, and the departments handed over to their new executive heads, Grover Cleveland began a régime simple enough to delight the heart of a Thomas Jefferson, honest enough to gladden the souls of a George Washington or an Abraham Lincoln, businesslike enough to give a thrill of pleasure to the genius of an Alexander Hamilton, but old-fashioned enough to be, to a generation educated by the modernism of Theodore Roosevelt, almost unbelievable. The President at first had no stenographer, and a single telephone answered the calls of the entire White House establishment. At the end of the regular hours of business, when the clerks and attendants had retired, its imperious summons was often answered by the President himself if William, the steward and general domestic head of the establishment, happened to be out of earshot; for these two shared the distinction of being the members of the establishment who kept no hours. According to Mr. Cleveland's philosophy, all of the President's time belongs to the public, without reservation.

Within the domain of his lawful tasks, William was allowed undisputed sway and he exercised his authority rigorously. Once, when a very young bride and groom were the only guests at the White House, the President, having noticed a worn and shabby dress suit laid out ready for him to put on, inquired of William why he had not selected a better one. William's laconic reply was: "It is plenty good enough for the occasion." And the President, without further protest, put it on and went down to dinner.

Such encounters were by no means infrequent, but the President had long ago committed himself to the political doctrine of division of powers, and he felt that, after all, William was within his rights. Upon one sultry spring evening, the President suddenly became aware of the fact that he was wearing a very heavy winter coat which his factotum had hung on the rack for him. As he mopped his brow, he remarked: "He is the most economical man I have ever known. He is bound I shall get a few more wears out of this coat before the hot weather comes."

The luxurious dinners prepared by the White House *chef* were usually accepted by the President in the same resigned spirit, though he sometimes rebelled, and insisted upon simpler fare. Wine was never served, unless guests were at the table. "What do you suppose I did the other day?" he once asked an intimate friend who was visiting the White House. "We sat down to a very delicious dinner, but it did not appeal to me. All at once, through the open window, there came an old and familiar odor. I said, 'William, what is that smell?' 'I am very sorry, sir,' he replied, 'but that is the smell of the servants' dinner.' 'What is it—corned beef and cabbage? Well, William, take this dinner down to the servants and bring their dinner to me,' I said. And I had the best dinner I had had for months." *"Bœuf corné au cabeau"* was his French for this dish.

When the first of each month came, the President insisted upon performing in person the unnecessary labor of making out checks for personal and household expenses, and going over the accounts with William. If Senators or other dignitaries called at this inauspicious moment, they had to submit to postponement. "I guess I have to take time to pay my bills," he would remark to William, and continue the work.

The glamour of his surroundings impressed him little, except to accentuate his feeling of loneliness, and even this was enlivened by his unfailing sense of humor. "It is nearly one o'clock," he wrote Bissell. "Colonel Lamont is gone and William too. If I did not keep one of the waiters here, I should be absolutely alone in the upper part of the house. That's splendor for you, sleeping alone in the White House."

He was averse to the idea of employing public property for his personal enjoyment, and never made any use of the *Dispatch,* a yacht which had been looked upon as the President's pleasure boat. When he went fishing, as he often did when confronted by any particularly difficult problem, he used a lighthouse tender, and insisted upon paying all expenses out of his private purse.

"The President's life," wrote the Baltimore *Sun* correspondent in July, 1887, "is . . . very much like that of any active business man having large and important interests committed to him. There is a difference, however, in the fact that Mr. Cleveland does an amount of work much in excess of that performed by the average first-class business man.

"The President's whole indoor life is under one roof. He transacts all the affairs of this great nation which come under his jurisdiction separated only by a few feet from the apartments where he eats, sleeps, and is supposed to enjoy his rest. The business man who has an immense manufacturing establishment, a great railroad, a bank, or other large interests in his hands, no matter how engrossed he may be or how much time he devotes, finds at last the hour when the door of the counting room or the office is closed upon him, and he can go home— home not infrequently miles away, where business and business cares can be shut out, and the tired brain can solace itself in the lighter joys which cluster around the home which is free from invasion. Not so with the President. He is never free from interruption until his head is on his pillow, the lights are out and the doors barred."

Mr. Cleveland had always been an early riser, and this habit continued at the White House. Eight o'clock in winter, and often a much earlier hour in summer, found him at breakfast, and by nine he was at his desk. From nine to ten he devoted himself to his able and accomplished private secretary, Dan Lamont, later Secretary of War, who understood, far better than did his Chief, the art of disposing of the piles of letters important enough to require the President's personal attention.

Each Wednesday, Friday, and Saturday, from ten until one, and Tuesdays and Thursdays from ten to twelve, he received, like the old Roman tribunes of the people, all those demanding an audience, giving precedence, however, to cabinet members, heads of bureaus, and members of Congress. In addition, except in warm weather, he held three public receptions a week, devoting to them nominally the half hour from one-thirty to two; but he invariably insisted that the period should be extended so as not to disappoint anyone who had entered the line before the hour of two. Mondays he reserved for cabinet officers, being on that day accessible to them at any hour. His regular cabinet meetings were set for noon on Tuesdays and Thursdays, and they rarely adjourned before three. In these meetings there were no set speeches, and no votes were taken, the President's theory being that in a cabinet there are many voices, but one vote. Each member was free to express his views; but when the illumination of frank comment and informal discussion was over, it was the President who must make the decision.

Luncheon was a necessity which had to adapt itself to more important matters; but his luncheon hour, in theory at least, was two o'clock, and before three he was back at his desk, disposing of the miscellaneous accumulations of the morning. During those strenuous early afternoon hours, visitors were rigorously excluded, cabinet officers excepted. At five or six, if all went well, it was his habit, often only a theoretical habit, to go out for a breath of air in preparation for dinner at seven. Regular exercise was a human frailty in which he never indulged, even theoretically. During public receptions he was always on his feet, moving from one group to another, and his right arm had scant opportunity to lose its cunning as it daily resisted the grip of a multitude. But within his quarters there were no dumb-bells, Indian clubs, punching-bags, or even masters of massage, and the many stories purporting to be descriptions of the President's exercises to reduce his weight were pure inventions.

A Washington correspondent of the period informs us that the President's breakfast consisted of "rolls and steak, ham and eggs, fish, chops, and coffee, preceded by the fruits of the season, and oatmeal and cream." That he covered the whole of this menu at any one meal is highly improbable, but his selections were undoubtedly generous in scope, as nature had endowed him with a robust appetite and a liking for heavy dishes. This fact was responsible for most of the physical discomforts of his life. His menu was heavy, his work was heavy, and he took no exercise. He was, therefore, often racked with pains which played agonizingly throughout the broad regions of his vast frame. Had he been more prudent, he might have preserved unimpaired the marvelous constitution with which nature had endowed him, but busy men with perfect constitutions seldom think of such things until too late.

During his first year at the White House, being unmarried, he kept his social engagements at a minimum. Public dinners, with himself as the honored guest, he abhorred, for he hated incense, and despised the semi-intellectual exercise of after-dinner speaking. The evenings he, therefore, almost invariably spent at his desk. He had entered the White House resolved that each day's work should be finished before the hour of retirement, and in consequence that hour not infrequently failed to come at all. His ordinary working day extended till two or three in the morning, but dawn often crept in through the east windows of the White House to find the people's servant still intent upon the people's business.

# CHAPTER VI

## FACING THE POLITICAL BREAD-LINE

*"Reward for partisan activities is one mode of misappropriation of public funds."*
—GROVER CLEVELAND.

LOUIS XIV once remarked that when he bestowed an office he made one ingrate and an hundred malcontents. The first part of this statement was doubtless unjust, but the second is in the nature of a general proposition, even truer of republics than of autocracies. The expectant official is the pest of politics, the thorn in the side of every President, of whatever character, theory, or party. The poor of politics, he is ever at hand. "His work begins at God knows when, and his work is never through." Lincoln found him almost unbearable. Garfield, after only a brief experience of his persecutions, cried in despair: "My God! what is there in this place that a man should ever want to get into it?" But for Grover Cleveland, the first Democratic Chief Executive since the days of James Buchanan, he provided a fearful testing. From the moment that the electoral colleges were chosen, awaiting neither the formal election of January nor the inauguration of March, he came by the thousands, pleading service, pleading poverty, pleading fitness, advancing every argument which could conceivably affect the mind or stir the emotions of the dispenser of patronage. At times he was blunderingly camouflaged, at times blatant, and often so illiterate as to be almost unreadable.

Here a Congressman urges the appointment of some faithful, incompetent henchman, "not on his account personally, but for the good of the department." There a man asks to be made a minister as "I do not care to lead an idle life," and adds: "Mrs. ———, too, wishes to go abroad as our daughter . . . requires treatment which can be best obtained in Europe." In answering this letter Mr. Cleveland might well have adapted the famous reply of Lincoln to a similar plea: "I'm sorry that there are eight other applicants for that place and they are all sicker than your man." Another, desirous of "a place in the Treasury," and fearful of the miscarriage of the "answer by return of male, because I need the office quick as I have a wife with seven children for support and I am out of menes and money too," enclosed an envelope marked, "in case you could not spel my name correctles I send you a invelope."

Within two weeks of his arrival at the White House Mr. Cleveland had received several hundred such applications for positions, including the following:

My Lord

I, the undersigned come most humbly and most respectfully to the feet of Your Most Gracious Majesty's throne, to offer this humble petition of mine to Your Most gracious Presidential Majesty. . . .

Your Most Gracious Presidential Excellence that so worthily and so gloriously occupying the throne of His forefathers, shines as the brightest star in the Heavens, among the crowned Heads of this World. . . .

Receive me, My Lord, as your soul-son.

Please to train this poor flower in one of your most celestial gardens, to blossom there, till the end of his life.

Dear Mr. President:

Permit me to Salute, Greet, Love and Congratulate you. I have the honor of applying to Your Excellency to a place in the due exercise of your high prerogative to humbly ask Your Excellency for an assignment after your private secretary or a position as Master of Ceremonies, Steward, or Door Keeper. I am a single man and was never married—prematurely Snowy headed and Bearded, I wish to live in Washington and make myself agreeable with everybody that I come in contact with, and will serve you with a perfect heart without vanity, egotism or anything else, with truth, integrity and probity. All I write is strictly true.

To the President:

As old father Time rolls his leaden car along, I learn that it behooves a lady left as a landmark of her posterity, 'mid the worlds' treacherous environments, to turn the leaves that are empowered with intelligence and glistening with embellishment: therefore I am impelled to ask, will our noble President give ear to another applicant for his bounteous aid to position? The humble writer, is an orphan, without kindred—literary by nature.

Der and respctble sir

Thrusting in hope I will be so free to ask your Honor for a situation. I have receive a good eddication. In other respects I am willing to render myself usful. I doubt not but that I shall be able to fulfil any duties assigned him more intelegent than most.

President Cleveland

It is verry dull out here. There is nothing to enliven things except the possibility of being impaled alive by a live Indian and I dont want to be impaled. I aint got any money to pay Rail Road fare and I want to get out of this. I thought if you could give me an office, I then could get a pass I voted the Republican ticket last fall but if you think there will be any chance of your being elected another term I will vote for you that is if I get an office.

Dear Sir:

Would you please appoint a man to some good office who has never taken a drink of whiskey in his life and who has never used tobacco in any way or been a politician or swore

Dear Sir:

I have made up my mind to ask you For an Employment if you Have anything that is suitable for a man that never was in the United States business but have filled Lodge Offices Promptly and correct if so as you could acomadate me Mr. Cleveland I will also be dutiful to my Occupation

Dear Sir

I am a young man wich I would like to beter my self. The buisnes I am at is Junk buisness, but I would rather have the buisness in the govment, either in the Cabnet or as watchman

Sur j would like to have the ofice of secetary j think j wold sute you j have a meligant desise all so j have the chills so j cant labor fur my liven. Send me the law so j will no what a secetery will bea.

The old-style Democrats, faithful to the spoils ideal, euphemistically termed "rotation in office," of course demanded a clean sweep. For a quarter of a century the pleasant fields of Federal patronage had been closed to them, and when now, at last, victory crowned their banners, they eagerly demanded the spoils of victory. The Mugwumps, on the other hand, fearing treason to the pledges and practices which had won their support, insisted that there be no sweep at all.

There was, of course, nothing new in this, for although the first forty years of our history were singularly free from the spoils system, with the coming of Andrew Jackson, "the man of perpetual fury," all this had been changed. Jackson frankly divided the spoils of political victory with his fellow Democrats and established a precedent which successive administrations, Democratic, Whig, and Republican alike, had eagerly followed, till slowly, but with terrible certainty, the partisan conception had grown into a system, generally accepted as an unavoidable incident of popular government.

There had, of course, always been indignant protestants. Calhoun, in 1835, declared: "So long as the offices were considered as public trusts, to be conferred on the honest, the faithful and capable, for the common good, and not for the benefit or gain of the incumbent or his party, and so long as it was the practice of the Government to continue in office those who faithfully performed their duties, its patronage, in point of fact, was limited to the mere power of nominating to accidental vacancies or to newly created offices, and would, of course, exercise but a moderate influence either over the body of the community or over the office holders themselves; but when this practice was reversed—when offices, instead of being considered as public trusts, to be conferred on the deserving, were regarded as the spoils of victory, to be bestowed as rewards for partisan service—it is easy to see the certain, direct, and inevitable tendency . . . to

convert the entire body of those in office into corrupt and
supple instruments of power, and to raise up a host of
hungry, greedy, and subservient partisans, ready for every
service, however base and corrupt."

But Calhoun and the earlier opponents of the system
were opponents with no healing prescription, reformers
with no organized plan of reform. In politics as in all
practical affairs mere idealism, however earnest, accom-
plishes nothing. To be of value, it must carry with it a
definite program which the ordinary citizen can understand, and no such program was brought forward until
1867, when Congressman T. A. Jenckes of Rhode Island,
recommended to Congress that certain classes of appointments hitherto regarded as party spoils be henceforth
made upon the basis of competitive examination, and
that the appointees be given a tenure independent of
political changes. From this suggestion there slowly
grew up an organized reform movement, and four years
later Congress authorized the President to appoint a Civil
Service Commission, and to carry out such rules as it
might decide upon relative to admission into government
employ. With this plan established, civil service reform
became a movement to be reckoned with by party leaders.

It fell to General Grant, as President, to choose the
first Civil Service Commission; but the clamor of spoilsmen was loud, and the General was no stoic. It was not
very long, therefore, before he suspended the operation
of the civil service rules, on the ground that Congress,
under the leadership of James G. Blaine, refused appro-
priations requisite for conducting the examinations. Thus
the spoils system again flourished like a green bay tree,
and again the spoilsmen, in the manner of the slaveholding
philosophers of old, wove cunning webs of logic to prove
their system "born of God." Immediately after this set-

back a Civil Service Reform Association was organized in New York, with George William Curtis as President. Theodore Roosevelt later became an active member of this association, which soon developed into the National Civil Service Reform League, and set itself the task of educating the people upon the necessity of reform.

Much of the needed education had been already given by the unprecedented corruption of Grant's second term, and the Democratic party had registered its pretended conversion in the national party platform of 1876, which declared: "Reform is necessary in the Civil Service. Experience proves that efficient, economical conduct of the Government business is not possible if its Civil Service be subject to change at every election, be a prize fought for at the ballot box, be a brief reward of party zeal, instead of posts of honor, assigned for proven competency and held for fidelity in the public employ." The Convention of 1880 reiterated these views in words of violence: "We execrate the course of this Administration (Hayes) in making places in the Civil Service a reward for political crime, and demand a reform by statute which shall make it forever impossible for the defeated candidate to bribe his way to the seat of the usurper by billeting villains upon the people."

The assassination of President Garfield at the hands of a disappointed office seeker had further emphasized the need of reform, and a solid foundation for its development was finally laid in the famous Pendleton Act of January 16, 1883, which empowered the President to bring under a merit system such groups of Federal employees as he should decide upon, and prohibited political assessments upon Federal office holders. This law gave hope of speedy regeneration for the public service, and Mr. Cleveland as Mayor of Buffalo, when the Pendleton

Bill was still merely proposed legislation, had freely com
mitted himself to its provisions. As Governor of New
York, he had been a tireless worker for reform and, amid
conditions discouraging in the extreme, had finally secured
a state law requiring the passing of civil service examina
tions by applicants for office.

In view of these actions, the reformers had worked
for his election to the Presidency, and had tipped the
balance in his favor; and on December 20, 1884, in order
to get his views squarely before the country, the National
Civil Service Reform League had asked him to prepare
a statement on the subject. Mr. Cleveland's reply is his
Civil Service confession of faith:

Albany, *Dec. 25, 1884.*

HON. GEORGE WILLIAM CURTIS,
President, &c.

Dear Sir:

Your communication dated December twentieth, ad
dressed to me on behalf of the National Civil Service
Reform League, has been received.

That a practical reform in the Civil Service is de
manded, is abundantly established by the fact that a
statute, referred to in your communication, to secure such
a result, has been passed in Congress with the assent of
both political parties; and by the further fact that a
sentiment is generally prevalent among patriotic people
calling for the fair and honest enforcement of the law
which has been thus enacted. I regard myself pledged
to this, because my conception of true Democratic faith
and public duty requires that this and all other statutes
should be in good faith, and without evasion enforced
and because in so many utterances made prior to my
election as President, approved by the party to which

I belong and which I have no disposition to disclaim, I
have in effect promised the people that this should be
done.

I am not unmindful of the fact to which you refer,
that many of our citizens fear that the recent party change
in the National Executive may demonstrate that the
abuses which have grown up in the Civil Service are
ineradicable. I know that they are deeply rooted, and
that the spoils system has been supposed to be intimately
related to success in the maintenance of party organization; and I am not sure that all those who profess to
be the friends of this reform will stand firmly among
its advocates, when they find it obstructing their way to
patronage and place. But fully appreciating the trust
committed to my charge, no such consideration shall
cause a relaxation on my part of an earnest effort to enforce this law.

There is a class of Government positions which are
not within the letter of the Civil Service statute, but
which are so disconnected with the policy of an administration, that the removal therefrom of present incumbents, in my opinion, should not be made during the
terms for which they were appointed, solely on partisan
grounds, and for the purpose of putting in their places
those who are in political accord with the appointing
power. But many now holding such positions have forfeited all just claim to retention, because they have used
their places for party purposes, in disregard of their duty
to the people, and because, instead of being decent public servants, they have proved themselves offensive partisans, and unscrupulous manipulators of local party management. The lessons of the past should be unlearned;
and such officials, as well as their successors, should be
taught that efficiency, fitness and devotion to public duty

are the conditions of their continuance in public place
and that the quiet and unobtrusive exercise of individua
rights is the reasonable measure of their party service.

If I were addressing none but party friends, I shoulc
deem it entirely proper to remind them that, though the
coming administration is to be Democratic, a due regarc
for the people's interest does not permit faithful party
work to be always rewarded by appointment to office
and to say to them that while Democrats may expect al.
proper consideration, selections for office not embraced
within the Civil Service rules will be based upon sufficient
inquiry as to fitness, instituted by those charged with
that duty, rather than upon persistent importunity or
self-solicited recommendations, on behalf of candidates
for appointment.

Yours very truly,

GROVER CLEVELAND.

This letter promised reform, but it did not promise
the impossible. Even at this early stage of his Federal
career, Mr. Cleveland was conscious that his Mugwump
friends were preparing to insist that he perform miracles
of healing, and he knew that he could perform no miracles. To his severely practical mind the business of
government was to seek increased efficiency, and to that
end honesty and ability on the part of all officials were
essential. But to reverse this order, as some of the reformers demanded, and make of government a sort of
moral crusade, he felt to be unwise, deeply as he resented
the spoils system in all of its aspects.

As Francis Lynde Stetson expressed it, "If, upon the
accession of President Cleveland, he had found, as he
did find, every appointive office in the possession of a
Republican, and if he had found, as he did not find,

every one of these incumbents to be fully competent and
worthy . . . it is inconceivable that he should have been
expected to reappoint all of such officers upon the expiration of their terms.  He had never given any promise or
pledge with reference to reappointments, and the principle of civil service reform would have become odious
to the great mass of the people had it been so practically
applied as to indicate that it was intended to continue
exclusion from office of all members of the Democratic
party."

Mr. Cleveland planned to be, not a civil service reformer with Democratic tendencies, but a President of the
United States, believing in civil service principles. "Those
who have complained," he once declared, "have enter-
ained a very different understanding of what is meant by
civil service reform from that which the law required me
to observe and that it was practicable to carry out.  The
President is clothed with many and various responsibilities.  He is expected, primarily, to do all in his power
to secure good government.  That imposes upon him the
exercise of discretion in making many appointments.  It
is admitted that in filling many places the importance of
securing persons in sympathy with the political views of
the dominant party is properly to be considered.  My
civil service friends have sometimes seemed to think that
the Government was to be conducted merely for the purpose of promoting civil service reform.  To me the importance of general administrative reform has appeared
to be superior to the incidental matter of civil service
reform.  Good government is the main thing to be aimed
at.  Civil Service Reform is but a means to that end."

A few days after his inauguration he received a long
letter from Carl Schurz reminding him, in specific terms,
of what the reformers expected, and ardently pleading

for the retention of the Republican Postmaster of New York: "The reappointment of Mr. Pearson," the letter declared, "is . . . regarded as a test of your policy." By failing to keep him in his position, you "would disappoint the hopes of those of your supporters who have the success of your endeavors to reform abuses and to purify the political atmosphere, most earnestly at heart. They cordially appreciate the noble resistance you have offered to the pressure of the spoils politicians, and they would be much pained at seeing that record blurred. . . . Owing . . . to the fact that your performances have always gone beyond your formal promises, public expectation is now higher than it has ever been before. . . . If now, in spite of your own inclination . . . considerations of a partizan character . . . maintain their ascendancy, keeping the field open for a future revival of spoils politics, the disappointment would indeed be great." Doubtless Mr. Cleveland was better able than even Mr. Schurz to estimate the effect of such a policy, as he had cautiously presented the problem to the public, through inspired leaders in the press, and had watched the reaction, a practice quite common with him.

The effect on the spoilsmen had been immediate and violent. One wrote to Lamont: "You are aware of the President's civil reform declarations and the amount of capital the Republican papers and members of the party are making out of it. . . . Not less than twenty of our best workers here, come right out and say, if Mr. Cleveland proposes to retain the republicans that are in office, throughout his administration, they will go back on the party forever. I have no doubt but what this same feeling exists throughout the state. . . . Should Mr. Pearson be reappointed Postmaster in N. Y. City, it would make the greatest commotion, and would cause the loss of not less than 10,000 votes in this state."

A few days after this letter was written, the wily Tammany leader, John Kelly, wrote to Charles P. Britton: "I am under the impression that President Cleveland will be successful in administering the Government of the United States, as he undoubtedly was in discharge of the duties of the office of Governor of this State. He is calm, dignified, thoughtful, and acts after mature deliberation. Besides, he possesses the qualification of listening, and saying but very little, although he is very agreeable, social and is fond of interchanging views and opinions as any person can be holding the dignified and important position of President of the United States. Of course it is a great gift to be able to listen and analyze and draw conclusions from what may be said of him by the various persons who appeal to him, from time to time, for place or favor of some kind."

Evidently Mr. Kelly felt that Tammany must adopt a course different from that pursued in the case of Senator Grady, if they were to get their part of the spoils of victory. At the end of the letter, clearly designed for transfer to the President's own hand, Kelly added this sentence, eloquent when taken in connection with the idea of Mr. Pearson's reappointment as Postmaster of New York: "Besides, his (the President's) ambition is not so great as to inaugurate measures that would cause great discussion and violent opposition. I wish him every success in life, and hope that he may succeed in discharging the duties of the Presidency of this country to the entire satisfaction of the people."

In view of the threat that by persisting in Mr. Pearson's reappointment the President would lose "not less than 10,000 votes" in New York, Mr. Kelly's plan was adroit; and, as the Tammany leader had doubtless expected, Mr. Britton promptly sent Kelly's neat words of praise to Lamont, with the following suggestive comment, bearing date, March 22, 1885: "I note by the papers that Mr. Kelly is in Washington to-day . . . and I presume he will call at the White House. . . . I trust that both you yourself and the President will receive him with great cordiality, for I assure you from positive knowledge that *personally* he *desires it,* and he is just the man (and I presume in just the state of mind) to *appreciate* magnanimity on the part of President Cleveland, and this too without a thought as regards patronage for his henchmen. For them, individually or collectively, I care nothing; but for him, personally, I have great respect. I *know* what he did for us during the campaign against an opposition that would have crushed an ordinary man. . . . *It is of the utmost importance to us, in our future work, that the entente cordiale be established at once between the President and Mr. Kelly."*

But neither the consideration of 10,000 votes in New York, nor the sweet reasonableness of John Kelly could save the New York Post-office for the Democrats. Pearson's name went to the Senate, and to the press went the following inspired leader, the manuscript of which is in Mr. Cleveland's own hand:

"A gentleman very near the President and undoubtedly speaking from actual knowledge, reports that the reappointment of Mr. Pearson was made after a most patient examination of all the facts connected with the charges against him and his answer to the same, which was yesterday submitted and read by the President. The appointment therefore may be considered a complete vindication of the postmaster.

"It is further stated that the reappointment of Mr. Pearson will constitute a notable exception to the course which the President may be expected to pursue. The New York post-office is the largest and most important in the country and of interest to all the people and especially to the vast business enterprises centered in the metropolis. It is to-day a complete illustration of the successful application of civil service reform principles to an immense governmental establishment. This condition has been brought about very largely by the intelligent effort of Mr. Pearson, and he is thus identified in the closest manner with this example of the success of the reform. To retain him insures faith and confidence in the movement, which would receive a shock from his removal. His retention was earnestly requested by a large number of business men of the city, both Democrats and Republicans, and very generally by the Independent Republicans who did such good service in support of the Democratic candidates in the last campaign.

"This act of the President must not be regarded as indicating that in other cases those opposed to the party of the President will either be appointed or retained after the expiration of their terms of office.

"In answer to the suggestion that the reappointment of Mr. Pearson might cause great dissatisfaction in the ranks of his party, the President is represented as saying: 'The Democratic party is neither hypocritical, unpatriotic or ungrateful—they will understand the whole matter and be satisfied.' "

At each new venture along the line of reform, to which not he alone but his party, was committed, similar protests poured in upon him; but they failed to dominate him. Some old political supporter would find his appli-

cation for a minor Federal appointment denied on the
ground that it was covered by the civil service law. This
he could endure; but when he saw an active secretary of
a Blaine and Logan club, whose name happened to stand
high on the eligible list, awarded the coveted post by the
President whom he had helped to elect, his submission
was turned to rage, which rage was not lessened by the
Republican taunt, "You got your President, but you can't
get your Postmaster." Nor was the fact that the taunt
was true calculated to make disappointed Democrats love
the grim figure in the White House, who was heroically
facing the task which they had assigned him.

The more radical reformers, headed by Schurz, continued to urge him to "aim straight at the non-partisan
service," but, in so urging, asked more than could have
been reasonably expected. Mr. Cleveland believed that
the chief object of civil service reform is not to prevent
removals from office, but to supply a body of competent
persons, tested by examinations, from whom appointments can be made. He believed that if the incompetent
should be weeded out there would be ample opportunity
to gratify the natural desires of the Democrats for recognition, without dropping any, of whatever party, who had
shown special fitness for their places. This was a perfectly fair standard, and one which could be adhered to
without complete disregard of party obligations. Chosen
by a party which had known, not seven lean years, but
more than two lean decades, Mr. Cleveland knew that a
purely non-partisan plan for the distribution of patronage would mean suicide in office and a fruitless administration.

At times he made serious mistakes, or was led into
error, but in the light of new evidence he did not hesitate
to reverse his decisions, offend whom it might. Not long

after he had ordered the appointment of James Blackburn of Kentucky as Collector of Internal Revenue, his attention was called to a letter written by Mr. Blackburn during the war:

Abingdon, Va., *October 2, 1861.*

MY DEAR WIFE,

I have left you and our children in the land of the despot, but God grant that I may soon be able to make the Union men of Kentucky feel the edge of my knife. From this day I hold every *Union traitor* as my enemy, and from him I scorn to receive quarter, and to whom I will never grant my soul in death; for they are *cowards* and villains *enough.* Brother Henry and I arrived here without hindrance. I have had chills all the way, but I hope to live to kill forty Yankees for every chill that I ever had. I learn that Hardee is still in the Arkansas lines, inactive, and if this proves true I will tender my resignation and go immediately to Kentucky. I hope that I will do my duty as a rebel and a free man. Since I know the *Union men* of Kentucky, I intend to begin the work of murder in earnest, and if I ever spare one of them may hell be my portion. I want to see Union blood now deep enough for my horse to swim in.

Your husband,

JAMES BLACKBURN.

The President sent for some of Blackburn's friends to inquire if the letter as printed was authentic, and found that it was admitted to be genuine. He then consulted with the members of the Cabinet, and the order was given to cancel the appointment. Mr. Blackburn's friends and political sponsors pleaded, clamored, threatened, but in vain.

That he was sincere will hardly be doubted by one who has read the following letter, written not for public perusal, not for campaign use, but for the eyes of a trusted and beloved friend, Wilson S. Bissell:

Executive Mansion, Washington.
*June 25, 1885.*

DEAR BISSELL:

It is nearly 12. o'c. Lamont just brought in your letter (we have a mail at 11 o'c now) and after reading it, I have put aside my work to reply.

Somehow this letter has impressed me with the suspicion that in one quarter at least there is an idea that I owe something to friends for political aid, which I am not ready enough to acknowledge. Perhaps this is true. At all events I tell you now, with the utmost sincerity, that I cannot rid myself of the idea that I owe so much to the country, that all other obligations shrink almost to nothingness before it—though I must confess that sometimes I am much comforted by the reflection that I may serve the country well and still serve my party. My ability to do either of these things depends of course upon the approval of the people. The people I have to deal with—that is the people of the country—are not perhaps just what I wish they were, and they perhaps have ideas which are not useful or correct, but their ideas to a very great extent must be met or my efforts to do good must miscarry.

Your letter indicates that you appreciate partly the extent and perplexity, as well as the delicacy of my work. For three months I have stood here and battled with those of my party who deem party success but a means to personal advantage. They have been refused and disappointed; and you are able to-day to write as you do, that my administration is strong and popular, because those thus refused and disappointed cannot say that I have refused them in order to make place for personal friends, and have bestowed patronage in payment of personal political debts.

I have often thought how solemn a thing it is to live and feel the pressure of the duties which life—the mere existence in a social state—imposes; but I have never appreciated the thought in its full solemnity till now. It seems to me that I am as much consecrated to a service, as the religionist who secludes himself from all that is joyous in life and devotes himself to a sacred mission.

I think you know how much of all that has had anything of comfort in my life has grown out of my love for my friends and the hope that I had earned some real unselfish attachments. And if, in carrying my present burden, I must feel that friends are calling me selfish and doubting my attachment to them and criticising the fact that in the administration of my great trust I am not aiding them, I shall certainly be unhappy, but shall nevertheless struggle on. The end will come; and if on that day I can retire with a sure consciousness that I have done my whole duty according to my lights and my ability, there will be some corner for me where I can rest.

You must not think that I am always blue and always unhappy. In the midst of all I have to do, daily and hourly come the assurances from the people in all parts, that they are satisfied and pleased. If I could only, by giving up all I have or expect, liquidate the debts and obligations to my friends, a terrible load would fall from my shoulders. You say they were very few and could be counted upon the fingers of one hand. I am sure five thousand have claimed that they were spent in my behalf to an extent that can never be compensated. What a nice thing it would be if my *close* friends could see a compensation in my successful administration.

Of one thing you may be certain. I shall bear with me to my dying day a heart full of gratitude for all that you have done for me.

Yours faithfully,<br>
GROVER CLEVELAND.

He was painfully conscientious in searching for the best candidates for office and painfully alert to avoid misrepresentations. "I have fallen into the habit lately of wrestling very hard with this cursed office-filling in my dreams," he wrote to Charles W. Goodyear, on June 16th. And, a month later, he describes himself as "pitching about half asleep and half awake, trying to make postmasters." But despite his caution, he was occasionally misled, at times deliberately, by men who wished either to accommodate friends, or to shift the burden of refusal to the President's shoulders. To one such, who had ventured to express surprise at the appointment of a candidate whom he had himself thus recommended, the President wrote, in unmeasured condemnation:

Executive Mansion, Washington,<br>
*August 1, 1885.*

DEAR SIR:

I have read your letter of the 24th ult. with amazement and indignation. There is but one mitigation to the perfidy which your letter discloses, and that is found in the fact that you confess your share in it. I don't know whether you are a Democrat or not; but if you are the crime which you confess is the more unpardonable. The idea that this administration, pledged to give the people better government and better officers, and engaged in a hand-to-hand fight with the bad elements of both parties, should be betrayed by those who ought to be worthy of implicit trust, is atrocious; and such treason to the people and to the party ought to be punished by imprisonment.

Your confession comes too late to be of immediate use to the public service, and I can only say that while this is not the first time I have been deceived and misled by lying and treacherous representatives, you are the first one that has so frankly owned his grievous fault. If any comfort is to be extracted from this assurance you are welcome to it.

Yours truly,<br>
GROVER CLEVELAND.

The pressure for office coming from his Buffalo friends was hardest to bear, and their complaints caused him keen distress, but they did not cause him to swerve from the rigid standards of public duty which he had set himself. To Charles W. Goodyear he thus unburdened his heart:

Executive Mansion, Washington.<br>
Aug. 6, 1885.

DEAR CHARLEY:

I return you Bissell's letter, and am exceedingly surprised at it, as also by the statement in your letter, that you have wanted to tell me "of ——, ——, ——, ——, and others who were your (my) warm hearted friends," etc., etc. I think I understand it; and the truth that I have been attempting to crowd back, is forced upon me. What have these friends to complain of?

Has —— made up his mind that he is justified in withdrawing his friendship, because he was not appointed as a member of the Cabinet or Consul to London? These two things he will see some day were impossible; and from one he withdrew himself. I would not demean myself to speak of the pleasure it has given me to do every other thing which I thought he wanted.

Is —— offended because I forgot to insist in the Cabinet (and I would not have done it if I had remembered it) that the banking business should be continued in the hands of the most pronounced Republicans, who were fleecing the Government right and left?

Has —— ceased to be a friend because I did not appoint him to a place in the diplomatic service, and thus offend my party and give the lie to my declaration that the administration was to be Democratic, and weaken myself by giving public places to reward personal friends?

Has —— made up his mind that our long friendship should be broken and interrupted, because I did not insist upon his taking the Paris Consulship, or because I am now hesitating about an attempt to find something of personal and professional interest to him, which I am convinced by my present lights ought not to be done?

I can think of nothing else which should interfere with the relations I have been so delighted to maintain with these gentlemen. Of all the 60,000,000 people in the country, high or low, my Buffalo friends when here have been treated with the utmost consideration and hospitality, so far as I have been able to do it, and so far as my knowledge of proper and handsome treatment went. It may be that public business has prevented my devoting as much time to them as I desired, but I did the best I could.

I have been here five months now, and have met many people who had no friendship for me, and were intent on selfishly grabbing all they could get, without any regard to the country, the party or to me; but I have managed to get along with them apparently as well as with my Buffalo friends. And now I am done. I feel sick at heart. I don't want to let these friends go; but I am tired of this beating about the bush and all this talk about "second-handed invitation" and "holes in a plank" and that sort of thing. If people lie in wait for me to discover things that may be construed into slights and offenses, they will find plenty of them. I am not much on my guard with friends.

I have no complaints to make. Of course I thought it a little strange that with the hundreds of invitations, to visit hundreds of places during my vacation, my friends in Buffalo did not seem to care to see me; but I am not going to say that I can get along without Buffalo or Buffalo friends. I care much—very much—for the latter. But by God! I have something on hand here that cannot be interfered with; and if my Buffalo friends or any other friends cannot appreciate that, I can't help it.

I am getting in that condition where any demonstration of kindness touches me deeply; and therefore I thank you for your kind words and offer to attend to any matter for me in Buffalo.

I hope to receive the tin box very soon; and after that I will try to be real good and make as little trouble as possible.

For God's sake, Charley, don't think that I am [in] any way out of sorts with you.

                              Yours faithfully,
                                   GROVER CLEVELAND.

Such a letter, certainly unjust in many of its implications, and that to men whom he really loved, showed that nerves were giving the danger signal, and he eagerly welcomed the long-looked-for vacation in the woods, with the leaping trout, the rippling streams, and the soothing comradeship of Dr. Bryant, his devoted physician and still more devoted friend.

Thanks to Lamont's scrapbook, the following Presidential movie of a Cleveland fishing trip is preserved. It was written by a Chicago *Tribune* reporter on August 21, 1885, and shows Mr. Cleveland at play:

" 'I think,' said the Doctor, as he and the President emerged from the tent after luncheon, 'that we can't do better than try the pools up the creek for pickerel. I saw a big fellow lurking under the shadow of the bank yesterday, and I'm confident we shall have sport. It's a good afternoon for fishing. What do you say to it, Mr. Cleveland?'

" 'I don't believe we can do better, Doc,' was the reply.

"The two shouldered their poles and started off up the creek. Arriving at what seemed a likely spot for pickerel, the question of what bait was best came up, and the Doctor advocated live frogs. 'I know you object to killing an old bullfrog,' he explained, 'because of your sentiments expressed yesterday, but the kind we shall use for bait will be the little brown hoppers. If there's anything a pickerel just delights in, it's a small, fresh frog.'

"Two active little frogs were easily caught, the hooks were baited by passing the steel through the skin on the frogs' back, leaving them alive and with power of movement, and then, seating themselves on the bank a few yards apart, the President and the Doctor began fishing. Little was said, and each, lighting a cigar, smoked away placidly awaiting a bite. It was not long before there was a rush in the water, a swirl, a struggle, and a little later the Doctor had landed a fine pickerel on the sward behind him. The President looked enviously at the dappled sides of the fish and watched his own line with increased interest, but it did not stir. Again and again was the Doctor successful, but his companion had no luck. The hours passed, but the President caught no fish. He became listless.

" 'I don't see how it is, Doc,' said he finally, 'that you catch so many fish while I don't get even a nibble. I used to be a successful fisherman when I was a boy. Ah, those were good times!' and he sighed deeply. 'Dinner always had a relish in those days, and there was enjoyment in everything. I can see it now—the hard, white road, winding between green fields, and the wooden bridge over the creek in the hollow. There were always fish in the deep water under the bridge and in the pools above and below it. We fished with pin hooks, we boys, and we brought out every fish with a yank, to prevent his falling off the hook, but we generally had good luck. I know I always went home with more chubs and shiners than they liked to cook.

" 'It was a triumphal march home with my catch, up the long clay road and into the front yard—why don't they have such front yards nowadays?' he soliloquized. 'There is a fashion in country front yards, imported from New England, I think. There was a plank or gravel walk from the gate up to the front door, and on either side of the walk were the flowers—not such flowers as are raised now, but old-fashioned flowers. There were larkspurs and a bed of China asters, and then one of the old style of pinks, next to a great bunch of phlox, and then dahlias. Up against the house would be hollyhocks, and between them, at their feet, "bouncing Betty's" and "old hen and chickens." Oh, I know those old-fashioned gardens! But'—and here he suddenly recollected himself— 'I haven't had a bite yet, and you've caught a lot more pickerel! I've got the same kind of frog on my hook that you have. Why don't they bite at him? By the way, there's a good frog for bait on that stump across the creek. See it, Doc?'

" 'That's so,' said the Doctor; 'I believe if you had that fellow on your hook the pickerel would bite.'

" 'I'm going to try to get him,' said the President, and he began to reel in his line preparatory to crossing the creek at a shallow place further up. The line became gradually taut, though the President did not at first notice it, his eyes being fastened on the frog, until that little animal began to scramble and cling to his perch for dear life, as if something were pulling at him. The President, in astonishment, stopped reeling, and by a coincidence the frog appeared at peace again. The President looked at his pole, then along his line, then at the Doctor, then back to the frog. A light dawned upon him. He uttered a single word:

" 'Jehoshaphat!'

" 'What is it?' exclaimed the Doctor. 'What's the matter?'

" 'Don't speak to me,' replied the President. 'I'll be hanged if that isn't my frog on the stump! He's swum across and climbed the stump, hook and all, and here I've been sitting waiting on him all the afternoon—waiting for pickerel to bite! Great Scott!'

"The sympathizing Doctor crossed the creek and prepared to toss the frog and hook back into the water, but the President said he guessed he wouldn't fish any more that day. The frog was released with all care, and subsequently tossed into a puddle.

" 'I don't blame him much,' said the President. 'I ought to have attended to business. I've been day-dreaming.' "

Perhaps daydreams were not unnatural in a President who had just escaped for a time the eager political bread-line, and knew that he must soon return, not to it alone, but to the as yet untried business of dealing with Congress.

It was his physical salvation, during the trying years of conflict that followed, to be able, when the strain grew unbearable, to take down his beloved rod, or sling over his shoulder his shotgun—modestly named "Death and Destruction"—and seek the restoring balm of God's glorious solitude. They might slander him, as they did; they might trick him with cunning, deceive him with lies, torture him with reproaches of ingratitude and of unfriendliness to friends; but no one could rob him of his duck marshes, or prevent the shy trout and agile blue-fish from turning his mind away, for a time, from all worries. God made him a sportsman, and the instinct served him as the protective coloring serves the wild things in the great, free world of outdoors.

Early in September he returned to the White House, conscious that the clamor for office had not diminished nor would for many weary months. His heart had been lightened, however, by the discovery, made during the summer, that he was mistaken in his judgment concerning his Buffalo intimates of whose unfriendliness he had so bitterly complained to Goodyear. As soon as he reached his desk he wrote acknowledging that misjudgment and, incidentally, recorded his general distaste for the life of a President:

"I feel that I am in the treadmill again and look forward to the time when another respite shall be due to me and all that must take place between now and then with the gravest concern. If it were not for the full faith I have in the Higher Power that aids honest, faithful endeavor, I should be frightened by all I see before me. But I have not a particle of real fear, though I confess to anxiety, because so much depends upon me. It's a curious state of mind to be in, when all the value of life is measured by its relation to other persons and other things, and when the natural desire to live for the sake of living and enjoying life is nearly gone."

In his absence, King Leopold of Belgium had sent him a formal announcement that the mandatory of the Congo, which the Powers had recently conferred upon Belgium, "will hereafter form the independent state of the Congo," and that he had "taken . . . the title of Sovereign" of that new state. Mr. Cleveland's reply was a formal recognition of conditions in the creation of which he had had no part, and for the cruel and unforeseen outcome of which, "the horrors of the Congo," he can be held in no degree responsible.

ESTEEMED AND GREAT FRIEND:

I have had much pleasure in receiving your Majesty's letter of the 1st of August last, announcing that the possessions of the International Association of the Congo will hereafter form the Independent State of the Congo, and that your Majesty, under the authorization of the Belgian Legislative Chambers, and in accord with the association, has assumed the title of Sovereign of the Independent State of the Congo. I observe your Majesty's further statement that the convention between Belgium and the new State is exclusively personal. This government at the outset testified its lively interest in the well being and future progress of the vast region now committed to your Majesty's wise care, being the first among the Powers to recognize the flag of the International Association of the Congo as that of a friendly State;

and now that the progress of events has brought with it
the general recognition of the jurisdiction of the association and opened the way for its incorporation as an independent and sovereign State, I have great satisfaction in
congratulating your Majesty on being called to the Chief
Magistracy of the newly formed government.

The Government and people of the United States,
whose only concern lies in watching with benevolent
expectation the growth of prosperity and peace among the
communities to whom they are joined by ties of friendship, cannot doubt that under your Majesty's good government the peoples of the Congo region will advance in
the paths of civilization and deserve the good-will of all
those States and people who may be brought into contact
with them.

I am, my esteemed and great friend, your faithful
friend.

GROVER CLEVELAND.

Done at Washington, this 11th day of September,
1885, by the President.

T. F. BAYARD,
Secretary of State.

Once more in harness, the President again faced the
political bread-line. The Pendleton Law already covered some thirteen thousand five hundred offices, but
there remained subject to Mr. Cleveland's appointment
forty-nine thousand fourth-class postmasters, and five
thousand miscellaneous posts mostly packed with Republicans. For each there were at hand many expectant
Democratic officials, backed by not less expectant Democratic politicians hunting votes. These were they who

had ranted on the stump, organized gigantic torchlight parades, "gathered the coin," or fed the columns of a party press during the late campaign. They could see no excuse for a President who would not fill vacancies with the faithful, or make vacancies where none existed, and shrieked traitor at each non-partisan appointment, however excellent.

On the other hand, Republicans who had fed the fires of personal slander, had cheered themselves hoarse at the mention of the name of James G. Blaine, and had ransacked the political garbage cans for new filth to hurl at the then Governor of New York, loudly cried hypocrite at each removal, however necessary, while despite his honest and persistent fight for reform against an increasingly powerful faction in his own party, many even among civil service reformers looked upon the President as a betrayer of their confidence, a wolf in sheep's clothing, a champion spoilsman camouflaged. This was his penalty for leadership of a party not yet regenerate. Over and over again his friends broke party pledges in the belief that the President would never know. They made partisan removals in such numbers as to justify the complaint that the Democrats were no more attached to reform than the Republicans had been, and the reckless manner in which Congressmen, Senators, and others high in office lent their names to undesirable candidates caused the President to wonder whether any recommendation could be considered of value. "The Vice-President, and at least half the Democratic Senators, and nearly all the Democrats of the House," commented the *Commercial Gazette,* "[have] banded themselves together to break down the President and his Cabinet, and force him to do their bidding. . . . The first surprise of the President was as nothing compared with his amazement over the later features of the office-seekers' raid."

Yet the more judicial reformers knew that he was reforming, slowly, cautiously, practically, but really; working as one who knows the limitations of executive power must work if permanent results are to be attained. "Since the spoils system was first generally introduced into our national administration," wrote George William Curtis, after watching the new President for only five months, "no President has given such conclusive evidence both of his reform convictions and of his courage in enforcing his convictions as Grover Cleveland." And, during the same summer, Gladstone remarked to Theodore L. Cuyler, who was visiting England: "Cleveland is the noblest man that has filled the Presidential chair since Lincoln."

The President's frank and uncompromising methods made for him relentless enemies who, in various sections of the country, poured vitriol into a personally conducted press, causing it to produce many stories more interesting than authentic. In turn, he generalized too freely, and his sweeping denunciations appealed to the *esprit de corps* of editors, disposed, and not unjustly, to resent blanket indictments of their order. They busied themselves making and printing collections, built on the line of modern three-foot shelf libraries, to show the public "how the people's President slanders the people's press." The newspaper clippers, who in those days were employed to make presidential scrapbooks, filled volumes with their gleanings, letters many of which the President had written for private, not public eyes.

One example, which the newspapers spread broadcast over the country, will suffice to show why Grover Cleveland was not beloved of the press:

To Joseph Keppler, Esq.,
New York City.
My dear Sir:

I just received your letter, with the newspaper clipping which caused you so much annoyance.

I don't think there ever was a time when newspaper lying was so general and so mean as at present, and there never was a country under the sun where it flourished as it does in this. The falsehoods daily spread before the people in our newspapers, while they are proofs of the mental ingenuity of those engaged in newspaper work, are insults to the American love for decency and fair play of which we boast.

I hasten to reply to your letter that the allegation contained in the slip you send me, to the effect that you ever asked a personal favor of me, is entirely and utterly false. You have never in the slightest manner indicated a wish, claim, or preference touching any appointment to office, or any official act of mine, and the only occasion I remember when I ever had any conversation with you was during a short and very friendly call you made upon me in Albany, during my term as Governor. If I ever received a letter or message from you on any subject I have forgotten it—a thing I should not be apt to do.

While I am sorry that any friendliness you may have felt or exhibited for me has been the cause of embarrassment to you, I cannot refrain from saying that if you ever become a subject of newspaper lying, and attempt to run down and expose all such lies, you will be a busy man, if you attempt nothing else.

Hoping that the denial which I send is sufficiently explicit, I am

Yours very sincerely,

Grover Cleveland.

Under such conditions it is not remarkable that the public was for a time deceived concerning the real nature of the man whom they had chosen President, and that the slanders of the campaign of 1884 were kept alive in the minds of the people. His critics, for the most part, either failed to understand what he had promised, were misinformed as to his actions, or intentionally misrepresented him. By refusing to go to one extreme with the reformers, he lost their confidence; by refusing to go to the other extreme with the spoilsmen, he lost theirs. But he yielded to neither, considering that his duty lay between, in which position he became the target of both.

The months, as they passed, brought no cessation of the conflict. "All this time, like a nightmare," he wrote to Charles Goodyear, "this dreadful, damnable office-seeking hangs over me and surrounds me," and to Bissell he used even stronger language: "The d—d everlasting clatter for offices continues . . . and makes me feel like resigning and hell is to pay generally."

The Bacon-Sterling case, which had just been disposed of and which had irritated the President for the past three months, was responsible for a considerable part of the exasperation which this letter expresses. It had begun late in the summer when Hedden, Collector of the Port of New York, removed Captain Bacon, chief weigher of the Brooklyn customs district, with a service of sixteen years behind him, and put George H. Sterling, a local political leader, in his place, without requiring of him a civil service examination, the Commission having ruled that one was not necessary for appointment to the post of weigher. Sterling was believed by the reformers to be the man of "Boss" McLaughlin of Brooklyn, who in turn rejoiced in the title "political henchman of David B. Hill." The office was politically important as it controlled over three hundred laborers with votes, and a mayoralty campaign was on in Brooklyn.

"The change," commented the New York *Times* of September 16, 1885, "has no apparent motive except the control of laborers' votes by a Democratic weigher." The *Evening Post,* the *World,* the independent papers of Boston, and many others, also loudly condemned the act, and civil service reformers, Democratic, Republican, and Mugwump alike, without stopping to investigate, raised an indignant protest. Henry Ward Beecher wrote to the President: "The ousting of Capt. Bacon and the appointment of Sterling in his place, is most unfortunate for all who desire to work with you, in a purification of government. A faithful soldier, and a singularly honest and efficient man displaced by a pot-house politician, himself a liquor dealer!—It disgusts all temperance men, it wounds patriotic citizens—and is a blow in the face to all who abandoned the Republican party in order to establish a purer administration—Of course, you cannot know personally every subordinate candidate or appointee. But, in a case so flagrant as this, you cannot escape knowledge and responsibility, and I earnestly hope, for the cause which we both serve, that it will seem to you a duty to interfere in this matter before it is too late."

On September 16th the Executive Committee of the Civil Service Reform Association voted to send a representative to point out to the President wherein the civil service laws had been violated by Hedden, and invited Edward M. Shepard, then President of the Young Men's Democratic Club of Brooklyn, to act in this capacity; but Mr. Shepard declined, preferring to send a personal appeal to the President, in which he wrote:

"I do not know Mr. Sterling personally; but he is certainly widely supposed to be a corrupt man. He is not now a weigher—and his experience as a weigher, if he ever had it, was very long ago and was not of an importance to fit him to be the executive head of three hundred employees. He is a liquor-dealer, whose associates are reputed to be of a very rough character. To place to a considerable degree, in his charge, the enormous commercial interests of the warehousemen along the Brooklyn water front and their customers would be an official act, if adopted by the Administration, which would be a lasting and most serious burden upon its friends."

There followed many pages in justification of his complaint, and the letter ended with the declaration that the President should "without delay and in the most emphatic way revoke Mr. Sterling's appointment, and restore Captain Bacon, unless there be proven charges against him."

Collector Hedden, on the other hand, stoutly defended the change, on the ground that neither the letter nor the spirit of the civil service regulations had been violated, that Bacon had been a highly unsatisfactory official, lending his office to political exploitation, and that Sterling was "a man of integrity, and particularly skilled in the work of the office to which he was appointed."

Under such conditions, it was necessary for the President to discover the truth for himself before expressing an opinion. He therefore requested his brother-in-law, E. B. Yeomans, to visit the district in question and to report upon the facts, while in order to protect the service he directed that Sterling's appointment be revoked until a final decision could be properly rendered. Yeomans's report, which covered seventeen sheets of foolscap, was distinctly favorable to Sterling, and tended to justify his appointment to succeed Bacon, although it declared that Sterling kept a liquor saloon.

The President next wrote the following letter:

Executive Mansion, Washington.

*Sept. 29, 1885.*

EDWARD M. SHEPARD, ESQ.,
Dear Sir:

I was glad you wrote to me regarding the Bacon-Sterling affair. Since the receipt of your letter I have caused the suspension of Sterling pending an examination. I cannot afford to be unjust even towards a man so promptly and vigorously assailed. In such cases as this we are all apt to go a little fast. I want you now in cooler moments to help me investigate this affair—and especially the character of Sterling. The rest I can attend to.

I have received letters from very excellent sources representing that Sterling is and always has been a good son to a widowed mother and exemplary as a husband and father, and much more very much to his credit.

I wish you would take a little pains to enquire concerning him and his associates and all that will aid me in making up a judgment. and write to me the result of your investigation.

Mr. James How of the Union White Lead Manufacturing Company knows him well, and he had the endorsement of Arbuckle Bros. and other prominent business houses before he was appointed. Vicar General Keegan knows him well, and I think can say something of his life and habits.

The people I have mentioned are no doubt ready to speak well of him. It is in your power to give me the names and opinions of others perhaps who speak ill of him.

You can readily see that I am not in position to act now on general denunciation.

Yours sincerely,
GROVER CLEVELAND.

Mr. Shepard's report is a frank acknowledgment of the fact that his first impressions had been wrong. On September 19th he had insisted that Sterling was manifestly unfit, and that Captain Bacon should be instantly restored to office, unless facts "justifying his removal" are known to the Administration. By October 12th careful investigation had convinced him that Sterling was "a man of considerable native vigor and brightness, having some practical knowledge of weighing and a fair knowledge of figures, and perfectly competent to direct gangs of men," and that "although personally an upright and intelligent man, Captain Bacon has had no great success, either in vigorously directing his subordinates, or in preventing in years past occasion for grave objections to their partisan employment in the politics of Brooklyn."

But President Cleveland had not waited for Mr. Shepard's report. Although upon the basis of the evidence already before him it was clear that nothing had been proved against Sterling, sufficient to warrant his rejection upon personal grounds, the arguments of the civil service reformers had convinced him that his retention would injure the reform movement. He therefore consulted with the Commissioners, and a re-examination of their decision in regard to the status of weighers under the law resulted in an agreement that their prior decision was wrong and that weighers should be examined and passed before appointment. The examination was held, and Sterling was twenty-second out of forty-five candidates. The first man on the list, John W. O'Brien, was therefore made weigher. The Democrats of the Second Ward passed resolutions denouncing this "mean and cowardly treatment of Mr. Sterling" and sent them to "the Mugwump President, the vacillating Secretary of the Treasury, and the weak-minded Collector, Hedden." And so the affair passed into history.

In view of the bitterness which the Bacon-Sterling case had engendered, and of the approaching New York Democratic Convention which was to nominate a Governor, cautious politicians felt that it would be wise for the President to "soft-pedal" his reform views. Clearly, his party in New York was not with him upon this subject. Powerful organizations of New York Democrats had frankly declared bitter hostility to the principles and practices of civil service reform, and influential Democratic newspapers had urged that the convention either condemn the movement openly, or pass it over with a silence which would be interpreted as dissent. Most of the New York Democratic leaders who had made any comment had either condemned the law, which they contemptuously called the "Snivil Service Reform Act," or had construed it in a manner calculated to make it no longer the foe of the spoils system. The gifted Tammany orator, Bourke Cockran, had painted for the benefit of the faithful a heartbreaking picture of the inevitable wreck of democratic equality, should America ever allow to prevail that "pernicious system . . . that erects and creates irresponsible boards or commissions to control or limit the powers conferred by the Constitution on the elect of the people." And the faithful had shouted a glad Amen! They were weary of Cleveland and reform.

At this point Mr. Cleveland chose to imitate his beloved friend, the salmon, which rejoices to swim against the fiercest current. On July 27, 1885, Commissioner Eaton had offered his resignation, and the President, in the face of predictions of calamity, deliberately selected the critical moment in the meeting of the New York Democratic Convention to make public his own letter, dated September 11, 1885, accepting the resignation, and reaffirming his determination to press forward the civil service reform movement.

Coming as it did between the nominations of the two parties in New York, and accompanied as it was by the suspension of Sterling, this letter attracted more attention than either of the platforms adopted at Saratoga, but it did not bring victory to the reform element in New York. David B. Hill, backed by Tammany Hall, the old canal ring, and other highly un-reform-like elements, was master of the convention. His hungry eyes were on the White House, and the hungry eyes of the disappointed spoilsmen of New York were on David B. Hill, who had shown that he understood how to give them "their meat in due season." His nomination caused many of the Independents who had supported Cleveland in 1884 to gravitate toward the Republican candidate, Davenport, who, as Carl Schurz expressed it, "represents the best tendencies, not only in his own, but in both political parties, and Mr. Hill the worst."

These defections, together with the desertion of many Democrats, due in part to Hill's nomination and in part to the belief that President Cleveland was opposed to his election, greatly disturbed the New York Democratic leaders. On October 5, 1885, Alton B. Parker, Chairman of the Executive Committee, therefore, made an appeal to the President, declaring that the only thing necessary to insure the election of Hill and his fellow New York Democrats was a word from Mr. Cleveland in their favor. This he promptly received; for, as a party man, Mr. Cleveland felt that he must support the party ticket; and he contributed a thousand dollars toward the campaign fund, although conscious that many of Hill's friends were daily denouncing and misrepresenting him.

"If I thought," he wrote to Parker when making his contribution, "that you needed any advice I should strongly urge upon you to enjoin upon any person pretending to desire the success of the ticket, and at the same time howling about the Administration and claiming that it should *speak out,* that campaigns are successfully fought by pushing the merits of candidates and principles, and not by a foolish attempt to discredit an Administration which is doing all that is possible to assist the canvass. I think the greatest enemy to the success of your ticket to-day is the man and the paper which is constantly yelling to the Administration to come to its rescue. And if you know of anybody that has any influence with the N. Y. *World* you should, I think, ask that the manifestation of its unfriendliness to the Administration be restrained till after election. As for the professed friends of the ticket who are constantly drumming at the Administration, their motives and purposes ought not to be misunderstood and they should not be permitted to conceal their misdeeds by the cry of 'stop thief.' You see I do not claim any decent treatment for myself, though I am not able to see where I have forfeited it."

Hill won a sweeping victory, his plurality over his Republican opponent being more than ten times as large as that of Cleveland over Blaine in 1884, and his total vote falling only sixty-one thousand below the New York Democratic presidential vote in that year. It was a victory most pleasing to the Cleveland partisans who were not in a position to read its true meaning; but to the President himself, gifted with the seeing eye, it was far from being a victory in praise of Grover Cleveland, friend of civil service reform.

Never given to self-adulation or smug complacency, he was conscious then, as he was made more conscious later, that, despite his best efforts to lead his party in the right direction, a great and dangerous political machine composed of Federal office holders was slowly fastening its grip upon the party, with the purpose of perpetuating Democratic control, and that David B. Hill was increasingly regarded as a coming Moses, fit to lead them out of the wilderness of non-partisan government and exasperating reform. The progress of the new year, 1886, saw this tendency steadily increasing; and Hill's references in his inaugural address to New York Governors who had become national leaders, indicated the workings of his ambition.

In view of this fact, and in view of the lessons of his Eaton letter, Mr. Cleveland might have been pardoned, had he maintained a discreet silence regarding the growing evil of official interference in partisan politics. Indeed, he might have escaped the censure of others had he set his mind toward the building of a personal machine of office holders. Instead, however, he astonished the machine men, delighted the reformers, and threw consternation into the ranks of his closest partisan advisers by issuing the following drastic executive order:

Executive Mansion, Washington,
*July 14, 1886.*

I deem this a proper time to especially warn all subordinates in the several departments and all office-holders under the General Government against the use of their official positions in attempts to control political movements in their localities.

Office-holders are the agents of the people—not their masters. Not only is their time and labor due to the Government, but they should scrupulously avoid in their political action, as well as in the discharge of their official duty, offending by a display of obtrusive partisanship their neighbors who have relations with them as public officials.

They should also constantly remember that their party friends from whom they have received preferment, have not invested them with the power of arbitrarily managing their political affairs. They have no right as office-holders to dictate the political action of their party associates or to throttle freedom of action within party lines by methods and practices which pervert every useful and justifiable purpose of party organization.

The influence of Federal office-holders should not be felt in the manipulation of political primary meetings and nominating conventions. The use by these officials of their positions to compass their selection as delegates to political conventions is indecent and unfair, and proper regard for the proprieties and requirements of official place will also prevent their assuming the active conduct of political campaigns.

Individual interest and activity in political affairs are by no means condemned. Office-holders are neither disfranchised nor forbidden the exercise of political privileges, but their privileges are not enlarged, nor is their duty to party increased to pernicious activity by office-holding.

A just discrimination in this regard between the things a citizen may properly do and the purposes for which a public office should not be used is easy, in the light of a correct appreciation of the relation between the people and those intrusted with official place, and a consideration of the necessity, under our form of government, of political action free from official coercion. You are

requested to communicate the substance of these views
to those for whose guidance they are intended.

GROVER CLEVELAND.

With the autumn campaign came the inevitable test
case, and for once the cautious President was found in-
cautious, the careful investigator of facts spoke without
a knowledge of the facts, thus inviting ridicule and insult
which his many enemies gave freely, gladly, exultantly.
Two Federal District Attorneys, Benton of Missouri, a
Democrat, and Stone of Pennsylvania, a Republican, had
made campaign speeches and President Cleveland, without sufficient inquiry into the facts, suspended both. At
once Benton, the Democrat, pleaded for restoration on
the ground that his speeches had in no way interfered
with his official duties. Convinced upon this point, Mr.
Cleveland ordered that Benton be restored to his post.
At the announcement of this decision, the other suspended
District Attorney, Stone, appealed for restoration on the
ground that his suspension had been for the same reasons
as that of Benton. "I made but two speeches prior to the
receipt of the order of suspension," he said, "nor . . .
did I in any particular neglect the duties of my office."

After carefully weighing Stone's plea, President
Cleveland drafted a refusal in these words:

Executive Mansion,

*Nov. 23, 1886.*

HON. A. H. GARLAND, Attorney General.

Dear Sir:

I have read the letter of the 18th inst. written to you
by William A. Stone, lately suspended from office as
District Attorney for the western district of Pennsylvania,

and the subject matter to which it refers has received my careful consideration. I shall not impute to the writer any mischievous motive in his plainly erroneous assumption that his case and that of M. E. Benton, recently suspended and reinstated, rest upon the same state of facts, but prefer to regard his letter as containing the best statement possible upon the question of his reinstatement.

You remember, of course, that soon after the present administration was installed, and, I think, nearly a year and a half ago, I considered with you certain charges which had been preferred against Mr. Stone as a federal official. You remember, too, that the action we then contemplated was withheld by reason of the excuses and explanations of his friends. These excuses and explanations induced me to believe that Mr. Stone's retention would insure a faithful performance of official duty; and that whatever offensive partisanship he had deemed justifiable in other circumstances, he would, during his continuance in office at his request under an administration opposed to him in political creed and policy, content himself with a quiet and unobtrusive enjoyment of his political privileges. . . .

Mr. Stone, when permitted to remain in office, became a part of the business organization of the present administration, bound by every obligation of honor to assist, within his sphere, in its successful operation. This obligation involved not only the proper performance of official duty, but a certain good faith and fidelity which, while not exacting the least sacrifice of political principle, forbade active participation in purely partisan demonstrations of a pronounced type, undertaken for the purpose of advancing partisan interests, and conducted upon the avowed theory that the administration of the government was not entitled to the confidence and respect of the people.  There is no dispute whatever concerning the fact that Mr. Stone did join others who were campaigning the State of Pennsylvania in opposition to the administration.  It appears, too, that he was active and prominent with noisy enthusiasm in attendance upon at least two large public meetings; that the speeches at such meetings were largely devoted to abuse and misrepresentation of the administration; that he approved all this and actually addressed the meetings himself in somewhat the same strain; that he attended such meetings away from his home for the purpose of making such addresses, and that he was advertised as one of the speakers at each of the said meetings.

I shall accept as true the statement of Mr. Stone that the time spent by him in thus demonstrating his willingness to hold a profitable office at the hands of the administration which he endeavored to discredit with the people, and which had kindly overlooked his previous offenses, did not result in the neglect of ordinary official duty.  But his conduct has brought to light such an unfriendliness toward the administration which he pretends to serve and of which he is nominally a part, and such a subsequent lack of loyal interest in its success, that the safest and surest guaranty of his faithful service is, in my opinion, entirely wanting. . . . Mr. Stone and others of like disposition are not to suppose that party lines are so far obliterated that the administration of the government is to be trusted in places high or low to those who aggressively and constantly endeavor, unfairly to destroy the confidence of the people in the party responsible for such administration. . . . Upon a full consideration of all I have before me, I am constrained to decline the application of Mr. Stone for his reinstatement.

I inclose his letter with this, and desire you to acquaint him with my decision.

Yours truly,

GROVER CLEVELAND.

Upon the publication of this letter, the anti-Cleveland press opened their largest vials of wrath, declaring the discrimination against Mr. Stone to be "a presidential sop to the Bourbon Cerberus of the spoils system." This criticism was unfair, as no rules have ever been operative in this or any other country whereby a subordinate is protected in office while openly seeking to deprive his superior of public confidence. President Cleveland had generously continued Stone in office, despite the fact that he had been an active anti-Cleveland campaigner in 1884; but the warning of July 14, 1886, had been specific and should have been sufficient. Stone had flagrantly disregarded it, and his removal was, therefore, entirely just.

The weakness of the President's position lay in the fact that, in his effort to differentiate the two cases, he had incautiously assumed that Benton, being a Democrat, had spoken in defense of the Administration. "I did not intend," he wrote in ordering Benton's restoration, "to condemn the making of a political speech by a Federal official . . . if the speech itself was decent and fair." When the full body of evidence became available, however, it appeared that Benton had attacked President Cleveland's dearest policies quite as violently as any Republican could have done. "I heard Colonel M. E. Benton's speech, October 11th," wrote the editor of the *North Missourian,* on November 27th." . . . Among other things Colonel Benton said: "Democracy is the

poor and ignorant party of this country—the great bare-
footed, unwashed, dirty-socked party. . . . I don't agree
with Mr. Cleveland in everything. I don't believe in his
Civil Service humbuggery. . . . I don't agree with Mr.
Cleveland on the silver question. He was raised east of
the Alleghany Mountains, and he gets his ideas from that
region. He never has been west of Buffalo, and has not
any more idea of the great west . . . than the mere
schoolboy who learns it from studying geography. He
gets his ideas on finance from the gold bugs of Wall Street,
who once demonetized silver and had it—the dollar—
stricken from the coinage act clandestinely. . . . He
learns his financial theories from Wall Street, the leeches
that suck the blood of the honest yeomanry of the west,
like vampires." In view of such facts it is clear that Mr.
Cleveland's mistake was not in refusing to restore Stone,
but in restoring Benton without first making certain that
he had been "decent and fair."

That this was a mistake is beyond question, and it
shook the ranks of Mr. Cleveland's Mugwump followers.
At the suggestion of a number of Cleveland Independent
leaders, Carl Schurz wrote to the President, with brutal
frankness: "Until recently . . . the worst things tied to
your charge were construed as mere errors of judgment,
and occasionally a certain stubbornness of temper in stick-
ing to an error once committed. But . . . this confiding
belief has been seriously shaken by your action in . . .
the Benton-Stone case. This was not a mere mistake as
to the character or qualifications of a person, or an error
owing to misinformation. This was a retreat from a position of principle—a backdown apparently for partisan
reasons or under partisan dictation. The letters with
which that retreat was sought to be covered made the
matter only worse, and the subsequent revelation of the

fact that the Democrat, Benton, had really attacked your administration while the Republican, Stone, had cautiously abstained from doing so, has poured over all professions of principle or impartiality in the proceeding a flood of ridicule which is even more hateful than severe, serious criticism. . . . This one step has greatly diminished the number of those who were confident that, whatever you did, if not always well done, was at least always well meant. . . . It seems no exaggeration to say that your action in the Benton-Stone case is the worst blow the Democratic party has suffered since 1884. It has been received with jubilant shouts by your worst enemies, such as the New York *Sun,* who wish not only to defeat but to disgrace you."

But the tasks of a President are many, and mistakes are inevitable, while it is also inevitable that even friends will at times impute motives which the facts do not justify. The interpretation of the Independents was unfair to the President, who was honestly striving to live up to his pledge, and, being only human, was failing, at times.

Perhaps an even sounder point of criticism was the fact that, despite Mr. Cleveland's wise declaration in the order of July 14, 1886, that "the influences of Federal office holders should not be felt in the manipulation of political primary meetings and nominating conventions," the nominating conventions and primaries of 1886 had witnessed again the effects of that type of pernicious partisanship, far more dangerous to free government than is mere participation in open campaigning, and there had been no dismissals upon that charge. It was indeed true, as his enemies vociferously asserted, that the punishment he had imposed had been for the lesser offense; for if the people can be left free to make their own nominations, in unbossed, unpacked conventions, the master hand of officialdom being kept from interfering, they will be little injured by listening to campaign speeches by officials.

# CHAPTER VII

## THE INDEPENDENCE OF THE EXECUTIVE

*"It is not the mere slothful acceptance of righteous political ideas, but the call to action for their enforcement and application, that tests the endurance and moral courage of men."*
—GROVER CLEVELAND.

FROM the beginning of the history of popular government to the present day there has gone on a ceaseless conflict between the Executive and those whose "advice and consent" was essential to effective administration. Indeed, it is not too much to say that the history of the phrase "advice and consent" is the history of the gradual evolution of the British Parliament from the Anglo-Saxon Witenagemot, or Assembly of Wise Men, and the Norman Great Council of the Realm. Go back into English history as far as constitutional documents permit, and always, in every period, written in Latin, in French, or in English, appear the words "with the advice and consent."

In 759 King Sigiraed gave lands to Bishop Eardwulf "with the advice and consent of my principal men." In 774 Alcred, King of Northumbria, "by the advice and consent of all his people . . . exchanged the majesty of empire for exile," according to a contemporary chronicle. Henry II issued the Forest Assize of 1184 "by the advice and consent of the archbishops, bishops, barons, earles, and nobles of England." The Wicked King John acknowledged that his subjects were to be taxed "by the common advice and assent of our Council." Henry III ascended the throne "by the common advice and consent of the said king and the magnates," and Bracton, the prince of mediæval lawyers, declares: "The laws of England cannot be changed or destroyed without the common advice and consent of all those by whose advice and consent they were promulgated." During all those centuries the people through their representatives, a term of increasing definiteness of meaning, struggled with the crown, first to win power, and later to defend and enlarge it. By "the glorious revolution of 1688" they became supreme, and at once the Crown devised a system of patronage by which the executive power could control, by indirection, a legislature no longer amenable to the direct control of earlier days.

Meanwhile the English colonies in America had naturally fallen into the ancient formula, performing their simple acts of government "by and with the advice and consent" of whatever their legislative branch happened to be called. The old statute book of North Carolina opened with the phrase: "Be it enacted by his Excellency Gabriel Johnston, Esq., Governor, by and with the advice and consent of his Majesty's Council and General Assembly." And New York, Delaware, Maryland, South Carolina, and Georgia prefaced their statutes by that selfsame phrase.

After the Revolution, when the weak articles of confederation were leading the new nation toward anarchy, the Constitutional Convention of 1787 assembled at Philadelphia to prepare for a more perfect union. Every lawyer there had thumbed the English statute books, reading each time the ancient phrase, "by and with the advice and consent." And many of the delegates were accustomed to its use in their state constitutions. It was natural, therefore, that the convention, when seeking a phrase to describe the proposed action of the Senate to which was to be given the right of passing upon executive appointments, should have provided that "he (the President) shall nominate, and by and with the advice and consent of the Senate shall appoint ambassadors, other public ministers, and consuls, etc." Thus the power of appointment was definitely assigned to what at first sight appears a combination—the President, with the advice and consent of the Senate sitting in executive session. The word "advice," however, soon lost its independent meaning and became "merged in 'consent,' " as Wharton informs us, and thus consent alone was left to the Senate, which could check the President's power of appointment, but could not properly claim to share it.

The question of whether removals from office were to be made by the President alone, or by the President with the consent of the Senate was unfortunately left undetermined. In the beginning it was generally recognized that the power of removal rested with the President, independently, the first Congress having affirmed this principle after a conflict which Senator Evarts later characterized as "the most important and best considered debate in the history of Congress." But little importance attached to the matter, however, during our first forty years under the Constitution, as there were, during that period, less than a hundred removals. Washington, although frankly declaring that he would never, knowingly, appoint a man opposed to the policies of his administration, would have scorned the suggestion that he should remove an officer so opposed, in order to give his post to one who professed agreement. John Adams was almost equally generous, although the bitterness of recently developed party politics made his temptations far greater. It is true that when Jefferson became President, after what he termed "the Revolution of 1800," and found the offices packed with Federalists, he exclaimed: "If a due participation of office is a matter of right, how are vacancies to be obtained? Those by death are few, by resignation none. Can any other mode than that of removal be proposed?" But despite the apparent menace of the words, he contented himself with displacing thirty-nine officials, and his three immediate successors each fell short of this record.

When Andrew Jackson and his new-style democracy swept into power, however, this condition was suddenly and ruthlessly altered. Feeling the need of places for his followers, Jackson suggested that all civil service posts be put under the four years' law, a change which would have produced executive pandemonium every four years. And when the Senate refused to countenance this plan, he made places by wholesale removals, two thousand official heads falling within the first year. At once the Senate, realizing the political power represented by the control of removals upon such a scale, showed a disposition to share it with him; but they found Jackson like a lion in the path, and promptly desisted.

Against the weaker Presidents who followed Jackson, senatorial encroachment was comparatively easy. Each Senator had only to let his fellow Senators know that he would help confirm appointees from their states in return for reciprocal favors, and lo! in their joint control lay the patronage of the nation. It mattered not that both removals and nominations must come from the President. Confirmations must come from the Senate, and the President soon found himself obliged to make his nominations fit the cogs of senatorial local machines, or the executive national car would not move. "The courtesy of the Senate," as its inventors euphemistically termed this sim-

ple scheme of silence and division, enabled the Senate
to extend its constitutional right of confirmation so as to
make it cover also removals from office. By an ingenious
expansion they argued that before they could know
whether Mr. Y. was worthy of being confirmed for a
Federal office, they must be shown that Mr. Y.'s predecessor had been properly removed from that office.

The climax of this interesting development of senatorial encroachment upon powers long admitted to be
purely executive, came in 1867. By one audacious enactment, the Tenure of Office Act, the Senate grasped complete control of both appointments and removals, and
reduced the executive branch of the Government to the
humiliating position of a mere executive agency, bound
to ask leave of the Senate when called upon to deal with
its own subordinates. This law limited the executive
power of removal to suspension which, even during congressional recess, could be only for "misconduct . . . or
crime," which misconduct or crime must be reported to
the Senate with the evidence and reasons for the President's action, within twenty days after the reconvening
of that body. If the Senate refused to approve the action
of the President, the suspended official was at liberty
forthwith to return to his post. Thus, by action of a
co-ordinate branch of the government, the great presidential office, which in Jackson's time had invented the
spoils system, was deprived of its power of appointment,
as well as its power of removal. The United States Senate
had fulfilled to the letter the prediction which James
Wilson had made in the Convention of 1787: "The President will not be the man of the people, but the minion
of the Senate."

The use made of this inflated senatorial power of
patronage was demoralizing in the extreme. United

States Senators became autocrats in state politics, "spoiling" their way to re-election by the not too subtle power of the plum. And before the days of reconstruction were ended, indignant public opinion and more indignant executive protest compelled a revision of the Tenure of Office Act which, by the law of April 5, 1869, was shorn of its most obnoxious features. The sections of the act regulating suspensions were entirely repealed, and provisions were substituted which, instead of limiting the causes of suspension to misconduct, and crime, expressly permitted such suspension by the President "in his discretion," and abandoned the requirement that he report to the Senate "the evidence and reasons" for his action.

The amendment, however, failed to restore to the Executive the full freedom of removal which he had enjoyed in early days, and as such was far from satisfactory to succeeding Presidents. Under it the President, while free to make removals, not mere suspensions, was required, "within thirty days after the commencement of each session, . . . to nominate persons to fill all vacancies." If the Senate rejected a nomination, the President was expected to make another, and to proceed thus until an agreement was reached. But the officer dismissed was not free to resume his office, however long the disagreement between President and Senate.

Against these remaining limitations President Grant vigorously protested, declaring in his first annual message that their provisions were "inconsistent with the faithful and efficient administration of the Government" and should be totally repealed. President Hayes made a similar demand; and Garfield, during his brief period as head of the nation, bitterly denounced "the usurpation by the Senate of a large share of appointing power," declaring: "The President can remove no officer without

the consent of the Senate . . . unless the successor is
agreeable to the Senator in the state where the appointee
resides—a power most corrupting and dangerous." It
was, furthermore, the frank opinion of most of the lawyers, both in and out of the Senate, that the Tenure of
Office Act, even in its altered form, was unconstitutional
But the question was not passed upon by the courts and
although the House of Representatives upon three occasions declared for the repeal of the laws, the Senate
would not concur.  And so until the days of President
Cleveland successive Presidents vainly fretted because
of what they considered legislative encroachments, desirous of freeing themselves from the remains of the
Tenure of Office Act, but unable to do so.

In all the realm of political theory, in which indeed
he wandered but little, there is no doctrine which Mr.
Cleveland reverenced more highly than that of the separation of powers.  That this was not due to any personal
craving for power is shown by the fact that he was always
ready, in the interest of civil service reform, to part with
the control of patronage, the very essence of political influence.  It was due rather to his belief that in the definite
division of powers lay the hope of efficient government.

At the very beginning of his administration he received from political supporters definite and frequent
warnings of the Senate's intention to encroach in the matter of removals.  With the impending conflict in mind,
Bayard wrote:  "I do not see how the President can better serve the Country than by keeping the lines of his
official duties and powers clearly defined, neither stepping
beyond them, nor allowing intrusion by anyone."  And
again:  "If the discretion of Congress is to be substituted
for that of the Executive the anomaly will appear of de-

priving the only officer having the duty and power and opportunity of supervision . . . of all control."

These warnings confirmed Mr. Cleveland's own fears, and in his opening message to the Forty-ninth Congress he sounded a note which was dangerously like a warning to the Senate. "It is well," he said, "for us to bear in mind that our usefulness to the people's interests will be promoted by a constant appreciation of the scope and character of our respective bodies as they relate to Federal legislation. . . . Contemplation of the grave and responsible functions assigned to the respective branches of the Government under the Constitution will disclose the partitions of power between our respective departments and their necessary independence, and also the need for the exercise of all the power entrusted to each in that spirit of comity and co-operation which is essential to the proper fulfilment of the patriotic obligations which rest upon us as faithful servants of the people."

This statement set forth in unmistakable terms the theory by which he proposed to conduct his administration; and those who knew him realized that the co-ordinate branch was expected to order its affairs in accordance. He regarded it not as his own political theory, but as the theory upon which the people had constructed their state. He had studied the law, and was formally expounding it to his fellow workers, in order that needless friction might be avoided. Furthermore, it was his mature conviction that removals from office were not intended by the Constitution to be in any way subject to the will of the Senate, and he was determined to guard the prerogatives of his department, cost what it might, offend whom it might. A conflict with the Senate was thus inevitable.

Within the legal limit of a month after the assembling of his first Congress, President Cleveland sent to the

Senate the names of the persons whom he had selected to take the places of officials suspended during vacation. There were six hundred and forty-three in all, and at once members of Senate committees prepared to insist that the President give his reasons for the removal of the officers whose places he was thus proposing to fill. That concession made, the Senate would again be in the saddle. They first asked the heads of executive departments for reasons for the removals. At the direction of the President, this request was refused on the ground that "the public interest would not be thereby promoted" or that "the reasons related to a purely executive act." Requests of this character at last became so numerous that a set form of reply was prescribed by the President.

This mild method of encroachment having failed, the Senators prepared to turn the screw which had so often brought from Executives a reluctant submission. "If we can't get the information we want," declared one prominent Republican Senator, . . . "we can let some of the appointees broil a while in fear that they will get no salaries." This suggestion the Senate promptly adopted. They left the President's nominations to slumber in the senatorial committees to which they had been referred and, diplomatically but definitely, intimated that they would at once confirm every nomination if he would publicly declare that he had made removals and appointments for political reasons. Their object was, of course, to induce him to repudiate his reform pledges, and by thus discrediting the party to which he belonged, increase the strength of the opposing party which controlled the Senate. Equally, of course, the plan was a failure. The President would not barter.

To argue as did the New York *Tribune* that the Senate was acting in the interest of publicity for the facts concerning removals was manifestly to flatter that body. Their aim was not publicity, but control of removals. Such matters as confirmations they themselves considered far from openly.   At any moment, upon demand of two Senators, the galleries would be cleared, the doors locked, and the publicity-loving Senate would settle down to a quiet game of office trading.

Convinced at last that neither by appeals to heads of departments nor by holding up appointments could they bring the President to an acknowledgment of their right to control removals, the senatorial majority tried another tack.   On July 17, 1885, President Cleveland had removed George M. Duskin from his post as Federal Attorney for the southern district of Alabama, and had appointed John D. Burnett to the place thus vacated.   In ignorance of the fact that Duskin's term had expired on December 20, 1885, and that for that reason his was a poor test case, Senator Edmunds, Chairman of the Committee on the Judiciary, on December 26th requested the Attorney General of the United States to submit to it all information and papers relating to the nomination of Burnett, and to the removal of Duskin.

On January 11, 1886, the Attorney General sent the former documents, but declared that he had received no direction from the President which would justify him in sending those relating to the suspension of Duskin. Within a few hours the Senate Judiciary Committee took up a discussion of the question, and that evening Senator Vest wrote to the President:

"I think you should be apprized of what occurred this morning. . . . A letter from the Attorney General was read. . . . I then inquired of Mr. Edmunds, the Chairman, whether the Committee proposed to obtain the reasons of the President for removals and suspensions. That for myself I denied any such right in the Committee—that we had the right to examine the qualifications of persons nominated, but not the President's reasons for suspension.

"Mr. Edmunds replied that he did not claim the right to know the President's reasons for suspension, but that committees of Congress had never been refused such courtesy by the President, etc. No one of the Republican senators present dissented from this position. Mr. Edmunds clearly conceded the point, that the President had the exclusive Constitutional power to make removals and suspensions, for reasons satisfactory to him, without consulting the Senate."

Despite this opinion, the Republican majority organized a movement to force the President to yield to the demand of the Senate and contrived to make it appear that Mr. Cleveland refused the information required because he dared not allow his reasons to be known. "His refusal," declared one of the leaders of the movement . . . "is enough to show that he has departed from his idea (of reform) and is now acting simply on the old-fashioned spoils system."

Mr. Cleveland, while fully conscious of the purpose of the senatorial majority and determined to defend the prerogatives of his office, was equally determined to force his antagonists to become the open aggressors. He therefore allowed the heads of departments to continue unable to grant the requests of the Senate and waited for requests to become demands. At that point actual strife between the Senate and the President would begin, and a farsighted press predicted that the end of that strife would be the repeal of what remained of the Tenure of Office Act.

On January 25, 1886, that point was reached. On that

day, in the face of the best legal opinion, the Senate definitely directed the Attorney General "to transmit . . .
copies of all documents . . . filed in the Department of
Justice since the 1st day of January, A. D. 1885, in relation
to the conduct of the office of District Attorney of the
United States for the Southern District of Alabama."

Affairs being thus brought to a head, the President
took up with his advisers the question as to the precise
form of refusal which the Attorney General should send
to this demand. Mr. Cleveland's papers contain a number of drafts, the most interesting of which is the following, written wholly in his "copper-plate."

"I have to reply that all documents and papers relating to the appointment of a District Attorney for the
Southern District of Alabama have already been transmitted to the Judiciary Committee of the Senate. I am
directed by the President to reply to that part of the
resolution of the Senate adopted in Executive session calling on me to transmit all papers and documents touching
the conduct of said officer, that it is not deemed consistent
with the good of the public service to transmit to the
Senate in executive session all the papers and documents
without regard to their character which are in the possession of this department in relation to the management
and conduct of the office of District Attorney of the
Southern District of Alabama."

The reply actually sent by the Attorney General differed considerably from this draft, though its meaning
was identical with it: "I am directed by the President
to refuse your demand." This was a challenge to battle,
and the Senate Committee on the Judiciary promptly laid
before the Senate a report censuring the Attorney General
—and in effect the President—for his refusal, though a

minority presented a dissenting report agreeing with the position of the Executive.

Up to this time the exchange of communications had been confined to committees of the Senate and heads of departments, neither the Senate itself nor the President being directly involved. But this resolution was a challenge to the President himself upon the issue, whether the Executive is or is not invested with the right to remove officials without interference from the Senate. Upon that question, President Cleveland entertained no doubts. Freely as he recognized the duty of the Executive to avoid encroachments upon legislative power, he was no less clear that he was bound to transmit unimpaired to his successors the prerogatives of the executive office, which he considered "pre-eminently the people's office."

"The only thing that gives me any real anxiety," he told a Boston reporter, on January 28th, "is that the people may get a false idea of my position, and imagine that I have done anything which I have the least ground to cover up. I have nothing to conceal, and am conscious that in exercising the power of suspension I have in every case been governed by a sense of duty and a regard for the good of the public service. Any and every proper inquiry, made in good faith and with a regard to the courtesies that have always prevailed . . . would have been answered. But that is not what is sought." And he added, deliberately, "I shall not submit to improper dictation."

Soon rumors of a coming conflict between President and Senate formed the center of society gossip, newspaper speculation, and cloakroom conversations, throughout Washington, and gradually throughout the country. Letters poured in from every direction, full of advice, full of warning, full of solicitude. James Schouler, the historian, wrote: "The firm stand which it is understood that you intend taking against permitting the Senate to inquire into the reasons for your suspensions, I believe to be just, constitutional, and politic. . . . I do not see how any papers bearing upon such cases could be furnished as a rule, without requiring some further explanation of reasons. And if you were once to put your high prerogatives before the present Senate, in any deprecating tone, they would not show magnanimity in return."

Other and more cautious friends pleaded with him not to become involved in conflict with the Senate, but to no purpose. In vain did Carl Schurz ply him with pages of fatherly advice, urging him to yield. "The Republican Senators," wrote the latter, "are not going to let this matter rest. Some of them are in possession of cases of removal which have an ugly partisan look. You refuse all information about them. They contrive some way of investigating them, and they certainly have the power, and are likely to do that. Some of the cases in question are brought out before the public as removals on mere partisan grounds, in direct violation of your pledges. Suppose this contingency—in what light will it leave you?"

It was characteristic of Mr. Cleveland that he paid very little attention to the question "In what light will it leave you?" His fight was for principle, not for personal prestige. After reading this letter, and many like it, he turned, quite unmoved, to the task of drafting his message of March 1, 1886, which frankly avowed the opinion that in censuring the Attorney General the Senate Committee had in reality censured the President. "These suspensions are my executive acts . . ." he said, "I am wholly responsible." "The letter of the Attorney General . . . was written at my suggestion and by my direction." "I am not responsible to the Senate, and I am unwilling to submit my actions . . . to them for judgment."

In elaborate detail he argued the question of the independence of the Executive in matters of removals. He drew a clear distinction between documents official in character, and documents purely unofficial and private. The former he declared himself ready and willing to transmit to the Senate on demand; the latter he declined to deliver, regarding them as "having reference to the performance of a duty exclusively mine."

He made it abundantly clear that he disputed, unequivocally, the right of the Senate, by the aid of any document whatever, or in any way "save through the judicial process of trial by impeachment," to revise the acts of the Executive in the suspension of Federal officials. Vigorously he protested against the Senate's attempt to revive, after "nearly twenty years of almost innocuous desuetude," the laws which had hampered Andrew Johnson. Baldly he declared the opinion that both the repealed and the unrepealed parts of the Tenure of Office Act were unconstitutional, and scornfully asked: "Why should the provisions of the repealed law . . . be now in effect applied to the present Executive, instead of the law afterwards passed and unrepealed, which distinctly permits suspensions by the President 'in his discretion'?"

He declared that the scores of demands which had been presented to the departments "have had but one complexion. They assume the right of the Senate to sit in judgment upon the exercise of my exclusive discretion and executive function, for which I am solely responsible to the people. . . . My oath to support and defend the Constitution, my duty to the people who have chosen me to execute the powers of their great office and not to relinquish them, and my duty to the Chief Magistracy which I must preserve unimpaired in all its dignity and vigor compel me to refuse compliance. . . ."

His remark about Andrew Johnson and impeachment was no chance reference. He knew the temper of the Republican majority of 1886 better perhaps than Johnson had known that of the Republican majority of 1868, and yet he dared thus to flaunt the idea of impeachment in the very face of his enemies.

This message reiterates President Cleveland's fighting faith in the theory of the separation of powers, and his conception of the scope of those belonging to the office of President, a conception which in later years he thus compressed into a paragraph: "The members of the Convention (which formed the Constitution) were not willing . . . that the executive power which they had vested in the President should be cramped and embarrassed by any implication that a specific statement of certain granted powers and duties excluded all" others. "Therefore . . . the Constitution supplements a recital of the specific powers and duties of the President with this impressive and conclusive additional requirement: 'He shall take care that the laws be faithfully executed.' This I conceive to be equivalent to a grant of all the power necessary to the performance of his duty in the faithful execution of the laws."

This view of the President's powers is closely akin to that later formulated by President Roosevelt in the words: "My belief was that it was not only his right but his duty to do anything that the need of the nation demanded unless such action was forbidden by the Constitution or by the laws. . . . I did not usurp power, but I did greatly broaden the use of Executive power. In other words, I acted for the public welfare, I acted for the common well-being of all our people, whenever and in whatever manner was necessary, unless prevented by direct Constitutional or legislative prohibition."

There is, however, one striking difference between the theories of these two Presidents: Mr. Cleveland felt that the Executive must carefully avoid encroachments upon the legislative power; while Mr. Roosevelt professed no such view. "In theory," the latter wrote in his autobiography, "the Executive has nothing to do with legislation. In practice, as things are, the Executive is or ought to be peculiarly representative of the people as a whole. As often as not the action of the Executive offers the only means by which the people can get the legislation they demand and ought to have. Therefore a good Executive . . . must take a very active interest in getting the right kind of legislation, in addition to performing his executive duties." In other words, Mr. Cleveland's interpretation was that the President is free to perform in the executive field functions of any character not specifically forbidden; Mr. Roosevelt's interpretation was that he is thus free in both executive and legislative fields.

For two weeks the Senate debated Mr. Cleveland's message of March 1, 1886, the majority leaders fiercely attacking, and a minority vigorously defending. Senator Edmunds, in urging that the message be referred to the Committee on the Judiciary, used the suggestive words: "It very vividly brought to my mind the communication of King Charles I to Parliament, telling them what, in conducting their affairs, they ought to do and ought not to do." When at last the vote was taken, by a majority of thirty-two to twenty-five, the Attorney General, and by implication the President, was formally censured for withholding the documents which the Senate had demanded, as being an act "subversive of the fundamental principles of the Government." At this critical moment, the President calmly pointed out that as Duskin's term had expired before the controversy opened, the only question requiring action by the Senate was whether Burnett should be confirmed as his successor. As there was no special reason for displacing Burnett, who had now been several months in office, the confirmation was made and the immediate conflict was over.

But in the sequel lies the chief result of the President's determined fight. Senator Hoar, one of the leaders of the anti-Cleveland forces in this conflict, himself "took the first opportunity to introduce a bill repealing the provisions of the statute relating to the tenure of office . . ." as his autobiography declares, "so that we might go back again to the law which had been in force from the foundation of the Government." The bill was introduced in December, 1886, and on the third of the following March received the ready approval of the President. Looking back, in reminiscent mood, in 1904, Senator Hoar wrote: "I do not think a man can be found in the Senate now who would wish to go back to the law."

Thus ended, in a manner wholly satisfactory to Mr. Cleveland, the most important and far-reaching of the many conflicts of his first administration. The time-honored boundaries of executive power were restored, and Presidents were again free to deal with their subordinates without senatorial suspension or control. Once more the mountain had labored; but it had this time produced something more than the traditional mouse. It has been said with truth that in the field of political theory Grover Cleveland left no monuments; but in his reassertion of the independence of the Executive he left a restoration more valuable than many a new creation.

Long before his fight for the independence of the Executive was over, Mr. Cleveland had willfully and deliberately compromised it for all future time by persuading the beautiful Frances Folsom, daughter of his former law partner, Oscar Folsom, to fix the second day of June as her wedding day. Soon after her graduation from Wells College, in June, 1885, Miss Folsom and her mother had sailed for Europe, not to study the social machinery of court life, as the newspapers later informed an interested public, but to travel and study. Although the engagement had taken place before the boat sailed, the secret had been jealously guarded and had not been suspected by the public. A *bon voyage* telegram from the President, which the operator generously sent broadcast over the country, had for the time being set the tongues of gossip wagging, but they wagged more slowly as the months passed without bringing further news. Indeed, they had almost ceased altogether when there came a letter from the bride-elect to a friend announcing in confidence her engagement. The injunction to secrecy was, however, not in the beginning, but in a later paragraph, and the recipient read the letter aloud at the breakfast table, only stopping when she reached the command for silence.

A few days later, the President was driving with an old friend and her daughter when the latter called his attention to a newspaper clipping which intimated that the President was going to marry Mrs. Folsom. To which the President promptly answered: "I don't see why the papers keep marrying me to old ladies all the while—I wonder why they don't say I am engaged to marry her daughter." It was natural that gossip should connect his name with the handsome widow of his former friend, rather than with the beautiful daughter of twenty-two, to whom, since the death of her father, he had stood almost *in loco parentis*. During her father's life he had been an ever welcome guest in the house, had supplied her with her first baby carriage, and after Mr. Folsom's death, he had, as administrator of the estate, won the heart of the little girl of thirteen by allowing her to copy certain legal papers connected with her father's affairs. He had encouraged her to call him "Uncle Cleve," and had given her a frisky bull-terrier puppy. When she entered college, Mayor Cleveland, of Buffalo, had asked permission to write to her, being conscious for the first time that she was now a woman, and had kept her college room bright with flowers.

When Mr. Cleveland was notified of his nomination for Governor of New York, "Frank," as he always called her, had attended with her mother. Later, she had occupied the Governor's box upon public occasions, and had received visits from him upon his frequent trips to Buffalo, upon one of which she had annoyed His Excellency by keeping him waiting for a reception. She had not been able to attend his inauguration as President, but had gone with her mother to pay him a visit at the White House a few months later.

On the whole, the only relationship of which the public was aware was something very much like guardianship, although Mr. Cleveland had never been her legal guardian. By degrees that relationship had changed, and before her commencement day she had given her consent to become "the first lady of the land." It was his wise counsel which had carried her through to the degree; and it was in accordance with his wishes that she made her trip to Europe.

Upon her arrival in New York, Miss Folsom was an object of such enthusiastic interest that, in order to avoid reporters, she was transferred to a tender and landed at an uptown pier. But the next morning small newsboys, with characteristic disregard of fact and chronology, went about the streets calling, "Here's your morning *Sun;* all about the President's wife." Before the end of that day a definite announcement appeared.

On June 2, 1886, the wedding took place, according to schedule, in the Blue Room of the White House, the Reverend Dr. Sunderland officiating, and using a ceremony written especially for the occasion, but materially revised and condensed by the President. In it the bride is made to promise "to love . . . honor, comfort, and keep." The papers delighted in the fact that the bride's veil was six yards long; the President, that the list of guests was so short as to avoid the sensation of a function, there being all told only thirty-one persons present, including the bride and groom. A host, however, was represented by urgent requests that certain garments forwarded to Miss Folsom be worn at the wedding and returned as souvenirs. Amid the deluge of letters inevitable to such an event was the following, from Joe James, a Chinese resident of Philadelphia:

Mister President:

I am glad you marrie to bear plenty good fruits to the nation, and I congratulate to your marriage all enjoy yourself. I read your letter you so kind to our Chinese living here, and instruct the Government to protect the Chinese and be please to live everywhere. So I thank your kindness ever so much. I heard you on June 2d to be marrie. So I send a little present to you and the bride. I hope you enjoy yourself to received it. One china ivory fan, with sandalwood box, for the bride; one ivory card-case for the President, all sent by mail. I hope God bless you in prosperity in all things.

The letter bears the writer's signature in Chinese as well as in English. A few days later Joe James's Oriental heart was made glad by an autograph letter of thanks from the President of the United States.

Immediately after the wedding, the President and his bride repaired to Deer Park, in the mountains of Maryland; and it was not long before they were experiencing, to a painful degree, the sensation of being exploited before an eager public. A President on a honeymoon was something of a gold mine to ambitious reporters with eyes on space. No incident of the life at the Deer Park lodge could be too trivial for use, and the President and his wife were literally compassed about with reporters. The persecutors erected a whispering post opposite the cottage and, armed with powerful field glasses, settled down to the task of telling the public how a newly married President of the United States passes his time.

"They have," wrote Mr. Cleveland to the New York *Evening Post,* "used the enormous power of the modern newspaper to perpetuate and disseminate a colossal impertinence, and have done it, not as professional gossips and tattlers, but as the guides and instructors of the public in conduct and morals. And they have done it, not to a private citizen, but to the President of the United States, thereby lifting their offence into the gaze of the whole world, and doing their utmost to make American journalism contemptible in the estimation of people of good breeding everywhere."

But Mr. Cleveland was mistaken if he thought that the people were not interested in his affairs. The newspapers, while certainly sufficiently contemptible in the President's eyes, were merely doing their best to live up to the expectations of their readers. Every item of news or gossip concerning the august couple was eagerly scanned by an interested public. When the Elmira *Gazette* declared: "President Cleveland is not dead-heading during his honeymoon. He pays for his special train to Deer Park, pays for his cottage, pays for his board, and pays for his horses. That is the kind of President he is," its readers were grateful for the information. When the *Union* adorned its columns with the words: "The word 'obey' was not included in the vows," another worthy group was gratified. And when the Springfield *Republican,* with an eye to local glory worthy of a professional western town boomer, called attention to the fact that the bride and groom were both descended from early settlers of Springfield, it scored a scoop in that section of the country. "In the land granted by the town to the men of about 1640," it said, "the lot of Henry Burt, Mr. Cleveland's ancestor, lay next to the lot of John Harmon, Mrs. Cleveland's ancestor. The Burts and Harmons lived out their allotted days in humdrum fashion; the children came and the old folks died, the years went on, and in due time President Cleveland married Miss Folsom. And so two family trees that were planted side by side in Springfield branched out until they are now entwined in the White House."

The Honorable Chauncey M. Depew, writing to Dan Lamont, as Republican politician to Democratic politician, gave this practical view of the meaning of a bride in the White House: "My only regret about it is that it will be so much harder for us to win against both Mr. and Mrs. Cleveland."

But winning was little in the President's thoughts. He had won.

# CHAPTER VIII

## CLEVELAND AND THE VETERANS OF THE CIVIL WAR

*"I have considered the pension list of the Republic a roll of honor."*
—GROVER CLEVELAND.

IT has ever been easy to arouse popular excitement upon the subject of the treatment of wounded or disabled soldiers, and this noble sentiment has been often played upon by designing men. Moreover, the Democratic party has always been compelled to deal with more than usual caution with the question when it affected soldiers who served in the Federal ranks during the Civil War, as any unwillingness to pass pension bills for such soldiers was certain to be interpreted as reflecting sympathy for the lost cause. For this reason Grover Cleveland, as he looked over the pension system of the nation of which he was the chosen President, must have summoned all his courage. To allow the scandals which had developed to pass unrebuked was impossible for a man with his views of the duty of a President; to attempt to end them was to bring down more abuse from his enemies in both political parties.

Under a just system of army pensions the maximum of expenditure on account of any war is reached within eight or ten years of its close. Thereafter death steadily diminishes the number of legitimate pensioners, and the size of the disbursement on their account. In 1866 there had been 126,722 pensioners drawing from the public treasury, all told, about thirteen and a half million dollars annually. As the years passed these numbers steadily increased until, in 1873, there were more than 238,000 names on the roll, which called for some $29,000,000 a year. From that time, mortality should have materially reduced the number of pensions; and if the congressional demagogues had kept their hands off, this would certainly have happened.

But on January 25, 1879, was passed the Arrears of Pensions Act, which allowed every successful claimant to recover the amount to which he would have been entitled if the pension had been granted at the time the disability occurred. This placed a tremendous premium upon deception and fraud. Old soldiers whose wounds were long since healed began to discover that, after all, their injuries had been very serious. Men who had had an attack of fever in the army persuaded themselves that every ill they had since suffered was due to it. Before the passage of the act, the average of new claims had been 1,597 monthly; after its passage the average leaped to more than 10,000 a month, while thousands of claims already rejected were revived and pushed through. As a result, by the year 1885, when Grover Cleveland became President, there were 345,125 pensioners, drawing yearly more than sixty-five and a half million dollars, and the list was being steadily extended by the addition of names which represented only the most fantastic claims upon public bounty.

Here, then, was a subject worthy of a President's best efforts. For to reform such a system would be not only to stop the robbery of the public treasury, but would remove from a noble body of heroes a stigma which the selfish designs of unworthy schemers had fastened upon it. To be an honored list, a veteran pension roll must be a pure list, and every name entered by fraud is an injury which all honest soldiers resent.

Mr. Cleveland, while anxious that the country should show not only a just but a generous appreciation of the services of the country's defenders, was determined that so far as was possible the money appropriated for pensions should be devoted to those who had suffered in the nation's service, and that such men should never find themselves "side by side on the pension roll with those who have been tempted to attribute the natural ills to which humanity is heir to service in the Army." In his first annual message to Congress he used the words: "It is fully as important that the rolls should be cleansed of all those who by fraud have secured a place therein, as that meritorious claims should be speedily examined and adjusted." For he was conscious of the existence of practices which must be attacked as soon as the full body of facts was in his possession.

These facts were of a character that would not bear the light of day. Conscienceless profiteers, intent upon coining into gold a noble public sentiment, had adopted the practice of disregarding the decisions of the Pension Bureau, and taking spurious claims directly to Congress in the form of private pension bills, which dishonest manipulators or too sentimental patriots steered through, as secretly as the rules would allow. It was a practice safe as well as profitable, for few politicians dared to resist, lest they be regarded as unpatriotic.

Mr. Cleveland was not in an ideal position to become a champion of the people against this insidious form of corruption; for, lurking in the shadow, ready to be again brought forward at a moment's notice, was the figure of a certain George Brinski, native of Poland, who had served in the ranks of the Federal Army as the hired

substitute of one Grover Cleveland, Assistant Distric
Attorney of Erie County. It mattered not at all that M
Cleveland's action in avoiding military service had bee
above reproach, in strict accord with law, and in respons
to the demands of filial duty. The circumstances wer
clear in his own memory, and they left his conscience voi
of offense: a widowed mother, watching her three son
"draw straws" from the family Bible to decide which o
the three should remain at home to bear the unromanti
burdens of bread-winner—this was the picture which
mention of the Civil War first called to his mind. The
came the memory of the draft, the hiring of a substitut
when he might properly have pleaded exemption; an
then the slanderous attacks of 1884 which had exhibite
him as little better than a deserter. Well he knew tha
any attempt on his part to check the easy flow of fraudu
lent pensions would cause the old fires to burn again wit
the light of new slanders, but he knew that he must mak
the attempt.

According to the habit which had made him a terro
to the evildoers of Buffalo and Albany, he turned hi
attention to a study of the pension system in general, an
of the individual bills presented for his signature. The
results were amazing. Hundreds of bills had been passe
by Congress on the most fantastic and fraudulent claims

Cuthbert Stone had been voted a pension on the
ground that he had incurred a pensionable disability during his "long and faithful service" in the Army. The
records of the War Department, however, showed that
he enlisted October 25, 1861, and was reported as deserted
from December 31st of that year until November, 1864.
He was mustered out with his company some two months
after the latter date, with no evidence of disability, and
had filed no claim for pension until 1881, when he al-

eged that he contracted a disability in the winter of 1863. He subsequently changed this date, and alleged that the disease was contracted "while he was being carried from place to place as a prisoner, he having been tried by court martial in 1862, for desertion, and sentenced to imprisonment until the expiration of his term of enlistment." It thus appeared by his own admission that Cuthbert Stone had spent most of his time in desertion, or in imprisonment for desertion; and yet a committee of Congress reported in favor of granting him a pension on account of the "long and faithful service and the high character of the claimant"! Mr. Cleveland withheld his consent, on the ground that "the allowance of this claim would, in my opinion, be a travesty upon our whole scheme of pensions, and an insult to every decent veteran soldier."

William Bishop had hired himself as a substitute in March, 1865, and had been mustered out in May of that year, having spent more than a month of the intervening time in hospital with the measles. Congress passed a bill, giving him a pension, which Mr. Cleveland vetoed with the remark: "This is the military record of this soldier, who remained in the army one month and seventeen days, having entered it as a substitute at a time when high bounties were paid. Fifteen years after this brilliant service and this terrific encounter with the measles, and on the 28th day of June, 1880, the claimant discovered that his attack of the measles had some relation to his army enrollment, and that this disease had 'settled in his eyes, also affecting his spinal column.' This claim was rejected by the pension bureau, and I have no doubt of the correctness of its determination."

Another bill proposed to grant a pension to one Charles Glamann, who left the service in 1865 without having made any claim of disability, but fifteen years later alleged that he had been struck with a brick by a comrade with whom he had got into a row, and injured in the left arm. Mr. Cleveland concludes his veto in this case with the remark: "I believe that if the veterans of the war knew all that was going on in the way of granting pensions by private bills, they would be more disgusted than any other class of our citizens."

Still another was the case of Mary A. Van Etten, who was allowed a pension because of the drowning of her husband in 1875. To which Mr. Cleveland objects: "It is claimed that in an effort to drive across that bay in a buggy with his young son the buggy was overturned and both were drowned. The application for pension was based upon the theory that during his military service the deceased soldier contracted rheumatism, which so interfered with his ability to save himself by swimming that his death may be fairly traced to a disability incurred in the service. . . . He was mustered out in 1863, and though he lived twelve years thereafter, it does not appear that he ever applied for a pension; and, though he was drowned in 1875, his widow apparently did not connect his military service with his death until ten years thereafter. It seems to me that there is such an entire absence of direct and tangible evidence that the death of this soldier resulted from an incident of his service that the granting of a pension upon such a theory is not justified."

Of one Wilson he wrote: "Whatever else may be said of the claimant's achievements during his short military career, it must be conceded that he accumulated a great deal of disability."

One of the vetoes which caused the most violent abuse of Mr. Cleveland was that of a bill giving a pension to Sallie Ann Bradley, who had been presented as a candidate for governmental support as being the very mother of heroic sacrifice. According to her petition, her husband and her four sons had been Union soldiers. Two of the sons were pictured as slain on the field of battle, a third had his arm torn off by a shell, and the fourth lost an eye in the gallant defence of his country. Her husband was described as a fighting member of a fighting regiment, the 24th Ohio, later transferred to the gallant 18th Ohio, only to fall, terribly wounded, in "Pap" Thomas's fight before Nashville. Maimed, but still heroic, he had dragged out his shattered life until 1880, drawing the pitiful pittance of four dollars a month; and then, worn out by wounds that would not heal, had passed to the other shore, leaving his wife, poor, broken by sorrow and sickness, and compelled to live on charity as an inmate of the County Infirmary, because her surviving sons were too crippled to earn enough to sustain her in her declining years.

Upon the face of the facts as stated, Sallie Ann Bradley certainly merited a liberal pension, as the widow of a hero whose death had been due solely to wounds received in battle. All she asked was eight dollars a month, and Congress had approved her prayer; but the President, having taken the trouble to investigate the facts, vetoed the bill, and was promptly denounced. The Clinton County *Democrat* of Wilmington, Ohio, on July 29, 1886, having investigated the case, sustained the President, giving its readers the following summary of the actual facts, as gathered from the neighbors of the widow, and from an inspection of what remained of her shattered family:

"The husband's name was T. J. Bradley. *He was not in the battle of Nashville,* and could not, therefore, have fallen terribly wounded in 'Pap' Thomas's fight. *He choked to death on a piece of beef when gorging himself while on a drunken spree,* and, therefore, did not go to

camp on the other shore when worn out with wounds and
old age.  So much for the old man.

"There were four sons who were in the service, viz.:
Robert, John, Carey, and James.  *They all came home
from the war,* so that two of them could not have been
shot dead on the battle field.  Two of them, John and
James, are living, so that they could not have been the
ones who are said to have been shot dead.  Of the others,
*Robert died of yellow fever in Memphis several years
after the war, while Carey committed suicide when on
a spree a few years ago* at his home in Bentonville, Adams
County, Ohio.  They were not shot on the battle field.

"Now for the eye and arm story.  John is the one
about whom the anecdote is told that he had his eye shot
out. . . . He is a shoemaker by trade, and the Democratic postmaster of Bentonville, *and lost his eye while
working at his trade from a piece of heel nail striking it*
when repairing a pair of boots.  James *was shot in the
arm at Nashville, but it was not torn off by a shell.*  Mrs.
Bradley *never was in the County Infirmary,* and her boys
are not unable to support her by reason of disabilities
produced from wounds received in the army.  *The Republican Senate twice rejected the bill to pension Mrs.
Bradley,* one of the bills having been introduced by that
valiant lover of the soldiers, Alphonso Hart.

"These are the facts, as can be vouched for by hundreds of persons in Adams County.  If Mrs. Bradley
is entitled to a pension because she is poor and in need,
there are thousands and tens of thousands of similar cases
in the United States, equally needy, who should be pensioned.  If her case is put upon that ground, she is no
better than all the other poor and needy widows in the
country, and if one of them is to be pensioned, there
should be a bill passed to put them all on the list.  But

it is not from any love of Sallie Ann Bradley that all this bluster is being made, nor because she is any more worthy of a pension, but because it is hoped that by misstating the facts a little political capital may be made."

House Bill No. 155 bestowed a pension on a man who never left the state in which he enlisted, and deserted while there. He was finally discharged on a surgeon's certificate for disability, incurred by a fall from his own wagon, the certificate bearing the endorsement: "Never did a day's duty—is utterly worthless and unfit for the veteran reserve corps." This, too, the President vetoed, supplying the public with a full bill of particulars, drawn with his unfailing frankness.

In another case, Mr. Cleveland declared that the "injury complained of existed prior to . . . enlistment," adding the scornful comment: "The proposed beneficiary, after all these disabilities had occurred, passed an examination as to his physical fitness for re-enlistment, and actually did enlist, and served till finally mustered out at the close of the war."

Another bill he indignantly rejected because the name of the soldier in question "is not borne upon any of the rolls of the regiment he alleges he was on his way to join," when injured. "If the wounds were received as described," another veto announced, "there is certainly no necessary connection between them and death fourteen years afterwards from neuralgia of the heart." In refusing a grant to a widow, he wrote of the departed husband: "He never did a day's service," and was "drowned in a canal six miles from his home" after having deserted from the army. "Those who prosecute claims . . . have grown very bold when cases of this description are presented for consideration." "It is stated that about five years ago," another message declared, "while the claimant was gathering dandelions . . . his leg broke . . . [but] it is not evident that the fracture had anything to do with . . . military service." And he summed up both his point of view and his exasperation in the cutting phrase: "We are dealing with pensions, and not with gratuities."

All these bills and many similar ones President Cleveland vetoed, thus giving proof of heartless indifference to claims on the public treasury of men bearing a strange variety of singularly unheroic and unmilitary wounds, or of women demanding compensation for the unpatriotic deaths of husbands, little cherished during life.

Month after month, the dreary process went on, the President striving, amid a myriad of imperious calls upon his time, to do justice to the men who deserved well of the state, by refusing to allow their money to be given to those who merited only contempt. But even his unusual capacity for work was insufficient for the task. "There have lately been presented to me on the same day," he once declared, ". . . nearly 240 special bills granting and increasing pensions, and restoring to the pension list the names of parties which for cause have been dropped." And upon another occasion he indignantly wrote: "During the present session of Congress, 493 special pension bills have been submitted to me, and I am advised that 111 more have received the favorable action of both houses of Congress and will be presented within a day or two, making over 600 of these bills which have been passed up to this time during the present session, nearly three times the number passed at any entire session since the year 1861. . . . I have now more than 130 of these bills before me awaiting executive action. It will be impossible to bestow upon them the examination they deserve, and many will probably become operative which should be rejected."

This was, of course, true. It was physically impossible for him to study each bill presented with the care necessary for a sound judgment upon its merits, but he did so study and veto 108 between March 10 and August 17, 1886, and in the case of each prepared, with his own hand, a set of reasons for its rejection. These Mss. lie before me as I write, a monument to the conscientious care with which Grover Cleveland guarded the interests of the men who saved the Union.

In January, 1887, Congress passed a pension bill which threatened worse results even than those of the Arrears Act of 1879. Under the latter it was still necessary for a claimant to show that his present disabilities were directly due to service in the army. Under the proposed Dependent Pension Bill any man who had served ninety days in the army during any war need only to claim that he could not earn his living, and the Government would give him from six to twelve dollars a month. This bill received the votes of an overwhelming majority in the Senate and the House, and an energetic and influential section of the Grand Army of the Republic strongly urged the President to approve it.

Instead, he sent to Congress, on February 11th, a veto message denouncing the measure as placing a premium upon fraud, by tempting honest men to quit work and seek to live by public charity. He declared himself unwilling to believe that the vast army of Union soldiers who, "having been disabled by the casualties of war, justly regard the present pension roll on which appear their names as a roll of honor, desire . . . to be confounded with those who through such a bill as this are willing to be objects of simple charity." He declared that "the race after the pensions offered by this bill would not only stimulate weakness and pretended incapacity for labor, but would be a further premium on mendacity and dishonesty."

The next day Horace White wrote:

My dear Mr. Cleveland:

I once knew a clergyman who, on being asked what his forte was, replied that he was 'happy at funerals.' I think that you are happy at vetoes, and of all your vetoes that I have seen that of the Pauper Pension Bill is the happiest and weightiest.

Charles Francis Adams later commended this veto in the picturesque paragraph:

"We had seen every dead-beat, and malingerer, every bummer, bounty-jumper, and suspected deserter . . . rush to the front as the greedy claimant of public bounty. If there was any man whose army record had been otherwise than creditable . . . we soon heard of him as the claimant of a back pension . . . or as being in the regular receipt of his monthly stipend. . . . We therefore felt a keen sense of relief when, in February, 1887, President Cleveland sent in his veto of the Dependent Pension Bill, which put a premium on self-abasement and perjury."

But while it is true that President Cleveland used the veto to a greater extent than any other President, and while it is true that but one pension bill had been vetoed before his administration, it is also true that more pension bills became laws by his signature than by that of any other President up to that time. During the years 1886 and 1887 he approved 863 private pension acts, being 77 more than Presidents Grant and Hayes approved in twelve years, and 127 more than Presidents Garfield and Arthur approved in four years. In addition he approved an act which increased to twelve dollars a month the pensions of some 80,000 widows, minor, and dependent relatives, of Union soldiers, and an act which increased the pensions of 10,030 crippled and maimed Union soldiers. It was also with his approval that more than 33,000 Mexican war veterans or their widows were placed upon the lists.

The net gain to the pension rolls is thus graphically summed up in a memorandum found among Mr. Cleveland's papers:

"On July 1, 1883, there were upon the pension rolls 303,658 pensioners of all classes.

"On July 1, 1885, there were . . . 345,125 . . . a net gain during the last two years of Republican rule . . . of 41,467 pensioners.

"On the first day of July, 1887, . . . there were upon the pension rolls 402,000 pensioners . . . of all classes.

"Here is a net gain to the rolls in two years under Democratic rule of 56,875, as against a net gain of 41,467 pensioners during the last two years of Republican rule, or 15,408 to the advantage of the Democratic administration and this, too, in the face of the fact that the clerical force of the Bureau of Pensions has been reduced 124 within the past two years, and that the death rate among the old soldiers is rapidly increasing."

Mr. Cleveland himself was justly proud of his record in regard to veterans, and confident that the soldiers themselves would appreciate the meaning of his vetoes if given a chance to read them. "He told me," wrote Richard Watson Gilder, in one of those curious little pencil memoranda which he kept of his conversations with the President, that "he would want no better campaign document than a pamphlet containing all his pension vetoes placed in every G. A. R. post."

But Mr. Cleveland's record was not placed in G. A. R. posts. Instead, attention was diverted from the facts by spectacular accusations. The papers teemed with abuse. He was the enemy of the veteran, the foe to the cause that triumphed, the shirker who had avoided his duty during the war that saved the nation.

In the meantime Mr. Cleveland exposed himself to attack from another angle, and in so doing proved again his broad-mindedness and his courage. On April 30, 1887, Adjutant-General Drum wrote to Secretary Endicott:

SIR:

I have the honor to state that there are now in this office, stored in one of the attic rooms of the building, a number of Union flags captured in action, but recovered on the fall of the Confederacy and forwarded to the War Department for safekeeping, together with a number of Confederate flags which the fortunes of war placed in our hands during the late Civil War.

While in the past favorable action has been taken on applications properly supported for the return of Union flags to organizations representing survivors of the military regiments in the service of the Government, I beg to submit that it would be a graceful act to anticipate future requests of this nature, and venture to suggest the propriety of returning all the flags (Union and Confederate) to the authorities of the respective states in which the regiments which bore these colors were organized, for such final disposition as they may determine. . . .

Very truly yours,

R. C. DRUM,<br>Adjutant-General.

Anxious always to restore harmony between the North and the South, and feeling that this suggestion offered a chance to show his spirit of conciliation, the President gave his verbal assent, without taking the precaution to examine the law as to his powers in the matter. To his mind it was a course so manifestly wise and proper as to be beyond question. On May 26, 1887, therefore, Secretary Endicott returned the proposition to the Adjutant-General, endorsed, "The within recommendation approved by the President."

There seemed no reason to suppose that there would be much opposition. General Drum, who had made the proposal, was a Republican and a member of the Grand Army of the Republic. The idea was clearly in line with the developments of recent years. It was true that in 1872 the Massachusetts Legislature had formally denounced Senator Sumner for having offered in the United States Senate a resolution providing "that the names of battles with fellow citizens shall not be continued in the Army Register, or placed on the regimental colors of the United States." But it was also true that fourteen months later that same legislature had rescinded the censure, thus acknowledging its error, and illustrating the trend of the times, which was toward a policy of conciliation and friendship with the South.

Since that time, the number of those whose aim it was to chisel deeper the record of civil strife had presumably grown steadily smaller and the custom of summoning the veteran organizations of North and South to joint celebrations upon former battle fields had become encouragingly common. At it chanced, less than a month after sanctioning the return of the flags, President Cleveland received an invitation to just such a joint celebration, to be held at Gettysburg, and his answer shows the spirit in which he had met General Drum's suggestion:

Executive Mansion, Washington.

*June 24, 1887.*

Mr. John W. Frazier,
Secretary, &c.

My dear Sir:

I have received your invitation to attend as a guest of the Philadelphia Brigade, a reunion of Ex-Confederate soldiers of Pickett's Division who survived their terrible charge at Gettysburg, and those of the Union Army still living, by whom it was heroically resisted.

The fraternal meeting of these soldiers, upon the battle field where twenty-four years ago in deadly fray they fiercely sought each other's lives, where they saw their comrades fall and where all their thoughts were of vengeance and destruction, will illustrate the generous impulse of brave men and their honest desire for peace and reconciliation.

The friendly assault there to be made will be resistless because inspired by American chivalry; and its result will be glorious because conquered hearts will be its trophies of success. Thereafter this battle field will be consecrated by a victory, which shall presage the end of the bitterness of strife, the exposure of the insincerity which conceals hatred by professions of kindness, the condemnation of frenzied appeals to passion for unworthy purposes, and the beating down of all that stands in the way of the destiny of our united Country.

While those who fought and who have so much to forgive, lead in the pleasant ways of peace, how wicked appear the traffic in sectional hate, and the betrayal of patriotic sentiment.

It surely cannot be wrong to desire the settled quiet which lights for our entire Country the path to prosperity and greatness; nor need the lessons of the war be forgotten and its results jeopardized, in the wish for that genuine fraternity which insures national pride and glory.

I should be very glad to accept your invitation and be with you at this interesting reunion; but other arrangements already made, and my official duties here, will prevent my doing so.

Hoping that the occasion will be as successful and useful as its promoters can desire, I am,

Yours very truly,

GROVER CLEVELAND.

Conscious of his own desire to see the "wounds that once were" healed by a new sense of brotherhood between the North and the South, the Unionist and the Confederate, he was clearly entitled to count upon a simliar feeling throughout the nation, and as clearly under obligation to do what he could to foster it. The suggestion of General Drum had appeared a case in point, and his approval had been hearty and generous. But President Cleveland's ceaseless activity for civil service reform, and for the purification of the pension rolls, had made for him and for his administration a body of enemies who eagerly seized upon the incident of the flags as a rallying cry. His act was denounced as a recognition of the

"Lost Cause." Letters of protest and resolutions of denunciation poured in. "For this," said one of the Southern papers, "the cry of treason rang out upon the air, and the noble impulses of a loyal and patriotic heart have been denounced by those who would perpetuate sectional prejudices and the passions of war to the detriment of the common good."

It was, unfortunately, true. The cry of rage was taken up by leaders whose vision was too narrow and whose prejudices were too dominant to enable them to understand such an action. Governor Foraker of Ohio announced, "No rebel flags will be surrendered while I am Governor," and the friends of a belated war spirit applauded him to the echo. General Sherman, who should have realized that the war was over, scornfully declared that Drum, as a noncombatant who had never captured a standard, could not be expected to understand what it means to a veteran: "He did not think of the blood and torture of battle; nor can Endicott, the Secretary of War, or Mr. Cleveland."

Mr. Cleveland was not, it is true, thinking of "blood and torture," he was thinking of a reunited nation; but he now realized that, in his eagerness, he had gone beyond the limits of his constitutional powers. Technically, the captured rebel flags were the property of the nation, not to be alienated without the consent of Congress.

Among Mr. Cleveland's private papers is the following memorandum, written in his own hand, evidently a press notice:

"The right of the Department to make the return being questioned by the President, such right was distinctly asserted and precedents alleged, and therefore his verbal assent was given to the proposed action. The matter was dismissed from his mind until comment thereupon within the last day or two brought it again to his attention, when upon examining the law and considering the subject more carefully he satisfied himself that no disposition of these flags could be made without Congressional action, whereupon he directed a suspension of operations by the letter above published."

That letter reads as follows:

Executive Mansion, Washington.
*June 15, 1887.*

To
THE SECRETARY OF WAR:

I have today considered, with more care than when the subject was orally presented to me, the action of your Department directing letters to be addressed to the Governors of all the States, offering to return, if desired, to the loyal States the Union flags captured in the War of the Rebellion by the Confederate forces and afterwards recovered by Government troops, and to the Confederate States the flags captured by the Union forces, all of which for many years have been packed in boxes and stored in the cellar and attic of the War Department.

I am of the opinion that the return of these flags in the manner thus contemplated is not authorized by existing law nor justified as an Executive act.

I request, therefore, that no further steps be taken in the matter, except to examine and inventory these flags and adopt proper measures for their preservation. Any directions as to the final disposition of them should originate with Congress.

Yours truly,
GROVER CLEVELAND.

This was, of course, the proper step under the circumstances. His impulse had been right, but his action had been in excess of the constitutional limits of his power. Unintentionally, he had encroached upon the domain of the legislative branch of the Government, and he therefore publicly acknowledged his error. The spirit of his action, and the spirit of his recantation, should have disarmed criticism.

But his bitter enemies were in no frame of mind to appreciate the one, or to forego the opportunity of making capital out of the other. Again the press and the platform teemed with violent, unreasoning abuse. "May God palsy the hand that wrote the order! May God palsy the tongue that dictated it!" screamed General Fairchild, Commander of the Grand Army of the Republic, in a meeting in Association Hall in Harlem. And less conspicuous veterans, fired by his unholy spirit, poured in upon the President a volley of insulting letters, calling him "viper," "traitor," "contemptible politician," "unworthy to breathe the air of heaven," "a skulker," "a hater of Union soldiers," "the oppressor of the widow and the fatherless."

In comment upon this senseless abuse, the *Nation,* on June 23, 1887, declared, in language more just than discreet:

"The awful cursing in which Gen. Fairchild indulged on hearing the news at the meeting of a Grand Army post last week in this city, gives a foretaste of the use which will be made of the order, in spite of its having been revoked. He shouted for God Almighty to help him in this matter by killing the President with two strokes of paralysis, one in the hand and the second in the brain, as if God Almighty had not done enough in this line by permitting the slaughter of 300,000 young men in the four years between 1861 and 1865. We suggest now that if there has to be any further loss of life in this quarrel,

Gen. Fairchild should do his own killing. If he or any other veteran thinks the President ought to die for restoring the captured flags, he must not blasphemously call on God to slay him, but step up like a man and assassinate him himself. If anything can justify the President's course, however, it would be talk like this."

Governor Foraker insultingly announced that, with these cries ringing in his ears, the President "sneaked like a whipped spaniel." But the President did not "sneak"; he only admitted—reluctantly and a little sadly —that it was still too soon for open generosity to the conquered South.

It is only just to say of the flag incident, as Mr. Cleveland himself said of the question of pension vetoes, that had the Grand Army posts been fully aware of the facts, they would have had little sympathy with these bitter denunciations of their President. That great, patriotic organization had been in existence for twenty-two years. It embraced the best class of veterans of the Civil War, men of every political faith, every religious sect, every calling. It commanded universal respect, not alone in the North, but in the South as well. Founded upon a patriotic impulse, its general aim was the promotion of brotherhod among the brave. It distinctly discarded partisan politics, and taught that the broadest independence of the citizen is the best training for the loyal soldier. But Grand Army posts had been deliberately and maliciously fed upon falsehood. Demagogues within and demagogues without the order had steadily misled their veteran brothers regarding the attitude and the methods of Mr. Cleveland, thus turning the organization into the forbidden path of party politics. "Little by little, step by step," commented the Philadelphia *Times* of July 9, 1887, "such political brawlers as Fairchild and

Tuttle crawled into responsible leadership," and they so poisoned the minds of many worthy veterans that the very sound of the President's name threw them into a fury of resentment.

The annual encampment of the Grand Army of the Republic was an event of national importance, worthy of the sacrifice of the nation's time which the presence of a chief executive always involves. Before the incident of the flags had occurred, the President had tentatively accepted an invitation to visit the Grand Army at its next encampment, to be held in St. Louis in the month of September. The committee had been hearty and generous in extending the invitation, and the President had accepted upon the assumption that they expressed the desires of the organization. No sooner did it become publicly known, however, that Mr. Cleveland was to be present, than a howl of rage arose from certain members who believed, or pretended to believe, that the President was the enemy of the veteran. Some announced, with explanations more eloquent than seemly, that they would not go to the reunion if Grover Cleveland was to be there; others proclaimed their intention to see that the President was properly insulted if he ventured to come, while the more lawless threatened personal violence.

At first the reason, or pretext, for such statements was his pension record, and later the affair of the flags gave new ammunition, which his enemies fired recklessly. Mitchell Post No. 45 drew up resolutions declaring that, by his order to return the Confederate flags, the President had forfeited the esteem of every faithful Union soldier and given unpardonable offense to the loyal patriotic people of the country; that by this act he had given evidence, either of his sympathy with the rebellion, or of his utter inability to appreciate the motives which induced patriots to enlist for the maintenance of the Union; that by this act he had taken away from the rising generation one incentive to loyalty and patriotism, proving thereby that treason is not to be regarded as dishonorable, and that, though men may plot the overthrow of the Government, they are, after all is over, to be held in as high repute as patriots; "that Catiline may sit side by side with Cicero; that Arnold may rear as proud a crest as Washington, and that Davis may be canonized in the affections of the people as well as the martyr, Lincoln. . . . *Resolved,* that in view of the expected presence of President Cleveland during the National Encampment of the G. A. R. at St. Louis, the chief authorities of our Order be requested to remove the Encampment in September next from St. Louis to some other city. . . ."

On June 24th, a committee appointed by the "Sam Rice Post" sent him a set of fiery resolutions. "The undersigned were appointed a committee," declared the accompanying letter, "to transmit to you the enclosed resolutions of the post, with an appropriate letter voicing, as fully as words may be made to do so, the feeling of the veterans who participated in the capture of the emblems of treason you so recently sought to place in positions of honor.

"We were instructed by unanimous vote to write these resolutions in burning letters of *red* on blood red paper, to enclose them in a blood red envelope and tie with crimson stained ribbon; thus emphasizing to you our heartfelt feelings symbolizing the burning loyalty which resents the sacrilege, and the field of blood from which these flags were snatched in the tumult of war. In the crimson hued band which binds this package we desire you to see the stream of blood ebbing from the heart of a loyal soldier as he leaped upon the rebel line, grasped the rebel flag, furled and passed it to his comrades as he fell lifeless on the field, pierced by a traitor's bayonet or ball, thus with this blood red band binding together all loyal hearts and hands and glistening and brightening as year after year sheds its historic light on the pages of time. But you have undertaken to undo all this by your mad act, conceived no doubt in a spirit of pique against the Grand Army of the Republic. You had no thought of, at least no regard for, the patriotic sentiment that warms the hearts of loyal soldiers.

"We would excuse you if this were simply your own private act, for we know full well that a man who performed his duty to his country in its time of peril by a *substitute* cannot enter into the true meaning of such a monstrous act as yours . . . as you could . . . had you heard with us the oft repeated 'Rebel Yell' that meant death or wounds and groans and shattered limbs; or had you met disease and seeds of consuming death on the field, march, and bivouac, or been placed face to face with the lipless mouth of gaunt relentless famine as it mocked at want and stalked unrebuked in southern prison pens with these flags floating over them in haughty defiance of the nation's power and the common rules of civilized warfare; or had you in search of freedom, aye, of bread, been hunted through southern swamps and woodlands by savage bloodhounds and listened to their horrid baying as they drew nearer and nearer on your track, set on by men who carried these same flags. . . .

"We desire that you may realize with us that the return of these flags, which do not represent property so much as principle, is deadly and destructive to every patriotic impulse. These flags can now have no other meaning than a representation of treason. There ought to be in this land to-day no one who would own them. Of value they have none, save as dishonored, hidden, disowned, they are visible warnings for the future: but placed as you propose, in the hands of those who carried them in war, who have been slowly learning to feel the shame of their treason, to be held in reverence and as sacred relics as of a just cause and their reception to be made as they say 'a season of rejoicing,' is to insult the Union dead, the loyal living, to give approval to treason and in fact to say to them, you can still adore treason, worship the heroes and relics of secession, declare your cause just and teach your children to hold in higher regard the 'stars and bars' of disunion than the 'stars and stripes' of the Union, and still fulfill the duty of a loyal citizen. . . .

"No, Mr. President, loyalty is not dead, it slumbereth not, nor does it sleep on its posts, and its watch fires are brightly burning. 'The penalty of treason is death.' It is and shall be made odious. The great Grand Army of the Republic have sworn it."

There was much more, equally violent, equally foolish, in the letter; but the "Resolutions," actually typewritten on blood-red paper, enclosed in a blood-red envelope and tied with a crimson-stained ribbon, though, for obvious reasons, not written in burning letters of red, represent the Mt. Everest of insult:

"*Be It Resolved by Sam Rice Post G. A. R. Department of Iowa:* That we do hereby protest against the surrender of the rebel flags to the men who bore them in their mad attempt to destroy the country, either by the president of the United States or by Congress.

"That the recent attempt to do so by the unauthorized act of the president was but an attempt to accomplish through him what they failed to do on the field of bat tle [re-capture the flags]. . . .

"That by this act of truculency and subserviency to treason Grover Cleveland has forfeited all claim to respect from those who fought to capture these emblems of treason, and from all who respect the valor and sacrifice of the Union soldiers, and that he has shown himself by this act more plainly, if possible, than before, that he is not only no friend to the Union soldier, but that what love and sympathy his nature is capable of goes out to the soldiers of the other side, and that in his readiness to serve them and solidify the Southern feeling, he has even violated his oath of office, and shown himself wholly unworthy of the trust reposed in him as chief magistrate of the Nation. . . .

"That in view of this bold attempt of a leader of a great party to break down all barriers and destroy all distinctions between loyalty and treason, patriotism and disunion, between government and anarchy, we recognize with ten-fold more force than ever the need of keeping alive the posts of the Grand Army of the Republic in which none can enter on whom the stain of treason rests, as schools of loyalty, and to sow the seeds of true patriotism. . . .

"That we heartily approve the action of our Department Commander in entering his early protest against the great vetoer's presence at the National Encampment as an invited guest, and in his protest at this resurrection of rebel trophies, and also the protest from Iowa's loyal Governor in this behalf, as formerly, when the old flag was assailed, Iowa is at the front."

In August, at a reunion of the Army of West Virginia, at Wheeling, a huge banner of the President was suspended across the street down which the parade was to pass. It was inscribed, "God bless our President, Commander-in-Chief of our Army and Navy." When the head of the first division, composed of Pennsylvania veterans, reached the picture, Post No. 41, which led the advance, went squarely under the flag. The succeeding posts, however, crowded into the gutter to avoid passing under the banner, and either drooped their colors or trailed them along the ground as they passed. As organization after organization went by in this manner, the excitement among the vast throng of spectators became intense, and cheers and hisses were alternately given as the banner was passed. During a halt caused by the great length of the column the action of some of the veterans became more marked, and curses and epithets were hurled at the picture. Meanwhile news of what was going on was spread far and wide, and soon the street was blocked with an excited mass. Democratic members of the G. A. R. began to tear off their badges and leave the ranks, while many officers of the marching posts hurried to and fro, urging their men over to the side of the street and commanding that the flags be trailed.

The excitement reached its height when an encampment of the Union Veterans' Legion of Pittsburgh reached the spot. The crowd had filled all the breadth of the street, leaving but a narrow lane along one curb for the column. The Legion, two hundred and fifty strong, struck a bee-line down the center of the street, the officers in front, clearing the way, and as they passed under the Cleveland banner with upright flag-staffs many of their members took off their hats and saluted. Immediately pandemonium was let loose, and while most of the G. A. R. men and their friends filled the air with hisses and groans, the Democrats cheered until they were

hoarse, while threats of violence were freely inter
changed. However, the column passed on, and all dange
was over, though during the remainder of the day th
excitement was very great, and threats to tear down th
flag were heard on all sides.

But the G. A. R. were not all hostile to the President
One veteran from the West, more friendly than literate
wrote:

My dear Sir:

. . . I served four years and six months in the rebellion. . . . My weight is 240. My Collor is 18 inches
and in all this Flesh of mine I never seen such utter
foolishness as some of the G. A. R. is making over the
encampment: and to have one of our leeding statesmen
Ex Gov Fairchild a man we all loved as a comrad to tak
the stand he has take I must say I am uterly astoned of
him and the Boodle Comrades he has with him . . .
Pardon my boldness in writing and I would not do it
ownly to show you that the G. A. R. is not all trying to
make fools of the selves.

Despite such encouragement, however, it was evident to the President and his friends that the presidential
office would certainly suffer insult, if indeed the President himself were not subjected to personal violence, if
the intended visit to St. Louis were made. It was not
easy, however, to recall the acceptance without giving
countenance to the accusation, certain to be made, that
Mr. Cleveland was afraid to go. The correspondence
among his friends upon this delicate point is full of solicitude. "I want him to avoid having them say afterwards
that he was frightened," wrote Secretary Whitney to
Colonel Lamont, adding: "That's what the *World* and

the rest of that ilk will say unless between now and Monday morning there should come a general demand of public sentiment against it. I think it will come and the President can then peacefully yield to it if he thinks it judicious not to go. . . . I write this because I know the President begins to feel it his duty to the country to keep himself safe. It is his duty . . . but . . . until there is apparent a great deal of public demand against it, not in this little teapot of Washington, but from outside, he should adhere to his decision. Give out the fact that he is urged not to go, etc." And in a postscript he added, "Let the solicitude for his personal safety grow. . . . Don't check it, for Heaven's sake." From the point of view of "good politics," this was doubtless the wise method of handling the situation; but Mr. Cleveland's ideas were different. As soon as he was convinced that the visit would imperil the dignity of his great office, he sent Mayor Francis an open letter containing a straightforward statement of the facts, and flatly declaring his determination to remain at Washington, not in order to avoid personal danger, but that the office of Chief Executive might not be publicly insulted.

Passions aroused by civil war die hard, and almost two decades passed before a Republican President, Theodore Roosevelt, acting in harmony with a Republican Congress, realized Grover Cleveland's aim by restoring the Confederate flags. In February, 1905, a bill to that effect, and substantially identical with the one for which Mr. Cleveland had been so violently attacked, passed both houses unanimously, and without the formality of the yeas and nays.

# CHAPTER IX

## CLEVELAND AND THE WARDS OF THE NATION, THE AMERICAN INDIANS

*"The conscience of the people demands that the Indians
be fairly and honestly treated as wards of the Government."*
—GROVER CLEVELAND.

WHEN Grover Cleveland became President, the status of the North American Indian was chaotic indeed. A few Indians had from time to time been admitted to citizenship, but as a whole the Indian was a man without law, a wild thing whose relationship to the soil which nourished him was like that of the bear, the wolf, or the coyote. The laws dealt with "the pack," not with the individual, and the rights of "the pack" were little regarded, even those which rested upon Indian treaties. From the beginning of the American Federal Union to the year 1871, when such formalities were abandoned, almost four hundred Indian treaties had been made; but they had seldom, if ever, been allowed to interfere with the plans of the white men.

The Supreme Court of the United States had frequently declared that an Indian title "was not inconsistent with the fee simple, the absolute ownership, being in other persons." Upon that theory the white man had seized the continent, and upon that theory he had administered it, despite frequent appeals from successive Presidents for justice to the red man. In his seventh annual address, Washington had called the attention of Congress to the fact that "to enforce upon the Indians

218

the observance of justice, it is indispensable that there shall be competent means of rendering justice to them"; and most, if not all, of his successors had made similar pleas. With equal regularity successive Congresses had failed to respond, the few instances in which either house proposed such laws proving abortive by virtue of a refusal of the other house to concur.

In theory, the tribe was sovereign within certain areas; in fact, membership in a tribe meant only such security as increasing tribal weakness, savagery fighting civilization, could guarantee, a quantity slowly but certainly tending from the first toward the absolute zero. This process, as inevitable as fate itself when backward races with decadent tribal institutions occupy land needed for expanding civilization, implies little more malicious wickedness than any other natural application of the law of the survival of the fittest. Did not this law operate, primitive races would be left in non-productive enjoyment of lands capable of supporting fifty times their populations; and all that can be hoped, even by the most idealistic friends of primitive peoples, is that the inevitable crowding-out process shall be conducted with as much consideration as just laws and generous administrations can afford.

By 1830, this crowding-out process, for lands east of the Mississippi River, had reached its inevitable result, and with solemn and not intentionally misleading promises that the new lands beyond the Father of Waters should be theirs and their tribes' forever, and without a hint that compulsion was contemplated by the enacting Congress, arrangements had been made to remove the Indians into the great, unorganized west. The argument was made to them that, while remaining in their old homes, they were under the control of the states in which those homes lay, and therefore not within reach of the kindly friendship of the National Government. Thus tribe after tribe was persuaded to exchange its lands in the east for lands in the west, where the "Great Father" would see that their rights were protected. Established in their new homes, the Indians had been, for a time, allowed to enjoy the sense of independent sovereignty; and some, notably the Cherokees, Choctaws, Creeks, Chickasaws, and Seminoles, for whom the beautiful Indian Territory was set aside, had developed some capacity for self-government and became known as the Five Civilized Tribes. For years before Mr. Cleveland's appearance in Federal affairs, however, the conception of a savage tribe as a separate nation had been slowly giving place to the idea that the Indians were definitely under the control of the United States; and on the very day before his inauguration a Federal statute began to operate, which asserted full jurisdiction over Indians upon reservations, thus justifying in a measure the Indian's definition of Heaven as "the place where white men lie no more."

In his inaugural address President Cleveland clearly stated his views regarding the use to be made of that full jurisdiction. "The conscience of the people," he declared, "demands that the Indians . . . shall be fairly and honestly treated, as wards of the Government." Such an opinion from such an executive could only be interpreted as meaning that the President was determined to secure for the Indian the rights to which he was entitled under treaty stipulations.

Among such rights was that of occupying reservations free from the presence of white invaders. That this would not be easily obtained for them Mr. Cleveland knew. The question had always been a complicated one, and it had been recently rendered still more difficult by an act of President Arthur who, five days before surrendering the executive office, had issued an order that on the first of the following May the Winnebago and Crow Creek lands should be opened for settlement. Thus were those Indians robbed of 500,000 acres granted to them by treaty with the United States.

Without waiting for the designated day to arrive, a rush for the new lands had begun. By March 5, 1885, it was said that two thousand persons were already making their homes in the to-be-opened reservations, that one quarter of the claims had been taken, and that houses were going up by the hundreds. Other and more prudent settlers waited on the border-land. The Payne Colony rendezvoused at Arkansas City, preparing to move at the appointed time. Of its 10,000 members, twenty-five hundred expected to be ready with arms and provisions to descend upon the promised land by May first. Another strong organization waited at Coffeyville; still another at Kansas City.

The Indian agent at Crow Creek, Major Gassman, sent his Indian police on the rounds to warn such settlers as had already arrived that, as the reservation was not yet open for settlement, all persons found on the lands were trespassers, legally bound to withdraw and remove their property. The highest excitement immediately prevailed, the whites declaring that if the Indians molested their property they would defend it. Sixteen companies of cavalry and two of infantry, under the command of General Hatch, were next stationed on the border of the territory, with orders to prevent the entry of all not legally entitled to admission. They were instructed not to let the "boomers" in under any circumstances, and to use force, if necessary, to carry out their orders.

The new President saw his duty clearly. He had taken an oath which required him to see justice done, without fear or favor, to white men, black men, red, brown, and yellow. The opening of these reservations to white settlers appeared to him the very essence of injustice, in view of the history of the Indian titles. A careful study of the records, and frequent consultations with his Attorney-General, had furthermore convinced him that Arthur's action was *ultra vires,* setting aside treaty rights by mere executive proclamation. Accordingly, nine days after his inauguration, he issued the following proclamation: "Whereas, it is alleged that certain individuals, associations of persons, and corporations are in the unauthorized possession of portions of the territory . . . recognized by treaties and laws of the United States, and by the executive authority thereof as Indian lands; now, therefore, for the purpose of protecting the public interests, as well as the interests of the Indian nations and tribes . . . I, Grover Cleveland, President of the United States, do hereby warn all and every person or persons now in occupation of such lands, and all such person or persons as are intending, preparing, or threatening to enter . . . that they will neither be permitted to enter . . . nor, if already there, to remain."

This proclamation was hailed as an indication that, with the coming of Grover Cleveland, a new leaf was to be turned in the history of "a century of dishonor," as Helen Hunt Jackson had named our dealings with the Indians. Mrs. Jackson herself, then in her last illness, wrote to the President: "From my deathbed I send you messages of my heartfelt thanks for what you have already done for the Indians. I am dying happier for the belief that I have that it is your hand that is destined to strike the first steady blow toward lifting the burden of infamy from our country and righting the wrongs of the Indian race."

Within a month conditions developed which served to test the President's sincerity. The operations of the "cattle kings," men who had leased Indian lands at nominal prices and established upon them herds of cattle, were causing serious outbreaks and disorders. The savages were slaughtering cattle and terrorizing ranchmen, whom they charged with fraud and extortion. The invaders were pleading the existence of their Indian contracts and demanding protection, although conscious that these contracts, even had they been legal from the point of view of the United States, could have little meaning in the eyes of Indians, most of whom had no understanding of individual land tenure.

Determined to have the facts in hand before deciding upon any course of action, President Cleveland sent General Sheridan to Indian Territory to diagnose the case and suggest a remedy. The General reported that the cause of the disorder was the grass leases, by which the ranchmen agreed to pay a certain sum a year per acre for the privilege of grazing their cattle on the land set apart by the government for the Indians. These leases had been made without the consent of the government, in spite of the fact that the contract between the latter and the Indians stated that any lease which the Indians might make would not be legal without such consent. In this way, four million acres of grazing land, or about nine-tenths of the land of Indian Territory, was leased at from one to two cents a year per acre. Upon this land were fed hundreds of thousands of head of cattle. The cattle owners paid no taxes of any kind, and maintained no roads. Moreover, the Indians were liable to the ranchmen for the loss or injury of cattle, and the value of such loss was deducted from the rentals. Thus white cupidity and Indian ignorance were parties to contracts which the latter were in no position to understand, and by which their just and lawful rights were taken from them.

Such, in essence, was General Sheridan's report, and in the light of it President Cleveland, on April 17, 1885, issued a second proclamation which formally declared that President Arthur's order opening these lands was inoperative and void, and again warned all persons who had entered, or were preparing to enter, that they would not be allowed to remain. To such as under cover of Arthur's executive order were already within the Indian reserves, the proclamation gave sixty days in which to vacate, adding significantly: "All the power of the Government will be employed to carry into proper execution the treaties and laws."

This was a strong position, reversing as it did the deliberate action of his presidential predecessor, but one which appealed to such Americans as were interested in seeing justice done. The Mohonk Conference of friends of the Indian expressed their conviction that the President was "entitled to the thanks of the nation for his prompt, firm and energetic action"; and one of its speakers alluded to "the awakened conscience of the American people expressed in the executive will of President Cleveland."

The cattle men, however, believing the proclamation to be a mere play to political galleries, proceeded to bring pressure. Accompanied by a United States Senator, a Congressman and the editor of a leading Democratic newspaper, their committee proceeded to

Washington, confident that a President with a second term unwon would not dare to stand against them and their great interests, for the sake of a few thousand politically impotent Indians. And so they went up to the capital city as gaily as though assured in advance of a favorable reception, and an order suspending the removal of their cattle until an entirely convenient season.

Arrived at Washington, they were courteously received by the President, and encouraged to plead their case. This they did, fully and at leisure. They told him of the magnitude of their interests and the extent of their influence. They descanted upon the tremendous hardship it would be to them were they obliged to leave the territory upon which they had entered.

Mr. Cleveland listened patiently and then replied— and in replying he was at his best. He knew well how to break down the barriers of sophistries that a ring erects, for he had been a ring fighter all his life. He told them that they had talked much about their interest, and nothing about that of the public. The public interest was what he represented, and would represent. They had enlarged much on hardships which were of their own making, and not at all upon rights that had been violated. Bad faith had been at the bottom of this and most other Indian troubles. Public peace and public honor had been sacrificed to enrich the trespassers and impoverish the Indians. Of the sixty days given them in which to leave, they had sacrificed twelve in an endeavor to get him to back down. They had made no effort to obey the law. They must leave, and had best begin to go at once. The command to remove their cattle would not be withdrawn. The policy would not be changed. The time would not be extended, except in specific cases where it had been proven that every endeavor had been

made to go within the allotted time, and then only for
the purpose of insuring the removal, not for the purpose
of postponing or preventing it.

At this new proof of his determination to see justice
done, a volume of letters poured in upon him, some containing expert approval of his position, from men familiar with the situation at first hand; some voicing
pleas, more ardent than intelligent, for even greater
severity. Mediums, claiming to be controlled by "Tecumseh," "Miantinoma," or "Black Eagle," plied him
with pages of advice upon Indian policy. Enticing
pictures were drawn for him of the spirit land where
the departed braves and heroic chieftains "speak and
travel and do good to the whites."

One enthusiastic spiritualist from New York wrote:
"You would not scorn to see those Indians on the other
side, as I so often see them. They are among our most
talented and beautiful spirits—violet and fawn." Bushy-
head, "Principal Chief" of the Cherokee nation,
submitted a brief of nine typewritten sheets, most un-
chieftain-like in character, being full of citations from
Supreme Court decisions and excerpts from congressional
statutes. And the Woman's National Indian Association of western Pennsylvania described his proclamations
as marking the dawn of a new Indian policy. It was a
weary burden, when added to his myriad other responsibilities, to weigh, study and decide the questions presented; and Mr. Cleveland doubtless echoed the
sentiment of a correspondent who remarked that the
President must regret that "any cattle came out of the
ark."

The most constructive of these communications, however, while approving the President's brave insistence
upon the enforcement of law, and his demand for cor-

rections in the interest of even-handed justice, questioned the Government's entire policy of segregation. They argued that every reservation blocked the way to enterprise, and that what was needed was a new policy calculated to absorb the Indians into the civilized life so resistlessly pressing their reservations on all sides.

The conditions which in the past had made the reservation system measurably effective in guarding Indian lands from white encroachments had passed forever. Large and populous states had developed, side by side with the reserved areas; and the tendency to invasion of the unused lands was irresistible. "It is no longer possible," wrote an Indian commissioner, "for the United States to keep its citizens out of these territories. It has been demonstrated that isolation is an impossibility, and that if possible it could never result in the elevation or civilization of the Indan."

These views, repeated in many reports and letters laid before the President, were reinforced, late in the autumn of the same year, by a delegation from the Mohonk Conference, which visited him at Washington. After hearing their arguments, the President declared himself in accord with their general position. "Ultimately," he said, "lands must be given in severalty and the Indians thrown upon their own resources, but the question is meantime how best to prepare them for independence. . . . I should desire to do much and to place it among the achievements of my administration, yet probably I can only make a beginning. But I want that to be right, and I want to know what is the most useful thing that now can be done." Upon that matter the delegation was a unit. They desired a general law which would empower the President to grant lands in severalty to such

Indians as he thought ready, at the same time giving them American citizenship.

Before Mr. Cleveland, following his habitually deliberate course, had fully decided what he should do by way of carrying this suggestion into effect, reports of Indian agents intimated that certain tribes were disposed to press by war for rights which he was planning to secure for them by the surer methods of peace. The agent at Santa Fé predicted, "An Indian war is as sure to come next spring as that the sun will shine to-morrow," not a very convincing analogy for some sections of the country, but fairly conclusive when spoken in New Mexico.

In order, if possible, to prevent such an outbreak, President Cleveland prepared the following instructions for General Sheridan:

LT. GENERAL P. H. SHERIDAN.
Dear Sir:

In view of the possible disturbances that may occur among the Indians now in the Indian Territory, and the contemplated concentration of troops in that locality, I deem it desirable that you proceed at once to the location where trouble is to be apprehended and advise with and direct those in command, as to the steps to be taken to prevent disorder and depredation by the Indians and as to the disposition of the troops.

Your acquaintance with the history and the habits and customs of the Indians leads me also to request that you invite a statement on their part, as to any real or fancied injury or injustice towards them, or any other causes that may have led to discontent, and to inform yourself generally as to their condition.

You are justified in assuring them that any cause of

complaint will be fully examined by the authorities here, and if wrongs exist they shall be remedied.

I think I hardly need add that they must be fully assured of the determination on the part of the government to enforce their peaceful conduct, and by all the power it has at hand, to prevent and punish acts of lawlessness and any outrages upon our settlers.

Yours truly,

GROVER CLEVELAND.

Already, however, acts of lawlessness had been committed, and were being increasingly multiplied by the Apaches, who for three hundred years had been a scourge to northern Mexico, Arizona, and New Mexico. In May, they had begun to leave their reservation in small bands and, breaking over the borders, were leaving a trail of murder, arson, and pillage behind them.

General Crook had at once opened pursuit upon what he termed these "tigers of the human race," and the local authorities had vigorously seconded him, adopting methods so ferocious as to cause Mark Twain to send the following protest to the President: "You not only have the power to destroy scoundrelism of many kinds in this country, but you have amply proved that you have also the unwavering disposition and purpose to do it." As convincing proof that scoundrelism existed among the chosen guardians of Indian lands, he enclosed the following official notice from the *Southwest Sentinel* of Silver City, New Mexico:

## $250 Reward

The above reward will be paid by the Board of County Commissioners of Grant County to any citizen of said county for each and every hostile renegade

Apache killed by such citizen, on presentation to said board of the scalp of such Indian.

By order of the Board, E. Stine, Clerk.

Mark Twain's appeal, however, fell upon deaf ears. Sensitive as he was to the cry of injustice and inhumanity, Mr. Cleveland was equally conscious of the demands of law and order. His was not the type of character to spin theories of justice while neglecting to provide that indispensable prerequisite to justice, the protection of life and property. The Indians had appealed to the sword. To this, as he saw it, but one reply was possible: "Those who take the sword shall perish by the sword." He therefore made no effort to stay "the hand that smites."

On April 20, 1886, General Miles, who had succeeded Crook in the command of the border, issued his field order No. 7, and the last of the Indian wars was begun. Thereafter, for months, Captain Henry W. Lawton and his fighting doctor comrade, Captain Leonard Wood, scoured the borders and the recesses of upper Mexico in search of Geronimo and his Apache followers. On July 13th, the camp of Geronimo was surprised, and the capture of the rebel Apaches soon followed.

When the round-up came, the vanquished warriors, with all their tribe, were transported first to Florida and later to Mt. Vernon Barracks, Alabama, where, though well cared for, they were prisoners at large, held in restraint in defense of the rights of the majority, which they had violated. The result of this removal was to give peace and safety to New Mexico, Arizona and the whole Mexican border. War had been used to prevent a greater war.

Despite this, and one or two similar instances of stern measures in defense of law and order, the general policy of Mr. Cleveland's administration was one of peace. The Commissioner for Indian Affairs, at the end of the year 1886, reported that the "practical trial of this humanitarian and peace system only adds cumulative testimony to the superiority of its methods of Indian civilization over any others ever yet tried."

In September, 1886, Senator Dawes of Massachusetts prepared a general act embodying the fundamental ideas which the Mohonk Conference had elaborated, and which President Cleveland had approved in substance in the autumn of 1885. Having received the approval of both houses of Congress, it was signed by the President on February 8, 1886.

This law, which has been called the Indian Emancipation Act, made possible the disestablishment of the reservation system, and the transforming of the Indians from wards of the government into men in a world of men. It dealt chiefly with two questions: the Americanization of the Indian, and the allotment to individual Indians of lands hitherto held as the property of tribes. It authorized, but did not require, the President to allot the lands in fixed quantities to such Indians as made application according to a prescribed form, providing, however, that if at the end of four years there should be any Indians who had not accepted allotments, the Secretary of the Interior should arrange for someone to act for them. In all cases the land taken was made inalienable for twenty-five years. It was evident that in most reservations, after each Indian, man, woman and child, had received a designated share, amounting to from forty to three hundred and twenty acres each, there would be left much land to be accounted for. This the President was authorized to purchase from the Indians, depositing the purchase money in the United States treasury, to be used for the education and civilization of the Indians on the reservation concerned.

The other chief item of the bill gave the right of citizenship to such Indians as had already left their tribes and adopted "the habits of civilized life," truly a vague and difficult term, for the habits of civilized life are varied and hard to define. The right of citizenship was also conferred upon every Indian who received land, under this or any other law or treaty. Citizens thus made ceased automatically to be wards of the government, and became, as other citizens, amenable to the jurisdiction of the state or territory in which they should reside.

"The law," declared Senator Dawes, with a just pride of achievement, "confers upon every Indian in this land a homestead of his own; and, if he will take it, it makes him a citizen of the United States, with all the privileges and immunities and rights of such a citizen, and opens to him the doors of all courts in the land upon the same terms that it opens them to every other citizen. . . . Two hundred thousand Indians have been led out, as it were, to a new life, to a new pathway." A pathway, he added, with a caution which the circumstances fully warranted, "which is to them all a mystery; they do not know whither it leads or how to travel it. In the darkness they are groping about, and they are wandering away. They do not embrace this new life as by magic, and come out citizens of the United States."

This was perfectly true. The law had enacted an opportunity and nothing more. It made it possible, furthermore, for an unwise President to push forward the process too rapidly, thus aggravating, rather than relieving, the ills of the Indian.

Mr. Cleveland, fully realizing the vital importance of caution, told Senator Dawes, when signing the bill, that he did not intend to apply it to more than one reservation at first, for he knew, as the Senator quaintly phrased it, that the "hunger and thirst of the white man for the Indian's land is almost equal to his hunger and thirst after righteousness." The President added the assurance that, in selecting agents to carry out the processes of the bill, he would consult the friends of the Indians, knowing full well that a commissioner working in the interest of those desiring to secure the best lands could easily put the Indians upon the most inhospitable and unproductive sections, and sell the good sections to white men. In this cautious spirit, conscious of the pitfalls which yawned to punish precipitation or mistake, Mr. Cleveland studied the Indian question with astonishing care and patience, gave frequent audiences to committees, teachers, and missionaries, and, by autumn, had designated twenty-seven reservations as fields for experimentation in land allotments.

From the first, although a few tribes were favorable to the change, the greater number resented the appearance of allotment agents, even as the Englishmen of early days had resented the king's demand that they send representatives to consult with him regarding the making of laws. As the agents entered a reservation they were likely to see a cloud of dust in the distance, marking the course of the warriors taking to the woods, in order to avoid the hated process of being given a plot of ground with its attendant evil of American citizenship.

In both cases reluctance registered the conviction that what was planned was of sinister import. The Indians no more understood what private ownership of land might mean to them than did the early English understand what the representative idea, if accepted, would mean to them. To the Indian the allotment was danger to the ancient tribal system, and to the early English subject the summons to elect representatives meant only a new tax. But despite these difficulties, the work of allotment progressed, slowly but steadily.

The pressure of expanding white population, on the other hand, advanced with great rapidity, making the opening of new lands imperative. A few weeks after Mr. Cleveland left the White House, in 1889, the extent of this pressure was graphically illustrated by the opening of Oklahoma to white invasion, despite the fact that the Seminole Indians had sold it to the American nation with the express understanding that no white settlers were to be allowed to acquire lands therein. It was the old story repeated.

Most of the good farming and grazing country available for homesteads had by that date been assigned, and the news that Oklahoma was to be opened caused a stir among the pioneer element. To avoid the preliminary rush, President Harrison's proclamation contained this paragraph: "Warning is hereby . . . given that no person entering upon and occupying said lands before said hour of 12 o'clock noon of the 22d day of April, A.D. 1889, . . . will ever be permitted to enter any of said lands or acquire any rights thereto."

But even so dire a threat could not prevent premature invasion, and the rich valleys of Oklahoma were alive with eager trespassers days before the signal was given. The greater host, however, encamped on the borders; and at the sound of the bugle they invaded with one mad rush, which between the morning and the evening shadows of that single day settled an empire. Towns which at dawn had been only blue prints, closed the day with the population of small cities. By December the reserved territory boasted 60,000 inhabitants, with schools, churches, newspapers, and much needed jails. Less than a year later, the same scene was enacted upon the Sioux reservation in South Dakota when its broad acres also were added to those which by presidential proclamation were made available for white settlers.

It was the boast of President Harrison's Secretary of the Interior, John W. Noble, that during a single term he had opened to settlement more Indian reservations than all of his predecessors combined. And before Mr. Cleveland's second election these kaleidoscopic changes had produced, among the five civilized tribes of Indian Territory, conditions which made necessary there also the speedy destruction of the tribal system.

In defiance of American law, but often with the eager connivance of the Indians whose property that law was designed to protect, negroes and white settlers had invaded the territory, until they outnumbered the Indians six to one. Moreover, just beyond their boundaries lay the recently opened regions, full of new settlers, many of them lawless, desperate men, who robbed trains, murdered travelers, and otherwise plied the profession of knights of the road with comparative impunity. When too hard pressed by the officers of the law, these desperadoes "jumped the borders" into one of the five Indian "republics" where, in view of the lack of extradition arrangements with the United States, they remained as free as Robin Hood, and twice as lawless.

Of course, such a situation could not be tolerated. A short time before the inauguration of March 4, 1893, a committee of the Senate declared: "Their system of government cannot be continued. . . . It cannot be reformed; it must be abandoned and a better one substituted." And Mr. Cleveland, as Chief Executive, was expected to point the way.

This was an extremely difficult task, as the five civilized tribes, each with a kind of constitutional government of its own, held themselves sovereign, and desired to remain so, an ambition which Congress had recognized as legitimate by specifically exempting them from the operation of the Dawes bill. Moreover, the desire was not unnatural, in view of the large sums of money which were from time to time distributed among them as the result of land sales.

The day before Mr. Cleveland's second inauguration, Congress provided for the appointment of three commissioners to negotiate with the five tribes for the purpose of extinguishing their tribal titles. Mr. Cleveland selected as this commission Henry L. Dawes, M. H. Kidd, and Archibald S. McKennon, instructing them to act only with the willing approval of the Indians—instructions which seemed to doom the negotiations to certain failure.

The Dawes Commission received scant encouragement among the five civilized tribes. Wisely holding their peace as to the limitation of their power, they conferred with the chiefs and commissioners of each tribe, explaining the President's wish that lands should be allotted in severalty, and tribal governments changed into territorial governments. They could make no progress. A general conference of four of the tribes was then held, the Seminoles taking no part. This conference lasted three days, and conditions had begun to appear favorable for an agreement when information reached the Indians that they were free to act as they pleased, the commission having instructions to do nothing without the consent of the tribes. This knowledge put an effectual check upon the disposition to negotiate, and the only result of the conference was the adoption by the Indians of resolutions strongly condemning any change.

The general conference having failed, the commission returned to the original plan of conferences with the chiefs of each tribe in turn.  In private conversations, many of the Creek citizens expressed a disposition to accept the government's proposition; but, after listening to the address of a chief who warned them that they would each receive a lot of land only four by eight feet, the council again decided in the negative.

A year or more of weary wrangling got the commission no nearer their goal, and on November 20, 1894, they reported: The tribes "have demonstrated their incapacity to . . . govern themselves, and no higher duty can rest upon the Government that granted this authority than to revoke it when it has so lamentably failed."

The President's view, however, did not accord with this drastic suggestion.  He still believed that, with patience, the Indians could be brought to see their own interests and to negotiate.  On May 4, 1895, he wrote to Hoke Smith, Secretary of the Interior:

MY DEAR SIR:

As the commission to negotiate and treat with the five civilized tribes of Indians are about to resume their labors, my interest in the subject they have in charge induces me to write you a few words concerning their work. As I said to the commissioners when they were first appointed, I am especially desirous that there shall be no reason in all time to come to charge the commissioners with any unfair dealing with the Indians, and that whatever the results of their efforts may be the Indians will not be led into any action which they do not thoroughly understand or which is not clearly for their benefit.

At the same time I still believe, as I have always believed, that the best interests of the Indians will be found in American citizenship, with all the rights and privileges which belong to that condition. The approach of this relation should be carefully made and at every step the good and welfare of the Indian should be constantly kept in view, so that when the end is reached citizenship may be to them a real advantage, instead of an empty name.

I hope the commissioners will inspire such confidence in these Indians with whom they have to deal that they will be listened to, and that the Indians will see the wisdom and advantage of moving in the direction I have indicated. If they are willing to go immediately so far as we may think desirable, whatever steps are taken should be such as to point out the way and the results of which will encourage these people in future progress. A slow movement of that kind fully understood and approved by the Indians is infinitely better than swifter results gained by broken pledges and false promises.

Yours very truly,<br>
GROVER CLEVELAND.

In the end, the facts justified his patience. Early in February, 1897, he received from a commission of Chickasaws and Choctaws an elaborate memorial explaining their refusal to accept his propositions sent through the commission and, while arraigning the United States upon the question of honesty, consenting under certain conditions to the terms proposed.

"We fear," they declared, "that should our two nations *voluntarily convey* the fee-title to our lands to the United States, that, when done, it would be claimed by the railroads . . . and, perhaps in the end [the Indians] lose their homes. For this reason, more than all others, we . . . have refused to sign said agreement. . . . We are now ready to agree to the allotment of all the public domain belonging to the Choctaw and the Chickasaw people . . . provided the fee-title remain in the respective tribes until the allotments are completed and each allottee placed in peaceable possession of his or her allotment, and all other persons removed therefrom." As a preliminary condition they demanded "payment of the arrears of interest long since due on our trust fund . . . for we know from experience that it usually requires about two generations and a large amount of money, to prosecute to final judgment an Indian claim against the United States."

Less than a month later, Mr. Cleveland left the White House forever, conscious that the Indian problem was in a fair way to solution, and conscious also that the savage wards of the nation had received at his hands that justice which he ever strove to give to rich and poor, powerful and powerless alike, in equal measure. Sixty thousand Indians, not counting those in Indian Territory, had taken lands in severalty, and become American citizens, and the process was still in progress. On February 1, 1898, the Board of Indian Commissioners reported that Choctaws, Chickasaws, Creeks, and Seminoles had signed agreements, and the condition of *imperium in imperio* was at an end.

# CHAPTER X

## CLEVELAND, BISMARCK, AND SAMOA

*"I do not believe that nations any more than individuals*
*can safely violate the rules of honesty and fair dealing."*
—GROVER CLEVELAND.

FROM the point of view of permanent achievement in the field of foreign affairs, Mr. Cleveland's presidential career is generally labeled "not particularly successful." The Alaskan fisheries produced friction with England, and his treaty designed to remove the cause of the difficulty was rejected by the Senate, which thus forced him to resort to temporary expedients such as never fully satisfied his really constructive mind. Lord Sackville-West, British Minister at Washington, by an indiscreet letter, caused him annoyance, which incident he himself erected into a question of international importance by peremptorily dismissing the offender and inviting insult in return from Downing Street. And even in Samoa, despite his best efforts to preserve Samoan sovereignty, Germany in the end succeeded in her persistent and well-laid plans of conquest.

At first glance, therefore, the sum of his achievements in this field looks strangely like zero. But, if actual accomplishment was small, the influence of his persistent struggle against what he considered German imperialism in Samoa, American imperialism in Hawaii, and British imperialism in Venezuela, was certainly considerable. He dared to stand for the rights of weak and helpless

240

nations at a time when it was, internationally, the fashion to disregard them, and in so doing committed the nation to a policy as creditable as it was unusual.

The glory of America, in her dealings with helpless nations, in general, has been that we have given rather than taken; and Mr. Cleveland's foreign policy, even in its failures, helped to establish this ideal. It placed America before the world as a nation which would neither practice herself, nor countenance in others, the ancient methods of the international highwayman, however strong his arm, and however determined his purpose.

In writing the sentence, "We have a moral right to expect that no change of native rule shall extinguish the independence of the islands," Secretary Bayard stated for the President, not an abstract ideal, but a concrete program, which Mr. Cleveland insisted upon, not only from other nations but from his own as well; not only with reference to the Samoan Islands, but with reference to Hawaii and Venezuela, for in each instance he believed himself to be the defender of a threatened and impotent sovereignty. His decisions were not always correct, but they were always courageous, always unselfish, always the result of patient study.

"The Athenians know what is right, but the Lacedæmonians practice it," runs a famous Greek sentence; and it may be as truly said that, while many Presidents have talked of self-determination, and of the duty of strong nations to respect and defend the rights of weaker ones, few, if any, have so fearlessly and so persistently practiced these noble conceptions as did Grover Cleveland. To him, therefore, history must give a portion of the credit which has come to America from the international altruism which she has since shown, notably in her dealings with China, with Cuba, and with the Philippine Islands.

Prior to the Spanish War of 1898, which gave America her first insular possessions, the United States was hardly a world power. Her traditional doctrine of avoiding entangling alliances had kept her apart from most of the great international problems which vex nations that indulge in foreign alliances. For that reason Grover Cleveland's letters, messages, and speeches contain comparatively little regarding foreign affairs. One is constantly struck, upon comparing his papers with those of Theodore Roosevelt, with the astonishingly small place occupied by questions of foreign policy. Mr. Cleveland discussed foreign affairs very little, not because he was provincial-minded, but because he was the head of an isolated republic. Theodore Roosevelt discussed foreign affairs almost incessantly, not because he was world-minded (though he happened to be), but because he had inherited the world problems which had become America's problems in the epochal era of William McKinley, George Dewey, John Hay, and Elihu Root.

The rise of American interests in Samoa had been very gradual. In early days adventurous merchants from the west had entered the islands in pursuit of a trade which at first was casual. But in 1872 a guileless Samoan chief, guileless because ignorant of the Frankenstein image which he was invoking, granted to United States merchants the permanent right to use the harbor of Pago-Pago in the island of Tutuila. There followed promptly and properly the demand for laws that would secure life and property, and in 1875, after a conference in which an American adventurer, A. B. Steinberger, the foreign consuls, and the missionaries joined, Samoa adopted her first constitution. In certain respects it was an imitation of the Constitution of the United States; but it gave the Samoans only the semblance of representative government, since under it the premier was practically supreme, and Steinberger was premier. From the point of view of Steinberger, this was doubtless an admirable arrangement, and it was certainly of advantage to American traders. But it seemed to lead in the direction of ultimate annexation to the United States, and there were those present who were disposed to regard such an outcome as undesirable.

To Samoa had come other merchants and adventurers, from Germany, from Great Britain, and from other Western nations, holding out the hand, but demanding rather than asking similar concessions. These, too, were granted, and with the new babel of voices there entered the islands those twin brethren who sail upon every trading vessel, be it Occidental or Oriental, white owned, black owned, brown, or yellow—jealousy and deceit. By degrees, therefore, there arose a complication of treaty agreements, not alone with Samoa, but among the nations which had developed trade relations with her. England had her agreements with Samoa, Germany had hers; but each had also agreements, bargains, understandings, with the other and with America, and each had her secret plans and ambitions, not too much centered upon the welfare of Samoa and her only partly civilized people. An American special agent, later sent to Samoa by President Cleveland, registered the opinion that the missionaries are "the only class who are in Samoa for the benefit of the natives, and who . . . have no interests of their own to serve."

By 1878 British, German, and American rivalries had become so intense as to threaten open conflict. By virtue of a treaty which Secretary of State Evarts signed with

Samoa during the summer of that year, America obtained one advantage. The treaty opened to American commerce, without import or export duty, not alone Pago-Pago, but other ports of the Samoan Islands, and established a guarded exterritoriality, by the provision that Americans should be judged "according to the laws of their country," and Samoans, "pursuant to Samoan laws."

Of course existing jealousies were increased by the negotiation of such a treaty; but in 1879 they were soothed to rest by an agreement between England, Germany, and the United States, that no one of them would attempt to appropriate the islands. They also signed, on September 2nd, a "municipality convention" establishing a sort of composite government for the town and adjacent territory of Apia, the port and commercial center of Samoa. Delegates of the native government here united with the consuls of the interested foreign governments to preserve order, protect property, and make life secure. As a matter of courtesy, rather than as an acknowledgment of actual power, the native flag was suffered to float over Apia and the Samoan government buildings. Outside the area of this municipality convention there remained the ordinary Polynesian system of government—assembled chiefs, led by a head chief called by the ambitious title, "King of Samoa."

Five years later a new convention was signed between Samoa and Germany. This treaty seriously menaced Samoan independence, and that it was accepted by the Samoan king, Malietoa, without a knowledge of its provisions and under duress, was made abundantly clear by a passionate letter of protest written by him to the German Emperor a few weeks after its publication:

"I humble myself and beg and entreat Your Majesty to listen to my complaint. The first thing concerning which I wish to make known my complaint to Your Majesty is this: the agreement made on the 10th November between the Government of Germany and the Government of Samoa. The means by which that agreement was procured were unjust, for we did not want it and we were not permitted to deliberate and consider well concerning it. I wrote to the German Consul to give me a copy of that agreement in order that we might understand clearly the words in the agreement. But he was unwilling . . . unless we should first accept it, after which he would deliver up a copy to me and to my Government. But the reason for my accepting it and for writing our names . . . was on account of our fear through our being continually threatened."

From this time on, Germany secretly encouraged a Samoan faction attached to a chief, Tamasese, in their rebellion against King Malietoa, hoping thereby to bring in "the day" when Germany could declare herself master of Apia. On January 23, 1885, "the day" arrived. Upon the pretext that the Samoans had failed to carry out treaty engagements, the German Consul General seized Apia and the peninsula of Mulinuu, upon which the Samoan government was established, and raised over the internationalized district the imperial flag of Germany. Such was the situation when President Cleveland entered upon his duties as Chief Executive of the United States.

For more than a year King Malietoa failed to discover any method by which to recover his lost rights. At last, however, he bethought himself of the American treaty, which appeared to him to contain a promise of protection applicable to his existing distresses. He accordingly dispatched to the American consul, Greenebaum, the following appeal:

Apia, *May 10, 1886.*

SIR: In conformity with the treaty between this Government and the United States, dated January 17, 1878, Article V, I hereby ask that my flag be hoisted under the protection of the United States, until existing difficulties are settled.

SULU,
Secretary of State.

MALIETOA,
King of Samoa.

Article V, to which appeal was thus made, declares: "If, unhappily, any differences should have arisen, or shall hereafter arise, between the Samoan Government and any other Government in amity with the United States, the Government of the latter will employ its good offices for the purpose of adjusting those differences upon a satisfactory and solid foundation." There was nothing in this or in any other article of the treaty which required such action as Consul Greenebaum instantly set on foot. Without the knowledge or authority of the President, he extended to Malietoa and his domain the formal protection of the United States. The German Consul General at once gave "notice to all men" that "it is quite impossible that protection can be extended over the government of Samoa by the American Consul before such instructions have been received from his own government," and warned the Samoans to place no trust in such promises. The representatives of Great Britain quite properly sustained this contention.

Thus was created a situation demanding very definite and constructive action on the part of the Administration. Merely to repudiate Greenebaum's act would be of little value, for the problems arising from Germany's acts would still remain. Accordingly, Secretary Bayard invited Great Britain and Germany to join with the

United States in a conference designed to select "a competent and acceptable Chief" to rule as King of Samoa under the joint protectorate of the three powers, each of which should bind itself neither to annex Samoa nor to establish a separate protectorate over it. Both England and Germany readily consented, the latter suggesting, however, that no date could as yet be fixed as, owing to the lack of telegraphic communication with Samoa, some time must elapse before Germany could communicate with her consul. Opposite these words in the dispatch is written, in Mr. Cleveland's handwriting, this question, denoting suspicion: "Was this a pretext for time?"

But although the plan of tripartite control in Samoa came from Mr. Cleveland and Mr. Bayard, two staunch friends of the ancient American policy of steering clear of permanent foreign alliances, it is clear, from the instructions given to their special agent sent to investigate conditions in July, 1886, that they did not for a moment contemplate a policy which would make permanent any form of foreign control over Samoa. Their aim was to "insure stable government in which native interests shall be under autonomous native control." Germany, however, had other ideas, and slowly her true attitude became evident. She took no steps to relax her hold on Apia, and, while encouraging the idea that every detail for settlement would be left for the tripartite conference, secretly gave ear to her nationals in Samoa who were pleading that the islands be received into the number of the German South Sea colonies.

The months between July, 1886, and February, 1887, were used by the three governments to ascertain the facts, in preparation for the tripartite conference. The German agent reported in favor of a German protectorate, arguing, by means of statistics, the authenticity of which the British agent flatly contradicted, that conditions made it necessary for Samoa to "be placed in the hands of but one of the treaty powers," and that Germany must be that one. The report of the American special agent, made even clearer Germany's imperialistic plans and purposes, revealing with the aid of numerous documents the long history of her intrigues in Samoa. It also showed how fully Great Britain's special agent, J. B. Thurston, sympathized with the American purpose of avoiding a permanent protectorate and establishing an effective, autonomous native government in Samoa.

In addition, from the American vice-consul at Apia, President Cleveland learned that Germany was steadily fostering rebellion among the natives, and secretly furnishing arms to the rebels, at the very moment when she was solemnly taking counsel with England and America. When this became quite clear, Mr. Bayard sent to the German minister, von Alvensleben, the following letter:

DEPARTMENT OF STATE, WASHINGTON.

*March 2, 1887.*

SIR:

It is proper I should acquaint you with the purport of a dispatch just received at this department and dated January 31, 1887, from the American Vice Consul at Apia. It is stated in substance that Mr. Brandeis, lately connected with the German consulate at Apia, has been sent under pay and with the title of general, to give military instruction to Tamasese in promotion of his rebellion against the government of Malietoa. The Vice Consul further states that this action has been made the subject of earnest remonstrance by Malietoa to the Imperial German Government.

I trust that the just and benevolent plan of co-operation by the three powers will not be allowed to be impeded by any such inconsistent and maleficent action as has been so reported, and if any such steps have been taken, that your government will promptly check such action by its officials and under color of their approval.

Accept, Sir, etc.

**T. F. BAYARD.**

In his reply, dated April 11, 1887, von Alvensleben blandly denied all knowledge of Mr. Brandeis' activities in the interest of Samoan rebels, and disclaimed, on behalf of his government, all responsibility for them.

During the meeting of the tripartite conference which was held at Washington in June and July, 1887, Germany steadily pressed her mandatory scheme, and England suddenly reversed her entire policy by sustaining Germany. Perhaps the item needed to explain this change may be furnished by the following, copied in the *Berliner Tageblatt* of October 23, 1887, from a recent issue of the Sydney *Morning Herald:*

"It has not escaped observers that the Germans support an uncommonly strong fleet in the Australian waters —a fleet which bears no proportion to the interests which they have to protect—and even if one believes that they will not at present attempt to oppose the wishes of England in reference to the scheme of South Sea annexation, nevertheless the fact that they are represented with such a force must occupy the attention not otherwise than very seriously of all interested parties. Taken ship for ship, they surpass the English fleet in these waters, and control a greater number of men. The *Nelson,* our strongest ship, has a speed of about 14 knots, and is partially armored. In the *Bismarck, Olga, Carola,* and *Sophie,* the

Germans possess a quartette which can reach a speed of 13 to 14 knots, and is armed with modern Krupp's breech-loaders. All the ships of the royal navy which are here, with the exception of the *Rapid* carry old-fashioned muzzle-loaders, and not a single one of them could contend with the Germans under even tolerably equal conditions. Besides the ships already named, the Germans have in these waters also the corvette *Adler,* and the gunboat *Albatross,* so that their force consists of six ships, which carry about 52 guns and 2,000 men."

England knew, therefore, that Bismarck had a thoroughly modern colonial policy, a policy of plunder backed by superior engines of force. And England, while never carrying white feathers in her kit, had been long enough a member of that brotherhood of European powers —robber-barons from the point of view of weak or backward nations—to prefer the peaceful ways of diplomacy to the more costly ways of war. With great difficulty she had adjusted her imperialistic plans to the new ambitions of the Hohenzollerns, and she preferred not to disturb that adjustment, which, only on the sixth day of April, 1886, had been perfected in a formal agreement, whose astonishing terms recall the earlier papal line of demarcation.

Secretary Bayard thus describes this document: It "contemplated the absorption by those two powers of almost all the independent territory in that part of the Pacific Ocean called the West Pacific . . . which had not already been occupied by some foreign power. Through that part of the Pacific a line of division was drawn to mark the respective spheres of British and German influence, and annexation; and each joint declaration agreed not to make any acquisitions of territory, nor to establish protectorates, nor to oppose the operations of the other, in the sphere of action respectively assigned to it." It is true that under this marvelous declaration of a purpose to monopolize world-wide plunder, Samoa was an exception; but exceptions not infrequently cause more danger than rights falling within the rule.

It is, therefore, by no means remarkable that the ministers of Great Britain, deeply as they sympathized with Mr. Cleveland's idealistic policy of saving for the natives themselves those few bits of territory still unmarked by the world's great plunderers, should have been inclined to humor Germany in her plan for annexing Samoa, provided that result could be accomplished by methods already consecrated by first-class nations intent upon expansion. It is also fair to assume, in view of such facts and of later open German aggressions, that, in agreeing to the tripartite conference, Germany was merely camouflaging her real plans, which were to annex Samoa. This is the more evident when we recall the fact that the tripartite conference opened with the clear understanding that, pending its deliberations, affairs in Samoa should remain in *statu quo*.

As soon as the conference adjourned, the more ruthless side of Germany's plans began to appear. On August 29th, Alvensleben informed Secretary Bayard that the imperial government had found it necessary to declare war upon King Malietoa, and complacently referred to Great Britain's favorable attitude toward Germany's ambition for a protectorate. There can be no doubt that this boast was justified by the facts. Speaking of an interpellation of the ministry on the subject of Samoa, the London *Times* thus reported the spokesman of the ministry: "A word fell from the honorable gentleman as to the presence of Germany in those seas. Our own country has been engaged in the work of colonization. He

did not think we could expect that other nations which
had a similar desire for expansion would not also seek
to find colonies. . . . He did not think we ought to view
with jealousy the advent of the civilized powers to
colonies to some extent adjacent to our own. (Cheers.)
If we sought to do so we should be pursuing a selfish
policy."

An equally frank avowal appears in the *Berliner
Tageblatt* of a month earlier: "These little groups of
islands cannot . . . remain independent forever, and it
is therefore to be urgently wished that Germany should
not exhibit too much delicacy with respect to Samoa, but
take it while it is to be had. . . . America would have
no serious objection to such a course, for her motto is
'Trade, no dominion'; and England would joyfully give
her assent, if she were permitted in payment therefor to
lay her hands on the Tonga Islands."

But while Great Britain and Germany stood together
upon this general platform, Germany's methods soon
alienated British sympathy, her war upon King Malietoa
being conducted in a manner highly distasteful to Great
Britain. "Not only has Tamasese (the rival chief) been
installed as king," wrote the American Consul General
on September 10, 1887, "but the Germans have driven
Malietoa and his government from the capital. On the
19th a German squadron of four ships commanded by
Commodore Heusner arrived. On the 23rd a money
demand was made upon the king; the same day he replied, asking for time to consult his government and
people. Early the next morning war was begun. On
the morning of the 25th Tamasese was brought here [to
Apia], saluted as king, his flag raised at Mulinuu and
over the government house where it now flies. . . . A
letter from the German consul now informed me that

his government recognized Tamasese as King of Samoa. Immediately the British pro-consul joined me in a proclamation to the effect that we and our governments continued to recognize Malietoa, and advised Samoans not to fight, but to await quietly the result of the conference." The natives, however, did fight for a time. They had had the greatest reverence for Germany and the German Emperor, but this same German Emperor had robbed them of their king and of their liberty. His demands had been barefacedly without excuse and no time had been given Malietoa to decide the question.

The first demand had been that Malietoa should pay a large sum as indemnity for alleged insults inflicted upon the German Emperor and his people, prior to the appointment of the commission by the three powers. The second was that he should perform *ifu* to Germany. The act of *ifu* is one whose degradation cannot be surpassed in the Samoan mind. It consists in "approaching the conqueror with the face of the conquered in the dust, and crawling upon the belly upon the ground to the feet of the victor."

In describing the scene W. L. Rees writes: "The 17th of September will long be remembered by the Samoans. On that day Malietoa came down from the hills and sat with his chiefs beneath the telea tree in front of Government House. . . . It was from that tree that the Samoan flag had flown until it was torn down by German officers and seamen . . . there it had again been hoisted beneath the Stars and Stripes when the German fleet had sailed away; there the people had come in long array to pay their tribute; there the king had received . . . the representatives of great nations; and there he now sat upon the grass, surrounded by a crowd of weeping friends, to take a sad farewell before he delivered himself into the hands of his enemies. The Germans did not interrupt him. Tamasese kept far away. And while he spoke his last words of advice to his loving people, the tears flowed freely from all eyes. . . . At two o'clock the farewell speeches were ended. Malietoa then rose, and, accompanied by his chiefs and a large number of Europeans, went to the German barracks and gave himself up.

"An hour afterwards the German consul came out with Malietoa, and they marched together to the wharf, where a boat waited to take them to the *Bismarck*. As Malietoa proceeded the crowds followed him. Many voices cried out in tones of grief, his friends clung about his person, his servants sought to touch, if possible, his hand. . . . At length the exile disengaged himself from the embraces of his people, and having lifted his hands to bless them, sat down in the boat and was swiftly rowed to the German man-of-war. Next morning he was transferred from the *Bismarck* to the *Adler*. All night the people watched the ships, and in the morning they saw him taken from one vessel to the other, which latter got up steam and left the harbor. Thousands of eyes, blinded with tears, watched the retreating form of the German ship until the last wreath of its smoke sank beneath the horizon. Then they dispersed to their homes. That day and for many days afterwards there was bitter sorrow throughout Samoa."

Malietoa's farewell letter to the British and American consuls is a pathetic arraignment of those nations which had apparently acquiesced in his dethronement: "I was repeatedly told by the representatives of the British and American governments that they would afford me and my government every assistance and protection if I abstained from doing anything that might cause war among the Samoan people. Relying upon these promises, I did not put down the rebellion. Now I find that war has been made upon me by the Emperor of Germany and Tamasese has been proclaimed King of Samoa." These facts were doubtless in the mind of Mr. Bryce when, during an interpellation of the British ministry on its Samoan policy, he declared that the British Government "had played a sorry part in Samoa."

Meanwhile the Germans were masters, not alone in the regions which had been under native rule, but within the internationalized area of Apia. Early in October, Sewall, our consul, 'sent the following cryptic cable: "Tamasese German aid usurps municipal government. Americans unprotected." At once the American naval vessel *Adams,* with Commander Kempff in command, was ordered from Hawaii to Apia. She made the journey in fourteen days, and upon her arrival found four German vessels anchored in the harbor. On January 29th, Rear-Admiral Kimberly, commander of the American naval force on the Pacific station, arrived at Apia to relieve the *Adams,* and a few days later informed Secretary Whitney that "King Tamasese is governed by a German named Brandeis, who is sustained by the German men-of-war *Olga* and *Adler.*"

Of course such a travesty upon native government created increasing discontent; and Mataafa, King of Atua, who had inherited most of the followers of the exiled king, Malietoa, began to hope for a successful revolution which would make him king, and many of the native chiefs, deserting the government "made in Germany," joined him.

At this point Brandeis, the kingmaker, overplayed his hand, and influential followers of his "king," Tamasese, demanded his dismissal. But Brandeis threatened that with him would go the protecting German vessels, and with them, peace.  Rebellion would at once be upon Tamasese, with no arm to help him.

So Brandeis remained, the German warships remained; but peace did not remain, nor was it intended that it should.  On September 15th the American State Department received the following cable: "Apia, Samoa, September 4, 1888. . . . Samoans at war.  General revolt against Tamasese.  Affairs more serious than ever. BLACKLOCK, Vice-Consul."

The next document in the story is an example of the German policy with which the world has become distressingly familiar in recent years—*Schrechlichkeit*. It is a proclamation, dated September 5, 1888, and declares: "By authority of His Majesty Tamasese, the King of Samoa, I make known unto you all that the German man-of-war is about to go, together with a Samoan fleet, for the purpose of burning Manono, on account of their secret actions. . . . If you do not obey, then all your villages will be burnt down the same as Manono.  These instructions were made and set forth in truth.  In the sight of God in the Heaven, Chiefs, I am, BRANDEIS, The Chief Leader of the Government."

This brutal announcement was instantly challenged by the American naval commander, R. P. Leary, of the *Adams*.  "Being the only other representative of a naval power now present in this harbor," he wrote to Captain Fritze of the *Adler*, "for the sake of humanity I hereby respectfully and solemnly protest, in the name of the United States of America, and of the civilized world in general, against the use of a national war vessel for such services."  Captain Fritze's reply has the one merit of frankness, and it shows clearly that he recognized his orders as imperial: "I am neither obliged to interfere with political affairs nor to inquire whether a requisition

rom the diplomatic representatives of the German Em-
ire directed to me is lawful or not."

In America, public feeling registered in the form of
congressional appropriation of half a million dollars
or the protection of American interests in Samoa; and
1 Samoa, native sentiment ranged itself upon the side of
Mataafa with the result that Tamasese and his German
naster, Brandeis, soon found their following reduced to
our native chiefs, with which sparse backing they were
net and defeated by Mataafa on September 27th. At
nce America announced her intention of recognizing
he victor as king by the choice of the Samoan people.

As the months passed, however, it was increasingly
vident to the President, now nearing the end of his first
erm of office, that his fight for Samoan autonomy was
till unwon. Germany had evidently not abandoned hope
f annexing Samoa, and Mr. Cleveland, still unshaken in
iis determination to thwart her obvious designs, ordered
Admiral Kimberly back to Samoa. This done, he turned
o the task of drafting his final message regarding the
ituation. On January 16, 1889, it was delivered to Congress. It is a brief summary of the history of his efforts
o protect American interests and save Samoa from for-
ign domination. That it does not fully represent his
houghts upon the subject of German aggressions, how-
ver, is shown by the manuscript of another message
ound among his private papers. Had this document
been sent at that critical moment, it would doubtless have
aroused Germany as his later Venezuela message aroused
England:

To The Congress:

I transmit herewith the translation of a dispatch a
copy of which was left at the State Department on the

28th of January instant (1889) addressed by Count Bis
marck to the German minister at this capital.

This dispatch is sent to Congress as containing an
unequivocal statement of the manner in which the re
cent conflict between the native Samoans and a force from
the German vessels stationed in Samoan waters [was car
ried on] and an authoritative declaration of the attitude
of the German Government toward that part of the
Samoan natives alleged to be guilty of the attack upon the
Germans.

The correctness of the narrative of this affair and the
causes leading to it cannot in the light of dispatches re
ceived at the State Department be conceded. . . .

The dispatch of Count Bismarck which accompanies
this message makes it certain the war will be prosecuted
by the great power of Germany against the natives of
Samoa who are held responsible upon the facts assumed
by the Government of Germany for the attack upon Ger
man forces in said dispatch referred to.

It is also entirely apparent that such warfare will
be directed against the followers of Mataafa, one of the
chiefs now engaged in the civil war at Samoa and that
as an incident to such warfare the forces of Tamasese,
the chief opposed to Mataafa, will become the allies of
Germany.

Nor is there any reason to doubt that if Germany
and her allies succeed in destroying or subjugating
Mataafa and his adherents, the Government which will
be established will be one perhaps native in name, but
German to all intents and purposes.

Thus will be accomplished the purpose which Ger
many, in my opinion, has long had in view, being nothing
less or different than the inauguration of a condition of
government in the Islands of Samoa entirely in accord

with German interest and standing for German supremacy. This purpose has colored any proposition of adjustment made by Germany and furnishes the key to all her
acts.

And still at all times the profession has been made
by German representatives that the autonomy and independence of Samoa shall be maintained and our treaty
rights respected. . . .

On March 4, 1889, Benjamin Harrison became President, and at once, in response to public demand, laid
plans for the strengthening of the navy, conscious that
war with Germany was by no means a remote possibility.
Meanwhile Admiral Kimberly was on his way to Apia.

"By the second week in March," wrote Robert Louis
Stevenson, then living in Samoa, "three American ships
were in Apia Bay,—the *Nipsic,* the *Vandalia,* and the
*Trenton,* carrying the flag of Rear-Admiral Kimberly;
three German,—the *Adler,* the *Eber,* and the *Olga;* and
one British,—the *Calliope,* Captain Kane. . . . The
army of Mataafa still hung imminent behind the town.
The German quarter was still daily garrisoned with fifty
sailors from the squadron. What was yet more influential, Germany and the States, at least in Apia Bay, were
on the brink of war."

But a hand stronger than the hand of war suddenly
intervened. On March 16th, in the midst of this triple
preparation, a hurricane of unprecedented fury swept
the harbor of Apia, overwhelming the ships at their
moorings. Only one vessel, the British steamer *Calliope,*
escaped unharmed. And the returning Oriental sun
shone upon a peaceful Samoa.

"Thus," concludes Stevenson, . . . "within the duration of a single day, the sword arm of each of the two

angry powers was broken; their formidable ships reduced to junk; their disciplined hundreds to a horde of castaways. . . . The so-called hurricane of March 16th made thus a marking epoch in world-history; directly, and at once, it brought about the Congress and Treaty of Berlin; indirectly, and by a process still continuing, it founded the modern navy of the States."

This Berlin Congress, proposed by Bismarck himself, was merely a reconvening of the old conference. It began its sittings on April 29th, a few weeks after Mr. Cleveland's retirement from the White House. J. A. Kasson, William Walter Phelps, and G. M. Bates represented the United States, and the new Secretary of State, James G. Blaine, a man not to be overawed by "the Iron Chancellor," stood back of them. When they cabled the fact that Bismarck flew into terrible rage whenever they opposed his evident determination to have the conference recognize Germany's domination in Samoa, Blaine sent back the now famous reply: "The extent of the Chancellor's irritability is not the measure of American rights." Thus supported, the American and the British commissioners stood firm in their demand for a triple control instead of a German dominion in Samoa, and on June 14th, the three powers and Samoa entered into a treaty, guaranteeing the autonomy of the islands, restoring the banished Malietoa to his throne, and providing a tripartite protectorate with the powers of the protectors lodged in a chief justice and a president of the municipality of Apia appointed by them.

This was not what Germany desired, nor was it her intention to accept it as the end of her dream of annexation; but Bismarck, for the moment, acquiesced, and with such good grace as to create the impression of a change of heart. He abandoned King Tamasese, withdrew his German prop, Brandeis, the kingmaker, and returned the dethroned Malietoa, thus fully meeting the more obvious demands of the treaty. The result was to leave Mataafa, whom the Cleveland government had regarded as the choice of the Samoan people, to wander in the shadows, plotting the rebellion which would give Germany her next chance.

From the first the plans so carefully outlined by the three powers at Berlin failed. It was January, 1891, before the chief justice, Conrad Cederkrantz, arrived in Samoa, and it was another four months before the President, Baron Senfft von Pilsach, joined him; but even then nothing happened. "The curtain had risen; there was no play," wrote Stevenson. But there was work. Within a month after the arrival of the Prussian president, ex-King Mataafa altered his course and assumed regal state. The grim trappings of war were seen again in the islands, bearing the inscription "Made in Germany," as intimated by Stevenson. "The voice of the two whites," he wrote, "has ever been for war. They have published at least one incendiary proclamation, they have armed and sent into the field at least one Samoan war-party. . . . Into the question of motive I refuse to enter; but if we come to war in these islands . . . it will be a manufactured war, and one that has been manufactured . . . by two foreigners." Such was the German change of heart, being in reality only a change of method. In the triple alliance she saw a new pathway to German control. Having been thwarted in her attempts to annex by one method, she resorted to another, content to see a German Samoa at the end of a somewhat longer vista.

Membership in the triple alliance, entered by the United States in disregard of the warnings of Grover Cleveland, meant that for the first time since Washington issued his farewell warning against "entangling alliances," we were involved in just such an alliance. By the irony of fate, it worked well enough to tide over the four years of President Harrison who, on March 4, 1893, returned the executive office to Mr. Cleveland with the Samoan question again demanding attention.

As the restored President looked over the situation, he found that the Germans had not abandoned their plans for the acquisition of Samoa, and that they regarded him with an intense antipathy, as the author of their earlier defeat. He saw also that the triple alliance was a failure, and urged Congress to withdraw "on some reasonable terms not prejudicial to any other existing rights." To the judgment of Congress, however, he appealed in vain. If Congress had any wisdom to spare, it failed to lend it to the Executive in aid of a solution to his perplexing problem. And so the Samoan question rested. The triple protectorate remained an unredeemed failure, Germany, backing now one native aspirant for royal honors, now another, with America and Great Britain always in joint opposition.

By 1900, when Grover Cleveland was again a private citizen, conditions at last brought the day of German success. The Berlin treaty was abrogated, and Great Britain withdrew all claims within the Samoan group in return for German concessions in other parts of the world, while the United States confined her sphere of influence in the islands to Tutuila and the harbor of Pago-Pago, which she had held, to all intents and purposes, in 1872. The remainder of the beautiful Samoan group passed not to the sovereignty of its own people, but to the hands of the Hohenzollerns, the iron masters of the German Empire.

German persistence had won at last, but during the

conflict Grover Cleveland had tied the American people
a little more closely to the doctrine of the future—the
doctrine that among nations no less than among individuals, the strong have a duty to respect the rights of the
weak, and to see that others respect them. "The chief
historical significance of the Samoan incident," writes
John Bassett Moore, "lies less in the disposition ultimately
made of the islands, than in the assertion by the United
States, not merely of a willingness, but even of a right,
to take part in determining the fate of a remote and semi-
barbarous people."

# CHAPTER XI

## THROWING AWAY THE PRESIDENCY

*"What is the use of being elected or re-elected unless you stand for something?"*

—GROVER CLEVELAND.

POLITICAL prophets, with minds set upon approaching presidential elections, are always deeply interested in congressional elections and in local political sentiment. These are the straws which show the direction of political winds. Early in July, 1886, Texas held her first congressional convention and renominated Crane of the seventh district. Incidentally, the convention resolved: "That we recognize in Grover Cleveland a Democrat and patriot, who, under the heavy cares of his great office, has displayed masterly ability, unimpeachable integrity, and heroic courage; and that we commend the fidelity with which he has fulfilled his pledges to the people in the face of great pressure to violate them."

The Galveston *News,* the leading Democratic paper of the state, stamped this resolution as representative, not of the seventh Texas district alone, not of Texas alone, but of the entire South, declaring that nine Democrats out of ten in that part of the country and exclusive of office-seekers, were perfectly satisfied with Cleveland's administration, and that, if the national convention were held immediately, the South would be solid for his renomination. But the fact that the South stood ready to renominate the only Democrat who had occupied the White

House since the Civil War was, after all, not very significant, especially as great metropolitan journals like the New York *Sun* and the New York *World* longed to see the President's political scalp drying in the sun, before Tammany Hall, or any other long house. Their attacks were incessant and very bitter.

"Not long ago," said *Public Opinion,* on March 5, 1887, "the New York *Sun* advocated the passage of the interstate commerce bill, but no sooner was it passed and approved by the President than that journal found numerous objections to it, and actually condemned the President for not vetoing it. The same paper contained column after column of editorial matter exposing the job known as the dependent pension bill, and called on the President to veto it. The President did veto it, and the *Sun* at once makes the veto an occasion for another stab at its author. The New York *World* took the same position in regard to the pension bill, and called on the President to veto it, but no sooner did he do so than the *World* makes the remarkable discovery that public sentiment is not as it represented it to be, but that among the G. A. R. there is a 'practically unanimous call from New York and other states for Congress to override the veto.' The *Courier-Journal* advocated the civil-service bill, indorsed a plank in the Democratic platform demanding the enforcement of the civil-service system, applauded the President's pledge that he would enforce it, and then turned suddenly to denounce bitterly both the law and the President for respecting it. It is highly complimentary to the President that these ingenious and pestiferous critics can find no other ground to justify their abuse of him than his adherence to his pledges and his enforcement of the law. After all their enterprise and busy zeal, they are left without a pretext for their hostility, except what is found in the fact that the President has simply done what, at one time or another, they demanded of him. It is the old story over again of the lamb who muddies the water below the wolf, except that the President is somewhat of a wolf himself when he has a mind to be."

But despite such attacks President Cleveland continued to follow his own judgment, demonstrating more and more every day that he was as ready to act without party support as with it, when convinced that his course lay in the line of duty. Such an attitude bred increased resentment on the part of Democratic politicians, although optimistic Democratic sheets labored hard to prove that gossip in the Republican press about differences between the President and the leaders of the party was the sheerest folly.

More and more definitely, as the months passed, was the rift apparent. The Democratic politicians did not like Grover Cleveland: he could not be counted upon to "play the game." If there were dreams of a second term, it was not they who dreamed them, and in their narrow abuse they utterly failed to appreciate the impression which his honesty and fidelity in the discharge of duty had made upon the masses of the people. The Democratic politicians were against the President, but the Democratic people were for him.

"I have seen," declared ex-Senator Thurman of Ohio, "a good many Presidents in my long life. I have known several of them personally, and I have read the history of the administration of them all. I have seen and I know—and I think I know him full well—Grover Cleveland, our President of the United States; and on my honor as a man who is bound to tell you the truth, if ever a man was bound to tell the truth to his fellow-man, I don't believe that a more honest, braver, truer man ever filled the Presidential chair of the United States." This opinion the people shared.

How much they were for him appeared in his tour of glory of that autumn, his swing round the circle. He visited a dozen or more of the chief cities in the Middle West and South, and everywhere was greeted with the applause of expectant throngs. He won his audiences, not by the discussion of public issues, for he rarely discussed them, but by the personal and friendly manner of his approach to his fellow citizens in each city that he visited. In St. Paul, for example, where Mrs. Cleveland had once been for a short time in school, he wrote into his address this telling paragraph:

"My visit to you being a social one, and trusting that we have a sort of friendly feeling for each other, I want to suggest to you a reason why I am particularly and personally interested in St. Paul and its people. Some years ago, I won't say how many, a young girl dwelt among you and went to school. She has grown up and is my wife. If anyone thinks a President ought not to mention things of this sort in public, I hope he or she does not live in St. Paul, for I don't want to shock anybody when I thank the good people of this city because they neither married nor spoiled my wife; and when I tell them that I had much rather have her than the Presidency."

In October he returned to his executive duties, conscious that in the South and Middle West at least he was a President with prospects. The country was prosperous, and understood how false had been the dire prophecies of those who had hailed the return of Democracy as the beginning of a long calamity.

With a presidential year almost in sight, it was the part of the wise politician to say nothing definite, arouse no new animosities, and so drift again into power. But Cleveland's masterful conscience was driving him onward toward quite another course. By degrees he had become convinced of the iniquities of the existing tariff laws and of his duty to open an uncompromising attack upon them. This conviction had come slowly, but with a controlling definiteness.

When first chosen President he had considered himself unequipped to form an opinion upon the tariff question. Having had no responsibility for the tariff, save that which falls to the lot of every citizen, he had not felt called upon to study the subject as he always studied every subject which came within the range of his official duty. And being devoid of pretense and of the pride of erudition, he frankly confessed to his friends his need of help, following unconsciously but literally the advice which Charles Dickens once gave a group of students: "Admit ignorance of many things and thus avoid the more terrible alternative of being ignorant of all things."

Carl Schurz has left this account of a conversation which he had with Mr. Cleveland shortly after the latter's first election:

"With characteristic directness [he] asked me what big questions I thought he ought to take up when he got into the White House. I told him I thought he ought to take up the tariff. I shall never forget what then happened. The man bent forward and buried his face in his hands on the table before him. After two or three minutes he straightened up and, with the same directness, said to me: 'I am ashamed to say it, but the truth is I know nothing about the tariff. . . . Will you tell me how to go about it to learn?'

"Of course I said I would. So I gave him a list of books to read. Did he read them? Indeed he did, and came back for more. Nobody ever worked harder to master a new subject than the determined Cleveland worked to master the tariff."

Realizing the strength of the arguments upon each side of the problem, the President at first halted between two opinions; but by slow degrees he grew to feel that a protective tariff, in the sense in which that term had been interpreted since the Civil War, was iniquitous, involving favoritism for the few at the expense of the many. At times, during the two decades since Lee's surrender, Congress had shown signs of similar views, and had moved in the direction of reducing the war tariffs; but the perserverance of the saints had been denied them, and the tariffs had one by one reappeared. Even when President Arthur's tariff commission, which consisted entirely of protectionists, had drawn up a bill aiming at a twenty per cent reduction, Congress had stilled its conscience, or its political forebodings, by cutting down this reduction to three or four per cent. Thus, despite many professions, the tariffs remained practically undisturbed until President Cleveland's day, not for the sake of revenue, as the treasury surplus was a great embarrassment; not for protection merely, as such rates were far in excess of those required to equalize the difference in wages between the United States and other manufacturing countries, but, as Mr. Cleveland's study convinced him, in order that the manufacturer should enjoy a rich subsidy at the expense of the consumer.

In his first annual message Mr. Cleveland ventured upon the general suggestion that, as the revenues were greatly in excess of the actual needs of an economical administration, they ought to be reduced in such a way as not to injure or destroy "interests which have been encouraged by such laws" and with a view to the protection of American labor. During the year following he sought the advice of many men learned in tariff history—cabinet members, Congressmen, Senators, and unofficial experts. As a consequence, the tone of his second annual message was more definite and more aggressive regarding the maintenance of war tariffs in time of peace. He pointed out the fact that the income of the government was greatly in excess of public necessities, receipts having increased by about fourteen million dollars, of which almost twelve million came from customs, and declared that "When more of the people's substance is exacted through the form of taxation than is necessary to meet the just obligations of the Government and the expense of its economical administration . . . such exaction becomes ruthless extortion and a violation of the fundamental principles of a free government."

It was not tariff to which he objected, but tariff in excess of the needs of the Government. He was no idealist thinking free trade thoughts in a world of nations devoted to protection, but a practical, honest trustee insisting upon administration in the interest of the people. His increasingly bitter denunciations of the robber aspect of the tariff, as then administered, recall the picture of the Moorish pirate, Taric, Tarik, or Tariff, hovering about the entrance of the pillars of Hercules, forcing merchant vessels to share their cargoes with him. Historically, the word tariff means, in the language of frank piracy, the share of imported goods or money equivalent, which a government exacts as the price of admission. To Grover Cleveland, in that autumn of 1887, existing American tariff laws conjured up the vision of the grim Tarik plundering his helpless victims.

As he watched the mounting surplus, bringing with it the inevitable evils of extravagance and inefficiency, he conceived the idea of bringing the facts to the notice of the public by devoting his entire message to this one topic. This, being an absolutely new departure, would in itself focus the attention of the country and cause comment and discussion of the issue which he was so urgently recommending. The facts, if once understood, would constitute sufficient argument in favor of reform.

The average rate of tariff paid upon imports during the year 1887 had been exceeded only thirteen times in the history of the United States, and the amount so collected during the fiscal year was over fifty-five million dollars above the requirements of current expenses, while the estimated surplus for the succeeding year was vastly larger. Congress had refused to revise the tariff. The President would bring the pressure of public opinion to bear upon Congress.

His political advisers for the most part opposed the plan. To them it seemed sheer political suicide to force such an issue in the face of a presidential campaign. But the outcome of that campaign was to the President a small matter compared with the duty which he saw before him. When one alarmed political prophet warned him that his defeat lurked in a too bold deliverance upon this subject, he replied: "I would stultify myself if I failed to let the message go forward from any fear that it might affect my election." To another he answered: "What is the use of being elected or re-elected, unless you stand for something?" And so, in defiance of warning, and in the face of friendly dissuasion, he prepared the now famous tariff message, which sacrificed his immediate political future, and made of the tariff a living issue.

On December 6, 1887, the message went to Congress, carrying consternation among his followers and jubilation into the camp of the enemy. It was not a radical document and not a free-trade document. "Our progress toward a wise conclusion," it declared, "will not be improved by dwelling upon the theories of protection and free trade. This savors too much of bandying epithets. It is a condition which confronts us—not a theory."

With the precise language of a definite mind, he called attention to the fact that "while comparatively few use imported articles, millions . . . purchase and use things of the same kind made in this country, and pay therefor nearly or quite the same enhanced price which the duty adds to the imported articles. Those who buy imports pay the duty charged thereon into the public treasury, but the great majority of our citizens, who buy domestic articles of the same class, pay a sum at least approximately equal to this duty to the home manufacturer."

At once blessings and curses descended upon his head. Henry George sent a cordial letter of congratulation; and the anti-protection journals were ecstatic in praise. The *Nation* pronounced it "the most courageous document that has been sent from the Executive Mansion since the close of the Civil War," laying down "a platform for the next national campaign as clean cut as any high-tariff politician could possibly desire." The *Post* declared: "This message . . . makes the revenue question the paramount and controlling one in American politics." The protectionist journals, on the other hand, were bitter and at times indecently insulting. "Free-trade, cant, and humbug," commented the headlines in the Chicago *Journal*. "Ignoramus, dolt, simpleton, idiot—firebug in public finance," were the epithets employed by the *Commercial Gazette*.

James G. Blaine, then in France, cabled an interview designating the message as "Free trade," and intimating that it was in the interest of Great Britain, which cable the New York *Tribune* interpreted in the phrase: "Mr. Blaine in Europe speaks as an American. Mr. Cleveland in America speaks as a British manufacturer, anxious to be admitted without any charge to a share of the best and largest market in the world." And some of the London papers, by their enthusiastic praise of the message, made easier the task of those seeking to convict the President of unholy British sympathy. The London *Morning Post* of December 12th, after praising "that remarkable state document," and the wisdom and high courage of the man who had dared to deliver it, ventured upon the prediction that "sooner or later this Congress will recognize the wisdom of the President's advice and resolve to reduce the Federal revenues." But no such flash of wisdom followed. There followed instead cries of indignation from thousands of Irish voters, susceptible to the faintest suspicion of pro-British sympathy on the part of an American public man; and thus the chief aim of the distortion was secured.

In Congress an abortive attempt was made, under the leadership of Roger Q. Mills, to push through a bill providing for a reduction of tariff revenues by about $53,-000,000, with other reductions amounting to a quarter of a million. The measure was conceived in a partisan spirit, and did not fairly represent the reform for which the President had pleaded.

Round this Mills Bill raged the great tariff debate of 1888, Mills and Carlisle crossing swords with McKinley and Reed. The opponents of the President, including ex-Speaker Randall, rang the changes upon Blaine's suggestion that the Democrats were playing into the hands of the British merchant. Reed of Maine interpreted the policy of the administration in the following words: "A nice little dog . . . trotted along happy as the day, for he had in his mouth a nice shoulder of succulent mutton. By and by he came to a stream bridged by a plank. He trotted along, and, looking over the side of the plank, he saw the markets of the world and dived for them." He emerged, said Mr. Reed, "the most muttonless dog that ever swam ashore." The Democrats, however, had a safe majority in the House, and on July 21st, they passed the Mills Bill, by a vote of 162 to 149, fourteen not voting.

The Republican Senate, under the leadership of Allison and Aldrich, promptly produced a substitute as narrow and partisan as the Mills Bill itself. In the conflict which ensued both bills were blocked, and the tariff question, still unsettled, remained the dominant issue for the elections of 1888. Thus Mr. Cleveland's message forced the two great parties to adopt definite positions upon the tariff, and to those positions they have in general adhered since that day. It also accomplished what Mr. Cleveland's friends had predicted, disaster to all dreams of his re-election in 1888.

Indeed, many Democrats high in party councils, and a few with well-defined ambitions for the succession, hoped that the tariff message had made impossible even the renomination of President Cleveland. Others sought to add to this longed-for disqualification the unquestioned fact that in his letter of acceptance of 1884, he had said: "We recognize in the eligibility of the President for re-election a most serious danger to that calm, deliberate, and intelligent political action which must characterize a government by the people." They believed, or professed to believe, that that statement bound Grover Cleveland to a single term. Such was not, however, a fair interpretation. Mr. Cleveland had merely suggested the idea that Presidents should be rendered ineligible for second terms.

But no such law had been passed, no such action taken, either by Congress or by the people. Had the public responded to his suggestion, it would have found him ready to co-operate. Having failed to do so, it left him free to seek a second term, should he so desire.

Had he followed his own very strong inclination, as repeatedly expressed to his intimate friends, he would have refused a second nomination and spent the remainder of his days as a private citizen, but circumstances rendered such a course difficult. Fellow Democrats assured him that by such a refusal he would endanger party supremacy and party associates who had served loyally under his banner. He also knew that a public statement of an intention to retire at the end of his first term would weaken, if not destroy, his usefulness, and imperil the success of his policies. In this knowledge his political enemies shared, and had even ventured to make such a statement for him, and to sign his name to it. Early in February, 1888, the Albany *Times* had bloomed out with the following specific and singularly clumsy communication, palpably a forgery, which Lamont promptly denounced as such:

Executive Mansion, Washington.
*February 6, 1888.*

MY DEAR FRIEND:

You have been correctly informed as to my fixed purpose to decline a renomination to the Presidency, and I am only awaiting a fitting occasion to make this purpose known to the country without seeming to decline in advance what might never have been tendered me. Perhaps the meeting of the National Democratic Committee here on the 22nd inst. may furnish as good an opportunity as any.

The few friends to whom I have communicated my determination in this matter have without exception, and with great strenuousness, tried to dissuade me from it, and have used the same arguments in substance as those urged in your friendly letter. But, while the arguments are highly flattering to me personally, they are not at all convincing, and I do not feel that I ought to yield to them. There are several reasons entirely conclusive to my mind why I should not permit myself to be a candidate for renomination.

In my letter accepting the nomination nearly four years ago, I took, as you know, strong ground against a second term; I have good and substantial reasons for my position, which are as strong now as they were then. I even went to the extent of advising an amendment to the Constitution prohibiting the election of anyone to the Presidency for a second term. Now, if there is one thing the people specially dislike it is the man, whether physician or politician, who refuses to take the dose that he prescribes for others. "Practice what you preach" is an injunction that all honest men have a right to rigidly impose upon those who assume to advise the people.

Again, you are well aware that the strongest opposition I have had to encounter from my own party during my Administration has arisen from the fact that I insisted upon standing by my pledges and by the platform of the convention that nominated me in their entirety. I refer especially to Civil Service Reform and the distribution of patronage. I am told—and I have no doubt it is true—that most of those who have criticised this feature of my Administration are opposed to my renomination and are doing all they can to thwart it. Now, suppose I were to accept a renomination. Do you not see in what an extremely selfish and hypocritical light I should be placed before these men and before the world?

"Here is a man," they would say, "who was extremely punctilious and conscientious about breaking any pledges or violating any planks in the platform that were calculated to benefit Democrats and reward the men who worked to elect him, but when it comes to his own personal interest, and he sees a chance to perpetuate himself in office, he has no scruples about breaking any pledges or smashing any plank in the platform, even though it was voluntarily framed by himself and recommended for incorporation into the Constitution."

This kind of criticism, as you must admit, would be unanswerable, as well as just, and I can not consent to stand in such a light as it would place me before my countrymen. But independently of these considerations, is it not true that the one-term principle is the right principle after all? Has it not, in fact, become almost a fixed principle in the Democratic creed? Our party made it a specific and distinctive feature of its platform in 1872. In 1876 Samuel J. Tilden, in his letter accepting the nomination to the Presidency, said: "No reform of the Civil Service in this country will be complete and permanent until its Chief Magistrate is disqualified for re-election."

Not only in its platforms, but in the practice of its candidates, has the Democratic party for half a century adhered to the one-term idea. Since the days of General Jackson no Democratic President has sought a renomination, except his immediate successor, Mr. Van Buren, and he was overwhelmingly defeated. Even Washington, who it is claimed set the example for a second term, was personally in favor of a single term, and had, as he says in his Farewell Address, prepared an address to the people declining a renomination, but was persuaded to reconsider it solely on account of the then "perplexed and critical posture of our affairs with foreign nations."

No such exigency in the foreign or domestic affairs of our Government exists at present, or ever has existed since the time of Washington, except, perhaps, on the occasion of Lincoln's renomination. Certainly there is not now, nor is there likely to be in the next four years, any condition of public affairs in this country that can not be fully met and successfully dealt with by scores of Democrats in our party who have had far more experience in public life than myself, and who have also stronger claims on the gratitude of their countrymen.

Finally, I can see no good and substantial reason why I should consent to be a candidate for re-election, while I can see a great many reasons why I should not. My only regret is that I did not announce my determination in respect to a second term in my inaugural address. It would have saved me a great deal of unkind, as well as unfounded, criticism that has been indulged in during the last six months with regard to my alleged objects and intentions. It was only by an oversight that it was omitted from my inaugural, for my purpose in this regard was fixed then as it is now, and has been ever since I wrote my letter of acceptance.

With sincere regard, your friend,

GROVER CLEVELAND.

In the state of New York Mr. Cleveland's prospects were distinctly unfavorable. There his political enemies of Democratic persuasion, including his perennial foes of Tammany Hall, had long since planned his elimination. More than a year earlier George F. Spinney wrote: "I want to say that there are politicians high in the

Democratic party in this state who actually believe that they can secure a majority of the New York delegation at the next national convention and thus seize a nomination for a gentleman who is without training in national affairs, and, I may truthfully add, does not possess the confidence of that very large portion of our intelligent citizens . . . who are anxious for your reelection and who will heartily support you at the polls if they are not robbed of that opportunity by the intriguers of your own party. Governor Hill has about him, I regret to say, some reckless advisers, men who are tainted with fraud and who scruple at nothing in the game of politics. Unless these men are checked, and that very speedily, they will, in my judgment, succeed in so blocking the way that your own friends within the party must go to the wall; and with their retirement must be abandoned the hope that the management of our national affairs will be continued in honest hands another presidential term.

"It is with many pangs of regret that I here record the prediction that unless judicious action is promptly taken, within six months your enemies will have secured the State Committee and will have so fortified themselves for carrying the state for their own candidate the following year, that it will be impossible for your friends to prevent their carrying out their plans. And when I say your friends, I mean the more decent portion of the Democratic party. True, these intriguers may pull the temple down upon themselves and enrich some western state with a presidential nomination. They may be so shortsighted as not to take that fact into consideration. Even if they did, they are so ambitious and reckless that they will take any chances.

"As I know and as others know, you were already beaten when your friends went quietly to work for you

in the spring of 1884. I need not recall the Herculean
labors which they performed. I was an observer and saw
much. Others who were participants have told me more.
To-day, as matters stand, you are beaten in the State of
New York, and no one can more sincerely regret the admission than myself."

For over a year Spinney had shot such letters into
Washington, laying bare what he believed to be a plot
between Hill, Murphy, and the Blaine men to defeat
President Cleveland, while making certain that Hill
would be re-elected Governor of New York and made
presidential timber by his demonstrated ability to control
the Empire State. Being himself a shrewd judge of men,
Mr. Cleveland could not have failed to form a fairly
accurate conception of the man who had succeeded him
as Governor of New York, and who had been later elected
to that same high office, chiefly through the support of
Democrats with scant sympathy for reform movements
in politics.

David B. Hill was a master politician of a none too
subtle character, a scientific manipulator of no mean
cunning, who had studied for a career in politics as some
men study for holy orders. His school had taught him
the art of forming alliances, the science of effective combinations. It had not taught him the humanities of
politics. He was cold, he was harsh, he was masterful;
but he was financially above reproach. He could inspire
fear, at times even admiration, but never affection. Thus
he was forced to lure rather than to lead, to tempt rather
than to inspire. But he was shrewd enough to be liberal
in distributing the spoils when the victory was won.

Mr. Cleveland's personal and political relations with
him had been cordial, at times almost intimate, despite
frequent warnings from friends that the Governor was

planning to supplant him. Not himself eager to stand
for a second term, Mr. Cleveland showed little resentment at Hill's apparent attitude. If the Governor had
ambitions, Mr. Cleveland saw no reason to resent them;
for Hill was clearly entitled to ambitions, even should
they rise to the high office which he himself held. "I
am quite fully convinced," he wrote to Bissell, "that
schemes are on foot for an anti-administration control in
New York . . . but you know my feeling well enough
to be satisfied that it will not keep me awake at night.
I do think, however, that a move ought to be made toward
organization for the sake of the best interests of the party
—whatever they are."

In the same strain he wrote to his friend James
Shanahan:

"I hardly think that you will be surprised to hear that
my feelings, tastes, and inclinations are such that if I felt
justified in following their lead and doing precisely as I
personally desire, I would insist that my public life
should end with the fourth of March next; and if any
person authorized to speak for our grand party would
to-day give me my discharge to take effect on the day I
have named, I should be a very happy man. But I am
daily and hourly told that the conditions are such that
such a course is not open without endangering the supremacy of the party and the good of the country. Occupying the position I do on this subject, having no
personal ambition, willing to obey the command of my
party and by my own act being in no man's way, I confess
I cannot quite keep my temper when I learn of the mean
and low attempts that are made by underhand means
to endanger the results to which I am devoted. And
when I see such good staunch friends as you with their

coats off and sleeves rolled up, I feel like taking a hand with them.

"Much of what you say in your letter corroborates what I have heard before concerning certain parties and influences which you mention. Many friends have been here since the Albany meeting of the committee and I think plans have been pretty well made in different parts of the State. There is no slumbering and if the Albany fiasco did nothing else it roused up a lot of first-rate men and led them to see the danger of inaction. . . . There has been enough of lying since the meeting of the State Committee to damn the world; and it has amused us a good deal here to see certain people protesting either that they had nothing to do with some queer transactions or that they didn't mean anything. Ex-Mayor Grace was here and said to me, 'Don't let them give you any sleeping doses'—and I have not. I think I know a man who will before a great while be asking such men as you for the nomination for Governor and will be protesting that all his manipulation was for the general good and for the purpose of keeping certain discontented persons in line, &c., &c.

"I have written very frankly to you and said more about my feelings and inclinations than I intended; and some of what I have written is, of course, intended for you alone. My position is this: I should personally like better than anything else to be let alone and let out; but although I often get quite discouraged and feel like insisting upon following my inclinations, I shall neither go counter to the wishes of the party I love and which has honored me, nor shall I desert my friends."

Feeling that Governor Hill's growing prospects of renomination were a very serious menace to Mr. Cleveland's own political future, his friends urged the President to use his influence in the gubernatorial contest. But Mr. Cleveland declined absolutely to interfere in the matter. He would not attempt to read his New York enemies out of the party.

But despite this disposition to view with good-humored tolerance movements designed to eliminate him from consideration for a second term, he was determined that his record as President should not be misrepresented at the New York State Convention. Accordingly, just before that body assembled, he wrote the following frank commendation of his own administration, as a guide to those of his friends who should become members of the platform committee:

"The representatives of the Democratic party in the state of New York, assembled for the purpose of selecting delegates . . . direct thoughtful attention to the fact that all the pledges and assurances made at the Democratic Convention of 1884 have been fully kept and realized. The allegiance and adherence of the State Democracy to the principles announced by that Convention and the State Convention of 1887 are hereby again declared, with an explicit approval of the doctrines contained in the last annual message of the President to the Congress that the people should not be unnecessarily taxed under a pretext of Governmental necessity; that in promotion of the public welfare and in the interest of American labor and the healthful condition of our established industries and enterprises, taxation for the mere purpose of unfairly benefiting the few at the expense of the many, is a perversion of governmental power; and that a large surplus in the National Treasury drawn by vicious taxation from the channels of trade is a dangerous and indefensible abuse.

"The Democracy of the State is justly proud of the

fact that one of its members was selected to carry to a successful issue in the last national campaign, the contest for the supremacy of the principles of popular government and for the defeat and destruction of the false theories and corrupt practices which threatened the happiness and welfare of the American people. His wise guidance and administration of public affairs as Chief Executive of the Nation have exhibited to the Democracy of the Land and to all our citizens, the value and the beneficent results of a faithful discharge of public duty. During his incumbency our system of government has been restored to the honest simplicity impressed upon it by its founders; integrity and ability have been substituted for artifice and incapacity in public places; the Civil Service has been purified, elevated and improved; economies have been inaugurated, useless offices have been abolished and business methods have been introduced in the management of governmental affairs; millions of acres of the public domain have been wrested from the grasp of foreign and domestic speculators and returned to settlers seeking homes; the waste and corrupt misuse of funds appropriated for the rebuilding of our navy have been exposed and corrected and the scandals arising therefrom no longer offend the moral sense of the people; thousands of names of deserving veterans have been added to the pension rolls; the rights of every citizen have been maintained at home and abroad; sectional hate has been discouraged and friendly relations among all our people have been promoted.

"In the light of such achievements, in recognition of faithful public service, to the end that reforms already inaugurated may be fully completed, and in strict obedience to the mandate of the Democratic and Independent voters of the State, the delegates selected by this Conven-

tion are instructed to present to the National Democratic
Convention the name of Grover Cleveland as their candidate for President of the United States. And said delegates are further instructed to act as a unit in all matters
entrusted to their charge, said action to be in accordance
with the preference of a majority of said delegates."

From now on, echoes of the old slanders of 1884 began to appear, coupled with new and astonishing ones;
and most ingenious devices were resorted to to get them
before the public. Mrs. Cleveland herself received the
following letter written, apparently in good faith, by one
eager to know the truth about these matters of vague
rumor:

Worcester, Mass.,
*May 29/88.*

MRS. CLEVELAND.
Dear Madam:

You will no doubt be surprised to receive this communication, but as it is of interest to yourself only, and
not the writer, I know you will pardon the intrusion. To
explain. The City in which I at present reside, is in a
state of agitation over an item which appeared in one of
the daily papers this morning, in regard to the uncongenial state of affairs at the White House. I can't credit
such statements as are there made, and feel it to be my
duty to give you an opportunity to deny them, which I
do by sending the enclosed items, that you may read them
as they appear. I myself think this is only a ruse to lead
those who favor Mr. Cleveland, to change their views,
and I think from what I have heard today that it will
not fail in its object unless authoritatively denied. I re-
sided in Wash. up to within a year or two ago and failed
to learn what this paper says has been an open secret

for some time. It would gratify me very much to have you answer this, as I wish to convince some friends with whom I conversed today, that the whole thing is a falsehood.

I remain Respec'ly

MRS. MAGGIE NICODEMUS.

Mrs. Cleveland's reply was immediate and convincing:

Executive Mansion, Washington,
*June 3, 1888.*

MRS. NICODEMUS:
Dear Madam:

I can only say in answer to your letter that every statement made by the Rev. C. H. Pendleton in the interview which you send me is basely false, and I pity the man of his calling who has been made the tool to give circulation to such wicked and heartless lies. I can wish the women of our Country no greater blessing than that their homes and lives may be as happy, and their husbands may be as kind, attentive, considerate and affectionate as mine.

Very truly,

FRANCES F. CLEVELAND.

This denial had little effect, for it was not truth that interested the President's persecutors. The tales continued to circulate, advantage being taken of every incident susceptible of misinterpretation. Did Mrs. Cleveland but go for a day or two to New York or Philadelphia, on a visit or to shop, the report flew over the country that she had been obliged to leave the President and would not return. Time and again the lie was circulated that Mr. Cleveland's inhuman treatment had caused her to leave the White House in the middle of the night and seek shelter at the home of friends.

In vain did Mrs. Folsom, Mrs. Whitney, Mrs. Greely, Miss Willard, and others in a position to know the facts about the President and his wife deny the baseless slanders. The stories grew from bad to worse, were whispered in every ear that would listen, were hawked about hotel corridors and newspaper offices, were written in private letters to individuals, till well-nigh the whole of America had heard them. No effective method could be found either to stop the slanders, or to fix the responsibility upon the authors. With diabolical ingenuity, cruel falsehood was sent abroad through the channels of the innocent. The Baptist ministers, at a conference in Washington, were charged with it before they left for their homes, and spread it in their congregations and through letters to their professional brethren. Children were told of it at the Sunday schools. In one case it was actually carried around from house to house by a female colporteur, who used to weep in telling it. At dinner tables in the cities it was freely repeated, and always on the authority of someone else who was present at some horrid scene.

On June 4, Silas W. Burt wrote to Colonel Lamont of certain "mysterious intimations in the air that an awful scandal about the President would be launched soon after his nomination. I could not learn its purport until Saturday, since which time it has reached me from several sources and my friendship and attachment for the President urges me to write to you about it. It is so absolutely absurd and ridiculous that I could not conceive it possible that it would be uttered, were it not for the campaign libels of '84 and the malignant and vile abuse spewed out by Ingalls. The new lie is that the President gets drunk and beats his wife so that she makes every pretext to be away from him. In the long list of foul calumnies that have been hatched by partisan rancor in the past I can recall none so utterly base as this. . . . It may be that this lie is to be uttered not openly but whispered about in secret detraction and it has already gained some currency in that way, though in every instance that I have heard of, it has been treated with absolute disbelief and disgust. Is it possible that Ingalls' recent vituperative diatribe sets the keynote of the Republican campaign? If so, it will be certainly disagreeable but will make the failure of that side more overwhelming."

Nor was the scandal confined to newspapers and private individuals. It echoed even in the halls of Congress, often in language most unbecoming a representative of the United States. After a particularly flagrant attack, a reporter said to Mr. Cleveland: "People are sometimes curious to know, Mr. President, how you regard these congressional assaults made on you personally." To which Mr. Cleveland replied: "In regard to personal assaults made upon me by my political opponents, I am free to say I care little for them. I know they are not true, and I believe they are meant to be understood— by myself at least—in a Pickwickian sense. I confess that the speeches of some of the Senators surprise me, for I look upon the Senate of the United States as the most dignified body in the world, and certainly there have been speeches delivered there which do not comport with that dignity. But if they can stand it I can. I am a little amused, though, sometimes that these very Republican Senators who are the most bitter against me have no hesitation in asking very particular favors at my hands."

The Republican press generally denied any part in the wretched business. "The country knows," wrote one

incensed editor, "that the Republican press has not circulated any of these vile stories or discussed the subject."
And he added: "Without exception, the stories . . .
were originated by Democrats, and further than this, by
Democrats whose names are known throughout their
party. And further still, the very worst talk of all originated among Democrats who were active and prominent
in the headquarters of the National Democratic Committee of New York."

Slander, like the proverbial cat, has nine lives; but
slander of the great has ninety times nine. Despite de-
nials, despite disproof, despite the softening touch of
time, the poison of those slanders concerning Grover
Cleveland's domestic life have outlived the generation
which witnessed their unholy birth, in the "earth slime"
of filthy politics.

On the fifth day of June, the Democratic National
Convention assembled at St. Louis. From the first it was
evident that Mr. Cleveland must be the nominee. A
repudiation of him would be equivalent to a confession
by the Democratic party that their only President since
Buchanan had been a failure. The New York delegation, however, appeared far from secure. Murphy was
apathetic and one faction, at least, of Governor Hill's
followers was using every conceivable means to discredit
President Cleveland. For this purpose a scurrilous pamphlet designed to operate in the interest of Governor
Hill's presidential ambitions was printed and circulated
in the convention. A more disgraceful collection of
slanderous vituperation can scarcely be found, among
the political pamphlets of our country, from Freneau and
Callender down.

"Cleveland, W. R. Grace and W. C. Whitney—A Pair
of Thieves—How They Run the Administration and

Knife the Governor of the Empire State," runs the title.
Throughout its eighteen almost unbelievably brutal pages
one evident purpose runs: to glorify Hill, "our deliberate
choice as our Democratic Chief," and the memory of
the late John Kelly, "Tammany's greatest head," "whom
Grace and Whitney were still hounding in the last hours
of his protracted fatal illness"; and to hold up to contumely President Grover Cleveland, "the Beast of
Buffalo."

But wisely disregarding the slanders of factional opposition, the placard "The Republican prayer—Renominate Cleveland," and other bids for his defeat, the convention accepted the inevitable and nominated Grover
Cleveland. So complete was his victory that no ballot
was taken, the nomination being made by acclamation
and without the appearance of a serious rival.

When Lamont brought the news, he found the President in his library looking over a set of textbooks designed
for Indian children on government reservations. Mr.
Cleveland glanced at the telegram, and turned again to
his textbooks. Apparently the news excited him very
little. He had felt certain of the result, and hardly
needed to be told what had been formally enacted. Every
vital detail of the convention had been carefully planned,
and, barring accidents, the outcome had been assured in
advance. Even the platform had been drawn by the
President more than a week before the assembling of the
convention, and his friends had been strong enough to
secure its adoption, almost without change.

According to E. V. Smalley, the well-known journal-
ist, Mr. Cleveland connived with Senator Gorman to secure the passage of the tariff plank, whose wording he had
made so clear as to constitute a direct refutation of Mr.
Blaine's charge that Mr. Cleveland was a disciple of free

trade. When the document was in exactly the form in which he desired it to appear in the platform, Mr. Cleveland summoned Senator Gorman and gave it to him with the request that he see it through. Gorman, without revealing its authorship, showed it to Mr. Randall, who remarked that it suited him but that "the Cleveland crowd would kick." Gorman said he thought he could manage them, and accordingly entered the convention, where the two labored to get it adopted. The resolution endorsing the Mills Bill, however, does not appear in President Cleveland's draft, and the evidence shows that he did not desire to see it included. Indeed, Senator Faulkner is responsible for the statement that the President strongly urged upon Senator Gorman the importance of having no such indorsement.

The excitement of the conflict over, President Cleveland viewed his success with no great personal satisfaction. He was fully conscious that his nomination had not come willingly from the Democratic politicians, but had been wrung from them by a combination of the popular demand, the difficulty of repudiating a leader already entrenched, and the skillful maneuvering of his managers. But he was entitled to a glow of satisfaction at the remarkable enthusiasm with which the convention had done what he had planned, being blissfully unconscious that he had planned at all.

In the Republican convention, which followed on June 19th, the striking feature was the listlessness with which the unexpected was done. Blaine had been confidently regarded as the nominee, but for some reason he insisted upon standing aside. In cable messages from Europe he repeatedly declined to allow his name to be used in connection with the nomination. Despite his expressed wishes, however, on the first ballot he was seventh in the list of nineteen candidates, John Sherman, Walter Q. Gresham, Chauncey M. Depew, Russell A. Alger, and Benjamin Harrison leading him by large majorities. On the eighth ballot, Harrison, clearly the choice of the convention, was nominated by a rising vote, generously labeled unanimous, and thus Grover Cleveland faced not James G. Blaine, but a new leader, a human iceberg, as his associates called him.

At first glance the chances for a Democratic victory seemed excellent, but the politically weatherwise, even within the Democratic ranks, knew better. Richard Croker expressed the belief that Harrison would be hard to beat, and intimated that, in view of this fact, he would "do absolutely as Washington wants" in the matter of a Democratic nomination for Governor of New York. Upon that subject the President still declined to express his desires. His New York political followers again besieged him to join with them in preventing Hill's nomination. Ex-Mayor Grace threatened that if Hill were made the standard bearer he would bolt the ticket; and he added the opinion that D-Cady Herrick, Frederic R. Coudert, and many other prominent Cleveland Democrats would do the same.

Again, Mr. Cleveland's reply was an unequivocal refusal to have anything to do with the matter. "I am surprised," he wrote, "that you should suppose that I ought to control or dictate the nomination in New York State. . . . I am isolated here, full of public duties and at the same time much perplexed with political questions which are presented to me daily. . . . A crisis is upon us involving such immense considerations that they must occur to every thinking man, among which my personal defeat is insignificant. Judgment should rule the hour—carefully made up and uninfluenced by passion or prejudice. The exercise of such judgment in the formation of tickets &c &c must be left to those in whose hands party organization has placed it.

"I appreciate fully the very great value you and Mr. Herrick are in the canvass, and cannot but hope that, in view of the great interests at stake, you will be found supporting the result of the judgment of the Democracy of the State even if it should not be in line with your own. In the meantime I am willing to trust it and I must abide by it. I beg you to think of the depressing influence which will result throughout the country from any coolness or defection in the State of New York. Perhaps I need hardly add that I have absolutely and persistently declined to interfere or express an opinion respecting the subject of your letter."

Three days later he wrote to Bissell: "I am determined to let the Gubernatorial question alone, but I am surprised to hear quite a number of people who have been strongly against the Governor say that they think his nomination would be the safest and best one. Indeed I think as at present advised that if it was desired it would be very difficult to change the current in his favor for renomination—some of it arising from personal and political attachment, and some of it from motives of political expediency. There are a good many voters, I am sure, who would rather vote for him than anybody else, and a good many who would not vote for anyone else on our side." Thus, leaving the local organization of New York, as of all the other states, to solve local problems, the President faced his double task of Chief Executive and Presidential Candidate, a combination which told heavily upon his wonderful but much overtaxed constitution. He worked each night until two or three o'clock, and by nine each morning was again at his desk.

His letter of acceptance reasserted the tariff views of his recent message, while scornfully and indignantly repudiating the Republican accusation that he was tilting in the lists as a free trade idealist. In congratulating the President on this letter Governor Hill wrote: "I can give it no greater praise than to say it expresses yourself. . . . It is just what was needed at this time, and its publication could not have been more opportune. Under the inspiration of this letter our state platform will confidently assure our friends throughout the Nation that New York will maintain her honorable place in the line of Democratic states."

So far as Governor Hill's own prospects were concerned, this confident prediction was fully justified; but from the point of view of President Cleveland and the national ticket, the case was quite otherwise. His enemies, especially in New York, were again appealing to the Irish vote on the plea that President Cleveland was a British tool "employed by Ireland's cruel enemy to aid her work of enslavement." To this end his extradition treaty was distorted into a scheme for placing all the machinery of the government in this country at the service of England for the suppression of defection in Ireland. To this end he was depicted as the man who had surrendered "the rights of American fishermen at the bidding of Joseph Chamberlain," as unfair an interpretation of Mr. Cleveland's conduct of the fisheries disputes as hostile ingenuity could have devised. The facts were as follows:

The controversy over the rights of American fishing vessels in Canadian waters and Canadian ports had been waged off and on ever since the foundation of the Government. Disputes had been constant, and in 1886 two American vessels had been seized by Canadians. The

Administration had made vigorous protests, characterizing the course of Canadian officials in terms of severe rebuke, and demanding the fullest redress. Within our borders many were the threats of war with Canada.

Had President Cleveland been less a patriot and statesman and more a demagogue and claptrap partisan, he would have met the issue, as the jingo policy of the period dictated, by an appeal to popular prejudice in the shape of prompt enforcement of non-intercourse and the possible disruption of peaceable relations with England. This would have disturbed commerce and trade; it would have spread distrust throughout the sensitive financial and business circles of the land, and it would have inflicted a large measure of injury upon our own people, but it would have been called good politics. He had, however, preferred to avow his faith in the intelligence and integrity of the American people by presenting the issue to the nation and to the world on the highest plane of statesmanship.

He had, therefore, appointed a commission who, with the British commission, had drawn up a treaty which went far beyond any of the four former treaties between the two countries in conceding privileges to our fishing vessels, and was calculated to put an end to disputes and relieve the relations of the United States and Canada from their one source of danger. Regardless of consequences to the relations of the country with a friendly power, or to the vast commercial interests involved in those relations, the Senate, by a strict party vote, had not only rejected the treaty, but by the same party vote had refused to allow it to be amended to meet real or pretended objections. Their criticism was of the kind which, finding fault, proposes no improvement. They had hoped to discredit the President before the country as an Execu-

tive unable to procure the ratification of his treaty, and
thus to end his career.

The peaceful method of dealing with the question
having failed of support, the President, determined as
ever to uphold the honor of the nation and the rights of
American citizens, had sent a message asking Congress
for power to make a retaliatory war upon the industry
of Canada. These were the facts in the case, and this
the magnanimous and statesmanlike treatment of the
situation which was interpreted to make the President
"the confessed ally of England," and by analogy "the
enemy of Ireland."

But most iniquitous of all the attempts to make Grover
Cleveland appear the tool of Great Britain, was the Sackville-West incident, staged long in advance of the campaign, and with unscrupulous cunning. On September 4,
1888, a letter from Pomona, California, signed Charles F.
Murchison, was addressed to the British Minister at
Washington, Sir Lionel Sackville-West, asking his opinion as to how a Britisher, loyal, though naturalized an
American, ought to vote if desiring to serve England.
With almost unbelievable folly, Sir Lionel took the bait,
and, over his own signature, wrote to his fancied com-
patriot that he held a favorable opinion of the friendly
disposition of the Democratic party toward England.

Fifteen days before the election, to the consternation
of the Cleveland camp, the press published this correspondence, certain papers printing the British Minister's
letter with a broad black mourning band around it. There
followed a flood of comment regarding the President's
duty in the premises. "If this letter is an audacious
forgery," said the New York *Sun,* "Lord Sackville should
denounce it as such without an hour's delay. If it is
genuine, Mr. Bayard should send him his passports be-

fore to-morrow night." This suggestion was laid before Sir Lionel by an enterprising *Tribune* reporter, who asked whether the letter was authentic, and if so whether his Lordship felt apprehensive of recall. Without hesitation the minister replied: "The man wrote me asking my advice . . . as he had a perfect right to do. I answered him giving him my views upon the matter, as I had a right to do. . . . I am not alarmed. . . . There has been so much said about me in the past that I have become indifferent to such comment. . . . I have done nothing that is at all prejudicial to my position or that is in violation of any international custom or courtesy." With this point of view, Secretary Bayard apparently agreed, as, on October 24th, he telegraphed from Georgetown that if the much discussed letter were marked "private" the Government would not be justified in noticing it.

The press, however, far from agreeing, insisted, in varied and picturesque language, that the offending minister must go. "It matters not," said the New York *Times,* "whether Lord Sackville is a fool or a knave; whether he was trapped, as he says, or whether he conspired with the politicians to arouse national prejudice in a presidential contest," he should be dismissed. Mr. Cleveland, no less incensed than were his friends that the representative of a friendly power should give advice as to elections, intimated to Lord Salisbury that Sir Lionel should be recalled, and upon receiving no satisfaction, curtly dismissed the offending minister, thereby arousing not only his ire, but that of his government as well. But the mischief had been done.

The autumn elections assured to the President the period of rest for which he had so often longed. Whitney brought the news of defeat. Entering the room where the

President and his young wife were awaiting the final verdict, he remarked: "Well, it's all up." Cleveland had received only 168 electoral votes out of 401, although his popular vote was almost a million larger than that of his successful rival.

On the other hand, Hill was re-elected Governor of New York by a plurality of 19,171, although the Republican candidate for President received, in the same state, a plurality of more than 14,000. This apparently unnatural discrepancy suggested to the minds of many Cleveland men the existence of a combination between Hill and the Republicans with a view to making more certain the elimination of Cleveland and the availability of Hill, in view of a future presidential campaign. Later, however, when heads were cool, they acknowledged the injustice of their inferences.

Writing almost twenty years later, after Hill had retired from public life, and when Mr. Cleveland was nearing his end, St. Clair McKelway, anti-Hill though he had always been, bore public witness to the mature opinion that Hill did not betray Cleveland in 1888. "Something should be said now which could not, for want of knowledge of the inside facts, be said before," he wrote in a Brooklyn *Eagle* editorial, on December 10, 1907. "Governor Hill was true to Mr. Cleveland in 1888. Mr. Cleveland lost this state then because many German Republicans, who voted for General Harrison, also voted for Governor Hill, Democrat, to beat Warner Miller, Republican candidate for Governor, on account of the rigorous excise views which Warner Miller had expressed. The slump from Miller to Hill of German Republicans who were for Harrison, anyway, made the vote for Hill larger than for Cleveland, but Governor Hill, though he benefited by that fact, did not promote it, and did all he could to get everybody who voted for him to vote for Cleveland also." Doubtless the Germans who voted for Harrison did so with an added relish since it was Grover Cleveland who had resisted Bismarck's design of annexing the Samoan Islands.

To Mr. Cleveland's mind no inferential accusations were necessary to explain his defeat. He had deliberately chosen his battle ground, had followed the dictates of his conscience with the full knowledge of what such a course might mean to his political fortunes, and having been beaten, he spent no time in nursing suspicions. "After all," he remarked to C. S. Cary two days after the election, "I would rather have my name to that tariff message than be President."

From the moment of defeat he began to rally his followers for another conflict. "Temporary defeat," he wrote to the Massachusetts Tariff Reform Association, on December 24th, "brings no discouragement; it but proves the stubbornness of the forces of combined selfishness, and discloses how the people have been led astray and how great is the necessity of redoubled efforts. . . . In the track of reform are often found the dead hopes of pioneers and the despair of those who fall in the march. But there will be neither despair nor dead hopes in the path of tariff reform, nor shall its pioneers fail to reach the heights. Holding fast to their faith and rejecting every alluring overture and every deceptive compromise which would betray their sacred trust, they themselves shall regain and restore the patrimony of their countrymen, freed from the trespass of grasping encroachment."

To other organizations he sent similar letters, urging above all systematic educational work to make the people understand the tariff issue. "The danger which we have to guard against," he wrote to the American Tariff Reform League, "is the misleading of our countrymen by specious theories, cunningly contrived, and falsely offering the people relief from personal burdens and the legitimate expenses necessary to secure the benefits of beneficent rule under the sanction of free institutions. The declared purpose of your league will not be attained until all those instructed in the economic question which is now pressed upon their attention are freed from all sophistries and clouding fallacies and until the subject of tariff reform is presented to them as a topic involving the relief of the plain people in their homes from useless and unjust expense."

A few days after this letter was written, William B. Hornblower called at the White House to pay his respects to the defeated President. "I was asked into his private reception room," writes Mr. Hornblower, "and found him sitting at his desk alone. After a few words of greeting, he spoke of his tariff message, which seemed to be on his mind. He said: 'My friends all advised me not to send it in. They told me that it would hurt the party; that without it, I was sure to be re-elected, but that if I sent in that message to Congress, it would in all probability defeat me; that I could wait till after election and then raise the tariff question. I felt, however, that this would not be fair to the country; the situation as it existed was to my mind intolerable and immediate action was necessary. Besides, I did not wish to be re-elected without having the people understand just where I stood on the tariff question and then spring the question on them after my re-election.' He paused a moment and then added, as if speaking to himself: 'Perhaps I made a mistake from the party standpoint; but damn it, it was right,' and he brought his fist down on his desk, 'I have at least that satisfaction.'

" 'Yes,' said I, 'Mr. President, it was right, and I want to say to you, that not only was it right, but that the young men of the country are with you and four years from now, we mean to put you back in the White House.' "

# CHAPTER XII

## RETIRES TO NEW YORK

*"I have just entered the real world, and see in a small child more of value than I have ever called my own."*
—GROVER CLEVELAND.

THE last months of President Cleveland's first term, like those of every defeated President, were tedious and difficult. The gloom of defeat was upon his followers; his enemies were little disposed to consider a discredited leader, as they chose to designate him; the people, a majority of whom had voted for him, had their faces turned toward the rising sun; and foreign nations approached him convinced that his day of power was forever gone.

England, in particular, resentful of the dismissal of Sir Lionel Sackville-West, made no attempt to conceal the fact that she was waiting, none too patiently, for the coming of another President, and was meanwhile content to leave American questions in the hands of a chargé, Michael H. Herbert, Second Secretary of Legation. Under these circumstances the American Minister at London, the Honorable E. J. Phelps, could not but feel the impropriety of his position. Frequent dinners of farewell were given him by well-intending friends who assumed that his stay would of necessity be brief, and that America, too, would place a subordinate in charge of her affairs. At last, on January 7th, he was granted leave of absence, at his own earnest request, and sailed for America, with no intention of returning. Secretary Bayard, while somewhat reluctantly consenting to Mr. Phelps's retirement, declined to accept his interpretation of the British attitude, stoutly insisting that England had meant no slight when failing to fill Sir Lionel's post. "I am most unwilling to believe," he wrote to Endicott, "that Lord Salisbury would sneakingly attempt to inflict a slight and yet seek to conceal from its recipient a knowledge of what was intended. The lion is the king of beasts, but such a course would reduce the British lion to the dimensions of a jackal." Whatever the motive, however, the fact was clear that Sir Lionel was not to be replaced so long as Mr. Cleveland remained in office. Like the rest, the British lion was waiting for the rising sun. In view of such conditions, it is strange that the American people have not long ago insisted upon a change which would release a retiring President and establish his successor within a reasonable time after the results of the election are known.

Upon the purely personal and domestic side, the task of leaving the White House involved the Cleveland family in many peculiar obligations. The household must remain until a definite hour, fixed by a combination of precedent and constitutional enactment, and be then ready to hand over the Executive Mansion to the Harrison family and a host of guests waiting to celebrate a new social era.

Before this hour provision had to be made for the disposition of the extraordinary collection of personal presents which had arrived at the White House during Mr. Cleveland's term of service. Although he had declined all gifts of intrinsic value, and returned many of little account, the attic was nevertheless filled with an odd assortment of strangely varied character. There were photographs by the thousands, including scores of pictures of presidential namesakes, and hundreds of other baby pictures sent because it was known that Mr. Cleveland loved children. The slaughter of these innocents which the move made necessary was a task in itself.

There were gallons of patent medicines and lotions; luck stones, rabbits' feet and other mascots *en gros;* bed quilts, sofa cushions, table covers, mats, and scarfs. There were boxes of cigars, sent with the best of intentions; baby's first teeth, baby's first shoes; fishing rods, flies, reels, sinkers, hooks and lines—every article ever dreamed of by Izaak Walton or any of his spiritual descendants. There was a veritable arsenal of firearms, with cartridges, hunting belts, stool pigeons, and game baskets. There were manuscripts in prose, verse, and the reverse—of the latter an unbelievable mass; rhymes that could raise the goose-flesh upon the most seasoned editor, in which "the Cæsar of all the world" and "his fair, modern Helen" sported together "on sylvan pleasures bent," and without the least regard for the rules of the game, either as to meter, rhyme, rhythm, or the sacred rights of chronology. There was "a piece of gold dug up in Michigan," accompanied by a frank request that, upon receipt of it, the President would wire an offer for the land from which it came. The nugget was dusty with age, but the telegram was still unwritten. There was a rusty horseshoe, marked "please except"; and a shining silver-plated one from a winning foot of the famous racer, Nancy Hanks. There was "a genuine Virginia madstone"; a large tankard of "mad dog medicine" carefully inscribed "a remedy for internal fever, it is Plesen to Drink no bad tast"; and a dozen bottles of tempting "home made liniment." There was "a Panel painted in oil subject being roses," with a string attached in the shape of the following suggestion: "You might feel like sending me $100 and we will be quits." An admirer in Utah had contributed "a suit of endowment garments such as are worn by the High Priests of the Mormon Church."

All told there remained, to be disposed of, over three thousand presents, from the good and the great, the less good and the less great, and not a few from the great unknown who loved him and trusted him and who had taken their own peculiar methods of showing it. And in the midst of all these strange symbols of affection, or of ambition for office, standing as a painful reminder of the vanishing qualities of human greatness, was a noble bust of President Garfield done in soap.

At Oak View, the President's private country house outside of Washington, was a different kind of collection. There he had spent his summers since 1886, a couple of weeks only of each having been devoted to fishing and hunting in the Adirondacks; and thither his admirers had sent an odd assortment of living treasures. There were "two baby foxes," now no longer babies. There had been some white rats which had borne fruit after their kind; but one had bitten the finger of the first lady of the land, and all had shared his banishment. A youthful admirer had donated an Angora kitten; but it had long ago disappeared, having fallen over the banisters and broken its leg, thereby necessitating the simultaneous sacrifice of all nine of its lives. There were a dachshund, a French poodle, and a St. Bernard, which had partaken somewhat of the natures of their respective countries— the beagle and the French poodle continually drifting into war, and the neutral St. Bernard invariably intervening. There had come also a fine setter; but he had been returned to the giver with the characteristic explanation that, as a President has little time for hunting, to keep him "would not be fair to the dog."

Upon one occasion a sporting acquaintance sent a flock

of quail; and the President devoted much care to the construction of an elaborate pen for their accommodation, hoping that henceforth he could enjoy the whistle which brought back so many happy memories of dog and gun. By an error of judgment, however, the mesh of the wire selected was too large, and as soon as the birds were placed within, there came a familiar whir of wings, and the presidential carpenter, in speechless wrath, watched his hopes vanish in the distance, to seek for themselves a freer, if a less distinguished habitation.

With the exception of the foxes, such of these treasures as survived to the end of his term were carefully crated and marked "Grover Cleveland, Hotel Victoria, New York City," where Mr. Cleveland had engaged a commodious apartment on the second floor to serve as home until long-coveted leisure should enable him to select a private residence.

On the night before his retirement from the White House Mr. Cleveland heard the surging crowds pass and repass his doors, singing and shouting their comments upon the President who to-morrow would pass into oblivion. Again and again, from thousands of lusty throats, floated the popular refrain: "Grover's in the cold, cold ground." But he was thinking little of his departure. He was thinking rather of the freedom that awaited him. The defeat he refused to consider his defeat. "It is not a personal matter," he told a New York *Herald* reporter. "It is not proper to speak of it either as my victory or as my defeat. It was a contest between two great parties battling for the supremacy of certain well-defined principles. One party has won and the other has lost—that is all there is to it."

Furthermore, he cherished no bitterness toward Governor Hill, no tendency to agree with those who accused

Hill of treachery to the head of his party. When asked by a reporter to what cause he attributed the loss of New York, he replied, with a smile: "It was mainly because the other party had the most votes." But gravely and with evident conviction, he added: "I have not the slightest doubt of Governor Hill's absolute good faith and honesty in the canvass. Nothing has ever occurred to interrupt our kindly relations since we ran on the ticket together as Governor and Lieutenant Governor."

Arrived in New York, Mr. Cleveland resumed the practice of the law, as a member of the distinguished firm, Bangs, Stetson, Tracy, and MacVeagh. Here he again exhibited the indifference to fees which had so often astonished his earlier law partner, Wilson S. Bissell. "I am now closing up a case of Cleveland's which has been running for years," Bissell once wrote to a friend, "during all which time he has paid all disbursements, such as costs of entry, witness fees, etc., out of his own pocket, because the man was too poor to meet these necessary expenses." And he often remarked that the ex-President deserved no praise for incorruptibility in office since money had never had power to tempt him.

This indifference was not due to that "private fortune brought from the White House" of which the newspapers so often spoke; for Mr. Cleveland left the executive office little richer than he had entered it. He had saved a little—the New York *Sun* later kindly fixed the amount at $25,000 a year—but he had not multiplied these savings, as he might readily have done, by particularly fortunate investments, for he refused to speculate or even to hold stocks concerning which he had any special knowledge, feeling, as he often said, that "a man is apt to know too much in my position that might affect matters in the least speculative."

It is quite possible that he would have fared worse, however, had he been less scrupulous; for he had not the gift of prophecy which makes a successful speculator, and was by no means skillful in questions of stocks and bonds. At times he was singularly childlike in his requests for specific directions as to how to sell certain stocks, frankly pleading lack of understanding of such matters. On one occasion he wrote to Commodore Benedict, his chief adviser in regard to private investments: "If you and I were speculators instead of steady-going investors, I think I would suggest that one of us buy a moderate amount of something, and having thus prepared the way for a decline, that the other sell a large quantity of the same thing short, and divide the profits. It must be that such a scheme would work." But he never bought on margin, always insisting that what was purchased for him should be paid for in full.

His return to the bar, after four years in the White House, was not a mere pretense. Politics had not lifted for him the curse of Cain, and work was not a pastime, but a necessity.

The leisure to which he had looked forward long and eagerly proved far from leisurely. The stern sense of duty which had been so heavy a taskmaster in the White House did not relax its grip, and his life in New York was almost puritanical in its rigid, laborious simplicity. A walk downtown in the early morning was his only regular exercise, almost his only diversion, for he declined to learn golf, studiously avoided dinners—especially such as seemed likely to involve his pet abhorrence, after-dinner speaking—and regarded the theater as an indulgence to be but sparingly enjoyed.

In the autumn of 1889, after his usual fishing trip in the Adirondacks, he established himself at 816 Madison

Avenue, living, like St. Paul, in "his own hired house," as he expressed it. He reveled in his home, the first unofficial one he had ever possessed, played cribbage to his heart's content, and enjoyed his friends as he had never been able to enjoy them. He was enthusiastic about New York as a place of residence, and when he received from Chicago friends an urgent invitation to make his permanent home in that city he replied:

"I beg you to remember that I too have a State and City—great in their progress and achievements—imperial in their standing among American States and Cities, and grand in their history and traditions. I have spent my life since early boyhood in the State of New York. I have stood at the head of her State Government. I am now happy and contented as a resident of the City of New York, and am daily the grateful recipient of the kindness and consideration of her citizens. You have a wonderful City and I am glad that the people of Chicago cannot monopolize the pride, due to every American, arising from her prosperity and growth. But New York State and New York City are very dear to me and I should not know how to entertain the thought of living elsewhere.

"I have made an unnecessarily long response to what was intended as merely a kind expression. I should like to say a word in reply to what you write in regard to the 'favorite son.' I will resist the temptation and only say that whatever the State of New York does will be rightly done. In all circumstances you and I can congratulate ourselves and each other on being residents of the greatest Cities our Country can boast, on being citizens of the grandest land on Earth, and on belonging to a party which seeks to protect the rights and further the prosperity and happiness of the American people."

Satisfied with his life and work, Mr. Cleveland gave no indication of a desire to enter again into the turmoil of politics; although from the first his political followers set themselves the task of keeping him before the country, with a view to a renomination in 1892. "I am," he wrote to L. Clarke Davis, "in a miserable condition—a private citizen without political ambition, trying to do private work, and yet pulled and hauled and importuned daily and hourly to do things in a public and semi-public way which are hard and distasteful to me. I have never made a speech or written a letter except in compliance with importunities which I could not resist from those engaged in some good work, or from those entitled to claim my consideration on party grounds. To refuse, as I am obliged to, the many requests presented to me is as wearing and as perplexing as it was to refuse applications for office at Washington. . . . I often have a pretty blue time of it, and confess to frequent spells of resentment, but I shall get on in a fashion."

When forced to speak, he refused to heed the advice of his political friends constantly urging caution, and fearlessly declared his convictions. While Governor Hill was meditatively balancing the popularity of free silver, Grover Cleveland was alarming his supporters by frankly and unequivocally denouncing it upon every proper occasion. And when warned that the nomination was coming and that Hill had ambitions, he replied: "D—— the nomination. I will say what I think is right."

He made no attempt to defend his stewardship as President; presented no excuses, no apologies, beyond the simple statement: "No man can lay down the trust which he has held in behalf of a generous and confiding people, and feel that at all times he has met in the best possible way the requirements of his trust; but he is not derelict in duty if he has conscientiously devoted his efforts and his judgments to the people's service." He knew that he had performed his public duties faithfully, uncongenial as many of them had been. He had neither faltered before duty, quailed before threats, nor fallen captive to the enervating whisper, the politician's Lorelei, "This will be popular."

Early in October, 1889, when the Democratic Society of Pennsylvania pleaded with him to address their first general assembly, he declined. His simple letter of regret, however, was used, in lieu of the desired address, to arouse political enthusiasm for the "brave and stainless leader" who had suffered "electoral defeat" in the face of "moral and popular victory." The chairman of the meeting, Chauncey F. Black, painted an inspiring picture of this champion of the masses, this challenger of the classes, "cut down by venal treachery . . . and overwhelmed by the tide of monopoly's corruption." And he brought the assembly to its feet with the words: "We are for tariff reform. From the high ground to which our great captain led us last year, we will not retreat one inch."

In December Mr. Cleveland made his first address of large political importance since his retirement from the Presidency. It was delivered at a dinner of the Merchants' Association of Boston, to over four hundred business men assembled to honor the ex-President. A Republican, Governor Ames, sounded the keynote in the sentence: "If wicked Democrats speak as well of me when I retire from office as Republicans now do of you, I shall be abundantly satisfied," while James Russell Lowell's letter of regret expressed the feeling of the guests with the unerring instinct of a man of genius:

Elmwood, Cambridge, Mass.
*10th Dec. 1889.*

DEAR MR. QUINCY:

I regret very much that I cannot have the pleasure of joining with you in paying respect to a man so worthy of it as Mr. Cleveland.

> Let who has felt compute the strain
> Of struggle with abuses strong,
> The doubtful course, the helpless pain
> Of seeing best intents go wrong;
> We, who look on with critic eyes
> Exempt from action's crucial test,
> Human ourselves, at least are wise
> In honoring one who did his best.

Faithfully yours,
J. R. LOWELL.

JOSIAH QUINCY, ESQ.

The choice of the subject for his own address, ballot reform, had, as usual, caused Mr. Cleveland many restless hours; its preparation had given him many wretched days. But its reception at the hands of this distinguished non-partisan company fully compensated for all.

As we read the address to-day, it is difficult to understand how so commonplace a production could have made so striking an impression upon such an audience. But this was doubtless due in part to the personal popularity of the speaker, and to the skill with which he was staged by men far more anxious than he regarding this politically planned non-political appearance, this camouflaged opening gun in a campaign to make Mr. Cleveland, for a third time, the Democratic nominee for President. Mr. Cleveland, said Andrew Carnegie in the closing address of the meeting, has "demonstrated one answer to a question of his own asking,—what to do with ex-Presidents. He has shown that one good thing to do with them is to invite them to all banquets; and in this connection the question occurs to me—why not run them again?"

Although this idea now began to be widely discussed, Mr. Cleveland himself rather discouraged than welcomed it. Living in the metropolis of the nation, close to the most powerful of all Democratic machines, he rarely met its leaders, and never cultivated them. His mind was upon the people, and his appeals were to public opinion through infrequent addresses and personal letters. He sought to influence public opinion, not to use it. He was willing to serve the nation should the nation call, but was determined not to "consent to be the candidate unless on a basis of honest principle." He would not accept leadership at the hands of machine men.

But though indifferent to the praise or blame of politicians, the letters of appreciation from admirers, known or unknown, which came in quantities from every section of the country, pleased him enormously, and his appreciation took the effective form of an answer to each, written in his own hand. To friends who protested against such an apparently useless expenditure of energy he replied: "If a fellow takes the trouble to write to me, the least I can do is to answer him."

In the early autumn the Albany *Argus* published an interview with Mr. Cleveland which made it abundantly clear that the ex-President must be regarded as permanently enlisted in the fight for tariff reform, ballot reform, civil service reform, and all other reforms calculated to relieve "the positive distress daily threatening our people's homes under the operation of a new and iniquitous tariff law," and other "reckless enactments which stifle the results of the people's suffrage." "The party that knew no discouragement in 1888," he concluded, "will not waver nor falter in 1890." This statement greatly cheered the hearts of his followers, for they knew that, after giving it forth, Grover Cleveland would not himself waver nor falter if asked to lead the greater fight of 1892.

The November elections showed a tremendous drift back to Democracy, in the East as well as in the West, although the western victories were so associated with the Farmers' Alliance movement as to be difficult of interpretation in the terms of Democrat and Republican. Many skillful political prophets denied indeed that they pointed to Democratic victory in 1892, unless the Democratic party should adopt the cherished schemes of the Alliance. In the East, however, the interpretation was clear. Here the fight had been won upon the policies of Grover Cleveland: tariff reform, civil service reform, economy, sound money, opposition to Federal subsidies and to improper interference in local affairs. "Reckoning on the result of the last November election," commented one pro-Cleveland paper, "the Democrats have 75 electoral votes east of Pennsylvania. They carried Connecticut, with its 6 electoral votes, Massachusetts with its 15 . . . New Hampshire with its 4, New Jersey with its 10 . . . New York with 36 votes, and Rhode Island with 4." The conclusion was obvious: as the East, in 1890, voted for Democrats because of Cleveland policies, she could be relied upon to vote for them in 1892, if Cleveland should be the nominee. The South could, of course, be counted upon, whoever was nominated. The only question, therefore, was—what of the West?

While pleased with election returns in general, Mr. Cleveland was uncertain concerning Governor Hill's wing of the Democracy, and how New York would interpret her duty in the pending contest for United States Senator which would show how far Hill was justified in his evident ambition to be the Democratic presidential nominee in 1892. "Of one thing you may be entirely certain," he wrote Bissell. "Hill and his friends are bent on his nomination for the Presidency, and failing in that, they are determined that it shall not come towards me. You know how I feel about this matter as a personal question; but if I have pulled any chestnuts out of the fire I want those who take them to keep civil tongues in their heads; and further . . . I don't want to see my hard work wasted and the old party fall back to shiftlessness and cheap expediency."

Mr. Cleveland was of the opinion that Hill's nomination would mean an end of the reforms toward which he himself had worked as President. The more carefully he considered the meaning of the senatorial contest in New York, the more thoroughly was he convinced that Hill ought not to be allowed to control it. On November 17th he wrote to Bissell: "What a glorious thing it would be if you could be elected to the Senate. I have been sounding about on the subject and find this to be the present condition of the thing: It is conceded in all quarters which my inquiries have reached, that Hill positively controls the situation. The gains in Legislative representation are mostly here and in Brooklyn. The members from these two localities can, if united, control the caucus within a vote or two, which of course they can easily obtain. I have not seen Weed at all, but I hear that he started in the canvass upon the supposition that Hill was pledged to his candidacy. This I believe is not now Hill's position; but instead of openly helping him he is fighting off, as I think, to pledge Weed and such friends as he has to his [Hill's] schemes. Some think that the result of the recent elections will cause Hill to turn his eyes toward the senatorship for himself as the best thing he can now see in sight."

But increasingly prominent as his political interest of necessity became, month by month, in view of elections which passed upon his policies, his chief delight was still his home and his family. This fact is avowed in his reply to the wedding invitation of a friend, John Temple Graves:

MY DEAR MR. GRAVES:

We received the card of invitation to your wedding a day or two ago, and I am glad that your letter—received only a few hours—justifies me, on behalf of my dear wife and myself, to do more than formally notice the occasion; and, first of all, let me assure you how much we appreciate the kind and touching sentiment you convey to us in our married state.

As I look back upon the years that have passed since God in his infinite goodness bestowed upon me the best of all his gifts—a loving and affectionate wife—all else, honor, the opportunity of usefulness, and the esteem of my fellow countrymen, are subordinated in every aspiration of gratitude and thankfulness.

You are not wrong, therefore, when you claim, in the atmosphere of fast coming bliss which now surrounds you, kinship with one who can testify with unreserved tenderness to the sanctification which comes to man when heaven-directed love leads the way to marriage. Since this tender theme has made us kinsmen, let me wish for you and the dear one who is to make your life doubly dear to you, all the joy and happiness vouchsafed to man.

You will, I know, feel that our kind wishes can reach no greater sincerity and force than when my wife joins

ne in the fervent desire that you and your bride may
nter upon and enjoy the same felicity which has made
ur married life "one grand, sweet song."

Very truly your friend,

GROVER CLEVELAND.

Most men begin the new year with good resolutions,
nd it seems likely that Mr. Cleveland faced the dawn of
891 with the resolution to do his duty by way of speech
naking. Otherwise, it is difficult to see why, in view of
is oft-repeated declaration to intimate and confidential
riends that he did not wish to be nominated again for
he Presidency, he consented to begin the new year with
political speech.

It was delivered in Philadelphia on the eighth of
anuary, at the annual celebration of the Battle of New
)rleans, and was one of his ablest addresses, breathing
hroughout that high moral standard which had charac-
erized his own public life. It was, moreover, a cam-
)aign document of no mean character, calculated to
.ppeal to the party pride of Democrats, and to rally them
o the defense of the great reforms for which his name
tood. In it, in one compact and illuminating paragraph,
ie recited as the principles of true democracy: "equal
.nd exact justice for all men; peace, commerce and honest
riendship with all nations—entangling alliance with
ione; the support of the State governments in all their
·ights; the preservation of the general government in its
vhole constitutional vigor; a jealous care of the right of
:lection by the people; absolute acquiescence in the de-
:isions of the majority; the supremacy of the civil over
he military authority; economy in the public expenses;
he honest payment of our debts and sacred preservation
)f the public faith; the encouragement of agriculture,

and commerce as its handmaid, and freedom of religion, freedom of the press, and freedom of the person."

The remainder of the address was an elaboration of each of these principles from the history of the two parties: the Democrats being painted—but not too shamelessly—as having in general observed them; while the Republicans, having in general disregarded them, were now listening "for the footsteps of that death which destroys parties false to their trust." "Thus," he declared, "when we see the functions of government used to enrich the few at the expense of the many, and see also its inevitable result in the pinching privation of the poor and the profuse extravagance of the rich; and when we see in operation an unjust tariff which banishes from many humble homes the comforts of life, in order that in the palaces of wealth luxury may more abound, we turn to our creed and find that it enjoins 'equal and exact justice to all men.'"

Of course no one could be really eloquent in a sentence of such length and complexity; but the speech represents near-eloquence and in some passages, weeded of the usual Clevelandesque verbiage, we catch the gleam of real eloquence. It is so with the brilliant sub-title, "principles enduring because they are right, and invincible because they are just." It is so with the paragraph which declares: "It is right that every man should enjoy the results of his labor to the fullest extent consistent with his membership in a civilized community. It is right that our Government should be but the instrument of the people's will, and that its cost should be limited within the lines of strict economy. It is right that the influence of the Government should be known in every humble home as the guardian of frugal comfort and content, and a defense against unjust exactions, and the unearned tribute persistently coveted by the selfish and designing. It is right that efficiency and honesty in public service should not be sacrificed to partisan greed; and it is right that the suffrage of our people should be pure and free."

In February, 1891, there came one of those choices between principle and expediency which always showed Mr. Cleveland at his best. The situation was typical of his career. The question had arisen as to what response he should make to an invitation of the Reform Club to attend a banquet at which the free coinage of silver was to be attacked. Most of his advisers thought he should keep silent on the subject, lest the chance of his nomination be injured. To these Mr. Cleveland's reply was characteristic: "I am supposed to be a leader in my party. If any word of mine can check these dangerous fallacies, it is my duty to give that word, whatever the cost may be to me."

He, therefore, used the occasion to denounce the free silver bill then pending before the Senate, and believed to be favored by almost every Democratic Senator, and by the great doubtful West. His letter, which Charles Francis Adams pronounced "one of the most creditable utterances that ever came from an American public character," reads as follows:

*February 10, 1891.*

E. ELLERY ANDERSON, Chairman:
Dear Sir:

I have this afternoon received your note inviting me to attend tomorrow evening the meeting called for the purpose of voicing the opposition of the business men of our city to "the free coinage of silver in the United States."

I shall not be able to attend and address the meeting

as you request, but I am glad that the business interest of New York are at last to be heard on this subject. I surely cannot be necessary for me to make a formal ex pression of my agreement with those who believe that th greatest peril would be invited by the adoption of th scheme, embraced in the measure now pending in Con gress, for the unlimited coinage of silver at our mints.

If we have developed an unexpected capacity for th assimilation of a largely increased volume of this cur rency, and even if we have demonstrated the usefulnes of such an increase, these conditions fall far short o insuring us against disaster if, in the present situation we enter upon the dangerous and reckless experiment o free, unlimited, and independent silver coinage.

Yours very truly,

GROVER CLEVELAND.

At once the cry went up from Democratic machine men all over the country that this was the end of Grove Cleveland. Hill's friends hastened to call the attention of "real Democrats" to the fact that, months before, Gov ernor Hill had declared for free coinage. The greates indignation was manifested throughout the South and West, where faith in free silver was large and increasing The more conservative East, however, applauded his wis dom and praised his courage. "It matters not," com mented the Philadelphia *Daily Evening Telegram* "whether such a man be of one party or another. It i enough that he is an American statesman to whom the welfare of the country is greater, more important, than self."

When a friend, years later, commented upon Mr Cleveland's courage in thus defying the clamor of the free silver element in his own party in the face of a presiden

al election in which he was to be a candidate, Mr. Cleve-
ınd replied: "It does not begin to be as hard as the stand
had to take, years ago, in Albany, relative to the five-
ent fare bill. I vetoed the bill and felt I had driven
ıe last nail into my political coffin."

The denunciations had not ceased when, in the sum-
ıer, he retired to Gray Gables for the quiet out-of-door
fe which he loved; and from this calm retreat he wrote
ɔ Gilder: "How little and frivolous all this seems to
ıe! Not because I do not realize the importance of
verything in the remotest way connected with the great
ffice of President, but because they appear to be indices
f the meanness and malice of men and politicians. So
ll this time I am wondering when the bluefish will be
bout and biting."

He kept a very watchful eye upon the anti-Cleveland
ıovement, nevertheless, and his comments upon Hill,
heehan, Tammany Hall, and the rest of the local "gang"
⸱ere frankly pugilistic, as he watched their clever schemes
ɔr his own elimination, and for the defeat of the policies
⸱hich he advocated.

On July 3d, he wrote to Lamont: "My only thought
bout politics is that we are great fools if we allow our-
elves to be hauled about by Hill and his gang. I know
hat I, who am doing next to nothing to prevent such a
ondition, ought not to expect others to inordinately exert
hemselves; but I do hope the thing will not be neglected
ɔ long as the pins will be fixed fast and strong against
.s. My information and my belief is, that Tammany
Iall will not aid us. They don't like me—never did and
ever will—and they will not help any movement with
⸱hich my name is associated. Of course you know I am
eady to take my discharge papers and be very obedient
nd faithful—except in one contingency." That contin-

gency, which seemed to him at the moment impossibl
was a nomination which would leave him free to serv
the people without any sense of obligation to seekers afte
spoils.

On October 8th, a great Democratic mass meetin
was held in Cooper Union, New York. Mr. Clevelan
had been prevailed upon to preside, and introduce Gov
ernor Hill and other Democratic notables. The audienc
was large, so large that the elated managers expressed th
regret that they had not taken Madison Square Garder
Mr. Cleveland's appearance was greeted with a tremer
dous ovation; and his brief introductory address, full c
caustic references to the Republican party and somewh;
unblushing praise for the Democrats, whom his privat
letters of late had not praised over much, was enthus
astically received. It was the speech of a man who, afte
heavy trials, sees the people at last turning their fac
back to him, and it was effective.

"Never has the irresistible strength of the principl
of Democracy been more fully exemplified," he sai(
"From the west and from the east come tidings of vi(
tory. In the popular branch of the next Congress, th
party which lately impudently arrogated to itself th
domination of that body will fill hardly more than on
fourth of its seats. Democratic governors occupy th
enemy's strongholds in Iowa, Massachusetts, Ohio, Wi
consin, and Michigan. In Pennsylvania the election of
Democratic governor presents conclusive proof of R(
publican corruption exposed, and Republican dishonest
detected." He also touched upon tariff reform, makin
it perfectly clear that, if Grover Cleveland were comin
back, he would come, like the ancient Roman Sibyl, witl
out abating one jot or one tittle of the demands which ha
been his political undoing in 1888.

But the thought of coming back was little in his mind those days. Five days before the Cooper Union meeting, his first child, Ruth, was born, and the glory of her advent completely dwarfed all else.

"The house is perfectly quiet," he wrote to Bissell, on October 21st. "I have just been up, to find my wife and child sleeping, and the nurse too. Only our mother-in-law awake.

"I feel an impulse to write to you. And I feel, too, that unless I make an effort, I shall write in a strange fashion to you. I who have just entered the real world, and see in a small child more of value than I have ever called my own before; who puts aside as hardly worth a thought, all that has gone before—fame, honor, place, everything—reach out my hand to you and fervently express the wish—the best my great friendship for you yields —that in safety and in joy you may soon reach my estate.

"I think a great deal about you and your dear wife just now. I think a little of your anxiety and suspense, a little of the cloud that must pass over her, but a great deal of the joy and happiness that will come to both of you when anxiety and suspense are over and the cloud is past.

"Give our love to Mrs. Bissell and let me know when you are made happy.

"Yours faithfully,
GROVER CLEVELAND."

# CHAPTER XIII

## AN UNPRECEDENTED RESTORATION

*"It's a funny thing for a man to be running for the Presidency with all the politicians against him."*
—GROVER CLEVELAND.

AS Grover Cleveland watched the winter deepen toward the Christmas season, his thoughts were less than usual thoughts of peace and good will. Reluctantly he had reached the conclusion that David B. Hill was wrecking the Democratic party by his methods in New York. "Hill's performances in Albany and the late proceedings of the State Committee," he wrote to Bissell on December 4th, ". . . convince me that we are either rushing to overwhelming defeat or the people are heedless of everything political that may happen. Was it for this that we braved temporary defeat in order that we might stand on principle? And what becomes of all our fine promises to the people? If we have much more of the work that is now disgracing us and the people do not resent it, I shall think the people are not worth saving or serving." And a week later he added: "I have every possible desire to see our party succeed on decent honest lines, and have a strong disinclination to being exhibited at the tail end of a procession which means the betrayal of the principles we profess and the deception of the people. It seems very ridiculous for the State of New York to claim any sympathy with the professed aims of the National Democracy, and to still be content to follow the lead of Hill, Murphy & Co."

The opening of the presidential year 1892 found him again laboriously preparing an address on Andrew Jackson. Of the real Andrew Jackson he knew little, as the not infrequent references to him in letters and speeches abundantly demonstrate. But of the "Andrew Jackson cult," the national Democracy annually worshiping at Jackson's shrine, he knew a great deal; and his speech was a skillful appeal to its votaries to exhibit the Jacksonian qualities—vigor, courage, honesty of purpose, steady persistency—in the coming elections. "We who are proud to call ourselves Jacksonian Democrats," he said, "have boldly and aggressively attacked a political heresy opposed to the best interests of the people and defended by an arrogant and unscrupulous party. The fight is still on. Who has the hardihood to say that we can lay claim to the least Jacksonian spirit if, in the struggle, we turn our backs to the enemy or lower in the least our colors?" This was good Jackson doctrine; but it was equally good Cleveland doctrine, for of each it may justly be said that, in a fight, his only use for a back was to put it against the wall.

While containing little of lasting value, this address made it clear, were there doubters, that the principles of the tariff message of 1887 were still the fighting issues of Grover Cleveland. If Democracy was ready again to march to battle for those principles, their leader would not fail them, if called upon. He was, however, still only a willing, not an eager, potential leader.

As it chanced, this January 8th marked the turning point. While Cleveland in New York was lauding Jackson, Democrats throughout the nation were reading the call for the assembling of their national convention, and the Hill-Murphy machine was planning a *coup* which would eliminate Grover Cleveland and give to David B.

Hill the entire New York delegation. In total disregard of precedent, and despite the fact that the Democratic National Committee had set June 21st as the date for the National Convention, they issued, upon short notice, a call for a state convention, to be held at Albany on February 22nd.

The meaning of such a move was not lost on the country. Everywhere it was interpreted as a scheme of machine men to beat the man they could not buy, and to train a New York boss with Tammany backing for the Presidency. The undemocratic character of the movement was denounced in headlines throughout the country as the "Snap Convention" idea. But the New York machine had the power, and could not be turned from its purpose to use it.

As early as September 26, 1891, C. S. Cary had sent to Mr. Cleveland a warning that "there is a combination between Croker, Hill, and Murphy to control the Democratic party of this State, by resort to the most outrageous methods that have ever been resorted to in the State." And now the facts were plainly fulfilling the prediction, although neither Murphy, Croker, nor Hill was the originator of the idea. Writing fifteen years after the event, St. Clair McKelway, who certainly knew the facts and who as certainly had no predisposition to guard the memory of Hill, declared: "The February 22, 1892, Snap State Convention was not brought about on Governor Hill's initiative. He was asked to bring it on by those who deserted him, when he complied with their request. The others were Senator Gorman of Maryland, Senator Palmer of Illinois, and Senator Voorhees of Indiana."

Gorman and Palmer, quite as really as David B. Hill, were seeking the Democratic nomination, but both had managed to conceal that fact from the watchful eyes of their astute associates in this important cold-storage enterprise. Murphy's eyes, while not venturing to seek the White House, gazed at New York's empty seat in the United States Senate, and tiger-like, he hunted silently, that other tiger, Richard Croker, treading softly at his side, knowing by experience that he would share the game when taken. But whoever deserves the doubtful honor of having invented the "Snap Convention" idea, it was Hill who paid the penalty. He alone took, openly and eagerly, the gambler's chance, only to find that it was not the hour of the gambler.

Just before the meeting of the State Committee, William C. Whitney penciled a protest against the idea of a Snap Convention, which Ellery Anderson, R. G. Monroe and others presented in person, but it produced no effect. As soon as the protestants retired, the call for the Snap Convention of February 22nd was issued. At once indignant Democrats, headed by Charles S. Fairchild, Frederick R. Coudert, William R. Grace, and Ellery Anderson, met at the Murray Hill Hotel, and denounced the plan, declaring that "the outcome of a convention selected in midwinter upon so short a call cannot be fairly and truly representative of the Democratic sentiment of the State, and would inevitably debar the mass of Democratic voters from the voice to which they are justly entitled in the selection of the Democratic candidates for President and Vice President and the framing of the party's platform."

This was the beginning of a determined fight against Hill and his political methods. Cleveland Democrats signed and circulated petitions denouncing the Snap Convention idea, to be themselves denounced by Chairman Murphy, but to be praised in press and in pulpit throughout the state and beyond. When the Snap Convention assembled, a committee headed by Mr. Fairchild appeared with another spirited protest against the proceeding. And when this protest too was unheeded, they at once carried out their contingent instructions to issue a call for a state convention, to be held at Syracuse in May, in order that a contesting New York delegation might find ready supporters when the National Convention should assemble.

While the Hill-Murphy clans were gathering at Albany, Cleveland was starting for Ann Arbor to make the Washington's Birthday address to the students of the University of Michigan. It was his desire to make the trip as unostentatiously as possible, but his political sponsors thought otherwise, and arranged for a special train, with all the camp following of an ex-President contemplating a speedy abbreviation of the title.

In the cars adjoining his was the standard collection of politicians, who passed the time in gloomy predictions regarding the pending fate of their leader at the hands of machine men, protective tariff men, silver men, pension men, and other especially horrific enemies, and who gravely prophesied with reference to the chances of Hill. Fresh in their minds was the memory of Mr. Cleveland's recent "injudicious" attack upon free silver, and of Hill's "more politic" utterances; and it was the general opinion that "the old man's done for." One said, "I begged him not to write that anti-silver letter, but he would do it, and it has killed him. It has caused such a split that nothing can be done."

But upon the platform at Ann Arbor the next day Mr. Cleveland showed that something could be done. He delivered a speech on "The Character of George Washington" which threw a flood of light upon the character of Grover Cleveland. A speech with less apparent political significance could hardly have been devised. But its almost childlike profession of faith in the homely virtues of truth, fidelity to duty, family affection, and trust in God, took hold upon the people as no learned discourse, no political invective, could have done.

His listeners felt, as did the millions who read the address or who heard echoes of its teachings, that here was a public man whose record entitled him to discuss ethical standards for public officials, standards which mean "the exaction of moral principle and personal honor and honesty and goodness as indispensable credentials to political preferment." "I know," he said, "that the decrees of God are never obsolete. . . . Do not surrender your faith to those who discredit and debase politics by scoffing at sentiment and principle, and whose political activity consists in attempts to gain popular support by cunning devices and shrewd manipulation."

It is quite apparent that the Snap Convention was in his mind when he wrote these lines, but he came no nearer to the discussion of pending political issues. He was content to deal with principles, believing that the people would themselves make the practical application at the proper time. "The people are not dead, but sleeping," he declared. "They will awaken in good time, and scourge the money changers from their sacred temple." Mr. Cleveland's friends, not satisfied to leave the awakening of the people solely to chance incidents, planned the publicity releases in such a way that the public read Cleveland's Ann Arbor speech and the incidents of the Snap Convention in the same issues of their local papers.

From a comparison of his methods with those of the Cleveland faction, Hill saw no reason to shrink. He had won his state delegation by the skillful use of means con-

secrated by generations of service, and no spiritual misgivings arose to cloud the sunshine of his satisfaction. "I
am a Democrat," was his oft-repeated phrase, and he was
satisfied that he had won his preliminary contest with
Grover Cleveland by methods which Democrats would
approve. Indeed, to his dying day he insisted that his
Snap Convention was entirely creditable. "I was," he
wrote to St. Clair McKelway sixteen years later, "a
candidate for the Presidential nomination in 1892. . . .
The New York delegation had been instructed for me
in its State Convention which had been duly called on the
usual thirty days' notice and in which there was not really
a contested seat, and I was entitled to the full vote of the
State in the National Convention."

Mr. Cleveland returned from Ann Arbor, well pleased
with the signs of favor shown him in the West and somewhat elated at the reception which his Washington's
Birthday address had received.

"I arrived home Thursday morning, quite tired and
with my hand a little lame, but feeling pretty well," he
wrote Bissell on March first. "My trip has started up a
number of invitations from colleges, &c., in different
parts of the country, but I intend to 'stay put' now for
awhile. I had a very warm invitation from Yale this
morning.

"The protesting movement seems to move on without
much abatement. It's wonderful how well the situation
in New York is understood in every corner of the land.
If things go on I shall not be surprised if Tammany Hall
hears some very plain language next June. The question
in my mind now is whether it would not be better for the
convention in May to send a *committee* to Chicago instead of *delegates* claiming admission. Within the last
day or two I have heard quite a little talk about my doing

something. Some want me to write a letter denying that
I have withdrawn, &c. Others rather hint that I should
do something still more pronounced. A letter might
be carefully written that would steer clear of anything
like self-assertion and which might still plainly present
the fact that I did not intend, for personal reasons and to
satisfy personal inclinations, to abandon those enlisted in
a cause to which they deem me useful. My personal
desire you fully understand, but I am going to tell you
how I think the matter may progress.

"Congress will do about all the fool things it can,
nearly, or quite (so far as they can), committing the party
to the silver craze and puttering with tariff reform until
it is tired and sick as an issue. When the Convention
meets the representatives of the party will perhaps see
the condition—that they have nearly lost the only issues
upon which there is the least hope of carrying the
Country. If they do, they will see that they must have a
man who in his person and record represents exactly the
things so nearly thrown away and the direct opposite of
all that they have tried to do.

"If such a man is nominated, the Democratic masses
and the honest men of non-Democratic affiliations will
feel so relieved and so happy in the prospect of political
salvation that an enthusiasm will be furnished to the campaign that will be irresistible. If matters should take on
such a complexion present politics would be brushed
aside without any ceremony. A good sound new man
might just fit the situation. The people in the eastern
states, especially Massachusetts, are very much roused and
I should not be surprised if they spoke quite emphatically
very soon. Every man in this state ought to be well
considered."

This letter makes it abundantly clear that Mr. Cleveland even yet did not have his heart set upon a return to the White House. It was, however, a private letter, written to an intimate and confidential friend, and as such not given to the press. It therefore did nothing to enlighten the thousands of eager friends and the thousands of even more eager enemies who were awaiting his declaration.

On March 9th, in reply to the oft-repeated question: "Will you be a candidate in 1892?" he wrote to the Honorable Edward S. Bragg, author of the slogan, "We love him for the enemies he has made":

MY DEAR SIR:

Your letter of the 5th inst. is received. I have thought until now that I might continue silent on the subject which, under the high sanction of your position as my "fellow-Democrat and fellow-citizen," and in your relation as a true and trusted friend, you present to me. If, in answering your question, I might only consider my personal desires and my individual ease and comfort, my response would be promptly made, and without the least reservation or difficulty.

But if you are right in supposing that the subject is related to a duty I owe to the country and to my party, a condition exists which makes such private and personal considerations entirely irrelevant. I cannot, however, refrain from declaring to you that my experience in the great office of President of the United States has so impressed me with the solemnity of the trust and its awful responsibilities, that I cannot bring myself to regard a candidacy for the place as something to be won by personal strife and active self-assertion.

I have also an idea that the Presidency is pre-eminently the people's office, and I have been sincere in my constant advocacy of the effective participation in political affairs on the part of all our citizens. Consequently, I believe the people should be heard in the choice of their party candidates, and that they themselves should make nominations as directly as is consistent with open, fair, and full party organizations and methods.

I speak of these things solely for the purpose of advising you that my conception of the nature of the Presidential office, and my conviction that the voters of our party should be free in the selection of their candidates, preclude the possibility of my leading and pushing a self-seeking canvass for the Presidential nomination, even if I had a desire to be again a candidate.

Believing that the complete supremacy of Democratic principles means increased national prosperity and the increased happiness of our people, I am earnestly anxious for the success of the party. I am confident success is still within our reach, but I believe this is a time for Democratic thoughtfulness and deliberation, not only as to candidates, but concerning party action upon questions of immense interest to the patriotic and intelligent voters of the land, who watch for an assurance of safety as the price of their confidence and support.

Yours very truly,<br>
GROVER CLEVELAND.

And so the die was cast, and from that moment Grover Cleveland stood before the country as a candidate for a third nomination.

Five days later came encouraging news from Nebraska, whose State Convention rejected, on a square vote forced by the able and brilliant Congressman, William Jennings Bryan, a resolution favoring the unlimited coinage of silver. Mr. Bryan's boundless personal popularity, which equaled in Nebraska Mr. Cleveland's popularity in the country at large, could not save him. He was on the floor, and in the lobbies of the convention; he was everywhere, with personal appeal for himself, and he was beaten—beaten by the power of a Cleveland wave which had swept over the state, inflaming public opinion with a desire to see the ex-President restored to the White House. Indeed, only the fear that New York would be lost should Cleveland be nominated, prevented the Nebraska Convention from instructing for him.

Mr. Cleveland was quite conscious of the growing power of the "silver heresy" and was determined that his nomination, if it came at all, should come with the clear knowledge that he was the implacable enemy of free silver. The idea of going down to defeat lashed to party planks of sound political principles caused him no alarm. To be beaten on account of unpopular principles was to him far preferable to winning a victory based upon unsound principles. This feeling he set forth in detail, in a letter to Mr. Justice Lamar:

"I have within the last few months passed through much that has been trying and perplexing to me. The office of president has not to me personally a single allurement. I shrink from everything which another canvass and its result involves. I know what another election means, and I know as well the dark depths that yawn at the foot of another defeat. I would avoid either if I should consult alone my peace, my comfort or my desire.

"My discomforts arise from a sense of duty to honest people and devoted friends. I am alone with my own thoughts and with the apparent trust and confidence of my countrymen. Am I mistaken in all this, and are my country and my party prepared to discharge me from service? One thing I know. Forces are at work which certainly mean the complete turning back of the hands on the dial of democracy, and the destruction of party hopes.

"Is it ordained that I am to be the instrument through which democratic principles can be saved, whether party supremacy immediately awaits us or not? If folly is to defeat us in any event, ought I to be called upon to place myself under the falling timber? This last consideration smacks a little of care for self, which perhaps ought to be discarded.

"You shall know, my dear friend, my inmost thoughts. I shall be obedient to the call of my country and my party. Whatever happens, no one shall say that I refused to serve in time of evil, or abandoned those whom I have been instrumental in calling to the field, when is waged the battle for democratic principle. If I am given my discharge I shall thank God most fervently. I can easily be disposed of, either by the selection of a candidate more available, or by the adoption of a campaign policy on the financial question which I am not willing to further. In the first case, I shall be a happy helper; in the second, I shall sadly await the announcement of a party defeat which will be predetermined.

"Our southern friends, if they persist, will be left alone with their free coinage heresy. The west is slipping away from their side. The danger is that another idea, and a charge of heedlessness for the public safety on the financial question will do service in the place of the memories of the civil war.

"The question is often and justifiably put by friendly southerners, 'Can Cleveland carry New York?' The answer is ready as to Cleveland or any other man, if the democracy is at all weak on the coinage question.

"As one who loves his country and believes that her interest is bound up in democratic supremacy, I am most uncomfortable and unhappy in the fear that the south will not see until too late the danger of their marring all."

This letter shows how clear was his conviction, even at this early date, that for the Democratic party to adopt the free silver heresy was to court certain defeat at the hands of the people—a remarkable instance of a vision ahead of his party, and in fact of both parties; for until the crisis of 1896 was over and the Democrats were committed to free silver, both parties were uncertain upon the question which in Mr. Cleveland's view was only one of common sense and common honesty.

In May Mr. Whitney returned from Europe and assumed the leadership of the Cleveland movement. He found that there were more delegates favorable to Cleveland than to Hill, but he found also that every New York delegate had signed a protest against the ex-President's renomination. As an experienced leader, Whitney knew this to be a heavy handicap, especially in the case of a candidate who had led the party twice already, the second time to electoral defeat. He was conscious also that the regulars regarded a Democratic victory in November as well-nigh certain, even should the convention choose a candidate unacceptable to the Mugwumps; for the country was weary of Republican rule and high tariffs.

When the contesting delegation, "the May delegates," as Mr. Cleveland called his "anti-snap" representatives, were ready to start for Chicago, Whitney took control, resolved not to fight to seat the "May delegates," but to win a nomination without their votes. To his mind it was no longer a question of disputing the control of New York with the Hill-Murphy machine, but of securing the nomination of Mr. Cleveland under conditions least likely to divide the party. In preliminary conferences with Cleveland men from every state Whitney checked up the Cleveland vote. Upon the basis of reports carefully probed, he decided that at least six hundred delegates would vote for Cleveland on the first ballot. Under these conditions, it was manifestly wise to avoid an open contest with the corporal's guard which had come prepared to vote for Hill.

In the meantime, Senator Gorman had made similar canvasses and had reached a similar conclusion. He therefore deserted the Hill camp and went over to the Cleveland forces, to be speedily followed by Senator Palmer, while Senator Voorhees, the third member of the trio which had launched the Snap Convention, retired to Indiana, leaving his followers to make such terms as they could with the Whitney-led forces of Grover Cleveland.

Mr. Cleveland was far less confident of victory than were his friends. On June 11th he wrote to Bissell:

"I am delighted to know that you are going to Chicago, for if my name is presented there and there is any danger of my nomination, I shall feel very safe and comfortable if a few such good and discreet friends as you are on the spot. . . . You may not understand, and perhaps will not entirely approve, the way the thing has drifted; but I have been fully convinced that nothing better could be done in this thing than to have Whitney pretty well to the front in the matter of management and organization. In point of fact, it has already gravitated to that point. Associated with him from N. Y. State I hope will be Bissell, Cady Herrick, Tracy, Stetson and such others as are like-minded and are wise and useful. . . .

"One reason why I hope the persons I have mentioned

will work together is found in my anxiety about the platform of the Convention. Of course as a Democrat I want a good platform for the success of our party; and if I should chance to be in any way related to it, it must be sound, especially in the money plank. If the nomination to the Presidency passes by me I shall be anything but disappointed or afflicted; but for the nomination, or for anything else, I cannot forego my opinions nor appear to shuffle or falter on the financial question. . . . While I want to do my duty to my party and the good people of the Country, I am still perfectly sincere in saying that the result which would bring to me the greatest personal gratification would be the nomination of some other good man and good Democrat. And this is quite consistent with my great satisfaction and gratitude for all that is done for me."

Among the things that had been done for him was the installation at his summer home of a telegraph operator, that to some extent the ex-President might follow, moment by moment, the developments in the convention. There were of course many details which could not be sent over the wire, much business being transacted in secret.

At Chicago, his friends, like those of every candidate since the convention system was inaugurated, conciliated, coaxed, promised, and bargained with those who controlled the floating votes. His enemies lurking in the corridors captured these same doubtful delegates as they left his friends and spread before them counter-promises, threats, and intimidations, pointing to past defeats and predicting future disasters if this man Cleveland should be again chosen to lead the party.

At the beginning of these conferences the anti-Cleveland men were jubilantly confident, but as they talked to delegation after delegation they began to see that a surprising number were from sections where the people had shown an unmistakable desire for Cleveland leadership. What was the explanation? They had played the dead march over him. But now, ears to the ground, they heard the sound of the "master's" voice—the people were speaking the name, Grover Cleveland. Why? They could not tell. He lacked the magic personality which had at times made anti-machine men irresistible. He was in no sense either dramatic or picturesque. He could not be looked upon as a campaigner, for he was opposed to the idea of a candidate for the Presidency pleading his own cause from the stump. As a public speaker, furthermore, he was as uninspiring as reluctant. He never spoke unless compelled by a sense of duty, and then with few of the arts of the orator. He promised no favors, courted no leaders, conciliated no mobs. Why such a man should defy the laws of politics, long accepted as immutable, and rise from his political grave to the discomfiture of the regulars, no regular could understand. But that he was to be the controlling force in that convention few doubted after the first few hours of preliminary skirmishing.

When at last the private wire in the gun room at Gray Gables began to click off the proceedings, moment by moment, the excitement of his companions—Mrs. Cleveland, Mr. and Mrs. William E. Russell, Mr. Joseph Jefferson and his two sons—became intense. Indeed, of that little company only one appeared entirely at ease, and that one was Grover Cleveland. Once he arose with the surprising statement, "I forgot to dry my lines," and retired to the garden to stretch his fishing line across the laundress's drying ground.

As the nomination speeches began, the gun room waited, breathless. The honor of naming Grover Cleveland had fallen to Governor Leon Abbett of New Jersey, not because of any particular Cleveland enthusiasm on his part, as he was an old-line politician with a sneaking sympathy for Hill, but because, in opposition to his wishes, the New Jersey delegation were under instructions "to vote for Mr. Cleveland so long as his name should be before the convention." When the roll call reached Arkansas, she yielded to New Jersey. "Governor Abbett is nominating Grover Cleveland," reported the private wire; and then followed the usual bewildering succession of speeches, lasting until midnight.

Shortly after twelve o'clock, the roll of the states complete, the weary delegates and the thousands of weary onlookers, including the select company in the gun room, were rallying their jaded minds for the long-expected first ballot, when the famous Tammany orator, Bourke Cockran, furnished a diversion. Apparently unconscious of the fact that more oratory was what the convention least desired, in the face of a tempest which was raging without and an anti-Tammany victory which was imminent within, he mounted the platform and for an hour and a half held his weary audience of hostile but charmed listeners by the eloquence of his attack upon Grover Cleveland and his support of Hill. When Cockran had finished his last rounded period and resumed his seat, the Cleveland men, without a word of reply, moved that a ballot be taken.

The vote came to the gun room, state by state, as the roll was called. Mr. Cleveland occupied a chair immediately in front of the window, and just opposite him sat Joe Jefferson, the rest of the little company being in the center of the room. Thus grouped, they had watched

night fall. Now sunrise was approaching, as they tabu-
lated the call of states. Six hundred and seven must be
registered in the Cleveland column before the traditional
two-thirds majority would be complete.

Glancing out of the window during one of the pauses
between reports from the operator, Mrs. Cleveland remarked that a little stream in the center of the landscape
had caught the crimson glow of dawn. Then came
another report, and another, and then, just as the first ray
of sunshine strayed through the window, touching Mr.
Cleveland's head, the operator gave the final touch to the
picture by announcing: "Mr. Cleveland is nominated."

That lone ballot tells the tale of the astonishing failure
of the Hill campaign, the Snap Convention, and the Tammany orator combined; and of the still more astonishing
strength of Grover Cleveland:

Whole number of votes.......... 909 1-2
Number necessary for 2-3 majority 607
Grover Cleveland of New York... 617 1-3
David B. Hill of New York...... 114
Horace Boies of Iowa .......... 103
Arthur P. Gorman of Maryland.. 36 1-2
Adlai E. Stevenson of Illinois.... 16 2-3
John G. Carlisle of Kentucky..... 14
William R. Morrison of Illinois.. 3
James E. Campbell of Ohio...... 2
William C. Whitney of New York 1
William E. Russell of Massa-
chusetts ................... 1
Robert E. Pattison of Pennsylvania 1

The platform, as at first reported by the committee,
was alarmingly stand-pat upon the vital issue of the tariff;

but Mr. Cleveland's friends fought it in open convention and won by the convincing majority of 564 to 342. As a result the platform ended with the following words, which might have been written by Mr. Cleveland himself: "We reiterate the oft-repeated doctrines of the Democratic party that the necessity of government is the only justification for taxation, and that whenever a tax is unnecessary it is unjustifiable; that when custom house taxation is levied upon articles of any kind produced in this country, the difference between cost of labor here and labor abroad, when such a difference exists, fully measures any possible benefits to labor, and the enormous additional impositions of existing tariff fall with crushing force upon our farmers and workingmen and for the mere advantage of the few whom it enriches, exact from labor a grossly unjust share of the expenses of the Government, and we demand such a revision of the tariff laws as will remove their iniquitous inequalities, lighten their oppression and put them on a Constitutional and equitable basis."

From returning delegates Mr. Cleveland received those unpublished secrets in which every convention abounds. At first the May delegates from New York had been anxious for a trial of strength with the Snap Convention delegates. But Mr. Whitney, confident of the soundness of his preliminary calculations, insisted that "they could not afford to split New York; that if Hill bolted, we would lose the state; that the one thing we were after was to have our candidate nominated and elected." He carried his point and also his program, and for that reason no fair criticism can be made of the way he handled the Cleveland interests. There was, however, much bitter criticism; but from the following letter to

Bissell it is evident that it received no encouragement from Mr. Cleveland:

Gray Gables,
Buzzards Bay, Mass.
June 30, 1892.

MY DEAR BISSELL:

I was delighted to receive your letter yesterday and thank you for it. I think the way you looked into my hand in the matter of dealing with certain parties is "perfectly lovely," as the ladies say. I will not attempt to tell you even a small part of what is in my mind and heart in the way of admiration and gratitude for all that was done at Chicago. All was superb, and it was almost uncanny to sit here at the end of a wire and see and hear and feel and know it all as it transpired. Of course my duty now is to be as good a candidate as possible, and do all I can to aid success.

I do not think Murphy or Sheehan should be at all prominent in the campaign. In point of fact, I think neither of them, nor any of that kind of thing, should have the least direction of it. But I do think—indeed I know —that Whitney should nominally, if not really and actively, be at the head of the Committee to manage the National Campaign. I have regarded it as exceedingly desirable on my own judgment, and the letters I have received within a few days and the expressions I have heard made convince me that it is more essential and vital to success than any one thing. . . .

I don't see how your baby got "them teeth." Ours could have plenty of them, I suppose, if she wanted them, but she don't eat any roasted beef or things of that kind —so what's the use? . . .

I have never received so many and such warm and

enthusiastic congratulations, but thus far not one from any state official in New York, and almost none from the Hill following. This is queer, and I think it will be a good thing to let them dwell a while with their *alleged* reasons and consciences.

I have written a queer kind of letter to Tammany Hall, to be read at its Fourth of July celebration. I shall watch and see how that takes.

God bless you and your dear wife and baby. We all send love to them and you. I hear Ruth crowing and carrying on now.

Yours faithfully,<br>GROVER CLEVELAND.

Mr. Cleveland faced the campaign with a solemn sense of responsibility, but with the grateful consciousness that the people had demanded his return, and that he was to be allowed to reopen the case which the election of 1888 had decided against him, and against the majority of the people. He had won a moral victory and one without gilt or tinsel. He had been nominated on his merit, not "by cunning devices and shrewd manipulation," against which he had so earnestly warned the students of the University of Michigan.

From the point of view of those trained to trust such methods, his return was a political miracle. They had discovered no machine adequate to so great a task, and the idea that his nomination was the natural result of a popular enthusiasm for an honest public servant was to them fanciful. That there had been a sort of machine they knew, of course. The Anti-Snappers had covered the land with their moral protest against the methods and aims of Hill and Murphy. But it was a machine designed to give the people the facts, not one organized to promise them offices, and its methods would have been entirely ineffective had not four years of sober second thought convinced the country that Grover Cleveland had been an honest public servant, fearless and painstaking, thinking first of duty and the people, and not even second of self.

There was still another element, of the existence of which his enemies had of necessity been ignorant. The thousands of personal letters which he had written during the brief period of his retirement had greatly strengthened his hold upon the public. Every man who had received such a letter faced the question of a party candidate with a sense of personal relationship with Grover Cleveland, and the convention delegates were made to appreciate this fact. Thus in almost every section of the country he possessed friends whose enthusiasm no local politician could cool, and who labored for his nomination, and later for his election, in a spirit rarely seen among political workers.

After some delay, the notification ceremony was set for Wednesday evening, July 20th, and Madison Square Garden was selected. The Philadelphia *Public Ledger* thus pictured Mr. Cleveland's appearance upon the occasion: "Whatever may have been his feelings, Grover Cleveland's face looked painfully sad as he stood on the platform and looked over the vast audience gathered to do him honor. Perhaps no other man ever experienced a greater personal triumph than he did at that time. Against all political precedent, and against bitter personal opposition, he had been nominated for the third time to the highest office in the world, and there he stood, in the biggest hall of the greatest city of the State which had voted against him at Chicago, and in the presence of his enemies, as well as of his friends, and amid the plaudits of 20,000 people was formally notified of his nomination. No Roman conquerer ever had a more notable triumph. No political leader in this country was ever welcomed by a grander audience.

"Yet there was not the slightest sign of triumph in his face. His countenance mirrored forth no exultation of soul, no pride of victory, no joy over the discomfiture of his enemies. He did not smile once from the time he entered the hall until he left it, but surveyed the scene of triumph with a face that showed more humility than pride, more sadness than joy. At one time indeed it seemed as if he were going to break down and shed tears— this man of iron will and nerves of oak.

"He seemed to regard the occasion with the feeling of a priest who is being consecrated for the holy services of bishop. But he never lost his self-possession and . . . repeated his speech from memory without the change of a single word. Reporters who held his printed speech in their hands and followed him word by word testify to this fact."

But a Democratic nomination is by no means an election, and as Mr. Cleveland watched the progress of affairs in Washington he grew uneasy lest the foolish in his own party, in their infatuation for the heresy of free silver, should give President Harrison an opportunity to seize the sound money standard as the Republican battle flag.

"If the Democratic House of Representatives," he wrote to Congressman Harter on July 7th, "permits a free silver bill to go to Mr. Harrison for his veto, those responsible for it will, in my opinion, stand a chance to gain the same splendid notoriety as the man who burned the Temple of Diana." On this question he felt as Daniel Webster had felt about the Democratic advocacy of the policy of the Wilmot proviso: "It is not their thunder."

In his brief response to the formal notification of his nomination, however, he failed to touch the subject of free silver, again devoting his attention chiefly to the task of flaying "the selfish schemes of those who seek through the aid of unequal tariff laws to gain unearned and unreasonable advantages at the expense of their fellows." He was determined that as he had against advice and warning led the party to defeat on the tariff issue, he would now lead it to victory upon that selfsame question.

The condition of the New York Democracy was constantly on his mind. "Fishing or eating, reading or drinking, asleep or awake," he wrote to Bissell, "my mind has been on one thing constantly, and that is the situation politically in the city, county and state of New York. *The thing is not right*—that is, in my judgment. I believe there is a lot of lying and cheating going on, and unless the complexion changes we shall wake up, I think, the morning after election and find that we have been fooled by as base a set of cutthroats as ever scuttled a ship.

"The one of my friends at the front in the city of New York is Mr. Whitney. He is as true as steel, and is devoting himself night and day to the work. But his labor is altogether in the line of pacification and everything he does tends to persuading the men of Tammany Hall and those who belong to their gang, to vote the Democratic ticket. In the meantime my friends are entirely ignored, or are treated as if they deserved punishment. This is on the theory, as he says, that my friends we have anyway, and the point should be to gain the support and votes of those who were not my friends at Chicago and who were 'beaten and humiliated.'

"The campaign is to be put in the hands of men who have solemnly declared that I cannot carry New York.

Do you suppose that Hill wants to see me elected? Look at the men through the state whom he has been building up for two years and who are on the local committees. They will, I suppose, insist stronger than ever upon managing the campaign in their localities, and when the disaster comes will lay it on the May Convention people. . . . You will see, when men are appointed to attend to political business in the campaign, that they will be Hill men unless such a thing is prevented. You will see Sheehan on the Executive Committee, and then I believe the effort will be to let the ticket drop and hide their responsibility for it. If this is the result, Whitney will be as badly fooled, or worse, than anybody else; but you see, when a man is thoroughly saturated with pacification he doesn't suspect these things. . . . It's a funny thing for a man to be running for the Presidency with all the politicians against him."

As the campaign proceeded it became more and more evident that Whitney's faith was indeed pinned to the policy of pacifying Tammany Hall. He knew that Tammany leaders held the vote of New York City in the hollow of their hands, and that they were disposed to use it for Mr. Cleveland's defeat. With Richard Croker, who had succeeded John Kelly as "Big Chief," Whitney had great influence, having ably defended him against the charge of murder. With characteristic fidelity to a friend, Croker remembered the service gratefully, and through that gratitude Whitney hoped to bring Tammany into line for the Democratic candidate.

Much as Mr. Cleveland admired Mr. Whitney, the methods of conciliation always irked him, and in the secrecy of a confidential letter to Bissell he again poured out his heart regarding Whitney's latest proposition.

Gray Gables,
Buzzard's Bay, Mass.
*August 10, 1892.*

MY DEAR BISSELL:

There is an old story which you have doubtless heard but which was fixed in my mind by the fact that it is the only story I ever heard Chapin of Brooklyn tell.

A frontiersman had occasion to leave his cabin and his wife and children for a number of days and nights. When he returned he found that his house had been burned and the mutilated and charred remains of his family were scattered about the ground. He leaned upon his gun in silence for a moment, and then remarked with earnestness: "Well, I'll be damned, if this ain't *too* ridiculous!"

I felt like saying just that when I read in the paper yesterday morning that Sheehan had been appointed Chairman of the Campaign State Committee.

My condition is not improved by receiving a letter from Whitney to-day in which he suggests the form of a most abject and humble letter for me to write to Murphy amounting to a prayer for his support. I'll see the whole outfit to the Devil before I'll do it. Somebody must be crazy, and unless the people of the State take matters in their own hands some people stand a right smart chance to get left—and I am one of them. I expect to see Whitney on Monday. I am glad it is not to-day, for I don't believe I could hold myself in.

Yours faithfully,
GROVER CLEVELAND.

Other Democrats also found it difficult to "hold themselves in" as they watched Whitney's constant overtures

to Tammany Hall. Many of Mr. Cleveland's follower
feared that by this course he would arouse antagonism
not alone in Mugwump and Independent circles, bu
among conservative Democrats as well; not only in New
York, but throughout the country, doing irreparable harn
in the close states, and perhaps causing Cleveland's de
feat. But Whitney was determined, his New York asso
ciates supported him, and during the rest of the summe
the candidate was constantly reminded that "Murphy ha
the votes." "It is no use to say not to trust any of them,'
Whitney wrote on August 22d; "we have got to trus
them. They have the organization and the power, anc
by trusting them we can make them pull straight. I wish
you would do as much reconciling of recalcitrants as you
see your way to do. You can do more with a word than
I can with a speech."

Again and again Mr. Cleveland expressed his pent-up
feelings, as these reminders came—to Bissell most freely
of all. On September 4th, he wrote from Gray Gables:

MY DEAR BISSELL:
  . . . I feel very gloomy and very much provoked and
am not sure that I ought to write to you in such a mood
The whole policy of truckling conciliation which ha
characterized the campaign thus far has resulted in it
legitimate fruit and I am urged now to send for Murphy
and Sheehan and conciliate them.

Whitney wrote me a letter he wanted me to send to
Murphy and I declined to do it—whereupon he wrote me
a very petulant and unpleasant letter. He was here yes
terday and we had a little talk—nothing unpleasant, bu
I can see that he is not satisfied and he seemed to be on
the point of exploding. He professes to feel that th
campaign is in a very dangerous shape and more than hal

intimates that unless I get into personal relations with these men I will be defeated.

I told him I would go to New York whenever he desired and meet them and be as agreeable as I could, but I would not pledge myself to do their bidding in case of success. I further told him I did not want to annoy him, but that I did not have a particle of confidence in Sheehan and that I thought he would use any money or power that was put into his hands for the election of members of assembly to the end that Flower might be made Senator and he Governor.

I believe Tammany and Kings will do as well as they can, that the electoral tickets will be neglected for the legislative tickets in the rural districts, and that if I am defeated in the State it will be claimed as further proof of my unpopularity, which will be urged as an explanation of the result. The neglect of everything except tickling these men amounts to a craze at headquarters, and in the meantime the campaign, it seems to me, limps and halts.

I curse myself for getting into this scrape, and would get out of it to-day if I could. I will not give up my old friends for the gang, and yet I do not see why the latter want me to conciliate them unless they mean by that an assurance which they will regard as a promise of exclusive favor and influence.

Cannot you come and see me for a day? We are easily reached from Boston.

Yours faithfully,<br>GROVER CLEVELAND.

Mr. Whitney's persistence having at last brought from Mr. Cleveland a grudging consent to come down from Gray Gables in order that conciliation might have a fair

trial, the latter arrived in New York, and went at once to
the Victoria Hotel, where Judge Herrick of Albany joined
him by appointment, finding the candidate in a condition
of unusual excitement.  Mr. Cleveland remarked that he
had been brought to the city to persuade the Democratic
organization to support him; that if the recognition of
that organization meant the ignoring of men who had
stood by him in the state, he was prepared to decline the
nomination and support any man substituted in his place;
but that if his friends agreed that he should not yield to
the organization, he was prepared to call mass meetings
in every county in the state and to inform the people that
the so-called Democratic organization had refused to support the regular Democratic nominee for the Presidency.

Judge Herrick replied that the organization ought
to be recognized; that there were many bright men in the
machine who could be given appointments abroad; that
others could be brought down to Washington and kept
under Mr. Cleveland's own eyes; that Mr. Cleveland's
friends could be appointed to Federal positions in the
state; and that in less than six months they would have
control of the organization.  At this point Mr. Whitney
came in, accompanied by Mr. Dickinson, and among
them they persuaded Mr. Cleveland to meet the Tammany chiefs, Murphy, Croker, and Sheehan, at a dinner
of reconciliation which was to be staged in the Victoria
Hotel.  Judge Herrick was urged to be present also, but
declined, feeling that he was *persona non grata* to the
Tammany leaders.

But Mr. Cleveland proved conciliatory only in the
going.  When the dinner was ended, and the hour for
discussion had arrived, he turned to the expectant machine
men and said:

"Well, gentlemen, what do you want?"

"We want pledges from you," replied Mr. Sheehan. "We want to know what you are going to do if you are elected. We want you to give us promises that will satisfy us that the organization will be properly recognized if you become President again."

Mr. Cleveland doubled up his huge fist and smote the table.

"Gentlemen," he said, speaking slowly and with almost painful distinctness, "I will not go into the White House pledged to you or to any one else. I will make no secret promises. I'll be damned if I will."

Again the big fist whacked the table.

"What are you going to do then?" inquired Mr. Sheehan cynically.

"I'll tell you what I'm going to do," said Mr. Cleveland as he rose to his feet. "I intend to address a letter to the public in which I shall withdraw from the ticket. I intend to explain my situation and to report what you have said to me here. I will tell the voters of the country that I cannot give any secret pledges, and that unless I do you will not support the Democratic ticket. I will tell the voters that I do not want to stand in the way of a Democratic victory. That is what I shall do. Then, gentlemen, you can pick out a candidate to suit you, and if he is a proper man and the candidate of the party I will vote for him."

There was a pause.

"But I'll tell you one thing, Mr. Sheehan," added Mr. Cleveland, as he turned to the now breathless Lieutenant-Governor, "in my opinion public indignation will snow you and your organization out of sight before the end of a week."

Mr. Croker leaped to his feet at this point, exclaiming: "This must stop, Mr. Sheehan; I agree with Mr.

Cleveland. He cannot make any pledges and it is no right to ask for them."

Thus did Mr. Whitney's policy of conciliation conciliate by conquering, and Grover Cleveland again faced the election a free man.

Meanwhile he was engaged upon the uncongenial work of preparing his letter of acceptance. The day it was completed, he wrote to Gilder: "Take my advice, my dear friend, and never run for President."

The letter itself did not satisfy him. His own productions rarely did. Nor can it be said that it was a literary composition of great distinction. It was marked, as were all his writings, by a ruggedness of style and an involved and cumbersome construction, but it made perfectly clear Mr. Cleveland's thought, and contained not one word of doubtful meaning. The greater part of the letter he devoted to a discussion of the necessity of reducing the tariff to a revenue basis, but he touched also upon sound money, and civil service reform. He promised "consideration for our worthy veteran soldiers, and for the families of those who have died," while contending anew that our pension roll should be a roll of honor "uncontaminated by ill desert, and unvitiated by demagogic use."

The campaign developed no new or startling features, except the unexpected growth of the Populist strength in the West and in certain Southern districts, a growth the full meaning of which appeared later.

The Republicans, conscious that their ticket, Benjamin Harrison and Whitelaw Reid, was not an inspiring one, trusted that the hopeless break in the New York Democracy might give them victory. They knew that Tammany's declarations of loyalty to the Democratic ticket meant little, and put their faith in the confident assertion of the Hill faction that Grover Cleveland could not carry New York.

During the campaign Mr. Cleveland received an invitation to pay a personal visit in Chicago at a time when Mrs. Harrison's illness compelled the Republican candidate to remain inactive. He replied: "I am unwilling to take a trip which . . . would be regarded as a political tour made by a candidate for the Presidency. My general aversion to such a trip is overwhelmingly increased in this particular instance when I recall the afflictive dispensation which detains at the bedside of his sick wife another candidate for the Presidency."

As the end of the season approached, Mr. Cleveland prepared to leave Gray Gables and return to New York. He had leased from his friend, Commodore Benedict, an attractive residence, 12 West 51st Street; and, during the summer, workmen had been busy remodeling and redecorating it. The Commodore had spared neither trouble nor expense in his effort to make it worthy of its new tenant. Early in October Mr. Cleveland moved in, making preparations as for a permanent home, and seeming almost as unconcerned regarding the election as did his baby daughter, of whom he wrote to Dr. Wilton Merle Smith: "Ruth lives her sweet little life in the midst of it all as unconsciously as though it were not history."

Four nights before election Mr. Cleveland, contrary to his established rule, spoke at the last grand rally of the campaign, at Oakland Rink, Jersey City. There was a heavy fog abroad, and a steady drizzling rain was falling; but the Democratic political clubs marched, nevertheless. And when the rink doors were thrown open there was a rush of eager Democrats, who, within ten minutes, filled every seat in the vast structure. The appearance of the ex-President, accompanied by Senator McPherson, ex-Senator William Brinkerhoff, and William F. Harrity, Chairman of the Democratic National Committee, caused a pandemonium of enthusiasm which became almost hysteria as Mr. Cleveland rose to speak. With characteristic directness, he launched at once into his prime theme, tariff reform, but in a most un-Clevelandesque manner. The speech was rankly partisan throughout. Like any ward politician, he pointed with pride, he whitewashed, he coaxed, he cajoled. He painted the Democrats lily white and the Republicans a very inky black. He drew inspiring pictures of the good Democrats and horrific caricatures of the wicked Republicans who would not let the Democrats do their duty.

On election night, a few intimate friends gathered at the Cleveland home to receive the returns, which were favorable from the first. As results became more and more certain, more guests arrived. The throng in the street also increased in size and enthusiasm until, at midnight, the ex-President yielded to the necessities of the occasion and addressed a few words to them.

The definite announcement of victory was brought by Mrs. Whitney, whose husband had informed the President of his defeat in 1888. She came into the drawing-room breathlessly radiant with excitement. The wires had just announced the final verdict and the long tension was broken. At once pandemonium reigned, but the President-elect was very quiet, weighed down with a sense of responsibility, and when his friends departed, at five A.M., they left behind a solemn victor.

The full details of the astonishing results came by slow stages. Cleveland had carried every doubtful state, and his majority in New York was over 45,000. His total electoral vote was 277, an increase of 190 over that of 1888, and of 59 over that of 1884. His popular vote of

5,556,543 was 16,214 more than that of 1888, and 681,557 more than that of 1884. There could be no doubt that it was, to a large extent, a personal victory. More than five and a half million Americans had expressed the desire that the leader, once rejected, should again lead the nation.

"I care more for principle than for the Presidency," he had said to Richard Watson Gilder, and had added that he would "have the Presidency clean or not at all." He had put himself outside intimate party counsels. He had enraged Democratic spoilsmen by his persistent refusal to pay party debts with public offices. He had disappointed the reformers who insisted that reform should be the only consideration. But, incidentally, he had laid deep the foundations of his place in history. And as a consequence he had, as William H. Taft later expressed it, "led his party to the greatest victory in its history."

But victory meant not peace but a change of battle front, for Edward Murphy, Jr., promptly announced his desire to represent New York in the United States Senate, an ambition abhorrent to the President-elect. Mr. Cleveland had known, of course, that Mr. Whitney's policy of conciliating the Tammany chieftains meant demands for compensation, the more difficult to resist the more effective the Tammany support should prove. But among all the horrible senatorial possibilities which he had discussed with his friends this one had never appeared. It seemed "too raw" even for Tammany, and he frankly said as much, first to Croker and Murphy, then to the general public. With that "eminent impartiality" to which his friend Bissell so often refers, he elaborated the reasons for his opposition, and entrusted them to the columns of the New York *World:*

"We need the best aid that we can procure . . . and the man who is selected as Senator from this state should be able, in the largest sense, to help the party fulfill its promises to the people. The people of our state who this year gave to the Democratic Electoral ticket a majority so large as to indicate that they expect much from Democratic supremacy, are entitled to a Senator who will not only represent their interests and their principles, but will be able to advance and defend them. We need in the Senate a man of training and experience in public affairs as well as a man of clear ideas concerning the important questions which confront our party. It seems to me that the selection of Mr. Murphy does not indicate a disposition to choose for the Senatorship a man of the kind that is needed at this juncture, and I fear that this first manifestation of the power put in our hands will give rise to a feeling of public disappointment such as our party ought not to be called upon to face."

The anti-Tammany press throughout the country also did what it could to defeat Murphy. The Philadelphia *Ledger* of December 30th declared: "If Mr. Murphy were elected Senator, the President would be expected to allow Mr. Hill and Mr. Murphy to divide the Federal offices of New York between themselves as spoils to their fellows, the Tammany henchmen. Mr. Murphy, like Mr. Hill, is an advocate of free silver, an enemy of civil service and of every other political reform of which Mr. Cleveland is the earnest, public-spirited supporter. If he refused to give the Federal offices to these two Senators, they would use all the advantages the office of Senator confers upon them to embarrass and annoy him and to defeat the wholesome efforts of the Administration to secure and maintain good government."

But Tammany Hall controlled the New York Legislature, in whose hands the Constitution then placed the choice of New York Senators, Croker and Hill controlled Tammany Hall, and Murphy became United States Senator.

# GROVER CLEVELAND
## THE MAN AND THE STATESMAN

### VOLUME TWO

# CONTENTS

## VOLUME II

| CHAPTER | | PAGE |
|---|---|---|
| I. | THE FIRST BATTLE WITH BRYAN—THE REPEAL OF THE SHERMAN LAW | 1 |
| II. | BLOCKING "MANIFEST DESTINY" IN HAWAII | 45 |
| III. | BREAKING THE ENDLESS CHAIN—THE FOUR BOND ISSUES | 74 |
| IV. | THE WILSON-GORMAN TARIFF | 107 |
| V. | THE PULLMAN STRIKE OF 1894 | 138 |
| VI. | THE VENEZUELAN AFFAIR | 173 |
| VII. | THE WARWICK OF 1896 | 203 |
| VIII. | THE FOUR LEAN MONTHS | 238 |
| IX. | RETIRES TO PRINCETON | 256 |
| X. | WATCHING THE GAME FROM THE SIDE LINES | 271 |
| XI. | THE TURN OF THE TIDE | 301 |
| XII. | THE ELECTION OF 1904 | 321 |
| XIII. | REORGANIZING THE EQUITABLE | 350 |
| XIV. | SUNSET DAYS | 365 |
| | INDEX | 417 |

# GROVER CLEVELAND

## CHAPTER I

### THE FIRST BATTLE WITH BRYAN—THE REPEAL OF THE SHERMAN LAW

*"Patriotism is no substitute for a sound currency."*
—GROVER CLEVELAND.

THE election of November, 1892, placed Grover Cleveland in a position unique in American history. He was the only President ever re-elected after a defeat. Furthermore, he was the first President-elect since 1840 who was manifestly a greater political figure than any man whom he could conceivably select for his Cabinet

Harrison and Tyler had been outclassed by many leaders in their own party. James K. Polk had his William L. Marcy, his Robert J. Walker, his George Bancroft; Zachary Taylor, his John M. Clayton, Reverdy Johnson, and Thomas Ewing; Franklin Pierce, to his own generation, looked small beside Marcy, Guthrie, and Caleb Cushing; and James Buchanan was clearly eclipsed by Lewis Cass. Lincoln started his presidential career with both Seward and Chase to overshadow him. Andrew Johnson was outclassed in the public mind by most of the Cabinet which he inherited from Lincoln. Grant, though eminent as a soldier, was politically of small stature beside Elihu Washburn or Hamilton Fish. Hayes was dwarfed by Evarts, Sherman, and Carl

Schurz. Blaine, as Secretary of State, completely over-topped both Garfield and Arthur, while Cleveland him-self in 1884 was far less eminent than either Tilden or Thomas F. Bayard. But with Grover Cleveland's resto-ration, the older and better tradition was resumed, for, with the single exception of Monroe's first term, every administration down to that of William Henry Harri-son had begun with a President more eminent than any of his advisers.

In addition to this personal prestige, Mr. Cleveland returned to power with the added advantage of being the first President since Pierce whose party was in a posi-tion to control both Senate and House. During his first term Congress had been Democratic; but the Re-publicans had controlled the Senate, and from that strong-hold had wrought havoc upon many of his cherished plans. Now, however, for a brief but satisfying period, he found himself riding the crest of the wave, his tri-umphant party eagerly hailing him chief, and even the Republicans admitting that he had "qualities."

In the House of Representatives he was entitled to expect the support of two hundred and nineteen out of a membership of three hundred and fifty-five, with one seat vacant. Out of a Senate of eighty-eight the Demo-crats numbered forty-four, while the three seats yet to be filled gave them hope of a majority, especially as the five Populist Senators might reasonably be expected to train with them. To all appearances, therefore, Mr. Cleveland could count upon the support of both Houses, and but for the break in his own party when the testing time came, he might have commanded the storm for many a day.

When ready to choose his Cabinet, Mr. Cleveland felt it wise to select new men who would bring new points of view and new suggestions to bear upon the problems confronting the country. And so, while freely seeking the personal advice of his old Cabinet associates, he persistently looked elsewhere for official advisers.

On January 25, 1893, he wrote to L. Clarke Davis:

"Bayard came to me night before last and left this morning. We had a very frank and unrestrained talk, as we have always had, and so far as he can do so, he has, like the good patriotic friend he is, left matters almost entirely in my control.

"I am dreadfully perplexed and bothered. I cannot get the men I want to help me, but strange to say, my greatest trials come through those professing to be near and attached friends, who expect things.

"I hope the skies will lighten by and by, but I have never seen a day since I consented to drift with events that I have not cursed myself for yielding; and in these particular days I think I curse a little more heartily than ever. This is strange talk and perhaps seems ungracious and unappreciative. It is nothing of the kind. It presents only the personal side of the matter; and sometimes when I feel that perhaps I may after all be the instrument of doing good to the American people whom I know I love, I am quite happy."

That night he offered Bayard's old post, the portfolio of State, to Judge Walter Q. Gresham, of Indiana, a man who, except for the year 1864, when he had been unable to go to the polls, had voted the Republican ticket at every presidential election since the party was organized. Gresham had served as Secretary of the Treasury for one month during Arthur's administration, and at the opening of the campaign of 1892, had been in the minds of many

anti-Harrison leaders, a possible Republican nominee
for the Presidency. Indeed, according to the memoir published by his widow, he had been actually asked to lead
the Republicans in a fight for the nomination, but had
answered: "I am out of politics, and have no political
aspirations." The People's party, too, had offered him
their nomination, and this also he had declined, declaring
to his son that he thought the thing for him to do was to
take the stump for Grover Cleveland, largely because of
the latter's tariff views. Gresham's support under such
.circumstances had been of great value to the Democratic
ticket, but the offer of the leading place in the Cabinet
came as a surprise, and he at first declined. Mr. Cleveland met his objections with the assurance that "prior
political affiliations matter not a bit." Whitney, Carlisle,
Henry Watterson, and other prominent Democrats added
their arguments, and Mr. Gresham finally accepted the
appointment. In acknowledging the acceptance, Mr.
Cleveland wrote:

*Confidential.*

Lakewood, N. J.

Hon. Walter Q. Gresham.                *Feby. 9, 1893.*

My dear Sir:

Your letter of the 7th instant came to hand two or
three hours ago, and causes me the greatest satisfaction.
I know perfectly well that only considerations of patriotism and duty have constrained you to accede to my wishes,
and I assure you this vastly increases my appreciation
of what you have done. . . .

I would certainly be exceedingly glad to have a chat
with you between now and the 4th of March, and hope
that your work will so close up as to enable you to come
to me.

I have settled, I think, on five members of the Cabinet. I mean to have Carlisle for the Treasury—Lamont for War—Bissell (of Buffalo, one of my oldest friends and former partner) for Postmaster General, and Hoke Smith, of Georgia (a very able representative of the new and progressive South), for Interior. This leaves Navy, Attorney General and Agriculture still to be selected. I want George Gray, Senator from Delaware, to accept the Attorney General's place, but he has thus far, strangely enough, declined. If there was a first-rate man in Alabama, Mississippi, or that neighborhood, I would like to consider him. If not, I am prepared to take a man from almost any quarter.

I offered Agriculture to Boies of Iowa; but he and his friends are reckoning on his making a successful canvass for United States Senator next fall, and he declined my invitation. The Navy ought not to be a very hard place to fill, but I have not just the man in view yet. It is barely possible that I may induce Senator Gray to take the Attorney Generalship after all, but I hardly expect it.

I would be very glad to receive any suggestions you may make concerning incumbents for these vacant places. Now that I have secured the head of my Cabinet, I feel that it should be completed as soon as possible.

If your leisure and convenience permit, I hope you will write to me. Please address me by letter or dispatch at this place.

Very sincerely yours,
GROVER CLEVELAND.

Disappointed in his hope of securing Senator Gray as Attorney General, Mr. Cleveland appointed Richard Olney, whom he had met but once, but whose qualifications he had carefully investigated. Mr. Olney's success as counsel for the Eastern Railroad in 1875, during a period of peculiar difficulty, had established his reputation as a lawyer, and he had ably sustained the reputation thus secured.

As Secretary of the Navy, Hilary A. Herbert, of Alabama, was finally selected, while Julius Sterling Morton, of Nebraska, accepted the post of Secretary of Agriculture. Thus the Cabinet was complete, and of the men chosen only Lamont had been associated with his first administration.

In describing his Cabinet to Richard Watson Gilder, the President-elect said of John G. Carlisle: "We are just right for each other. He knows all I ought to know, and I can bear all we have to bear." And already his daily mail showed many premonitory symptoms of what he would have to bear.

Office seekers of every conceivable type once more employed every means to impress upon him the duty of a President with power to bestow. Some of these appeals were pathetic, some patriotic; but the vast majority were grotesque, almost illiterate pleas for pay for alleged party service.

One bore the distressingly familiar ring, which had called forth so many pension vetoes during his first term: "I congratulate you with greetings of love. Forget not the noble soldier. Procrastinate not. Strike at once. Give pensions to all that fought."

Another of equally well-known purport ran: "Please send me immediately $1,000, to which you are indebted to me, to say nothin about the pain and sufferin endured, caused by a pure accident when celebratin your election."

A third mingled his good wishes with a request for $45, giving as his reason: "I had ben votin the Democrat ticket ever sense the War, and I have never received anything for my trouble. goin to the election whitch some of the Republicans has been payed for votin there own ticket."

"A young lady aged 17 years old," opened her epistle with the words: "Thou ruler of the United, as such you are and have a rite to be, bein Democratic." And a New Englander, less effusive but doubtless equally sincere, modestly apologized for the form of his congratulations in the words: "I am not very mutch on the writin and spelin but then you will excuse I bein Born in Maine."

Thus again Mr. Cleveland knew what the psychologists call "the reality feeling." The burden which he had shifted to another Atlas in 1889 was his again, and while grateful for the confidence of the people, he was far from elated. "Every feeling of jubilation," he wrote, "and even my sense of gratitude is so tempered as to be almost entirely obscured by the realization, nearly painful, of the responsibility I have assumed in the sight of the American people."

Although executive authority was not yet his, his sense of responsibility drove him ruthlessly. At his office in the Mills Building, New York, he received the brunt of the office seekers' attacks. At his retreat in Lakewood, he welcomed his friends and those political leaders whose advice and assistance he requested. But whether in New York or in Lakewood, he avoided no obligation, and worked at the people's problems as though he were already once more the people's sworn servant.

"I have just been to see Mr. Cleveland at Lakewood," wrote Thomas F. Bayard to Judge Lambert Tree, "and his self-abnegation and simple devotion to the great work which confronts him touch and impress me greatly. No small purpose has any right to be brought into view where he is concerned, and self-seeking should stand rebuked in his presence."

The month before inauguration Mr. Cleveland devoted largely to work upon his address, abandoning his office hour at the Mills Building. Toward the end of that period Dr. Wilton Merle Smith, pastor of a New York church which Mr. Cleveland frequently attended, paid a visit to Lakewood.

"Come into my den," said Mr. Cleveland, "I want to read you my inaugural speech." When he had finished the final paragraph: "Above all I know there is a Supreme Being who rules the affairs of men, and whose goodness and mercy have always followed the American people, and I know He will not turn from us now if we humbly and reverently seek His powerful aid," his visitor remarked, "I like it immensely and its conclusion best of all." "I will never forget," said Dr. Smith later, "the way this strong man then paced up and down the floor, and returned and returned, with these words, 'I suppose at times you will not approve many things I do, but I want you to know that I am trying to do what is right. I have a hungry party behind me, and they say I am not grateful. Sometimes the pressure is almost overwhelming, and a President cannot always get at the exact truth, but I want you to know, and all my friends to know, that I am trying to do what is right—I am trying to do what is right.' "

Shortly before the date fixed for Mr. Cleveland's departure for Washington, a number of his intimate friends presented him with a watch. In his letter of thanks to Mr. Gilder, he wrote: "I expected to see you this evening and did not suspect any such conspiracy as was developed when the beautiful gift sent to me by yourself and your 'pals' reached my hands. I don't know what to say to 'you fellows'—and no wonder, for I never had so fine a present before.

"I can only say that I am perfectly delighted, and that this reminder of real friendliness comes to me at a time when my surroundings do not indicate that all friendship is sincere and disinterested. I thank you from the bottom of my heart."

Cleveland took his second oath as President with the ground white with snow. Before him spread an audience in which appeared at points the glint of Indian costumes, denoting not real red men but Tammany tigers. Led by Richard Croker and other of Mr. Cleveland's ancient opponents, Tammany, for the moment, celebrated Cleveland's return.

As he faced the sea of upturned faces awaiting his inaugural address, he boldly resumed the topic which four years earlier had caused his defeat. "The verdict of our voters which condemns the injustice of maintaining protection for protection's sake," he declared, "enjoins upon the people's servants the duty of exposing and destroying the brood of kindred evils which are the unwholesome progeny of paternalism." The fact that in his message of 1887 he had doomed himself and his party to defeat by a frank avowal of the same view, induced no caution. To his mind, personal or party defeats were merely incidents in the operation of great forces. It was his intention to bring about a sweeping reform of the tariff, and his method was to let the country know it at the earliest possible moment.

To those Democrats who despite his previous utterances still hoped that Grover Cleveland would promise to "do something for silver," he presented an uncompromising front. And he as frankly disappointed those who had ventured to suggest that he would "soft-pedal" when touching questions of wastefulness, civil service, and pension reform.

His speech was a reiteration of his past speeches. Four years' relief from executive cares had altered none of his fundamental conceptions. Simply, frankly, and uncompromisingly, he declared not new views but old: "Nothing is more vital to our supremacy as a nation . . . than a sound and stable currency"; "the injustice of maintaining protection for protection's sake"; "a challenge of wild and reckless pension expenditures"; "the waste of public money is a crime"; "to secure the fitness and competency of appointees to office and remove from political action the demoralizing madness of spoils"; "legitimate strife in business should not be superseded by an enforced concession to the demands of combinations that have the power to destroy."

The address made a profound impression in Europe. The President of the Paris Council caused extracts from it to be printed for use in the public schools of France, and the Papal Nuncio declared that it was: "One of the grandest spectacles of modern times to see the head of a great nation inculcate such lessons of morality and practical religion."

No sooner was the ceremony of inauguration over than Mr. Cleveland encountered, with regard to almost every article of his creed, bitter and determined opposition, not only from the Republicans, but from his own party as well. In the lower House, which had been elected under the same popular inspiration which had restored him, the adverse current remained within bounds, thanks to the high-minded leadership of Mr. Wilson, of West Virginia, and many of his efforts to carry out the promises made to the people found a fair degree of party support.  But the Democratic contingent of the Senate was controlled by men who hated Cleveland and spared no pains to block his measures.  To such opposition the Republicans gave assistance, for to them Grover Cleveland was only the first successful leader of Democracy since the small years of the century, and their business was to add party opposition to personal opposition, that the days of his power might prove as few as possible.

Thus the new President soon saw that his expected majority in the Senate was not to be realized.  He was, in short, in the unenviable position of a leader determined to lead, at the head of a band of followers who refused to follow, and this at a time when the situation was most perplexing and difficult.

His party was pledged to tariff reform, but there seemed little chance of securing it in the face of such a combination.  Civil service, too, was part of its promise to the people, but the Democratic leaders, with reform ardor cooled by victory, found satisfying absolution in the fact that the Republicans had packed the federal offices with their henchmen as rapidly as vacancies had occurred, thus restoring the inequality which had prevailed for a quarter of a century before Mr. Cleveland's coming.

To upset this iniquitous situation, so at variance with the will of the people as expressed in the recent elections, they boldly declared a necessary preliminary to real reform.  They pointed out the fact that of the 200,000 employees in the civil service of the United States only 43,000 were classified according to the rules of civil service reform, and that of this 43,000 a large percentage were but examples of how a defeated party can, in the last few hours of its power, use civil service reform laws to furnish permanent berths for its members. Particularly did they denounce Amended Postal Rule No. 1, signed by President Harrison two months before his retirement, which brought some 7,500 federal employees of the free delivery post-offices within the protection of the civil service laws.

"This is perhaps the most important extension that has ever taken place under the civil service law," runs the Commissioners' annual report, signed by Theodore Roosevelt and Charles Lyman. ". . . It is needless to point out the very great benefit conferred upon the public at large and upon the cause of decent politics by this extension of the classified service."

Doubtless Mr. Roosevelt and Mr. Lyman were sincere in this opinion, but the minority report signed by the third Commissioner, George D. Johnston, gave a different interpretation, and one more favorable to the case of Democratic politicians desirous of removals. Writing to President Cleveland, on November 21, 1893, Johnston declared the action the very opposite of reform: "The extension of the classified service does not of necessity mean civil service reform. . . . When such an extension is ordered by an administration and goes into effect shortly before the government is turned over to another administration of different political faith and party affiliation, known to be friendly to the cause of civil service reform, it is difficult to reconcile it to fair-minded men of all parties as a non-partisan measure."

While inclined to accept the minority interpretation, Mr. Cleveland showed his confidence in Theodore Roosevelt by the announcement that he would be retained as Civil Service Commissioner, and this decision was hailed with enthusiasm by the reformers of both parties. Carl

Schurz declared it "A great event, and in itself a large program for the next four years."

Mr. Roosevelt fully agreed with the President's view that "public office is a public trust," but, being far more ardent in his desire to hold public office, was far more active in seeking it. "He who has not wealth owes his first duty to his family," he once declared, "but he who has means owes his to the State."

Mr. Cleveland, on the other hand, believed that a citizen should not court public place. The *Inter-Ocean,* of May 3, 1903, recalls a conversation between him and Mr. Roosevelt shortly after the latter's reappointment as Civil Service Commissioner. To the question, "Do you intend to remain active in politics?" Mr. Roosevelt returned an instant affirmative. "I am sorry to hear it," Mr. Cleveland replied. "It is enough to be a good citizen."

But though anxious to retain Roosevelt's services, Mr. Cleveland had no intention of allowing any one element, even the civil service reformers, to run the government. He believed that the Democrats, as the victorious party commissioned by the people, were entitled to control, and he did not scruple to appoint competent Democrats, chiefly because they were Democrats. Nor did he hesitate to appoint competent Republicans, whatever the opposition, when the situation demanded it. Incompetent candidates, whether Democrats or Republicans, he stoutly refused to appoint, however great the political pressure back of their applications. He was, moreover, always ready to correct injustice when convinced that injustice had been done, as is shown by the following correspondence between Mark Twain and the President's daughter Ruth, aged one.

"My dear Ruth,

"I belong to the mugwumps, and one of the most sacred rules of our order prevents us from asking favors of officials or recommending men to office, but there is no harm in writing a friendly letter to you and telling you that an infernal outrage is about to be committed by your father in turning out of office the best consul I know [Captain Mason, Consul General at Frankfort] (and I know a great many) just because he is a Republican and a Democrat wants his place."

Mr. Clemens then related what he knew of Captain Mason and his official record, and continued:

"I can't send any message to the President, but the next time you have a talk with him concerning such matters, I wish you would tell him about Captain Mason and what I think of a government that so treats its efficient officials."

Three or four weeks later Mr. Clemens received a tiny envelope postmarked Washington, in which was a note, written in President Cleveland's own hand. It read:

"Miss Ruth Cleveland begs to acknowledge the receipt of Mr. Twain's letter, and to say that she took the liberty of reading it to the President, who desires her to thank Mr. Twain for his information and to say to him that Captain Mason will not be disturbed in the Frankfort Consulate. The President also desires Miss Cleveland to say that if Mr. Twain knows of any other cases of this kind he would be greatly obliged if he will write him concerning them at his earliest convenience."

But despite his readiness to accept advice from disinterested sources, Mr. Cleveland took every step possible to strip from Congressmen and Senators the harness by which they were accustomed to draw the chariot of the spoils system. To this end, and to the indignation of Senators with expectant officials in tow, he issued the following executive order:

Executive Mansion,
*May 8, 1893.*

It has become apparent after two months' experience that the rules heretofore promulgated regulating interviews with the President have wholly failed in operation. The time which under those rules was set apart for the reception of senators and representatives has been spent almost entirely in listening to applications for office, which have been bewildering in volume, perplexing and exhausting in their iteration, and impossible of remembrance.

A due regard for public duty, which must be neglected if present conditions continue, and an observance of the limitations placed upon human endurance oblige me to decline from and after this date all personal interviews with those seeking appointments to office, except as I, on my own motion, may especially invite them. . . .

I earnestly request senators and representatives to aid me in securing for them uninterrupted interviews by declining to introduce their constituents and friends when visiting the executive mansion during the hours designated for their reception. Applicants for office will only prejudice their prospects by repeated importunities and by remaining at Washington to await results.

This did not, of course, solve the problem, but it did something to relieve the strain, leaving him a little freer to follow his conscience in matters which the Constitution had made his responsibility.

During the remainder of his term he worked slowly toward the ideal of the reformers, and by the end the 42,950 classified officers mentioned in the Commissioners' tenth annual report had grown into 84,000, while only 100 civil servants at the National Capitol were outside the graded service.

But the outstanding conflict of Mr. Cleveland's first year of restored power was not civil service but currency reform, the state of the nation's circulating medium when President Harrison surrendered the reins of government making prompt action imperative. The situation which culminated in the panic of 1893 had begun, long before Mr. Cleveland's restoration, with a widespread business prostration, the responsibility for which he laid at the door of those who had yielded to the oft-repeated plea: "Do something for silver." During his first term he had made clear his attitude toward what he called "the free silver heresy," and through his Secretary of the Treasury, Daniel Manning, had devoted himself whole-heartedly to conserving the gold balance in the Treasury. He had suspended for a time the bond purchases, discontinued the issue of $1 and $2 greenbacks, in order to increase the demand for silver certificates, and had sold to New York City bankers $5,915,000 worth of subsidiary silver coin, receiving gold in payment. These measures he had taken by executive action alone, existing conditions not being serious enough to justify an extra session of Congress.

In his first message, he had denounced the existing silver purchase law, the Bland-Allison Act in these words:

"Since February, 1878, the government has under the compulsory provisions of law purchased silver bullion and coined the same at the rate of more than $2,000,000 every month. By this process up to the present date, 215,759,431 silver dollars have been coined. . . . Only about 50,000,000 of the silver dollars so coined have actually found their way into circulation, leaving more than 165,000,000 in the possession of the government, the custody of which has entailed a considerable expense for the construction of vaults for its deposit. Against this latter amount there are outstanding silver certificates amounting to about $93,000,000.

"Every month two millions of gold . . . are paid out for two millions of silver dollars, to be added to the idle mass already accumulated.

"If continued long enough, this operation will result in the substitution of silver for all the gold the government owns applicable to its general purposes.

"It will not do to rely upon the customs receipts of the government to make good this drain of gold, because the silver thus coined having been made legal tender for all debts and dues, public and private, at times during the last six months, 58% of the receipts for duties has been in silver or silver certificates, while the average within that period has been 20%.

"This proportion . . . will probably increase as time goes on, for the reason that the nearer the period approaches when it will be obliged to offer silver in payment of its obligations, the greater inducement there will be to hoard gold against depreciation in the value of silver or for the purpose of speculating.

"This hoarding of gold has already begun.

"When the time comes that gold has been withdrawn from circulation, then will be apparent the difference between the real value of the silver dollar and a dollar in gold, and the two coins will part company. Gold, still the standard of value and necessary in our dealings with other countries, will be at a premium over silver; banks which have substituted gold for the deposits of their customers may pay them with silver . . . thus making a handsome profit; rich speculators will sell their hoarded gold to their neighbors who need it to liquidate their foreign debts, at a ruinous premium over silver, and the laboring men and women of the land, most defenceless of all, will find that the dollar received for the wages of their toil has sadly shrunk in its purchasing power.

"If this silver coinage be continued, we may reasonably expect that gold and its equivalent will abandon the field of circulation to silver alone. This, of course, must produce a severe contraction of our circulating medium, instead of adding to it.

"It will not be disputed that any attempt . . . to cause the circulation of silver dollars worth 80 cents side by side with gold dollars worth 100 cents . . . to be successful must be seconded by the confidence of the people that both coins will retain the same purchasing power and be interchangeable at will."

He was willing to concede that, with the concurrent action of the other great nations, the problem of maintaining a set ratio between gold and silver would present a different aspect; but all efforts in that direction had failed, "and still we continue our coinage of silver at a ratio different from that of any other nation. . . . Without an ally or friend we battle upon the silver field in an illogical and losing contest."

He reminded Congress that the five countries composing the Latin Union had not only refused, as had the leading countries of Europe, to join in a movement to maintain a fixed ratio between gold and silver, but had "just completed an agreement among themselves that no more silver shall be coined by their respective governments and that such as has been already coined . . . shall be redeemed in gold by the country of its coinage."

Such conditions, he concluded, make it the duty of the President to "recommend the suspension of the compulsory coinage of silver dollars, directed by the law passed in February, 1878." This recommendation had, however, not been heeded, and the mints had continued to turn out silver dollars, a large percentage of whose declared value was merely psychological. By December, 1886, there were in circulation 247,131,549 of these dollars, worth barely seventy-eight cents each.

By 1890 Mr. Cleveland's dire prophecies had begun to be realized. Prosperity was giving place to hard times. Cautious men were unloading securities, and values had begun to shrivel in the hands of holders. During the first six months of 1890 the mortgages of over a score of railroad companies were foreclosed, and the Barings' collapse in England later in the year caused widespread consternation.

Then there had appeared again, with their customary attendant disasters, two ancient heresies: the first, that when business languishes the enactment of a high tariff law will restore prosperity and bring financial stability. But the McKinley tariff, with its unprecedented protective features, failed to accomplish this result.

The other delusion is to the effect that a sure remedy for failing confidence and hard times may be found in a sudden increase in the volume of money, irrespective of the foundations upon which that volume rests. This remedy was also applied in 1890 by the enactment of the so-called Sherman Act, which made it imperative for the Treasury Department to purchase 4½ million ounces of silver each month. But the business decline was not stopped by the operation of the Sherman Act. On the contrary, those monthly purchases of silver only added to existing uncertainties the portentous question whether, if the issues of the government against silver purchases were continued, it would be possible to maintain the parity between gold and silver which the law required.

When retiring from office, at the end of his first term, Mr. Cleveland had turned over to Harrison a cash balance of $281,000,000 of which $196,689,614 was in gold. From Harrison he received back in 1893 only $112,-450,577 of which only $103,500,000 was in gold; and this gold reserve would certainly have been below the $100,-000,000 mark, the point fixed by the act of July 12, 1882, as the danger point, had not Secretary Foster during January and February, 1893, obtained several millions in gold from greenbacks sold to New York bankers, with the definite purpose of keeping the gold reserve secure, at least until the end of his period of direct responsibility. By such a makeshift, Foster had managed to keep the gold reserve above the $100,000,000 limit, but, as Mr. Cleveland clearly understood, now must come the deluge, unless he could find some way to check the financial forces which had so disturbed the last days of the Harrison administration.

Even before the repeal of the Sherman Law, far-sighted financiers had foreseen the necessity of issuing bonds in purchase of gold, if the gold standard was to endure, for they felt certain that it was hopeless to look to Congress for legislation sufficient to stem the tide which was setting so hard toward the disaster of a silver basis.

On February 28, 1893, August Belmont had written to the President-elect: "I have cabled to London very fully and hope for a reply which will enable me to bring before you the basis of an actual plan. The more I think the subject over, the more fully satisfied I am that not only will it be best to sell $50 million of bds., but it is essential that they should be sold abroad if they are to serve the purpose at all. . . . I am going to work to sound the Bank Presidents. I have two supporters already. Of course I have betrayed nothing.

"The difficulty is there is not 'anything in it' so to speak for the Banks in my plan."

Inauguration day found the President still searching a solution other than the issuance of bonds in time of peace.

"In our effort to meet the emergency without an issue of bonds," he wrote in after years, "Secretary Carlisle immediately applied to banks in different localities for an exchange with the government of a portion of their holdings of gold coin for other forms of currency. The effect was so far successful that on the twenty-fifth of March the gold reserve amounted to over $107,000,000, notwithstanding the fact that considerable withdrawals had been made in the interval.

"The slight betterment thus secured proved, however, to be only temporary; for under the stress of continued and augmented withdrawals, the gold reserve, on the twenty-second day of April, 1893, for the first time since its establishment, was reduced below the $100,000,000 limit—amounting on that day to about $97,000,000."

While this fact, which a generation of financiers had learned to couple with thoughts of inevitable financial collapse, was not followed by any sudden and distinctly new disaster, it had the effect of increasing the hoarding of gold and its exportation. Furthermore, gold almost ceased to come into the Federal Treasury through customs and other revenue charges.

During the anxious weeks in which the President had been seeking a remedy which would check these inroads upon the gold reserve, and avert disaster, he had let it be known that suggestions from men skilled in currency questions would be welcome, and advice now came in a deluge from men urging action, from men urging caution, from silver men, gold men, bimetallists, special pleaders for every conceivable type of currency reform. Henry Clews, an eminent figure in the world of finance, called the President's attention to the fact that "eighty-three cents per ounce or thereabouts in New York and thirty-eight pence in London is now recognized as the world's value for silver, being equal to in the neighborhood of twenty-five silver to one gold," and suggested that if the government would recoin its silver, allowing such a ratio, "silver certificates or silver coin dollars will be of equal value to gold certificates or gold coin dollars."

Mr. Clews also contributed a summary of facts regarding the existing currency: "There are now outstanding $346,000,000 of U. S. legal tender notes (called greenbacks), $328,226,504 legal tender treasury notes issued under the Bland Act, and $135,490,148 of notes issued under the Sherman 1890 Act, making in all $809,-716,652. All these notes are direct obligations of the government, all possess the legal tender quality alike; the three different acts authorizing their issue specify that they are payable at the U. S. Treasury in coin.

"Since the resumption of gold payments these notes have all been treated alike and have been redeemed in gold coin, not silver. Now it is feared that Secretary Car-

lisle intends to change their present status into two classes
—the $346,000,000 greenbacks to remain as gold notes,
and the $328,226,504 Bland notes, together with the
$135,490,148 issued under the Sherman Act, to be recog-
nized as silver obligations."

As the Sherman Act allowed the Secretary of the
Treasury to redeem the notes issued in payment of this
silver bullion "in gold or silver coin at his discretion,"
it would have been easy to establish the policy of paying them in silver, even to holders desiring gold, but
for the fact that the law declared it the established policy
of the United States to maintain the two metals at a
parity.

This clause, to quote Mr. Cleveland, "had the effect
of transferring the discretion of determining whether
these Treasury notes should be redeemed in gold or silver
from the Secretary of the Treasury to the holder of the
notes. Manifestly, in the face of this assertion of the
government's intention, a demand for gold redemption
on the part of the holders of such notes could not be
refused, and the acceptance of silver dollars insisted
upon, without either subjecting to doubt the good faith
and honest intention of the government's professions, or
creating a suspicion of our country's solvency. The
parity . . . would be distinctly denied, if the Secretary
of the Treasury persisted in redeeming these notes,
against the will of the holders, in dollars of silver instead
of gold."

At this point, the rumor was circulated that Secretary
Carlisle was nevertheless planning so to redeem them.
At once financial circles poured in upon the President a
flood of protest.

"The report . . . has created very grave alarm here,"
wrote L. Clarke Davis from Philadelphia. "I have just

received a letter from a leading banker, your friend Mr. Drexel, who . . . says: 'If the arrangement is made that the silver notes will only be paid in silver the result will be that all public dues will be gradually paid in those notes, in which case where will the gold accrue from to pay the gold interest on the public debt, as the receipts of the Sub-Treasury will all be in silver?  The feeling here is (in which I cordially join) that it will be far better to encroach upon the hundred million reserve if the department is not willing to sell bonds abroad.' "

A few hours before this letter was received, Secretary Carlisle issued a statement, designed but not calculated to relieve the public mind of doubt in this important regard.  It was so ambiguous as to increase rather than to quiet public apprehension, and made it necessary for the President himself to declare publicly that gold payments would continue so long as he remained President.  A letter from Andrew Carnegie, written two days after Carlisle's announcement, strongly urged this course:

"Let me assure you that in my opinion the decision to pay notes in gold saved this country from panic and entire confusion in its industrial interests.  From my own experience I can tell you that foreigners had taken alarm and had begun to withdraw their capital in gold.  Unless all doubt is put to rest, there is still great danger of the country being drained of its gold."

He urged the President to make a public declaration. "If I might suggest," he said, "the announcement should be somewhat like the following: 'As long as I am President of the United States, the workingman is going to be paid in as good dollars as the foreign banker is.' " Such a statement would be "good politics," he said, and added: "I have spoken to many Republicans, and without exception they agree that in standing for sound money, and the parity of gold and silver, you will receive almost the unanimous support of the Republican party."

On April 2d the President's public declaration was issued, in the spirit though not in the words which Mr. Carnegie had suggested:

"The inclination on the part of the public to accept newspaper reports concerning the intentions of those charged with the management of our national finances, seems to justify my emphatic contradiction of the statement that the redemption of any kind of Treasury notes, except in gold, has at any time been determined upon or contemplated by the Secretary of the Treasury or any other member of the present Administration.

"The President and his Cabinet are absolutely harmonious in the determination to exercise every power conferred upon them to maintain the public credit, to keep the public faith and to preserve the parity between gold and silver and between all financial obligations of the Government. . . ."

Such a declaration of executive intention, however, the President knew to be vain unless Congress could be induced to alter the laws responsible for the nation's financial plight, and the repeal of the Sherman Law thus became the first item on his program. This meant, of course, a special session of Congress, for which the sound money men of both parties and the general public were clamoring.

On May 12th, Carl Schurz wrote: "Before leaving Washington I had a conversation with Secretary Carlisle about the financial situation, in the course of which he expressed himself as more and more inclined to think that the earliest possible calling together of Congress—

earlier than September—would be advisable. I am very much of the same opinion. The financial situation of the country is becoming more critical every day. The failures and restrictions of credit which have already occurred are only a premonitory symptom. Whatever measures the Executive alone can take, will only be palliatives, temporary makeshifts. I fear you take too great a responsibility upon yourself for what may happen if the meeting of Congress is put off unnecessarily long."

August Belmont warned him of confidential news from England to the effect that the Indian mints were about to be closed to silver. "The race between India and the United States to get upon dry ground first," he said, "is all in favor of India, unless we act with the greatest promptitude."

Harvey Fisk and Sons issued a circular letter declaring "the actual intrinsic value of our present silver dollar is but fifty-three cents and growing less each day. Still this great American nation is obliged to calmly face inevitable ruin—the sweeping away of far more wealth than was involved in the great war between the North and the South, simply because its representatives are not called together, in accordance with the authority vested in its Chief Executive, and forced to remove from the Statute Books the law which is eating away the vitals of American honesty."

Hundreds of resolutions to the same effect were passed by chambers of commerce, business men's clubs, bankers' associations, churches, congresses of voters, mass meetings, etc., and sent by telegram, by special messenger, by solemn delegation. They warned, they coaxed, they threatened; but they did not cause the President to act hastily.

On June 4th, however, Mr. Cleveland intimated to a representative of the United Press that Congress would be speedily summoned and asked to stop the silver purchases. Again his letter pouch jumped to twice its normal size. Again prophecies of calamity came from free silver men, again gold men praised him for his sane financial views and clamored for the program of reform.

At this point, the President suddenly faced the appalling discovery that a virulent growth in the roof of his mouth menaced him with death unless an operation were immediately performed. Dr. W. W. Keen gives this account of the case: "On Sunday, June 18, 1893, Dr. R. M. O'Reilly—later Surgeon-General of the United States Army—the official medical attendant on officers of the government in Washington, examined a rough place on the roof of Mr. Cleveland's mouth. He found an ulcer as large as a quarter of a dollar, extending from the molar teeth to within one third of an inch of the middle line, and encroaching slightly on the soft palate, and some diseased bone."

A small fragment was subjected to the scrutiny of a pathologist and pronounced strongly indicative of malignancy. The President's personal physician and intimate friend, Dr. Joseph D. Bryant, was therefore summoned to Washington and, after a careful examination of the malignant area, urged an immediate operation. The President accepted the verdict, but insisted that absolute secrecy be observed, as he feared the effect which an announcement of his peril might have upon the already alarming financial situation.

With this in view, it was decided that the operation should be performed on Commodore Benedict's yacht, the *Oneida,* in which Mr. Cleveland had already traveled over fifty thousand miles, and which he could therefore board without arousing suspicion. As Dr. Bryant was of the opinion that he ought to be in condition to return to Washington within about five weeks after the operation, Mr. Cleveland prepared a proclamation summoning Congress to meet in special session on August 7th, to consider the repeal of the Sherman Law; and on the day of its publication, June 30, 1893, with every precaution for secrecy, he joined his surgeons on the *Oneida* in New York Harbor.

"I reached New York City in the evening," writes Dr. Keen, "went to Pier A, and was taken over to the yacht, which was lying at anchor at a considerable distance from the Battery. Dr. E. G. Janeway, of New York; Dr. O'Reilly; Dr. John F. Erdmann, Dr. Bryant's assistant; and Dr. Hasbrouck had also secretly gone to the yacht. The President, Dr. Bryant and Secretary Lamont, at a later hour, arrived from Washington, and openly drove to Pier A, whence they were taken to the yacht. . . . On arriving on the yacht, the President lighted a cigar, and we sat on deck smoking and chatting until near midnight. Once he burst out with, 'Oh, Doctor Keen, those office seekers! Those office seekers! They haunt me in my dreams!'"

For the time at least he was secure from their intrusion. Early the next morning, the *Oneida* weighed anchor and proceeded at half speed up the East River, the President, under nitrous oxide, stretched upon the operating table, the doctors performing the extremely delicate operation of removing "the entire left upper jaw . . . from the first bicuspid tooth to just beyond the last molar, and nearly up to the middle line. . . . A small portion of the soft palate was removed" also.

The operation was performed without external incision, and was completed at 1.55 P.M. "At 2.55 P.M. a hypodermic of one sixth of a grain of morphine was given—the only narcotic administered at any time."

Five days later the *Oneida* dropped anchor at Gray Gables, and the patient walked from the launch to his residence with little apparent effort.

A second slight operation twelve days later, and the surgical work was over. Dr. Kasson C. Gibson, of New York, then fitted Mr. Cleveland with an artificial jaw of vulcanized rubber and "when it was in place the President's speech was excellent, even its quality not being altered." "He was," concludes Dr. Keen's interesting monograph, "the most docile and courageous patient I ever had the pleasure of attending."

Upon this point there appears a difference of opinion. In an intimate letter to Colonel Lamont, Dr. Bryant laments the President's tendency to disobey orders regarding the medicines prescribed: "I . . . found him grunting as you know full well, suffering from an excess of medicine rather than the lack of it. He always believes that if a little will do some good, a bottle full must be of great advantage indeed. On that theory he had secured the full effects of the prescription I sent him, as well as some after effects."

To this we may add his wife's view of his docility as later expressed in a letter to Mrs. Joseph Jefferson: "He is hard at work on his letters. It is so dreadfully hard to do anything with him. This morning when no one noticed he got a peach and ate it. Wouldn't you think a *child* would have more sense after the narrow escape he had?"

In memory of his insubordination, Commodore Benedict sent him the following lines, which he greatly enjoyed:

"Friday sorry, yet defiant,
Next day, send for Doctor Bryant."

Mr. Cleveland, however, defended his defiance with
the words: "I am not so dreadfully heedless of the care
I owe myself (for others' sake) as is suspected of me;
and touching the Doctor's accusation of indiscretion, is
it not in the very nature of faithful, devoted, and anxious
medical ministrations to find patients indiscreet?"

At times also he expressed misgivings regarding the
science of healing. To Richard Watson Gilder he gave
the following enigmatical advice: "I hope that either
by following your Doctor's directions or defiantly dis-
obeying them (the chances probably being even in both
contingencies), you will soon regain your very best estate
in the matter of health. Don't forget at any time—whatever you do—that 'good men are scarce.' "

But though the President's docility is thus called into
question, none can doubt the justice of Dr. Keen's second
attribute—that of courage. Terribly weakened by loss
of blood, and believing himself still under the shadow
of death, Mr. Cleveland strove to prepare a message
for the pending special session of Congress. For some
time after the operation he received no visitors, until,
in view of the menacing condition of national finances,
he admitted Secretary Olney, who in a brief memorandum gives the story of his part in the preparation of Mr.
Cleveland's silver message:

"After an interval of a fortnight, more or less, during
which I made frequent attempts to see Mr. Cleveland,
I succeeded in having an interview. He had changed
a good deal in appearance, and lost a good deal of flesh,
and his mouth was so stuffed with antiseptic wads that he
could hardly articulate. The first utterance that I understood was something like this: 'My God, Olney, they

nearly killed me.' He did not talk much, was very much depressed, and at the same time acted, and I believe felt, as if he did not expect to recover."

After a painful attempt to discuss with Mr. Olney the great issue to be laid before the coming session, Mr. Cleveland produced the manuscript of the message upon which he was spending his remaining strength.

"There were perhaps twenty or thirty lines," writes Mr. Olney, "forming the first two paragraphs of the message as eventually sent to Congress. He was very depressed about the progress he was making and complained that his mind would not work, and, upon my suggestion that I might perhaps be of assistance, was evidently much relieved. In the course of two or three days I went to Gray Gables with a draft of a message, which was approved by Mr. Cleveland practically as drawn. . . . So far as I know, Mr. Carlisle was the only member of the Cabinet who saw the message before it was sent in."

A comparison of Mr. Olney's draft with the message as finally sent to Congress shows that only fifty-three lines out of one hundred and seventy-eight were adapted from the Olney draft. The body of the argument is clearly the President's own work and proves beyond question that, despite his forlorn appearance, he was still determined to write his own state papers.

Mr. Cleveland reached Washington on August 5th, prepared to give his personal direction to the launching of the movement to repeal the Sherman Law. Among his papers is a poll of Congress, name by name, designed to inform him of their attitude. It shows 114 silver men, 173 anti-silver men, and 69 marked doubtful, and bears testimony to the fact that he understood the very difficult task which awaited him.

His special message was read to Congress on August 8, 1893, and demanded "the prompt repeal of the provisions of the act passed July 14, 1890, authorizing the purchase of silver bullion." It is a document difficult to condense or epitomize, for it is itself an epitome, the compact argument of a singularly concrete mind. It is the case against free silver compressed into two thousand words.

"Our unfortunate financial plight is not the result of untoward events, nor of conditions related to our natural resources, nor is it traceable to any of the afflictions which frequently check national growth and prosperity. With plenteous crops, with abundant promise of remunerative production and manufacture, with unusual invitation to safe investment, and with satisfactory assurance to business enterprise, suddenly financial distrust and fear have sprung up on every side. Numerous moneyed institutions have suspended because abundant assets were not immediately available to meet the demands of frightened depositors. . . . These things are principally chargeable to Congressional legislation touching the purchase and coinage of silver by the general Government.

"Undoubtedly the monthly purchases by the Government of 4,500,000 ounces of silver, enforced under that statute, were regarded by those interested in silver production as a certain guarantee of its increase in price. The result, however, has been entirely different, for immediately following a spasmodic and slight rise, the price of silver began to fall after the passage of the act, and has since reached the lowest point ever known. This disappointing result has led to renewed and persistent effort in the direction of free silver coinage.

"The policy necessarily adopted of paying these silver

notes in gold has not spared the gold reserve of $100,-000,000 long ago set aside by the Government for the redemption of other notes. . . . Between the first day of July, 1890, and the 15th day of July, 1893, the gold coin and bullion in our Treasury decreased more than 132 million dollars, while during the same period the silver coin and bullion . . . increased more than a hundred and forty-seven million. Unless Government bonds are to be constantly issued and sold to replenish our exhausted gold, only to be again exhausted, it is apparent that the operation of the silver purchase law now in force leads in the direction of the entire substitution of silver for gold in the Government Treasury, and that this must be followed by the payment of all Government obligations in depreciated silver. . . . Our Government cannot make its fiat equivalent to intrinsic value, nor keep inferior money on a parity with superior money. . . .

"The people of the United States are entitled to a sound and stable currency, and to money recognized as such on every exchange and in every market of the world. Their government has no right to injure them by financial experiments opposed to the policy and practice of other civilized states."

Confidently, almost imperiously, in the interest of the whole nation, the message demanded the repeal of the Act of July 14, 1890, "condemned by the ordeal of three years' disastrous experience."

The appearance of this Cleveland-Olney message marks the stage in the silver conflict which placed Mr. Cleveland and Mr. Bryan squarely before the country as leaders of opposing factions in the Democratic party. Bryan was at that time a member of the lower house, elected as a Democrat, and abundantly willing to defend

the position that free silver was a proper article in the
Democratic creed.  Until after the launching of the
Cleveland boom of 1892, he had been a consistent Cleve-
land man; but a change had recently taken place in his
attitude toward his party chief.  In a letter to Jesse D.
Carr, dated May 22, 1903, Mr. Bryan wrote:

"I was an enthusiastic supporter of Mr. Cleveland
in 1884 and in 1888.  But between '88 and '92 I began
to study the money question, and when I came to understand its principles, I became an opponent of Cleveland's
renomination, but it required his second administration
to fully enlighten me upon the designs and methods of
Wall Street.  I have no doubt from my observation of
his course that the financiers put up the money that secured his nomination in 1892, and I know they furnished
large sums of money to secure his election.  His Committee spent $900,000 in the state of New York and
among the contributors to his campaign fund was the
Sugar Trust which gave $175,000.

"When he made up his Cabinet he deliberately
ignored the silver men who represented the majority of
the voters, and put gold men into the Cabinet.  When he
called Congress together in extraordinary session, he used
all the patronage in his possession to corrupt members
and he used important positions in the foreign service
to reward men who had betrayed their constituents.  He
was completely dominated by the banking influence in
New York City."

That "the interests" contributed largely to Mr. Cleveland's campaign of 1892 is unquestionably true, but the
innuendo that Mr. Cleveland sold himself to Wall Street
in order to win his way back to the White House is not

justified by a single line of evidence, and is most unquestionably untrue.

Though his own acts were often unfairly criticized, Mr. Cleveland himself habitually refrained from ascribing unworthy motives to his political opponents. "Because . . . views are various and conflicting, some of them must be wrong," he once wrote, "and yet when they are honestly held and advocated, they should provoke no bitterness nor condemnation." He did not doubt Mr. Bryan's loyalty to the country, but he did not think that this excused Mr. Bryan's financial heresies. As he himself expressed it: "Patriotism is no substitute for a sound currency." He acknowledged that free silver men could be loyal Americans, but he emphatically denied that they could be real Democrats, for he read into the Democratic party the principle of devotion to a currency system which would force no American to accept as a dollar that which was not intrinsically worth a dollar.

On August 11th, Congressman Wilson, of West Virginia, presented a bill to repeal the Sherman Law. With unfortunate lack of skill, if the aim was to rally Democrats, it was drawn in close imitation of a bill which Senator Sherman had presented to the Senate on July 14, 1892, a fact which made it easier for free silver Democrats to deny that it embodied Democratic doctrines.

Taking advantage of this fact, the free silver leader, Richard P. Bland, of Missouri, offered a substitute looking toward the free and unlimited coinage of silver at a fixed ratio; and over these rival measures, both Democratic in origin, there began at once a fierce debate, during which it speedily became evident that all calculations based upon titular party labels in the House were likely to prove misleading. Democrats who had been counted upon at the beginning of the administration to support the President, openly scorned his leadership, and the Populists sympathized with their insurgency. Most of the Republicans, on the other hand, showed marked sympathy with him. Thus party lines, already wavering and uncertain when the debate opened, grew more uncertain as it continued. If the question of the repeal of the silver purchase clause transcended old party lines, why might not the larger question of free silver be made the basis of new party lines?

That such a thought had entered Mr. Bryan's mind at an earlier date appears likely, and when he rose to speak, on August 16th, the thought of the fate of silver obliterated all thought of the fate of the Democratic party. Twice he had been elected to Congress as a Democrat, and had there won the right to regard himself as the man best fitted to lead the hosts of free silver. Richard P. Bland was manifestly too old to head a new movement; Grover Cleveland, the titular Democratic leader, did not count, for he, according to Mr. Bryan's judgment, had betrayed the party, deserted the people, and joined with the Israelites of Wall Street in the sacrilegious worship of the Golden Calf.

For almost three hours Mr. Bryan occupied the floor, the one hour limit allotted to each speaker being, by common consent, extended in his case. The magic of his personality, the unrivaled beauty of his voice, and the compelling eloquence, which were later to charm millions, were fully in evidence. The inspiration which Mr. Cleveland's message lacked breathed in every sentence of Mr. Bryan's impassioned speech. But the evidence of patient study and searching thought, which appears in every line of the President's argument, is missing from the Congressman's appeal. The one instructed the mind, the other played upon the emotions; the one appealed to reason, the other to sentiment; the one dealt in specific facts, the other in vague generalizations.

"Does any one believe," asked Mr. Bryan, "that Mr. Cleveland could have been elected President upon a platform declaring in favor of the unconditional repeal of the Sherman Law? Can we go back to our people and tell them that, after denouncing for twenty years the crime of 1873, we have at last accepted it as a blessing?" The answer to the first of these questions must remain purely speculative, although Mr. Cleveland's entire record had been a prophecy of the action which he was now taking, and if the voters of America had re-elected him in ignorance of his views on the Sherman Law, theirs was the fault, not his. As to the second question, the vote of the House, on August 28, 1893, repealing the debated clause by a majority of 239 to 109, answered it fully, making it necessary for every Congressman to return to his constituency with the news that Congress had agreed with Grover Cleveland that the "crime of 1873" had been but an example of sound finance.

On account of his weakened condition Mr. Cleveland had remained only five days in Washington, returning to Gray Gables on August 11th, weary, but confident of victory. When Congressman Wilson's telegram arrived announcing the vote of the House, he wired in return: "Please accept for yourself and associates in to-day's achievement my hearty congratulations and sincere thanks."

To those who had closely followed the situation, however, it was evident that the victory was the President's victory. "The country," wrote Jacob H. Schiff, on August 29th, "is to be congratulated that you, Mr. President, while others doubted and despaired, did not falter, and succeeded in carrying the adoption of the only measure which will restore the confidence at home and abroad which the country so sorely needs."

To the extreme silverites, however, the President's victory was susceptible only of sinister interpretation, and it goaded them to excesses of denunciation. *The Rocky Mountain News* of August 29, 1893, declared the repeal "John Bull's Work," its headlines announcing that "British Gold and Federal Patronage" had been used "to bribe the American Congress." Beneath the headline appeared a cartoon representing "Grover and J. Bull," unsteadily dancing together, with hands clasped and thick voices roaring the gin-house melody, "We won't go home till morning."

As the repeal had still to pass the Senate they again spread, with an energy worthy of a better cause, the story that Grover Cleveland was the hired agent of unscrupulous manipulators bent upon enslaving the masses of the United States.

Up to this time the secret of the President's operation had been kept from the press. But at this point appeared an announcement, fairly accurate in detail, as to what had transpired upon the *Oneida,* and though every effort was made by the President's friends to convince the public that it had no foundation in fact, the report soon spread over the country and to foreign lands.

On September 2d, Ambassador Bayard wrote to his daughter:

"I have been all along since I came abroad uneasy, feeling that all was not right with Mr. Cleveland. I have written to him, but neither expected nor desired that he should increase his labors by writing to me—but yesterday an English newspaper contained a statement from a surgeon dentist Dr. Hasbrouck detailing the very serious surgical operation which had been performed upon his mouth. I confess I bent my head and wept when I thought of the pain he had suffered & the danger to the country.

"Few know so well as I do the devotion of this plain true man to his great duties—what energies—what toil, what anxieties have been his in the high performance of his duties—and at last his natural force has abated— and his weak link in the chain of vitality has been found.

"Oh how ineffably base, mean, cruel & poor have been the assaults upon him—such wretched suspicions & surmises, when all the while he was struggling with disease & fighting the good fight for the welfare & honor of his country. Dear soul! how my heart goes out to him & how much I feel my absence from his side.

"I have just written to him what I feel about him, but I am deeply concerned & distressed. This pending issue of the currency is fraught with the most profound & farreaching results. You may remember how for years I have dinned it into the ears of those around me & how little it seemed to be comprehended. Now the poisonous effects have been felt of a false assertion of values— & it is to be hoped that the costly experience of this summer will bring men to their sober senses.—Should this struggle cost Mr. Cleveland his life, & also eventuate in the vindication of his wisdom & devotion he will be glorified in men's memories, & generations yet unborn will rise up & call him blessed."

Upon receipt of the letter mentioned by Mr. Bayard, the President sent his Ambassador the following characteristic compound of politics and family affairs:

*Private*

Executive Mansion, Washington.

*Sept* 11, 1893.

My dear Mr Bayard:

I received to-day your letter of Sept 1st and thank you for it as well as for two or three preceding it and thus far unacknowledged. I especially want to thank you for the splendid picture of yourself you sent. I think it is the best and most faithful likeness I have ever seen.

I can well believe how interested you are in the subject just now occupying the time of the Senate. The action of the House was wonderfully gratifying and the majority we secured was beyond our expectations and to me was a demonstration that behind these direct representatives of the people there was a sentiment that actually *drove* them to duty.

The Senate is making a shameful display, but no one doubts that we have a good sound majority when the vote comes. With this conceded by all, the result hangs on, keeping back the day of better things. I shall not be much surprised however if the break occurs and a vote is reached sooner than the most of us expect. Isn't it queer that Voorhees and Gorman should be the leaders in a cause in which I am so vitally interested? "Strange bedfellows!" They are I believe both working well but every day is an anxious one for me, fearing that something may occur to distract time and attention, from the pending topic. . . .

Day before yesterday (the 9th) my wife presented me with what is always called I believe "a fine baby." It's a little girl and they do say it's a healthy one. The mother is as well as she can be and Ruth thus far seems to think the newcomer's advent is a great joke. You were only one of many who were trapped by a fool of a newspaper man into the premature expression of kind congratulation. I laid yours away and applied it to the event of last Saturday.

The report you saw regarding my health resulted from a most astounding breach of professional duty on the part of a medical man. I tell you this in strict confidence for the policy here has been to deny and discredit his story. I believe the American public and newspapers are not speculating further on the subject.

The truth is, office seeking and office seekers came very near putting a period to my public career. Whatever else developed found its opportunity in the weakened walls of a constitution that had long withstood fierce attacks. I turned the corner to the stage of enforced caretaking almost in a day. And this must be hereafter the condition on which will depend my health and life. Another phase of the situation cannot be spoken of with certainty but I believe the chances in my favor are at least even.

I have learned how weak the strongest man is under God's decrees and I see in a new light the necessity of doing my allotted work in the full apprehension of the coming night.

You must understand that I am regarded here as a perfectly well man and the story of an important surgical operation is thoroughly discredited.

I think I never looked better and I am much stronger than I have lately been. You have now more of the story than any one else outside of the medical circle.

Mrs. Cleveland sends love to you and Mrs. Bayard and with mine added in plenteous degree I am

Yours very sincerely

GROVER CLEVELAND.

HON. T. F. BAYARD.

Meanwhile, free silver Senators were exhausting every known parliamentary device to prevent action. The entire machinery of obstruction, which in the hands of a skillful and determined minority has proved fatal to so many worthy measures, was called into play. With equal skill, and backed by the consciousness of a stronger following, sound money Senators worked for a speedy trial of strength, and John Sherman worked with the President's friends.

In a spirit of compromise, Sherman had given his name to the Sherman Bill, in order to prevent the enactment of a more extreme free silver law, and he was as eager as was the President himself to see it repealed. In this, as in many previous currency conflicts, he merited the praise which Mr. Cleveland bestowed upon him: "No man in public life, certainly no Republican, has rendered a greater service to sound finance than John Sherman."

These weeks of steady conflict and ceaseless anxiety told heavily upon the impaired vitality of the President. His letters breathe the spirit almost of despair, but in them one looks in vain for the slightest sign of surrender. "I know there is a God," he wrote to Richard Watson Gilder, on October 12th, "but I do not know his purposes, nor when their results will appear. I know the clouds will roll away, but I do not know who, before that time, will be drowned in their floods." And to L. Clarke Davis, two days later, he said: "I am growing very tired physically and if I did not believe in God I should be sick at heart.

"I wonder if the good people of the Country will see before it is too late the danger that threatens, not only their financial well-being, but the very foundations upon which their institutions rest.

"I suppose it is wrong, but sometimes I feel very despondent and very much deserted. I believe in the people so fully, and things are often so forlorn here, that I want to feel and hear my fellow Countrymen all the time. Are they still about me? I think so often of Martin Luther's 'Here I stand—God help me.'"

Two weeks later, Ambassador Bayard wrote to Frederic Emory: "Assuming that the miserable makeshift of Sherman shall be wiped out, it seems to me there could be no better time than now to recall the words of James Russell Lowell, addressed to President Cleveland in his oration at the 250th anniversary of Harvard, in Cambridge:—The pilot of Seneca, 'Oh! Neptune, you may sink me, you may save me, but I will hold my rudder true.'

"Were I a painter, I should depict the scene of confusion, insubordination, and selfishness on deck, and the calm, steadfast pilot at the helm with his eye on the pole star, keeping the ship in her unswerving course."

Fortunately victory came before the President's depleted vitality had collapsed under the strain of keeping his rudder true. On October 30th, repeal in the form of a Senate substitute for the House bill passed the Senate by 43 to 32, 23 Republicans voting yea. Two days later, by 194 to 94, the House accepted the Senate bill, and Mr. Cleveland had won a truce over the increasing hosts of free silver.

In the *Atlantic Monthly* of March, 1897, Woodrow Wilson, then Professor of Jurisprudence in Princeton University, thus interpreted the meaning of this Cleveland victory:

"It was the President's victory that the law was at last repealed, and everyone knew it. He had forced the consideration of the question; he had told Senators plainly, almost passionately, when they approached him, that he would accept no compromise,—that he would veto anything less than absolute repeal, and let them face the country as best they might afterwards.

"Until he came on the stage, both parties had dallied and coquetted with the advocates of silver. Now he had brought both to a parting of the ways. The silver men were forced to separate themselves and look their situation in the face, choose which party they should plan to bring under their will and policy, if they could, and no longer camp in the tents of both.

"Such a stroke settled what the course of Congressional politics should be throughout the four years of Mr. Cleveland's term, and made it certain that at the end of that term he should either have won his party to himself or lost it altogether. It was evident that any party that rejected the gold standard for the currency must look upon him as its opponent."

From the point of view of the peace and effectiveness of the new administration, it was a costly victory. The necessities of the conflict had forced the President to cut across his own party and its Republican opponent, forming thereby a temporary coalition, dangerous alike to party discipline and party solidarity. He had, furthermore, admitted by his actions that the Republicans were nearer to soundness upon the great question of the hour than were the representatives of his own party. And by these actions he had won the bitter and lasting resentment of a vast body of Democrats who now denied, not only that Grover Cleveland was a Democrat, but even that he was an honest man, and who henceforth dedicated themselves to the task of reading him out of the party.

# CHAPTER II

## BLOCKING "MANIFEST DESTINY" IN HAWAII

*"I mistake the American people if they favor the odious doctrine that there is no such thing as international morality; that there is one law for a strong nation and another for a weak one."*

—GROVER CLEVELAND.

FEW of Mr. Cleveland's public actions have been more bitterly denounced, more needlessly misunderstood, or more deliberately misrepresented, than was his attitude toward the Hawaiian situation. Yet in refusing to connive at the annexation of Hawaii by methods sanctified by long usage, he but sounded, in the nineteenth century, the note which is the hope of the twentieth, the right of men everywhere "to choose their own ways of life and of obedience." As in the case of Germany and Samoa, he had uncompromisingly opposed a powerful nation in the interests of a helpless one, so in the case of the United States and Hawaii he took a ground no less just and impartial, although this time the aggressor was his own nation.

It would have been easy, had he been fitted with a less exacting conscience, for President Cleveland to allow the process of Hawaiian annexation to go smoothly on to its culmination. Instead, however, he invited conflict, which he hated, solely in the interest of international justice, solely that another weak and defenseless people might remain free. It was not annexation that he opposed, but conquest disguised as annexation.

From the beginning of our contact with the Hawaiian Islands, many Americans had felt that control by the United States, perhaps annexation, was inevitable. But until the days of President Harrison, the actions of American statesmen were in the main considerate of the sovereign rights of the Hawaiian people. In 1851 a menacing move on the part of France caused King Kamehameha III to deliver to Mr. Severance, American Commissioner in Honolulu, an executed deed of gift, granting the islands in full sovereignty to the United States, and requesting him to take possession as soon as it should become evident that the king could not resist the French encroachments.

Instead of taking advantage of this situation to establish an American control over the islands, as he might easily have done, our Secretary of State, Daniel Webster, to the credit of the nation, directed that the deed be returned to the Hawaiian government, and notified France that it was the intention of the United States to keep her "naval armament . . . in the Pacific Ocean in such a state of strength and preparation as shall be requisite for the preservation of the honor and dignity of the United States and the safety of the government of the Hawaiian Islands."

In 1854 President Pierce's Secretary of State, William L. Marcy, marred this record by negotiating a treaty providing for the annexation of the islands, but the death of the Hawaiian king upset the scheme, and Hawaii was still free.

Meanwhile, commercial connections between the two countries grew rapidly. American merchants and planters immigrated in considerable numbers, and, in 1875, the United States and Hawaii entered into a treaty of commercial reciprocity. In this treaty appeared no menace to Hawaiian independence, save the provision which bound her not to alienate any of her territory to nations other than the United States. In 1884 a supplementary convention was negotiated by which Pearl Harbor was set aside for the exclusive use of the United States and her commerce.

Owing to delay in ratification, this supplementary convention was still pending when Mr. Cleveland first became President; and, after carefully studying its provisions, he strongly advised the Senate to approve it.

"I express my unhesitating conviction," he declared in his second annual message, "that the intimacy of our relations with Hawaii should be emphasized. As a result of the reciprocity treaty of 1875, those islands, on the highway of Oriental and Australasian traffic, are virtually an outpost of American commerce and a stepping-stone to the growing trade of the Pacific. The Polynesian island groups have been so absorbed by other and more powerful governments that the Hawaiian Islands are left almost alone in the enjoyment of their autonomy, which it is important for us, should be preserved. Our treaty is now terminable on one year's notice, but propositions to abrogate it would be, in my judgment, most ill-advised. The paramount influence we have there acquired, once relinquished, could only with difficulty be regained, and a valuable ground of vantage for ourselves might be converted into a stronghold for our commercial competitors. I earnestly recommend that the existing treaty stipulations be extended to a further term of seven years."

The treaty was proclaimed on November 9, 1887, and in the meantime the Bayonet revolution in Hawaii had forced the Hawaiian king to consent to a liberal constitution, enfranchising his numerous Western guests and making of himself a limited monarch. The character of this constitution was clearly the work of American minds, and is evidence that the Republic of the West was rapidly coming into control in Hawaii in the persons of men bred to American law and American ideals of government.

And so, when President Cleveland retired from office in 1889, although the sovereignty of the Hawaiian Islands was unimpaired, and her form of government entitled her to be called a constitutional monarchy, the process of peaceful penetration was well advanced, and it was evident to all men trained in the arts of imperialistic expansion that the days of Hawaiian independence were numbered.

Had the annexationists exercised patience, and respected the sovereign rights of the Hawaiian people, they might have reached their goal without the opposition which Grover Cleveland later accorded them. He saw no crime in annexation, should it come to be the free choice of the inhabitants of the islands, and while he perhaps never definitely approved, there is no indication that he ever disapproved the views of his Secretary of State, Thomas F. Bayard, who later declared: "The obvious course was to wait quietly and patiently, and let the islands fill up with American planters and American industries, until they should be wholly identified in business interests and political sympathies with the United States. It was simply a matter of waiting until the apple should ripen and fall."

Unfortunately, the administration which superseded Mr. Cleveland had not Mr. Cleveland's patience, and it was not long before our Minister to Hawaii, John S. Stevens, began consciously working by political means in the direction of the annexation of the country to which he was accredited, while the American Secretary of State failed to rebuke, if he did not actually encourage, this ambition. "The near future," Minister Stevens wrote to Secretary Blaine, on March 20, 1890, "is to show conclusively that only the strong pressure and continual vigilance of the United States can enable American men and American ideas to hold ascendency here and make these islands as prosperous and valuable to American commerce and to American marine supremacy in the north Pacific as the isles of the Mediterranean have been and are to its adjacent nations." Eagerly Stevens awaited the psychological moment for a brilliant stroke which would land the islands in the lap of his own country—waited, worked, and planned.

In 1891, King Kalakua died while on a visit to the United States, and his sister, the Princess Liliuokalani, ascended the throne by virtue of the twenty-second article of the Hawaiian Constitution of 1887. The new queen, imbued, as had been her late brother, with autocratic theories and possessed of a despotic temperament, was out of harmony with the liberal tendencies clearly manifest in her kingdom and specifically embodied in the constitution under which she reigned, and which she had sworn to defend.

This constitution was too modern for Queen Liliuokalani, who hated the white intruders, hated the missionaries, hated all the paraphernalia of what the West had labeled progress, and dreamed of reaction to the dark old ways of primitive autocracy. What she and her reactionary advisers longed for, was to be freed from the shackles of the constitution theory. This done, it would be easy to drive out the white man, confiscate his property, if necessary take his life.

Within a month after her accession, the ill-advised queen attempted to force the resignation of her ministers, and to select a cabinet composed of her tools. The opium ring, the lottery ring, and other parasites that flourish best upon autocracy, were pressing upon her plans, which they knew would have scant shrift should the American element gain control, and she was readily countenancing their advances, conscious that she needed their support in her contemplated return to the ways of earlier times. On January 14, 1893, professing to act under pressure of popular demand, she declared her intention to overthrow the constitution which had enfranchised the hated foreigner, and to substitute another more in accordance with her temperament and aspirations. But Hawaii had progressed beyond the point at which a restoration of autocracy was possible. The monarchy was a shell, ready to crumble at a touch of opposition, and the Queen's action was at once interpreted by Stevens and the small but powerful minority of annexationists as abdication, an interpretation based on ideas purely Western.

As soon as Liliuokalani understood the interpretation put upon her autocratic threat by her dangerous guest-citizens and their fellow disciples of Western law, she issued a recantation. But it was already too late. A committee of safety had been organized, and plans had been made for arming those who resented her disloyalty to the Constitution. It was revolution, and the days of Hawaiian royalty were over.

It is an interesting fact that Minister Stevens was not in Honolulu when the revolution broke. On January 4, 1893, he had sailed on the *Boston* for a cruise to Hilo, a hundred miles away. It is still more interesting to discover that he returned just as the revolution needed the support of American marines, and that, ten months before, he had written to Secretary Blaine: "I have little doubt the revolutionary attempt would have been made ere this but for the presence here of the United States ship-of-war. I still incline to the opinion that the revolutionary attempt will not be made so long as there is a United States force in the harbor of Honolulu."

As soon as the *Boston,* with the American Minister on board, re-entered the harbor, Mr. Stevens was asked by the leaders of the revolution to land the marines, and he at once complied. Admiral Skerrett later commented that: "the American troops were well located if designed to promote the movement for the Provisional Government, and very improperly located if only intended to protect American citizens in person and property."

The revolution moved rapidly. Before the close of the seventeenth of January, the monarchy was declared at an end, Stevens had recognized the Provisional Government, and the latter had assumed full control "until such time as terms of union with the United States of America should have been agreed on. Two weeks later, at the request of President Dole of the Provisional Government, Stevens raised the American flag over the government buildings, and thus established a protectorate pending annexation.

These facts furnish an excellent basis for what the theologians term "argument from design." They tally also with the defense which Murat Halstead later made of Stevens: "He was an American himself, with a partiality for white folks, and, we presume, had the common American sentiment that the islands belonged to us, and our title would be perfected some day," and Stevens' own dispatches, both the published and the unpublished, make it quite clear that he gloried in the belief that manifest destiny had thus marked Hawaii as American property.

Meanwhile the Provisional Government had dis-

patched five commissioners, four Americans and one
Englishman, to request President Harrison to annex the
islands of the Hawaiians to the United States. They were
received, on February 4th, by Secretary of State Foster,
and eleven days later Harrison sent to the United States
Senate a treaty providing that: "the government of the
Hawaiian Islands hereby cedes . . . absolutely and without reservation to the United States forever all rights of
sovereignty of whatever kind in and over the Hawaiian
Islands and their dependencies." The document bore
six signatures—John W. Foster, Lorin A. Thurston,
William R. Castle, William C. Wilder, Charles L. Carter, and Joseph Marsden. There was not one Polynesian
name on the list.

In his accompanying message President Harrison informed the Senate that "the overthrow of the monarchy
was not in any way promoted by this Government," and
this President Harrison unquestionably believed, having
been so informed by the promoters of "Manifest Destiny," that ancient altar piece which the annexationists
were employing to give sanctity to their plans and value
to their plantations.

As President Harrison's term was drawing toward
its close, friend and foe of the pending annexation treaty
began to speculate what would be the policy of the returning President, Grover Cleveland. But the latter,
while watching carefully the progress of the annexation
movement, scrupulously avoided any expression of opinion upon the subject until the responsibility should again
become his.

In the absence of facts, the newspapers, of course,
published fiction. The day before the inauguration, the
Omaha *Bee* confidently assured its readers, upon the basis
of that most untrustworthy witness, "good authority,"

that Mr. Cleveland could be counted upon "to promote as far as possible the 'Manifest Destiny' doctrine which contemplates the ultimate extension of the United States over the entire North American continent and the absorption of whatever 'outposts' it may be found expedient or desirable to possess."

This illusion was soon dispelled by the new President. Within a week after his inauguration, he sent to the Senate a curt message of five lines: "For the purpose of re-examination I withdraw the treaty of annexation between the United States and the Provisional Government of the Hawaiian Islands now pending in the Senate, which was signed on February 14, 1893, and transmitted to the Senate on the 15th of the same month; and I therefore request that said treaty be returned to me. Grover Cleveland."

He was not content that Hawaii should be annexed upon the mere assurance of annexationists that "the overthrow of the monarchy was not in any way promoted by this Government." Beneath the insistent demand for immediate annexation, in order that there might be, as Harrison had expressed it, "decent administration of civil affairs," might lurk the ancient Anglo-Saxon thirst for empire. Perhaps in Hawaii his own nation had been guilty of the very sin which he was seeking to prevent the German Imperial Chancellor from committing in the Samoan Islands—the ruthless subversion of a weak and helpless nation.

As he studied the documents in the State Department he became increasingly suspicious. To annex the islands in response to the free will of their population would be entirely justifiable, but to annex them in response to the desire of American officials would be something quite different. What he had learned of the history of Hawaii's

recent past inclined him to give ear to an appeal lately
received from the dethroned queen herself, a passionate
appeal for justice, based upon the contention that the
revolution had been planned and carried out by Americans, chief among whom was the American Minister:

To His Excellency
Grover Cleveland
President Elect of the
United States.
My great and good friend:

In the vicissitudes which happened in the Hawaiian
Islands and which affect my people, myself and my house
so seriously, I feel comforted the more that beside the
friendly relations of the United States, I have the boon of
Your personal friendship and good will.

The changes which occurred here need not be stated
in this letter. You will have, at the time at which it
reaches You the official information, but I have instructed
the Hon. Paul Neuman whom I have appointed my
representative at Washington, to submit to You a precis
of the facts and circumstances relating to the revolution
in Honolulu, and to supplement it by such statements
which you may please to elicit.

I beg that You will consider this matter in which
there is so much involved for my people, and that you
give us your friendly assistance in granting redress for
a wrong which we claim has been done to us under color
of the assistance of the naval forces of the United States
in a friendly port.

Believe me that I do not veil under this a request to
You the fulfillment of which could in the slightest degree
be contrary to Your position, and I leave our grievance

in Your hands confident that in so far as you deem it proper we shall have Your sympathy and Your aid.

I am Your good friend

LILIUOKALANI.

Looking only upon the surface, it seemed reasonable to accept the vociferous assurances of the annexationists that Stevens had landed the marines only for the entirely legal and proper task of protecting American lives and American property. But in his study of the documents, Mr. Cleveland soon became convinced that Stevens had deliberately furthered the revolution in order the sooner to make Hawaii American territory. "To a minister of this temper, full of zeal for annexation," he later informed Congress, "there seemed to arise in January, 1893, the precise opportunity for which he was *watchfully waiting* . . . and we are quite prepared for the exultant enthusiasm with which, in a letter to the State Department dated February 1, 1893, he declares: 'The Hawaiian pear is now fully ripe, and this is the golden hour for the United States to pluck it.' "

Having withdrawn the treaty from the Senate, President Cleveland next sent the Honorable James H. Blount, recently Chairman of the House Committee on Foreign Affairs, as his special personal agent to Hawaii to discover the facts. In his testimony before the Senate Committee at a later date, Blount made under oath the statement that President Cleveland never gave him the least intimation as to what his own views regarding the situation in Hawaii were. "I was impressed," he said, "with the belief that he wanted information."

Pending Blount's report, the President of course received information from Minister Stevens, whose new dispatches presented the history of the revolution in the most favorable light, and made it quite clear that the landing of troops, in Stevens's opinion, had insured its final success.

"The supporters of the Provisional Government," he wrote, on April 4, 1893, "having had little or no military experience, an organized military force could not be created at once. Time was absolutely necessary. The presence of the few United States soldiers with their country's flag was of incalculable importance to the only existing and the only possible government for Hawaii. When the men of the *Boston* went to their ship April 1st, the Provisional Government had at its command a military force of four hundred men,—the most effective ever known in the islands, and an organized police with a tried and efficient man at the head. The remarkable change accomplished in seventy-five days had been without the loss of life or the destruction of property. Had the United States Minister and the Naval Commander not acted as they did, they would have deserved prompt removal from their places and the just censure of the friends of humanity and of civilization."

Thus Stevens's own dispatches justified the President's uneasy suspicions. But when Blount's report of July 17th reached him, it changed suspicion into a sense of certainty. After studying it and numerous items of documentary evidence furnished by his personal agent, Mr. Cleveland reached a definite conclusion. Stevens and certain American associates were the real authors of the Hawaiian revolution, made with the express purpose of annexation. "Mr. Stevens," Blount boldly declared, "consulted freely with the leaders of the revolutionary movement from the evening of the 14th. These disclosed to him all their plans. They feared arrest and punishment. He promised them protection. They needed the troops on shore to overawe the Queen's supporters and government. This he agreed to and did furnish. . . . The leaders of the revolutionary movement would not have undertaken it but for Mr. Stevens's promise to protect them against any danger from the government. . . . But for this no request to land troops would have been made. Had the troops not been landed no measures for the organization of a new government would have been taken.

"The American Minister and the revolutionary leaders had determined on a new addition to the United States and had agreed on the part each was to act to the very end."

Blount's report made it further evident that the revolution rested little upon the wishes of the native Hawaiians. "If the votes of persons claiming allegiance to foreign countries were excluded," he confidently informed Mr. Cleveland, "it (annexation) would be defeated by more than five to one." And this view was independently confirmed by Charles Nordhoff, a veteran Washington correspondent, whom the New York *Herald* sent to Honolulu to check up Blount's statements and report to the American people, and whom the Provisional Government vainly tried to silence.

"No one unprejudiced," declared the New York *Herald's* leading editorial of November 22, 1893, "can read Mr. Blount's report without the conviction that it goes into the archives of the State Department at Washington as the darkest chapter in the diplomatic annals of this country."

The New York *Times* declared, editorially, that it "reveals a conspiracy . . . which if not repudiated by this nation, would sully the honor and blacken the fair name of the United States."

"The people of this country," said the Savannah
*Morning News,* "if they accept Mr. Blount's report,
cannot do otherwise than sustain the position taken by
the President and his Cabinet. The only way to create a
sentiment against that position is to show that Mr.
Blount's report is not correct."

This suggestion the annexationists promptly adopted.
Blount was accused of working for a verdict against the
white "crusaders of Democracy," and in favor of "the
lady who looks like the inside of a package of Arbuckle's
coffee"; he had seen only the queen's friends; he was
the man who had hauled down the American flag. But
Blount's work had been conscientiously and intelligently
done, his facts were in the main identical with those
presented by Nordhoff and other disinterested spectators,
and the attempts of the annexationists to prove the contrary met with little success.

The Cleveland press challenged Stevens or ex-President Harrison, or any one else to point to a statement in
the report which was not true. "Mr. Stevens," declared
the Chicago *Herald,* "was asked to show wherein Mr.
Blount has misstated facts. Mr. Stevens had a peremptory engagement out of town for several days. . . . Ex-
President Harrison was also invited to show that Blount
erred in any statement of fact. The ex-President diplomatically avoided the issue."

A few days later, however, Stevens sent forth from
his retreat in Maine an elaborate reply to Blount's report;
and the Hawaiian Minister, Lorin A. Thurston, in columns of argument, denounced what he termed Blount's
"gross inaccuracies." But Stevens was now in the position of a deposed official, and Thurston was regarded as
merely a special pleader paid for the work.

The New York *Tribune,* in its issue of November 22,

1893, ventured upon a psychological argument designed to discredit Mr. Cleveland's policy. "The secret springs or motives are out of sight, hidden in personal relations," it impressively declared, ". . . In this, as in a great many other things, the unwritten, personal factor is potential. It is easily stated. The present Secretary of State (Mr. Gresham) has been for many years the personal enemy of ex-President Harrison, as he was also of the late Secretary Blaine. . . . Minister Stevens was an intimate personal friend of Mr. Blaine. He was an appointee of President Harrison. The policy he pursued in Hawaii was approved by the Harrison administration."

And so Grover Cleveland had faced his own nation and thwarted a movement which strongly appeals always to the strain of Anglo-Saxon blood, in order that Secretary Gresham's personal hatreds might be avenged. To such strange lengths will party spirit go, even in great affairs. And this is one of the dangers of democracies.

With little attention to disputes regarding his methods or motives, President Cleveland now faced the difficult question of action. One thing was clear to his mind: Whatever the cost, he must see justice done to the sovereignty of Hawaii.

In his search for a method by which the United States could undo the wrong which had been done by men serving in her name, the President suggested that Secretary Gresham ask specific advice from the members of the Cabinet. The opinion furnished by Attorney General Richard Olney anticipates in essential features the plan finally adopted. After a convincing summary of the American origin of what he terms "the Stevens Government," Mr. Olney suggested:

"1. All the resources of diplomacy should be exhausted to restore the *status quo* in Hawaii by peaceful methods and without force.

"2. If, as a last resort, force is found to be necessary . . . the matter must be submitted to Congress for its action.

"3. In addition to providing for the security of the queen's person pending efforts to reinstate the queen's government . . . the United States should require of the queen . . . authority to negotiate and bring about the restoration of her government on such reasonable terms and conditions as the United States may approve and find to be practicable.

"Among such terms and conditions must be, I think, full pardon and amnesty for all connected with the Stevens government who might otherwise be liable to be visited with the pains and penalties attending the crime of treason."

In the light of this and other opinions, Secretary Gresham wrote to the President an elaborate summary of the case. His recommendations were less specific than Olney's, but their general tenor was the same. And he added a moral interpretation which he knew would strike a responsive chord in the President's heart: "Should not the great wrong done to a feeble but independent state by an abuse of the authority of the United States be undone by restoring the legitimate government? Anything short of that will not, I respectfully submit, satisfy the demands of justice. . . ."

A consultation followed and that evening Secretary Gresham wrote to inform the new Minister, Albert S. Willis, of the President's decision, and to give confidential instructions for his guidance:

"You will . . . inform the Queen that, when reinstated, the President expects that she will pursue a mag-

nanimous course by granting full amnesty to all who
participated in the movement against her. . . . Having
secured the Queen's agreement . . . you will then advise
the Executive of the Provisional Government and his
ministers of the President's determination of the question . . . and they are expected to promptly relinquish
to her her constitutional authority." In case of failure
to accomplish a peaceful settlement by agreement, Willis
was ordered to report the facts and await further
directions.

From this and many subsequent letters, it is evident
that Mr. Cleveland had no idea of attempting by force
to restore the queen of Hawaii. On the contrary, on
December 3d, Secretary Gresham again wrote to Willis:
"Should the Queen ask whether if she accedes to conditions, active steps will be taken by the United States to
effect her restoration or to maintain her authority thereafter, you will say that the President cannot use force
without the authority of Congress." And Blount, in his
sworn testimony before the Morgan Committee, later declared: "I never heard it [the idea of a restoration by
force] suggested until my return to the United States."

A busy press had, however, already managed to interpret the necessary operations of the navy as proof that
armed intervention in favor of Liliuokalani was the
President's program. The Newport, R. I., *Herald* had
informed its readers, on November 16th, that "it is said
on good naval authority that as soon as the United States
ships, *Ranger* and *Mohican* . . . can be made ready for
sea the Secretary of the Navy will order their comman-
ders to proceed direct to Honolulu. . . . The combined
crews of the *Ranger* and *Mohican* would enable the landing of a larger marine force than from the *Philadelphia*
(already there)."

Upon the basis of this evidence of heroic intent, the enthusiastic colored citizens of Newport met and dispatched to the President a letter of congratulation that in his blow for justice he had not regarded color, nor been prejudiced by the fact that "the sun has blared heavily upon the dark skin Queen's ancestry."

As it chanced, on that very sixteenth of November, Minister Willis was preparing a dispatch containing the discouraging details of his first interview with the dethroned queen: "In the forenoon of Monday . . . [November 13th] the Queen, accompanied by the Royal Chamberlain . . . called at the Legation. . . . After a formal greeting, the Queen was informed that the President . . . had important communications to make to her, and she was asked whether she was willing to receive them alone and in confidence. . . . She answered in the affirmative.

"I then made known to her the President's sincere regret that through the unauthorized intervention of the United States, she had been obliged to surrender her sovereignty, and his hope that with her consent and co-operation, the wrong done to her and her people might be redressed. To this she bowed her acknowledgment.

"I then said to her: 'The President expects and believes that when reinstated you will show forgiveness and magnanimity.' . . . To this she made no reply.

"After waiting a moment, I continued: 'The President not only tenders you his sympathy but wishes to help you. Before fully making known to you his purposes, I desire to know whether you are willing to answer certain questions which it is my duty to ask.' She answered: 'I am willing.'"

The Minister then asked whether, if restored to her

throne, she would grant full amnesty to those concerned in her overthrow.

"She hesitated for a moment and then slowly and calmly answered: 'There are certain laws of my government by which I shall abide. My decision would be, as the law directs, that such persons should be beheaded and their property confiscated.' "

The Minister, dumbfounded at so frank a statement, asked: "Do you fully understand the meaning of every word which I have said to you, and of every word which you have said to me?" The queen replied: "I have understood and mean all I have said. . . . These people were the cause of the revolution and Constitution of 1887. There will never be any peace while they are here. . . ."

Immediately after this interview, Willis telegraphed to Washington: "Views of first party so extreme as to require further instructions."

These facts were, of course, not made public and, with the newspaper stories of a projected forcible restoration of the queen in mind, the President's annual message was eagerly awaited. When, on December 4, 1893, it came, it was disappointingly lacking in dramatic quality. Simply, unimpassionedly, Mr. Cleveland informed Congress that he was conscientiously seeking "to undo the wrong that had been done by those representing us and to restore, as far as practicable, the status existing at the time of our forcible intervention." More than that he was not yet ready to say.

A fortnight later, the President received from Willis a list of perplexing questions: ". . . Assuming the restoration of the Queen, with the temporary acquiescence of the Provisional Government, what next? If left to itself it would fall to pieces like a card house. Would it be just to restore her and have another revolution at once—

which seems probable? If restored, would she not be
entitled to our protection until she was securely seated?
How long would this require, and what immediate announcement (after restoration) if any, should be made?

"Shall our Government suggest to the restored
queen (in the interest of peace and good government)
that the Constitution of 1887 should not be overturned
except as therein provided? Shall anything be said about
the opium license law and lottery law which have been
repealed by the Provisional Government and the passage
of which had as much to do with the late uprising as the
threat of the Queen to promulgate a new Constitution?

"In restoring the status ante shall men like Mr. Dole
be put back on the Supreme Bench? Shall vacancies (as
now intimated) be declared because of participation in
the Queen's overthrow? . . .

"If the Queen should, while under our quasi protection, again promulgate a new Constitution, shall we make
no remonstrance? This question is uppermost in Hawaiian hearts."

Such questions asked by the perplexed Minister
reached far beyond the realm which the Constitution had
assigned to the executive branch of the Government. The
President, therefore, decided to mass his evidence regarding the origin and meaning of the Hawaiian revolution into a special message to Congress, and thus force it
and the nation to face squarely and without the distraction
of other topics what he conceived to be a great moral
issue. On December 18th, this special Hawaiian message was sent to Congress. It is a document of arraignment, of denunciation, ballasted by carefully substanti-
ated facts. Never, not even in his suppressed message
concerning Germany's secret intrigues against Samoan
independence, nor in his later and more famous arraign-

ment of what he believed to be the British disregard of Venezuela's sovereign rights, did he denounce a foreign government more uncompromisingly than he here denounced his own government.

It mattered not to him that expansion into the Pacific was a popular policy; that the American public could not easily be aroused to sympathy with a dethroned, dark-skinned Oriental queen; that the wrong which he denounced was an accomplished fact, and that it requires more than courage and a good cause to set back the hands of time. He poured his withering scorn upon a great and powerful nation which will stoop to countenance intrigue on the part of its own officials, that a few more acres of soil, a few more harbors and clear lagoons may be added to its vast estate. "The control of both sides of a bargain," such were his words, ". . . is called by a familiar and unpleasant name when found in private transactions."

In acknowledging his failure to secure justice to Hawaii, although executive power had been employed to the full, he laid before Congress his vision of a foreign policy worthy of a great, powerful Christian nation. In begging that justice be done, he urged upon them a standard than which no loftier has ever been presented to that body, whether by President, Secretary, or duly elected Senator or Representative:

"It has been the boast of our Government," he said, "that it seeks to do justice in all things, without regard to the strength or weakness of those with whom it deals. I mistake the American people if they favor the odious doctrine that there is no such thing as international morality; that there is one law for a strong nation and another for a weak one, and that even by indirection a strong power may with impunity despoil a weak one of its territory. . . . The law of nations is founded upon reason and jus-

tice, and the rules of conduct governing individual rela
tions between citizens or subjects of a civilized state ar
equally applicable as between enlightened nations.

"The considerations that international law is withou
a court for its enforcement and that obedience to its com
mands practically depends upon good faith instead o
upon the mandate of a superior tribunal only give addi
tional sanction to the law itself and brand any deliberat
infraction of it not merely as wrong, but as a disgrace
A man of true honor protects the unwritten word which
binds his conscience more scrupulously, if possible, that
he does a bond a breach of which subjects him to lega
liabilities, and the United States, in aiming to maintai
itself as one of the most enlightened nations, would do it
citizens gross injustice if it applied to its internationa
relations any other than a high standard of honor an
morality. On that ground the United States cannot b
properly put in the position of countenancing a wron
after its commission any more than of consenting to it i
advance. On that ground it cannot allow itself to refus
to redress an injury inflicted through an abuse of powe
by officers clothed with its authority and wearing its uni
form; and on the same ground, if a feeble but friendl
state is in danger of being robbed of its independence an
its sovereignty by a misuse of the name and power of th
United States, the United States cannot fail to vindicat
its honor and its sense of justice by an earnest effort t
make all possible reparation."

Henceforth, while diligently furnishing to Congres
all information which reached him, the President was n
longer the chief actor. As it chanced, on the very da
when his Hawaiian message was presented, Quee
Liliuokalani capitulated, sending to Mr. Willis a lette
which declared: "I must not feel vengeful to any of m

people. If I am restored by the United States, I must forget myself, and remember only my dear people and my country. . . ." With it she sent a solemn pledge promising, in the event of her restoration, full pardon and amnesty to all who had taken part in the revolution.

The same day brought to Minister Willis, from President Dole, the curt inquiry: "Will you inform me if . . . you are acting in any way hostile to this government?" Willis's reply was a demand that the Provisional Government restore to the queen the authority of Constitutional Monarch of Hawaii, upon which the Provisional Government declared that, even if the revolution had been made possible by the assistance of American troops and American officials, which was stoutly denied, "the President was not thereby given the least right to control the actions of the *de facto* government of Hawaii," a proposition which Mr. Cleveland would have been the last to controvert.

Willis here ventured upon dangerous ground. In order to test the courage of the Provisional Government he resorted to the menace of violence, and in so doing violated the whole spirit of his instructions. Taking advantage of the arrival of the revenue cutter, *Corwin,* with dispatches from the State Department the nature of which was of course unknown to the Provisional Government, Willis had the troops drawn up on the decks of the *Adams* and the *Philadelphia,* as though preparing to land an attack. "He had the guns of our ships pointed at the palace in Honolulu," reported the San Francisco *Evening Bulletin* of January 10, 1894, "but he did not succeed in scaring anybody. . . . The Provisional Government did not come down. . . . President Dole . . . knew just how far Willis dared go. It would have been as much as his official neck was worth to have done more than beat the tom-tom."

This incident served to give the enemies of the administration a shadowy pretext for circulating the report that the President was invading the precincts of Congress, by presuming to menace a friendly sovereign nation with a war which Congress had never sanctioned. The cry of impeachment was raised, was gravely re-echoed on the floors of Congress, only to sink into deserved oblivion; for those who knew the facts knew that the President had never contemplated force in Hawaii, but only an honorable settlement by mutual agreement.

Meanwhile, Congress, to whose wide discretion he had committed the task, as too large for mere executive control, was unsteadily but certainly yielding to "Manifest Destiny." The House of Representatives, while condemning the filibustering which had brought on the Hawaiian revolution, and declining to sanction annexation under such conditions, was naturally unwilling to take steps to restore the deposed queen by force; while the Senate felt that the United States should let Hawaiian affairs alone, insisting that other nations do the same. This was equivalent to allowing the revolution to stand, and annexation to await a more convenient season.

During the six months which followed, the Hawaiian revolution developed into the Hawaiian Republic, which was formally proclaimed on July 4, 1894. The stability of this new government becoming clear, President Cleveland, before the end of the month, withdrew the American vessels from the harbor of Honolulu and, on August 7th, sent to President Dole a formal letter of recognition. He thus accepted in its fullness the logic of the facts. Dole and his fellow white men in Hawaii had succeeded in establishing an orderly government, demonstrably able

to fulfil the obligations of statehood. They were, therefore, entitled to the legal recognition which alone could
make them responsible agents among the nations of the
world.

In recognizing the new republic President Cleveland
logically committed himself to the proposition that it was
able to speak with the voice of Hawaiian sovereignty.
His subsequent refusal to countenance annexation at its
request was, therefore, illogical and of doubtful wisdom.
Had he not thus refused, the revolt of 1895 might have
been avoided. As it was, the Royalists made a final effort
to re-enlist him in their now hopeless cause, soon to end
in a bloody defeat. They sent to Washington a commission
to plead for his assistance. But when the date set for
the audience arrived, Mr. Cleveland was ill in bed. He
therefore sent them the following address, with which
they were forced to depart:

Executive Mansion, Washington.

Gentlemen:

You must permit me to remind you that this interview is not an official one, and that instead of receiving
you in any representative capacity, I meet you as individuals who have traveled a long distance for the purpose of laying a certain matter before me.

You ask if there is any hope of my "doing anything
for the restoration of the Constitutional Government of
the Hawaiian Islands." I suppose that this question is
largely prompted by the fact that soon after the over-
turning of the late Government of the Queen, I investigated that transaction and was satisfied that there had
been such an unjustifiable interference in aid of that
movement, on the part of representatives of the Government of the United States in its Diplomatic and Naval

service, as to call for correction, not only to rectify what seemed to be a wrong done to others, but also through that rectification to ward off what appeared to be a danger to American honor and probity.

"Fully appreciating the constitutional limitations of my Executive power and by no means unmindful of the hindrances that might arise, I undertook the task. Having failed in my plans, I committed the entire subject to the Congress of the United States, which had abundant power and authority in the premises. The Executive branch of the Government was thereby discharged from further duty and responsibility in the matter unless moved thereto by Congressional command. The Congress has, both by its action and its omission to act, signified that nothing need be done touching American interference with the overthrow of the Government of the Queen.

"Quite lately a government has been established in Hawaii which is in full force and operation in all parts of the Islands. It is maintaining its authority and discharging all ordinary governmental functions. Upon general principles and not losing sight of the special circumstances surrounding this case, the new government is clearly entitled to our recognition without regard to any of the incidents which accompanied or preceded its inauguration.

"This recognition and the attitude of the Congress concerning Hawaiian affairs of course lead to an absolute denial of the least present or future aid or encouragement on my part to an effort to restore any government heretofore existing in the Hawaiian Islands."

When the Republican platform of 1896 was sent broadcast over the country, it contained these words: "The Hawaiian Islands should be controlled by the

United States." No one could question the fact that Hawaii was now in a condition quite different from that of the days of the revolution. Her republic was firmly established, her Constitution in effective operation, and she had demonstrated her ability to preserve order at home and to fulfil her obligations abroad. Furthermore, the friends of annexation unhesitatingly urged two most effective arguments, and urged them through the medium of organized propaganda. These were first, commercial interest, and second, fear of Japan.

Almost ninety-three per cent of Hawaii's trade, declared one of their propaganda leaflets, is with the United States. China and Japan have only about two and a half per cent, although they number in the islands over forty thousand out of a total population of a hundred and ten thousand. "We can prevent Chinese occupying our beautiful country . . . but it is not so with Japan. . . . Japan wants colonies and possessions. From the Japanese press and from what her people say here, it is evident that Japan intends to possess Hawaii. . . . While you are maintaining your policy of 'hands off' and 'let Hawaii alone' . . . the Japanese will quietly and peacefully pour into Hawaii till they simply overwhelm us by their numbers. . . . When Hawaii is full of Japanese, of whom many will be educated and just as intelligent and capable of self-government as our present electors, can it be supposed that we can prevent them from voting? Never! and by a single election all will be changed. . . . In place of the beloved Stars and Stripes, our ports will be filled with ships carrying the bright field and proud sun flag of Japan."

In response to such appeals President McKinley, on June 16, 1897, submitted to the United States Senate a new treaty of annexation. And three days later Mr.

Cleveland wrote to Mr. Olney: "Did you ever see such a preposterous thing as the Hawaiian business? The papers I read are most strongly opposed to it and there ought to be soberness and decency enough in the Senate to save us from launching upon the dangerous policy which is foreshadowed by the pending treaty; but I am prepared for almost anything."

For a time the opposition in the Senate proved stronger than Mr. Cleveland had dared hope. The expected ratification failed to materialize, and on February 16, 1898, Mr. Cleveland, now a private citizen, wrote confidently to Olney: "All the influence of this administration appears unable thus far to bring to a successful issue the Hawaiian monstrosity." But the annexationists bided their time, which now was not far off. On April 25, 1898, came the declaration of war against Spain, and for a time it seemed that the annexation question would have to wait upon more pressing matters. "Hawaii," wrote Mr. Olney to Mr. Cleveland, with the intimacy of an old comrade in arms, "seems to be in the soup."

That "soup," however, offered unforeseen advantages to the cause of annexation, for the new government of Hawaii soon won further favor in the United States by openly violating international law in allowing American ships of war to coal in Honolulu and to use the islands as a sort of naval base, thus giving a graphic illustration of the vastly increased importance of annexation, now that American guns had made for us a Philippine problem.

About a month after Admiral Dewey's victory at Manila Bay (May 1, 1898), President McKinley remarked to Mr. Cortelyou: "We need Hawaii just as much and a good deal more than we did California. It is Manifest Destiny." Two months later he signed a joint resolution of both houses annexing the islands, and on August 12th, the very American flag which Grover Cleveland had caused to be hauled down was raised again in token of American sovereignty. "Manifest Destiny" had triumphed at last.

After reading the newspaper account of the closing scene in the long drama, Mr. Cleveland sadly wrote to Mr. Olney: "Hawaii is ours. As I look back upon the first steps in this miserable business and as I contemplate the means used to complete the outrage, I am ashamed of the whole affair."

The world's past struggles toward liberty and equality have had as their goal liberty and equality among those of the white race. Its struggles to come lie along the pathway that leads to liberty and equality among all peoples, whether white or black, red, brown, or yellow. In the Hawaiian affair Grover Cleveland made many minor mistakes, but in holding that far-off goal before the eyes of his fellow-citizens, he was, in a very real and a very heroic sense, a world-pioneer.

# CHAPTER III

### BREAKING THE ENDLESS CHAIN—THE FOUR BOND ISSUES

*"There is a vast difference between a standard of value and a currency for monetary use."*

—GROVER CLEVELAND.

WHAT our nation needs—and sorely needs," Mr. Cleveland said, when speaking in honor of the great American, Carl Schurz, "is more patriotism that is born of moral courage—the courage that attacks abuses and struggles for civic reforms, single-handed, without counting opposing numbers or measuring opposing forces."

Had these words been written for Grover Cleveland himself, they could not have better described his attitude toward the duties which go with office. His public life was a succession of such conflicts. Before one storm was over, there always appeared on the political horizon another cloud the size of a man's hand, prophesying another deluge. When thinking of his public life, he instinctively thought of conflict, and his writing regarding his two administrations deals wholly with the history of major struggles in the interest of what he conceived to be the honor of the Republic and the safety of its people.

Four years before his death, in outlining a course of lectures regarding his second term, to be delivered at Princeton University, he wrote: "The members of that administration who still survive, in recalling the events of this laborious service, cannot fail to fix upon the years 1894 and 1895 as the most troublous and anxious of their incumbency." He enumerated as the chief incidents of

74

that testing time the following leading conflicts: (1) "Unhappy currency complications [which] compelled executive resort to heroic treatment for the preservation of our nation's financial integrity, and forced upon the administration a constant, unrelenting struggle for sound money." (2) "A long and persistent executive effort to accomplish beneficent and satisfactory tariff reform." (3) "A very determined labor disturbance [which] broke out in the City of Chicago." (4) "Executive insistence upon the Monroe Doctrine [which] culminated in a situation that gave birth to solemn thoughts of war."

The first and most pressing of these questions was but the recurrence, in a slightly different form, of the struggle which had resulted in the repeal of the Sherman Law, on November 1, 1893. Almost immediately after that repeal it became apparent that the President had won not a victory but an armistice, and that another trial of strength was inevitable. This was precipitated neither by Mr. Cleveland nor by his free silver opponents, but by the operation of economic law, menacing the country with the banishment of gold and the consequent establishment of a silver standard of value.

Despite the opposition which he offered to the free coinage of silver, President Cleveland never objected to the free use of silver as money. What he feared, and fought, was the substitution of a silver basis of value for our established gold standard, and the repeal of the Sherman Law had done little to quiet his fears. He was still responsible for the impossible task of keeping the two metals at a parity, which meant that still he must be ready to pay a gold dollar whenever a Treasury note, representing only a deposit of about sixty cents worth of silver, was presented with a demand for gold.

To do this it was essential that the gold reserve, designed to cover only greenbacks, be maintained at a strength sufficient for this added strain upon it. But, despite the fact that he had stopped the monthly increase of Treasury notes by repealing the Sherman Law, his gold reserve was melting away. The combined attack of the outstanding $450,000,000 of United States notes and greenbacks was working ruin, for, when redeemed for gold, they had to be reissued, only to return and draw out more gold.

Thus, in an endless chain, the paper money ran, dragging the gold reserve ever downward, and bringing the country ever nearer to the point where gold payment must be refused. Gold, furthermore, was being exported to an extent that added to the President's alarm. As the total amount of gold in the country was now only $597,697,865, it was not difficult to foresee the end.

The only available means of replenishing the gold reserve was through the issue of government bonds, as authorized by an act of January 14, 1875. But the practical value of this method was greatly lessened by the fact that such bonds could not be made payable in gold. To persuade the public to buy for gold five per cent ten-year bonds, four and a half per cent fifteen-year bonds, or four per cent thirty-year bonds "payable in coin," was certain to prove difficult, as the purchaser must take the chance of having them redeemed in depreciated silver at the end, should the Treasury Department so order.

In forcing the repeal of the Sherman Law, President Cleveland had, therefore, taken only the first step in his monetary reform, and he now prepared for the second, the issuing of bonds to secure the gold necessary to maintain the gold reserve.

At once the free silver men of both parties formed plans to block the program.

Congressman William Jennings Bryan was especially active in opposition. On January 5, 1894, Secretary Morton wrote to Henry T. Thurber, Private Secretary to the President:

"Find herewith enclosed a Washington dispatch taken from the Omaha *Daily Bee* of Tuesday, January 2. Mr. Heath, who signs it, is rather a careful and conservative man, and, I think, incapable of willing misrepresentation. Therefore, I send the article to you, that the President may see precisely how Mr. Bryan represents himself to his people in Nebraska, upon the issuance of bonds, which are vital to the good credit of our common country.

"Very truly yours,
"J. STERLING MORTON."

The enclosed clipping declared: "Bryan comes uppermost. . . . Fate of the bond issue in his hands. . . . Bryan, after all, appears to hold the whip hand upon the administration, and will be heard from and felt in such a way as to compel President Cleveland to respect if not fear him. He is a member of the Ways and Means Sub-committee having in charge the subject of the public debt. To this sub-committee, composed also of McMillin, of Tennessee, and Whiting, of Michigan, will be referred the bond question. The administration is very anxious for authority to issue $200,000,000 or more of bonds, with which to meet current expenses, fill the deficiency vacuum and replenish the gold reserve. Mr. Bryan is opposed to a bond issue for any purpose, and so are his two colleagues. . . . It looks as though a bond issue may be defeated."

A later paragraph throws light upon Mr. Bryan's political methods: "In view of Mr. Bryan's new accession of strength by virtue of the proposed bond issue, it will create no surprise if he hereafter gets his full share of the Nebraska federal patronage. He is now confident of being able to name the postmaster at Lincoln. . . . If the Morton-Castor combine cuts him out of this piece of local patronage, it can confidently be expected that Mr. Bryan will make the fur fly on the bond issue problem."

There is nothing to indicate that President Cleveland ever contemplated the issue of $200,000,000 of bonds at any one time, although the total amount of the bonds actually issued by him, in his fight to preserve the gold standard, greatly exceeded that amount, and the statement that he designed to employ the proceeds of the bond issue to meet current expenses was palpably untrue. The Treasury Department had no authority to issue bonds for such a purpose, and the President later assured Congress that "at no time . . . has there been any consideration of the question."

By January 17th, the gold reserve stood at $70,000,000, and the public was showing itself more and more distrustful of the government's will or ability to furnish gold upon demand. The same day Secretary Carlisle announced that $50,000,000 in ten-year five per cent bonds, redeemable in "coin," would be on sale for gold until the first of the following February. But he warned all prospective purchasers that no bid would be considered which did not offer a fraction over seventeen per cent premium, thus reducing the yield to three per cent.

The bond sale worked far less smoothly than did the endless chain. Buyers were so alarmingly few that the President, fearful lest the issue fail, despatched Mr. Carlisle to New York to confer with a number of well-known financiers, an unwelcome expedient for one who had often declared that "the government ought not, regardless of any public purpose, to identify itself with private business or speculation." The financiers, fully conscious of the danger, rallied to the support of the government, and "barely in time to prevent a disastrous failure of the sale," as Mr. Cleveland later explained. The gold realized from this sale amounted to $58,660,917.63, thus raising the reserve to $107,440,802, and the crisis was over for the moment.

The President knew, however, that it was only for the moment, and therefore toward the end of March he sent to Congress a message which urged "the desirability of granting to the Secretary of the Treasury a better power than now exists to issue bonds to protect the gold reserve." In view of the composition of that body, prudence demanded that, pending its answer, he should avoid any action likely to lead to conflict. But, unfortunately, such a course was impossible. The Seigniorage Bill which Congress had just passed was waiting his signature, and sign it he could not.

Seigniorage is the gain accruing to the government by the purchase of bullion at a price less than the value stamped on the metal when coined. It represents the difference between a silver dollar and a dollar's worth of silver. The Seigniorage Bill provided for an addition to the currency of approximately 50,000,000 silver dollars, coined from the Seigniorage in the Treasury, and worth intrinsically about fifty per cent. of their face value. Congressman Bland of Missouri—"Silver Dick," his admirers called him—was its sponsor, and it was the darling project of the free silver men, who regarded it as the test to determine whether or not the President was an irreconcilable enemy of silver.

The receipt of the Seigniorage Bill, therefore, placed

the President in serious embarrassment. Many of his sound money supporters assumed that he would veto it. Carl Schurz wrote: "Put your heel on this seigniorage humbug and save the country's honor."

On the other hand, many friends as ardently "sound money" as Mr. Schurz, urged him to sign the bill, arguing that the amount of silver was so small as to add little to the danger of the situation, and that the enmity which would be aroused by a veto would greatly weaken his chance of being given the power needed for an effective bond issue. Among these Secretary Gresham was conspicuous, and no one could question the fact that he was the soundest of sound money men. Still others urged him to sign the bill in the interest of party unity. "If you veto it," wrote David R. Francis, "the party will be so irreparably divided and demoralized that defeat will ensue."

But the latter argument only angered the President. He could not comprehend how sound money men could hope to purchase party unity by consenting to an increase of unsound money. By the terms of the bill, the seigniorage was to be coined "into legal tender standard dollars," the fiat of the government being substituted for real value.

William Elroy Curtis, then Washington correspondent for the Chicago *Record,* gives this account of an interview in which the President expressed his views upon the ethics of the situation:

"The president lost his temper yesterday while a party of western and southern congressmen were trying to persuade him to sign the silver bill. . . . After discussing the financial side of the question they brought up the political end of it, and one of them told the president that unless the bill became a law there was no hope for the democrats' getting a majority in the next congress. He added, by way of a clincher, that it would be scarcely possible for him and several others of the gentlemen present to be re-elected.

"Whereupon the president turned on him and remarked that he supposed that was the reason why the bill got so many votes in the house, and proceeded to give his opinion of members of congress who pandered to the delusions of the people and voted for all sorts of legislation in order to keep themselves in office. He said that the credit of the government and the condition of the national finances were too important to be treated from that point of view, and that he had a decided contempt for anyone who would ask him to aid in such legislation for such a reason."

Having considered the bill wholly upon its merits, and with reference to the public interest, Mr. Cleveland returned it to Congress with his veto, on March 29, 1894, the very day when he asked Congress for "a better power than now exists to issue bonds."

Had it been possible, the President would doubtless have swallowed his pride and his personal opinions and signed, in order to win support for the demand for power which he had just made upon Congress, but he considered the Seigniorage Bill a concession to dishonesty and as such he could not sign it. This his veto message made perfectly plain:

"My strong desire to avoid disagreement with those in both Houses of Congress who have supported this bill would lead me to approve it if I could believe that the public good would not be thereby endangered and that such action on my part would be a proper discharge of official duty. Inasmuch, however, as I am unable to satisfy myself that the proposed legislation is either wise or opportune, my conception of the obligations and responsibilities attached to the great office I hold forbids the indulgence of my personal desire and inexorably confines me to that course which is dictated by my reason and judgment, and pointed out by a sincere purpose to protect and promote the general interests of our people."

In the face of this veto Congress refused to grant the extra powers for which the President had pleaded, and the latter was forced to make shift to defend the gold standard with the powers already possessed. For this he saw no chance, save a succession of bond issues, likely to give only temporary relief.

So hopeless was the situation that he at times indulged the thought that he had made a mistake in consenting to return to office. "I do not mind confessing to you," he wrote to one of his former New York law partners, Howard Van Sinderen, on April 6th, "that my position at 15 Broad Street was an easier one than I now occupy, and I occasionally wonder if it was not quite as useful."

Within three months of the close of the first bond sales, the gold reserve stood at $78,693,267, and was still sinking, while domestic hoarding and exportation of gold were on the increase, and the customs revenues brought practically no gold into the Treasury. The time had come for another issue or a silver basis.

With state and congressional elections almost in sight, this was a hard alternative, but Mr. Cleveland showed no hesitation. "An obedient regard for official duty," he later explained, "made the right path exceedingly plain."

Unfortunately for the President, and for the party

which he led, this plain path of duty made plain also the path of opportunity for Hill, Sheehan, and Murphy, in New York, and for like-minded politicians throughout the land. So sinister was the interpretation given by his enemies to the bond issue and its approaching duplicate that many of the President's former supporters turned against such of the party candidates as remained his friends, and supported those who were openly antagonistic to him. The Democrats of New York assembled in a rollicking convention at Saratoga on Monday, September 24th, and staged an anti-Cleveland scene which recalls the description of Revolutionary Boston, as a place where the King's enemies went about in homespun and his friends in tar and feathers. They nominated David B. Hill for Governor and equally dear enemies for other important state offices.

The folly of this course was soon evident. The Reform Democrats, revolting from Hill, nominated Everett P. Wheeler for Governor, thus insuring the election of Levi P. Morton, candidate of the Republicans and Independent Republicans. William L. Strong, Republican and Union Anti-Tammany candidate for Mayor of New York, won an overwhelming victory, while, in the country at large, there was a veritable landslide toward Republicanism. "The latest returns," declared the New York *Tribune* of November 8, 1894, ". . . show that there have been elected to the next House of Representatives 234 Republicans, 117 Democrats and 5 Populists." Even the solid South was broken, not one but many Southern states returning Republican Congressmen in considerable numbers: West Virginia 4, Maryland 3, Kentucky 4, Virginia 2, North Carolina 3, Tennessee 4, Missouri 7, Delaware 1, and even Texas 1.

On November 14th, eight days after the elections, the second bond issue was announced, $50,000,000 of five per cent bonds being again the proposition presented to the public. But the public was no more disposed than formerly to part with gold in exchange for bonds. Once more bidding was dishearteningly slow and insultingly low.

At last came a bid "for all or none" from a combination of thirty-three banking institutions and financiers of New York. Their offer being more advantageous to the government than all previous bids, it was accepted, and the President had the satisfaction of seeing $58,538,500 added to the gold reserve.

In view of the unkind and ungenerous interpretation which has been so often put upon this transaction, it is only fair to quote the words of Mr. Cleveland, written ten years later: "The President . . . of the United States Trust Company . . . rendered most useful and patriotic service in making both this and the previous offer of bonds successful. . . . He afterward testified under oath that the accepted bid for 'all or none,' in which his company was a large participant, proved unprofitable to the bidders."

In calmer days even the New York *World* acknowledged that: "The first two bond issues by the Cleveland administration . . . were made with full publicity and entire propriety."

When on December 3, 1894, Congress heard the President's annual message, it listened to no vague generalities written to conciliate hostile factions, or disarm jubilant political opponents. He painted the financial situation in somber colors, and suggested the cure in specific terms. But neither his pleas, his arguments, nor his lucid explanations produced the slightest effect upon his enemies, who rejoiced at his discomfiture and declined to give him the authority which he demanded.

In January, 1895, the gold withdrawals amounted to $45,000,000, and again the end of gold payment was not far off unless Congress would consent to act or the President should for the third time issue bonds. On the 28th, he again appealed to Congress, but again his plea was disregarded, and by February 8th the gold reserve was less than fifty per cent of the traditional level of safety.

Meanwhile, many of his most trusted advisers were eagerly urging him to invoke expert aid from Wall Street again, but with little success. While bitterly resentful toward Congress, he was disposed to blame the bankers also, and declined to hold further conference with them. Finally, however, less in concession to friendly advice than because he had become convinced that the public would not purchase more government bonds, he agreed to see J. P. Morgan, though he was still firmly resolved that any new issue of bonds should be first offered to public subscription. In commenting upon this decision, a prominent banker declared: "If a man needs beef, he goes to a butcher; if he needs gold, he goes to a banker. If he needs a great deal of beef, he goes to a big butcher; if he requires a great deal of gold, he must go to a big banker and pay his price for it."

The story of the now famous interview between the President and Mr. Morgan was later thus related by Mr. Cleveland himself:

"On the evening of the seventh day of February, 1895, an interview was held at the White House with J. P. Morgan of New York. . . . Secretary Carlisle was present nearly or quite all the time; Attorney General Olney was there a portion of the time, and Mr. Morgan and a young man from his office and myself all the time.

"At the outset Mr. Morgan was inclined to complain of the treatment he had received from Treasury officials in the repudiation of the arrangement which he thought he had been encouraged to perfect in connection with the disposal of another issue of bonds. I said to Mr. Morgan [that] whatever there might be in all this, another offer of bonds for popular subscription, open to all bidders, had been determined upon, and that there were two questions I wanted to ask him which he ought to be able to answer: one was whether the bonds to be so offered would probably be taken at a good price on short notice; and the other was whether, in case there should be imminent danger of the disappearance of what remained of the gold reserve, during the time that must elapse between published notice and the opening of bids, a sufficient amount of gold could be temporarily obtained from financial institutions in the City of New York to bridge over the difficulty and save the reserve until the Government could realize upon the sale of its bonds.

"Mr. Morgan replied that he had no doubt bonds could be again sold on popular subscription at some price, but he could not say what the price would be; and to the second inquiry his answer was that, in his opinion, such an advance of gold as might be required could be accomplished if the gold could be kept in the country, but that there might be reluctance to make such an advance if it was to be immediately withdrawn for shipment abroad, leaving our financial condition substantially unimproved.

"After a little further discussion of the situation, he suddenly asked me why we did not buy $100,000,000 in gold at a fixed price and pay for it in bonds under Section 3700 of the Revised Statutes.

"This was a proposition entirely new to me. I turned to the Statutes and read the section he mentioned. Secretary Carlisle confirmed me in the opinion that this law abundantly authorized such a transaction, and agreed that it might be expedient if favorable terms could be made.

"The section of the Statute referred to reads as follows: 'Section 3700. The Secretary of the Treasury may purchase coin with any of the bonds or notes of the United States, authorized by law, at such rates and upon such terms as he may deem most advantageous to the public interest.'

"Mr. Morgan strongly urged that, if we proceeded under this law, the amount of gold purchased should not be less than $100,000,000; but he was at once informed that in no event would more bonds be then issued than would be sufficient to provide for adding to the reserve about $60,000,000, the amount necessary to raise the fund to $100,000,000. . . .

"The position of Mr. Morgan and other parties in interest whom he represented was such in the business world that they were abundantly able not only to furnish the gold we needed, but to protect us . . . against its immediate loss. Their willingness to undertake both these services was developed during the discussion of the plan proposed."

Mr. Morgan also announced that he and his associates would be glad to accept bonds bearing three per cent instead of four per cent if they were made payable in gold instead of in coin, but the power to authorize such a transaction lay wholly with Congress, and the House of Representatives had just declined to sanction such a change. Mr. Morgan then suggested that ten days be allowed in which to induce Congress to change its decision, as the government could thus save $16,000,000. But Mr. Cleveland knew that such a delay would avail nothing, and so, again to quote his words:

"After careful consideration of every detail until a late hour of the night, an agreement was made by which J. P. Morgan & Co., of New York, for themselves and for J. S. Morgan & Co., of London, August Belmont & Co., of New York, for themselves and for N. M. Rothschild & Sons, of London, were to sell and deliver to the Government 3,500,000 ounces of standard gold coin of the United States, to be paid for in bonds bearing annual interest at the rate of 4% per annum, and payable [in coin] at the pleasure of the Government after thirty years from their date, such bonds to be issued and delivered from time to time as the gold coin to be furnished was deposited by said parties in the Sub-Treasuries or other depositories of the United States.

"At least one half of the [gold] coin so delivered was to be obtained in Europe, and shipped from there in amounts not less than 300,000 ounces per month, at the expense and risk of the parties furnishing the same; and so far as was in their power they were to 'exert all financial influence and make all legitimate efforts to protect the Treasury of the United States against the withdrawals of gold pending the complete performance of the contract.'"

"The conference lasted some hours," writes John G. Milburn, "under conditions so tense as to be almost indescribable. I remember Mr. Morgan's describing how he held a large unlighted cigar in his hand, and at the end of the conference he found it was gone, having been unconsciously ground into powder under the excitement of the occasion."

But, despite this excitement, Mr. Morgan's outward appearance was quite calm, and Mr. Cleveland later commented upon his "quiet, masterly way of coming to the rescue."

The conference over, the President retired to prepare a message for the opening of the congressional session on the morrow, leaving to Secretary Carlisle, Attorney General Olney, and the bankers the task of reducing the agreement to writing.

The Morgan-Cleveland bond contract was a bold move; indeed it is doubtful whether a bolder could be found in our financial history, and the message sent to Congress the next day was not less bold. In barely one thousand words, Mr. Cleveland explained, not a plan, but an action. He informed Congress that, as they had failed to grant him the power needed to defend the public credit, he had acted "in pursuance of Section 3700 of the Revised Statutes" and concluded an agreement "with parties abundantly able to fulfill their undertaking."

Five days later the President wrote to his British Ambassador:

Executive Mansion, Washington.
*Feby. 13, 1895.*

My dear Mr. Bayard:

First of all I want to thank you, from the bottom of my heart, for several very kind and very comforting letters I have received from you. I have been dreadfully forlorn these many months and sorely perplexed and tried.

Think of it!! Not a man in the Senate with whom I can be on terms of absolute confidence. Our Wisconsin friend and former associate seems somehow to be cowed, and our Delaware friend has only spasmodic self-assertion and generally is in doubt as to the correctness of what I do or want to do. Not one of them comes to me on public business unless sent for and then full of reservations and doubt. We are very far apart in feeling and, it seems to me, in purposes. I am on the whole glad you are not among them. Your efforts to stem the tide would only hurt and grieve you. And yet I must not forget the opportunity you would have to add glory to your patriotic career and raise the hopes and inspire the faith of your Countrymen. I am sorry the malevolent change in our public life since you and I worked together here, has been made known to me. I am sure you cannot fully realize it.

I have at my side a Cabinet composed of pure-minded, patriotic and thoroughly loyal men. I sometimes feel guilty when I recall the troubles I have induced them to share with me. In our hand to hand conflict our triumphs are many but I am afraid as we triumph our party loses and the Country does not gain as it should; and yet what would the condition be without us?

You may be surprised to learn that in all the darkness I have never lost the feeling that the American people and I have a perfectly fair understanding.

I do not believe you will think me vain and foolish if I say to you that I ought to be and am profoundly grateful for a guidance which has thus far kept me from pitfalls. God knows I cannot bear mistakes now.

Our friends at the Capitol have blindly wandered into a close trap on the financial question. To-day the House Ways and Means Committee expect a bill for gold bonds, and the Senate is thrashing about in a way that is pitiable. In the meantime the administration is lightened from a heavy load by our last arrangement for the procurement of gold. I have not a doubt that we shall be free from anxiety on that score for a good long breathing spell.

That trouble over, another looms up. I do not see how I can make myself responsible for such a departure from our traditions as is involved in an appropriation in the Diplomatic bill, for building a cable by the Government to Hawaii. The Senate has thus amended the House bill. The House will stubbornly oppose and resist it and I hope it will be disposed of in conference and rejected. If it is not, another conflict will be forced upon me. I hear to-day that the claim is made that I have heretofore expressed myself favorably towards such a scheme. I suppose this claim is based upon references to the usefulness of telegraph communication between us and Hawaii in my annual messages of 1886 and 1888. Whatever inferences are attempted to be drawn from those expressions I do not believe we should in present circumstances boom the annexation craze by entering upon Government cable building.

I long for the 4th of March to come with no necessity in sight for a special session. We shall not need it for the purpose of making another effort to bridge or cure financial troubles.

I need not say to you that I shall be delighted at all times to hear from you. I am surprised to see how sensibly the English papers treat our situation as manifested by the clippings you sent me.

I trust you will be alert to discover any growing inclination in England to deal with the silver question internationally, and advise us if you see a propitious opening.

Mrs. Cleveland and the babies are well. God be praised for that! I often think that if things should go wrong in that end of the house, I should abandon the ship.

If she were not in bed and asleep, Mrs. Cleveland

would send her love to you and Mrs. Bayard. Mine
goes anyway.

Yours very sincerely,

GROVER CLEVELAND.

HON. T. F. BAYARD,
  U. S. Embassy,
    London, England.

As the opposition studied the situation created by the
Morgan contract and the President's message, it saw how
cleverly Mr. Cleveland had chosen his position. There
now appeared no hope of defeating his main purpose,
for the bonds had been sold and $65,116,244.62 had been
thereby secured for the gold reserve. But the presentation of a joint resolution, designed to make the new bonds
specifically payable in gold, and known to be of executive
origin, offered them a chance to present their views, and
to balk him of complete success. Attack upon this joint
resolution was rendered easier by the fact that Congress
had rejected a similar proposition a few hours before the
Morgan-Cleveland interview.

In describing the debate, the New York *Herald* correspondent wrote: "Mr. Bryan, of Nebraska, amused the
House by offering himself as a martyr to the cause of free
coinage and cheap dollars, declaring that he would willingly give up his life to secure the defeat of the pending
resolution." He declared that the President's suggestion
to make the bonds payable in gold was the first instance in
which a bribe had been offered to our people by foreign
money lenders. "They come to us," he said, "with the
insolent proposition, 'We will give you $16,000,000, pay-
ing a proportionate amount each year, if the United States
will change its financial policy to suit us.'"

In this opposition Mr. Bryan was joined not only by

silver Democrats, silver Republicans, and Populists, but also by some sound money men, who objected either to the terms of the Morgan-Belmont-Rothschild contract itself, or to the idea of such a contract, whatever its terms. When the vote came, therefore, it was a crushing defeat for the President's policy, 94 Democrats, 63 Republicans, and 10 Populists constituting the opposition in a vote of 167 to 120. In consequence, the bonds of the syndicate issue bore four per cent instead of three per cent interest; though the premium allowed under the contract made the interest, in effect, only three and three quarters per cent, and the United States paid $549,159 a year for thirty years, or a total of $16,474,770, as the price of William Jennings Bryan's first victory over Grover Cleveland.

After consultation together, the President and the Secretary of the Treasury decided not to insist upon the literal fulfilment of the Morgan promise, that "at least one half of the gold . . . be supplied from abroad"; "but the remainder of the contract," to quote Mr. Cleveland himself, was "so well carried out . . . that during its continuance the operation of 'the endless chain' . . . was interrupted. No gold was, during that period, taken from the Treasury to be used in the purchase of bonds, as had previously been the case, nor was any withdrawn for shipment abroad."

As soon as the bonds came into the possession of their purchasers, Morgan, Belmont, and the Rothschilds, the lack of confidence which had forced the United States Government to sell its second issue at a rate lower than its first disappeared. Indeed, the public, confident that the bonds were now secure of payment in gold, showed an astonishing eagerness to purchase them.

The original syndicate formed a second syndicate,

taking in certain other prominent banks, international bankers, and gold importers. This second syndicate took over the entire issue of bonds and, on February 20th, offered them for public sale, the bidding beginning in London and New York at the same hour. The scenes recall the one in Philadelphia, when shares of the first United States Bank were offered to the public by Secretary of the Treasury, Alexander Hamilton. Men crowded, cursed and struggled for a place in the line of those eager to pay 118½ for bonds which their indifference had forced their President to sell to the syndicate at 104½ only a few days before. Mr. Morgan personally supervised the bids at his office, and in twenty-two minutes gave the signal that the sale was over; but for hours thereafter men held their places in the hope that they might yet be able to purchase. In London a similar scene was enacted, Rothschild & Sons receiving fifteen times as many applications as they were able to fill. Thus the bankers, as a result of the confidence which their confidence had restored, reaped a full harvest.

These operations resulted, of course, in bitter denunciations of the President, who was assailed as the friend of robbers, enriching himself from the treasury of the nation over which he was called upon to rule, and opening its vaults to the sinister influence of the great unscrupulous banking concerns of the world. His enemies seized every item which could be distorted into a pretext for abuse. His friendship with Commodore Benedict, of the Chicago Gas Trust, was cited as a suspicious circumstance, and as wild tales spread throughout the land, Populism grew in the West in exact proportion as they were believed, Bryan's spiritual kinsfolk whispering the alarming rumor that Grover Cleveland was not a Democrat, but a Republican, a rich spoilsman dividing the spoil with the strong.

But the third issue of bonds could no more permanently save the financial situation than had the second, and soon the "endless chain" again began to work. In his third annual message (December 2, 1895), therefore, the President again pleaded with Congress for a law which would make the gold standard safe, but he pleaded in vain.

In his anxiety to find some way to restore public confidence, he suggested: "The only thorough and practicable remedy . . . is found in the retirement and cancellation of our United States notes, commonly called greenbacks, and the outstanding Treasury notes issued by the Government in payment of silver purchases under the [Sherman] Act of 1890. I believe this could be readily accomplished by the exchange of these notes for United States bonds, of small as well as large denominations, bearing a low rate of interest." He urged also that authority be "given to the Secretary of the Treasury to dispose of the bonds abroad for gold if necessary to complete the contemplated redemption and cancellation."

As the cancellation of so large an amount of currency would produce a dangerous financial stringency unless its place were immediately filled by some other kind of money, he suggested that "the currency withdrawn . . . might be supplied by such gold as would be used on their retirement or by an increase in the circulation of our national banks." And he added a suggestion, which shows how little he objected to silver dollars as currency or to the coining of the seigniorage under safe conditions: "I do not overlook the fact that the cancellation of the Treasury notes . . . would leave the Treasury in the actual ownership of sufficient silver, including seigniorage, to coin nearly $178,000,000 in standard dollars. It is worthy of consideration whether this might not from time to time be converted into dollars or fractional coin and slowly put into circulation."

The moment another bond issue was suggested, the campaign of misrepresentation and recrimination began again. Not satisfied with the vast proceeds of deals already made with the robber barons, his opponents declared, he is now planning again to open the people's treasury to their exploitation. At this critical moment the situation was suddenly rendered far more critical by the Venezuelan crisis. On December 17, 1895, President Cleveland's startling Venezuelan message went to Congress, and the menace of war accelerated the flight of gold.

In view of the situation thus complicated almost beyond precedent, the President urged Congress not to take a Christmas recess until they had done something to put the country upon a solid financial basis. But the hour for recess was at hand and, as Mr. Cleveland later scornfully commented, "it should not have been expected that members of Congress would permit troublesome thoughts of the Government's financial difficulties to disturb the pleasant anticipations of their holiday recess." Without giving the least heed to the President's plea, Congress dispersed for its brief Christmas recess, leaving him to cope with the situation as best he could.

But Wall Street, less eager for vacation, worked while Congress celebrated. On Monday, December 23d, Robert Bacon, of the firm of J. P. Morgan & Co., made a trip to Washington, accompanied by the President's late law partner, Francis Lynde Stetson, to be joined within a few hours by Mr. Morgan himself.

"During my visit," Mr. Morgan later explained,

". . . no negotiations for a loan were commenced or even suggested, nor was there then or since any agreement or request that I should take any steps preparatory to making a contract. The result of my visit was that I came to the following conclusions:

"First.—That the President and Secretary of the Treasury were determined to use every power at their command to restore and maintain the gold reserve.

"Second.—That no steps would be taken or even any preparatory negotiations commenced until it was ascertained what action, if any, Congress would be likely to take in response to the appeal of the President for adequate and improved means for making such restoration.

"Third.—That the Executive Department would prefer, if possible, to secure $200,000,000 of gold in order to avoid any probable necessity for similar negotiations before the meeting of the new Congress in 1897.

"Fourth.—That it was absolutely certain that no adequate relief could be obtained from Congress, and that no bill could be passed through the Senate for the improvement of the monetary system of the country.

"Upon my return, appreciating to the full the gravity of the situation, and keenly alive to the fact that early action was essential, and in order that I might be prepared, if called upon to act promptly, I took steps to ascertain to what extent it would be possible to secure the co-operation of capitalists, institutions, and others in forming a syndicate which would agree to sell to the United States Government $200,000,000 of gold coin.

"In my efforts, while far from sanguine as to the result, the ready acquiescence of James Stillman, Esq., President of the National City Bank, New York, Edward D. Adams, Esq., with full power representing the Deutsche Bank of Berlin, Germany; John A. Stewart,

Esq., President [of the] United States Trust Company, Pliny Fisk, Esq., of Messrs. Harvey Fisk & Sons, and others . . . encouraged me to proceed.

"The contract, as prepared and signed by the participants, did not stipulate whether the purchase should be by private contract or by public offer. The only proviso (in addition to the important one that no gold should be withdrawn from the Treasury) was that the minimum amount of the contract should be $100,000,000 and the maximum . . . not exceeding $200,000,000. . . . At the end of three or four days the total of $200,000,000 was reached, and I had in my hands full authority which would enable me, whenever and however the Executive might decide to act, to secure that amount of gold for the Treasury reserve in exchange for United States Bonds. . . .

"The formation of the syndicate being completed, I commenced negotiations for the permanent placing of a portion of the loan by public issue in Europe, should a contract with the Government be made."

News of Mr. Morgan's negotiations was soon abroad, and was wrongly interpreted by many of the papers of the country as evidence of a secret agreement between the President and Wall Street.

The New York *World* of January 3, 1896, under the heading, "Grover Cleveland's Golden Opportunity, Smash the Ring," declared: "This bargain has been made with a suspicious secrecy which has been guarded by a picket line of falsehoods put forth for the misleading of the people. It is a bargain between yourself in your official capacity and your near friends. It promises to give princely millions of the people's money to those friends, and that without any need. . . . You must see, Mr. Cleveland, that secrecy of negotiation under such cir-

cumstances is bound to excite suspicion. You must realize that men are already saying things which the newspapers as yet hesitate to print."

The editorial further announced the *World's* readiness to purchase one million of the bonds on a three per
cent basis, and ventured to assure the President that there
were thousands of others willing to take a similar course,
if given the opportunity. "Trust the People, Mr. Cleveland! Appeal to them! Smash the gold ring!" it urged.

This attitude of the *World,* far from helping matters,
made more difficult the task of accomplishing the purposes of the Government, and the next day Mr. Morgan
addressed to the President the following letter, which
shows how far the *World* was from a knowledge of the
facts:

New York, 219 Madison Avenue.
*January 4, 1896.*

To the President,
    Washington, D. C.
Sir:

It is with great hesitation that I venture to address
you in relation to the present financial situation.

As you are doubtless aware financial affairs are approaching a serious crisis, and the tension today is
extreme, and, whilst no outward evidences have developed, we are likely at any moment to reach the point,
and consequences, which it will then be too late to remedy.
The gravity of the situation must be my excuse.

The most important step at the moment is the restoration of Government credit, by placing the amount of
the gold reserve in the Treasury beyond question. This
once accomplished confidence both at home and abroad
in the stability of our currency will be restored.

After my recent visit to Washington I became convinced that any legislative action to improve the methods at the disposal of the Executive was unlikely, in fact impossible. I therefore took steps to ascertain whether it would be possible to obtain the coöperation of parties at home and abroad to an extent that would enable me to negotiate a contract with the Government for the sale of 11,500,000 ounces of gold approximating 200,000,000 of Dollars on about the basis of the contract of February 8th, 1895. In this effort I have been successful and am now in a position to make such a contract for the full amount.

I do not hesitate to affirm, in fact to urge, that such a contract would in every way be for the best interests of the Government and the people, and would be followed by less derangement of the money market, of trade, in fact of all interests, including foreign exchanges, which until recently were in such an increasingly prosperous condition, and I urge your serious consideration of such a contract.

At the same time I recognize the effect of legislation which has been proposed and the discussions thereupon in both houses of Congress, all of which might lead you to hesitate to make a private contract, and, consequently, in view of the gravity of the situation, I feel bound to say, that if after a conference, in which I can more fully lay the matter before you, and without expressing any confidence in such a mode of procedure in face of previous failures of similar attempts, but recognizing as I do that the responsibility of decision lies with you, I pledge to you every influence and effort in my power to assist the Government in its endeavor to make successful a negotiation by public advertisement which shall result in the sale to the Treasury of 11,500,000 ounces United States gold coin ($200,000,000), and further, I will so far as I possibly can, take such steps as will enable the Syndicate which I represent to join in making the negotiation successful to its full amount.

Awaiting the indication of your pleasure, I remain,

Respectfully yours,

J. PIERPONT MORGAN.

Meanwhile, the Christmas recess over, Congressmen and Senators returned to their seats, armed with copies of the *World's* attack upon the President, and there began a strange debate, a strife of words with a sensational newspaper article as the chief arsenal from which was drawn ammunition for both offense and defense. Senator Sherman declared that "while Congress has, perhaps too hastily, but with entire unanimity, supported the President in maintaining the interests and honor of our country in the field of diplomacy, it has not and will not approve his recommendations on the more important subject of our financial policy, and especially of our currency. It will not approve his secret bond syndicate contract." Senator Elkins, of West Virginia, introduced a resolution "directing the disposal of bonds by public sale to the highest bidder," his speech in defense of this insult being frankly based upon hearsay and newspaper history. Senator Hill, in defense of what he supposed to be the intentions of the administration, questioned whether the public would purchase the bonds if offered to them. "There have been assertions," he cried, "but assertions are not backed with proof. Let these people who want bonds come forward and say so. Where are they? The sole person to come forward so far is Mr. Pulitzer of the *World*. So far so good. Where are the persons to take the other $49,000,000 of a loan?" This defense was gravely answered by Senator Henry Cabot Lodge, who spoke *World* in hand, and without the thorough knowledge of the facts which the country was entitled to expect from this scholar-statesman.

After reading with astonishment the debates concerning his reputed intentions, Mr. Cleveland sent to Senator Caffery the following statement:

Executive Mansion, Washington.
*Jan. 5, 1896.*

My dear Senator:

I have read to-day in the Congressional Record the debate in the Senate on Friday concerning the financial situation and the bond issue. I am amazed at the intolerance that leads even excited partisanship to adopt as a basis of attack the unfounded accusations and assertions of a maliciously mendacious and sensational newspaper.

No banker or financier, nor any other human being, has been invited to Washington for the purpose of arranging in any way or manner for the disposition of bonds to meet the present or future needs of the gold reserve. No arrangement of any kind has been made for the disposition of such bonds to any syndicate or through the agency of any syndicate. No assurance of such a disposal of bonds has been directly or indirectly given to any person. In point of fact, a decided leaning toward a popular loan and advertising for bids has been plainly exhibited on the part of the administration at all times when the subject was under discussion.

Those charged with the responsibility of maintaining our gold reserve, so far as legislation renders it possible, have anxiously conferred with each other, and, as occasion permitted, with those having knowledge of financial affairs and present monetary conditions as to the best and most favorable means of selling bonds for gold. The unusual importance of a successful result, if the attempt is again made, ought to be apparent to every American citizen who bestows upon the subject a moment's patriotic thought.

The Secretary of the Treasury, from the first moment that a necessity for the sale of another issue of bonds seemed to be approaching, desired to offer them, if issued, to the people, by public advertisement, if they could thus be successfully disposed of. After full consideration he came to the conclusion, with which I fully agree, that the amount of gold in reserve, being now $20,000,000 more than it was in February last, when a sale of bonds was made to a syndicate, and other conditions differing from those then existing, justify us in offering the bonds now about to be issued for sale by popular subscription. This is the entire matter, and all these particulars could have been easily obtained by any member of the Senate by simply inquiring.

If Mr. Morgan, or anyone else, reasoning from his own standpoint, brought himself to the belief that the government would at length be constrained to again sell bonds to a syndicate, I suppose he would have a perfect right, if he chose, to take such steps as seemed to him prudent to put himself in condition to negotiate.

I expect an issue of bonds will be advertised for sale to-morrow, and that bids will be invited, not only for those now allowed by law, but for such other and different bonds as Congress may authorize during the pendency of the advertisement.

Not having had an opportunity to confer with you in person since the present session of Congress began, and noticing your participation in the debate of last Friday,

I have thought it not amiss to put you in possession of
the facts and information herein contained.

Yours very truly,

GROVER CLEVELAND.

That same day the New York *World* sent 10,370 telegrams to leading bankers of America, asking whether
they would buy if the loan were thrown open to popular
subscription, and 5,300 replies were received, ranging
in length from 300 to 600 words each. They filled three
full pages of the *World,* printed in the finest type. Some
answered yes, some answered no, but the question remained: Who will pay the highest price? And even the
New York *World* could not answer.

On January 6, 1896, Secretary Carlisle announced a
new thirty-year four per cent loan, not for $200,000,000
as Mr. Morgan expected, but for $100,000,000. This
made the syndicate contract available only to bid for all
or none, owing to the minimum therein set. Therefore
Mr. Morgan, "unwilling to make such a bid under present circumstances," as he told his associates, decided to
dissolve the syndicate. Feeling, however, that the knowledge of its existence would tend to make this popular
loan a success, he did not actually effect the dissolution
until January 14th, when, as he informed the bankers concerned, "the subscriptions by individuals and others, including many of the syndicate whom I have encouraged
to subscribe, from present indications, will insure the
complete success of the issue."

The test of public faith came, however, with the bidding. A month was allowed for the process, during
which 4635 bids were received from forty-seven states
and territories. As the advertisements had promised, the
bonds were awarded to the highest bidders, but only 827

proved higher than J. Pierpont Morgan and Co. To these accordingly was awarded $62,321,150 worth of bonds. The rest of the issue went to Mr. Morgan and his associates, not by the will of the President, but by the will of the people who had failed to display the faith in the nation's bonds which the bankers displayed. Nor were the gains of the bankers excessive, especially as, had the gold standard failed, their bonds would have been paid in silver, worth only fifty cents on the dollar. In subsequent hearings before a Congressional Committee, it was shown that they made five per cent upon their actual investment.

This transaction successfully ended one of the most remarkable experiments in the history of finance. Had the run on the Treasury continued one month longer, the possibility of gold payments would have ceased. On the last day of January, 1896, the gold reserve had dropped below $50,000,000. At the end of February it stood at $124,000,000. By a single issue of bonds $111,000,000 had been added to the gold reserve.

Thus, during that second term, which Senator Stewart, to the delight of his Populist friends, pronounced probably the worst that ever occurred in this or any other country, President Cleveland accomplished what he himself and most of his countrymen later considered his greatest service to the American people, and the credit belongs almost exclusively to him. Congress had refused help, the Democratic and Populist parties had withheld sympathy, and the Republicans had cynically avoided responsibility. But by an ingenious interpretation of executive power based upon laws which could not be repudiated, Mr. Cleveland had, within two years, added all told $293,000,000 of gold to the reserve fund by the creation of a debt of only $262,000,000.

The fourth bond issue was the last ever made in time of peace, for so thoroughly was the work accomplished that even the panic which swept over the country during the political crisis of the following summer could not again drag the gold reserve to the danger point. The endless chain was broken.

# CHAPTER IV

## THE WILSON-GORMAN TARIFF

*"A tariff for any other purpose than public revenue is public robbery."*

—GROVER CLEVELAND.

THOUGH forced by circumstances to fight the first great battle of his second administration in the interest of sound money, Mr. Cleveland had not for a moment lost sight of the fact that he had been restored to power upon the basis of a definite pledge to overthrow the McKinley tariff and substitute one built upon the opposite principle. The very platform upon which he had won his second term denounced protection as fraud, and the McKinley tariff as "the culminating atrocity of class legislation." That this tariff had brought not prosperity but hard times, the President, in his first annual message (December 4, 1893) attempted to prove, citing the estimates of the Secretary of the Treasury which forecast a deficit of $28,000,000.

The Republicans, on the other hand, pointed with pride to a surplus of over two and a quarter millions for the year ending June 30, 1893, and attributed the failing revenue and hard times to a general distrust of Democratic rule. They felt it wise also to await the results of the repeal of the Sherman Law before complicating the situation by "tinkering with the tariff." Their pleas for further delay, however, were discounted by the President as selfish attempts to continue the McKinley system of special favors, despite the recent verdict of the people, and in this same first annual message he squarely faced the new Congress with a statement of its duty:

"If there is anything in the theory of a representation in public places," he declared, ". . . if public officers are really the servants of the people . . . our failure to give the relief so long awaited will be sheer recreancy. Nothing should intervene to distract our attention or disturb our effort until this reform is accomplished."

Mr. Cleveland was confident that sufficient revenue could be collected under a tariff allowing free raw materials to American factories, and only the necessity of revenue justified the imposition of tariff duties, according to his economic creed. He argued that free raw materials would mean cheaper necessities, greater regularity of employment, a wider market, and a settled prosperity, thus enabling the people easily to supply the revenue needed for an economical administration of the government.

"Even if the oft disproven assertion could be made good that a lower rate of wages would result from free raw materials and low tariff duties," he said, "the intelligence of our workmen leads them quickly to discover that their steady employment, permitted by free raw materials, is the most important factor in their relation to tariff legislation." With his customary care for the strict fulfillment of all governmental obligations, by whomsoever incurred, he warned Congress against such a revision of the tariff as would suddenly endanger interests built upon faith that protection would remain, and begged that "unselfish counsel" and a "willingness to subordinate personal desires and ambitions to the general good" might prevail.

A tariff bill, designed to embody these ideas, and later famous as the Wilson Bill, had been already prepared, in consultation with the President, and was ready to be presented to Congress when the President's message of December 4th was read. It was not a free trade measure, but it was a step in that direction. Lumber, coal, iron, and wool were placed on the free list, and sugar, both raw and refined. The duty was cut down on woolens, linens, and cottons, in the shape of manufactured goods. This bill the President commended to the favorable attention of Congress, declaring that it dealt with the subject of tariff "consistently and as thoroughly as existing conditions permit." To the clause providing for "a small tax upon incomes derived from certain corporate investments," he had, however, given only a reluctant assent, as necessary to provide against temporary deficiencies.

Forty-nine days after the repeal of the Sherman Law, this bill was presented to the House of Representatives by William L. Wilson, chairman of the Ways and Means Committee, and, as he had expected, Mr. Cleveland found himself facing another major conflict. The free wool item alienated the farmers, as it materially reduced their profits from flocks of sheep. Free iron ore offended the mine owners. Free refined sugar was a blow at the sugar trust, to which the McKinley Bill gave a subsidy, and which desired to keep the duty upon refined sugar, while admitting raw sugar free. On the other hand, the growers clamored for a duty on raw sugar to protect their crops from the cheap products of foreign countries, and so, by placing both classes of sugar on the free list, the bill added both the sugar trust and the sugar growers to the enemies created by the income tax clause and other specific provisions.

As the discussion in the lower house proceeded, however, it became evident that even such a combination of opponents could not defeat the Wilson Bill. Richard Croker instructed the Tammany Congressmen to stand by the President's policy, and to fight aggressively for the bill. The President's more regular supporters urged upon their colleagues in Congress the expediency of keeping the party's pre-election pledges, and warned them of the inevitable consequences incident to their betrayal. On February 1, 1894, the House passed the Wilson Bill by a vote of 182 to 106, sixty-one Congressmen being absent or otherwise avoiding the record, and cheers from the Democratic side indicated the belief that victory for tariff reform was in sight.

But the Senate was yet to act, and Mr. Cleveland knew that there his plea for a "willingness to subordinate personal desires and ambitions to the general good" would fall upon many deaf ears. There, as the President had learned to his sorrow, the interests stood intrenched. There, the administration majority was in effect nonexistent, and there was little in the Wilson Bill likely to win supporters.

When the Populist Senators voted with the Democrats, they could together muster a majority of nine. When the Populist support went with the Republicans, the Democrats were left with a bare majority of three. But upon questions directly interesting the President, as did this, there were certain to be serious Democratic defections. The free silver Senators were still smarting under their defeat in the repeal of the Sherman Law. The spoilsmen hated him as the President who refused to "divide the spoils," and the Senators of special interests saw in him only a difficult person who could not appreciate their arguments.

What the President saw in the Senate is indicated by a story which went the rounds, doubtless invention but fairly representing his opinion: One night Mr. Cleveland was roused from a heavy sleep by his wife, who whispered, "Wake up, Mr. Cleveland, wake up, there are robbers in the house." "Oh, no, my dear," replied the President, turning heavily, "I think you are mistaken. There are no robbers in the House, but there are lots in the Senate."

To the Senate, indeed, the President's plea for unselfish counsel was like a whisper in the teeth of a north wind. Protection they understood; free trade they feared; but unselfish counsel they ridiculed. Louisiana Senators saw their duty through the sugar house; Maryland, West Virginia, Alabama, and Pennsylvania Senators looked at theirs from the mouth of the mine; Senator Hill felt that his line of greatest political usefulness was in the defeat of the income tax clause, which touched his constituency most closely; while his colleague, Senator Murphy, despite Tammany's instructions, indulged in an enthusiasm for high duties on collars and cuffs, the chief desire of the leading political manipulators of his senatorial district. Senators Gorman and Brice were open to conviction regarding the President's tariff bill; but conviction waited upon the assurance that the measure would be kind to certain interests which had been kind to them.

"The truth is," later declared the Republican Senator Cullom, "we were all—Democrats as well as Republicans —trying to get in amendments in the interest of protecting the industries of our respective states."

Thus did the United States Senate, whose glorious history had justified the claim that it was "the most august deliberative body in the world," approach the task of tariff revision, not to subordinate personal desires and ambitions to the general good, but to subordinate the general good to personal desires and ambitions. In a spirit of live and let live, each Senator was allowed his slice, and as a result the Wilson Bill lost its character so shamelessly as to become almost unrecognizable.

The President watched, with consternation, the process by which the Senate was writing "private" upon a public measure, designed to fulfill a public pledge.

"When I came here," he wrote to L. Clarke Davis on February 25th, "I knew perfectly well that there were schemes, ideas, policies, and men with which and with whom I should be obliged to do battle, and hard and trying battle. I thought the right must win and perhaps I relied too sentimentally upon the right to win. I thought the men who professed to be willing to fight with me were sincere and earnest.

"I still believe that right will win but I do not now believe that all the men who loudly proclaimed their desire for better things were in earnest.

"At any rate not a few of them are doing excellent service in the cause of the worst possible political methods and are aiding in bringing about the worst and most dangerous political situation."

When at last on July 3d, the Wilson Bill passed the Senate, by a vote of thirty-nine to thirty-four, with twelve Senators silent, it carried back to the House and to its indignant sponsors, 634 alterations, many of them fundamental in character. The free raw material idea, the very essence of the President's plan, had been well nigh annihilated. Coal, sugar, and iron ore had been removed from the free list, which wool, lumber, and copper were left to grace alone.

There followed the usual Committee of Conference which, however, failed to agree; and when, on July 19th, Mr. Wilson rose to report and repudiate that which he had proudly called his own, he presented to Congress a letter which the President had sent him just as he was entering the conference, and which he requested the clerk to read to the House. In it Mr. Cleveland boldly denounced the Senate amendments, the basis of the conference, as indicative of party perfidy and party dishonor. "Every true Democrat and every sincere tariff reformer," he declared, "knows that this bill in its present form and as it will be submitted to the conference, falls far short of the consummation for which we have long labored, and for which we have suffered defeat without discouragement." And he warned the conferees of the dangers which lay in the pathway of those guilty of "the abandonment of Democratic principles."

There can be no doubt that by this letter Mr. Cleveland designed to aid the defeat of the Senate's amendments. Although his whole political philosophy was opposed to executive interference in pending legislation, he felt that his party in the Senate had entered into a conspiracy to violate a promise, made to the people, and that it was his duty to thwart them, or at least to let the people know that he had not connived with them. His disclaimer was answered by Senators Gorman, Jones, and Vest, who insisted in open Senate that the President had approved the changes which the Senate had made in the bill.

In commenting on Senator Gorman's defense of the amendments, Mr. Dickinson wrote to the President on July 23d:

"My dear Mr. President:
"The Gorman defense will carry the hangers-on . . . but will not impress the strong men. . . . Summing it up, it is a clever confession that the Senate bill is a sacrifice of principle and a surrender of everything we fought for in 1892. He avoids [responsibility] by urging that a compromise was necessary to pass *any* bill; but the

country knows that, with the votes of his coterie, a bill in entire harmony with the platform would have met with the approval of the Senate months ago. A compromise was only necessary because *he* stood in the way, and *he* is the man who demanded the concessions which he deplores in his argument. His witnesses on the other point—that they did this thing because you approved it—remind one of Tony Weller's 'halibi.' Unspeakably weak, and unspeakably infamous is his appeal to the lawless and the unreflective on your action in the late labor troubles.

"Whatever the outcome at present, it remains that for the sake of your supporters and friends, for the cause you have led since 1884, for your own place in history, and for your own fame, it was absolutely necessary for you to make the record that you have made on the pending measure."

The outcome was far from satisfactory to Mr. Cleveland, however. The will of the Senate prevailed upon every disputed point, the House yielding after long and stubborn resistance.

As soon as the Wilson-Gorman Tariff Act, as it was now called, reached the President's desk, advice was offered him from every side. The soundness of the bill, its unspeakable unsoundness, and a hundred other contradictory points were urged, and as he gave no public indication of his intentions regarding it, human ingenuity was soon taxed to the utmost in an effort to show contempt. Among other insults, he received ninety-odd letters suggesting that he sign the tariff bill with the quill of a crow.

On August 23d Senator Palmer warned him:

"Your message of 1887 made Tariff reform the leading issue. . . . The present Tariff bill contains all that your true friends in Congress were able to obtain. . . . If you . . . conclude to veto the bill, they can defend you. . . . If you sign the bill, you thereby retain the leadership of the Democratic party. The party can defend you and itself by comparing the measure with the McKinley Bill. They can point to free wool, free lumber, and the large reductions upon the woolen, cotton and other schedules, and to the abolition of the sugar bounty. . . .

"If you allow the bill to become a law without your signature, you abdicate the leadership of the Democratic party on the issue that made you President. . . . The commander of an army and the leader of a party must alike share the fortunes of their followers. The present Tariff bill is a Democratic measure."

The President, however, did not agree with Mr. Palmer. The day before the expiration of the ten days allowed him by law for consideration of the bill, he sent to Congressman Catchings the following analysis of the problem as it appeared to him:

Executive Mansion, Washington,
*August 27th, 1894.*
Hon. T. C. Catchings,
My dear sir:—
Since the conversation I had with you and Mr. Clark of Alabama a few days ago, in regard to my action upon the tariff bill now before me, I have given the subject further and most serious consideration. The result is I am more settled than ever in the determination to allow the bill to become a law without my signature.
When the formulation of legislation which it was hoped would embody Democratic ideas of tariff reform

was lately entered upon by Congress, nothing was further from my anticipation than a result which I could not promptly and enthusiastically endorse.

It is therefore with a feeling of the utmost disappointment that I submit to a denial of this privilege.

I do not claim to be better than the masses of my party, nor do I wish to avoid any responsibility which, on account of the passage of this law, I ought to bear as a member of the Democratic organization. Neither will I permit myself to be separated from my party to such an extent as might be implied by my veto of tariff legislation, which though disappointing, is still chargeable to Democratic effort. But there are provisions in this bill which are not in line with honest tariff reform, and it contains inconsistencies and crudities which ought not to appear in tariff laws or laws of any kind.

Besides, there were, as you and I well know, incidents accompanying the passage of the bill through the Congress, which made every sincere tariff reformer unhappy, while influences surrounded it in its latter stages and interfered with its final construction, which ought not to be recognized or tolerated in Democratic tariff reform counsels.

And yet, notwithstanding all its vicissitudes and all the bad treatment it received at the hands of pretended friends, it presents a vast improvement to existing conditions. It will certainly lighten many tariff burdens that now rest heavily upon the people. It is not only a barrier against the return of mad protection, but it furnishes a vantage ground from which must be waged further aggressive operations against protected monopoly and governmental favoritism.

I take my place with the rank and file of the Democratic party who believe in tariff reform and who know what it is, who refuse to accept the results embodied in this bill as the close of the war, who are not blinded to the fact that the livery of Democratic tariff reform has been stolen and worn in the service of Republican protection, and who have marked the places where the deadly blight of treason has blasted the counsels of the brave in their hour of might.

The trusts and combinations—the communism of pelf —whose machinations have prevented us from reaching the success we deserved, should not be forgotten nor forgiven. We shall recover from our astonishment at their exhibition of power, and if then the question is forced upon us whether they shall submit to the free legislative will of the people's representatives, or shall dictate the laws which the people must obey, we will accept and settle that issue as one involving the integrity and safety of American institutions.

I love the principles of true Democracy because they are founded in patriotism and upon justice and fairness toward all interests. I am proud of my party organization because it is conservatively sturdy and persistent in the enforcement of its principles. Therefore I do not despair of the efforts made by the House of Representatives to supplement the bill already passed by further legislation, and to have engrafted upon it such modifications as will more nearly meet Democratic hopes and aspirations.

I cannot be mistaken as to the necessity of free raw materials as the foundation of logical and sensible tariff reform. The extent to which this is recognized in the legislation already secured is one of its encouraging and redeeming features; but it is vexatious to recall that while free coal and iron ore have been denied us, a recent letter of the Secretary of the Treasury discloses the fact that both might have been made free by the annual surrender of only about seven hundred thousand dollars of unnecessary revenue.

I am sure that there is a common habit of underestimating the importance of free raw materials in tariff legislation, and of regarding them as only related to concessions to be made to our manufacturers. The truth is, their influence is so far-reaching that if disregarded, a complete and beneficent scheme of tariff reform cannot be successfully inaugurated.

When we give to our manufacturers free raw materials we unshackle American enterprise and ingenuity, and these will open the doors of foreign markets to the reception of our wares and give opportunity for the continuous and remunerative employment of American labor.

With materials cheapened by their freedom from tariff charges, the cost of their product must be correspondingly cheapened. Thereupon justice and fairness to the consumer would demand that the manufacturers be obliged to submit to such a readjustment and modification of the tariff upon their finished goods as would secure to the people the benefit of the reduced cost of their manufacture, and shield the consumer against the exaction of inordinate profits.

It will thus be seen that free raw materials and a just and fearless regulation and reduction of the tariff to meet the changed conditions, would carry to every humble home in the land the blessings of increased comfort and cheaper living.

The millions of our countrymen who have fought bravely and well for tariff reform should be exhorted to continue the struggle, boldly challenging to open warfare and constantly guarding against treachery and half-heartedness in their camp.

Tariff reform will not be settled until it is honestly and fairly settled in the interest and to the benefit of a patient and long suffering people.

Yours very truly,

GROVER CLEVELAND.

Within twenty-four hours after this letter was written, the Wilson-Gorman Bill became a law (August 28, 1894), but without the signature of Grover Cleveland.

Writing in commendation of the President's stand in this matter, Wayne MacVeagh, formerly a member of the Garfield-Arthur Cabinet, and a frequent critic of Mr. Cleveland, said:

*Personal* Embassy of the United States, Rome.

*September 10, 1894.*

My dear Sir:

I have just received your letter to Mr. Catchings by today's mail and I must at once thank you *for every word of it.*

I sometimes wonder if you have any true conception of the services you have been enabled to render to your country. You have made, no doubt, many mistakes—some perhaps grievous ones. You know how I regretted the "Higgins" appointment in your former term, and how I regretted your decision not to call the extra session as soon as you were inaugurated this last time and postpone as far as possible all questions of office until the tariff was revised and the Sherman bill repealed. No doubt I failed to see the arguments on the other side in both instances and I only recall these differences of opinion now as evidence that I have not been in the habit of giving indiscriminate approval to whatever you did.

But I do wish you to appreciate, to some extent at

least, what you have done for the country as a whole in the last eighteen months—in spite of wholly unequaled and wholly undeserved opposition in your own party—and what is far more weighty to my mind, in spite of the inevitable opposition your ideas and standards of public duty encounter in the Senate without regard to party. There many men of *both* parties have persuaded themselves that they are at liberty to serve themselves before their party, and their party before their country—while you reverse this order. Then a good many Democrats in the Senate—a great many indeed—had had their pride as "practical politicians" sorely wounded by your renomination and re-election against their well-known predictions and wishes.

Yet what have you not accomplished? You have put the nation's foreign affairs upon the sound basis of respect for the rights of others while exacting from others respect for our own—and criticism on that subject has absolutely disappeared.

You have made every dollar circulating in the United States as good as a gold dollar and, whoever may "fret or fume," that great work will never be undone.

You suppressed at almost no cost of blood and not much in money, a hideous outbreak of lawlessness which threatened to unsettle men's minds as to the respect due to law. Consider the value of that precedent alone in the immediate future.

And now for the first time in an entire generation—since 1861—you have turned a revision of the tariff away from higher to lower duties. For the first time in that long period trade is to be freer and the people's burdens less heavy.

And to crown all, you have written this last letter—*the bravest and best thing it seems to me you have yet done.* Those who were willing to misrepresent, were able to distort the plain meaning of your allusions to the sugar schedule in the letter to Mr. Wilson—but these last words are incapable of such abuse.

And then it summons both the party and the country to continue the inevitable struggle for still greater commercial freedom and still fewer and less heavy taxes to be levied by the protected interests upon their less favored fellow citizens. In the long run—nay, even in a short run—*free wool means all raw materials free.*

I know what discouragements you have encountered and how dark and hopeless the path before you must often have seemed; but if ever man did, you have served your country not only well but *effectively* since March 4, 1893.

Don't on any account answer this—get all the rest you can.

Sincerely yours,

WAYNE MACVEAGH.

To
HON. GROVER CLEVELAND.

A few weeks later Mr. Carnegie wrote:

New York, N. Y.,
5 West 51st St.,
*December 14, 1894.*

To HIS EXCELLENCY,
THE PRESIDENT of the
UNITED STATES.
Dear Sir:

I venture to address you, because a letter to the highest official will attract most attention, and also because of my respect for you personally.

There is great trouble in regard to the national

finances owing to a serious falling off in the Government's revenues. Permit me to lay a suggestion before you, which has nothing whatever to do with Free Trade or Protection, and is not in any possible sense a party question since neither party has ever acted upon the policy I am now about to suggest.

In 1892 the tariff duties were collected from foreign imports of the luxuries of the rich as follows:

| | |
|---|---|
| Wool manufactures | $34,293,609 |
| Silk manufactures | 16,965,637 |
| Cotton manufactures | 16,436,733 |
| Flax manufactures | 10,066,636 |
| Glass and china manufactures | 10,339,000 |
| Wines, liquors, etc. | 8,935,000 |
| Tobacco, cigars | 11,882,557 |

Here are $108,000,000 of revenues from seven classes of luxuries; and here are a few others which netted over six millions more—jewelry, artificial flowers, clocks, brushes, paper, perfumeries, musical instruments, making 114 millions, or two thirds of the total collected from imports—174 millions.

Now Mr. President, you have only to enquire to find that the masses of the people use none of these articles to speak of. As far as silk and woolen cloths are concerned, the home manufacturer supplies the masses. In regard to linens, common grade tablecloths are imported, but even in regard to these the poorer classes use cotton tablecloths of domestic manufacture.

Under the present tariff law these articles have been greatly reduced, and the main work of the Wilson Bill is this reduction of the luxuries of the rich, which yield two thirds of all the revenue collected. That the originators of the present tariff intended any such result, is not to be believed. The movement against the tariff, begun

by you, was to meet the question of a surplus when reductions were required to limit the exactions of revenue
from the people to the actual wants of the Government.

When the "condition and not the theory which confronts you" has changed, the statesman who regarded the
condition and not the theory, may be expected to leave the
theory to-day and deal with the new conditions. Such
would be consistency in the highest sense, although genius
cares little for consistency and is only concerned to do
what is best at the time.

My suggestion therefore is that a short bill be passed
increasing for two years the duties upon these articles de
luxe, used only by the extravagant few, at least 50 per cent.
I should go even beyond this, but this increase would
yield, say fifty millions of additional revenue, and not one
workingman or his family, nor a man upon a small salary
would be affected to the extent of one dollar.

It is a mistake to suppose that foreign imported
articles, which are really articles de luxe used by the rich,
can be either greatly diminished or greatly increased by a
change in duties, because cost is not the first consideration
with the purchasers, taste, fashion, being potent. But to
guard against the belief that these imported articles were
used to any extent by the masses, the proposed additional
duty should be placed upon cloths of certain grades and
value. This would allow the masses to use these articles
upon as favorable terms as now, but believe me Sir, they
do not use imported articles at all.

You no doubt have it within your power to ascertain
whether this be true or not, may I beg you so to ascertain.
I believe you will agree with me that if this be true, you
have here the best remedy possible, and the easiest to
carry, for our present trouble.

This is neither free Trade nor Protection, neither party has ever treated these luxuries simply from a revenue point of view, the Republican bills have been protective, and the Democratic bills in the direction of lower duties. This is neither, but simply the best means of raising more revenue, and I submit for your consideration that if this can be raised upon the extravagances of the pleasure-loving luxurious-living few, and it is for the best interests of the masses of the people that this should be done. The Income Tax could readily be abandoned, and yet the increased duties proposed would come as exclusively as the Income Tax will from the few having more than four-thousand dollars income per annum, and require no increase of officials or entail additional cost; besides these duties would yield double any estimate made of the Income Tax revenue.

It is a new policy Mr. President, and I cannot but think one worthy of you, and one which requires just such a man to propose and establish. I am Mr. President, with great respect

Very sincerely yours,

ANDREW CARNEGIE.

HIS EXCELLENCY, GROVER CLEVELAND, PRESIDENT.

Executive Mansion,

Washington, D. C.

P. S.

People generally do not quite understand to what extent foreign textile articles are for the rich only. Take wool, for instance: In 1890 the value of the home manufactured article was $338,000,000. The high-priced foreign fine woolens were imported to the value of only $35,500,000, their value per yard being much greater than that of the ordinary qualities produced at home; the number of yards probably was not beyond six or seven per cent of the total consumption. We have a similar result with cotton: The value of the home-manufactured product in 1890 was $268,000,000, and the total amount imported was valued at only $28,000,000. Even in regard to silks imported, the manufactured product of American mills in 1890 was valued at $69,000,000, the total imported silk manufactures $31,000,000 only. These are also of much higher value per yard than the home product. Since 1890 the silk manufacturers of America have gained greatly, and are constantly filling the home demands more completely.

If the foreign woolens, silks, and linens were classified as to fineness and value, it would be seen that goods of common grades, such as the people generally use, were no longer imported to any considerable extent, nor can they be under the present bill.

By limiting the bill to two years and confining the increased duties to the higher qualities, it could not be said that the measure was framed in the interests of the home manufacturer, because the finer qualities could not be successfully produced to any great extent in the short space of two years, and manufacturers would not invest capital for the necessary special machinery, etc.

The increased revenues thus obtainable with the decrease in pensions, and the natural increase of revenues from increase of wealth and population would give the last year of the Administration a splendid record, and the President would pass into history as a Statesman who met an emergency by a heroic and original measure. At the same time, its close would be graced by a reduction of duties by the expiration of the temporary act.

The Republican party, of course, could be relied upon

to favor this measure, and surely a sufficient number of
the Democratic party would see its wisdom.

A. C.

Disappointed as they were in the final form of their
tariff bill, the Democrats were somewhat comforted by the
presence of the income tax clause, but their satisfaction
was of short duration, for Senator Hill of New York
promptly attacked the constitutionality of the latter, denouncing it as a direct tax not based on population, and
quite beyond the power of the Federal Government. He
denounced it also as continuing in a period of peace
measures which had been accepted by the people only as
a stern war necessity.

In 1861 a three per cent tax had been imposed on
incomes over eight hundred dollars. In 1862 the rate had
been increased to five per cent on incomes between six
hundred and five thousand dollars, and to seven and a
half per cent on incomes between five thousand and ten
thousand dollars. Incomes over ten thousand a year had
been taxed ten per cent. In 1864 another change was
made, providing for the taxing at five per cent of all
incomes between six hundred and five thousand dollars,
all over five thousand being called upon to pay ten per
cent. But these war taxes had expired in 1872, and
Senator Hill protested against their re-enactment in time
of peace. He also denounced the exemption of four thousand dollars as making the measure class legislation and
therefore contrary to the spirit of free government. He
pointed out indignantly that it was unjust and sectional
in its provisions, bearing more heavily upon the East
than upon the West and South. Despite protests, however, the Treasury sent out blanks and got ready for the
collection of the tax, while its opponents selected cases

which were sent to the Supreme Court, in order that the question of constitutionality might be judicially determined.

Pending a decision, Mr. Cleveland, while by no means an enthusiastic supporter of the income tax, prepared to meet the requirements of the law in his own case. "The President," reported a Washington dispatch, "has filed his income tax returns and has included his salary, although the law expressly stipulates that no act of Congress shall increase or decrease the compensation of the President of the United States during his term of office, and the income tax certainly does decrease his salary to the extent of $920 a year. There would be no question concerning its application to the salary of his successor in office, but he seems to have desired to set a good example to the people by construing a doubtful question in the law against himself and in favor of the government." He was, however, not called upon to pay the $920, as by a decision of the Supreme Court on May 20th, the income tax clause of the Wilson-Gorman bill was declared unconstitutional.

This opinion was the more remarkable in view of the fact that fifteen years earlier the Supreme Court had rendered the opposite decision by unanimous consent. It now reversed that decision by the narrow majority of one vote, Associate-Justices Harlan, Brown, Jackson, and White voting to uphold the law, Associate-Justices Brewer, Field, Gray, Shiras, and Chief Justice Fuller voting to declare it unconstitutional.

As a sequel to the defeat of Mr. Cleveland's efforts to keep faith with the people over tariff reform, we find two incidents showing his breadth of vision and unusual magnanimity of spirit. When the Wilson Bill left the House, sugar, both raw and refined, was upon the free list. In the Senate, however, the sugar Senators secured protective rates satisfactory to the Trust, and the question had been not inappropriately raised as to how this protection of an industry certainly in no sense "infant" was secured. Recriminations followed, and an investigation.

The investigating committee, composed of two Democratic Senators, two Republican Senators, and one Populist, unearthed scandal enough to justify even the most radical preachers against the trust evil. Henry O. Havemeyer, President of the Sugar Trust, admitted on the stand that the Trust regularly contributed to the campaign chest of the party most likely to serve their interests in any particular state, and concealed these under the head of "expenses" on their books. He also admitted that sugar lobbyists had been kept in Washington when the Wilson Bill was pending, to influence the people's representatives in the interest of sugar. Senator Quay defiantly admitted that while deliberating on the tariff on sugar, he had been buying and selling sugar stock, and boldly proclaimed his intention to continue to do so.

The Committee's report, signed by every member, deprecated the "pressure to which Congress and its members are subjected by the representatives of great industrial combinations whose enormous wealth tends to suggest undue influence."

Had there been anything vindictive in the President's nature, he would have been disposed to interpret every subsequent case in a manner unfavorable to these sugar barons. Instead, he was as scrupulously fair in interpreting the law when touching them as he was with reference to any other citizen, as is shown by the following letter to Attorney-General Harmon:

Gray Gables,
Buzzard's Bay, Mass.
*July 31, 1895.*

My dear Mr. Attorney General

. . . I am a good deal annoyed by the situation of the sugar bounty question and Comptroller Bowler's position in relation to it.

I have always expressed the opinion that in view of the fact that the McKinley law provided that the bounty should be paid for a certain number of years—in so many words or in effect—that sugar producers had more than an ordinary right to rely upon the payment of the bounty during that time. Having relied upon the permanency, of the bounty to the extent provided by the limit fixed in the law, it has always seemed to me that when the bounty was swept away in the midst of the producing season and after expense had been incurred on the faith of the promised bounty, equity and justice dictated some reimbursement of the loss sustained by reliance upon the promise of the Government. I don't call this a bounty but a *reimbursement*. I hold the belief that the money appropriated by way of such indemnification should be paid, and I am very earnest in this belief and I think I am perfectly consistent in claiming at the same time to be one of the strongest opponents of bounties in the Country.

I have no idea that there is any constitutional objection in the way of the Government's doing a thing so clearly in the line of equity and good conscience, as is this indemnification to the sugar producers who have incurred expense they would not have incurred except for the Government's invitation.

I thought the question all out before approving the appropriation; and while I esteem Mr. Bowler as an excellent and careful officer, I do not think that in this case

he is called on to override the Congress and the President
on a question so entirely judicial as the constitutionality
of this provision.

Even if he should think it his duty to take up the judicial question of constitutionality, I am by no means certain that he would find in the decision of the District
Court of Appeals justification for deciding against the
appropriation. Before he assumes such a responsibility
(if in any case he should assume it) he should have, it
seems to me, the judgment of the highest court upon the
exact point. He certainly has not the former and I do
not believe the judgment of the Court of Appeals covers
the phase of the bounty question now presented.

I cannot but feel the greatest anxiety on this subject;
for I have been an openly avowed advocate of this measure of restitution; and until I get new light, shall continue
my efforts to bring it about whoever withstands.

I am not at all adverse to Mr. Bowler's knowing my
views.

                    Yours sincerely,
                            GROVER CLEVELAND.

HON. JUDSON HARMON,
    Attorney General,
        Washington.

Even more surprising was his selection, in the heat of
the sugar conflict, of one of his strongest opponents,
Senator White, of Louisiana, to a vacant place upon the
Supreme Bench. That vacancy, caused by the death of
Associate Justice Samuel Blatchford, had already
brought the President much trouble, and not a little
humiliation. Soon after Mr. Blatchford's death, Mr.
Cleveland had nominated William B. Hornblower, of
New York, a man admirably equipped for the post, but

unfortunately possessed of powerful political enemies, chief among whom was the New York Senator, David B. Hill.

Hill had not forgotten that Hornblower had been one of the committee of nine, appointed by the Association of the Bar of the City of New York to investigate the conduct of Isaac H. Maynard, attorney and counsel for the Board of State Canvassers, and accused of illegal action in the senatorial count of 1891. At that time, Maynard had been Deputy Attorney General of New York State, acting under the general direction of Governor Hill. The committee had reported that Maynard had committed one of the gravest offenses known to the law, that of falsifying election returns, and had recommended, by unanimous consent of its nine members, Frederic R. Coudert, James C. Carter, John E. Parsons, Clifford A. Hand, Edmund Randolph Robinson, John L. Cadwalader, William B. Hornblower, Elihu Root, and Albert Stickney, that: "A copy of this report be transmitted to the Senate and Assembly, and that those bodies be respectfully requested to consider whether the conduct of Judge Isaac H. Maynard therein mentioned does not demand an exercise of the power to remove judges vested by the Constitution in the Legislature." Hill's resentment against the committee was great, and against Hornblower it was especially bitter, as the latter had been appointed on the committee at the suggestion of Judge Maynard's counsel, and was therefore, according to Hill, Maynard's representative. His acquiescence in the verdict Hill therefore regarded as treason.

When Mr. Hornblower's nomination to the Supreme Bench came before the Judiciary Committee of the United States Senate, Hill, now a Senator from New York and a member of the committee, marked it for slaughter. He managed to delay action until the end of the extra session during which the President had made the nomination, and let it be understood that he would fight it if presented during the regular session. Conscious of Mr. Hill's powerful opposition, and unwilling to embarrass the administration, Mr. Hornblower made known his willingness to withdraw his name. Mr. Cleveland's reply was characteristic: "Tell Hornblower that his name will go into the Senate the first day of the regular session of Congress and will stay there until confirmed."

Confirmation, however, proved impossible. The Judiciary Committee reported the nomination to the Senate, where it met determined opposition. Some of the Senators resented the fact that Mr. Hornblower had been nominated without previous consultation with the Judiciary Committee; some felt that well established custom had been slighted by the President's failure to discuss the question with the Senators from New York before presenting a New York man for so important a position; some were eager to express their antagonism against Mr. Cleveland in order to show their loyalty to the Silverites. Others, but not enough, echoed the statement of Senator Morgan: "I hate the ground that man [Cleveland] walks on, but I do not believe in turning down a good man for the Supreme Court for the purpose of rebuking Cleveland." When at last the vote was taken, Mr. Hornblower failed to secure the majority necessary for confirmation.

After the defeat of Mr. Hornblower, the President nominated Judge Wheeler H. Peckham, against whom also Senator Hill turned his poisoned arrows. In his eagerness to secure Peckham's confirmation, Mr. Cleveland sent the following appeal to Joseph H. Choate, recognized leader of the New York bar:

Executive Mansion, Washington.
*January 27, 1894.*

My dear Mr. Choate,

You can do what I deem to be a great service to the Country and add very much to the prospect of a high honor coming to the Bar of New York if you will immediately write a letter to Senator Hoar representing to him the good things you know concerning Wheeler H. Peckham's fitness for a place on the bench of the Supreme Court.

You can hardly conceive what little and mean things have been and will be resorted to in an effort to defeat him. One pretext is that he has an infernally bad temper, and there is an inclination in certain quarters to hide behind this pretext. I suppose, of course, there is nothing in this allegation. If I am right in this supposition I wish you would negative the charges and speak of Mr. P's ability in such a way as your knowledge of the man justifies.

Let me suggest that it would be very well indeed if you could convey to Senator Hoar, or have presented to him, Mr. Evarts' good opinion of Mr. Peckham, as well as your own. I wish Mr. Carter would also write.

I desire Mr. Peckham's confirmation,

    1st  On account of his merits and fitness, and

    2nd  Because I want the appointee to come from the New York Bar *and I have no names in reserve which represent it.*

    Yours very sincerely,

        GROVER CLEVELAND.

JOSEPH H. CHOATE, ESQ.,
  New York City.

But nothing could save Mr. Peckham, in view of the curse, called senatorial courtesy, which "Dave" Hill wielded against him, and in view of the number of Mr. Cleveland's own senatorial enemies. The President next urged Mr. Frederic R. Coudert to allow his name to be sent in, but the latter declined on the grounds of personal obligations to clients. Thus, long before the conflict over the Wilson Bill was ended, the opposition Senators boasted that President Cleveland could nominate no man whom the Senate would confirm as Associate Justice. A mocking phrase to that effect, by Senator Chandler of New Hampshire, coming to Mr. Cleveland's ears when the debate upon the sugar sections of the Wilson Bill was at its hottest, the latter remarked: "I'll name a man to-morrow whom the Senate will unanimously confirm, and for whom that pestiferous wasp will himself be compelled to vote."

To those who watched the sugar debate in the Senate, few names would have seemed less likely to be thus employed than that of Edward Douglas White, Senator from Louisiana. Mr. White was a member of the Gorman-Brice alliance, and through it was seeking to restore duties upon sugar, iron ore, coal, and other raw materials which the House had put on the free list. His standing before the country, however, was not shaken by his activities in the interest of his constituency, and it would have been hard to find a representative man in any party ready to credit against him the charge, so effective against others, of being "Senator from Havemeyer."

Although, of course, conscious of the high regard in which he was held, Senator White did not suspect that the President, whose cherished plans he was so effectively opposing, was considering him in connection with the much-discussed vacant Associate-Justiceship. Indeed it is said that when he received a request to call at the White House he remarked to a friend that this would probably

be his last call upon President Cleveland. To his astonishment, instead of reproaches for his anti-administration
activities, he was offered the vacant seat on the Supreme
Bench, and at once accepted. The Senate unanimously
confirmed the appointment, on February 19, 1894, without even the formality of a reference to a committee, and
America witnessed the remarkable sight of a soldier of
the lost cause, a man who had raised his hand against the
Stars and Stripes, first sitting with the Court in whose
hands lies the interpretation of the Constitution, and later
presiding over it as the universally loved, honored, and
trusted Chief Justice.

It is characteristic of Mr. Cleveland that when,
eighteen months later, Mr. Justice Jackson died, he again
contemplated a trial of strength with the Senate by the
nomination of Mr. Hornblower, but the following letter
rendered such a course impossible:

875 Madison Avenue, New York.

*Nov. 9/ 95.*

Dear Mr. President,

I observe that the newspapers are again mentioning
my name as a possible nominee to succeed Mr. Justice
Jackson. I have been meaning for some time past to
write you, asking you to leave me out of the question, as
I have definitely made up my mind that in justice to my
family I ought not to make the pecuniary sacrifice involved in giving up my professional income for a judicial
salary, and that I should therefore feel constrained to
decline a nomination, if tendered me, even if confirmation by the Senate were certain to follow and without protracted delay.

I have hesitated to write, however, lest I should seem

to assume—as of course I had no reason to assume—that you were considering the possibility of my nomination.

When you named me two years ago to succeed Mr. Justice Blatchford, I allowed the high honor of the appointment and the congeniality of judicial work to outweigh the consideration of pecuniary sacrifice; but further reflection has led me to look upon the matter differently.

With best regards, I remain,

Yrs very sincerely,

WM. B. HORNBLOWER.

To the
HON. GROVER CLEVELAND,
Pres. of the U. S.

The President then turned again to Mr. Coudert, who again refusing, he named Rufus W. Peckham, brother of Wheeler H. Peckham and, in order to forestall hostile action on the part of Senator Hill, sent the following letter:

Executive Mansion, Washington.
*Nov. 18, 1895.*

My dear Senator:

Secretary Lamont has shown me your letter to him, and I appreciate your willingness to come to Washington to confer with me if thought desirable. There is only one matter which I desired to talk with you about that I think, to save you the trip here, and especially in view of your expected absence from the opening of Congress, I ought to write you about. All other things will as you say "keep" until you arrive here.

I have been a good deal bothered about a nomination to the U. S. Supreme Court—not because I have had much personal doubt as to the best selection under all the circumstances, but on account of other considerations outside of absolute fitness.

Of course I want to nominate a New Yorker; and my mind has been constantly drawn to Judge Peckham as the best choice. It seemed to me a short time ago that I ought to know whether or not he would accept the plan, and I wrote to him asking the question. After some reflection he replied in the affirmative. So you see I am committed to the nomination. I think the place should be filled by a confirmed nominee as early as practicable and I want to send in the name as soon as the Senate meets.

I suppose in your absence and with a lack of knowledge on the part of the Committee as to your feeling in the matter, it might and would be laid over until your arrival.

Have you any desire as to the time of sending in the nomination?

I think the court needs him and I would be glad to have him qualified very early if you could find it consistent and agreeable to pave the way for it in your absence.

I need hardly say to you that this is entirely confidential except as you may see fit to confer with Judge Peckham himself.

Yours very truly,<br>GROVER CLEVELAND.

HON. DAVID B. HILL,
Albany, N. Y.

This time Senator Hill proved amenable, possibly owing to the fact that another presidential year was at hand, with Grover Cleveland at last out of the running. The opposition was called off, and Mr. Peckham was confirmed.

# CHAPTER V

## THE PULLMAN STRIKE OF 1894

*"The real interests of labor are not promoted by a resort to threats and violent manifestations."*
—GROVER CLEVELAND.

IF some ingenious mind could invent a process by which labor would instantly recognize its friends, the problems of the world would be immeasurably simplified. No President was ever more vilified by labor than was Grover Cleveland, and yet, in view of his public acts and private papers, it is fair to say that no President ever sympathized more sincerely with its every just and honorable ambition. On the other hand, no President ever saw more clearly the duties and obligations which belong to labor, and the supreme necessity, in the interest of capital and labor alike, of maintaining law and order as the only basis of society.

To reconcile opposing positions, not to take sides with one or the other of opposing factions, he felt to be the line of promise in labor disputes. He therefore refused to become the partisan of labor in order to conciliate the labor vote, and was equally careful not to allow himself to be branded with the mark of capital. In this way he stood free to act for the nation when these two contended, and, in consequence, he was especially loved by neither. To-day, however, as we review his career from the vantage point of a generation freed from the passions engendered by his many conflicts, it is clear that his paramount sympathy was for those who depend upon their physical labor for the necessities of life, and that, while fully conceding and loyally defending the legal rights of capital, he felt himself, in a more special sense, the champion of the majority. "The capitalist can protect himself," he often declared, "but the wage earner is practically defenseless."

That reconciliation was necessary between these two genii of the lantern, he attributed more to the sins of capital than to the sins of labor, although he saw with clear eyes the many sins of both. Communism, he said, is "a hateful thing and a menace to peace and organized government"; but he added, "The Communism of combined wealth and capital, the outgrowth of overweening cupidity and selfishness which assiduously undermines the justice and integrity of free institutions, is not less dangerous than the Communism of oppressed poverty and toil which, exasperated by injustice and discontent, attacks with wild disorder the citadel of misrule."

He eagerly welcomed every suggestion which offered a prospect of bridging the chasm between employer and employee; and one of the reasons for his great admiration for Andrew Carnegie was that the steel magnate showed a zeal equal to his own in the search for the germ of reconciliation.

In acknowledging an autograph copy of Mr. Carnegie's volume, *The Gospel of Wealth,* Mr. Cleveland said: "I am by no means in a despairing mood; but I am afraid that there is danger in the fact that you are nearly the only man, able experimentally to preach the 'Gospel of Wealth,' who is attempting to lessen a gulf by going nearer to those who cannot hope to climb nearer to him." And in commenting upon a manuscript received from the same friend, he wrote:

"I have thought for a long time that there must be a way to so weld capital and labor together that the distressing result of their quarrels and misunderstandings would be prevented; and now I am wondering if your address does not point that way.

"Perhaps a plan could now be evolved from the theories and facts you suggest, that would adjust itself to all conditions; but you state the rule which must underlie any effective remedy, when you say: 'You must capture and keep the heart of the original and supremely able man before his brain can do its best'—but I am sure your own experience justifies you in further saying: 'You must capture and keep the heart of any *working man* before his *hands* will do their best.' "

This idea of reconciliation runs through his labor discussions of every period. In accepting the nomination as Governor of New York, and the first nomination as President, in his first inaugural address, and in his earlier presidential utterances, it appears and reappears. And with it is seen, with ever increasing definiteness, his conviction that arbitration is the only sane method of reconciliation.

"The proper theory upon which to proceed," declared his special message of April 22, 1886, "is that of voluntary arbitration as a means of settling these difficulties. But I suggest that instead of arbitrators chosen in the heat of conflicting claims, and after each dispute shall arise, for the purpose of determining the same, there shall be created a Commission of Labor, consisting of three members, who shall be regular officers of the Government, charged among other duties with the consideration and settlement, when possible, of all controversies between labor and capital. . . . In July, 1884, by a law of Congress, a Bureau of Labor was established and placed in charge of a Commissioner of Labor. . . . The Commission which I suggest could easily be engrafted upon the bureau thus already organized." Out of this suggestion grew the

Springer Bill, which President Cleveland approved on October 1, 1888, and which provided special federal machinery for the arbitration of labor disputes.

Reconciliation, however, was not his supreme theory. That place of honor belonged to the idea of enforcement of law; and its testing was not far off.

Labor troubles had been brewing since the beginning of Mr. Cleveland's second term, due, he believed, chiefly to the effects of the McKinley tariff and free silver legislation. In the summer of 1893 the situation was rendered more acute by the Columbian Exposition, which brought 12,000,000 people to Chicago, and tested to the utmost the extraordinary railroad facilities of the country.

When the great event was over and the well-to-do sightseers had departed, Chicago was left to deal with the derelicts of many lands and of many tongues, who had drifted to the scene of the world's interest, and had not been able to drift out again. Caught by the panic of 1893, their plight was rendered far more desperate than it would normally have been. Soup kitchens and charity organizations of all kinds did their futile best to relieve the distress; but such are only weak anæsthetics, able to deaden pain for but a moment, and discontent grew apace.

Moreover, Chicago was but one center of a disease which reached from ocean to ocean. A party rendered careless by long power had sown the wind and another party was called upon to reap the whirlwind. Such at least was the President's interpretation. Throughout the country an army of discontent, the unemployed of a nation, victims of circumstance, and products of vicious habits, were facing that hard winter with a feeling that government had failed.

By spring, discontent had hardened into purpose. Dreaming of wealth by the operation of government printing presses, shouting for an issue of five hundred million dollars of unreal, inconvertible paper money, with which to relieve their very real needs, Coxey, Kelly, and Frye, generals of a horde gathered from all parts of the country, marched on Washington.

On April 28th the "Army of the Commonwealth of Christ," led by Coxey, reached the city, a depleted, bedraggled retinue of tramps, and, straggling across the lawns of the Capitol, ended their glorious march in the lock-up for having disregarded the sign: "Keep off the grass." But though the project ended ridiculously, it indicated a dangerous failure of free government in America. If jest, this great uprising was a solemn jest, for so vast an army of unemployed is a real problem in any age and in any land. There was, moreover, another army, the greater army of the employed, preparing to exhibit a similar spirit of discontent and protest against a free government that had failed of full success.

The history of organized labor has been a short history, though sporadic attempts to combine in self-defense have marked many ages in the world's progress. Capital, on the other hand, has long understood the art of combination for class protection. Indeed, it has usually contemplated far more than mere protection, effecting in addition plans for the exploitation of labor. Thus these two, twin brethren by nature, have too commonly faced one another as enemies—alert, suspicious, and at frequent intervals openly hostile.

Expedients labeled "welfare work," "employer's generosity," or what not, have at times been used in the hope of keeping labor content with an unfair division of the common gains, but labor, though it has generally taken what was offered, has done so sullenly, desiring not gratuities, but partnership.

The Pullman Palace Car Company had gone the full distance in its attempt to make labor physically comfortable. Its magnates had provided a village near Chicago, with good cottages, well paved streets, excellent sanitary arrangements, and beautiful parks. They had acted with uncommon generosity, and they looked for gratitude and contentment in the village.

But they looked in vain. "Happy Pullman Town" was neither grateful nor satisfied; it was a seething mass of discontent. And why? Partly, no doubt, because the comforts which men's hands had earned were handed out to them as though they were gratuities, partly because their rents were from twenty to twenty-five per cent higher than corresponding rents in Chicago. Moreover, the ears of employers were keen. Whispers of discontent or criticism seemed in some mysterious way to connect with the distant chambers where sat the owners of the company, in whose eyes criticism was ingratitude and when discovered meant for the workman the dusty road and the black list.

During the spring of 1894, four thousand of the Pullman village residents joined the American Railway Union, which had been organized the year before to protect railway workers against the General Managers' Association, an organization representing forty-two railroads, and aiming to control labor. The growth of this union had been phenomenal. Between August, 1893, and June, 1894, it had enrolled 150,000 members from all classes of railway employees, and was, as Mr. Cleveland later expressed it, "the most compact and effective organization of the kind ever attempted."

In May, 1894, the Pullman Company declared a reduction of twenty per cent in the wages of their employees, the denizens of the lovely village, and dismissed a number of them as being no longer necessary in view of the state of the market. At once a committee of the villagers called on President Pullman, and requested that the wages be restored to their original standard. This request was refused, and soon after, three of the committee were discharged, contrary to the promise given by Mr. Pullman. At this point five sixths of the inhabitants of the village struck, and they, too, were discharged, and with them the one sixth who had not joined the strikers.

Had the lowering of wages been accompanied by a corresponding lowering of dividends and of officers' salaries, the men would have had little cause for resentment; but salaries and dividends remained unchanged, and, as the Company refused to arbitrate, the cause of the strikers was taken up by the Railway Union, which forbade its members to operate trains with Pullman cars attached.

How far the leaders of the Union were from plans of violence when the strike started is shown by the following proclamation issued by Eugene V. Debs, its President:

"To all striking employees:

"In view of the report of disturbances in various localities, I deem it my duty to caution you against being a party to any violation of law—municipal, State or national—during the existing difficulties. We have repeatedly declared that we respect law and order, and our conduct must conform to our profession. A man who commits violence in any form, whether a member of our order or not, should be promptly arrested and punished, and we should be the first to apprehend the miscreant and bring him to justice.

"We must triumph as law-abiding citizens or not at all. Those who engage in force and violence are our real enemies. We have it upon reliable authority that thugs and toughs have been employed to create trouble, so as to prejudice the public against our cause. The scoundrels should be made in every case to pay the full penalty of the law.

"I appeal to you to be men, orderly and law-abiding. Our cause is just. The great public is with us, and we have nothing to fear. Let it be borne in mind that if the railroad companies can secure men to handle their trains, they have that right. Our men have the right to quit, but their right ends there. Other men have the right to take their places, whatever the propriety of so doing may be. Keep away from railroad yards or rights of way, or other places where large crowds congregate. A safe plan is to remain away entirely from places where there is any likelihood of being an outbreak.

"The railroad managers have sought to make it appear that their trains do not move because of the interference of the strikers. The statement is an unqualified falsehood, and no one knows this better than the managers themselves. They make this falsehood serve their purpose of calling out the troops. Respect the law, conduct yourselves as becomes men, and our cause shall be crowned with success."

It was not long, however, before the strikers were openly boasting that they would, if necessary, "tie up and paralyze the operations of every railway in the United States, and the business and industries dependent thereon," and were emphasizing their meaning by intimidation and violence. Just when and at whose instigation violence was begun, it is not easy to determine. Some writers have concluded that the change was due to secret machinations of the railway managers, who realized that thus would the strikers weaken their own cause. Others have traced it to the human driftwood whom the World's Fair had left stranded in Chicago, while many have laid the blame at the door of President Debs himself. But there can be no doubt that almost from the first the strikers were guilty of what the courts later described as a "conspiracy to prevent the railroad companies . . . from performing their duties as common carriers," and that, early in the strike, they succeeded in many sections of the country.

As early as June 28th, news reached Mr. Cleveland that on the Southern Pacific system the mails were completely obstructed, and similar complaints poured in from other sections of the West and South. To each in turn, at his direction, the Attorney-General wired the message: "See that the passage of the regular trains, carrying United States mails in the usual and ordinary way . . . is not obstructed." On June 30th the Superintendent of the Railway Mail Service at Chicago telegraphed to his chief at Washington: "No mails have accumulated at Chicago so far. All regular mail trains are running nearly on time with a few slight exceptions." But on the same day the District Attorney for the Chicago District warned the President that violent interference with transportation was imminent, and urged that the marshal be instructed to place special deputies upon all mail trains, with orders to protect the mails.

The desired order was sent at once, with the addition, "Action ought to be prompt and vigorous"; and the Attorney-General followed it the next day by the appointment of Edwin Walker as special counsel for the United States, and by the suggestion that an injunction be secured from the Circuit Court of the District forbidding in advance those acts of violence which the government had reason to fear. As yet, if we may accept the testimony of Mr. Debs, later given under oath, there was no actual violence anywhere; but Mr. Olney was convinced that violence was at hand and the injunction was intended to prevent it.

Such an injunction was clearly within the competency of the Federal Courts under general principles of law, and, in addition, the Constitution specifically places the United States mails and Interstate Commerce under the exclusive care of the federal government. Moreover, by an act of July 2, 1890, Congress had provided that conspiracies in restraint of trade or commerce among the several states were illegal, and had instructed the Circuit Courts of the United States to prevent and restrain such conspiracies. Furthermore, the law left no doubt of the President's power in the premises, section 5298 of the Revised Statutes of the United States containing these words: "Whenever by reason of unlawful obstructions, combinations or assemblages of persons, or rebellion against the authority of the United States, it shall become impracticable in the judgment of the President to enforce, by the ordinary course of judicial proceedings, the laws of the United States within any State or Territory, it shall be lawful for the President to call forth the militia of any or all of the States, and to employ such parts of the land or naval forces of the United States as he may deem necessary."

Whether, however, it was wise, at such a time, to invoke so unrestrained a power as a blanket injunction which meant, if effective, the immediate end of the strike, was even then questioned by farsighted men, some of whom had themselves handled this two-edged sword to their regret. On July 14, 1894, Henry M. Shepard, Presiding Justice of the First District of the Illinois Appellate Court, wrote to Judge Gresham:

"I don't remember, if I ever knew, how you have, when on the bench, ruled with reference to operating the

Government through a writ of injunction . . . but I do think some of the Judges have run wild over the question. I did once, and I guess about the first, undertake to execute all the functions of government—Executive, Judicial, and perhaps Legislative—in putting down a switchman's strike on the Lake Shore road, some eight or ten years ago, by an injunction writ, and I am now pretty certain I ought to have been impeached. I would have given a hundred dollars to a fund for the employment of a lawyer for the switchmen to present a motion to dissolve the injunction within a week after I granted it (*ex parte*), but no one came and I sent two poor devils to jail on the theory in my own mind that so long as the order stood it must be obeyed. It broke up the strike, or had a tendency to do so, but I concluded I was exercising very dangerous powers."

The idea of an injunction was naturally resented by the strikers, who saw that it would force them either to abandon the strike or defy the court, and they regarded the appointment of Walker as indicating that the federal government was on the side of the railroads. Governor Altgeld later summed up the objections to Walker in these words: He was "one of the most prominent corporation lawyers in the country . . . the hired attorney of one of the railroads involved in the strike, and . . . at the time personally engaged in fighting strikers, and therefore had an interest in the outcome. Yet this man was clothed with all the powers of the government and he brought to the use of himself and his clients, without expense to them, the service of over 4,000 United States marshals, of a specially picked United States Grand Jury, of several United States judges, and of the United States army. Never before were the United States government and the corporations of the country so completely blended, all the powers of the one being at the service of the other, and never before was the goddess of justice made a mere handmaid for one of the combatants."

The injunction was promptly prepared by the court, to be ready for use when needed. It commanded "all persons . . . absolutely to desist and refrain from in any way or manner interfering with, hindering, obstructing, or stopping any of the business of any of the following named railroads [a list of which was inserted] as common carriers of passengers and freight between or among any States . . . and from in any way or manner interfering with, hindering, obstructing or stopping any trains carrying the mail."

To ask Mr. Debs and his fellow leaders to bow to so drastic an injunction at a moment when blood was hot, and when victory seemed to them assured, was a stern test of their sweet reasonableness. "The railway managers were completely defeated," Debs later explained. "Their immediate resources were exhausted, their properties were paralyzed, and they were unable to operate their trains." But to expect Grover Cleveland to demand less than complete obedience to law was to ask the impossible, in view of his oath of office, and of his conviction that he must act in the interest of the public, which belonged neither to the General Managers' Association nor to the American Railway Union. Their mail and their commerce were being hindered in lawful transit. Their lives and their property were being jeopardized. Their President must interfere, cost what it might, offend whom it might.

On July 2nd news reached the White House that the injunction had been issued to restrain Debs and his fellow officials, together with parties of names unknown, and that the writs would be served that same afternoon. The President was, furthermore, warned that the temper of the strikers was such as to indicate that troops might be required, "if the United States mails were to be kept moving and the injunction respected."

"IF the United States mails were to be kept moving" was a proposition which Mr. Cleveland never harbored. His method of reasoning on such a subject was not in conditional clauses. There were no "ifs" or "buts" in his attitude toward lawlessness. The United States mails *would* be kept moving. Interstate commerce *would* be kept open, whoever opposed. His special council had appealed for troops, and troops he should have. Accordingly General Nelson A. Miles, Commandant of the Department of Missouri, was warned to "expect orders at any time."

This dispatch had scarcely touched the wires, when startling news arrived: "When the injunction was granted . . . a mob of from two to three thousand held possession of a point in the city near the crossing of the Rock Island by other roads, where they had already ditched a mail train, and prevented the passing of any train, whether mail or otherwise. . . . I . . . believe that no force less than the regular troops of the United States can procure the passage of mail trains, or enforce the orders of the courts." The dispatch bore the signatures of Edwin Walker, Thomas E. Milchrist, and Judge P. S. Grosscup.

In reply District Attorney Milchrist was informed that "While action should be prompt and decisive, it should of course be kept within the limits provided by the Constitution and laws," and orders were issued through the War Department which brought Colonel Crofton's regiment to Chicago, where General Miles himself assumed command.  The day, as it chanced, was July 4th.  The outlook was so alarming that before the day closed Miles requested more troops for Fort Sheridan, and in reply the War Department authorized him to draw six companies from Fort Leavenworth and two from Fort Brady.

When Benjamin Franklin was informed of George III's intention of sending redcoats to Boston to put down rebellion, he replied, "If sent they will not find a rebellion, but they will create one."  This was a true prediction, and a similar one might have been made regarding the immediate effect of the arrival of federal troops in Chicago.  For the time at least, they bred not peace but war.  Governor Altgeld interpreted their presence as a threat against local self-government, and his indiscreet utterances deepened the resentment of the strikers and their friends.  General Miles reported an increase in the size of the sullen mobs, a bolder series of lawless attacks upon trains, mingled with occasional instances of outrages upon persons or property.  "The injunction of the United States Court," he declared, "is openly defied, and unless the mobs are dispersed . . . more serious trouble may be expected."

Such was the state of affairs when Governor Altgeld addressed to President Cleveland the following telegram of protest:

Executive Office, State of Illinois.
*July 5, 1894.*

The HON. GROVER CLEVELAND,
President of the United States,
Washington, D. C.

Dear Sir:

I am advised that you have ordered federal troops to go into service in the State of Illinois.  Surely the facts have not been correctly presented to you in this case or you would not have taken the step, for it is entirely unnecessary and, as it seems to me, unjustifiable. Waiving all questions of courtesy, I will say that the State of Illinois is not only able to take care of itself, but it stands ready to-day to furnish the Federal Government any assistance it may need elsewhere. Our military force is ample and consists of as good soldiers as can be found in the country. They have been ordered promptly whenever and wherever they were needed. We have stationed in Chicago alone three regiments of infantry, one battery and one troop of cavalry, and no better soldiers can be found. They have been ready every moment to go on duty and have been and are now eager to go into service. But they have not been ordered out because nobody in Cook County, whether official or private citizen, asked to have their assistance, or even intimated in any way that their assistance was desired or necessary.

So far as I have been advised, the local officials have been able to handle the situation. But if any assistance were needed the State stood ready to furnish one hundred men for every one man required, and stood ready to do so at a moment's notice. Notwithstanding these facts, the Federal Government has been applied to by men who had political and selfish motives for wanting to ignore the State government. We have just gone through a long coal strike, more extensive here than in any other state, because our soft-coal field is larger than that of any other state. We have now had ten days of the railroad strike, and we have promptly furnished military aid wherever the local officials needed it.

In two instances the United States Marshal for the southern district of Illinois applied for assistance to enable him to enforce the processes of the United States courts, and troops were promptly furnished him, and he was assisted in every way he desired. The law has been thoroughly executed and every man guilty of violating it during the strike has been brought to justice. If the Marshal for the northern district of Illinois or the authorities of Cook County needed military assistance they had but to ask for it in order to get it from the State.

At present some of our railroads are paralyzed, not by reason of obstructions, but because they cannot get men to operate their trains. For some reason they are anxious to keep this fact from the public, and for this purpose are making an outcry about obstructions in order to divert attention. Now, I will cite to you two examples which illustrate the situation: Some days ago I was advised that the business of one of our railroads was obstructed at two railroad centers, that there was a condition bordering on anarchy there; and I was asked to furnish protection so as to enable the employees of the road to operate the trains. Troops were promptly ordered to both points. Then it transpired that the company had not sufficient men on its line to operate one train. All the old hands were orderly, but refused to go. The company had large shops in which work a number of men who did not belong to the railway union and who could run an engine. They were appealed to to run the train, but flatly refused. We were obliged to hunt up soldiers who could run an engine and operate a train.

Again, two days ago, appeals which were almost frantic came from officials of another road, stating that at an important point on their lines trains were forcibly obstructed, and that there was a reign of anarchy at that place; and they asked for protection so that they could move their trains. Troops were put on the ground in a few hours' time, when the officer in command telegraphed me that there was no trouble and had been none at that point, but that the road seemed to have no men to run trains; and the sheriff telegraphed that he did not need troops, but would himself move every train if the company would only furnish an engineer. The result was that the troops were there over twelve hours before a single train was moved, although there was no attempt at interference by anybody. It is true that in several instances a road made efforts to work a few green men, and a crowd standing around insulted them and tried to drive them away; and in a few other places they cut off Pullman sleepers from trains. But all these troubles were local in character and could easily be handled by the State authorities. Illinois has more railroad men than any other state in the Union, but as a rule they are orderly and well behaved. This is shown by the fact that so very little actual violence has been committed. Only a very small per cent of these men have been guilty of any infractions of the law. The newspaper accounts have in many cases been pure fabrications, and in others, wild exaggerations.

I have gone thus into details to show that it is not soldiers that the railroads need so much as it is men to operate trains, and that the conditions do not exist here which bring the cause within the Federal statutes, a statute that was passed in 1881, and was in reality a war measure. This statute authorized the use of Federal troops in a state whenever it shall be impracticable to enforce the laws of the United States within such states by the ordinary judicial proceedings. Such a condition does not exist in Illinois. There have been a few local disturbances, but nothing that seriously interfered with the administration of justice, or that could not be easily controlled by the local or state authorities, for the Federal troops can do nothing that the state troops cannot do.

I repeat that you have been imposed upon in this matter, but even if by a forced construction it was held that the condition here came within the letter of the statute, then I submit that local self-government is a fundamental principle of our Constitution. Each community shall govern itself so long as it can and is ready and able to enforce the law, and it is in harmony with this fundamental principle that the statute authorizing the President to send troops into states must be construed. Especially is this so in matters relating to the exercise of police power and the preservation of law and order. To absolutely ignore a local government in matters of this kind, when the local government is ready to furnish assistance needed and is amply able to enforce the law, not only insults the people of this state by imputing to them an inability to govern themselves or an unwillingness to enforce the law, but is in violation of a basic principle of our institutions. The question of Federal supremacy is in no way involved —no one disputes it for a moment—but under our Constitution Federal supremacy and local self-government must go hand in hand, and to ignore the latter is to do violence to the Constitution.

As Governor of the State of Illinois, I protest against this and ask immediate withdrawal of the Federal troops from active duty in this State. Should the situation at any time get so serious that we cannot control it with the State forces, we will promptly and freely ask for Federal assistance; but until such time I protest with all due deference against this uncalled for reflection upon our people, and again ask the immediate withdrawal of these troops.

I have the honor to be,

Yours respectfully,

JOHN P. ALTGELD, Governor of Illinois.

This lengthy statement, Mr. Cleveland later declared, "so far missed the actual condition as to appear irrelevant and, in some parts, absolutely frivolous." "It was probably a very fortunate circumstance that the presence of United States soldiers in Chicago at that time did not depend upon the request or desire of Governor Altgeld."

The President's reply was immediate and definite, but its sure, unargumentative tone was calculated, though not designed, to exasperate the Governor still more:

> Washington,
> *July 5, 1894.*

HON. JOHN P. ALTGELD,
Governor of Illinois,
Springfield, Illinois.

Federal troops were sent to Chicago in strict accordance with the Constitution and laws of the United States upon the demand of the Post Office Department that obstruction of the mails should be removed, and upon the representations of the judicial officers of the United States that process of the Federal courts could not be executed through the ordinary means, and upon abundant proof that conspiracies existed against commerce between the states. To meet these conditions, which are clearly within the province of Federal authority, the presence of Federal troops in the city of Chicago was deemed not only proper but necessary, and there has been no intention of thereby interfering with the plain duty of the local authorities to preserve the peace of the city.

> GROVER CLEVELAND.

As printed in the Chicago *Times,* the letter closed at this point. An autograph copy found among the Lamont papers, however, adds this postscript, which clearly shows how far Mr. Cleveland was from serving the cause of the railway management:

"Mr. McNaught should be informed that whatever arrangement is made by the Company with its employees must positively be made without relying upon the Government for any guarantee whatever. The Military power of the Government refuses to be drawn into any relation with the details of railroad management.    *G. C.*"

That Mr. Debs was even yet determined to avoid violence is evident from the following paragraph from his pen, printed in an anti-Debs Chicago newspaper on July 5th: "We hold the position that we can win without even the semblance of violence, and if we cannot I prefer to lose rather than tolerate violence. Let me repeat: There is but one well-defined estimate of the situation, and that is, we hold the railroads cannot get men sufficient to run their trains. On that proposition we win or lose. We shall not interfere with any man who wants to work. We have not done so and shall not. A man has a legal right to quit work, and it is not the part of the troops or the civil officers of the law to arrest them for so doing, though I am informed such an arrest was made today. The American Railway Union will protect its men from the penalties of such arrests."

It is only fair to add that Governor Altgeld sent out many orders directing the sheriffs of the various counties of Illinois to see that the traveling public was protected and that trains were kept moving. It is also true that he insisted that "the reports . . . as to actual conditions in Chicago during the strike were malicious libels upon the city." But he later admitted that from July 4th to July 14th $355,612 worth of property was destroyed.

It was clearly the duty of both President Debs and Governor Altgeld to continue to preach peace and obedience to law, even in the face of the injunction; unfortunately, however, they chose another course, and one which compelled the hand that still held the olive branch to change it for the sword. Debs now defiantly resisted the injunction, and encouraged others to do likewise, while Altgeld flayed it in the words: "A Federal judge, not content with deciding controversies brought into his Court . . . proceeds to legislate and then administer. He issues a ukase which he calls an injunction forbidding whatever he pleases . . . and he deprives men of the right of trial by jury when the law guarantees this right, and he then enforces this ukase in a summary and arbitrary manner by imprisonment, throwing men into prison not for violating a law, but for being guilty of a contempt of court in disregarding one of these injunctions." In the following open telegram he added further fuel to the flame of lawlessness:

*[July 6, 1894]*

The HON. GROVER CLEVELAND,
    President of the United States,
        Washington, D. C.
Sir:
    Your answer to my protest involves some startling conclusions, and ignores and evades the question at issue, that is, that the principle of local self-government is just as fundamental in our institutions as is that of Federal supremacy.
    1. You calmly assume that the Executive has the legal right to order Federal troops into any community of the United States, in the first instance, whenever there is the slightest disturbance, and that he can do this without any

regard to the question as to whether that community is able to and ready to enforce the law itself. And inasmuch as the Executive is the sole judge of the question as to whether any disturbance exists or not in any part of the country, this assumption means that the Executive can send Federal troops into any community in the United States at his pleasure and keep them there as long as he chooses.

If this is the law, then the principle of local self-government either never did exist in this country or else has been destroyed, for no community can be said to possess local self-government if the Executive can at his pleasure send military forces to patrol its streets under pretense of enforcing some law. The kind of local self-government that could exist under these circumstances can be found in any of the monarchies of Europe and is not in harmony with the spirit of our institutions.

2. It is also a fundamental principle in our government that except in times of war the military shall be subordinate to the civil authority. In harmony with this provision the state troops when ordered out act under and with the civil authorities. The Federal troops you have ordered to Chicago are not under the civil authorities, and are in no way responsible to them for their conduct. They are not even acting under the United States Marshal, or under any Federal officer of the State, but are acting directly under military orders issued from military head-quarters at Washington, and in so far as these troops act at all it is military government.

3. The statute authorizing Federal troops to be sent into states in certain cases contemplates that the state troops shall be taken first. This provision has been ignored, and it is assumed that the Executive is not bound by it. Federal interference with industrial disturbances

in the various states is certainly a new departure, and opens up so large a field that it will require a very little stretch of authority to absorb to itself all the details of local government.

4. You say that the troops were ordered into Illinois upon the demand of the Post Office Department and upon representations of the judicial officers of the United States that process of the courts could not be served and upon proof that conspiracies existed. We will not discuss the facts, but look for a moment at the principle involved in your statement. All of these officers are appointed by the Executive. Most of them can be removed by him at his will. They are not only obliged to do his bidding, but they are, in fact, a part of the Executive. If several of them can apply for troops one alone can, so that under the law, as you assume it to be, an Executive, through any one of his appointees, can apply to himself to have the military sent into any city or number of cities, and base his application on such representations or showing as he sees fit to make. In fact, it will be immaterial whether he makes any showing or not, for the Executive is the sole judge and nobody else has any right to interfere or even inquire about it. Then the Executive can pass on his own application. His will being the sole guide, he can hold the application to be sufficient and order troops to as many places as he wishes, and put them in command of any one he chooses and have them act, not under the civil officers, either Federal or State, but act directly under military orders from Washington, and there is not in the Constitution or laws of the land, whether written or unwritten, any limitation or restraint upon his power. His judgment, that is, his will, is the sole guide, and it being purely a matter of discretion, his decision can never be examined or questioned.

This assumption as to the power of the Executive is certainly new, and I respectfully submit that it is not the law of the land.

The jurists have told us that this is a government of law, and not a government by the caprice of individuals; and, further, instead of being autocratic, it was a government of limited power. Yet the autocratic Russia could certainly not possess nor claim to possess greater power than is possessed by the Executive of the United States, if your assumption is correct.

5. The Executive has the command not only of the regular forces of the United States, but of the military forces of all the states, and can order them to any place he sees fit, and as there are always more or less local disturbances over the country, it would be an easy matter, under your construction of the law, for an ambitious Executive to order out the military forces of all the states and establish at once a military government. The only chance of failure in such a movement could come from rebellion, and with such a vast military power at command this could be readily crushed, for, as a rule, soldiers will obey orders. As for the situation in Illinois, that is of no consequence now, when compared with the far-reaching principle involved. True, according to my advices, Federal troops have now been on duty for over two days and, although the men were brave and the officers valiant and able, yet their very presence proved to be an irritant because it aroused the indignation of a large class of people who, while upholding law and order, had been taught to believe in local self-government and therefore resented what they regarded as an unwarranted interference.

Inasmuch as the Federal troops can do nothing but what the state troops can do there, and believing that the state is amply able to take care of the situation and to enforce the law, and believing that the ordering out of the Federal troops was unwarranted, I again ask their withdrawal.

JOHN P. ALTGELD.

At the same time, General Miles and other officers and officials reported riotous assemblies, violent mobs, and stealthy dealings in arson and murder. One of General Miles's telegrams declared: "Of the twenty-three roads centering in Chicago only six are unobstructed in freight, passenger and mail transportation. . . . Large numbers of trains moving in and out of the city have been stoned and fired upon by mobs, and one engineer killed. There was a secret meeting to-day of Debs and the representatives of labor unions considering the advisability of a general strike of all labor unions. About one hundred men were present at that meeting." Miles later telegraphed: "Men who were in secret meeting last night say that all labor union men will be called out Monday. In meantime all labor men have been advised to get Winchester rifles and pistols. They hope to have one hundred thousand men in this city. They decided to support . . . strike in every way. . . . I recommend immediate concentration of troops near Chicago . . . to be ready any emergency Monday."

In view of such facts, and they were but representative of many, the Governor's "rather dreary discussion of the importance of preserving the rights of the States," as Mr. Cleveland later described his lengthy telegram, only exasperated the President. "I confess," he declared, "that my patience was somewhat strained, when I quickly sent the following dispatch . . .":

Washington,
*July 6, 1894.*

HON. JOHN P. ALTGELD,
Governor of Illinois,
Springfield, Ills.

While I am still persuaded that I have neither transcended my authority or duty, in the emergency that confronts us, it seems to me that in this hour of danger and public distress discussion may well give way to active effort on the part of all in authority to restore obedience to law and to protect life and property.

GROVER CLEVELAND.

Attorney-General Olney was equally contemptuous. To the Washington *Post* he said:

"It is hardly worth while to discuss at length the false premise and the illogical *non-sequiturs* of the Altgeld manifesto. As a campaign platform, it is a safe prediction that the author will be found to be the only person to stand upon it.

"The soil of Illinois is the soil of the United States and, for all United States purposes, the United States is there with its courts, its marshals, and its troops, not by license or comity, but as of right. The paramount duty of the President of the United States is to see that the laws of the United States are faithfully executed, and in the discharge of that duty he is not hampered or crippled by the necessity of consulting chief of police, Mayor, or even Governor. In the present instance nothing has been done and nothing ordered which the most captious critic can condemn as any invasion of State rights.

"The action of the national executive has been simply and exclusively directed to the enforcement of the United

States laws, the execution of the orders and processes of the United States courts, and the prevention of any obstruction of the United States mails.

"The notion that the territory of any State is too sacred to permit the exercise thereon, by the United States government, of any of its legitimate functions never had any legal existence, and, as a rule of conduct, became practically extinct with the close of the civil war."

Two days later, the President issued his famous Proclamation of July 8, 1894:

"Proclamation
"By the President of the United States
"Whereas, by reason of unlawful obstructions, combinations and assemblages of persons, it has become impracticable in the judgment of the President to enforce, by the ordinary course of judicial proceedings, the laws of the United States within the State of Illinois and especially in the city of Chicago within said state; and,

"Whereas, for the purpose of enforcing the faithful execution of the laws of the United States and protecting its property and removing obstructions to the United States mails in the state and city aforesaid, the President has employed a part of the military forces of the United States:

"Now, therefore, I, Grover Cleveland, President of the United States, do hereby admonish all good citizens and all persons who may be or may come within the city and state aforesaid, against aiding, countenancing, encouraging or taking any part in such unlawful obstructions, combinations and assemblages; and I hereby warn all persons engaged in or in any way connected with such unlawful obstructions, combinations and assemblages to disperse and retire peaceably to their respective abodes on or before twelve o'clock noon on the ninth day of July instant.

"Those who disregard this warning and persist in taking part with a riotous mob in forcibly resisting and obstructing the execution of the laws of the United States or interfering with the functions of the Government and destroying or attempting to destroy the property belonging to the United States or under its protection cannot be regarded otherwise than as public enemies.

"Troops employed against such a riotous mob, will act with all the moderation and forbearance consistent with the accomplishment of the desired end; but the stern necessities that confront them will not certainly permit discrimination between guilty participants and those who are mingled with them from curiosity and without criminal intent. The only safe course therefore for those not actually unlawfully participating is to abide at their homes, or at least not to be found in the neighborhood of riotous assemblages.

"While there will be no hesitation or vacillation in the decisive treatment of the guilty, this warning is especially intended to protect and save the innocent.

"In Testimony Whereof I have hereunto set my hand and caused the seal of the United States to be hereto affixed.

"Done at the city of Washington this eighth day of July, A.D., in the year of our Lord One Thousand Eight Hundred and Ninety-four, and of the Independence of the United States of America the One Hundred and Eighteenth."

Upon reading this proclamation, Mr. Debs declared it "a plot to place Chicago under martial law at the instigation of the railway companies in furtherance of the latter's plan to destroy public sympathy. This cannot be done. This meeting to-night will in all probability last until daylight. I am certain that every union represented, numbering over 100,000 laborers, will vote to strike tomorrow."

With the coming of the morrow, however, came new evidence of the President's determination. He issued a second proclamation which recognized the conflict as nation-wide, and warned the good people "at certain points and places within the States of North Dakota, Montana, Idaho, Washington, Wyoming, Colorado, and California, and the Territories of Utah and New Mexico, and especially along the lines of such railways traversing said States and Territories as are military roads and post routes and are engaged in Interstate commerce and in carrying United States mails," to "retire peaceably to their respective abodes on or before 3 o'clock in the afternoon on the 10th day of July instant."

These proclamations had the desired effect, though indirectly. Debs and his associates having failed to "retire peaceably," at the command of the Court, were "in contempt." They were accordingly arrested on July 10th, and their arrest ended the strike.

But Mr. Cleveland was not yet entirely satisfied. Having carried into effect his primary policy—the enforcement of law—he announced the intention of appointing a commission to investigate the questions which had caused the strike. Of this announcement Mr. Debs declared: "We have no doubt that the board will be composed of men of high character and ability, and that they will be able to locate the right or wrong involved in the existing controversy, by virtue of which a satisfactory settlement will be reached. It is to be hoped that the board will be promptly appointed and organized, that its work will be prosecuted vigorously to the end of a speedy settlement of the existing conflict. We are of course for arbitration, and have been from the very beginning, and had this principle been recognized this strike would have been avoided."

The next day, he and his fellow prisoners sent the President the following telegram:

*July 13, 1894.*

The HON. GROVER CLEVELAND,
  President of the United States,
  Washington, D. C.

Dear Sir:

We the undersigned beg to advise you that we have just submitted the following proposition to the Railway Managers, and if it meets with your approval we respectfully request that you take such action as you may deem proper to influence its acceptance:—

Chicago, Ill., *July 13, 1894.*

To the Railway Managers
Gentlemen:

The existing troubles growing out of the Pullman strike having assumed continental proportions, and there being no indication of relief from the widespread business demoralization and distress incident thereto, the Railway employees, through the Board of Directors of the American Railway Union, respectfully make the following proposition as basis of settlement: They agree to return to work in a body at once, provided they shall be restored to their former positions without prejudice except in cases, if any there be, where they have been convicted of crime —this proposition looking to an immediate settlement of the existing strike on all lines of railway is inspired by a purpose to subserve the public good. The strike, small and comparatively unimportant in its inception, has kindled in every direction until now it involves or threatens not only every public interest but the peace, security and prosperity of our common country. The contest has waged fiercely. It has extended far beyond the limits of interest originally involved and has laid hold of a vast number of industries and enterprises in no wise responsible for the differences and disagreements that led to the trouble. Factory, mill, mine, and shop have been silenced. Widespread demoralization has sway. The interests of multiplied thousands of innocent people are suffering. The common welfare is seriously menaced. The public peace and tranquillity are in peril. Grave apprehension for the future prevails. This being true, and the statement will *not* be *controverted,* we conceive it to be our duty as citizens and as men to make extraordinary efforts to end the existing strife and avert approaching calamities whose shadows are even now upon us. If ended now the contest, however serious in some of its consequences, will not have been in vain. Sacrifices have been made but they will have their compensations. Indeed, if lessons shall be taught by experience the troubles now so widely deplored will prove a blessing of inestimable value in the months and years to come. The differences that led up to the present complications need not now be discussed. At this supreme juncture every consideration of duty and patriotism demands that a remedy for existing troubles be found and applied. The employees propose to do their part by meeting their employers half-way. Let it be stated that they do not impose any condition of settlement except that they be returned to their former positions. They do not ask the recognition of their organization or of any organization. Believing this proposition to be fair, reasonable and just, it is respectfully submitted with the belief that its acceptance will result in the prompt resumption of traffic, the revival of industry, and the restoration of peace and order.

Respectfully,

EUGENE V. DEBS, President

GEO. W. HOWARD, Vice-President

SYLVESTER KOLIHER, Secty.,

American Railway Union.

But Mr. Debs no longer had anything to offer. The strike was over, and all that remained was for the courts to decide upon the penalty. He and his associates refused to give bail, scorning to wear the martyr's crown without bearing also the martyr's cross, as their admirers claimed; or, perhaps, as Mr. Cleveland less charitably suggested, "intending by such an act of martyrdom either to revive a waning cause, or to gain a plausible and justifying excuse for the collapse of their already foredoomed movement."

By July 22d Mr. Debs seems to have entirely changed his attitude. From Cook County jail, Chicago, contemptuously christened by the pro-Pullman press "Headquarters of the American Railway Union," he sent out the following declaration:

"We propose to continue this strike against the Pullman Company through good and evil report and without regard to consequences, until justice shall be done. We will use every available means to press the contest. Dungeons shall not daunt us. The struggle is for humanity and against the most cruel tyranny, and, unless we are dead to every impulse of mercy and fellow-feeling, must be crowned with success."

On July 26th, Mr. Cleveland announced his commission, Carroll D. Wright, John D. Kernan, and Nicholas E. Worthington, and directed them to "visit the State of Illinois and the city of Chicago and such other places in the United States as may appear proper . . . make careful inquiry into the causes of any pending dispute or existing controversy, and hear all persons interested therein."

While Mr. Debs and his fellow prisoners awaited trial, this commission carried forward its investigations, examining all told one hundred and nine witnesses. According to the testimony, the railroads lost in property destroyed, hire of United States Deputy Marshals, and incidental expenses, at least $685,308. The loss of earnings to these roads was estimated at $4,672,916. As estimated also, the 3,100 employees at Pullman lost $350,000 in wages, and the 100,000 employees upon the twenty-four railroads centering in Chicago paid at least $1,389,143 for their part in the strike. The Commission found also that during the strike the number shot and fatally wounded was 12, number arrested by police, 515; number arrested under United States statutes and against whom indictments were found, 71. The arrests made by the police were for murder, arson, burglary, assault, intimidation, riot, and lesser crimes. The cases passed upon by the United States Grand Jury were for obstruction of the mail, conspiracy in restraint of trade, and conspiracy to injure, oppress, threaten, or intimidate. It further found that, "The conditions created at Pullman enable the management at all times to assert with great vigor its assumed right to fix wages and rents absolutely, and to repress that sort of independence which leads to labor organizations and their attempts at mediation, arbitration, strikes, etc."

On December 10, 1894, the President transmitted the full report to Congress. Four days later the Illinois Circuit Court decided that these facts did not justify Mr. Debs and his companions in their course of resistance to organized authority and defiance of a federal injunction. It sentenced Mr. Debs to six months' imprisonment, and his associates to three months each, "for contempt of court." The decision was based upon the Sherman Anti-Trust Law of 1890, "an act to protect trade and commerce against unlawful restraint and monopolies"—an interesting development in view of the fact that the controversy had proceeded from a strike of laboring men against the unjust exactions of the Pullman Palace Car Company, one of the most perfect monopolies ever devised, which Mr. Debs hyperbolically characterized as "remorseless as a man-eating tiger."

An appeal was taken to the Supreme Court, President Debs and his fellows applying for a writ of habeas corpus on the ground that the facts found by the Circuit Court did not constitute disobedience to the writs of injunction served upon them. The case was argued on March 25 and 26, 1895, and on May 27th a decision was handed down, sustaining the verdict of the Circuit Court and completely vindicating the legality of President Cleveland's course. The decision declared:

"The United States may remove everything put upon highways, natural or artificial, to obstruct the passage of interstate commerce, or the carrying of the mails. . . . It is equally within its competency to appeal to the civil courts for an inquiry and determination as to the existence and the character of any of them, and if such are found to exist or threaten to occur, to invoke the powers of those courts to remove or restrain them, the jurisdiction of the courts to interfere in such matters by injunction being recognized from ancient times and by indubitable authority. . . .

"The complaint filed in this case clearly shows an existing obstruction of the artificial highways for the passage of interstate commerce and the transmission of the mails, not only temporarily existing, but threatening to continue, and under it the Circuit Court had power to issue its process of injunction.

"Such an injunction having been issued and served upon the defendants, the Circuit Court had authority to inquire whether its orders had been disobeyed, and when it found that they had been disobeyed, to proceed under Rev. Stat. § 725, and to enter the order of punishment complained of."

By this prompt and determined course, Mr. Cleveland had made it clear, not only that law must be obeyed, but that the nation is paramount and state lines only geographical expressions when the welfare of the country is at stake. He prized the decision of the court, not because it vindicated his dignity, but because, to quote his own words, it established "in an absolutely authoritative manner, and for all time, the power of the national government to protect itself in the exercise of its functions."

# CHAPTER VI

## THE VENEZUELAN AFFAIR

*"The rules of conduct governing individual relations are
equally applicable as between enlightened nations."*
—GROVER CLEVELAND.

WHEN Grover Cleveland became President, few of
his contemporaries would have classed among the
most important of the great outstanding questions which
confronted him a boundary dispute which for almost
three quarters of a century had periodically caused friction between Venezuela and Great Britain. Yet such was
the case.

In 1814, Great Britain, by her treaty with the Nether-
lands, acquired the provinces of Essequibo, Demerara,
and Berbice, which under her rule came to be known as
British Guiana. In 1840 Mr. (later Sir) Robert Schomburgk, an English engineer, was sent by England to survey
and delimit its boundaries, as a preliminary measure, and
report to the British Government. He took particular
care to fortify himself with the history of the case, from
actual exploration and information obtained from the
Indians and from the evidence of local remains, and on
such data he based his report.

At Point Barima, where the remains of a Dutch fort
still existed, and at the mouth of the Amacura, he placed
two boundary posts. At the urgent entreaty of the Venezuelan government these two posts were afterwards removed, but the concession was made with the distinct
understanding that Great Britain did not thereby in any

way abandon her claim to that position. In fact the Schomburgk line, as finally drawn, was a great reduction of the boundary claimed by Great Britain as her right and its proposal originated in a desire on her part to come to a friendly arrangement with a weaker power with whom she desired to remain in cordial relations.

As soon as Schomburgk's report was submitted to the Venezuelan government, the latter objected, with a statement of her own claims—claims starting in such obsolete grounds as the original discovery by Spain of the American continent, and supported by quotations more or less vague from the writing of travelers and geographers. She adduced no substantial evidence of actual conquest or occupation of the territory claimed.

Lord Aberdeen, then Secretary of State for Foreign Affairs, pointed out that it would be impossible to arrive at any agreement if both sides brought forward pretensions of so extreme a character, and announced certain concessions which Great Britain was prepared to make "out of friendly regard to Venezuela," on condition that the Venezuelan government would agree that no part of the territory proposed to be ceded should be alienated at any time to a foreign power, and that the Indian tribes residing in it should be protected from oppression. No answer to this note was ever received from the Venezuelan government, and in 1850 Her Majesty's Government informed the British Chargé d'Affaires at Carácas that as the proposal had remained for more than six years unaccepted, it must be considered as having lapsed, and instructed him to make a communication to the Venezuelan government to that effect.

Venezuela subsequently permitted projects to be set on foot for the occupation of Point Barima and certain other disputed positions, and the British Chargé d'Affaires was instructed to inform the government of Venezuela "that, whilst on the one hand Great Britain had no intention of occupying or encroaching upon the disputed territory, she would not, on the other hand, view with indifference aggressions on that territory by Venezuela." To which the Venezuelan government replied that Venezuela had no intention of occupying or encroaching upon any part of the territory in dispute, and that orders would be issued to the authorities in Guiana to abstain from taking any steps contrary to this engagement.

For a generation thereafter the question received little consideration, Venezuela being the victim of absorbing revolutions; and when at the end of that time it began again to be discussed, it had grown more difficult, owing to the value of the gold fields lying between the admitted dominions of the two contestants and claimed by both. Venezuela protested that Great Britain had moved the line of her pretensions westward, appropriating some 33,000 square miles of Venezuelan territory; and British statesmen indignantly denied the accusation.

In 1876 Venezuela requested American intervention in her behalf, and a few months later suggested to Great Britain that the justice of the respective claims of the two nations might readily be determined by the discussion of historical proofs, or, if Great Britain preferred, that "a conventional line fixed by mutual accord" might be agreed upon. Neither idea, however, secured the desired results. Our Secretary of State did not intervene; and Venezuela refused to accept the line suggested by Lord Salisbury.

After various other proposals, Venezuela requested that the question be submitted to arbitration, but the reply of Lord Granville, now Secretary of State for Foreign Affairs, wholly disregarded the request, and further insistence met curt refusal at the hands of the British ministry.

Early in the year 1885, it seemed that a settlement had been provided by the negotiation of a general treaty between Great Britain and Venezuela, which specified that all differences should be arbitrated, should the method of friendly negotiation fail. But Lord Salisbury, who had succeeded Lord Granville in the Foreign Office, repudiated the treaty in a note of July 27, 1885.

In December of the following year, Secretary Bayard offered the co-operation of our government to England, to the end that the question might be decided by arbitration, but Lord Salisbury refused the offer. By February, 1887, the controversy had become so heated that Venezuela, in protest against what she termed "acts of spoliation," suspended diplomatic relations with Great Britain. Secretary Bayard, during the following year, called attention to the fact that Great Britain had apparently enlarged her boundary claims, thus committing the United States to a position of sympathy with Venezuela; but no action was taken. And so the affair stood until 1890, when Lord Salisbury, to the astonishment of the Venezuelan government, declared that, while Great Britain would not waive her title to any of the territory comprised within the Schomburgk line which, despite the objections of Venezuela, she still believed to be correct, and within which many English had now long been established, she would be willing to refer to arbitration her claims to certain territory west of that line.

Here matters rested for the remainder of President Harrison's term. Fifty-two years of intermittent controversy had done nothing to settle the question. The United States, when she had ventured to touch the matter at all, had done so with so uncertain a hand as to produce results negligible or worse. Fish, Evarts, Blaine, Frelinghuysen, and Bayard, all able Secretaries of State, had considered the subject. All had commented upon its relationship to the Monroe Doctrine; but, with the exception of Secretary Bayard's offer of arbitration, no one of them had made any definite contribution toward its solution.

England's position, as later defined by Lord Kimberley, was that the negotiations between the two countries had led to no results because "Venezuela has insisted on maintaining a claim extending beyond the River Essequibo and including a large portion of long settled districts of the Colony of British Guiana. On the other hand, Great Britain has throughout been prepared to make large abatements from her extreme claim although Her Majesty's Government has been continually accumulating stronger documentary proofs of the correctness of that extreme claim as being their inheritance from their Dutch predecessors."

Upon his return to power in 1893, Mr. Cleveland faced the question in a new spirit, conscious that if further neglected it might prove serious, in view of the tendency of the nations of Europe to seek an extension of their territory at the expense of weak and backward peoples, and of the equally apparent tendency of South American countries to use the name of the United States as a shield against Europe in times of danger, while insisting upon absolute freedom of action when no danger threatened.

Mr. Cleveland was by nature disposed to suspect strong nations of designs against weaker ones, a tendency which his experiences with Germany in Samoa and the United States in Hawaii had not lessened. He was also a firm believer in arbitration as a means of settling international disputes; but, in the case of Venezuela, England had shown little disposition to consider that method, and he felt that the time had come when the question must be settled, peacefully if possible, but settled. Secretary Gresham was also an enthusiast for arbitration, while Thomas F. Bayard, now Ambassador to the Court of St. James, felt that America and Great Britain were committed to this principle. In the hands of these three men rested the decision of America's course regarding the Venezuelan boundary. All three believed that powerless nations are entitled to the same rights as are powerful nations, and that it is the duty of the latter to see that these rights are respected. All three believed in the special responsibility of the United States to see that the American continent be left in the freest enjoyment of the right of self-determination as guaranteed by the Monroe Doctrine. If it were true, as Secretary Bayard had said, that the United States had a moral right to protect the sovereign independence of the distant, dark-skinned peoples of the far Pacific, then was it more than a moral right, it was a moral duty, to see that nations covered by the Monroe Doctrine were similarly protected.

Shortly after Ambassador Bayard took up his post in London, he wrote to Secretary Gresham that the time was ripe for a settlement of the Venezuelan boundary dispute: "Great Britain has just now her hands very full in other quarters of the globe. The United States is the last nation on earth with whom the British people or their rulers desire to quarrel, and of this I have new proofs every day in my intercourse with them. The other European nations are watching each other like pugilists in the ring." To the diplomatic mind of our Ambassador, England's necessity was America's opportunity, and the determination to force arbitration upon a hard-pressed, friendly nation at a moment when she was considered not free to refuse, was both ungenerous and unfair, especially in view of the fact that Great Britain had as her Ambassador at Washington Sir Julian Pauncefote, a man whom Secretary Gresham himself described as candid, fair, and an open fighter, although "a firm supporter of British interests."

On December 1, 1894, Gresham instructed Bayard to open the question by pointing out to the British government that "England and America are fully committed to the principle of arbitration and this Government will gladly do what it can do to further a determination in that sense." As Bayard proceeded, the old difficulties reappeared. In a confidential dispatch of April 5, 1895, he reported that Lord Kimberley had shown him a map of the disputed territory "on which were delineated, in different colors, the three lines of delimitation. The line coloured in pink was the Schomburgk line, one of the terminal points of which was a short distance inside the mouth of the Orinoco, and which His Lordship stated was conclusively proven and established as a British possession, and would not be submitted to arbitration, but that the ownership of the territory intersected by the other two lines, they would be willing to submit to arbitration."

Upon the receipt of this dispatch, Gresham began the preparation of a report for the guidance of the government during the negotiations, but before the work was completed, death intervened. His loss was a severe blow to Mr. Cleveland, both personally and officially. On the train in which the remains were taken to the widow's home in Chicago, he showed the depth of his grief. He sat for a long time absorbed in thought. At length he asked one of the members of his Cabinet to escort him forward to the baggage car where the coffin was carried, and, arriving there, indicated a wish to be left alone. An hour or so later, as he had not returned to his stateroom,

two members of the Cabinet went forward to the funeral
car, fearing that he had been overcome by the heat or that
some accident had happened. They found the President
on his knees by the bier of the dead Secretary, his arms
resting upon the coffin, his eyes full of tears. Apparently
he had no notion of the flight of time. He was assisted
to rise to his feet, and was then escorted back to his stateroom. In this apartment he remained during the remainder of the journey, and a servant who went to take the
President's orders found him lying in his berth, his face
buried in the pillows.

Ten days later, Attorney-General Olney was made
Secretary of State. He spent the remainder of the month
in Washington, studying the documents upon which Secretary Gresham had been intent at the time of his death.
As a result, early in July, he went to Gray Gables, and
left with the President the draft of a letter written to
Ambassador Bayard regarding the Venezuelan question.
It was a statement of startling boldness, which, after careful consideration, Mr. Cleveland approved, conditionally,
in the following letter:

> Gray Gables,
> Buzzards Bay, Mass.,
> *July 7, 1895.*

My dear Mr. Olney,

About five hours ago our family was augmented by the
addition of a strong plump loud voiced little girl. Mother
and daughter doing well—also the "old man."

I want to thank you for the rubber gloves which came
last night. If the blue fish will hang around here a little
while longer I will test their effectiveness.

I read your deliverance on Venezuelan affairs the day
you left it with me. It's the best thing of the kind I have

ever read and it leads to a conclusion that one cannot escape if he tries—that is if there is anything of the Monroe Doctrine at all. You show there is a great deal of that and place it I think on better and more defensible ground than any of your predecessors—*or mine.*

Of course I have some suggestions to make. I always have. Some of them are not of much account and some of them propose a little more softened verbiage here and there.

What day after Wednesday of this week can you come and spend a few hours with me so that we can go over it together? Mrs. Cleveland sends love to Mrs. Olney.

Yours sincerely,

GROVER CLEVELAND.

HON. RICHARD OLNEY,
    Falmouth, Mass.

After a conference between Olney, Herbert, Carlisle, Harmon and Lamont, the letter was again revised, put on official State Department paper, was dated the 20th, and forwarded. The "verbiage" had been somewhat softened, but was still far from soft. Indeed, so strong were its terse paragraphs that Mr. Cleveland later christened it "Olney's twenty-inch gun."

It followed the line of facts which Secretary Gresham had worked out, but it did not follow his views regarding procedure. To Isidore Straus, who suggested, "Mr. Olney has stolen your husband's thunder," Mrs. Gresham replied: "No, there was to be no ultimatum as my husband had prepared it, and Mr. Olney and President Cleveland are entitled to all the credit for such a state paper." That the credit was, or should be real, Mr. Cleveland never doubted. Seven years before his death, speaking in Princeton, he declared: "In no event will the American principle [the Monroe Doctrine] ever be better defined, better defended, or more bravely asserted than was done by Mr. Olney in this dispatch."

For several months, the British Foreign Office remained silent, and when the time came for Mr. Cleveland's third annual message, he had nothing new to report. He, therefore, contented himself with the statement that the general conclusions of the Olney dispatch "are in substance that the traditional and established policy of this Government is firmly opposed to a forcible increase by any European power of its territorial possessions on this Continent . . . ; that as a consequence the United States is bound to protest against the enlargement of the area of British Guiana in derogation of the rights and against the will of Venezuela; that considering the disparity in strength of Great Britain and Venezuela, the territorial dispute between them can be reasonably settled only by friendly and impartial arbitration." In view of these facts, he informed Congress, "the dispatch in question called upon Great Britain for a definite answer to the question, whether it would or would not submit the territorial controversy . . . in its entirety to impartial arbitration."

Clearly he did not regard his action as involving any new principle. He was merely preparing to protect another impotent sovereign power, menaced, he believed, as had been Samoa and Hawaii, by a nation strong enough to work her will if left unchallenged. Moreover, unlike Samoa and Hawaii, Venezuela was within the area covered by the Monroe Doctrine, and he felt that any European nation, suspected of an attempt to control the destinies of an American state, either by forcible invasion or by the no less effective method of extending boundary lines, should submit her course to the investigation of impartial arbiters. He felt also that it was entirely proper to call upon her to do so. Whether or not she would consent, he made no attempt to predict.

The message off his mind, he decided to pay a visit to the wilderness where, free from the exactions of official routine, he might think out alone a course of conduct to be pursued when Lord Salisbury's long delayed answer should arrive. He therefore wrote to Olney:

Executive Mansion, Washington.<br>
Dec. 3, 1895.

Dear Mr. Olney,

I want very much to go away this week Thursday and stay until next week—say Friday or some such matter.

Can I do so? I will have all the nominations to go in signed and they can be sent in by instalments during my absence.

The only thing I am hesitating about is the state of some things in your Department.

You cannot receive anything from Bayard or Sir Julian before the early part of next week. Why can you not put the thing in your pocket, so that no one will know you have heard it read or at least that you have it in possession, until I return? In the meantime if its transmission should be accompanied by any particular message you can, if you have time, be blocking it out.

If I were here I would not be hurried in the matter even if the Congress should begin grinding again the resolution-of-inquiry mill.

Yours very sincerely,<br>
GROVER CLEVELAND.

HON. RICHARD OLNEY,
    Secretary of State.

A few days later John Bassett Moore, a loyal supporter of Mr. Cleveland's, sent to Postmaster General

Wilson a twelve-page letter of protest against the President's position.

"I am apprehensive," he said, "that, unless great judgment is exercised, the President's announcement will prove to have started us on a course that involves not only the abandonment of all our traditions, but also our participation in numberless quarrels.

"The statement that the question can be reasonably settled only by such arbitration as Venezuela proposes, certainly was not based on any examination of the merits of the subject.

"The whole system of arbitration presupposes that nations will be reasonable in their claims. The claim of Venezuela to all territory west of the Essequibo is not a scrupulous claim. . . . Instead of asserting that arbitration is the only reasonable way of settling the question, I should say that it would be a very unsatisfactory way of attempting it; and in so saying I do not forget that Lord Granville once consented to lump boundary and all other questions in a general arbitration.

"We have arbitrated boundary disputes and so has Great Britain, but never, so far as I am informed, where a line had not previously been agreed upon by direct negotiation. Governments are not in the habit of resigning their functions so completely into the hands of arbitrators as to say, 'We have no boundaries; make some for us.' . . . It would be at least unusual to leave it to arbitrators to make a boundary. . . .

". . . Boundaries in South America have almost universally been settled on the basis of the *uti possidetis,* as the only practicable basis of peaceful adjustment."

The opinion of Mr. Moore (and his is an opinion

which all nations will be disposed to treat with consideration), was extremely unfavorable to Venezuela.

"For twenty years," he continued, "Venezuela, instead of settling her boundary dispute, has in various ways, some of them obviously dishonest, been trying to drag the United States into the dispute, and the United States has progressed good-naturedly step by step, without examining the merits of the case, till at length with a sudden impulse it leaps over the precipice blindly. And what is the position we now hold? It is substantially this: 'When a weak American republic asserts a claim to territory in America as against a strong European occupant, and offers to submit its claim to arbitration, the European power, if it refuses the offer, is to be considered as holding the territory by force, and as infringing the Monroe Doctrine.' This is the sum and substance of our position. . . .

"We now address Venezuela substantially thus: 'You are an American republic, and in your claims against European powers we back you. True you settled your southern boundary directly, on the basis of the *uti possidetis,* but this principle, though applicable everywhere else in South America, is inapplicable to your eastern boundary. Even the great doctrine of prescription, recognized by every publicist from the time of Grotius, and the very foundation of the peace of nations, is not applicable to that boundary. Claim what you will, and propose arbitration of it, and I will step in and say that it shall be settled in no other way. I know nothing of the merits of the controversy. I am simply backing you. This is according to the Monroe Doctrine.' Of course, the President never intended to say any such thing, but when we examine the facts, we find that it is precisely what he has said."

In concluding his letter, Mr. Moore expressed the

belief that President Cleveland would "not be willing to launch his country on a career as mad and as fatal as that on which France was started by Louis XIV."

But the President had definitely decided, before sending the Olney dispatch, that light must be thrown upon the British claims. Should the British Foreign Office refuse to throw the light, he would be compelled to have it thrown for her by the United States. This decided, he "cut bait," and waited.

While Mr. Cleveland pondered, Mr. Olney studied two dispatches from Lord Salisbury, dated November 26, 1895, which Sir Julian Pauncefote had delivered soon after the President's departure. In the first, while declaring that the Monroe Doctrine had "received the entire sympathy of the English Government," his Lordship frankly declined to accept Mr. Olney's interpretation of that doctrine as applicable to the boundary dispute between Great Britain and Venezuela, "a controversy with which the United States have no apparent practical concern." He emphatically denied our right to demand, "that when a European power has a frontier difference with a South American community, the European power shall consent to refer that controversy to arbitration," and insisted that Secretary Olney had misapprehended the meaning of America's historic policy.

His second dispatch was an historical brief in justification of England's course with reference to the Venezuelan boundary line, from the conquest and military occupation of the Dutch settlements in 1796. In general terms he designated the territory to which her Majesty's government was entitled as being embraced within the lines of the claim which she had presented from the first, and added: "A portion of that claim, however, they have always been willing to waive altogether; in regard to another portion they have been and continue to be perfectly ready to submit the question of their title to arbitration. As regards the rest, that which lies within the so-called Schomburgk line, they do not consider that the rights of Great Britain are open to question. Even within that line they have on various occasions offered to Venezuela considerable concessions as a matter of friendship and conciliation and for the purpose of securing an amicable settlement of the dispute. If, as time has gone on, the concessions thus offered have been withdrawn, this has been the necessary consequence of the gradual spread over the country of British settlements, which Her Majesty's Government cannot in justice to the inhabitants offer to surrender to foreign rule."

In conclusion Lord Salisbury asserted that his government had "repeatedly expressed their readiness to submit to arbitration the conflicting claims of Great Britain and Venezuela to large tracts of territory which from their auriferous nature are known to be of almost untold value. But they cannot consent to entertain, or to submit to the arbitration of another power or of foreign jurists however eminent, claims based on the extravagant pretensions of Spanish officials in the last century and involving the transfer of large numbers of British subjects, who have for many years enjoyed the settled rule of a British colony, to a nation of different race and language, whose political system is subject to frequent disturbance, and whose institutions as yet too often afford very inadequate protection to life and property."

In commenting on these dispatches, Mr. Bayard wrote to the President on December 4th: "The replies of Lord Salisbury to your Venezuelan instructions are in good temper and moderate in tone. Our difficulty lies in the wholly unreliable character of the Venezuelan rulers and

people, and results in an almost undefinable, and therefore dangerous, responsibility for the conduct by them of
their own affairs.  I believe, however, that your interpretation of this boundary dispute will check efficiently the
tendency to 'land grabbing' in South America, which is
rather an Anglo-Saxon disposition everywhere."

To Secretary Olney, however, Lord Salisbury's dispatches were far from satisfactory, and by the time the
President returned to Washington Mr. Olney had formed
definite ideas as to the reply which should be sent and had
embodied them in a set of suggestions for a special message to Congress as strong and unyielding as had been his
"twenty-inch gun."  He advised the President to ask for
an appropriation to meet the expenses of a commission to
determine what the true line between Venezuela and British Guiana should be, and added significantly: "When
such report is made and accepted, it will be the duty of
this Government to communicate to Great Britain the
boundary line thus ascertained and to give notice that any
appropriation of territory or exercise of jurisdiction by
Great Britain beyond that line (except with the consent
of Venezuela) will be regarded by this Government as a
wilful aggression upon the rights and interests of the
United States which this Government cannot suffer to go
undefended."

Armed with this document, Mr. Olney met the returning President, was closeted with him for a few hours,
and retired.  Mr. Cleveland spent the remainder of the
night at his desk, and by dawn had the draft of a message
ready for the copyist.  At ten o'clock he received a fair
copy, which he revised, and by noon his most famous
state paper was ready.

In the message as finally sent to Congress on December
17, 1895, about ninety per cent of Mr. Olney's sentences

were discarded; but his most menacing phrases were retained, and explain the later contention that the Venezuela Message was "a New England document, written by a New Englander." It was, however, Cleveland's in the same sense in which Monroe's most famous message was Monroe's, although drafted by John Quincy Adams, and as Washington's Neutrality Proclamation was Washington's, although showing traces of the pens of more than one eminent man of the time. In each case the responsibility rested upon the President, and upon him alone.

The message itself was brief. It is summed up in the words:

"The answer of the British Government . . . claims that . . . a new and strange extension and development of this [the Monroe] doctrine is insisted on by the United States; . . . that the reasons justifying an appeal to the doctrine . . . are inapplicable. . . .

"If a European power by an extension of its boundaries takes possession of the territory of one of our neighboring republics against its will and in derogation of its rights . . . this is the precise action which President Monroe declared to be 'dangerous to our peace and safety,' and it can make no difference whether the European system is extended by an advance of frontier or otherwise. . . .

"The dispute has reached such a stage as to make it now incumbent on the United States to take measures to determine . . . the true division line between the Republic of Venezuela and British Guiana. . . . When such report is made . . . it will . . . be the duty of the United States to resist by every means in its power . . . the appropriation by Great Britain of any lands . . .

which after investigation we have determined of right belong to Venezuela.

"In making these recommendations I am fully alive to the responsibility incurred and keenly realize all the consequences that may follow. . . . There is no calamity which a great nation can invite which equals that which follows a supine submission to wrong. . . ."

With the text of the message, the press received also the texts of Secretary Olney's note and of Lord Salisbury's two replies. There was no attempt to conceal from the people the extreme gravity of the situation.

Thus was the issue squarely drawn between the United States and Great Britain, and for once the President had the practically unanimous approval of the members of both houses of Congress, regardless of politics.

In his account of the reception of the message by Congress, the New York *Herald's* Washington correspondent telegraphed: "All the traditions of the Senate were cast to the winds when the message was read in that body, for the chamber rang with applause, in which the Republicans seemed to take even a more hearty part than the Democrats. In the House, the President's vigorous expressions were cheered to the echo . . . Republicans . . . as enthusiastic . . . as their political opponents. It is long since any President's message has had such a reception."

The first British mail brought an anxious letter to the President:

*Personal*

Embassy of the United States, London
*Dec. 18, 1895.*

Dear Mr. President:

With this note I send you the *Times* of this morning—in order that you may perceive the tone of *average*

*British comment* on your message to Congress and position in relation to the Venezuelan-Guiana boundary dispute and claim of right and duty under American policy as laid down by President Monroe to insist upon a submission of questions, touching the territorial jurisdiction of South American states to international arbitration—

I send to the Secretary of State fuller—or rather more numerous—public expressions on the subject—which while varying in phrase and tone—are entirely at one on the main point, i.e., of opposition to the propositions laid down in your message, and the instructions of the State Department conveyed to this Embassy—

In my correspondence while I was Secretary of State —also with Judge Gresham since I came here—and personally with you—my opinions have been genuinely stated—and as the Venezuelan transactions and history are unfolded I am not able to shake off a grave sense of apprehension in allowing the interests and welfare of our Country to be imperilled or complicated by such a government and people as those of Venezuela.

It is not needful that I should repeat these views—and I now wish to study carefully and deliberately the situation as it exhibits itself under the light suddenly cast upon this profoundly important question—which includes in its principles and treatment every European claim of ownership and control of soil in the western hemisphere—

May peace, happiness and health dwell in your home —and throughout the country you have served so unselfishly and faithfully—

Sincerely yours

The President
of the United States.

T. F. BAYARD.

Mr. Bayard's letter showed that he was mystified and uncertain regarding the exact position of the President, whose views he was to interpret to the British government and to the British people. Mr. Cleveland therefore sent the following reply:

Executive Mansion, Washington.
*December 29, 1895.*

My dear Mr. Bayard:

I thank you sincerely for the hunting stool you kindly sent me, and I hope I may have abundant occasion to recall by its use your thoughtfulness.

I am very sorry indeed that I cannot fully understand your very apparent thought and feeling on the Venezuelan question; and you must believe me to be entirely sincere when I say that I think my want of understanding on the subject is somehow my own fault.

You cannot fail to remember my inclination, during my former incumbency of this office, to avoid a doctrine which I knew to be troublesome and upon which I had nothing like your clear conception and information. I knew that your predecessors for many years, and you as well, regarded the Monroe doctrine as important, and I supposed that when it was frequently quoted by you and them in treating of this very question of Venezuelan boundary, it was so quoted because it was deemed to have relation to that question. Not being able to perceive how a doctrine could have any life or could do any good or harm, unless it was applicable to a condition of facts that might arise, and unless when applied all consequences must be appreciated and awaited, I was quite willing if possible within the limits of inexorable duty, to escape its serious contemplation.

I remember too how kindly and considerately you used to speak of and treat the people and the governments of South America, though fully understanding their weaknesses and faults, and how much, through your treatment of them these countries became attached to the Administration. Very few incidents attended my last coming to Washington, more pleasing than the heartiness with which the representatives of Central and South America welcomed me. These considerations are not, however, of importance since in an application of the Monroe doctrine, though another country may give the *occasion,* we are I suppose not looking after *its* interests but *our own.*

Events accompanying the growth of this Venezuelan question have recently forced a fuller examination of this question upon me and have also compelled us to assume a position in regard to it.

I am entirely clear that the doctrine is not obsolete, and it should be defended and maintained for its value and importance *to our government and welfare,* and that its defense and maintenance involve its application when a state of facts arises requiring it.

In this state of mind I am positive that I can never be made to see why the extension of European systems, territory, and jurisdiction, on our continent, may not be effected as surely and as unwarrantably under the guise of boundary claims as by invasion or any other means. In 1888 you called Mr. Phelps' attention to the apparent enlargement of Great Britain's boundary claims between the years 1877 and 1887, and I think within a year you have referred us to the same or other enlargements. I have not failed to notice the stress laid by Lord Salisbury upon the fact that settlements have been made by British subjects whose allegiance might be disturbed if England's insistence was found to be incorrect.

We do not say, either that Great Britain's boundary claim is false, nor that the enlargement of her claims toward the centre of Venezuela as now known, is unjustifiable beyond a doubt, nor that the settlements upon the territory claimed by Venezuela, have been brought about or encouraged while delay in settling the boundary has been prompted or permitted; nor do we attach too much prejudicial importance to other facts and considerations within our view, but we do say that these things and others furnished a controversy in which we were interested, that this controversy was complicated by facts so disputed that it presented a case which of all cases that can be imagined should be subjected to the sifting and examination which impartial arbitration affords.

The refusal to refer the question to such determination was intensely disappointing.

It was disappointing because we cannot see the force of the reasons given for refusal.

After a little hesitation, just here, I shall mention another reason for disappointment and chagrin, which I believe to be entirely irrelevant to the case and which has had absolutely nothing to do with any action I have taken. It would have been exceedingly gratifying and a very handsome thing for Great Britain to do, if, in the midst of all this Administration has had to do in attempts to stem the tide of "jingoism," she had yielded or rather conceded something (if she called it so, which I do not) for our sake. In our relations with her we have been open, honest and fair, except as to settling or providing for the adjustment of claims for Behring Sea seizures. I am ashamed of the conduct of Congress in that matter but it is understood everywhere how persistent the Administration has been in efforts to have the right thing done.

The insistence upon a principle or the assertion of a right should be the same in the case of England as Chili; and I do not see, the necessity actually arising, that former relations or anything of that sort should prevent action or change the course of action, except that good relations, etc., might induce a nation to acquiesce in arbitration when not obliged to do so, in aid of the ascertainment of facts which a friendly power felt should be developed to relieve it from embarrassment.

Great Britain says she has a flawless case. Our interest in the question led us to ask her to exhibit that case in a tribunal above all others recognized as a proper one for that purpose; and this was done to avoid a wrong procedure on our part in a matter we could not pass by.

Great Britain has refused our request. What is to be done? We certainly ought not, we certainly cannot abandon the case because she says she is right, nor because she refuses arbitration. We do not threaten nor invite war because she refuses—far from it. We do not propose to proceed to extremities, leaving open any chance that can be guarded against, of a mistake on our part as to the facts. So instead of threatening war for nor arbitrating, we simply say inasmuch as Great Britain will not aid us in fixing the facts, we will not go to war but do the best we can to discover the true state of facts for ourselves, with all the facilities at our command. When with all this, we become as certain as we can be, in default of Great Britain's co-operation, that she has seized the territory and superseded the jurisdiction of Venezuela—that is a different matter.

I feel that I would like you to know precisely what is in my mind and therefore I have hastily written you, without the least hint of it to any person whatever and without the least consultation.

It seems as if all the troubles and perplexities that can

gather about the office I hold, were just at this time, making a combined assault.

As ever

Your sincere friend,

GROVER CLEVELAND.

HON. T. F. BAYARD,
    Ambassador, &c., &c.,
      London.

The President's message fell like a crash of thunder upon English ears, attuned to the precision of diplomatic language, and made familiar by the history of "thin red lines of heroes" with the meaning of war. The *Annual Register* summed up its opinion in the following words: "The President's extraordinary proposal was believed to have been made in view of the approaching Presidential election, in which the American-Irish vote would be an important factor; and this belief was strengthened by the eagerness of Republicans and Democrats alike to associate themselves with a policy which affected to appeal to a sentiment of patriotism. For several days politicians in the United States, with a few exceptions, gave themselves up to a delirium of jingoism, and had that feeling continued and been reciprocated by the English press and the English people, the two countries might really have drifted into war."

Englishmen of whatever party, however, restrained their language, and hoped for an adjustment. In a speech at Bristol, two days after the publication of the message, the Chancellor of the Exchequer, as spokesman for the British Cabinet, confidently and courteously predicted that when the "case of Great Britain . . . was laid before the people, either on this side of the Atlantic or on the other, the result would be happy, peaceful, and honorable to both parties."

In contrast to such expressions from British statesmen, the manners displayed in the American Congress left much to be desired, needlessly complicating an already delicate situation by language as uncalled for as it was unparliamentary. Outside, in the street, the theater, and the market place, men of even lesser minds caught the infection. Jingoes shrieked for war; American yellow journals fanned the flame, and one gallant orator, climbing to the giddy peak of exaggerated patriotism, toppled over with the impious prayer that he might live to "guide center forward" against "my ancient enemy."

In opposition to this senseless war clamor, the New York *World* stood out conspicuously, earning the right to public gratitude by cabling to certain leading men of England for "a word of peace" with which to stem the tide of war.

Mr. Gladstone replied: "I dare not interfere. Common sense only required. I cannot say more with advantage."

The Prince of Wales, disregarding the convention which normally kept his name out of international disputes, answered that both he and the Duke of York "earnestly trust, and cannot but believe, that the present crisis will be arranged in a manner satisfactory to both countries, and will be succeeded by the same warm feeling of friendship which has existed between them for so many years."

John Redmond, on the other hand, sent a reply calculated to fan the war flame, and to encourage his Irish kinsmen across the sea: "You ask for an expression of opinion from me, on the war crisis, as a representative of British thought. In this, as in all other matters, I can speak only as a representative of Irish opinion. If war results from the reassertion of the Monroe Doctrine, Irish national sentiment will be solid on the side of America. With Home Rule rejected, Ireland can have no feeling of friendliness for Great Britain."

Congress having authorized the appointment of the commission "to determine . . . the true division line between the Republic of Venezuela and British Guiana," Mr. Cleveland selected the following distinguished citizens to act as that commission: David J. Brewer, Associate Justice of the Supreme Court of the United States, Richard H. Alvey, Chief Justice of the Court of Appeals of the District of Columbia, Andrew D. White, ex-President of Cornell University and ex-Minister to Russia, Frederic R. Coudert, one of the counsel for the United States in the Behring Sea Arbitration, and Daniel C. Gilman, President of Johns Hopkins University.

Their appointment apparently had the effect of arousing Great Britain to the need of a less dangerous method of settlement, for a few days later Ambassador Bayard sent the following cipher telegram to Secretary Olney, containing the plan for an adjustment by which neither Great Britain nor Venezuela would be called upon to abandon long established settlements:

Translation of cipher telegram sent from the Embassy *January 13, 1896*.

Olney, Secretary, Washington.

Lord Playfair, lately Liberal Cabinet Minister, came confidentially yesterday to my residence, at the request of Lord Salisbury and Secretary of State for Colonies, expressing earnest desire of both political parties here Venezuela dispute should not be allowed to drift, but be promptly settled by friendly co-operation. Suggests as solution, United States should propose conference with United States of European countries now having Colonies in American Hemisphere—Great Britain, France, Spain, Holland, to proclaim the Monroe Doctrine—that European Powers having interests in America, should not seem to extend their influence in that Hemisphere. If the United States would propose this, Great Britain would accept Monroe Doctrine, and it would become international law between countries named. Assuming from the President's Message, that any settlement of boundary satisfactory to Venezuela, would be unobjectionable to United States, friendly arbitration is suggested. There being no Venezuelan settlements inside Schomburgk line, and no British settlements beyond that line; therefore, irrespective of that line, mutual condition be accepted, that all British and all Venezuelan settlements be excluded from arbitration, but all country between the settlements be settled by a Court of Arbitration drawing a boundary line, which should be accepted by both countries. Such Court of Arbitration to consist of two or three Commissioners from England, two or three from Venezuela, and two or three from present United States Commission, to represent knowledge they have acquired. Under this principle, districts already settled by Venezuela or British Government or people, would not be referred to by arbitration, and there would be no difficulty in settling line by friendly arbitration. I will write you fully next Wednesday mail. But desire to express positive judgment, that proclaimed recognition of Monroe Doctrine as international law between Powers named would make it binding, not only on them, but practically on all other European Powers, and would end all contemplated plans of future conquest, or intermeddling alliances, in the Western Hemisphere, by European Powers, under any pretext.

BAYARD.

After carefully considering these suggestions, Mr. Cleveland and Mr. Olney decided against calling a conference of European powers to pass judgment on the Monroe Doctrine, declaring that they preferred to deal with Great Britain alone. To this Lord Salisbury readily consented.

Meanwhile the American Commissioners continued the work for which the President had appointed them. Confident of the British sense of fair play, they applied to the British government for aid, and on February 11th, the Honorable A. J. Balfour, First Lord of the Treasury, and Conservative Leader of the House of Commons, reported to Parliament: "We have promised to give them all the information we are able to give at the earliest possible moment." (Cheers.) "No false pride or diplomatic punctilio will be allowed to stand in the way of a settlement, as far as we are concerned. Whatever other conclusions the Commission may arrive at, it will most assuredly reach the conclusion that no desire to push beyond the due limit of the frontier of this empire has ever been the animating cause which moved British diplomacy in this long-drawn-out controversy." Lord Salisbury followed with the conciliatory announcement: "I do not think that the invoking of the Monroe Doctrine was, controversially, quite unnecessary," and admitted that satisfactory results would have come less rapidly had not the United States interfered. "I have had an increasing belief during the past few weeks that we shall . . . find some satisfactory settlement, and all danger of a rupture of relations between the two nations be entirely removed." (Cheers.)

By the middle of May both countries were intent upon the preparation of plans, and on the 22nd Lord Salisbury sent a definite proposal for the substance and form of a treaty for the creation of the joint arbitration committee. Seven weeks later Mr. Olney, acting in accordance with England's own suggestion to that effect, as expressed in Bayard's dispatch of January 13th, asked whether Great Britain would consent to unrestricted arbitration of the whole matter, "provided it were made the rule of the arbitration that territory which had been in the exclusive, notorious, and actual use and occupation of either party for sixty years should be held to belong to such party." This suggestion, differing from that of the British proposal only in that it specified the period of sixty years as the term of occupancy, was accepted by Lord Salisbury.

And so, in his fourth annual message, Mr. Cleveland was able to announce: "The Venezuelan boundary question has ceased to be a matter of difference between Great Britain and the United States, their respective Governments having agreed upon the substantial provisions of a treaty between Great Britain and Venezuela submitting the whole controversy to arbitration. The provisions of the treaty are so eminently just and fair that the assent of Venezuela thereto may confidently be anticipated."

On February 2, 1897, one month before President Cleveland's retirement, such a treaty between Great Britain and Venezuela was signed at the State Department in Washington. It was a strange, if not a unique instance of treaty making, American State Department officials having taken the leading part in the negotiations, although Great Britain and Venezuela were the signatories. Articles I and II provided for an arbitral tribunal to consist of five jurists, two on the part of Great Britain, two on the part of Venezuela (one named by President Cleveland and one by the Justices of the United States Supreme Court), and the fifth to be selected by these four. Article III empowered the tribunal to "determine the boundary line between the Colony of British Guiana and the United States of Venezuela"; while Article XIII bound the signatory powers "to consider the result of the proceedings of the tribunal of arbitration as a full, perfect, and final settlement of all the questions referred to the arbitrators." On October 3, 1899, the award was presented to the British Parliament, and the controversy was at an end.

That an adjustment, honorable alike to both England and America, was reached is to the credit of both; but the biographers of Lord Salisbury may safely add to his many achievements the fact that it was his proposal, transmitted through Ambassador Bayard's dispatch of January 13, 1895, which enabled America to abandon her independent study of the Venezuela boundary and opened the way to a peaceful settlement.

# CHAPTER VII

## THE WARWICK OF 1896

*"Our fealty to party rests upon something higher and better than an instinct to blindly follow adventurous leadership, regardless of consequences."*

—GROVER CLEVELAND.

SOME time before the assembling of the National Conventions of 1896, Mr. Euclid Martin, Chairman of the Nebraska State Central Committee, wrote to President Cleveland from Omaha: "We held our primaries day before yesterday in this city for the purpose of selecting delegates to a Democratic State Convention. The issues were many. Upon one side was Democracy and the administration. Upon the other was Free Silver, Populism, Bryanism, Strikism and a very large sprinkling of Church. The ambition of those who oppose the administration seemed to be to combine all of the elements, and they were apparently successful. . . . The Populists who wanted a Populist Governor were willing to play upon the prejudices of the Catholic Church because the Republican nominee is supposed to be a member of a secret organization antagonistic to their church, and the Honorable William Jennings Bryan was in it for all there was in sight for himself. . . . *Circumstances* and *treachery* of those who should *owe* you allegiance, without calling names further, played an important part in the result. Add to this a craze for which I cannot account, and which I am pleased to say is abating to some extent, for Mr. Bryan, and the results are before you."

At the same time William Lynde Stetson warned him that the New York Democracy was in the hands of its worst enemies, and that the silver men "are making plans for 1896, when the silver party shall have swallowed the Populists, as the Republicans did free silver." Evidently, despite Mr. Cleveland's many battles in its behalf, the gold standard was not yet safe and could be permanently decided only by a national referendum in a presidential election. To educate the people upon this question before it was too late, therefore, appeared to the President the imperative need of the hour, and he began to urge upon those still in sympathy with his views the necessity of informing the public upon the dangers inherent in an unsound currency. With this in mind he wrote to a group of Chicago business men:

"If the sound money sentiment abroad in the land is to save us from mischief and disaster, it must be crystallized and combined and made immediately active. It is dangerous to overlook the fact that a vast number of our people, with scant opportunity thus far to examine the question in all its aspects, have nevertheless been ingeniously pressed with specious suggestions, which in this time of misfortune and depression find willing listeners, prepared to give credence to any scheme which is plausibly presented as a remedy for their unfortunate condition.

"What is now needed more than anything else is a plain and simple representation of the argument in favor of sound money. In other words, it is time for the American people to reason together as members of a great nation, which can promise them a continuance of protection and safety only so long as its solvency is unsuspected,

its honor unsullied, and the soundness of its money unquestioned.  These things are ill-exchanged for the illu-
sions of a debased currency and groundless hope of
advantages to be gained by a disregard of our financial
credit and commercial standing among the nations of the
world.

"If our people were isolated from all others and if
the question of our currency could be treated without
regard to our relations to other countries, its character
would be a matter of comparatively little importance.
If the American people were only concerned in the
maintenance of their physical life among themselves they
might return to the old days of barter, and in this primitive manner acquire from each other the materials to
supply the wants of their existence.  But if American
civilization were satisfied with this, it would abjectly fail
in its high and noble mission.

"In these restless days the farmer is tempted by the
assurance that though our currency may be debased,
redundant, and uncertain, such a situation will improve
the price of his products.  Let us remind him that he
must buy as well as sell; that his dreams of plenty are
shaded by the certainty that if the price of the things he
has to sell is nominally enhanced, the cost of the things
he must buy will not remain stationary. . . .

"It ought not to be difficult to convince the wage
earner that if there were benefits arising from a degenerated currency they would reach him least of all and
last of all.  In an unhealthy stimulation of prices an
increased cost of all the needs of his home must long be
his portion, while he is at the same time vexed with the
vanishing visions of increased wages and an easier lot.
The pages of history and experience are full of this lesson.

"An insidious attempt is made to create a prejudice against the advocates of a safe and sound currency by the insinuation, more or less directly made, that they belong to financial and business classes, and are therefore not only out of sympathy with the common people of the land, but for selfish and wicked purposes are willing to sacrifice the interests of those outside their circle.

"I believe that capital and wealth, through combination and other means, sometimes gain an undue advantage, and it must be conceded that the maintenance of a sound currency may, in a sense, be invested with a greater or less importance to individuals according to their condition and circumstances. It is, however, only a difference in degree, since it is utterly impossible that anyone in our broad land, rich or poor, whatever may be his occupation, and whether dwelling in a center of finance and commerce or in a remote corner of our domain, can be really benefited by a financial scheme not alike beneficial to all our people, or that anyone should be excluded from a common and universal interest in the safe character and stable value of the currency of the country. . . .

"If reckless discontent and wild experiment should sweep our currency from its safe support, the most defenseless of all who suffer in that time of distress and national discredit will be the poor, as they reckon the loss in their scanty support, and the laborer or workingman as he sees the money he has received for his toil shrink and shrivel in his hand when he tenders it for the necessaries to supply the humble home. Disguise it as we may, the line of battle is drawn between the forces of safe currency and those of silver monometalism."

Two weeks later, he wrote to Governor Stone of Mississippi:

Executive Mansion, Washington, D.C.
*April 26, 1895.*

HONORABLE J. M. STONE, Governor
My dear Sir:
    . . . .

If we, who profess fealty to the Democratic party, are sincere in our devotion to its principles, and if we are right in believing that the ascendency of those principles is a guarantee of personal liberty, universal care for the rights of all, non-sectional, American brotherhood and manly trust in American citizenship in any part of our land, we should study the effects upon our party and consequently upon our country of a committal of the national democracy to this silver aberration.

If there are Democrats who suppose that our party can succeed upon a platform embodying such a doctrine, either through its affirmative strength or through the perplexity of our opponents upon the same proposition, or if there are Democrats who are willing to turn their backs upon their party associations in the hope that free, unlimited and independent coinage of silver can win a victory without the aid of either party organization, they should deceive themselves no longer, nor longer refuse to look in the face the results that will follow the defeat, if not the disintegration of the Democratic party upon the issue which tempts them from their allegiance. If we should be forced away from our traditional doctrine of sound and safe money our old antagonists will take the field on the platform which we abandon, and neither the votes of reckless Democrats nor reckless Republicans will avail to stay their easy march to power. . . .

Yours very truly,
GROVER CLEVELAND.

From that time until the assembling of the Democratic Convention, the warfare between the Free Silver
Democrats and the followers of Grover Cleveland grew
ever fiercer, each faction maneuvering for position in
the coming battle. From Bryanism in the West and
South, from Gormanism in Maryland, from Vest and
Jones, Bland and Voorhees, from New York's Tammany-
ized Democracy, despite its normal sound money sympathies, he knew that he and his sound money allies could
expect only vituperation and insult, despite the fact that
the end of his political career was close at hand. Even
had they not differed with him on this vital subject, they
and the myriad other enemies, bred of many conflicts,
were eager to send him forth at the end of his public
service repudiated, like the ancient Hebrew scapegoat
upon whose fleecy back the highpriest laid the sins of the
people.

Meanwhile the voice of the scandalmonger was again
heard in the land, fashioning ever new lies. Indignant
at the utter baseness of their attacks, Don M. Dickinson
wrote to the President:

666 Jefferson Avenue.

My dear Mr. President:

I want to thank you not only for your note of the 19th
inst., but also for your good letter of the 18th ulto., of
which I expected when in Washington, to have had an
opportunity to speak to you but did not.

No one has a clearer realization of the situation than
I, no one has seen what you have passed through with a
keener or more sensitive appreciation of the general
demoralization and prevailing madness, and of your
situation in the midst of it. History will set down your
four years as the most difficult period—war work

excepted—in the life of this government, for its Chief Executive, and history will surely set down against the epoch, that the Chief, standing alone, was great in his place, equal to every occasion, a patriot always, and in and of himself the bulwark that turned back the flood of destruction.

Surely you hold up the only beacon. Outside and around, God and Truth and Right and Honor seem a dream. Self-sacrifice, bravery, loyalty, friendship, seem to have left you alone on the field. *Friendship!* it sneaks or whispers its professions in hiding. *Friendship!* in public and in private, it listens to insult with lowered eyes, or covertly smiles or winks at the enemy at the vilest ribaldry at the expense of a friend. One is not to challenge any vile spawn from the mouth of "rank" (rank save the mark) for fear of getting into the papers and being lied about. Who stays the liars and the mouthers of billingsgate from saying and printing broadcast the foulest screeds under the sanction of "high" official station? A man who is so bound that he cannot move, so held, that he cannot speak, is attacked by none of the human race except the digger Indian. But he who stands by and sees a digger Indian do it is meaner than the digger. Democrats, yes, but they are among the rank and file. I am glad I am among them. If I had been in office in these times I would have fought myself back to the ranks in some highly improper way, no doubt.

The people, not as Democrats or Republicans, but the American people, a part of the great mind of the Infinite, *do* understand and *do* appreciate, and will accord, not mere justice, but reward of merit; of this I have no more doubt than I have the sun shines. In the meantime I can only emulate Smollett when he said:

"Thy spirit, independence, let me share,
    Lord of the lion heart and purpose high.
Thy steps I follow with my bosom bare,
    Nor heed the storm that howls along the sky."

Faithfully yours,
DON M. DICKINSON.

Commodore Benedict wrote in the same strain, and
to him Mr. Cleveland replied: " . . . Such expressions
are my only comfort, except my wife and babies, in these
troublous, perplexing days. The next week will be
especially harassing and anxious, and what will follow
may add to my burdens. Do you know, my dear Commodore, that I have never been so sure as now that there
is a high and unseen Power that guides and sustains the
weak efforts of man? I feel it all the time and somehow I have come to expect that I shall find the path of
duty and right, if I honestly and patriotically go on my
way. I should be afraid to allow a bad, low motive to
find lodgment in my mind, for I know I should then
stumble and go astray."

But though often discouraged, he kept up the fight for
popular enlightenment. On May 20th, he wrote to a
conference of New York Democratic newspaper editors:

"There is a temptation now vexing the people in different sections of the country which assumes the disguise
of Democratic party principle, inasmuch as it presents a
scheme which is claimed to be a remedy for agricultural
depression and such other hardships as afflict our fellow
citizens. Thus, because we are the friends of the people
and profess devotion to their interests, the help of the
members of our party is invoked in support of a plan to

revolutionize the monetary condition of the country and embark upon an experiment which is discredited by all reason and experience, which invites trouble and disaster in every avenue of labor and enterprise, and which must prove destructive to our national prestige and character.

"When a campaign is actively on foot to force the free, unlimited and independent coinage of silver by the government at a ratio which will add to our circulation unrestrained millions of so-called dollars, intrinsically worth but half the amount they purport to represent, with no provision or resource to make good this deficiency in value, and when it is claimed that such a proposition has any relation to the principles of Democracy, it is time for all who may in the least degree influence Democratic thought to realize their responsibility.

"Our party is the party of the people, not because it is wafted hither and thither by every sudden wave of popular excitement and misconception, but because while it tests every proposition by the doctrines which underlie its organization, it insists that all interests should be defended in the administration of the government without especial favor or discrimination.

"Our party is the party of the people because in its care for the welfare of all our countrymen it resists dangerous schemes born of discontent, advocated by appeals to sectional or class prejudices, and reinforced by the insidious aid of private selfishness and cupidity.

"Above all our party is the party of the people when it recognizes the fact that sound and absolutely safe money is the life blood of our country's strength and prosperity, and when it teaches that none of our fellow citizens, rich or poor, great or humble, can escape the consequences of a degeneration of our currency."

In such letters, sent to leading Democrats throughout
the nation, President Cleveland sounded the call, before
the measure of his second term was more than half
accomplished. And it was this educational feature which
later made the campaign of 1896 unique in our history.
His alarm increased as the months passed, and his language strengthened with his sense of danger. In July
he wrote to Dickinson: "The devils that were cast out
of the swine centuries ago have, I am afraid, obtained
possession of some so-called Democratic leaders. Good
times and justification of Democratic policy, with gifts
in their hands, are driven out from the Democratic camp.
If there was a penitentiary devoted to the incarceration
of those who commit crimes against the Democratic
party, how easily it could be filled just at this time."

While such views more and more infuriated the silver
men, they created among sound money men of whatever
party the feeling that Grover Cleveland was the safest
man in public life. "The amount of third term feeling
that exists in New York is amazing," wrote William
Elroy Curtis. "President Cleveland seems to be the only
man in the Democratic party, and although there is
general dissatisfaction with the financial and foreign
policies of the administration, the same people who condemn them predict that he will be the next candidate for
president.

"I sat the other day in a business house which is very
prominent in the South American trade, and where all
the five partners are Democrats, some of whom have
been very active in politics. They condemned the administration for revoking the reciprocity treaties, for preventing the annexation of the Hawaiian Islands, for permitting Great Britain to blackmail Nicaragua, for not
interfering in the Cuban revolution, for the Venezuela

boundary dispute, for enforcing the payment of the
Mora claim, for permitting Chile to get the better of us
in the recent claims commission, and for almost everything else that has been done or omitted in our foreign
relations, and declared the Cleveland administration had
done more to injure our foreign trade than years of careful cultivation could correct.     Then when we began to
talk of the future every one of them declared his belief
that the President would be nominated for a third term
and would be the strongest candidate the Democrats
could offer to the country.

"Nor is this an exceptional instance.   You hear the
same talk everywhere—at the hotels, at the clubs and
restaurants, in the banks and brokers' offices and wherever
men who talk politics gather together."

The more the third term idea gained in strength, the
more violent were the denunciations heaped upon the
President by political opponents.   "I have never felt so
keenly as now the unjust accusations of political antagonists," he wrote to Dickinson, on February 18, 1896,
"and the hatred and vindictiveness of ingrates and traitors
who wear the stolen livery of Democracy. .   . You
know my supreme faith in the American people.   While
I believe them to be just now deluded, mistaken and
wickedly duped, they will certainly return to sound principles and patriotic aspirations; and what I may suffer
in the period of aberration is not important.   I have
studied laboriously to discover or imagine what, if anything, is in the minds of those who assume the rôle of
Democratic leaders.   Hatred of the administration seems
to be the only sentiment that pervades their counsels.

"It is absolutely certain that this issue [free silver]
will not wear during the campaign nor lead to success.

It will be the irony of fate, if in the hour of defeat, thus invited, the air is filled with democratic clamor accusing me of destroying party prospects. And yet this is precisely what I expect.

"I have a consciousness within me, however, and an experience behind me that will permit me to bear even this injustice with resignation; and I will patiently wait for the final verdict of my countrymen, which will certainly in due time be returned.

"I cannot be mistaken in believing that if the Democratic party is to survive, its banner upon which shall be inscribed its true principles and safe policies, must be held aloft by sturdy hands which even though few, will in the gloom of defeat, save it from the disgraceful clutch of time-serving camp followers and knavish traitors."

A few weeks later, he wrote again to Dickinson:

Executive Mansion, Washington,
*March 19, 1896.*

My dear Mr. Dickinson

I was made very happy yesterday by the receipt of the painting you sent me of the duck hunter. It is a very *relieving* picture to look at and every time my eye falls on it in these dreadfully dark and trying days, I say to myself, "I wish I was in that old fellow's place."

Two things I am longing for—the adjournment of Congress and the 4th day of March, 1897.

I honestly believe the present Congress is a menace to the good of the country if not to its actual safety. If the Democratic party was in proper condition and inclined to half behave itself the wildness and recklessness of this Republican Congress would turn many thousands of recruits to our party; but every day develops more and more plainly the seeming desperation and wickedness of those in the Senate and House for whose conduct our party will I suppose be held responsible.

I am positive there is but one chance for future Democratic successes—a perfectly and unequivocal sound money platform at Chicago. If this means the loss of votes, present defeat, or even a party division, the seed will be saved from which I believe Democratic successes will grow in the future.

But I must not be morbid on this subject—all the same it is outrageous that Democracy should be betrayed "in its hour of might."

Hoping that your short rest has done you good, I am

Yours very sincerely

GROVER CLEVELAND.

HON. DON M. DICKINSON,
Detroit, Mich.

Although determined that under no circumstances would he consider the idea of a third term, his letters of this period show a more eager interest in the coming presidential campaign than he had shown regarding the three contests in which he himself had figured as a candidate. Visions of disaster to his party, if seduced to error by the growing free silver wing, haunted him, and he eagerly watched the progress of state elections, those gauges which indicate the direction of the winds of politics. To Dickinson he wrote on May 1st:

Executive Mansion, Washington,
*May 1, 1896.*

My dear Mr. Dickinson

I steal a moment from working hours to write this, because I feel that I cannot longer refrain from expressing my thanks as a citizens and a democrat, to you and

those who worked with you, for the splendid achievement . . . in Michigan.

Whatever else may be done before July 7th to save
the country and the party, the result of the Michigan
Democratic State Convention will be, *must* be, looked
upon as the most important incident of all that will crowd
the intervening time. I know you do not want the least
invidious mention, when so many have done so well, but
I must tell you how much prouder than ever I am of
your friendship, and how glad I am to know more of
the splendid material in Stevenson's construction. No
two men in the country have better cause for self-
congratulation.

New York hangs fire and delays speaking, though she
can say but one thing, and though she now owes that
speech to the party and the cause. I am much humiliated and ashamed that she should be thus kept in the
background by the same dickering, petty, ignoble,
criminal figuring that will confront us "in our hour of
might" at Chicago. The treacherous cry of harmony
and the false pretense of compromise will still I fear be
in the path of those who may fight valiantly and well as
you have done.

Thanking and trusting you, and with sincere remem-
brances to Mr. Stevenson, I am

Yours very sincerely

GROVER CLEVELAND.

HON. DON M. DICKINSON.

President Cleveland was working for no mere temporary party victory. He already distinguished "the true
Democracy" from the body of death which was slowly
donning its livery. "We can survive as a party without
immediate success at the polls," he wrote to Dickinson,

"but I do not think we can survive if we have fastened upon us as an authoritative declaration of party policy, the free coinage of silver."

As the date of the Democratic National Convention drew near, however, it became increasingly difficult for him to believe that the Democrats would refuse the silver bait. The party was unmistakably being prepared for the transformation which would make of it the Free Silver party, and Mr. Cleveland was compelled to face, however reluctantly, the question, "What then?" He knew that he could not serve a free silver party, even as a private in the ranks. On the other hand, the Republican party offered no allurements, even had he been able to forget the McKinley tariff which had stamped it forever, in his mind, as the party of the interests. Moreover, McKinley, though now the leading candidate for the Republican nomination, had as yet recanted none of his silver views, and the chance seemed not too remote that the Republicans would sidestep the issue.

Under these circumstances he could but cling to the hope that the Democratic National Convention might after all be controlled by sound money men. "I am praying now," he wrote to L. Clarke Davis, on May 14th, "that the prevalent infection may pass away, leaving life and hope of complete recovery. In the meantime, the brood of liars and fools must have their carnival." Should the Democratic Convention declare for free silver, the only chance for the gold standard lay in the adoption by the Republicans of an uncompromisingly sound money platform, for he still believed that there were gold money men enough to elect a President if only they could have a party through which to express their views.

During the early months of the year, President Cleve-

land and Colonel Lamont had arranged to have the body
of the late Secretary of State removed to a place of honor
in Arlington Cemetery, and in May, Mrs. Gresham and
her son, Otto Gresham, accompanied the remains to the
new resting place. During his few days' visit to Washington Mr. Otto Gresham had frequent talks with the
President on the currency question. "During these conversations," writes Mr. Gresham, "the President confidently declared that 'if the Democrats should adopt a
free silver platform, that is silver at 16 to 1, and the
Republicans straddle, silver would win, because no sound
money Democrat would vote for a silver Republican
for President, and the silver Republicans will vote for
16 to 1.'"

Mr. Gresham left Washington convinced of the
soundness of this prophecy, and convinced also that the
President, too, would bolt the Democratic ticket if the
coming convention should father the free silver heresy.
On his way back to Chicago, he stopped at Indianapolis
to give the Indiana Democratic leaders the benefit of
Mr. Cleveland's views, and sought out as well his father's
old friends in the Republican camp.

According to his own account of his interviews, his
most fruitful conversation was with Charles W. Fairbanks, who showed him the keynote speech which he had
prepared for the coming Republican National Convention, of which Mr. McKinley had asked him to be temporary chairman. The speech was at best a straddle,
Mr. Gresham writes: "He quoted from McKinley's
speeches in favor of the Bland-Allison act, and in support of silver propaganda looking to some measure to
take the place of the Bland-Allison act, as it was expiring
by limitation. After he had finished reading it, he asked

me what I thought of it. I told him it would not do at all."

For a time they argued the situation, Fairbanks, a sound money man at heart, but planning a keynote speech controlled by considerations of political expediency, and Otto Gresham, a sound money enthusiast, filled with faith in Cleveland's prediction that a straddle on the part of the Republicans would mean a free silver President. "Mr. Cleveland," finally declared Gresham, "is going to bolt to your side, provided you give him something to bolt to. The silver Republicans will leave you and go to the silver Democrats if you straddle; the only chance for you to win is to get on a sound money platform." After a few moments' hesitation, Mr. Fairbanks replied: "I see it. You are right. I will tear this speech up, and write another one."

This second speech, duly delivered at the opening of the St. Louis Convention, gave notice that the Republican party, so long complacent toward the free silver heresy, was now ready to stand four-square for the gold standard. "We protest," it declared, "against lowering our standard of commercial honor. We stand against the Democratic attempt to degrade our currency to the low level of Mexico, China, India and Japan. The present high standard of our currency, our honor and our flag will be protected and preserved by the Republican party."

This change, in the opinion of Mr. Gresham, would not have been made had Mr. Fairbanks not "learned Mr. Cleveland's opinion. . . . He had unbounded faith in Mr. Cleveland's judgment and patriotism. . . . I am just as sure as I am of anything that I did not personally participate in, that Fairbanks sent McKinley Grover Cleveland's views as I brought them." "I have no doubt," he later declared, "that it was Grover Cleveland's views, financial and political, that switched William McKinley from . . . soft money to hard money in 1896."

While not too nearly akin to McKinley's own ideas, as interpreted by his past actions, these views were identical with those of Mark Hanna, McKinley's political manager. Hanna, a "gold bug" from the beginning, felt certain that McKinley could be nominated, but wished to be equally sure that if nominated he would stand upon an out-and-out gold platform. He therefore allowed the Platform Committee to debate the silver question for two days, and waited to be approached by the gold men, whom he had purposely left in doubt as to his position. At last they came, with an ultimatum. He must within one hour side with the gold wing or they would fight McKinley on the floor of the convention. Within the limits of the hour, the gold plank which Hanna had brought ready prepared with him to the convention was in the hands of the triumphant gold men, and William McKinley was secure of a place in history as the leader of the sound money crusade of 1896.

Upon the adoption of the platform, as sound in its financial plank as either Cleveland or Hanna could wish, the silver Republicans fulfilled to the letter Mr. Cleveland's prediction. Headed by Senators Teller, of Colorado, DuBois, of Idaho, Pettigrew, of South Dakota, and Cannon, of Utah, they marched, thirty-four strong, out of the Republican house of gold to find honored places in William Jennings Bryan's Democratic house of silver.

Such is the strange story of the influence exerted by a Democratic President upon a Republican campaign program, as told by one who saw matters from the inside. It is confessedly only a section of the picture, for, as Mr. Gresham's memorandum fully recognizes, many other leaders had their parts in the work of writing sound money principles into the Republican platform of 1896. Thomas C. Platt, for example, has modestly confessed: "In 1896 I scored what I regard as the greatest achievement of my political career. This was the insertion of the gold plank in the St. Louis platform." But Thomas C. Platt has confessed other things, and still others have been confessed for him, and therefore the world will not accept his voice as the voice of Clio, the muse of history, even though it accepts the fact that he played an important rôle in this drama, in company with a host of others: Herrick, Payne, Morrison and Lodge, Reed, Allison, Morton, Depew, and many more. Mr. Kohlsaat and Senator Foraker has each blushingly confessed himself the *deus ex machina,* and their part none can question. But the truth, while including them all, shows also the dominant figure of Grover Cleveland, the man who played in both companies in the interest of neither, but that the people's honor should be above reproach.

But though thus able to influence the Republican National Convention, Mr. Cleveland knew how small was his chance of changing the sentiments of the National Convention of his own party. Four weeks before the assembling of the latter he wrote to Dickinson:

Executive Mansion, Washington.
*June 10, 1896.*

My dear Mr. Dickinson

I so fully approve of your suggestions concerning delegations of sound and solid men to attend the convention as non-delegates with a view of exerting a wholesome influence on delegate sentiment, that I immediately began to agitate the subject in quarters where I thought it would effect the best results. My ideas seemed to meet with approval and I had some assurances of co-operation, though I am bound to say to you that they were even then accompanied with that sort of reserved enthusiasm which seems to have for the most part characterized all movements in favor of sound financial policy. Since the receipt of your letter, however, events have occurred so discouraging to the cause of sound finance, that I am afraid the efforts promised will not be made. The fact is, people whom I see here who believe with us, appear to be thoroughly impressed with the idea that nothing can be done to stem the tide of silverism at Chicago.

I believe I am by nature an undismayed and persistent fighter and I do not believe in giving an inch until we are obliged to; and yet it is hard to call on friends to maintain a struggle which seems so hopeless.

It does not seem to me that there should be any relaxation in the effort to prevent our party from entering upon a course which means its retirement for many years to come. If we cannot succeed in checking the desperate rush, perhaps a demonstration can be made which will indicate that a large section of the party is not infected. I don't know how this can best be done, but I very much desire that we shall not all have to hang our heads when our party is accused of free silverism.

Of course I have never seen anything like this craze before, but my faith in the American people is so great that I cannot believe they will cast themselves over the precipice.

But there is our old party with all its glorious traditions and all its achievements in the way of safe and conservative policies, and its exhibitions of indestructibility. Is it to founder on the rocks? Will not sanity return before we reach the final plunge? While I am not completely discouraged, I confess the way looks dark.

The most astounding feature of all this matter is the lethargy of our friends and the impossibility of stirring them to action. Michigan seems to be the only state whose work was needed and was forthcoming.

Events sometimes crowd closely upon each other and much may be developed within even four weeks.

Yours sincerely

GROVER CLEVELAND.

HON. DON M. DICKINSON.

When the Democratic National Convention assembled at Chicago on July 7th, it was at once apparent that the free silver men would control. Senator Daniel was chosen temporary chairman of the convention, to the discomfort of David B. Hill, who was now prominent as leader of the gold Democrats. Another ardent silver leader, Senator White of California, was made permanent chairman; and pending the report of a platform, the convention listened entranced to eloquent proponents of a currency reform guaranteed to save the nation.

The adoption of a platform demanding the free and unlimited coinage of both silver and gold at the ratio of 16 to 1 without waiting for the aid or consent of any other nation; the rejection by a vote of 564 to 357 of a resolution commendatory of the Cleveland administration, which David B. Hill introduced with the gleeful consciousness that it would be overwhelmingly defeated, and the nomination of William Jennings Bryan on the fifth ballot made Mr. Cleveland's dethronement complete. "Never before in American history," wrote a correspondent who witnessed his eclipse, "has a President sunk so low as Cleveland has fallen. Never has a President been so held in contempt by the people. No one is interested enough to care what he does or says. . . .

Cleveland has been driven out of his party, and it was Hill who closed the door and double locked it with his resolution as Cleveland departed."

It was here that Bryan made his "Crown of Thorns and Cross of Gold" speech. Up to that time, Bland was the leading Democratic candidate for President, and had a majority of the delegates, but from the moment of the "Cross and Crown" speech, state after state planted its banner beside the Nebraska standard, until two thirds of the convention were so represented.

It was felt by many of the onlookers that the sound money men would bolt, but this conviction was not justified. Tammany Hall was apparently ready to depart, but the counsels of Mr. Whitney, Governor Russell of Massachusetts, and other sound money leaders prevailed, and Tammany sat in silent protest as the platform was adopted and Bryan was nominated. When the nomination was announced, Senator Vest remarked in a stage whisper: "Now we are even with old Cleveland."

In accepting the nomination, Mr. Bryan amplified the protest, already made in the platform, against federal interference in local affairs. Taking Article IV, Section 4, of the Federal Constitution as his warrant, he pledged himself against such interference as that to which President Cleveland had resorted when he sent troops to Chicago in 1894.

Nothing could have more graphically illustrated the determination of the Bryanized Democracy to repudiate the former chief, for it was the Honorable John W. Daniel, of Virginia, president of the convention which nominated Bryan, who had proposed the resolution unanimously passed by the United States Senate on July 12, 1894, that: "The Senate indorses the prompt and vigorous measures adopted by the President of the United

States and the members of his administration to repulse and repress, by military force, the interference of lawless men with the due process of the laws of the United States, and with the transportation of the mails of the United States, and with commerce among the States."

In commenting upon the subject, the eminent Democratic leader, Judson Harmon, wrote: It is "a far more serious matter than the money question or any of the other questions before the people, grave as they all are. If a candidate for President may properly pledge himself in advance, as Mr. Bryan has done, to do nothing to protect the property, maintain the authority, and enforce the laws of the United States, unless and until the officers of another government request or consent, then we really have no Federal Government, for a government which is not entirely free to use force to protect and maintain itself in the discharge of its proper functions is no government at all."

The results of the convention gave President Cleveland a new phrase. Instead of the "free silver heresy," his fight was henceforth against "Bryanism." An abstract idea which he abhorred had become incarnate. His indignation at this conquest of an organization, this appropriation of an honored name, was boundless. While Hill was content to follow the new banner, declaring, "I am still a Democrat, very still," Cleveland, acting upon his own maxim, "a just cause is never lost," prepared to bolt, advising his friends, however, to hold their peace until a definite plan of action could be agreed upon.

"I really do not see what I can properly do or say," he wrote to Colonel Lamont, a few days later. "Those who controlled the convention displayed their hatred of me and wholly repudiated me. Those who at the convention differed from them, seem to have thought it wise to ignore me in all consultation fearing probably that any connection with me would imperil success. I do not say they were not right. I only say that events have pushed me so much aside that I do not see how I can be useful in harmonizing or smoothing matters.

"I have an idea, quite fixed and definite, that for the present at least we should none of us say anything. I have heard from Herbert to-day. He says he has declared he will not support the ticket. I am sorry he has done so. We have a right to be quiet—indeed I feel that I have been invited to that course. I am not fretting except about the future of the country and party, and the danger that the latter is to be compromised as an organization.

"I suppose it has occurred to you that since the Chicago Convention there cannot be a fool stupid enough or malicious enough to attribute to the present administration any calamity that may befall the organization of the Democratic party. While I would be willing to incur that accusation to save or benefit the party in a good cause, what is the use of inviting such an accusation by saying something which at this time can have no influence for good? I feel well out of it by the condemnation I have received at the hands of those who have managed affairs, and by the nomination of men whose personal hatred of me seemed to be a prerequisite for convention honors. Others who fought on the other side were not anxious to see me gain anything from the outcome, whatever it might be.

"I am receiving a good many letters from all sorts of people, which confirm me in the belief that, whatever the rest think they ought to do, I ought to keep silence—at least until conditions change.

"In the meantime I am having some good fishing and promptly attending to all official work sent me."

But though fully conscious of his position in the party

at large, he believed that every member of his Cabinet
was with him. It was, therefore, a shock to receive from
Hoke Smith, Secretary of the Interior, the information
that he considered it his duty to support Mr. Bryan publicly in his paper. This appeared to Cleveland almost
incredible. The Atlanta *Journal* had been regarded by
sound money men as one of their chief instruments for
presenting the gold cause to the South, and an elaborate
sound money supplement was ready for the press when
it was suddenly decided to swing the paper over to the
support of Bryan. The cause of the swing, as Secretary
Smith confessed in a letter to Mr. Cleveland, was local.
"I consider the protection of person and property involved in the local Democratic success which can only
continue through Democratic organization. I would
strike my own people a severe blow if I repudiated a
nominee of a regular convention, thereby setting a precedent for disorganization. While I shall not accept the
platform, I must support the nominee of the Chicago
Convention."

After some delay the President sent the following
answer:

Gray Gables
Buzzards Bay, Mass.
*August 4, 1896.*

My Dear Mr. Smith.

I suppose I should have replied to your letter of July
20th before; but to tell you the truth I have delayed and
hesitated because I could not satisfy myself as to what
I should write.

I have determined to say to you frankly that I was
astonished and much disappointed by your course and
that I am by no means relieved by the reasons you present
in justification of it.

When you addressed the citizens of your state so
nobly and patriotically, you were discussing the silver
question alone; and when you assured them that you
intended to support the nominee of the National Convention you could certainly have intended no more than to
pledge yourself that in case you were overruled by the
convention *in the question under discussion* you would
accept your defeat and support the platform and candidates which represented that defeat. This—considering
your strong expressions on the silver question, your earnest advocacy of sound money and your belief in its
transcendent importance—was going very far.

You surely could not have intended to promise support to a platform directly opposed not only to sound
money but to every other safe and conservative doctrine
or policy, and framed in every line and word in condemnation of all the acts and policies of an administration
of which you have from the first been a loyal, useful and
honorable member. You could not have intended a
promise to uphold candidates, not only pledged to the
support and advancement of this destructive and undemocratic platform, but whose selection largely depended
upon the depth and virulence of their hatred to our administration. I say "our" administration because I have
constantly in mind the work we have done, the patriotism
that has inspired our every act, the good we have accomplished and the evil we have averted in the face of the
opposition of the vicious forces that have temporarily
succeeded in their revolt against everything good and
glorious in Democratic faith and achievement.

It is due to our countrymen and to the safety of the
nation that such an administration should not be discredited or stricken down. It belongs to them and should
be protected and defended, because it is their agency

devoted to their welfare and safety. None can defend
it better than those who constitute it, and know the sin-
gleness of purpose and absolute patriotism that have
inspired it. You say, "While I shall not accept the platform, I must support the nominees of the Chicago Convention." I cannot see how this is to be done. It seems
to me like straining at a gnat and swallowing a camel.

The vital importance of the issues involved in the
national campaign and my failure to appreciate the
inseparable relation between it and a state contest, prevent
me from realizing the force of your reference to the
"local situation." I suppose much was said about the
"local situation" in 1860.

I am perfectly satisfied that you have been influenced
in the position you have taken by the same desire to do
exactly right that has guided you in all your acts as a
member of the Cabinet. You know how free my association with my official family has been, from any attempt to influence personal action, and how fully that
association has been characterized by perfect confidence
and a spirit of unreserved consultation and frankness.

In this spirit I now write. I have no personal grievance that any one need feel called on to even notice. My
only personal desire is to make as good a President as
possible during the residue of my term, and then to find
retirement and peace; but I cannot believe that I will do
my duty to my countrymen or party—either as President
or citizen, by giving the least aid and comfort to the
nominees of the Chicago Convention or the ideas they
represent.

                    Yours very sincerely,
                         GROVER CLEVELAND.

HON. HOKE SMITH,
   Washington, D. C.

Before this letter reached him, Mr. Smith wrote again:

Department of the Interior, Washington,
*August 5, 1896.*

Mr. President:

I had the honor, on July 20th, of advising you that I felt it to be my duty to support the nominee of the National Democratic Convention, notwithstanding the declaration by that Convention adverse to the views I entertain on the financial question.

I felt then, as I do now, that, in view of the contrary position assumed by some of the members of the Cabinet, the proprieties of the occasion would be best subserved by stating these conditions of embarrassment, and leaving to your judgment any suggestion that would insure the unanimity of counsel which you might desire.

To that communication I have received no reply.

I am constrained to infer that the embarrassments suggested by my letter of the 20th ult. are recognized by you as existing.

I therefore tender my resignation as Secretary of the Interior.

Very respectfully,
HOKE SMITH.

This letter crossed in transit Mr. Cleveland's reply to Secretary Smith's first letter; and accordingly the Secretary wrote again:

*August 6, 1896.*

My dear Mr. President:

I was very much pleased to receive your letter of this morning, which passed mine on the road. I must admit that I was a little hurt by your continued silence, for I can scarcely tell you how much I would feel the loss of your confidence.

I can hardly expect you to see the situation as I do, and I shall not undertake further to present it. I hope to still contribute in part toward helping the people to appreciate the great, patriotic work of your administration, nor do I believe my opportunity to do so will be lessened on account of the course which I pursue. My New England and German blood do not fit me to show feeling, but none the less my admiration for the President has grown during the last three years into an attachment scarcely less than that I have for my immediate family. I hope I am sufficiently devoted to the nation, but in 1860 I should have gone with my state, and now I must stand by it.

Very respectfully,

HOKE SMITH.

For the Cleveland wing of the party, as for the President himself, neither Bryanism nor McKinleyism had any appeal. Of the two they preferred the latter, although McKinley's enthusiasm for sound money had come so late as to smack of opportunism. With no hope but the election by indirection of the Republican candidate, they organized the National Democratic party, that sound money and Clevelandism might not be without witnesses in the coming campaign.

On September 2nd, this third party, belated but determined, met in National Convention at Indianapolis. "This convention," declared their platform, "has assembled to uphold the principles upon which depend the honor and welfare of the American people, in order that Democrats . . . may unite their patriotic efforts to avert disaster from their country and ruin from their party."

Denouncing the heresies of "protection and its ally, free coinage of silver," it reaffirmed the doctrines which the Cleveland *régime* had striven to promote, and praised "the fidelity, patriotism, and courage with which President Cleveland has fulfilled his great public trust, the high character of his administration, its wisdom and energy in the maintenance of civil order and the enforcement of the laws, its equal regard for the rights of every class and every section, its firm and dignified conduct of foreign affairs, and its sturdy persistence in upholding the credit and honor of the nation."

Such praise at such a time was sweet even to so unegotistical a nature as the President's, and its sincerity was attested by the following telegram, which came the day the platform was adopted:

Indianapolis, Ind., *Sept. 3, 1896.*
To HON. GROVER CLEVELAND:

You will be nominated to-morrow unless you make a definite refusal. Strongly urge that you communicate privately to be used publicly if necessary with some friend on the ground. Otherwise every indication you will be nominated by acclamation.

D. G. GRIFFIN.

Mr. Cleveland at once telegraphed in reply:

Buzzard's Bay, Mass., *Sept. 3, 1896.*
To DANIEL G. GRIFFIN,
Chairman New York Delegation,
Indianapolis, Ind.

My judgment and personal inclinations are so unalterably opposed to your suggestion that I cannot for a moment entertain it.

GROVER CLEVELAND.

But his heart was with the Gold Democrats, although his name was withheld; and when news came that on the first ballot John M. Palmer had been nominated, the President thus confided his approval to Colonel Lamont:

"I am delighted with the result of the Indianapolis Convention. Its platform is the best possible statement of the true doctrines of Democracy and makes all those who believe in and love the grand old organization [feel] that they still have a home. I am gratified to know that you are willing to declare your sentiments and the quicker and stronger you and any other member of the Cabinet speak the better I shall like it. My notion is that the tone should be, or at least one note of it, that the Indianapolis platform and candidates are democratic and the Chicago platform and candidates are not.

"I am perplexed concerning the course I should pursue. My inclination, of course, is to join the chorus of denunciation, but I am doubtful as to the wisdom of such action, in the light of a chance that [it] might do more harm than good. My position cannot be misunderstood by any man, woman, or child in the country. I am President of all the people, good, bad, and indifferent, and, as long as my opinions are known, ought perhaps to keep myself out of their squabbles. I must attempt to co-operate with Congress during another session in the interest of needed legislation, and perhaps ought not to unnecessarily further alienate that body and increase its hatred of me, and if I take an active and affirmatively aggressive position it may aid the cause we have *not* at heart, in increasing the effectiveness of the cry of presidential interference. In addition to all this, no one of weight or judgment in political matters has advised me to speak out—though I shall be surprised if Palmer does not urge it soon.

"If you say anything, I do not care how plainly you present the inference that I am in accord with your views."

Mr. Cleveland's praise was for those who "loved the principles of their party too well to follow its stolen banners in an attack upon those national safeguards which party as well as patriotism should at all times defend." But he was too shrewd to cherish the hope that Palmer could be chosen. Thus he found himself, a Democratic President of the United States, hoping to see a Republican victory which would place McKinley at the head of the nation.

Although determined to take no active part in the coming campaign, he felt that he could, without violating this purpose, accept one invitation which reached him in the early autumn. The College of New Jersey was to celebrate on October 22d her Sesquicentennial, and to mark the passage of one hundred and fifty years of public service by taking the name of Princeton University. With the escort and dignity appropriate to his high office and to the importance of the occasion, he appeared at Princeton on the day appointed, and in the presence of a company of scholars from many lands, and of leading Americans from many sections, delivered one of the most carefully prepared addresses of his life. The glory of an educated citizenship; the duty of a college or university toward the state; the dangers latent in ignorance concerning the great natural laws upon which organized society rests—these were his themes. He spoke in terms suitable to a purely academic function; but many of his carefully phrased sentences turned the minds of his auditors, and of the millions who later read the address, toward the question of the hour: "the free silver heresy," never once mentioned, but always implied.

"When popular discontent and passion," he said, "are stimulated by the arts of designing partisans to a pitch perilously near to class hatred or sectional anger, I would have our universities and colleges sound the alarm in the name of American brotherhood and fraternal dependence. When the attempt is made to delude the people into the belief that their suffrage can change the operation of natural laws, I would have our universities and colleges proclaim that those laws are inexorable and far removed from political control. . . . When a design is apparent to lure the people from their honest thoughts and to blind their eyes to the sad plight of national dishonor and bad faith, I would have Princeton University, panoplied in her patriotic traditions and glorious memories, and joined by all the other universities and colleges of our land, cry out against the infliction of this treacherous and fatal wound."

While the newspaper men sent his speech broadcast, the President and Mrs. Cleveland gave themselves up to the enjoyment of the students' enthusiasm. Remembering that whatever the result of the coming election, he must seek a new home on the fourth of the coming March, he observed Princeton with the eye of a prospector, and the prospector became in spirit the intending settler as he stood with his wife that evening on the steps of Nassau Hall, where Washington had received the first French Ambassador.

The hour of the scholar, the statesman, the savant from many lands, had passed with the formal meetings. This was the hour of the undergraduate. The students had arranged a parade, dotted with illuminated transparencies, touched with the humor which is the ever-present asset of student life the world over. As the President and his beautiful wife gazed upon the passing show, they got a glimpse of a transparency bearing the inscription: "Grover, send your boys to Princeton." At that moment the Cleveland "jewels" consisted of three daughters: Ruth, Esther, and Marion, born, one in New York, one in the White House, and the third at the President's summer home at Gray Gables on Buzzard's Bay. No son had appeared. But there was the transparency, which, as they looked, moved forward and halted immediately in front of them: "Grover, send your boys to Princeton." The President had entered Princeton an admirer of the college. He left it a Princeton man, although he had declined the honorary degree which was offered him.

From the academic shades of the university he passed again into the hot furnace of political strife. The campaign was nearing its close. Mr. McKinley upon his front porch at Canton, Ohio, and Mr. Bryan from an hundred platforms throughout the land, had discussed the issue, which was now about to be submitted to popular vote.

With election day came a landslide. Mr. McKinley received over half a million more votes than Mr. Bryan, with the comfortable assurance that he would enter the Presidency with a Republican majority in both House and Senate. The fight had been made for principles that are too high for party property, and the fight was won. With a courage that few men in his situation have displayed, and a patriotism that will be honored in all coming time, Mr. Cleveland had resisted a pressure strong enough to have overwhelmed any man less ready to sacrifice self in obedience to conviction.

Mr. Bryan summed up the cause of Democratic defeat in one sentence: "I have borne the sins of Grover Cleveland." But Mr. Bryan had not borne the sins of Grover Cleveland. He had borne the sins of a fundamental financial heresy, in the making of which Grover Cleveland had had no part nor lot. And Mr. Cleveland, as he watched the celebrations of the triumphant goldbugs, knew that they were the rejoicings of sound money men of all parties, and was satisfied that, like the strong man, he had slain more in his last great effort than he had slain in his life. His enemies were tireless in abuse, but the noise and vaporings of the few were not the sentiment of the millions who were patriots before being partisans.

"When the history of the present time comes to be seriously written," declared the Baltimore *Evening News* of November 4, 1896, "the name of the hero of this campaign will be that of a man who was not a candidate, not a manager, not an orator; the fight which has just been won was made possible by the noble service of one steadfast and heroic citizen, and the victory which was achieved yesterday must be set down as the crowning achievement of his great record. . . . It is impossible to overestimate the value of the service Grover Cleveland has done through his twelve years of unswerving fidelity to the cause of honest money. . . . This is Cleveland's day, the vindication of his course, and the abundant reward of his steadfast adherence . . . to that principle of honor which he has held above self, above party, above expediency."

# CHAPTER VIII

## THE FOUR LEAN MONTHS

*"I have done my duty as I saw it. I feel that I need no defense."*

—GROVER CLEVELAND.

IN the life of every President there comes at last the trying period which, from the point of view of national leadership, might well be called the four lean months. During this time, which the Constitution, in obedience to former conditions of travel, allows for a retiring President to stand aside, he is in effect a broken vessel. If he has served the two terms fixed by custom as the limit of an executive's official days, he stands as a "has been," a leader who can no longer lead. If he has served but one term and has been defeated for reelection, he is an Ichabod, whose glory has departed.

But of all our Presidents, Grover Cleveland alone knew both these periods of political poverty. In 1888 he was a defeated President. Now he was to have the still more trying experience of a President repudiated by his own party, which had itself been defeated, and which, not without reason, blamed him for its defeat. And truly but little power remained to him. Either he was no longer a Democrat, or the Democratic party had shrunk to strangely small dimensions, for he was determined to acknowledge no kinship with William Jennings Bryan or the infatuated crowd which hailed him with the cry, "Bryan is our savior."

Grimly he accepted his position of "splendid isolation," rejoicing in the conviction that he had remained right, even when his party had gone wrong. He knew that what he termed "The True Democracy" was composed of his followers, not of the majority now worshipping strange gods and who, as he expressed it, had with "the blight of treason blasted the councils of the brave." Nor were Mr. Bryan and his friends less bitter. They, in their turn, denounced the President as one who had used his party for his own selfish gain, and sold it out to the enemy.

From time to time came rumors of impending magazine articles planned to interpret to the world outstanding incidents in his presidential career, but he viewed them lightly. To Mr. Gilder, who wrote him an anxious letter upon the subject, he replied:

Executive Mansion, Washington.
*November 20, 1896.*

My dear Mr. Gilder:

You are quite right. There are now three projects on foot to serve me up and help people to breast or dark meat, with or without stuffing. The one I have heard the most of was, when I last got a sight of it, running towards Professor —— the man who made *The Nation* at Princeton. I've forgotten his name. [Woodrow Wilson.]

I don't know in the shuffle what will become of me and my poor old battered name, but I think perhaps I ought to look after it a little. I shall probably avail myself of your kindness.

Yours sincerely,

GROVER CLEVELAND.

Mr. Gilder having offered his own brilliant pen in defense of the "poor, old, battered name," the President gratefully accepted the proffered service, despite his life-long aversion to biographical work with himself as the theme:

Executive Mansion, Washington.
*Dec. 27, 1896.*

My dear Mr. Gilder:

I was very much touched to receive on Christmas day, your beautiful and valuable gift, made more impressive by the sentiment suggested on the card accompanying it. Of all men in the world you know best that I do honestly try to "keep the compass true," and I am convinced that you appreciate, better than others, how misleading the fogs sometimes are. I frequently think what a glorious boon omniscience would be to one charged with the Chief Magistracy of our nation.

I can only thank you from the bottom of my heart, for this last, of many, proofs of your friendship, and assure you of the comfort and encouragement it has been to me. I should be afflicted if my barometer ever indicated anything but "clear weather" in our relations.

I have been afraid sometimes since I left you here a week ago, that you might not feel like bothering us too much in the preparation of the article you had in proof. I want to say to you that you must draw on us to any extent you desire, to make the article suit you. Of course your magazine instinct fits you to judge as to the items that will interest readers, but you must understand that everything, personal or otherwise, that would be at all suitable for such publication is at your disposal.

For example, I have been sometimes surprised and irritated by the accusation or intimation that I lacked in appreciation of friendship and did not recognize suffi-ciently what others did for me. Of course this is as far from the truth as it can be, and can only have its rise in a refusal on my part to compensate friends by misappropriation from the trust funds of public duty. To this I plead guilty on many charges; but no one is more delighted than I when friendship and public duty travel in the same way. Would it add a bit to the interest if the reader was given a little more of a peep at the home life and the sustaining influence of wife and children— working in the remark I have many times made, in dark and trying times of perplexing public affairs, in answer to inquiries after the welfare of my family: "They are as well as they can be. It is this end of the house that troubles me. If things should go wrong at the other end I would feel like quitting the place for good"? Having made these suggestions, I am so impressed that they are useless and foolish that I feel like telling you to utterly disregard them, except as they indicate my willingness to do anything you wish in the premises.

A few days ago Mr. Gardiner Hubbard and Mr. McClure (of *McClure's Magazine*) called on me and said Carl Schurz was to write an article for that magazine on the administration; and they wanted to know if Mr. Cox could take some pictures, etc. Of course I could not object, but the *Century* article was spoken of and Professor Wilson's too. They seemed to understand or to know about both, and thought Mr. Schurz could hold his own with anyone in the same field. I suppose his article will be far removed from the track of yours.

I was delighted in my late interview with Mr. Schurz to see that he had recovered from his Venezuelan scare and was quite satisfied apparently with the civil service reform situation. He is a good and useful man and I am always pleased to have him friendly, but as I told him once, he is "a hard master." I only hope he will gain

the best information attainable and be just. I know he
will try to be.

This is a horribly long letter. Give my love to Mrs.
Gilder and believe me

Sincerely your friend

GROVER CLEVELAND.

R. W. GILDER, ESQ.

But conflicts awaited him which related to pending
questions and which perforce took precedence over mere
matters of his own place in history. From the beginning
of his troubled life as President, with its not infrequent
threats of war, some undoubtedly induced by his masterful method of conducting foreign affairs, Mr. Cleveland had worked to secure the adoption of an arbitration
treaty between the United States and England. Mr.
Carnegie, already famous for his services to the cause of
arbitration, had pronounced him "as strong a supporter
of that policy as ever I met." But the ceaseless disputes
about fisheries, which had raged with ever-increasing
bitterness since the Senate's rejection of his treaty of
1888, had fostered emotions unfavorable to the project.
Now, however, beneath Secretary Olney's guiding hand,
the irritating question, "What are the rights of American
fishermen?" had given place to the greater question: "Are
we willing to agree that all matters in difference between
the United States and Great Britain shall be settled by
friendly arbitration?"

On January 11, 1897, a treaty to that effect, negotiated
by Secretary Olney and Sir Julian Pauncefote, was sent
by Mr. Cleveland to the Senate. It bound the two nations, for a period of five years, "to submit to arbitration,
in accordance with the provisions and subject to the
limitations of this treaty, all questions in difference be-

tween them which they may fail to adjust by diplomatic negotiations," and provided for the appointment of arbitrators. It was Mr. Cleveland's hope that this treaty might stand beside the pending Venezuelan treaty as his last great act of service, not only to England and America, but to the general cause of peace. "Its ultimate ensuing benefits," he said, "are not likely to be limited to the two countries immediately concerned. . . . The example set and the lesson furnished by the successful operation of this treaty are sure to be felt and taken to heart sooner or later by other nations, and will thus mark the beginning of a new epoch in civilization."

The publication of the message, with an outline of the treaty, was the signal for demonstrations of enthusiasm in both countries. The New York *Tribune,* after a canvass of the members of Congress, announced that: "From each came expressions of cordial satisfaction. There was not a discordant note." The London *Standard* declared that it was proof positive that the lessons of the panic that followed the Venezuelan Message had not been thrown away, and the London *Times* ventured to predict that the Senate would not "defeat a policy that has obtained a decided and unusual degree of approval among the American people." And indeed the whole country recognized the treaty not only as the crowning glory of Mr. Cleveland's administration, but as a fitting climax to the century of civilization that was drawing to its close. Chambers of Commerce, boards of trade, church congresses, and the leading newspapers throughout the length and breadth of the land were urgently insistent upon the ratification of this treaty of lasting peace between the two greatest nations of the world.

On February 2d, Senator Sherman, Chairman of the Committee on Foreign Relations, reported the treaty

favorably, five out of six Republican members of the
committee having voted in favor of such a report, while
three out of the four Democratic members had opposed it.
For six weeks thereafter it remained under debate in
executive session. Some Senators objected that such a
treaty, if ratified before the Clayton-Bulwer Treaty of
1850 was definitely abrogated, would amount to a surrender of the American dream of building and controlling a canal across the Isthmus of Panama. Others
devised amendments which brought on renewed discussion, while still others talked for the sake of passing the
time. Toward the end of the session, the treaty was referred back to the committee, and in consequence the end
of the Cleveland administration saw it still in the possession of that body, no vote having been taken in the
Senate itself.

On March 17th, when Sherman, now Secretary of
State, met the Senate Committee on Foreign Relations,
he was told that the Arbitration Treaty would be reported favorably on the following day, and this was done;
but more discussion was the only immediate result. At
last, on May 5th, it came up for decision and was lost,
only forty-three votes being cast in favor of what remained of it after months of senatorial amending had
left it a mere skeleton.

To Mr. Cleveland and Mr. Olney, now private citizens, this outcome was a bitter disappointment. "The
treaty," sarcastically declared the latter, "in getting itself
made by the sole act of the Executive, without leave of
the Senate first had and obtained, had committed the unpardonable sin. It must be either altogether defeated
or so altered as to bear an unmistakable Senate stamp—
and thus be the means both of humiliating the Executive
and of showing to the world the greatness of the Senate.

Hence, the treaty has been assailed from all quarters and by Senators of all parties, and although the present Executive advocated its ratification no less warmly than his predecessor. The method of assault has been as insidious as it has been deadly. . . . Before the treaty came to a final vote, the Senate brand had been put upon every part of it, and the original instrument had been mutilated and distorted beyond all possibility of recognition. The object of the Senate in dealing with the treaty—the assertion of its own predominance—was thus successfully accomplished and would have been even if the treaty as amended had been ratified." Its defeat was, Olney declared, "a calamity, not merely of national but of world-wide proportions."

The other subject which disturbed the closing months of Mr. Cleveland's public life, was that of the revolution in Cuba. In February, 1895, the Cubans had rebelled against their Spanish masters, and on September 25th of that year Secretary Olney had reported to the President: "The situation of affairs in Cuba seems to me one calling for the careful consideration of the Executive. The Spanish side is naturally the side of which I have heard, and do hear, the most. It is, in substance, that the insurgents belong to the lowest order of the population of the Island, do not represent its property or its intelligence or its true interests, are the ignorant and vicious and desperate classes marshaled under the leadership of a few adventurers, and would be incapable of founding or maintaining a decent government if their revolution against Spain were to be successful. . . . There are, however, grounds for questioning the correctness of this view. . . . The Cuban insurgents are not to be regarded as the scum of the earth . . . In sympathy and feeling nine tenths of the Cuban population are with them. . . . The property class to a man is disgusted with Spanish misrule, with a system which has burdened the Island with $300,000,000 of debt, whose impositions in the way of annual taxes just stop short of prohibiting all industrial enterprise, and which yet does not fulfill the primary functions of government by insuring safety to life and security to property."

As an illustration of Spanish methods, he cited "the short and effective way the government has of dealing with non-combatant suspects. A file of soldiers visits certain designated houses at night—the proscribed persons are carried off—but, partly for the torture of the thing, and partly because the noise of the firearms is to be avoided, they are not shot but chopped to pieces with the small axes that the Spaniards call *machetes*." He summed up his conclusions with the declaration that the Cuban revolution was "just in itself, commanding the sympathy, if not the open support, of the great bulk of the population affected, and capable of issuing in an established, constitutional government," and expressed the conviction that within a few months either Cuba would be smothered in its own blood, or be "in the market, for sale to the highest bidder," as Spain would never be able to suppress the rebellion. He warned the President that American "politicians of all stripes, including Congressmen," were "setting their sails, or preparing to set them, so as to catch the popular breeze," which blew in the direction of a recognition of Cuban belligerency.

Since then the soundness of Mr. Olney's observations had been amply demonstrated. Spain's weakness and increasing cruelty, the unconquerable persistence of the insurrectionists, and the drift of American public sympathy, all had revealed themselves with unmistakable clearness. Other dangers, too, had emerged. The rights of American citizens in Cuba had become manifestly unsafe, their lives manifestly in danger.

As these facts had appeared, Congress had shown an increasing tendency to seize control, or as Ambassador Bayard expressed it, had seemed "strangely inclined to reverse the order of the Constitution, and . . . send messages and information to the Executive—not to receive them from him." This undoubted tendency Congress had already expressed in a concurrent resolution declaring that Cuban belligerent rights should be promptly recognized, a resolution which Secretary Olney ironically characterized as "an interesting expression of opinion." It had, however, apparently made not the slightest impression either upon him or upon Mr. Cleveland, who insisted that the conduct of America's foreign affairs belonged by law to the Executive, and that while Congress had the right to declare war, it was the President's duty to maintain peace until war was declared.

The end of October brought developments which made the task of preserving peace vastly more difficult. On the 21st of that month, Valeriano Weyler, the Spanish Captain-General of Cuba, issued his order of reconcentration, and with it the Spanish policy of suppression became a policy of extermination. The simple peasants from the outlying districts, most of whom had shown sympathy for the rebellion, were driven into the fortified towns and there subjected to treatment which called pestilence to the aid of the sword for their destruction. Four hundred thousand *reconcentrados* were soon kenneled in these urban pens of disease and starvation, while the world looked on in horror. The situation thus created required firm and wise leadership, as a declaration of war was inevitable unless some new solution could speedily be made effective. Such a solution Mr. Cleveland believed to lie in the purchase of the island, though he held the mailed fist ready, should this or other peaceful methods fail to secure protection for American life and property.

In his last annual message of December 7, 1896, he made this fact clear, declaring that from thirty to fifty million dollars of American capital was involved in the fate of Cuba, and that the revolution had virtually ruined American trade in the island, and added: "It cannot be reasonably assumed that the hitherto expectant attitude of the United States will be indefinitely maintained. While we are anxious to accord all due respect to the sovereignty of Spain, we cannot view the pending conflict in all its features and properly apprehend our inevitably close relations to it and its possible results without considering that by the course of events we may be drawn into such an unusual and unprecedented condition as will fix a limit to our patient waiting for Spain to end the contest, either alone and in her way or with our friendly co-operation.

"When the inability of Spain to deal successfully with the insurrection has become manifest, and it is demonstrated that her sovereignty is extinct in Cuba for all purposes of its rightful existence, and when a hopeless struggle for its re-establishment has degenerated into a strife which means nothing more than the useless sacrifice of human life and the utter destruction of the very subject matter of the conflict, a situation will be presented in which our obligations to the sovereignty of Spain will be superseded by higher obligations, which we can hardly hesitate to recognize and discharge.

"Deferring the choice of ways and methods until the time for action arrives, we should make them depend upon the precise conditions then existing, and they should not be determined upon without giving careful heed to every consideration involving our honor and interests, or the international duty we owe to Spain. Until we face the contingencies suggested, or the situation is by other incidents imperatively changed, we should continue in the line of conduct heretofore pursued, thus in all circumstances exhibiting our obedience to the requirements of public law and our regard for the duty enjoined upon us by the position we occupy in the family of nations.

"A contemplation of emergencies that may arise should plainly lead us to avoid their creation, either through a careless disregard of present duty or even an undue stimulation and ill-timed expression of feeling. But I have deemed it not amiss to remind the Congress that a time may arrive when a correct policy and care for our interests, as well as a regard for the interests of other nations and their citizens, joined by considerations of humanity and a desire to see a rich and fertile country, intimately related to us, saved from complete devastation, will constrain our government to such action as will subserve the interests thus involved, and at the same time promise to Cuba and its inhabitants an opportunity to enjoy the blessings of peace." And he added this phrase, characteristically Clevelandesque: "The United States is not a country to which peace is necessary." This hint of possible intervention fanned the flame of public opinion, and encouraged Congress to hope that it might force the President's hand.

"I was with the President at Woodley, near Washington, one Sunday afternoon," says Mr. A. B. Farquhar, "when some members of Congress came in and said, 'Mr. President, we wish to see you on an important matter.' I got up, but he motioned me to keep my seat. They said,

'We have about decided to declare war against Spain over the Cuban question. Conditions are intolerable.'

"Mr. Cleveland drew himself up and said, 'There will be no war with Spain over Cuba while I am President.'

"One of the members flushed up and said angrily, 'Mr. President, you seem to forget that the Constitution of the United States gives Congress the right to declare war.'

"He answered, 'Yes, but it also makes me Commander-in-Chief, and I will not mobilize the army. I happen to know that we can buy the Island of Cuba from Spain for $100,000,000, and a war will cost vastly more than that and will entail another long list of pensioners. It would be an outrage to declare war.' "

Mr. Cleveland's belief that Spain might be induced to sell Cuba for $100,000,000 doubtless rested in part upon the information obtained in a letter kept among his private papers, and written from London by H. Plasson to Senator Call, of Florida. It is marked "the strictest secrecy," and declares that in 1892 a group of London bankers had raised £20,000,000, with which to purchase the independence of the island, provided Cuba would assume the responsibility of the debt, and that a negotiator had been sent to Madrid with this purpose in view. Mr. Plasson was cabled to join this agent, but two days before he reached the capital the Spanish Cabinet had fallen. At the close of the letter Mr. Plasson suggested to Senator Call: "If you think I can be of any use to you . . . I will undertake to group again the bankers referred to."

With the idea of purchase in mind, Mr. Cleveland summoned the well-known international lawyer, Frederic R. Coudert, in a note which shows that he had continued his custom of late working hours:

*Feb. 28, 1897.* (Sunday)

My dear Mr. Coudert:

Can you not call on me at some hour this evening to suit your convenience? Any time from 8 P. M. to 2 A. M. will do for me.

Yours sincerely,

GROVER CLEVELAND.

HON. F. R. COUDERT,
   Arlington Hotel.

When Mr. Coudert arrived, the President confided to him his fear that war with Spain was imminent unless an adjustment could be reached at once, and expressed the belief that such a war would be the result of the activities of Americans in Cuba. He mentioned the American Consul General, General Fitzhugh Lee, as their ringleader. He proposed that Mr. Coudert undertake a mission to the Spanish authorities in Cuba, and expressed the belief that, through his command of the Spanish tongue and his unusual knowledge of Spain and Cuba, war might yet be avoided.

Mr. Coudert objected that within a few days there would be a new President of the United States, and a new Cabinet, who would naturally wish to form their own policies and choose their own personnel in the face of the Cuban situation. To this the President replied that in his opinion Mr. McKinley, as a high-minded and patriotic American, would never enter an unnecessary war, and that if Mr. Coudert would accept the appointment, he himself would take up the matter with the incoming administration. Pressed at last to an immediate decision, Mr. Coudert answered that his health was so impaired that he would not dare to undertake so arduous and difficult a mission. And so, when the fourth of

March came, the Cuban situation remained unsolved, and with forebodings of impending conflict Mr. Cleveland was compelled to hand over this great responsibility to the new administration, to be by it handled in the interests of peace, and ultimately disposed of by the grim methods of war.

The last official hours of President Cleveland were spent in the same careful service to the public which he had always given. Patiently he waded through the accumulation of official business, making the greatest elective office in the world ready for the leader of the opposing party. He had known abuse, party treachery, malicious personal slander, and scarcely veiled contempt from many loyal Americans who should have recognized his greatness. All that, however, was now history, and as such did not concern him overmuch.

Three days before his retirement his friend, A. B. Farquhar, wrote a defense of the President and sent it to the White House with the request that it be endorsed for publication, and on March 4th, despite the excitement incident to his last hours in office, Mr. Cleveland answered:

My dear Friend:

In a few hours I will cease to be President. The people seem to have deserted me, and I would advise you to withhold this publication. Any defense of me will only hurt you, and since I have done my duty as I saw it, I feel that I need no defense.

Yours sincerely,

GROVER CLEVELAND.

The pæan of thanksgiving raised by the free silver and the Populist press expressed a far different opinion.

Their denunciations are reminiscent of those with which the extreme Democratic press greeted Washington's retirement in 1797. Human ingenuity for the coining of billingsgate was taxed to the utmost to invent phrases more insulting than those with which Benjamin Bache and his fellow scribes had daubed their pages as parting insults to the man who had made America. "Grover Cleveland will go out," declared the Atlanta *Constitution* on March 4, 1897, "under a greater burden of popular contempt than has ever been excited by a public man since the foundation of the government." "The Democratic party which he has deceived, betrayed and humiliated," said the Kansas City *Times* of the same date, "long ago stamped him as a political leper and cast him out as one unclean. The reproaches and contumely of the entire American people accompany him in his retirement." A Populist orator of Minnesota assured the Legislature of that State that Grover Cleveland would leave the White House "with the ignominious distinction that he is the first President who ever accumulated millions during his term of office." To this slander Lamont replied with the following statement: "The retiring President has property amounting all told to $300,000 or $350,000 acquired from salary during two terms, fees received during the period of New York law practice, and about $100,000 of profits from the purchase of real estate just outside Washington."

Before completing his arrangements for his final departure, Mr. Cleveland called William and told him to take the portrait by Eastman Johnson and put it in the attic. He saw no good reason why the White House should treasure his picture, and he had not vanity enough to wish to see it left there.

At the hour appointed for the inauguration cere-

monies, he joined the President-elect and drove with him
to the Capitol, and as he gravely greeted the crowds
which lined his pathway, or rather the pathway of the
President soon to be, he rejoiced in the thought that,
while his party had been defeated, his policies had won
a signal victory. Such also must have been his thoughts
as he stood a little behind his successor, with head bowed,
listening to the solemn oath of office administered by
Chief Justice Fuller.

It is doubtful whether a President and an ex-President of opposite political parties ever separated with such
cordial relations as did McKinley and Cleveland.
McKinley thanked the retiring President for all that
had been done to make things smooth for the new administration, and said: "Now, Mr. Cleveland, isn't there
something you would like me to do for you?" "No, Mr.
President," replied Mr. Cleveland, "there is nothing that
I want personally; but I beg you to remember that the
time may come again when it will be necessary to have
another union of the forces which supported honest
money against this accursed heresy; and for this reason
I ask you to use all your influence against such extreme
action as would prevent such a union."

McKinley answered that he fully appreciated the
danger and the necessity, and that he had already begun
to act in that direction in the make-up of his Cabinet.
Both were much moved and both spoke with deep feeling. Mr. Cleveland expressed the hope that the new
President, when it came his turn to go out, would not
have so many reasons to be glad. To this Mr. McKinley
replied courteously that his [Mr. Cleveland's] place in
history was assured.

The ceremony of handing over a nation being complete, Grover Cleveland, not President but simple citizen, joined Admiral Evans, Captain Lamberton, and Leonard Wood for a fortnight's outing. "I remember him as he came aboard the ship, immediately after the great inaugural parade," writes General Wood. "He was tired and worn from weeks of hard work and the strain of the long hard day, and as we were pulling off from the dock . . . he sat down with a sigh of relief, glad that it was all over. 'I have had a long talk with President McKinley,' he said. 'He is an honest, sincere, and serious man. I feel that he is going to do his best to give the country a good administration. He impressed me as a man who will have the best interests of the people at heart.' Then he stopped and added, with a sigh: 'I envy him to-day only one thing, and that was the presence of his mother at his inauguration.'"

For the next two weeks, by day in shooting boxes, by night in the cozy cabin of the ship, he enjoyed his liberty as only the true sportsman can enjoy it. "If he found himself in a poor position for shooting," said General Wood, "he would always insist on staying there, never permitting any of us to be displaced . . . nor would he allow anything to be done for him which would seem to give him an undue advantage." He scorned special privileges, and any suggestion of carrying his gun was certain to be rejected with the words: "On this expedition, every fellow does his own carrying."

At the end of the trip, when the last of his companions, Leonard Wood, left him on the platform of his home-bound train, Mr. Cleveland suddenly realized that he was alone, and again a free man. Waving his hand in farewell, he called gayly: "If you don't mind, just ask the conductor to roll me off at Princeton."

# CHAPTER IX

## RETIRES TO PRINCETON

*"I feel like a locomotive hitched to a boy's express wagon."*
—GROVER CLEVELAND.

WHEN the conductor "rolled him off at Princeton"
on March 18, 1897, his sixtieth birthday as it
chanced, Mr. Cleveland believed himself the most unpopular man in America, and there was some justification
for the belief. The Bryanites hated him for having
caused the defeat of their leader, while the triumphant
Republicans were not yet ready to give him any of the
credit for their success. Thus reviled by the one and
disregarded by the other, he was a man without a party.

He arrived in Princeton in a pouring rain and was
driven to his new home, "Westland," a substantial colonial
mansion of stone covered with stucco and set in spacious
grounds dotted with fine old trees. As he had made the
purchase without seeing the property, he was eager to
inspect it, but the rain prevented. But though he chafed
under this enforced restraint, he weathered the storm as
he had weathered so many before it, and frankly luxuri-
ated in the unaccustomed freedom from pressing responsibilities. "I am enjoying the first holiday of my life," he
remarked to an inquisitive reporter. "I have worked
hard. Now I am entitled to rest. My mission in life has
been accomplished."

Dropping at once into the spirit of the place, he
watched with interest the arrangement of his books, and
adjusted the angle of his desk with a critical eye to the

question of light. A careful survey of his accumulated volumes convinced him that there were many which would never interest him. There were books in unknown tongues, sent by foreign admirers, ignorant of the fact that Grover Cleveland's reading was all done in his native language. There were presentation copies of works on science, works on art, works on music, medicine, and mines, for which he saw no reason to provide house room. He accordingly telephoned to the University Library that if one of the librarians would come up he might choose such of these books as the University wished. One of the young assistants, Varnum Lansing Collins, later Secretary of the University, was accordingly dispatched. He found the ex-President friendly, cheerful, and of a disposing mind. "Come in," he said, "and take what you want." Then, selecting a large volume, gorgeously bound in red leather and inscribed in gold, he remarked, "This is the Bible in the language of Borneo. I seldom read it. Could the Library make use of that?"

The transfers made, the remaining volumes arranged according to his fancy, and the furniture adjusted to his taste, he began summoning the elect. To Dean West he wrote on March 23rd, "Unless I see you within a very brief period, I shall pull up stakes and clear out." To Commodore Benedict, "I want to play cribbage with you. We are settled enough to make you comfortable and I suppose I might lend you a nightshirt *again,* though it would probably be better for you to bring one." To Evans and Gilder, L. Clarke Davis and Dan Lamont, Joe Jefferson and the rest, he sent invitations expressed in terms of the kind of intimacy which he had with each. Into his letters there had crept again the spirit of banter which they had lacked of late. After the Commodore's visit he wrote: "I discovered after you left . . . a perfect wealth of fine cigars which you brought. I don't think you can afford that on $2 winnings."

Mr. Cleveland intended to make his "at homes" distinctly exclusive affairs, open only to the elect, among whom he included none of those priests of the limelight—newspaper reporters. To one of the latter who eagerly pleaded for an interview, on the ground that "a vast number of people are interested in knowing what you do," he replied, "Well, we'll see how they get on without knowing." He had no interest in headlines with his name as the central theme. What he wanted was the privilege of living his life as other men live theirs, the privilege of privacy so long and at times so insolently denied him, and above all the privilege of selecting his own companions, and of meeting them upon a basis of personal relations only. Long years of officialdom had made these things loom large among the rights of man.

In dress he chose to be informal. A brown slouch hat, loose clothes, not too fresh from the shop, and wide, comfortable shoes added greatly to his new-born sense of freedom. He studiously avoided everything calculated to make him resemble the traditional political magnet, supremely content to be what Andrew Jackson once declared Sam Houston: "A man made by God and not by a tailor."

His manner of receiving such visitors as he chose to see was bluff, hearty, sincere, and surprisingly informal; but his natural dignity and self-restraint served to protect him from undue familiarity, and he never lost the consciousness of what was due to the office which he had occupied.

Over all, however, and not to be shaken off, was the disturbing feeling that he had lost the love and confidence of the American people. It crept, unbidden, into his conversations, and stood out in clear relief in his intimate letters. Upon one occasion when Jesse Lynch Williams was calling at "Westland," his fine setter dog, excluded at the door, searched for and found another entrance. When he trotted triumphant into the drawing-room and laid his cold muzzle on the ex-President's hand, his owner rose to expel him. "No, let him stay," remarked Mr. Cleveland. "He at least likes me."

When asked why he did not use his leisure in the preparation of an autobiography, Mr. Cleveland answered: "There is no reason for my writing my autobiography. My official acts and public career are public property. There is nothing to say about them. What I did is done and history must judge of its value, not I. My private life has been so commonplace that there is nothing to write about." This idea he emphasized more strongly one evening when Dean West interrupted a shot at billiards to urge "at least a brief, dictated personal memorandum." "I tell you, I won't do it," replied Mr. Cleveland, "and I'll tell you why. The moment I began, the newspapers would cry: 'There goes the old fool again.'"

With freedom from conflict, there came more fully to light the gentler qualities of his nature, among which was his tender sympathy with children. One St. Valentine's Day his little daughters came home from school with excited stories of the giving out of valentines to the classes. "Isn't it a shame," remarked one, "that Jean was the only child who did not get a valentine?" Mrs. Cleveland glanced at her husband and to her surprise saw the tears coursing down his cheeks. He could not stand the thought of the disappointment of the little girl who had been inadvertently overlooked, and at once a messenger was dispatched to carry her a valentine from Grover

Cleveland. Nor could he bear to attend the Christmas
tree celebrations held each year in the Princeton church
which he attended, because the voices of the children
singing Christmas carols always brought the tears to his
eyes.

He passed his days in reading, planning additions and
changes in his new house, and always, when opportunity
offered, in fishing. The diaries which he kept during his
later years are fuller of fishing entries than of all others
combined, and his personal letters show an almost equal
interest in duck hunting. "I am more deeply interested
in the plans for preserving the fish and game of this community," he remarked to a friend, "than I ever was in
being President of the United States." When such sports
were out of season, cribbage supplied the want. The
stakes were "shiners," new dimes which changed hands
without material alteration in the relative financial positions of the contestants. The Benedict collection of
Cleveland letters is liberally supplied with these trophies,
which the Commodore never thought worth while to remove. The challenges sent by Mr. Cleveland were of
varied form, but always measurably insulting to the
Commodore's pride of conflict:

Commodore:

I've got ten more shiners. If you will come up
to-night and can win them, you can put them in the contribution box to-morrow.                                    G. C.

My dear Commodore:

I was glad to hear that you had received and squan-
dered the ten dollars I sent you and that you had returned
to sobriety and decency. . . . As far as cribbage is concerned, I am prepared for the fray and think I have some
new dodges.                                                 G. C.

Upon one occasion, in the practice of these new dodges, Mr. Cleveland won the Commodore's yacht, the *Oneida,* and, although this departure from the established policy of shiners was entirely fictitious, from that day Mr. Cleveland became "the Admiral" when the "Poverty Club" was in action. In one letter to "the Commodore," "the Admiral" declared: "You may be sure, my dear Commodore, that I shall not acquire the habit of abandoning old companionships, and means of transportation, in my journeys homeward from Gray Gables. I like them both too well." And suddenly remembering that he was "Admiral," he added: "Besides, the owner of a yacht that pays for other travel is, as you often say, like the man who keeps a cow and buys milk."

The students' sports furnished a never-failing source of interest and at important games seats were always reserved for the ex-President and Mrs. Cleveland. It was not unusual at one of these games to hear a commotion in the grand stand, accompanied by good-natured boos and cat-calls, and if a stranger inquired the cause of the trouble his student neighbor would reply laconically: "Some guy got into Grover's seat."

The manner of his life had thus completely changed, but his attitude toward Bryanism never altered, though his enthusiasm for McKinley cooled rapidly. A few weeks after his arrival in Princeton, he wrote to Mr. Olney: "I have been a little amused at the cackling over eggs that were substantially in the nest before we left the scene, like the release of Americans in Cuba, etc., but have been on the whole much gratified by the apparent conviction among the people, that the new administration after all could find but little to amend. You know what I hope will be the result of the Senate's tomfoolery in the arbitration treaty business. I am satisfied I can indulge in the hope I have expressed to you without the least unpatriotic feeling, and I do want this Senate to get the hot end of the poker as long as present influences control it."

A week later he added: "Of course you and I are too patriotic to gloat over the condition and you no doubt feel as much humiliated as I do by the silly exhibition our government is making in its conduct of foreign affairs. I am willing, however, to confess to enough of the 'old Adam' to feel a little bit of satisfaction in a situation that crowds this bitter dose down the throats of the dirty liars who attempted so hard to decry and depreciate your dignified, decent, and proper management of our foreign relations. The present administration must soon find that the Executive Department cannot drift through public duty on the wave of public applause and adulation and that the day comes when popular tickling and humbug will not do."

"The Dingley bill," he wrote later, "has not done anything for me yet, and therefore I am still 'agin it.' " Indeed, he gradually grew almost as much 'agin the Government' as 'agin' the leaders of the Democratic organization, which now composed the opposition. In replying to an invitation from Mr. Fairchild to speak at a dinner of the Reform Club, he wrote:

Westland, Princeton, N.J.
*April 2, 1897.*

My dear Mr. Fairchild:

Yours of March 30th is received. I am perfectly willing to say something at the dinner on the 24th if I can do any good in that way. . . . But to tell you the truth I am going to find it difficult, I am afraid, to be prudent and say just what I would like to say. I am very much disgusted with the silver Democratic leaders and am not inclined to credit them with sincerity or convictions. I am near the point of believing them to be conspirators and traitors and, in their relations with the honest masses, as confidence sharks and swindlers.

I don't suppose that the diners will all be Democrats and so a man can't cuss both parties as at present controlled, and yet it is not perfectly easy to see how a Democrat can condemn his party organization and steer clear of being struck in the face with the suggestion that the way out is to act with the Republican party. But we will have to get along with it somehow.

Yours sincerely,<br>GROVER CLEVELAND.

HON. CHAS. S. FAIRCHILD,
    New York City.

When the hour arrived, however, he did "cuss both parties," unhesitatingly proclaiming his friends "the true Democracy," and denouncing his enemies, whether Republicans or Democrats, as unprofitable servants. He described the Bryan organization as "born of sordid greed and maintained by selfish interest and partisan ambition," spending its energies in "inflaming those inclined to be patient with tales of an ancient crime against their rights, to be avenged by encouraging the restless and turbulent with hints of greater license, and by offering to the poor as a smooth road to wealth, and to those in debt as a plan for easy payment, and to those who from any cause are unfortunate and discouraged as a remedy for all their ills . . . cheap money." "It was a rude awakening . . . when the bold promoters of this reckless crusade captured the organization of a powerful political party, and, seizing its banners, shouted defiance to the astonished conscience and conservatism of the country. Hosts of honest men, in blind loyalty, gathered behind the party flag they had been accustomed to follow, failing to discover that their party legends had been effaced." "Let us . . . break through the influence of the mischievous leadership," he declared. "Let true Democrats meet the passion and bitterness of their former associates who have assumed the leadership of anti-Democratic wanderings, with firm expostulations, reminding them that Democratic convictions and Democratic conscience cannot be forced to follow false lights, however held aloft."

His appeal was for a return to "true Democracy, a party of noble origin and traditions, identified with the counsels of the nation from its earliest days, and whose glorious achievements are written on every page of our country's history. Always the people's friend, seeking to lighten their burdens and protect their rights, true Democracy has constantly taught conservatism, American fraternity, and obedience to law. . . . It enjoins the utmost personal liberty consistent with peace and order. It defends the humble toiler against oppressive exactions in his home, and invites him to the fullest enjoyment of the fruits of industry, economy, and thrift. . . . True Democracy declares that . . . there is a limit beyond which the legitimate results and accumulations of effort and enterprise should be denounced as intrinsically criminal. . . . Above all things, true Democracy insists that the money of the people should be sound and stable, neither shriveling in purchasing power in the hands of the poor, nor by its uncertain value driving enterprise and productive energy into hiding."

Nor did he spare those who in obedience to their fetish, party loyalty, had turned from the light to follow after darkness: "They are willfully wicked and stupid who believe that disaster waits upon the ascendancy of those forces, and yet turn away from the plain evidence of their dangerous strength." Defiantly, passionately, he repudiated "adherence to a party organization merely for the purpose of compassing governmental control," and declared that the only partisanship which could command his allegiance was "the support of certain principles and theories of government, and a co-operation and association in political effort and activity with others who believe in the same theories and principles." "It is an impeachment of the intelligence of the members of any political association to say that party management and discipline should at all times command implicit obedience, even when such obedience leads to the abandonment or radical perversion of party principles."

He scored the Republicans as men who, placed in power by splendid Democratic patriotism, had "returned in hot haste to their wallowing in the mire of extreme protection, offending millions of voters by their exhibition of a party's bad faith, and disgusting millions more by their unconcealed determination to repay partisan support from the proceeds of increased burdens of taxation placed upon those already overladen."

Upon his return to Princeton, Mr. Cleveland received an intimation that the honorary degree which he had declined as President was awaiting him as a private citizen, and having accepted the offer, he turned his mind to the pressing problem of his academic costume. On June 11th, he wrote to Mr. Gilder, in high glee:

"My gown and cap came to-day, and my wife says I look very fine in them. I suppose your wife gave you a like assurance. I shall look for you Wednesday morning and I mean to ask Professor West to-morrow if you won't be obliged to wear your toggery too. The fox that lost his tail tried to make all the other foxes believe that short tails were the fashion."

In similar vein, he wrote to Olney after the event: "You needn't put on any airs because you are settled on Cape Cod. I'll open up there myself in a few days— and I've got a degree that I'm going to bring with me. There may be others—I presume there are—but there are no rivals of my gown, hood, and cap: and the Latin investiture of the degree was to my certain knowledge faultless. I wonder if Brad and Jim Jones ought not to have some sort of a degree, so that you and I might feel a little more at ease with them."

His acknowledgment to President Patton who had performed the Latin investiture was in different vein; for as yet he did not understand how much his less formal thoughts would have been appreciated by that supremely humorous master of the Latin:

"I cannot forbear the expression of my profound appreciation of the honor just conferred upon me, and the assurance of my gratitude for the hearty welcome which has greeted my admission to the brotherhood of Princeton University. As I recall the commanding place which Princeton holds among the universities of our land, her glorious history, her venerable traditions, her bright trophies won on the field of higher education, and her sacred relation to the patriotic achievements which made us a nation, I am proud of the honor which has come to me through her grace and favor, and as I realize the sincere and friendly comradeship attached to this new honor, I cannot keep out of mind the feeling that an additional tie has this day been created binding me with closer affection and deeper delight to the home where I hope to spend the remainder of my days."

True to his promise, he took his degree to Buzzards Bay soon after Commencement, and at once became intent upon squeteague, tautog, and the fighting blue fish, which he insisted upon catching with a rod and reel, contrary to the custom of those who "do business in great waters." Automatically, Brad and Jim Jones, undoctored but unashamed, took the place vacated by Dean West and President Patton in his daily scheme of social intercourse, and his figuring concerned itself with boats instead of libraries. The language of his letters, too, became at times most unacademic, as valve trouble dimmed the consciousness of what was due to his new cap and gown.

"I am having the devil's own time with my launch," he wrote to the Commodore. "I have not had but one satisfactory time with her since I came and that was the day after I arrived when Brad ran her. I get so cursed mad every time I go out that I almost swear I'll never go in her again."

Politics seemed a long way off in those gloriously damp and salty days, and his letters, even to the men who had fought by his side against a varied foe, touched rarely upon public questions, save for occasional pointed thrusts called out by passing incidents. On August 1st he wrote to Colonel Lamont: "As far as I can see the tendency at present is to enjoy being humbugged by the administration now in power and to forget or decry all that was done by the last one. Of all weak, milksop things, it seems to me the Democratic press so far as it comes under my observation is a prize winner." And to Harmon two days later: "The administration seems at present to be so little

in the minds of the people and its achievements appear
to be so nearly forgotten that I feel like apologizing to
all the good and true men who cast in their lot with
it. . . . It seems to me that in Ohio better than anywhere
else the Bogus Democracy has turned itself up for a sound
spanking. The thing that strikes me with amazement
is the gullibility of Democratic newspapers and men that
want to be sound and yet do not see the mischief and
humbug of the Maryland platform. When anything
straight, honest or truly democratic emanates from Mr.
Gorman, neither you nor I will be there to see." "I am
such a political outcast these days," he wrote to Don M.
Dickinson on October 20th, "that the rôle of looker-on
seems quite a natural one; and yet I feel that matters are
brewing that may bring decent men into activity again."

On October 28th, Mr. Cleveland's first son was born
at Westland, and at once the Princeton students, remembering their transparency, "Grover, send your sons to
Princeton," formally adopted him by posting on their
bulletin board this notice: "Grover Cleveland, Jr., arrived
today at twelve o'clock. Will enter Princeton with the
class of 1919, and will play center rush on the champion-
ship football teams of '16, '17, '18 and '19." A deluge
of congratulations came from all parts of the land, and
from many lands, while the press cried "politics," as
they had done at every great achievement of his life.
The Pittsburgh *Leader* presented a picture of the ex-
President, dramatically pointing his oratorical finger at
a tiny white bundle in an old-fashioned cradle, and
soliloquizing: "If this doesn't mean a third term, nothing
does."

Mr. Cleveland's own comments seem meant to conceal
the emotion which he felt at the possession of a son. To
Olney he wrote: "I wish I could write something satis-

factory to the ladies of your household, touching our new boy. This I cannot do on my own responsibility, for I agree with you that when they can count but two weeks as the period of earthly experience, all babies are very much alike, both as regards their looks and conduct. As sort of second-hand information, however, I venture to say that the female members of our household declare that this particular child looks like his father, that he has blue eyes, a finely shaped head, and bids fair to be a very handsome and a very distinguished man. I have no doubt this is all true, because a neighbor lady who was to-day admitted to a private inspection of the specimen, told me that he was 'the loveliest thing' she ever saw. We have named him Richard Folsom—my father's first name and my wife's father's last name. Some good friends thought we ought to call him Grover Jr., but so many people have been bothered by the name Grover, and it has been so knocked about that I thought it ought to have a rest."

So far as he himself was concerned, however, there had already been rest enough, and he began to feel the need of active employment. To one friend who asked how he felt with no Senate to fight and no weight of official responsibility to bear, he replied: "I feel like a locomotive hitched to a boy's express wagon." Three years later, the position of Stafford Little Lecturer on Public Affairs was founded in his honor, and he became an organic part of the University. His duties consisted only in the preparation of one or two public lectures a year, but the task weighed heavily upon him. The honor pleased him; but the work appalled him. For months before each address his intimate letters were filled with lamentations and forebodings of evil; but he had a rich experience from which to draw, and the lectures at once became intellectual events in the life of Princeton.

The final step in his academic career was his election as trustee of the University, and the new duties thus added to the old he took with equal seriousness. "As a trustee of Princeton," writes Dr. Charles Wood, "where I sat at the meetings of the Board directly opposite him, he was a constant surprise to us all. He was an indefatigable attendant of all meetings, interested in the University details and speaking with the greatest simplicity and modesty, as if feeling that his opinion could not be of any great value, though no man in the Board was more convincing."

Every detail of University life, from football to social coördination, from entrance examinations to the standard of the degree of doctor of philosophy, received from his trusteeship as painstaking care as he had formerly given to currency, tariff and foreign affairs. When the trustees discussed the necessity of a social reorganization of the institution, Mr. Cleveland drafted an elaborate plan for correcting the evils of undergraduate club life. And when the graduate school committee proposed expansion, he wrote to his friend, Andrew Carnegie, a letter designed to secure for the project the financial support which he had refused to accept for himself. These things, together with his family and his friends, his rods, guns and hunting dogs, pleasantly filled his life.

# CHAPTER X

## WATCHING THE GAME FROM THE SIDE LINES

*"Your every voter, as surely as your Chief Magistrate, under the same high sanction, though in a different sphere, exercises a public trust."*

—GROVER CLEVELAND.

ALTHOUGH out of politics, Mr. Cleveland had not lost his interest in the affairs of the country and from his home in Princeton he watched the passing show, sometimes with approval—often with dismay. By the 1st of December, 1897, it was apparent that a crisis was at hand in Cuba. Spain had continued her cruelties, and the following January, in response to appeals from General Fitzhugh Lee, American vessels of war were ordered to occupy vantage points, to be ready should action become necessary.

The North Atlantic squadron took up its vigil at the Dry Tortugas within six hours of the Cuban shores. Captain Sampson, with a squadron of battleships and cruisers, sailed for Key West, and on the 25th the Spanish Government was notified that the second-class battleship, *Maine,* had been ordered on a friendly visit to Havana. Thus the stage was set for the tragedy of February 15, 1898, when the *Maine* was wrecked by an explosion, with the loss of two officers and 264 enlisted men.

Even this disaster, which was interpreted by many as a deliberate act of war on the part of Spain, did not alter Mr. Cleveland's opinion that "it would be an outrage to declare war." "If the President's backbone holds out," he wrote to Mr. Olney the next day, "our Cuban policy will, I believe, be fully justified." He was far from being a pacifist, but he was a firm believer in the doctrine that nations should mind their own business, and he did not consider the Cuban situation our affair. He deeply resented the use made of the *Maine* disaster by the press, and freely expressed this resentment. On February 28th he telegraphed to William Randolph Hearst:

*Feb. 28, 1898.*

To W. R. HEARST,
N. Y. *Journal*, New York.

I decline to allow my sorrow for those who died on the *Maine* to be perverted to an advertising scheme for the New York *Journal*.

GROVER CLEVELAND.

Week by week he sought to keep his faith in the ultimate success of the policy of "hands off." "Notwithstanding warlike indications," he wrote to Olney on March 27th, "I cannot rid myself of the belief that war will be averted. There will be infinitely more credit and political capital in avoiding war when so imminent than to carry it on even well. And then there is Spain's condition and the reflection that may come to her that 'the game is not worth the candle.'" And to Commodore Benedict he declared: "I wish the President would stand fast and persist in following the lead of his own good sense and conscience, but I am afraid he intends to defer and yield to Congress. I cannot yet make myself believe there will be war. If there is and it is based upon present conditions, the time will not be long before there will be an earnest and not altogether successful search by our people for a justification."

A few days later the ambassadors of six European countries ventured to intimate the same opinion in a note to President McKinley, expressing the hope that he would avoid war for humanity's sake. Mr. McKinley's reply, that if war came it would be a war for humanity's sake, sounded to the ears of these diplomats like cant and hypocrisy. And when, on April 25th, Congress, by unanimous consent of both houses, with the approval of President McKinley and the vast majority of the American people, declared war and pledged the nation to the altruistic policy of giving Cuba back to her own people, the Continent's sarcastic comment was that this was a gesture planned to prevent European interference with a scheme to annex Cuba. England, on the other hand, took the part of the United States. When news of the declaration of war reached London, crowds of Englishmen went to the American Embassy and cheered, and the Stars and Stripes were displayed in every part of the city. There had been talk of foreign intervention to stop the war, but at this attitude of England it quickly died down.

Mr. Cleveland's view, however, was not changed, although he felt, as he wrote to Commodore Benedict, that: "We, the people, have but one thing to do when the storm is upon us and that is to stand by the action of our government."

"With all allowances I can make . . . ," he wrote to Olney, "I cannot avoid a feeling of shame and humiliation. It seems to me to be the same old story of good intentions and motives sacrificed to false considerations of complaisance and party harmony. McKinley is not a victim of ignorance, but of amiable weakness not unmixed with political ambition. He knew, or ought to have known, the cussedness of the Senate and he was abundantly warned against Lee, and yet he has surrendered to the former and given his confidence to the latter. The Senate would not hesitate to leave him in the lurch, and Lee will strut and swagger, I suppose, as a Major General and the idol of the populace. Roosevelt, too, will have his share of strut and sensation, and Miles will be commissioned General of the army. In the meantime, we who have undertaken war in the interest of humanity and civilization, will find ourselves in alliance and co-operation with Cuban insurgents—the most inhuman and barbarous cutthroats in the world. I suppose the outrages to which we shall then be privy, and the starvation and suffering abetted by our interference will be mildly called the 'incidents of the war.'

"My only relief from the sick feeling which these thoughts induce consists in the reflection that it affects no one but myself, and in the hope, almost amounting to expectation, that we shall find Spain so weak and inefficient that the war will be short and that the result may not be much worse than a depreciation of national standing before the world abroad, and at home, demoralization of our people's character, much demagogy and humbug, great additions to our public burdens, and the exposure of scandalous operations."

On June 21st, in the height of the war spirit, Mr. Cleveland delivered the Commencement address at Lawrenceville, choosing as his subject "Good Citizenship," and in ringing sentences denouncing, not the war, but the spirit of imperialism which he feared would follow war:

"Never before in our history have we been beset with temptations so dangerous as those which now whisper in our ears alluring words of conquest and expansion, and point out to us fields bright with the glory of war. . . .

Our government was formed for the express purpose of creating in a new world a new nation, the foundation of which should be man's self-government, whose safety and prosperity should be secure in its absolute freedom from Old World complications and its renunciation of all schemes of foreign conquest. . . .

"If you believe these things, do not permit any accusation . . . to trouble you. If . . . the suggestion is made that the time has come for our nation to abandon its old landmarks and to follow the lights of monarchical hazards, and that we should attempt to employ the simple machinery of our popular and domestic government to serve the schemes of imperialism, your challenge of the proposition is entirely in order. If you are satisfied that foreign conquest and unnatural extension or annexation are dangerous perversions of our national mission . . . you will not necessarily be wrong. . . .

"It is difficult to deal with the question of war at this time and avoid misconception and misrepresentation. But we are considering American citizenship, and endeavoring to find its best characteristics, and how they can be most effectively cultivated and securely preserved. From this standpoint, war is a hateful thing, which we should shun and avoid as antagonistic to the objects of our national existence, as threatening demoralization of our national character and as obstructive to our national destiny. . . . If you believe this, you should stand bravely for your belief, even though a shower of stupid calls should fill the air."

As the problems of a short war merged into those of a victorious peace, he became more and more fearful that the United States had entered upon an era of conquest which would surely enroll her among the imperialistic nations. Among his papers is a faded manuscript, in his own hand, evidently written as his anti-imperialistic creed:

"We believe that the spirit of our free institutions, the true intent and meaning of the Constitution, and the interest and welfare of our people forbid either the absolute and permanent control of the Philippine Islands as colonies or dependencies, or their admission to the family of states; and we insist that a consistent adherence to the American idea of freedom and liberty, an honest and sincere belief that the consent of the governed is essential to just government, and a scrupulous and American regard for the obligations of good faith, demand that an occupation and control of these Islands shall only be for the purpose of leading their inhabitants to the establishment of their own government; that these inhabitants shall be at once reassured and pacified by an immediate declaration of such purpose, and that when with our friendly aid such purpose is accomplished, our control and occupation by force in the Isles shall cease—save only so far as they may be desired or be necessary for the maintenance of peace and order under the new government."

In this opinion he had the full sympathy of Mr. Bryan who, though he raised the 3rd Regiment of the Nebraska Volunteer Infantry for the war and became its Colonel, was as suspicious as was the ex-President of the aims of the McKinley administration, and as eager to lead a crusade against imperialism. Truly peace problems no less than politics make strange bedfellows, but Mr. Cleveland had no desire to make room for Mr.

Bryan, feeling, not without reason, that he was large enough to occupy the bed alone.

In letter after letter he poured out his distressed consciousness of his own unpopularity, his disapproval of the conduct of affairs under Republican administration, and his anxiety over the "prevailing American madness":

Westland, Princeton, N. J.
*Jan. 12, 1899.*

My dear Mr. Shepard:

. . . With a full realization of the fact that my relations with Mr. Bayard and my love for him should constrain me to join with enthusiasm in any movement to honor his memory, I have determined to decline participation in the meeting suggested. I cannot detail all my reasons for this conclusion; and I hope my justification does not require it.

I will say, however, that I have been controllingly influenced by a clear negative conviction on the following proposition contained in your letter to me: "Whether amid all the present din and noise, a worthy presentation of Mr. Bayard's career and services can be fittingly heard, is possibly open to doubt."

Unpleasant suggestions of "pearls" and "swine" *will* obtrude themselves.

My pride and self-conceit have had a terrible fall. I thought I understood the American people.

Yours very sincerely,

GROVER CLEVELAND.

EDWARD M. SHEPARD, ESQ.
New York.

"I am not the sort of man people want to hear these days," he wrote to Harmon. "My beliefs and opinions are unsuited to the times. No word that I could speak would do the least good and the announcement that I was to address my fellow countrymen on any subject whatever would be the signal for coarse abuse and ridicule. I am content in my retirement and am far from complaining of my elimination from public thought or notice; but I cannot see that I ought to uselessly give an opportunity to those who delight in misrepresenting and maligning me.

"You know me too well to imagine that such a consideration would have a feather's weight with me if over against it there was the slightest possibility of my being of service to the country in these perilous days. Indeed I would gladly do such service. The time may come when I can see such an opportunity, but I cannot now; and it may be that this opportunity will more surely come to me, if I am silent now."

To Dr. Ward he declared: "Those who delight in my elimination from popular thought and consideration have no need to struggle with a resisting victim. I go most willingly. The delights of life are way back of incidents or days related to political devotion or hate; and of these I cannot be robbed."

"Did you ever 'in all your born days,'" he inquired of Olney, "see such goings on as have been exhibited at Washington during the past year? I am in a constant state of wonderment, when I am not in a state of nausea. Sometimes I feel like saying 'it's none of my business,' but that's pretty hard for me to do, though it would be comfortable if I could settle down to that condition.

"The Democratic party, if it was in only tolerable condition, could win an easy victory next year; but I am afraid it will never be in winning condition until we have had a regular knockout fight among ourselves, and succeed in putting the organization in Democratic hands and reviving Democratic principles in our platform. I don't think the kind of 'harmony' we hear so much of will bridge over our difficulties, and I don't believe our people, notwithstanding the disgust the administration is breeding, are ready to accept Bryan and the Chicago platform; and if they are, what comfort is there in that for decent, sound Democrats?

"One thing I regard as absolutely certain: If the plans of those now in charge of our party management are not interrupted, the dishes served up to us will be Bryan and the Chicago platform. To suppose anything else will occur in the contingency suggested, is to ignore every indication in the political sky." Then, with an effort to turn his mind to happier themes, he added: "Other questions, however, of utmost importance confront us. Bryan is alive and his followers active, numerous, and determined; but is Jim Jones alive, and are the bass in Long Pond numerous, and will they in due time prove active and determined?"

Mr. Olney replied in the same vein:

Boston, *22 March, 1899.*

My dear Mr. Cleveland:

I have your last favor—to receive which is a pleasure of itself, while, as always, I find the contents full of interest. It was high time, I have long been thinking, that communication between us was restored, and as one or the other of us had to begin, I am greatly obliged to you for not waiting for the other feller.

I think my surprise—not to say consternation—at the

performances in Washington equals your own. While believing the policy of the government in its foreign relations might well be liberalized and broadened, and certainly should not be hampered by rules not made for present conditions, I have never been able to understand why McKinley wanted to rush upon problems so momentous and why he should conceive it to be either the interest or the duty of the United States to undertake the thankless and enormously expensive task of civilizing and Christianizing some seven or eight millions of Malays. I have been told on good authority—and I have seen some evidence—that the Methodists of the land labored with him in the line of the policy to which he seems to be inclined—although he evidently means to be in a position to disclaim having any policy of his own and to load the whole responsibility upon Congress. But while that is his attitude in his speeches, is he not in fact committing the country to a course from which retreat, even were Congress so disposed, will be well-nigh impossible?

By the way, I had quite a talk with Senator Hoar the other evening. He asserted with much warmth—what I suppose to be true—that but for Bryan and his influence with Democratic Senators, the treaty would not have been ratified. That being so, will it not be quite impossible for him to pose successfully as an anti-imperialist? . . .

But though I put this in type rather than in my own elegant handwriting, to save your eyes and time and patience, I fear I am taking advantage of your welcome note to inflict upon you a reply of most inordinate length. The really important thing, after all, is what you suggest —namely, how to get to Cape Cod and Jim Jones and the bass at the earliest possible moment. I shall get there as soon as my family will permit—probably early in June—and that Jones and the bass will be on hand with their customary cordial greetings I have no reason to doubt.

Have you noticed what a handsome start our Ambassador in London has made? If they take him seriously on the other side, what a nice sort of nation they will deem us to be.

I hear that the Zorn portraits of Mrs. Cleveland and yourself are most successful—also that they are coming on here soon for exhibition—and hope both rumors will prove to be well founded.

My best regards to Mrs. Cleveland and the children, with the same for yourself and, looking forward with eagerness to a personal meeting before many weeks, I am

Sincerely yours,

RICHARD OLNEY.

P. S.

Miles is here—called on me yesterday—to my disappointment in plain clothes and not in his gold uniform. What he wanted to find out or what he did find out, I don't know. I think I found that the presidential bee in his bonnet has swelled to the size of a full-grown peacock.

"The poor old Democratic party!" Mr. Cleveland lamented in reply. "What a spectacle it presents as a tender to Bryanism and nonsense. If there should be a glimmer of returned Democratic sense between now and the next National Convention, it might, as its best (or worst) result, ascend (or descend) from Bryan to Gorman—nothing better in my opinion."

As the currency question upon which Mr. Cleveland had broken with his party was no longer an issue, thanks

to the fact that the newly discovered gold fields of the
Klondike, the Nome district, Cooks Inlet, etc., had fully
met the demands of business, the Democrats began to
hope that the ex-President would return to the party fold
and work with Bryan to stem the tide of imperialism.
But Mr. Cleveland had no intention of fighting in ranks
headed by Bryan. He did not wish to command, but if
he followed it must be some other leader than the
Prophet of Free Silver. Of this his letters left no doubt.

"Don't you in these days," he wrote to Dickinson, on
November 11th, "sometimes pinch yourself to see if you
are awake, when you contemplate so-called Democratic
management? I actually find myself wondering whether
or not those who are leading us do not deliberately intend to assassinate the organization, and bury it completely out of sight and for all time."

Princeton, N. J.
*February 7, 1900.*

My dear Mr. Shepard:
    Your letter is just at hand. I have not sufficiently
recovered from a tedious disability to permit my attendance at the dinner appointed for next Saturday evening.
    Perhaps I ought not to add anything to this; and yet
I feel that I would not be candid if I suppressed the
further statement, that even though the obstacle I have
mentioned were not in the way, I should still be constrained to avoid appearing as a somber figure at the
feast. This is written under the influence of so strong
a desire to see true Democracy rehabilitated that it out-
weighs every other wish. It is written, too, I beg you
to believe, uninfluenced by the least feeling of personal
irritation or resentment.

Considered in the light of judgment and expediency, I am satisfied you are wrong in suggesting my presence at your meeting of conciliation. Thousands of those who have struggled to maintain the true Democratic faith, may be forgiven by the apostles of a newly-invented Democracy; but it seems that I am as yet beyond the pale of honorable condonation.

Prominent among your guests of honor, there will be those who lose no occasion, on the floor of Congress or elsewhere, to repudiate me as a Democrat, and to swell the volume of "jeers" and "laughter" that greet the mention of my name in that connection. Perhaps they are justified; but if I have sinned against Democracy, I am ignorant of my sin; and in any event, my love of country and party will not permit me to sue for forgiveness while being dragged behind the chariot of Bryanism. I know your motives are pure and your purposes exalted. Have I not written something, that should challenge your thought, in support of my opinion that I would be an ill-selected guest at your dinner?

If a movement shall be there inaugurated tending toward a revival of true Democracy, I shall be glad that I have taken no risk of interrupting it. If it should lead to loading more securely upon our party the fatal burdens of the Chicago platform and Bryanism, I shall be glad to have had no part nor lot in the matter.

Yours very sincerely,

GROVER CLEVELAND.

HON. EDWARD M. SHEPARD,
Brooklyn, N.Y.

His letters were equally denunciatory of McKinley and the Republicans who seemed to him, he said, likely "to get their feet into the trough and upset it." Even the signing of the Currency Bill on March 14, 1900, which legalized the gold standard, fixed the reserve at $150,-000,000, and authorized the Secretary of the Treasury to protect it by effective bond issues, did not restore his confidence in McKinley. It seemed only to deepen his resentment that it had been left to the Republicans thus to serve the country while his own party was "in the hands of charlatans and put to the ignoble use of aiding personal ambition."

"The political situation is too much for me—that is, I cannot put it before me in any shape for satisfactory contemplation," he wrote to Olney on June 25th. "I see Massachusetts' sweet-scented 'scholar in politics' played true to his despicable nature at Philadelphia. As for our own party, the old Adam occasionally dominates me, to the extent of prompting me to second the suggestion of a queer old woman who said a few days ago, anent the *Herald's* suggestion that I run for President, 'Let them that got into the scrape, get out of it.'"

And so, he sought to absorb his faculties in academic activities, and to hold aloof from politics. But politics, in one form or another, inevitably crept in, though sometimes unawares. Richard Watson Gilder has left this account of such an occasion:

"Stayed at Westland, Saty., 25th to Tues., 28th, '99.

"Sunday night I brought Prof. W. W. [Woodrow Wilson] down to the house, wanting him to talk with the President on the subject W. is thinking and writing about—namely, high politics and the relation of statesmanship to practical partisanship, etc. The Professor wants to arrive at a working theory—to set forth considerations which will make it easier for men of conscience to remain in touch with the machinery of party. G. C. said that it was sometimes perplexing to draw the line, to know how far one could go in yielding to the views of others. . . . After W. W. went, G. C. entered into details."

On June 29th, William Elroy Curtis drew the following picture for the readers of the Chicago *Record:*

"Ex-President Cleveland is living a quiet, dignified life at Princeton in a congenial atmosphere and apparent contentment. He has plenty of time for study and reflection; he can command the society of many learned and agreeable men whose political views are more or less sympathetic, if not similar, to his own; he can accept consultation cases from New York firms and corporations that pay big fees and thus make an income sufficient for his wants; he can receive a sufficient amount of deference, adulation, and honor to satisfy his pride and keep his name before the public, and can have all the fun he needs watching the pranks of the students—all this without going out of Princeton; and what more can an ex-President ask for? The chaplains pray for him; the university professors quote from his public papers in their lectures to the students and hold him up before them as an eminent example; he is himself a member of the faculty, occupies the chair of 'lecturer on public affairs,' and the students admit him to the general circle of fun and good fellowship, which is the most gratifying, no doubt, to a man of his sentiment and sense of humor of all his experiences here.

"Whenever anything happens to excite a demonstration the ex-President is always remembered. The other evening when the youngest class in college, having completed their annual examinations, were celebrating their promotion from freshmen to sophomores in a rather boisterous way, their procession marched from the residence

of President Patton to Mr. Cleveland's modest home.
He heard them coming—the entire town could trace their
movements by the unearthly noise they made—and was
standing on the veranda when they reached his house.
They gave him the college yell, as they always do, and
he responded with a pleasant little speech, congratulating them upon the onward step they had taken, wishing
them a successful course in the university and successful
careers in after life, and thanking them for calling upon
him.

"When the Princeton baseball nine defeated Yale the
entire body of students in their enthusiasm marched to
his house and let him congratulate them and the university upon the victory.   'I wish I could give the Princeton
yell, boys,' he said, 'but, as I can't, you must give it for
me.   Now, together, with a will!'   And thus he main-
tains an intimate and sympathetic relation with 1,200 or
1,500 boys that keeps him young and is good for both
sides. . . .

"On all formal occasions Mr. Cleveland appears with
the rest of the faculty in a mortar-board cap, a silk gown,
a hood lined with orange, which is the university color,
and a band of purple, which denotes a doctor of laws."

When the Democratic National Convention assembled at Kansas City on July 4th, it manifested little desire
to tempt the old leader from the enfolding academic
shades.   Instead it nominated Bryan by acclamation and,
although making anti-imperialism the chief issue, reaffirmed and indorsed the principles of the Chicago platform of 1896, specifically demanding "the free and unlimited coinage of silver and gold at the present legal
ratio of 16 to 1, and without waiting for the aid or consent
of any other nation."

So overwhelming was Mr. Cleveland's disappointment at this outcome, that for several months he ceased to discuss public questions, even with his intimate friends. During those dark days, the darkest of all his life, his fish and his family were his consolation. Day after day, he hid himself in some quiet cove of Buzzards Bay, starting at dawn, with "Brad" and some chosen companion, Joe Jefferson, Dean West, Professor McClenahan, the Commodore, or some other member of the Poverty Club, not too closely associated with political memories. When the last ounce of joy had been extracted from his favorite nooks where bottom fish abound, he would troll for blue fish until, wearied at last, he landed at his little wooden wharf, climbed the grassy knoll to the privacy of his home, a quarter of a mile from the nearest neighbor, and sought the never-failing cheerfulness of wife and children, who alone had power to make endurable his St. Helena.

Amid the sadness of that summer of 1900, each mail brought from his friends requests for political advice, and from his foes indignant demands that he aid the party which had thrice honored him with its highest honor, while the newspapers gossiped over the question, "Why does he not speak?" Though declining to enlighten his enemies, the general public, or the press, he continued to state his views to his intimate and trusted friends. To Harmon he wrote:

Gray Gables, Buzzards Bay, Mass.
*July 17, 1900.*
*Personal*
My dear Mr. Harmon:

I was very glad to hear from you—though it is difficult to write as full and frank a reply as I would like.

Letters similar to yours come daily to me from all classes and conditions of men, who still love the old faith, and who cannot plainly see the path of duty. So with the arrival of every mail I have a season of cursing the criminals who have burglarized and befouled the Democratic Home.

I have refrained from replying to those letters, because I have not been forgiven by Mr. Bryan for lack of support in 1896; and *pending his pardon,* have no standing in the new Democracy, and cannot therefore speak from that standpoint; and if I should speak according to the principles and teachings of the old Democracy, the notions of the rank and file of the party are so mistaken and confused, that the charge against me of ingratitude, and other accusations and abuse, would do as much or more harm than good.

Of course the "old Adam" rebels against the demagogue and insolent crusader, whose title to Democracy is far from unquestioned, but who notwithstanding assumes to say what Democracy is, and to grant certificates of membership. It is humiliating to feel that Democrats who were fighting its battles before Bryan was born should be obliged to sue to him for credentials; and as a condition of obtaining them forego all the political beliefs of former days. But personal feelings should be sacrificed if by doing so the country can be saved from disaster.

As between imperialism and a continued struggle against sound money, you and many other good and patriotic Democrats, see more danger in the first. The latter and much more trouble we would surely get with Bryan. How certain can you be that he would save you from imperialism? What did he do towards that end when the treaty of peace was before the Senate; and how do you know what such an acrobat would do on that question if his personal ambition was in the balance?

My feeling is that the safety of the country is in the rehabilitation of the old Democratic party. It would be a difficult task to do this, at the end of four years of a Bryan administration and its absurdities, for which the Democratic party would be held responsible. With the defeat of Bryanism and the sham Democratic organization gathered about him, and his and its disappearance in the darkness of aroused Democracy's scorn and contempt, the old guard untainted with either Bryanism or McKinleyism could gather together the forces—checking, through fear of the indomitable force of *true* Democracy, Republican excesses and promising to the country the conservation and safety of Democratic principles.

Bear in mind that McKinleyism has not so far committed itself concerning the treatment and disposition of our new possessions, that it could not be frightened into decency by the organization of an opposition resting upon sane principle, solid character, and substantial appeal to the sense and judgment of our people.

I am afraid that the Republicans cannot be dislodged until Bryanism and all in its train is abandoned if not expressly repudiated; this cannot be done until new men are at the helm of the party; and when such new men are called for, it seems to me those most useful and acceptable will be those who now decline Bryanism because it is not Democracy, and Republicanism because it is in every way and at all times un-Democratic.

When the collapse of Bryanism comes, the rank and file, who have been deceived and misled, will in my opinion look for just such leaders. I shall remain an

intensely anxious looker-on. The activities will fall on
such men as you.

I have written you my thoughts as I have to no other
person. I may be all wrong, but if I am I don't intend
to influence others to do wrong too. I am quite happy in
political exile—or should be if I did not love my country
so well. I will only add that I am not in favor of an
independent Democratic ticket; and further that what I
have written is for you alone.

Give our love to Mrs. Harmon and believe me

Yours very sincerely,

GROVER CLEVELAND.

HON. JUDSON HARMON,
Cincinnati, Ohio.

Early in the fall, the Baltimore *Sun* called his attention to the fact that Mr. Olney had expressed the view
"that the best interests of the country again require . . .
the triumph of the Democratic party, despite the defects
which he recognizes in its platform, and its leadership,"
and asked for Mr. Cleveland's opinion on the subject,
"strictly confidential, or as matter for publication, as you
may desire." The same mail brought an indignant letter
from John P. Irish: "Mr. Olney and Mr. Wilson may
lie down with Mr. Hearst and Morgan, Altgeld, Towne,
and Eugene Debs, if they wish. I decline, though I lie
alone. . . . I prefer that you shall go into history as the
last Democratic President of the Republic, rather than
that Bryan shall go there as the first Populist President.
. . . The party in whose conventicles your name is mentioned only to be hissed is not the Democratic party." At
once Mr. Cleveland answered the *Sun's* question, but his
reply was not for publication:

Buzzards Bay,
*Sept. 11, 1900.*

MESSRS. A. S. ABELL CO.

Gentlemen:

I hope that I have not grown heedless of any duty I owe my countrymen; but I am not inclined to declare publicly my thoughts and opinions on the political situation. This I supposed was quite clearly expressed in my note recently published in the New York *Herald*.

For a number of years I have been abused and ridiculed by professed Democrats, because I have not hesitated to declare that Bryanism is not Democracy. I have had the consolation of seeing those who professed my belief run to cover, and of noting a more headlong Democratic rush after anti-Democratic vagaries. My opinions have not changed, why then should I speak when bedlam is at its height? Perhaps I am wrong in my opinions; at any rate I should say unwelcome things; and all to no purpose except to add to the volume of abuse, which *undefended,* I have so long borne.

I received this morning a clipping from a German newspaper containing my note to the *Herald* with this comment: "That was wise. That part of the American people who most need instruction at this time would not listen to Grover Cleveland, but the only thanks they would give him for his well-meant advice would be to open upon him a new bombardment of poison and dirt; the other part do not need to be taught by anyone how to vote rightly next November." That's about it.

You are not, however, to suppose for a moment that I could be induced to do anything in aid of McKinleyism or any phase of Republicanism. I suppose it is a case of being "damned if I do and damned if I don't," but I have made up my mind that I am entitled to decline enlistment in the war between Bryanism and McKinleyism.

This communication is strictly confidential. It is written because I cannot ignore your letter.

Yours truly,

GROVER CLEVELAND.

Five days later he poured out his heart to Bissell.

Buzzards Bay,
*Sept. 16, 1900.*

My dear Bissell:

I was very glad to get your letter of the 8th. Somehow, in these days, I think I am more than ever glad to hear from old friends.

The President wrote me asking if I would accept the appointment as one of the arbitrators under the Hague Convention. In reply I wrote that my disinclination to assume any duty of a public nature was so great, that I should ask him to permit me to decline the proffered honor. He replied urging me to accept the place, and informed me that Ex-President Harrison had accepted, &c. Oscar Straus, who was then in Washington, also wrote seconding the President's request; and Secretary Gage wrote to Hamlin in the same way, and his letter was sent to me by Hamlin. Notwithstanding all this, I felt constrained to adhere to my determination; and a number of days before the receipt of your letter, I had definitely disposed of the matter, by writing to the President that upon a re-examination of the subject I failed to persuade myself that I ought to accept the appointment.

I think the conclusions arrived at by the Hague Conference were lame and disappointing ones. I did not care to be one of four men, the majority of whom would probably be quite under the lead of Mr. Harrison; and in my peculiar relation to the organization of my party, I thought it better not to hold a place under the appointment of the present administration.

The pending campaign has brought upon me much unhappiness. First there came numerous letters from apparently honest Democrats in every part of the country, asking my advice as to how they should vote. These have been largely succeeded by persuasions and demands from self-styled rock-ribbed Democrats, that I should publicly declare myself in favor of the ticket of the "party which has so greatly honored me"; and in many cases the insistence is made that a word from me would insure the success of the ticket. With these came appeals from anti-imperialists, asking all sorts of things.

Through all this I have maintained silence, except to say that I have nothing to say. To four letters, I think, from people I could not ignore, I have written my views. I cannot write or speak favorably of Bryanism. I do not regard it as Democracy. But many good party men do. I cannot conceive that anything I might say would better conditions or change results. It would, however, add to the volume of abuse which for a long time has been hurled at my "defenseless head," and by a bare possibility destroy an opportunity for usefulness in the future.

I have some idea that the party may before long be purged of Bryanism, and that the rank and file, surprised at their wanderings, and enraged at their false leaders, will be anxious to return to the old faith; and in their desire to reorganize under the old banners will welcome the counsel of those who have never yielded to disastrous heresy. This may never be; or it may be that, however complete the return, those who now refuse to aid in the struggle made in the name of Democracy, whether for right or wrong, will still incur Democratic hatred and discontent. Still it is worth all, to be conscious that at all times one has been consistent and patriotically Democratic.

I have seen Olney but once this summer. I put the matter before him as I have to you. He expressed his inclination to vote for Bryan, and suggested that those who did so might better secure the confidence of the party in the future. He may be right on this proposition, as *there may have been something more in his mind than there was in mine.* It seems to me strange that a man who in my judgment is largely responsible, through his *Atlantic* article, for the doctrine of expansion and consequent imperialism, should now be so impressed with the fatal tendency of imperialism, as to be willing to take Bryanism as an antidote. But the times are as full of strange and untoward things as they can be; and no one can foretell the issue.

I cannot believe Bryanism will win. I am sure Democracy if it was in the field would win; and in any event we shall the most of us, I think, be surprised at the number who will follow the spurious banner to the polls. . . .

Yours very sincerely,<br>GROVER CLEVELAND.

The idea of forming a third party he disapproved as probably unnecessary and certainly untimely. "I am a strong Democrat," he wrote to A. B. Farquhar, on September 20th, "and my great affliction is that the present so-called Democratic organization does not represent Democratic principles as I understand them. I am not, therefore, perhaps, a very good adviser in the premises. I believe, however, if the organization of a third party becomes hereafter a strong movement, and is thought necessary by strong men, the present effort will not be a factor, but will be entirely ignored and passed over. . . . If such an emergency should arise, I am afraid identification with an insignificant and inopportune movement *now,* might impair usefulness that would be greatly needed *then.* The projectors of the present effort have been so very unfortunate, and the time left for action is so short, that I do not see how any national good can result from it."

Toward the end of September, Mr. John S. Green, a gold Democrat of Kentucky, sent him a copy of the letter to Chicago business men, written on April 13, 1895, denouncing Bryan. With it came the questions: "Are you still opposed to the Chicago platform, and do you advise your old friends to support Bryan and his present platform?" To which Mr. Cleveland replied:

Buzzards Bay, Mass.
*October 7, 1900.*

John S. Green, Esq.
Dear Sir:

I have received your letter enclosing a copy of my letter written more than five years ago to the business men of Chicago. I had not seen it in a long time; but it seems to me I could not state the case better at this time if I should try.

I have not changed my opinion as then expressed in the least.

Yours truly,
Grover Cleveland.

This correspondence, having been given to the press by Mr. Green, was at once explained by the Bryanites as

referring to currency alone. Currency, they argued, is no
longer the vital issue; imperialism has taken its place, and
upon the question of imperialism Mr. Cleveland and Mr.
Bryan are one. Therefore Mr. Cleveland favors Mr.
Bryan over Mr. McKinley. This conclusion, though .
perhaps logical, was without a shred of justification, as
the following confidential letter makes abundantly clear:

Princeton, *Oct. 12, 1900.*

My dear Mr. Dickinson:

. . . I am still pestered to death nearly with appeals
"to come out for Bryan" and for advice "how to vote."
It is surprising how many letters I receive purporting
to come from people who opposed Bryan in 1896 and
are supporting him now. A comparative few of my
correspondents ask me to oppose Bryan publicly. Since,
however, I cannot do what the large majority desires,
and since I am very far from wishing to aid McKinleyism
affirmatively, I have thought I might satisfy my conscience and avoid the accusation of open and pronounced
ingratitude by keeping silence. This is a thing very hard
for me to do at a time when I am so clear in my convictions; and occasionally I am very restive. You see
there are millions of our fellow citizens who believe that
the organization now supporting Bryan is the same that
on three occasions nominated and supported me; and it
is hard for them to reconcile my silence, and would be
more difficult to reconcile my open and avowed opposition, with a proper appreciation on my part, of the honors
and favors freely accorded me by Democracy in the past.

On the other hand, the day I hope is not far distant
when sanity will succeed insanity and the Democratic
masses will cry out for deliverance from Bryanism and
a resurrection of true Democratic faith. If that day

dawns, there must be those untainted with heresy to hold aloft the standard. I do not assume for a moment that I shall or can be one of these; but perchance I may encourage and rejoice. You can hardly believe [how] deeply I am concerned lest I should miss doing that which is best for my country and—what in the present emergency seems to me almost the same—best for my party.

I know you will pardon this long uninvited letter. I would be glad if you could give me any advice or comfort.

Yours very sincerely,<br>GROVER CLEVELAND.

HON. D. M. DICKINSON,
Detroit, Mich.

If more evidence be needed, it is found in another letter to Dickinson, written a few days later, which declared: "I don't see how an honest man, holding the views I then expressed, can favor Bryanism now." Also when Eckles, his former Comptroller of the Currency, and close personal friend, wrote from Chicago: "The followers of Bryan . . . are attempting to deceive honest and respectable Democrats to the support of Bryan by saying you are so much against McKinleyism that . . . you are accepting Bryanism," he declined to publish a statement, and when the Democratic Headquarters in New York, on October 21st, sent him an S. O. S., he answered: "My silence is the best contribution I can make."

A few days before the election certain of his enemies played their last card. On October 29th, a reporter named Black brought to the office of the Philadelphia *Times* what he declared to be an interview recently granted him at Princeton by ex-President Cleveland. He asked no compensation for the article, which circumstance should have aroused suspicion, and in the absence of the editor, Mr. A. K. McClure, the interview was passed and printed. It startled both parties with its astonishing declarations:

"Grover Cleveland . . . in an interview which I had with him, predicted a landslide to William Jennings Bryan. . . . Mr. Cleveland said: 'My young man, you will see a landslide for Bryan the morning after election; of that I am confident.' To this I replied that the indications, according to Republican leaders, are favorable to McKinley, but he quickly retorted: 'Of course they are; that is policy. What I tell you is my private opinion.'"

There was much more in the same vein, intended to create the impression that Grover Cleveland was back in the Democratic fold, eagerly waiting a Democratic victory which would place Bryan in the White House.

When he saw the interview in the morning papers of October 30th, Mr. Cleveland issued a prompt denial: "The whole thing from beginning to end is an absolute lie without the least foundation or shadow of truth. I have never uttered a word to any human being that affords the least pretext for such a mendacious statement."

Upon which Black as promptly made the following deposition:

Philadelphia, *Oct. 30, 1900.*

I, Robert J. Black, had an interview with Grover Cleveland, on the 23rd day of October, 1900, in his home in Princeton, N. J., and during a lengthy talk with him in his parlor he told me that he favored Bryan, and said: "My boy, you will see a landslide for Bryan on the day after election," that he also said "Bryan was a great orator."

R. J. BLACK, Vinton, Iowa.

Witness: JOHN A. BRADLEY.

Sworn and subscribed before me this
   30th day of October, 1900.

JOHN A. THORNTON, Magistrate of Court No. 23.

During the remainder of the campaign, this pretended interview continued to be used by unscrupulous politicians, but there is no evidence that it was with the connivance of responsible national leaders of the Democratic party.

When the election of 1900 was over, the most competent critics felt that Bryan had led his last charge, and that as a candidate he was "without hope, unless the [next] convention should be made up of political lunatics," as a Washington correspondent of the New York *Times* phrased it.

Theodore Roosevelt, the newly elected Vice-President, expressed his personal appreciation of Mr. Cleveland's part in this result in the following letter:

*Private.*

State of New York,
Executive Chamber,
Albany,
*Nov. 22nd, 1900.*

HON. GROVER CLEVELAND,
   Princeton, N. J.

My dear President Cleveland:

During the last campaign I grew more and more to realize the very great service you had rendered to the whole country by what you did about free silver. As I said to a Republican audience in South Dakota, I think your letter on free silver prior to your second nomination was as bold a bit of honest writing as I have ever seen in American public life. And more than anything else it put you in the position of doing for the American public in this matter of free silver what at that time no other man could have done. I was delighted to find that Governor Shaw of Iowa had just the same feeling about it that I had and made an even fuller acknowledgment of the debt due to you in one of his speeches at which I was present. I think now we have definitely won out on the free silver business and therefore I think you are entitled to thanks and congratulations.

With regards, and best wishes both for Mrs. Cleveland and yourself, I am

Very sincerely yours,

THEODORE ROOSEVELT.

Mr. Cleveland, too, believed that McKinley's re-election meant an end of the menace of free silver; but, through the columns of the Atlanta *Constitution,* he assured his friends of the South that William McKinley and Theodore Roosevelt were not President and Vice-President by virtue of his vote. If, on the other hand, he voted for Bryan, he violated the conscience and the desire of Grover Cleveland, and it is, therefore, safe to assume that he cast no vote in 1900.

On April 27, 1901, he wrote to Dickinson: "It is a little comforting to see the end of Bryanism in politics, but on the Democratic side I am constantly asking, 'What next?'" Although living in Princeton, in almost daily touch with the only Democrat destined within a quarter of a century to stand as the victorious leader of Democracy, the idea that Wilsonism was next never crossed his mind.

# CHAPTER XI

## THE TURN OF THE TIDE

*"Unswerving loyalty to duty, constant devotion to truth, and a clear conscience will overcome every discouragement and surely lead the way to usefulness and high achievement."*
—GROVER CLEVELAND.

EARLY in September, 1901, a small company of childhood friends of Vice President Roosevelt received on their dahabeah on the Nile the startling news that President McKinley had been shot by a half-crazed fanatic at Buffalo. "He will not recover," remarked one of the party. "We all know the Roosevelt luck." A few days later, upon the assurance of the physicians that the President was making good progress, Colonel Roosevelt left Washington for a wilderness journey of rest and recreation in little frequented parts of the Adirondacks. On September 13th he reached Lake Colton, near the summit of Mount Marcy, accessible only by means of a human messenger. Toward noon one such arrived, a mountain guide sent to bring the news that the President was sinking rapidly.

Within a few hours Colonel Roosevelt had returned to the house where he had left his family, and by midnight, attended by none save the driver, he was descending the mountain in a buckboard, heedless of rain, darkness, and almost impassable roads. Before dawn he had covered the thirty miles to the nearest railway station, to find a special train awaiting him, and a despatch which announced that once more a Vice President had succeeded to the office of Chief Executive. When he reached Buffalo, the Cabinet was assembled, and within a few moments he had taken the solemn oath which made him, at the age of forty-two, the youngest of American Presidents.

From his retreat at Princeton, Mr. Cleveland watched the career of the new Chief Executive, at first with sympathy, but soon with growing trepidation. Although anxious to do Mr. Roosevelt justice, he found it difficult to appreciate his sterling qualities, being constantly offended by methods which he considered wholly out of keeping with the dignity that should surround the office of President. Nor did he come under the wonderful magic of the Colonel's personality. His own slower mind mistook Roosevelt's rapidity for superficiality, and he interpreted the latter's instinctively dramatic appeals to the people as the works of the demagogue. Temperamentally, the two were as far apart as the poles. Roosevelt was mercurial, Cleveland was phlegmatic. Roosevelt was quick to form friendships or to conceive enmities. Cleveland did nothing in haste. Roosevelt was ready of speech, whether written or spoken, while a speech to Mr. Cleveland was like a mountain in the pathway, to be laboriously surmounted. But both were courageous and resourceful in danger, loyal and true to the traditions of America in the face of temptation, not self-seeking in public work, and of sterling honesty.

President Roosevelt's admiration for Mr. Cleveland was almost boyish. "I always regarded him as a freshman regards a senior," he once declared, and when leaving instructions to his biographer, Joseph Bucklin Bishop, he said: "I wish you would put in all the letters of mine to him. I was very fond of the old fellow."

About a year after Mr. Roosevelt's accession to power,

began the great coal strike of 1902, which offered him a chance to employ Mr. Cleveland's personal influence for an important public service. On May 12th, 145,000 coal miners ceased work, in obedience to the call of the United Mine Workers of America, under the leadership of John Mitchell. Throughout the summer the owners sought in vain to replace the strikers and resume the work of mining. As August advanced it became apparent that a coal famine must follow unless effective action were taken, for, though the mine owners had an abundance of coal within easy reach of the public, they were deliberately holding it out of the market in the hope that public opinion would drive the strikers to submission. They "had banded together, and positively refused to take any steps looking toward an accommodation," as President Roosevelt expressed it. The sympathy of the public was with the strikers, and the opinion was freely expressed that the federal government should seize the mines and produce the coal.

As Mr. Cleveland watched conditions, he became increasingly uneasy, being uncertain what use President Roosevelt might make of such a situation. "If the coal strike and some other matters do not change soon," he wrote to Commodore Benedict on August 24th, "I believe there will be serious trouble before we are six months older. I don't like to see so many things depending on one man's nod." Far from assuming unauthorized power, however, President Roosevelt was as determined as Mr. Cleveland could have been to adhere to the strictest constitutional limitations. "I had in theory," he later wrote, "no power to act directly unless the Governor of Pennsylvania or the Legislature . . . should request me, as Commander-in-Chief of the United States, to intervene and keep order."

On September 26th, New York closed her schools to save her scant supply of coal, the price of which was already almost prohibitory. By October, retail dealers were demanding $30 a ton, and the President was being bombarded with prayers for federal intervention.

In the absence of an appeal from the governors of the coal states, however, Mr. Roosevelt decided to try the rôle of peacemaker. He accordingly sent to the presidents of the anthracite coal companies the following telegram:

I should greatly like to see you on Friday next, October 3rd, at 11 o'clock A. M., here in Washington, in regard to the failure of the coal supply, which has become a matter of vital concern to the whole nation. I have sent a similar despatch to Mr. John Mitchell, President of the United Mine Workers of America.

THEODORE ROOSEVELT.

The meeting was an excited one, and much strong language was used. Mr. Roosevelt himself said of it: "There was only one person there who bore himself like a gentleman and it wasn't I." Later, in his Autobiography, he stated that it was John Mitchell who "kept his temper admirably and showed to much advantage." Mitchell readily agreed to arbitration, stipulating only that the President should have power to name the Commission, but the operators refused to arbitrate, insisting instead that the President aid them in breaking the strike. The session lasted throughout the afternoon, and, at the end, the operators boasted that they had "turned down both the miners and the President."

The next morning, on his way from Gray Gables to Princeton, Mr. Cleveland read in the New York *Herald* an account of the conference, under the heading: "President's Coal Conference a Complete Failure; Operators Reject Mitchell's Arbitration Offer."

Arrived at Princeton, he sent the President the following letter:

Princeton, *Oct. 4, 1902.*

MY DEAR MR. PRESIDENT:

I read in the paper this morning on my way home from Buzzards Bay, the newspaper account of what took place yesterday between you and the parties directly concerned in the coal strike.

I am so surprised and "stirred up" by the position taken by the contestants that I cannot refrain from making a suggestion which perhaps I would not presume to make if I gave the subject more thought. I am especially disturbed and vexed by the tone and substance of the operators' deliverances.

It cannot be that either side, after your admonition to them, cares to stand in their present plight, if any sort of an avenue, even for temporary escape, is suggested to them.

Has it ever been proposed to them that the indignation and dangerous condemnation now being launched against both their houses might be allayed by the production of coal in an amount, or for a length of time, sufficient to serve the necessities of consumers, leaving the parties to the quarrel, after such necessities are met, to take up the fight again where they left off "without prejudice" if they desire?

This would eliminate the troublesome consumer and public; and perhaps both operators and miners would see enough advantage in that to induce them to listen to such a proposition as I have suggested.

I know there would be nothing philosophical or consistent in all this; but my observation leads me to think that when quarreling parties are both in the wrong, and are assailed with blame so nearly universal, they will do strange things to save their faces.

If you pardon my presumption in thus writing you, I promise never to do it again. At any rate it may serve as an indication of the anxiety felt by millions of our citizens on the subject.

I have been quite impressed by a pamphlet I have lately read, by a Mr. Champlin of Boston, entitled, I believe, "The Coal Mines and the People." I suppose you have seen it.

Very respectfully,<br>Your obedient servant,<br>GROVER CLEVELAND.

To the President.

A more detailed statement of the thoughts aroused by the situation is contained in the following undated manuscript found among his papers, and showing many revisions:

"The stubborn and serious disagreements that have broken out from time to time in our industrial localities between employers of labor and those in their service who work with their hands, have given rise to much discussion concerning their origin and the blame for their existence. . . . They must be regarded as the outcome of a persistent effort on the part of labor to secure at any cost, a larger share of the fruits of American opportunity, and opposition to these efforts by employers, as based upon demands unreasonable in substance and unjustifiable in method of enforcement. In the meantime the situation they invite and their frequent accompaniment of strike, lockout, boycott, paralysis of production and interruption of important undertakings, inflict loss and injury upon numerous citizens absolutely innocent of the least complicity in these contentions and utter strangers to all they directly involve. . . .

"Wherever our sympathies may be, we can hardly escape the conviction that labor has made demands, adopted policies and permitted if not encouraged conduct, which cannot be justified; nor can we safely deny that in too many instances, employers of labor have been heedless of the just and reasonable claims of their employees, regardless of their interest and disdainful of their presentation of grievances. . . .

"Manifestly it cannot be necessary to dwell upon the sad consequences visited upon the actual participants in these labor quarrels. Those who run may read these consequences, in the pinching deprivation that enters the homes of our working men; in their idleness and its malevolent influence on character and habits; and in the morbid discontent and irritation that comes from brooding over wrongs.—Nor is the depressing story less plainly read in the dispiriting loss and perplexity of employers; in their inability to meet contract engagements and trust expectations; in the hardening of their sympathy with the mass of working men, and in their blinding resentment against those whom they accuse of guilty responsibility for afflictive conditions. . . .

"With all our efforts to escape it, the consciousness is forced upon us that neither the liberality and equal advantages of our scheme of government nor the patriotism which is abroad among our people has been found sufficient to prevent the birth and existence of labor disturbances. . . . Human nature when left to its own devices can be so blinded by interest or prejudice, and so strongly led by stereotyped methods of thought, as to be unable, of its own motion, to pass a fair judgment upon the quality of its operations or to correctly define its springs of action.

"These suggestions lead us to recall the ease with which disagreements between individuals are frequently settled, when the parties are brought to a calm review of their differences by a trusted intermediary. . . . No reason can be given why such a course cannot be followed with the same good results when the dispute, instead of merely involving individuals, is between organized working men and their employers. . . .

"The method . . . certainly savors of interference, but only with the consent of the disputants; and in view of the broad interests involved, and the multitude of our people affected by labor disputes, surely as much interference as this ought to be allowed. . . . It is the only remedy within our reach. It embodies every effort but force; and force is not suggested as a real cure by anyone who has studied the situation. . . .

"Any intermediary attempting to bring the parties in difference together for amicable deliberation should be absolutely disinterested and impartial, and should possess the unqualified respect and confidence of all the parties concerned. . . . Beyond doubt some concessions might also be made in advance of conference, which would better prepare the contestants in labor quarrels for friendly discussion. It is quite generally believed by those who would be glad to see the rights and interests of our working men fully recognized, that labor organizations are much too radical in some of their demands and too far-reaching in the objects of their efforts. If these were so far reduced that the claims and demands of labor could be presented to unprejudiced reason as only such

as are relevant to its needs, and necessary to the exigencies
of its just protection, the way to a peaceful adjustment of
their complaints would be made very much easier; and
if these organizations could be freed from the suspicion
of taking advantage of pending necessities and emergencies in industrial conditions to enforce questionable
demands, it would give great encouragement to our
conservative citizens who approve the legitimate purposes
of labor unions. . . .

"Labor unionism is with us to stay; and whatever the
result may be, it has become a permanent element of our
industrial system. Its further development must be expected. It behooves us therefore to ask whether this
development will be in the direction of more reasonable
demands, less menacing methods, and a larger, more
conscientious conception of the wide and vital interests
affected by the movements of labor, or in the direction of
a more sullen insistence upon excessive demands, greater
heedlessness of the comfort and prosperity of our people
at large, and vindictive and revengeful conduct, instead
of protective precautions? . . .

"It has been suggested that it would be well for
employers to organize for the purpose of acting together
in dealing with labor disputes. Such organization would
be useful if prompted by a desire to facilitate pacification
and if not allowed to originate and stimulate obstructive
resentments, or to keep on constant exhibition an ugly
collection of real or supposed wrongs. . . . With organization on both sides of a labor dispute the field for
review and deliberation would be so enlarged, and such
an aggregate of varied and individual situations would
be presented that any conclusion arrived at in adjusting
the dispute would be more widely binding and more

easily enforceable than any that could be otherwise reached. . . ."

The operators having refused his attempts at mutual agreement, President Roosevelt formed a drastic plan, conceived upon the theory, as he later explained, "that occasionally great national crises arise which call for immediate and vigorous executive action, and that in such cases it is the duty of the President to act upon the theory that he is the steward of the people, bound to assume that he has the legal right to do whatever the needs of the people demand, unless the Constitution or laws explicitly forbid him to do it." Through Senator Quay, he arranged that the Governor of Pennsylvania, at a preconcerted signal, should request federal aid for the coal fields, and that Major-General Schofield should then promptly set troops in motion and seize the mines.

Wishing, however, to avoid this extreme measure if possible, he decided to threaten the operators first with an investigation by a commission so commanding in its personnel as to insure popular support for any verdict it should render. "Ex-President Cleveland's letter . . ." he explained, "gave me the chance to secure him as head of the Arbitration Commission. I at once wrote him, stating that I would very probably have to appoint an Arbitration Commission or Investigating Commission to look into the matter and decide on the rights of the case . . . and that I would ask him to accept the chief place on the Commission. He answered that he would do so."

After sending his reply, Mr. Cleveland proceeded to divest himself of the holdings which he had in the stock of certain coal-carrying railroads, as he was unwilling to be a judge in matters in which he had a personal interest. By this transaction he lost $2,500, and unnecessarily, as it developed.

Had the fictitious millions which the enemy press had brought with him from Washington been real millions, such a sacrifice would have meant nothing. But Mr. Cleveland felt that it was by no means negligible, as he regarded his savings as scarcely sufficient for the dignified maintenance of his family. That his more intimate friends had a similar view is shown by numerous letters offering financial aid, in manners more or less guarded. More than one had suggested nominal business posts with salaries attached, and Andrew Carnegie only a few months before had offered to solve the difficulty by direct financial aid, an offer which Mr. Cleveland declined in the following letter:

*Jan. 13, 1902.*

MY DEAR MR. CARNEGIE:

I was so touched and overcome by your last letter that it has taken me some time to fit myself to reply to it. You and I both began to really live late in life—that is to say we were late in knowing the blessedness and joy of wife and children, and the homes they made for us. When I remind you of this I have an idea you will understand me better than other friends would, if I say to you that it has been with much anxiety that I have looked the "course of nature" in the face, and contemplated the time when the mother of my children would have to bear the burden of their care and maintenance alone.

I have never written or said as much as this before; but somehow as I have read and reread your letter, it has seemed to me that something of the kind must have been in your mind, and that I ought to be thus frank with you.

So far as the present is concerned, I am getting on I think as well as I deserve. If the law lately introduced in Congress, providing an annuity for ex-Presidents should pass, I would be glad, and would without the slightest compunction avail myself of it. Indeed I think I should nearly feel that I had earned what such a law would give to me.

But how can I ever bring myself to accept the private benefaction you suggest? And how can I take it from you, who in no sense owe me anything, but have always been a disinterested and warm friend? I am asking things of you in these days. I have just asked you to allow me to decline a great honor you sought to confer upon me; and now I ask you to allow me to pull and worry along in my own way—with permission to go to you, when the Fates are so hard with me that I must have a strong friendly hand; and whether I have this permission or not, let me assure you that your kindness and what you have offered to do, will always remain among my most cherished possessions.

Yours most gratefully

GROVER CLEVELAND.

Armed with Mr. Cleveland's consent to accept a place on his Commission, Mr. Roosevelt now played his trump card. Selecting as his agent the ablest member of his Cabinet, Mr. Elihu Root, Secretary of War, he dispatched him to New York to interview J. Pierpont Morgan, the man best able to influence the actions of the operators. At ten o'clock on the evening of October 11th, a watchful reporter from the New York *Herald* saw a boat put off from the pier and five minutes later a glass showed the Secretary climbing up the side ladder to greet Mr. Morgan, who stood on the deck. But the glass could not give the conversation in which Mr. Root made known the President's plan of an arbitration committee, and announced that upon it among other distinguished names would appear that of a man "whose word would have the ear of the nation, Grover Cleveland."

This warning had the desired effect. The meeting was followed by a hurried gathering of operators, who, the next day, notified the President that they were ready to submit all matters involved to a commission, consisting of one judge of the United States Court, one engineer of the army or navy, one mining expert, one eminent sociologist, and one man experienced in mining and selling coal. As arbitration had been Mr. Mitchell's desire from the beginning, he readily consented, insisting only that one of the commissioners should come from the ranks of labor.

Mr. Cleveland being neither a judge, an engineer, a sociologist nor a mining expert, President Roosevelt sent him the following telegram and letter, and headed the list of commissioners with the name of Judge Gray:

White House, Washington, D. C.
*October 15, 1902.*

HON. GROVER CLEVELAND
Princeton, N. J.
*Strictly personal*

Deeply grateful for your letter. Propositions that have been made since have totally changed situation so that I will not have to make the demand upon you which three days ago it seemed I would have to for the interest of the Nation. I thank you most deeply and shall write you at length.

THEODORE ROOSEVELT.

White House,
  Washington.

                                          *October 16, 1902.*

*Personal.*

MY DEAR MR. CLEVELAND:

I appreciated so deeply your being willing to accept that it was very hard for me to forego the chance of putting you on the commission. But in order to get the vitally necessary agreement between the operators and miners I found I had to consult their wishes as to the types of men. Of course I knew that it was the greatest relief to you not to be obliged to serve, but I did wish to have you on, in the first place, because of the weight your name would have lent the commission, and in the next place, because of the effect upon our people, and especially upon our young men, of such an example of genuine self-denying patriotism—for, my dear sir, your service would have meant all of this. I do not know whether you understand how heartily I thank you and appreciate what you have done.

                         Faithfully yours,
                              THEODORE ROOSEVELT.

Hon. Grover Cleveland,
  Princeton, N. J.


President Roosevelt's views in regard to the influence of the ex-President's name were in no wise exaggerated. Even when the denunciations of his enemies had been loudest, Mr. Cleveland had had the staunch support of a great body of men who understood and appreciated his struggles to uphold the law of the land, and his public activities of the last few years had but added to the number of these admirers and increased the regard in which he was held by the country at large—political antag-

onists included. From many were beginning to arise the
whisper that Grover Cleveland was again coming back,
and that he would lead the Democratic ranks to victory
in 1904. "There appears to be a strong and steadily
growing sentiment in the Middle Western States in favor
of your nomination," wrote Joseph Garretson, of Cincinnati. "The *Times-Star* has made a great effort to
investigate this sentiment, and the general tenor of all
our correspondents is along the line that you are the only
logical candidate in the field."

But Mr. Cleveland brushed all such suggestions im-
patiently aside. To this letter and the plea for a few
words in reply, he sent the following note:

Princeton, February 6, 1903.

JOSEPH GARRETSON, ESQ.
Editor, &c
DEAR SIR:

I have received your letter of the 4th instant asking
me on behalf of the *Times-Star* for an expression regarding my intentions as related to the next Democratic nomination for the Presidency.

I cannot possibly bring my mind to the belief that a
condition of sentiment exists that makes any expression
from me on the subject of the least importance.

Yours very truly,<br>GROVER CLEVELAND.

This cryptic utterance was interpreted by the press
as indicating a spirit of submission should the people
call again. "His letter . . . to an Ohio newspaper,"
commented the New York *Times,* " . . . is taken as an
assurance that at the proper time the reformer Buffalo-
nian will enter the field." The papers in other sections,

too, took up the theme, and, lacking facts, printed fiction, some stating positively that he would run again, others as positively that he would not. To such as came to his notice Mr. Cleveland dealt out such stinging reproofs as the following:

"Words have been put in my mouth which entirely misrepresent my position in politics. I never said I had retired from active politics to act as the party's adviser. To be thus pictured as an old Brahmin seated in the background and aspiring to manage things my own way is alike distasteful to me and absolutely false as to my true position."

His true position was never in doubt among his friends, to whom he repeatedly declared that no conceivable condition could tempt him back into public life. "There is nothing that presents anything like the same allurement to me," he wrote to Commodore Benedict, "as a retreat somewhere that would give me freedom from nagging annoyances and exhausting importunities." And later: "It seems to me . . . that I have expressed myself with sufficient clearness to enable all who believe in my sincerity, to understand how settled is my determination to spend the remainder of my life in the ranks of private citizenship. I can understand why the dirty little scoundrel who is allowed to scatter filth through the columns of the Louisville *Courier-Journal,* and a few vile imitators, pretend to understand me; and I am not inclined to give them the satisfaction of plainer speech. I doubt if the time will ever come when a more explicit declaration will be necessary for the satisfaction of my friends and the decent people of the country. When in my judgment that time has arrived, such a declaration, in my own way, will be forthcoming."

Had he known, as others knew, that the tide of public

sentiment had turned toward him, he would doubtless have been more patient with those who persisted in the belief that he would be a candidate for the fourth time in 1904, for even Tammany Hall showed a realization of the fact that this political Samson's hair was growing. At the Jefferson banquet on April 13, 1903, eight hundred braves, who had evinced little interest when letters from Hill and Bryan were read, leaped to their feet with cheers for "the next President," when the toastmaster read a simple note of regrets from Grover Cleveland. The cheers of Tammany Hall, however, affected him no more than had its curses. He believed that the people's faces were turned from him, and the belief was gall and wormwood.

But a revelation was in store for him, and at no distant date. With great reluctance he had yielded to the demands of his friends and had promised to attend the opening of the Louisiana Purchase Exposition at St. Louis, on April 30th. Before leaving he wrote to ask Mr. Dickinson's advice as to whether the time had arrived to announce his determination not to run again. To which Mr. Dickinson replied: "I cannot say what you would like me to say. . . . I feel that it ought not to be said just now, much as you are assailed by the Ass of Nebraska and others less worthy than he. . . . Recently in the South, I heard his name spoken, and spoke it when not otherwise called out, and it was invariably received with a cuss. . . . Men of good standing . . . who were regular in 1896 and 1900, *as I know,* are saying that they have been Democratic all their lives but 'Bryanism was not Democracy and I helped kill it,' and so on. The President's popularity [too] is waning remarkably." The letter urged him not to drive his friends into the arms of the Republicans: "If you speak now," it declared, "just about that will happen."

Acting upon this advice, Mr. Cleveland continued to deny to the public any declaration of his intention, and on the appointed day started to St. Louis. All along the line, in the various states through which the train passed, the entire population seemed to have gathered to see and cheer the ex-President, but their enthusiasm only puzzled him; he did not know that the day of the shadow had passed. That knowledge was soon to come. Standing beside President Roosevelt on the platform at St. Louis, he received in one great thunder of applause the whole-hearted plaudits of his fellow countrymen, and the sound was a healing balm to his wounded spirit. The scene is described in the following editorial sent him a few days later from Electra, Texas.

"Mr. Cleveland so far overshadowed President Roosevelt in popular applause, when both stood on the same platform, as to make the latter feel aggrieved. With every department of the administration on the platform, and a former Republican National Committee chairman acting as the spokesman of the occasion; with Governor Odell, of New York, at his feet, and Senator Hanna at his back; and with a circle of distinguished Republicans all around him, Mr. Roosevelt, the President, ought easily to have drawn out the most vociferous and continued applause when he stood before the multitude at St. Louis last Thursday. Yet when he sat down and Grover Cleveland, the private citizen, arose, the crowd, on the platform, and out in front, so instantly and so vigorously applauded, and so wildly manifested delight, that the President's greetings a few minutes before seemed like a whisper compared with a long-continued peal of thunder. It was an unexpected, instantaneous, generous, unmistakable ovation. It indicated clearly the state of the public mind toward the ex-President. It was a revelation to the politicians. It was an eye-opener to the anti-Cleveland Democrats. It was a warning to the Roosevelt Republicans. It was plainly the voice of public sentiment, and it thrust Grover Cleveland to the front as the strongest man in American politics to-day."

This editorial bears the marks of contemporary politics, and is, therefore, unfair to the memory of the great statesman whom it sought to belittle in order to gain additional glory for another great statesman whom it rightly desired to honor. Mr. Roosevelt himself, several years later, described the scene with as frank an enthusiasm as that shown by the editor in question: "I was at St. Louis as President when Mr. Cleveland, then a plain private citizen, arose to make an address in the great hall of the Exposition; and no one who was there will ever forget the extraordinary reception given him by the scores of thousands present. It was an extraordinary testimony to the esteem and regard in which he was held, an extraordinary testimony to the fact that the American people had not forgotten him, and, looking back, had recognized in him a man who with straightforward directness had sought to do all in his power to serve their interests."

To Mr. Cleveland, more than to any other soul in that vast assemblage, this overwhelming reception at the hands of an audience gathered from every part of the world was a revelation. Suddenly, without a shaft of light to warn him of its coming, the full noonday sun had broken through the black clouds that for years had covered his sky from horizon to horizon. At last he knew that the tide had turned; that the people whom he loved, and whom he had served with so unselfish and so untiring a devotion were again his friends. The joy that came to him with the knowledge lasted throughout the remainder of his life. "From that moment," declared his wife, "he was a different man."

# CHAPTER XII

## THE ELECTION OF 1904

*"Men and times change, but principles—never."*
—GROVER CLEVELAND.

MR. CLEVELAND left the St. Louis Exposition with a new joy in the realization of the people's confidence, but with no new ambitions. He still did not desire the nomination, but he delighted in the effect of third term talk upon Mr. Bryan. On May 8th he sent Mr. Gilder a cartoon by McCutcheon, showing four successive expressions upon his own face as he was interviewed by four successive reporters. In the background stand the figures of Bryan and Watterson, whose expressions change as Mr. Cleveland's change. "I find in the situation," reads the accompanying letter, "two satisfactory things—the hopping and jumping in certain cages of Democratic zoological specimens, and the belief that the Democratic party will get a hint that no Bryanism or Bryan conciliation will get enough votes to do the business."

On that same day "the faithful" read in Bryan's newspaper, the *Commoner,* a two-page editorial of denunciation of the ex-President as "an office-boy in a Wall Street institution . . . the logical candidate for the Presidency in case the Democratic party returns to its wallow in the mire. . . . He has been faithful to the financial interests that made him and have kept him, and if those interests are to dominate the Democratic party it would be unfair to deny to him the honor of being their representative. The third-term objection will have no influence upon those who are in sympathy with Mr. Cleveland's masters, for those who see no objection to making the White House the rendezvous for financial conspirators against the public, who will not be disturbed by the fear of continued authority in one man, the men who are willing to risk imperialism to secure the gold standard, would keep a President in power for life if they thought it would keep the control of the government in the hands of the financiers. The logic of events is forcing Mr. Cleveland more and more into the leadership of the reorganizing element. The New York *World* suggested him some months ago, and now the Brooklyn *Eagle* has withdrawn Mr. Parker and suggested Mr. Cleveland as the proper presidential candidate."

This editorial served as the caisson from which the petty officers of "Bogus Democracy" at once drew ammunition for further attacks. In the opinion of the Cleveland Democrats, however, they drew "duds," and on May 13th Lamont gleefully wrote to St. Clair McKelway: "The more the papers and the politicians discuss Cleveland, the smaller Bryan will grow, and they will get the habit of demanding the Cleveland type of President. Therefore, I have written him, urging him to say nothing at present."

During the summer, amid the delights of Gray Gables, it was comparatively easy to say nothing about politics, for other and more attractive thoughts engaged his attention. On July 4th he wrote to Mr. Gilder: "I am waiting for a new census report of the Cleveland race, which I expect will be in order within the next two or three days." And to Commodore Benedict, eleven days later:

Buzzards Bay
*July 15, 1903.*

DEAR COMMODORE:

I received your letter a few days ago and was glad to know that we might expect to see you soon. I cannot refrain from saying to you, however, that there are two conditions now existing which I would like to see changed before you come. One is the state of expectancy and anxiety which the *hover of the stork* over our house creates; and the other is the abominable fishing here just at this time. Both of these conditions will, I hope, give way for better before very long.

We have not been on the Bay to fish since the Doctor arrived. The fishing is not good enough to be tempting, and I guess we both feel like keeping fairly near home. The Doctor has been working in the hay all day and I have been trying to keep warm at home.

We may go out a little while to-morrow morning and try Rocky Point near home for squeteague. I will keep you posted as to the fish and the other event; and when conditions assume a more favorable aspect I will promptly give you the word.

With love to Mrs. Benedict, I am

Yours very sincerely
GROVER CLEVELAND.

Com. E. C. Benedict
80 Broadway, New York

Within three days the stork had descended, and the ex-President, father of a second boy, wrote to Mrs. John Grier Hibben, wife of the future President of Princeton:

Buzzards Bay
*July 18, 1903.*

MY DEAR MRS. HIBBEN:

I sent you a telegram this morning that a tramp boy had trespassed upon our premises. He was first seen and heard at 10 o'clock A. M. (I hear him now), and I sent the dispatch a few moments thereafter, to Redfield where, according to the itinerary you sent me, you were to be from the 5th to the 20th instant. I have heard since that there was difficulty in transmitting the dispatch from Camden to Redfield; and I shall not be surprised if this letter or the newspapers give you the first information touching to-day's important event.

The shameless naked little scoundrel weighed over 9 pounds. Richard was very much tickled as long as he thought it was something in the doll line, and was quite overcome with laughter when he found it was "a real baby." He and I have been planning for the amusement of the newcomer when he shall arrive at Richard's present age. He denies with considerable warmth any intention of taking him by the hair and throwing him down. In point of fact we have agreed upon no particular line of conduct, except an engagement on Richard's part to teach the young brother to swim if all goes well.

The dear Mother is as well apparently, as possible; and seems to me very self-conceitedly happy—as if she thought she had done a good job.

She sends her love—and so do I. And we both include the Professor.

Yours very sincerely
GROVER CLEVELAND.

To his neighbors at Buzzards Bay he announced the good news with even more elaboration:

"It may possibly be that some of you are aware of a very recent event in my household which has increased by one the present population of the town of Bourne, and has also added another to the future fishermen in Buzzards Bay. This newcomer was weighed on the scales I use for weighing the fish I catch; and he registered nine pounds and a half. That's not a wonderful weight for a child. For a fish it would be all right and among fishermen no explanation need be made. But it was not a fish that was weighed, and others besides fishermen have an interest in the truthfulness of all that pertains to the vital statistics of Bourne Township. Therefore I take this opportunity to say that the nine and a half pounds registered on my fishing scales honestly means nine pounds—no more and no less. The extra half pound is a matter of special and private arrangement between me and the scales. By this statement I satisfy all my conscientious scruples and disdain any attempt to gain credit for half a pound more increase in population than I am entitled to.

"It must not be for a moment supposed that my fish weighing scales are unique in the particular referred to, nor that I am by any means the only fisherman who resorts to such a mechanical contrivance to substantiate his stories. The fact is, anything I have done in that direction may be regarded as frivolous when compared with other transactions of a like character. In proof of this let me cite an instance of a medical fisherman who, having provided himself with one of these fish story supporting appliances, was called while on a fishing trip in a remote region with a party of companions, to attend the wife of one of the few inhabitants of the locality in the pains and perils of maternity. The child, it was insisted by the parents and all cognizant of its advent, must be weighed; and no scales but the Doctor's fish scales were at hand. After some demur on his part they were finally pressed into the service, with the astounding result that quite an ordinary looking newborn infant was found to weigh nineteen pounds and a half."

Shortly after his return to Princeton, his most intimate friend, Wilson S. Bissell, died, and to Commodore Benedict he wrote: "Bissell's death is another reminder . . . that the shafts are flying." But, though saddened by the loss, he was by no means inclined to chronic melancholy, and his native wit often enabled him to baffle inquisitive reporters and maintain the sphinx-like silence enjoined by his friends. At Chicago, about the middle of October, when compelled out of consideration to his host, Mr. Eckels, to make some reply to a group of eager questioners seeking a headline concerning the coming presidential campaign, he told the following story:

"A friend of mine went with me on one of my recent duck-shooting expeditions. Two ducks rose over our heads. One had a white breast and the other a brown one. They were plainly marked. As I raised my gun to fire, my friend said:

" 'Mr. Cleveland, I have named one of those ducks Nomination.'

"I fired and one duck fell." Here Mr. Cleveland paused.

"Which duck came down?" demanded his hearers breathlessly. But Mr. Cleveland only smiled.

At length, however, he sent to St. Clair McKelway the following letter with leave to print:

Princeton, *November 25, 1903.*

MY DEAR DR. MCKELWAY:

I have waited for a long time to say something which I think should be said to you before others.

You can never know how grateful I am for the manifestation of kindly feeling toward me, on the part of my countrymen, which your initiative has brought out. Your advocacy in the *Eagle* of my nomination for the Presidency came to me as a great surprise; and it has been seconded in such manner by Democratic sentiment, that conflicting thoughts of gratitude and duty have caused me to hesitate as to the time and manner of a declaration on my part concerning the subject—if such a declaration should seem necessary or proper.

In the midst of it all, and in full view of every consideration presented, I have not for a moment been able, nor am I now able, to open my mind to the thought that in any circumstances or upon any consideration, I should ever again become the nominee of my party for the Presidency. My determination not to do so is unalterable and conclusive.

This you at least ought to know from me; and I should be glad if the *Eagle* were made the medium of its conveyance to the public.

Very sincerely yours,

GROVER CLEVELAND.

St. Clair McKelway, LL.D.
Brooklyn, N. Y.

Six weeks later, on January 6, 1904, his daughter Ruth, died of diphtheria, and his grief dwarfed all else. Her death was most unexpected, as his diary shows:

January 2d, "Ruth is a little sick with tonsillitis."
January 3rd, "Ruth still sick, but better."

January 6th, "Doctor said this morning Ruth had diphtheria . . . a trained nurse came at 5:25. Prof. West was here. Dr. treated us all with antitoxin and reported that Ruth was getting on well. Houghton Murray came in the evening and we played cribbage until 12. At 2 o'clock in the night word came . . . that Ruth was not so well. Dr. Carnochan came at 2:30 and Dr. Wykoff at 3:30. We had been excluded from Ruth's room, but learned that dear Ruth died before Dr. Wykoff came, probably about 3 o'clock A. M., Jan. 7th."

January 8th [in a trembling, almost illegible hand], "We buried our daughter, Ruth, this morning."

Deep natures suffer long, and the memory of that little grave in the old Princeton Cemetery haunted him, despite his deep religious faith. On January 10th, he wrote, "I had a season of great trouble in keeping out of my mind the idea that Ruth was in the cold, cheerless grave instead of in the arms of her Saviour." And the next day, "It seems to me I mourn our darling Ruth's death more and more. So much of the time I can only think of her as dead, not joyfully living in Heaven." On the 15th the diary declares: "God has come to my help and I am able to adjust my thought to dear Ruth's death with as much comfort as selfish humanity will permit. One thing I can say: Not for one moment since she left us has a rebellious thought entered my mind." "It seems so long since we buried Ruth," he wrote to Commodore Benedict, on February 20th, "and yet it is only six weeks yesterday. We are becoming accustomed to her absence. For the rest of it we have not a shadow of a doubt that it is well with the child."

So deep was the impression made by the loss of this daughter, whose intelligence and personal charm had made her the life of the household, that his friends advised him to divert his mind by re-entering politics. Nathan Straus wrote: "While I have all along been very much averse, purely through a friendly feeling, to your being again drawn into politics, I have changed my opinion since you have met with the misfortune that has visited you. Nothing but time can heal such a wound as you have received; but a change of scene, an active life, the compelling of thoughts in other directions would naturally leave you less time to dwell upon your sorrow. . . . A short time ago I met Mr. Carlisle and told him how I felt about the matter, and he agreed with me and expressed the same sentiments. Further than this, wherever I speak of it, and to whomever I speak of it, I get only one reply, that the only hope of the success of the Democratic party lies in you. I fully agree . . . that you are the only man the Democrats can elect against Mr. Roosevelt."

Mr. Straus also quoted a conversation between Mr. J. S. Cram, of Tammany Hall, and Mr. Stillman, in which the latter said: "If you will nominate Mr. Cleveland, I will personally see that there is a fund raised bigger than was raised at the time McKinley was elected, and you know when he ran they had more money than they could use."

Tammany's friendly attitude toward the idea was expressed by Murphy to Lamont, who in turn reported it to the ex-President:

Wednesday Evening, *February 10, 1904.*
2 West Fifty-Third Street

MY DEAR MR. PRESIDENT:

Murphy whom I had never seen before called on me yesterday afternoon. He came alone and said he wanted to get in touch with me so that he could confer with me about national politics. I was greatly pleased with him because he is evidently a man of sense and wants to put his organization to the front for the best in the party.

He is honest in his talk about you and says if it can't be Cleveland, "then let's get the nearest to him that can be found." I advised him to fight down any instructions and to take his delegation to the convention with the announcement that New York was there to confer and to bring about the strongest nomination possible. He gives out to-night just about what I said to him. He says you would be elected without question, and to some things I said to him in response to that he answered, "Then do ask Mr. Cleveland to do no further declining now. Let's have the benefit of his name to round up a Cleveland party and all will agree on a Cleveland candidate." He is opposed to Parker—because he says there is nothing in Parker to campaign on; he is against Gorman and he says he would have no idea of McClellan for such a place. Bryan he says should be absolutely turned down and ignored. . . . He has no patience with anybody who wants to placate Bryan. As for Hearst, he says he cuts no figure whatever.

I have never seen a leader of Tammany Hall talk as well about things as this man does. You will be interested in my story of his visit when I see you.

I hope you got home safely and that your trip did you no harm. I wish you would come oftener. The seeing you did us all great good, especially Mrs. Lamont. My love to all.

Sincerely yours,
DANIEL S. LAMONT.

The newspaper statement, to which Lamont refers, reads as follows:

"Charles F. Murphy to-day practically disposed of the Parker presidential boom, so far as New York is concerned. He volunteered a denial of reports that he was really for Parker, and declared emphatically that he would fight to a finish any plan to instruct the delegates from New York State to the Democratic National Convention. He also made it plain that Parker will not figure in the national convention as New York's candidate at any stage of the proceedings if he (Murphy) has anything to say about it; and he thinks he will have a great deal to say about it.

"Murphy was moved to talk about the Parker boom by reports from Albany that, at a dinner there last night, which Judge Parker attended, Tammany senators and assemblymen shouted for Parker and voted for him on a mock ballot. . . . The Tammany leader did not say it in so many words, but he plainly implied that nobody would have a chance to vote for Parker next November. . . . He volunteered this statement: 'I hear that it is reported up the State that I have been speaking favorably of Mr. Cleveland by agreement with certain persons, and that I am using Cleveland just now to conceal my purpose of bringing about the nomination of Judge Parker. I wish to say that these reports are absolutely untrue. As I have said more than once, I think Mr. Cleveland is the strongest man that could be named, and I mean it. I am not committed to Cleveland or anybody else, however, and I certainly have not made any agreement with anybody to send the New York delegation to the national convention with instructions to support Judge Parker. I am opposed to instructions by the convention for any candidate, and I will go into the convention and fight any effort to instruct. I don't believe in instructions. . . .'

"This declaration is plainly a notice served by Murphy on David B. Hill and his friends that Judge Parker cannot be put forward as New York's candidate at the spring convention, and that any attempt to do so will result in a fight in the convention. The outcome of such a fight, Murphy's friends say, would not be doubtful. They assert that he will have a considerable majority in the convention, and that the Parker boomers will be suppressed in quick order. It was also asserted at Tammany Hall to-day that if any attempt is made to instruct for Parker, Murphy will not permit David B. Hill to go to St. Louis as a delegate-at-large.

"The Tammany senators and assemblymen who shouted for Parker last night, under the influence of good cheer at a particularly cheery place—'The Tub'— will hear something not to their advantage by calling at Tammany Hall when they come down from Albany on Friday. Murphy does not seem to be able to appreciate the humor of that vote for Parker, and there is such a thing as 'discipline' in Tammany Hall."

A few weeks later, the Honorable James Smith, Jr., Democratic boss of New Jersey, called at Westland to urge the ex-President to enter the race; but he was met by a firm refusal.

Mr. Cleveland's letters and conversations of this period are full of hopes and fears, speculations, and at times lamentations, as he watched the uncertain progress of the party of his devotion struggling toward the light. In reply to Lamont's letter, he wrote:

Princeton, *Feby. 18, 1904.*

MY DEAR COLONEL:

I was very glad to learn from your letter that you had met Mr. Murphy and that your favorable impression of him agreed with that made upon me by a moment's chat with him a long time ago. It is exceedingly fortunate that he is at the head of Tammany at this critical time for Democracy, and so far as I can now see it is also fortunate that McClellan is Mayor, and our old friend McAdoo at the head of New York's Police Department.

Under all the circumstances Murphy's idea of an uninstructed New York delegation to St. Louis is very wise, and I hope he will inexorably insist upon it. I wish I could look differently upon Parker's candidacy, but what you write of Murphy's opinion on that subject, exactly expresses my feeling.

As matters now stand I hope to see a growth in the sentiment towards Olney or Gray.

I note what you write about the hope expressed in your interview with Murphy that I "do no further declining now."

I am willing to be silent up to the point that continued silence might be construed as indicating a departure from my expressed determination not to be a candidate, or until such silence will subject me to the accusation of misleading my good friends.

I see the *Herald* this morning publishes a part of my political article which is to appear in the *Saturday Evening Post.*

I have had some misgivings about the wisdom or propriety of that utterance; but I am entirely reassured when I hear so much about Bryan-Hearst nonsense and when I recall my right to have my position understood as uncompromisingly opposed to Democratic suicide.   I will have no part or lot in such a crime.

I enjoyed my visit with you very much indeed.   It seemed like old times; and I want to thank you for the time you spent for my convenience and comfort.

With love from Mrs. Cleveland and me to both you and Mrs. Lamont, I am

Yours faithfully<br>GROVER CLEVELAND.

Hon. D. S. Lamont
  No. 2 West 53d St., New York.

And ten days later:

DEAR COLONEL:

My notion is that if there is to be an effort to get our party in any kind of promising shape there ought to be a movement in a hard-headed sensible way.   Perhaps Parker has such a start that he would be the best one to concentrate on.   You know my idea has been that Olney or Gray would suit present conditions best.

I want you to tell all who talk "Cleveland" non-sense that it is a waste of time that might be profitably spent in other ways.

I would not accept a nomination if it was tendered to me—which of course it cannot be—and I don't want to be considered as a defeated candidate for nomination.

I am content.   I want to see the party succeed, but I hope there will be no idea of playing any kind of trick on me.

Yours faithfully,<br>GROVER CLEVELAND.

Hon. D. S. Lamont,
  2 West 53rd St., New York.

The insistence of his friends in no way affected his determination to remain on the side lines, but their pleading pleased him, and his eagerness for party success was intense.   He watched with expert eye the uncertain drifting of the bark once so steady in his own guiding hand, and his comments regarding possible candidates of both parties were frequent and specific.   "There is one thing about our young President which I think cannot be denied," he wrote to Lamont.   "He has but little idea of the proprieties that belong to his high office or, for that matter, to its incumbent. . . . There never was a time I believe when the country would be a greater gainer than now, by the clearing out of an administration."   And to Hornblower, eighteen days later:

Princeton, *March 29, 1904.*

MY DEAR MR. HORNBLOWER:

I thank you for the pains you have taken to put in my hands the book I need.   I expect to receive it to-day.

In reply to the other matter contained in your letter I have to say, that I have had doubts as to Mr. Parker's being the very best candidate in sight, considering all things; but I am not very strong in these doubts.   One thing is certain, I think.   He is clean, decent, and conservative and ought on those grounds to inspire confidence in quarters where it is sadly needed, if our party is ever going to be a political power again.

It is in my view immensely important that the sane portion of our party should be as united on a decent candidate as circumstances will permit—to the end that the movement now threatened in the direction of insanity and indecency may be run over and killed "beyond recognition."   In this view it should be taken into account that Parker's candidacy has such a start and has so many elements ready to support it in the convention, that he appears to present a better rallying point than anyone else.

Personally I would prefer Olney or Gray; but they do not seem to me to be under much headway.

I believe if I were in your place I would signify a disposition towards Parker.

> Yours faithfully,
>
> GROVER CLEVELAND.

Hon. Wm. B. Hornblower
New York.

His leaning toward Mr. Olney pleased the latter, but it did not imbue him with presidential longings. "I am fairly astounded at some of your intimations about politics," wrote Mr. Olney, on May 18th. "I esteem any opinion of yours in my favor as about as high a compliment as it is possible for a man to receive. But I am sure it would not be to my advantage to be President, while at the prospect of a candidacy, if actually presented to me, I should be perfectly panic-stricken. Can you think of anyone less fitted for such an ordeal? I am not really disturbed, however, because I refuse to take the matter in the least seriously. Everything done here in Massachusetts has been done without my consent either asked or given, and but for the peculiar conditions of the Hearst invasion I should have publicly and expressly forbidden the use of my name in the contest for delegates at the St. Louis Convention."

Judge Parker's attitude was far more receptive, and he was in a position to point to a record of consistent opposition to free silver, even when the party had stood upon the silver platform. When Mr. Cleveland, toward the end of May, sent word that he could be counted upon to help in case Mr. Parker were nominated, the latter replied:

Albany, *June 1, 1904.*

MY DEAR MR. CLEVELAND:

Mr. Teague of the *North American* called on me last evening, and conveyed to me your very generous message, at the same time showing me your interview as it appeared in the *North American.* In the papers I had seen only excerpts. I wish to thank you for your expression of confidence, and the manner of it. I would not have had you put my name before that of Olney and Gray if you could conscientiously have done so, and am glad that you pointed to the fact that "circumstances" put the lead where it is at present. Your generous offer to help if the nomination should come to me is most welcome, for in that event I shall need your advice, and shall be greatly gratified if I may consult you about a few of the more important matters.

May I be permitted to suggest that you draft such a platform as seems to you to meet the situation? Am sure it will prove of great help to the party if you can find the time to do it.

Again assuring you of my great appreciation, I am
Very sincerely yours,
ALTON B. PARKER.

The Honorable Grover Cleveland.

As the date of their National Convention approached, Mr. Cleveland watched with astonishment the operations of the Republicans who were wise enough to realize —as he did not—that in Theodore Roosevelt, the "accidental president," they had a leader of the first order. When the latter's nomination was announced, he sent

Mr. Olney a clipping headed, "Is Bryan for Olney?" at the same time threatening the latter with the Presidency.

Princeton, June 24, 1904.

MY DEAR MR. OLNEY:

You had better look out. I cut the attached bit of news from the *Sun* of this morning.

Did you ever see such a boyish, silly performance as the Republican National Convention which has just adjourned? Perhaps Lodge & Co. think they can safely calculate on the stupidity of enough of the people to elect "Teddy"; but if our party was in proper shape, I am sure the conglomeration of the apostles of all good would find themselves reckoning without their host.

Somehow I cannot at all times feel very confident of Democratic success; but I honestly think if the hint contained in the clipping I sent could lead to a practical result, there would be brighter hopes than in any other condition—I mean of course for the country and party and not especially for the comfort and peace of the gentleman referred to. . . .

Yours faithfully,<br>GROVER CLEVELAND.

Hon. Richard Olney,
　23 Court St., Boston, Mass.

When the delegates were preparing to start for the Democratic National Convention at St. Louis, Mr. Cleveland wrote to the Honorable James Smith, Jr., head of the New Jersey delegation:

Princeton, June 26, 1904.

MY DEAR MR. SMITH:

You will, I suppose, head the delegation from my state to the St. Louis Convention. I am well aware of the favorable opinion you originally entertained touching my availability as a candidate for the Presidency in the coming campaign; and I remember with great satisfaction the friendly spirit in which you accepted the reasons I advanced against that proposition, when we met here a long time ago. My public declaration made before our conversation and the apparent reception of my refusal to be considered a candidate as justifiably conclusive, by you and other friends, have led me to regard all discussion of the matter as ended.

I have heard and read some things lately that disturb me. Perhaps that is unnecessary, but I am very anxious that there should be no misunderstanding which can be chargeable to me or to anything I may do or omit to do.

In view of all the circumstances, I have ventured to write you this, and to ask you as representing the state of my residence, as my friend, to prevent the use of my name in connection with the presidential nomination at the Convention. I certainly could not accept it.

I cannot think that any occasion will arise calling upon you to do me this service; but as I am just leaving here for my summer vacation, I regard it as not amiss to provide against even a very slight or possible contingency.

Yours very truly,<br>GROVER CLEVELAND.

Hon. James Smith,
Newark.

To this Mr. Smith replied on June 30th:

"I remember well the reasons advanced by you at our meeting some months ago for not wishing your name presented, and I then fully agreed with you. Since that time events have so shaped themselves that the people of this country, without regard to politics, seem determined to have you again assume the duties of President. Of course I shall carry out your instructions in this matter, and will see that the New Jersey delegation does not present your name to the Convention. Should it become necessary, I will go further and say on the floor of the Convention that I have a letter from you in which you state that you cannot accept the nomination, provided this course meets with your approval; but should the time come when the Convention shall arise and demand your nomination, with almost unanimous voice, I think it would be unfair to ask me, as the head of the delegation from your state, to refuse to assent to such a demand. . . .

"Senator Hill's leadership of the Parker forces, to my mind, makes Judge Parker's election, if nominated, very doubtful. I have no personal feeling against either Senator Hill or Judge Parker, but I think it my duty, as a Democrat, to do all in my power to prevent the latter's nomination, as I am convinced that such an event would be disastrous to Democratic success."

In his keynote speech at the opening of the St. Louis Convention, the temporary Chairman, John Sharp Williams, declared that, through the dogged persistence and indomitable will of Grover Cleveland, in forcing the repeal of the silver-purchase clause of the Sherman Act in 1893, the gold standard was now an established fact. At the mention of Mr. Cleveland's name, the party which had deserted him in 1896, and scorned and insulted him in 1900, burst into applause which lasted so long that the speaker had twice to take his seat before it subsided.

In spite of this fact, however, Mr. Bryan, with the skill of a master of forensic oratory, once more pushed his fight for a declaration in favor of the free and un-limited coinage of silver at the ratio of sixteen to one. Again he charmed the galleries with his eloquence, but he could not charm the delegates. The St. Louis Convention had no mind to go before the country chained to a dead issue.

When the platform was at length adopted, it was silent upon the silver issue, but when the news of his nomination reached Judge Parker, he sent the following telegram which forced the Convention to the position consistently maintained by Grover Cleveland since his first battle with Bryan, in 1893:

HONORABLE W. F. SHEEHAN,
    Hotel Jefferson, St. Louis, Mo.

I regard the gold standard as firmly and irrevocably established, and shall act accordingly if the action of the Convention to-day shall be ratified by the people. As the platform is silent on the subject, my views should be made known to the Convention, and if it is proved to be unsatisfactory to the majority, I request you to decline the nomination for me at once, so that another may be nominated before adjournment.

A. B. PARKER.

Upon reading this message, the Convention, by a vote of 774 to 191, directed that the following reply be sent:

"The platform adopted by this Convention is silent on the question of the monetary standard. It was not regarded by us as a possible issue in the campaign, and only campaign issues were mentioned. Therefore, there is nothing in the views expressed in the telegram received which would preclude a man entertaining them from accepting the nomination on the said platform."

These telegrams, to Mr. Cleveland's mind, meant party redemption. "True Democracy" was again in the ascendant, after eight years of almost total eclipse; and for the moment he was again a Democrat in full and regular communion with the leadership of his party. For these long, bitter years, he had stood on the side lines. Now, at last, he was able once more to join the team. He sent a cordial telegram to Judge Parker, to which the Democratic nominee responded:

Rosemount<br>Esopus-on-the-Hudson

MY DEAR MR. CLEVELAND:

I am deeply grateful for your telegram of congratulations, and pleased beyond expression that my action meets with your approval.

May I have the liberty of consulting you occasionally about matters that seem of larger moment? I will not trouble you except on very important matters.

Very sincerely yours,<br>ALTON B. PARKER.

*July 11, 1904.*

Mr. Cleveland's reply was the letter of a Democrat who is able to endorse his party's actions heartily and without reservations:

Buzzards Bay, Mass.<br>*July 14, 1904.*

MY DEAR MR. PARKER:

I received your letter yesterday at this place, where I have been stranded for more than a week on my way to join my family in New Hampshire.

I am certain that no man living appreciates your situation and its perplexities better than I; and I am equally positive that no one is more anxious for your election. Of course this does not necessarily mean that I can be of any great service to you—I wish it did. I hope, however, that you will feel absolutely at liberty to command me in every way. I am not afraid you will ask me to do anything inadvisable, and if at any time I am too forward with advice or suggestions you must go your way without the least embarrassment. Your judgment is too good, I am convinced, to be interfered with by *any one*.

Our best campaign material just now is—YOU. I mean "You" as you are manifested to your countrymen in the despatch you sent to St. Louis. The spirit and sentiment aroused by this utterance of yours, should be kept alive and stimulated from time to time during the campaign. Occasions will present themselves, when you respond probably to the Committee on notification and when you write your letter of acceptance. I do hope that you will insist upon a free hand in meeting these occasions and that you will not hesitate to paraphrase or give your own language to our platform, to such an extent as to convince our people that you propose to keep the reins you have in hand and that your conception of Democratic obligations will constrain you to protect all legitimate rights, and to restrain all harmful trespass upon the privileges and opportunities promised to *all* our people under our plan of government—so far as such an exercise of power is within executive limits. For myself I do not think expediency demands of you the distortion of anything your judgment suggests, in deference to the South or the radicals of our party. Bryan is doing the cause much good in his present mood; and I for one hope it will continue. We need Indiana; and if the Taggart

Chairmanship will help us to get it, it might be well to remember that after all the Chairman of the Executive Com. of the N. Y. Headquarters is the important man.

I am bothered about the question of retaining your judgeship while a candidate for President; but I hope there will be a safe deliverance.

Yours faithfully,

GROVER CLEVELAND.

Hon. Alton B. Parker,
Esopus, N. Y.

"I am very much pleased with the outcome of the Convention as brought about by Providence and a gentleman living in Esopus," he wrote to Olney, on July 19th. "Such Democrats as you and I ought to be pretty well satisfied. Bryan and Bryanism are eliminated as influential factors in Democratic councils, true Democracy has a leader, and its time-honored and time-approved principles again are set before the people of the land without apology or shamefacedness.

"If we can only keep peanut methods out of our campaign management, I believe there is a good chance to rid the country of Rooseveltism and its entire brood of dangers and humiliations. At any rate, it seems to me there can be no excuse for lack of effort or half-heartedness on the part of any true Democrat who has waited all these years for party regeneration."

No sooner was the presidential nomination disposed of, than the demand was made that Mr. Cleveland allow his name to be used as candidate for Governor of New Jersey. "So many people have waited on me, as well as newspaper men, to urge your name," wrote James Smith, Jr., on July 22d. "I simply told them that while it would be a great pleasure to me to have you accept it, and that while it would insure the state for Democratic electors, I hardly thought that after refusing to accept a nomination for the Presidency, you were . . . 'patriotic' enough to accept Governor," a prediction which Mr. Cleveland's reply promptly justified.

As the campaign progressed, he grew more and more eager for Judge Parker's election, writing articles to that effect for *Collier's Weekly,* for *McClure's Magazine,* and for the *Saturday Evening Post,* after seeing one of which Judge Parker thanked him in the following letter:

> Rosemount
> Esopus-on-the-Hudson
> *July 22, 1904.*

My dear Mr. Cleveland:

I wish to thank you for your very kind letter of the fourteenth, for all the generous things you say, and for all the suggestions you make. I shall always be most grateful for any advice that comes from you, and it shall always have great weight with me.

I have read with very grateful appreciation your most generous article written for *Collier's Weekly.* It is by far, in my opinion, the most telling contribution to the cause.

Thanking you again, and with best wishes for you always, I am,

> Very sincerely yours,
> Alton B. Parker.

Mr. Cleveland's diary records the events of November 8th with laconic brevity: "Election day. Voted about 10 o'c . . . Began to receive returns abt. ½ past 7 I think. It took but a few reports to enable me to see that we the Democrats were dreadfully left. Went to bed a little after 10." When the count was finished, it was seen that Roosevelt was overwhelmingly elected. He carried every state except the solid South, and Missouri and Maryland followed him into the Republican fold. His popular vote was over seven and a half millions, and his plurality more than two and a half millions.

So great was Mr. Cleveland's disappointment that for weeks he was silent on political matters, replying when questioned: "My present state of mind does not permit me to do the subject justice." To Mr. Farquhar, however, he wrote, on December 12th:

A. B. FARQUHAR, ESQ.,
   York, Penna.
MY DEAR SIR:—

I was glad to receive your recent letter after so long a silence. The result of the election was so astounding that I have hardly sufficiently recovered my composure to contemplate the reasons which led to it or the results likely to follow it. I am such an intense and unalterable believer in the saving common sense of the American people, that I cannot yet believe that the tremendous Republican majority given at the last election should be taken to indicate the people's willingness to allow the principles and practices of Republicanism to be unalterably fixed in the affairs of our body politic. I believe that the next swing of the pendulum of public sentiment will be quite to the Democratic side of the dial, and that, if Democracy is prepared to do its duty, when that time arrives, it will become again the beneficent agent of the people's salvation.

A number of the incidents involved in the election have so surprised me that sometimes, for a moment, the idea has entered my mind that a change in the character of our countrymen has taken place. This is, however, only for a moment, and the second thought immediately reinstates me in the confidence which I have always had in our people's right thinking. How the rejuvenation of the Democratic party which seems to be absolutely essential, is to be brought about, I do not know; but I am certain that in due time a way will be made plain.

Yours very truly,

GROVER CLEVELAND.

The defeat of Judge Parker served incidentally to heighten the prestige of Grover Cleveland, who remained the only Democrat since Buchanan strong enough to carry a presidential election. The oft-rejected prayer of friends, that he prepare an autobiography, grew more and more insistent, and flattering offers came from publishers, who understood far better than he the interest which his own story from his own pen would excite. He rejected them all, declaring the task distasteful to him as smacking too much of what he called "self-conceit." He admitted, however, the value of biographies of great men: "There is no sadder symptom of a generation's bad moral health than its lack of faith in its great men, and its loss of reverence for its heroes; but let this belief be coupled with the reservation that those called great shall be truly great, and that the heroes challenging our reverence shall be truly heroic, measured by standards adjusted to the highest moral conditions of man's civilization."

In this class he placed Washington, whom he described as "one whose glorious deeds are transcendently above all others recorded in our national annals . . . the incarnation of all the virtues and all the ideals that made our nationality possible"; and Lincoln, "A supremely great and good man . . . more and more sacredly enshrined in my passionate Americanism with every year of my life." But Grover Cleveland he persistently refused to consider even as a candidate for greatness. While fully conscious of a power to endure labor, far beyond that of the average man, of a courage that permitted him to steer his course regardless of opposition, of a purpose bent upon things outside his own personal gain, and of many other qualities of the warp and woof of greatness, he claimed no pedestal, no place among the immortals, content with the thought that he was a citizen who had done his duty. He felt he was in the world for quite another purpose than being great, as Dr. Merle Smith once expressed it.

But though disinclined to hear with favor the pleas of historians eager to become his biographers, he bitterly resented what he deemed the misrepresentations of pseudo-historians. To Gilder he expressed the wrath which the efforts of some of the latter had kindled:

Princeton, *January 28, 1905*.

MY DEAR MR. GILDER:

I want to thank you for your trouble in attempting to set Mr. ——— right. (PROF. ——— God save the mark!) I never heard of him until Nelson mentioned him in connection with his stuff; and I don't care what else he is, it must be that he is a lover of falsehood, who had rather, in the cloak of history writing, put down something new and striking, than tell the truth. There is another coyote in Kansas who is cut off the same piece; and I suppose such yelping and snarling as theirs is history.

I honestly think, my dear Gilder, that there are things in my life and career that if set out, and *read* by the young men of our country, might be of benefit to a generation soon to have in their keeping the safety and the mission of our nation; but I am not certain of this, for I am by no means sure that it would be in tune with the vaudeville that attracts our people and wins their applause. Somehow, I don't want to appear wearing a fur coat in July.

Mr. McClure and all the forces about him have lately importuned me, in season and out of season, to write, say twelve autobiographical articles, offering what seems to me a large sum for them [$10,000]; but I have declined the proposition. I went so far (for I softened up a bit under the suggestion of duty and money) to inquire how something would do like talking to another person for publication; but that did not take at all. I don't really think I would have done even that, but the disapproval of merely a hint that the "I" might to an extent be eliminated, made it seem to me more than ever that the retention of everything that might attract the lovers of a "snappy life" was considered important by the would-be publishers.

There is a circle of friends like you, who I hope will believe in me. I am happy in the conviction that they will continue in the faith whether an autobiography is written or not. I want my wife and children to love me now, and hereafter to proudly honor my memory. They will have my autobiography written on their hearts where every day they may turn the pages and read it. In these days what else is there that is worth while to a man nearly sixty-eight years old?

Give my love to Mrs. Gilder and believe me

Yours faithfully

GROVER CLEVELAND.

R. W. Gilder, Esq.,

13 E. 8th St., New York.

# CHAPTER XIII

## REORGANIZING THE EQUITABLE

*"We can better afford to slacken our pace than to abandon our old simple American standards of honesty."*
—GROVER CLEVELAND.

DURING the first eight years of Mr. Cleveland's life at Princeton, many attempts were made to lure him into business, where his hold upon the confidence of the public would have been of inestimable value; but he resisted them all, despite the tempting financial offers of many of them. In 1905, however, there came a call to what Elihu Root later characterized as "distinctly a public service," and one which, as such, he did not feel free to refuse, although it meant leadership in a field wholly new to him.

The Equitable Life Assurance Society, an association designed to benefit its policyholders, had by slow stages been transformed into a gigantic engine for their exploitation. Its funds were in the hands of directors who did not direct; its policyholders had become the victims of officials who did direct; while factional differences within the board had brought about a condition in which a receivership was inevitable, unless a thorough reorganization could be speedily effected. As a step toward such reorganization, its President, James W. Alexander, had asked the directors to mutualize the society by extending the voting privilege to all policyholders; and, in March, 1905, the committee appointed to effect this change unanimously recommended that the charter be so amended

350

as to provide that a majority of the directors, 28 out of 52, be elected by the policyholders.

Before the change was actually made, however, Mr. Thomas F. Ryan purchased 502 of the 1000 shares of Equitable capital stock, a block which had belonged to Henry B. Hyde, and with it the right to cast the majority vote upon all questions. Mr. Ryan later gave the following explanation of the motives which led him to make this purchase, involving the payment of $2,500,000: "I saw in the virtual necessity of a receivership of the Equitable . . . disaster impending unless the factional differences in the company among the directors and the management should be radically changed. To avert this and to prevent the frightful losses that would occur from the violent breaking up of the Equitable, not only to the policyholders but to the financial community at large, as well as to myself, I thought that someone ought to take over the business."

For one man to intervene to protect the interests of six hundred thousand policyholders, interests amounting to $400,000,000, was a venture of enormous proportions, and Mr. Ryan knew that if his plan were to succeed he must secure as the head of the trustees, in whose hands he intended to place the administration of his majority stock, a man whom the public would fully trust, since with the majority stock went the full control of the Equitable Corporation. Ex-President Cleveland appeared to him the man best fitted for this task, and he accordingly sent him the following letter:

New York, *June 9, 1905.*

DEAR MR. CLEVELAND:

You may be aware that a bitter controversy exists regarding the management of the Equitable Life Assurance Society and that public confidence has been shaken in the safety of the funds under the control of a single block of stock left by the late Henry B. Hyde. This loss of confidence affects a great public trust of more than $400,000,000, representing the savings of over 600,-000 policyholders, and the present condition amounts to a public misfortune.

In the hope of putting an end to this condition and in connection with a change of the executive management of the Society, I have . . . purchased this block of stock and propose to put it into the hands of a board of trustees having no connection with Wall Street, with power to vote it for the election of directors—as to twenty-eight of the fifty-two directors, in accordance with the instructions of the policyholders of the Society, and as to the remaining twenty-four directors in accordance with the uncontrolled judgment of the trustees. This division of twenty-eight and twenty-four is in accordance with a plan of giving substantial control to policyholders already approved by the Superintendent of Insurance.

I beg you to act as one of this board with other gentlemen, who shall be of a character entirely satisfactory to you.

I would not venture to ask this of you on any personal grounds; but to restore this great trust, affecting so many people of slender means, to soundness and public confidence would certainly be a great public service, and this view emboldens me to make the request.

The duties of the trust would be light, as, in the nature of things, when a satisfactory board is once constituted there are few changes, and all the clerical and formal work would be done by the office force of the Company.

I have written similar letters to Justice Morgan J.

O'Brien, Presiding Justice of the Appellate Division in our Supreme Court, and to Mr. George Westinghouse, of Pittsburgh, two of the largest policyholders in the Society.

Very truly yours,

THOMAS F. RYAN.

Hon. Grover Cleveland
    Princeton, N. J.

After some hesitation, Mr. Cleveland answered:

Princeton, N. J.

*June 10, 1905.*

THOMAS F. RYAN, ESQ.,
DEAR SIR:

I have this morning received your letter asking me to act as one of the three trustees to hold the stock of the Equitable Life Assurance Society, which has lately been acquired by you and certain associates, and to use the voting power of such stock in the selection of directors of said Society.

After a little reflection I have determined that I ought to accept this service. I assume this duty upon the express condition that, so far as the trustees are to be vested with discretion in the selection of directors, they are to be absolutely free and undisturbed in the exercise of their judgment, and that, so far as they are to act formally in voting for the directors conceded to policyholders, a fair and undoubted expression of policy-holding choice will be forthcoming.

The very general anxiety aroused by the recent unhappy dissensions in the management of the Equitable Society furnishes proof of the near relationship of our people to life insurance. These dissensions have not only injured the fair fame of the company immediately affected, but have impaired popular faith and confidence in the security of life insurance itself, as a provision for those who in thousands of cases would be otherwise helpless against the afflictive visitations of fate.

The character of this business is such that those who manage and direct it are charged with a grave trust for those who, necessarily, must rely upon their fidelity. In those circumstances they have no right to regard the places they hold as ornamental, but rather as positions of work and duty and watchfulness.

Above all things, they have no right to deal with the interests intrusted to them in such a way as to subserve or to become confused or complicated with their personal transactions or ventures.

While the hope that I might aid in improving the plight of the Equitable Society has led me to accept the trusteeship you tender, I cannot rid myself of the belief that what has overtaken this company is liable to happen to other insurance companies and fiduciary organizations as long as lax ideas of responsibility in places of trust are tolerated by our people.

The high pressure of speculation, the madness of inordinate business scheming, and the chances taken in new and uncertain enterprises, are constantly present temptations, too often successful, in leading managers and directors away from scrupulous loyalty and fidelity to the interests of others confided to their care.

We can better afford to slacken our pace than to abandon our old simple American standards of honesty; and we shall be safer if we regain our old habit of looking at the appropriation, to personal uses, of property and interests held in trust, in the same light as other forms of stealing.

Yours very truly,

GROVER CLEVELAND.

On June 15th a deed of trust was executed transferring control of the Equitable Life Assurance Society from its one majority owner to Mr. Cleveland and his two co-trustees. At the same time Paul Morton, ex-Secretary of the Navy, and a son of J. Sterling Morton, of Cleveland's second Cabinet, was made President of the Equitable, but he was in effect a President without a Board of Directors, as the old board had nearly all resigned, and the new one was as yet to be created.

During the days which intervened between his appointment and his first formal meeting with his co-trustees, Mr. Cleveland set himself to the task of mastering the problems and the complicated machinery of the insurance business. He sought advice from neither Mr. Ryan himself nor from Mr. Ryan's able counsel, Mr. Elihu Root, although fully conscious of their skill in matters of large business. He had friends also on the Board of Directors, but he asked no help from them, declaring that they had made a mess of things, and that now he, by his own methods, must find his "own blundering way." Disregarding the summer heat, he worked at his task of discovering the facts, which he later summarized thus:

"A majority of the directors of this Company were each qualified as stockholders and directors, by a colorable holding of five shares of the stock of the Company, placed in their hands by its President and subject at any time to his recall, or such other disposition as he should request. Nearly all of them were men of such wealth and were so distinguished and prominent in business and financial operations that their names were familiar throughout the United States, and some of them throughout the world. All of them were connected with the control and management of other large companies, numbering in some cases twenty or more. Their honorable business reputations repelled any suspicion of deliberate wrongdoing or willful neglect of obligations. They were simply non-directing directors, holding their places at the request of the President of the Company, and doing what a vicious system dictates in such cases—precisely nothing except drift with the current. Thus it came about that before their eyes and within their reach, peculation and breach of trust flourished, scandals grew, the beneficent designs of the Company, pending its thorough reformation, were discredited, and its policyholders were distressed with fear and gloomy forebodings."

As soon as he had mastered the situation, he sent an announcement to the policyholders, informing them that the trustees had assumed their posts as representing the majority stock, and asking that suggestions be made or names proposed for the vacant directorships. Although he refused expert advice, he instinctively sought the guidance of popular opinion.

While the replies were coming in, the question of the salary of the Chairman of the Trustees was taken up by a committee of the directors, which, on June 20th, reported that in view of "the nature and extent of the services rendered by Mr. Cleveland . . . $1000 per month is a fair sum."

By June 27th, some two hundred suggestions had been received in answer to Mr. Cleveland's request, and on

that day the second meeting of the trustees was held, nine directors were chosen, and a longer and more elaborate address adopted, to be sent out under date of June 28th. Each of these documents was drawn with as much care as though it had been a presidential message to Congress. Paul D. Cravath, one of the counsel who had executed the deed of trust, recalls the following incident: "At his request I had drafted a statement or paper of some kind, I forget just what it was, for which he was to become responsible. One afternoon I went to Princeton to submit it to him. He seemed to like it. I went to bed at a normal hour, say eleven o'clock. When I came down to early breakfast the next morning Mr. Cleveland greeted me with an entirely new paper which he had prepared after I had gone to bed. He must have stayed up most of the night. It is needless to say that his paper was very much better than the draft which I had proposed."

By the end of June, the Society was reorganized, with a board of trustees ready to take the responsibilities of their trust in the spirit of the "old simple American standards of honesty," to which Mr. Cleveland always pinned his faith. As Chairman he had furnished men for vacant places, destroying the practice of furnishing places for vacant men. As each new director had been appointed he had called upon Mr. Cleveland, nominally to pay his respects, but really to receive his instructions. Each came from the interview with a clear vision of the dangers which beset directors, and with the knowledge that there was no room for dummy directors on the new board.

In his letter accepting the trust, Mr. Cleveland had said: "What has overtaken this Company is liable to happen in other companies." And, on July 20th, acting perhaps upon this hint, the New York Legislature made provision for a committee to investigate the entire business of life insurance within the state. Senator Armstrong was its Chairman, and its chief counsel was Charles E. Hughes.

Their report laid bare a sordid and humiliating situation in which senators, masters of industry, political machine-men, bankers, railroad presidents, and directors of insurance companies had wrought together to exploit a helpless public. But it emphasized the value of the changes which Mr. Cleveland had brought about in the Equitable before the Armstrong Committee had even been appointed, and forced other companies to make similar changes in the interest of the public.

In commenting upon the report, Mr. Cleveland said of Mr. Hughes: "No one can better know the causes responsible for such management than the able and fearless man who conducted the investigation which brought it to light. His universally conceded sincerity and his pre-eminent qualification as a witness give the weight of conclusiveness to the following words addressed by him to his fellow citizens in the state of New York: 'What is the vice in the conduct of those great enterprises which directly affect our interests? It is the vice of selfishness. It is the vice of setting up self-interest as against service. It is the vice of seeing how much we can get and keep, instead of seeing how much benefit can be bestowed!' "

No sooner had the affairs of the Equitable been set in order than there came a new call:

*Dec. 15th,* [1905]

120 Broadway, New York

MY DEAR MR. CLEVELAND:

I am authorized by The New York Life Insurance Company, The Mutual Life Company, and this Society to offer you $12,000.00 per year salary to act as the referee between the three companies in matters of dispute concerning the respective agents of the three institutions rebating the commissions they receive from premiums paid.

This will not be arduous work and I doubt if there will be many cases. They can be submitted to you at Princeton generally by correspondence and any expenses for clerk hire will also be allowed you.

You were the only man suggested for the position and I sincerely hope you will decide to accept it commencing January 1st.

Mr. Thos. B. Reed once held this same relation to these companies.

Respectfully yours,<br>PAUL MORTON.

To
Hon. Grover Cleveland
Princeton, N. J.

To this Mr. Cleveland replied:

Princeton, Dec. 19, 1905.

MY DEAR MR. MORTON:

I have duly considered your letter of the 15th instant in which, on behalf of The New York Life Insurance Company, The Mutual Life Insurance Company, and The Equitable Life Assurance Society you offer me the position of Referee to determine disputes that may arise between the organizations mentioned concerning the allowance by their respective agents of rebates on their premium commissions.

I believe this to be a vice that can have no place in well-conducted life insurance.

I accept the proposition contained in your letter; but in doing so I assume that those for whom you speak are seriously determined to present the claims referred to, and will unreservedly second every effort directed to that end.

Yours very truly

GROVER CLEVELAND.

Hon. Paul Morton
President of The Equitable
Life Assurance Society.

To the duties of these two posts, the Equitable trusteeship and this refereeship, there was added a year later a third, also in the field of insurance. The revelations of the Armstrong Committee having produced a nationwide tendency on the part of legislatures to make unnecessary and ill-advised attacks upon the insurance business, representatives of the larger companies came together and formed an organization for mutual protection: "The Presidents' Association of Life Insurance Companies."

As head of this new organization, and therefore in effect the titular head of life insurance in America, they selected Mr. Cleveland, offering him a salary, liberal though not large in comparison with those which Americans had come to associate with high insurance posts. The duty of this office was to examine and elucidate measures of legislation as they were presented, a duty for which his public experience had admirably equipped him.

For a time he hesitated, accepting at first, and later sending a telegram of refusal, which he explained in the following letter to Mr. Morton:

Princeton, *Feby. 6, 1907.*

MY DEAR PAUL:

I have just sent you a dispatch which has brought me a great deal of regret, and a consciousness that I have caused you disappointment and embarrassment. I am altogether to blame for these and confess my fault without any claim of mitigation. If I had taken a little more time to consider the matter in all its aspects and had trusted a little more thoroughly to the soundness of my first promptings, I should have saved you embarrassment and vexation, by declining the place you offered me, at the proper time.

My interest in insurance affairs, I now realize more than ever, is related exclusively to the success and prosperity of the Equitable, and my great desire to be of service to you and Mr. Ryan as well as to the company. It is such a different proposition to make this new connection and to be related to other companies and their officials whom I know nothing about and which have not enlisted any personal attachment, that I cannot, all things considered, bring myself to its acceptance.

*I know, too, that on the actual basis of service to be rendered*—that is, real work to be done, I would not earn anything like the salary offered me.

I fully appreciate the generous compensation paid me for past services; but I have had no very serious twinges of conscience on account of its acceptance.

Conditions have, however, so changed and the work which I might do in the future will be so much diminished that I insist upon an entire suspension of the compensation heretofore allowed me in connection with my trusteeship and refereeship, or the relinquishment of both positions.

Perhaps, if continued, I ought to be reimbursed

actual expenses and a fair compensation for such matters as should be submitted to me as referee.

I want you to understand that my interest in the Equitable and your success as its President and the satisfaction of my relationship with Mr. Ryan, is as strong as ever (and that means as strong as it can be); and I would be glad if I could continue a serviceable connection.

In my judgment the head of the Presidents' Association would more naturally be an insurance man. I believe you do not agree with me in this.

Finally, if you will let me off from this new engagement with as much complacency as you can muster, I will be glad to render any other possible service to the institution and the persons with whom I am already associated, on the conditions which I believe you understand.

Yours faithfully,<br>GROVER CLEVELAND.

Hon. Paul Morton,
President, &c.,
120 Broadway, New York.

Mr. Morton and his associates, however, persisted in their demand that Mr. Cleveland accept the proffered post, and in the end he yielded. The field of his activities was nation-wide, but his audience was world-wide; and the influence exerted by his carefully considered statements concerning the business of life insurance was comparable with that which he had so long exerted as a political leader. His method of pinning the crime on the criminal was employed as fearlessly as in the old days of Sheriff, Mayor, Governor or President. One of his addresses bore the title, "Directors Who Do Not Direct," and into it he put his philosophy of representative responsibility. When a bank has been looted, he declared, it is not enough for the Directors to tell the plundered depositors that "someone must be trusted." Their proper reply is, "Yes! but we have trusted you."

Despite his frank acknowledgment of the fact that the insurance idea had at times been used as a cloak to cover many crooked deals, his examination of the entire field confirmed his earlier view that insurance companies had rendered invaluable service to the great majority. And his frank approval of the system reassured many minds and helped greatly to restore the confidence so rudely shaken by the findings of the Armstrong Committee.

Thus, in the last years of his life, was he able to apply his statesmanship to big business, carrying through promptly, efficiently, and without seeking the spotlight, a series of reforms whose ultimate influence extended far beyond the field of nation-wide insurance. The abuses that had disgraced the insurance business had but reflected others in a hundred kindred lines; and the reforms wrought by the practiced hand of Grover Cleveland, not skilled in insurance but an expert in reform, reacted upon many of these businesses as well. Men had come to believe that the existing system of interlocking directorates was essential to the conduct of big business, because the men capable of managing such enterprises were considered few. This bubble vanished at the first prick of Cleveland realism, for within five weeks after beginning his work as Chairman of the Equitable Trustees he had found enough new men not connected with the insurance business to conduct successfully a great enterprise which had been brought to the brink of ruin by the older system. He had proved that there is no mystery about big business, and that there is no need to erect its leaders into a mystic priesthood.

"It has been interesting to me," declared Judge Day, who entered the Equitable during Mr. Cleveland's reorganization, and later became its President, "to see how life insurance was revolutionized. . . . The new owner's courage in buying a majority of the stock, and his act in divesting himself of any vestige of control over it, by turning it over to the one man in the country who would inspire confidence, has always seemed to me one of the striking events in modern business. . . . The immediate return of confidence, the success of the open appeal to the great public which at once carried its effects beyond the policyholders of the Society, marked it as an outstanding event." And he added, "the one predominant influence was the name and character of Grover Cleveland. . . . The value of Cleveland's services to the cause of sound life insurance in the days of its trial cannot be overestimated."

# CHAPTER XIV

## SUNSET DAYS

*"I have tried so hard to do right."*
—GROVER CLEVELAND.

MR. CLEVELAND'S sixty-ninth birthday found him in Florida, seeking the health which never would return. Although not old, he was aging fast. The physical strength which had made possible strenuous days and deliberately sleepless nights was gone, and he dared not face the penetrating dampness of a New Jersey March. To him in his retreat came, as usual, a deluge of birthday letters, some from intimate friends, some from mere acquaintances, and many from admirers who knew him only by his works. Commodore Benedict, in playful vein, sounded the bugle call of the 69th:

Indian Harbor, Greenwich, Conn.
*March 12, 1906.*

MY DEAR ADMIRAL:—

I am credibly informed that you are to join the Sixty-ninth regiment on the 18th inst., the day following St. Patrick's.

As I shall not be present to extend the glad hand, and, as it was my good fortune to join that disorganization something over three years ago, I have thought, perhaps, you might be interested to hear what I think of it after serving the full term of my enlistment, and what you may expect, based on my experience.

You must not be surprised to find at the very outset that you are the youngest member of the whole shooting match, but advancement is very certain, rapid, and continuous. You will not be obliged to carry the pail at the end of the procession for more than a few moments, so rapidly are younger members admitted. You will not be greeted with a display of shamrocks or shillalahs, the regiment is too busy admitting new members and burying older ones to indulge in such luxuries. Your enlistment will be for one year only, at the end of which, if you survive, you will be a veteran.

Although the memberships of this regiment extend throughout the world, you will be surprised to find how few of them you will meet, and, of them, but very few will be found in good marching order, most of them preferring slippers to seven league boots. Never before did you belong to a club, society, or organization which comprised such a lot of rickety humanity. An atmosphere of spring will be found lingering in some hearts, but the most of them will betray a spring halt in their legs or a movement as if getting ready for winter by practicing on snowshoes. And yet the few little boys you will find to play with, some of whom may have been companions of your youth, will all seem to be on their good behavior. They will flatter one another with all sorts of preposterous assurances of youthful looks and actions, and, after swearing off twenty years or so from each other's ages consult a pedometer and a mirror, with the result that, while each admits a claim to youthful feelings, will all agree that they are pretty good imitations of old people. They will be ever ready to give the latitude and longitude of all their wanderings, and, after touching upon a few joys, such as fishing and hunting—shouldering their guns and rods to show how game and fish have been won—will lapse into a state of ecstatic agony as they unload upon each other the stories of their various sufferings.

Not the least of the attractions of this regiment is the fair light guard of grandmothers who belong; for women, of course, are not only admitted, but, for the most part, are drafted in spite of many protestations. There will appear to be more of them than men; and then will dawn upon you, if it never has done so before, the fact that, in spite of a few scuttle-bonnet cripples among them, there are a whole lot who are exceedingly fascinating and attractive, a joy wholly denied us in youth, but fortunately reserved for age. So much for the Sixty-niners.

Your year of service ended, without booming of cannon, earthquakes, lightning, or thunder, you will quietly slide into the very aristocracy of age. All your life long you have wondered if you would live out your natural days. How strange it is that we should spend so many years in fear that we may never attain the seventieth birthday, yet always dreading the day when we will do so! However, this question settled, you will find yourself in the ranks of many great men, particularly in Biblical history, like King David; and later, Columbus, and still later, Mark Twain, who made a joke of the event. He must have had in mind the inscription on Gay's tomb in Westminster Abbey:—

"Life is a jest, all things show it;
I thought so once, and now I know it."

Then you can almost consider yourself honorably mentioned in the burial service. Looking back to the Sixty-niners, they appear like a marked down lot at Macy's. I find little depression of spirits on my side of seventy. I am on velvet, as the gamblers say. Besides, many compensations appear, not the least is to be able to walk into the office of the Commissioner of Jurors, as I have done, with my thumb on my nose and my fingers fluttering in the air. Your value as an antique has increased, and bumps of veneration come to your support on every hand and head.

But I am exceeding the objects of this letter. At this juncture in your career you might follow the advice given by the little Sunday School boy (in a story you told me, by the way). You remember when asked by his teacher —"What about hell and the Devil?" he answered, "Wait and see." Meanwhile, uniting with the congratulations of other friends, and, in the language of Robert Roosevelt, let me "wish that you may live as long as you want to and want to as long as you live."

Very sincerely yours,

E. C. BENEDICT.

Grover Cleveland.

Richard Olney avowed the opinion that, "On your 69th birthday you find yourself the object of higher and more general respect and esteem among your fellow countrymen than any other living American."

Mark Twain's tribute revamped the slogan of 1884: "We love him for the enemies he has made."

21 Fifth Avenue
March 6, 1906.

GROVER CLEVELAND, ESQ.
EX-PRESIDENT.
HONORED SIR:

Your patriotic virtues have won for you the homage of half the nation and the enmity of the other half. This places your character as a citizen upon a summit as high as Washington's. The verdict is unanimous and unassailable. The votes of both sides are necessary in cases like these, and the votes of the one side are quite as valuable as are the votes of the other. When the votes are all in a public man's favor the verdict is against him. It is sand, and history will wash it away. But the verdict for you is rock, and will stand.

With the profoundest respect,

S. L. CLEMENS.

(as of date March 18, 1906)

Woodrow Wilson thus acknowledged his personal debt to the teachings of the Sage of Princeton:

Princeton University
Princeton, N. J.

President's Room                              *5 March, 1906.*
MY DEAR MR. CLEVELAND:—

I should think that a birth-day would bring you very many gratifying thoughts, and I hope that you realize how specially strong the admiration and affection of those of us in Princeton who know you best has grown during the years when we have been privileged to be near you. It has been one of the best circumstances of my life that I have been closely associated with you in matters both large and small. It has given me strength and knowledge of affairs.

But if I may judge by my own feeling, what a man specially wants to know on his birth-day is how he stands, not in reputation or in power, but in the affection of those whose affection he cares for. The fine thing about the feeling for yourself which I find in the mind of almost everyone I talk with, is that it is mixed with genuine affection. I often find this true even of persons who do not know you personally. How much more must it be true of those who are near you.

With most affectionate regard and with a hope that you may enjoy many another anniversary in peace and honor and affection,

Faithfully yours,

WOODROW WILSON.

Honorable Grover Cleveland,
Princeton, N. J.

Illiterate or literary, commonplace or clever, each birthday tribute received its answer in his own hand-writing. To Richard Watson Gilder he wrote: "From the height of sixty-nine, I write to assure you that this is a happy day in my life, and to tell you how happy I am that you have made it so—more by your own loving message of congratulations than by those you have in-spired. I have been so deeply impressed by it all, that I have had many struggles between smiles and tears as I read the words of affection and praise that have met me at the gate of entrance to another year. Somehow I am wondering why all this should be, since I have left many things undone I ought to have done in the realm of friendship, and since in the work of public life and effort, God has never failed to clearly make known to me the path of duty. And still it is in human nature for one to hug the praise of his fellows and the affection of friends to his bosom as his earned possessions. I am no better than this; but I shall trust you to acquit me of affectation when I say to you that in to-day's mood there comes the regret that the time is so shortened, within which I can make further payment to the people that have honored and trusted me."

To Andrew Carnegie, he sent the following reply:

Stuart, Florida.
*March 20, 1906.*

MY DEAR MR. CARNEGIE:

Your exceedingly kind letter of congratulation touched me deeply, and I want to thank you for it from the bottom of my heart. With other like manifestations of good will from friends whom I also hold close in affection, I feel that it compensates not only for advancing age, but for all that has been hard and laborious in the past.

I avail myself of the knowledge of your address which your letter furnishes, to thank you for the package from Scotland which arrived in proper condition some time ago. Despite all fanatical medical advice, I insist upon it that at the age of sixty-nine, a man should know himself of at least one thing that meets his physical condition.

Ever since you told me something of your dear daughter's ailment, I have been exceedingly anxious to hear that you had been relieved of solicitude on her account.

Will you please convey to Mrs. Carnegie my dutiful regards and believe me

Faithfully yours
GROVER CLEVELAND.

Andrew Carnegie, Esq.
The Cottage
Dungeness, Fernandino, Fla.

His acknowledgment to the Rev. Wilton Merle-Smith, D.D., beautifully sums up his own high philosophy of life:

Stuart, Fla., *March 21, 1906.*

MY DEAR DOCTOR SMITH:

You don't know how much good your generous letter of congratulation has done me. It has enlivened my sense of gratitude for what I have been able to do in the past, for the joys of the present, and for such friendship and confidence as yours. I have quite often, lately, found myself longing for the rest of idleness, and the peace of inactivity; and I have sometimes even given entrance to the thought that these were my due. But you have written words to me that will help me to constantly appreciate the fact that God who has blessed me above all other men, and directed all my ways, deserves my service, and every good cause deserves my best endeavor, as long as my life and strength shall last.

I know as no one else can know my limitations, and how fixed and inexorable they are . . . but I shall trust God, as I have in the past, for strength and opportunity for further usefulness.

Yours faithfully,
GROVER CLEVELAND.

Rev. Wilton Merle Smith, D.D.
29 W. 54th St., New York.

His letter to Vilas, the only surviving member of his first Cabinet, he wrote, in reminiscent mood:

Stuart, Fla., *March 24, 1906.*

MY DEAR MR. VILAS,

In this rather secluded place where I have come to seek rest and recreation, many kind congratulations upon my sixty-ninth birthday have reached me. They have all been delightful and comforting to me; but none have touched me so deeply as yours. Twenty-one years is really a long time; and yet without dwelling upon their actual number how short a time it seems since on the 4th day of March, 1885, seven of the best and most patriotic men in our country joined me in the highest executive work. It would have been strange indeed if the national responsibilities and perplexities of the next four years—nobly shared by all—had not grappled us together by bands stronger and more enduring than steel. It is one of the most impressive thoughts that enter my mind in these days, that of all that circle you and I alone remain.

And so it is, that your letter recalling this, and bringing to my mind our free, frank and trustful association, and manifesting the same unrestrained affection as of old, comes so near my heart. . . .

With thanks for your continued kindly remembrance of me, and its beautiful expression just at this time, I am,

Faithfully your friend,

GROVER CLEVELAND.

Hon. Wm. F. Vilas,
Madison, Wis.

George Allen Bennett, aged nine, received this reply:

Stuart, Florida.
*March 30, 1906.*

MY DEAR LITTLE FRIEND:

I am very glad you wrote me a letter of congratulation and good wishes on my birthday. And I thank you for kindly thinking of me. We ought to be very good friends, if we were born on the same day of the month, though there is a difference of sixty years in our ages. The years seem to pass much more quickly, as a person grows older and when you arrive at the age of sixty-nine, as I have done, you will wonder at the short distance between nine and sixty-nine.

I think the 18th of March is the best day in all the year to be born on and I hope you do too. I wish for you a great many Happy Birthdays, and that as each one passes, there will be such increase in your mental and moral growth and such improvement in every way that you will be insured a life of honor and usefulness.

Your friend<br>GROVER CLEVELAND.

Master George Allen Bennett
North Ridgefield, Conn.

Mr. Cleveland loved children and this letter is the result of the natural impulse of that affection. One of his law partners in the old days in Buffalo has recorded the fact that in furnishing his bachelor apartments "his fondness for children was shown in a preponderance of children's pictures in the photographs scattered about." And another friend of early days recalls the fact that, while Governor of New York, he used to walk every day from his residence to the Capitol, and always greeted each child whom he met with "Hello, little one!" Not infrequently he received and always enjoyed the retort: "Hello, little one!" During one of Judge Hornblower's visits to Mr. Cleveland, when Ruth was a very new baby, he drew out from his overcoat pocket and displayed to the ex-President a sadly dilapidated doll which his daughter, Susie, aged five, had asked her father to take to little Ruth when she heard that the latter was ill. The conversation then turned to other matters, and when the Judge returned home he carried the doll with him, forgotten. The next day he received from Mr. Cleveland the following letter:

My dear Mr. Hornblower:

I scarcely do anything just now but read the kindest messages of congratulation and receive in every possible way manifestations of the kindness which pervades the people of the Land.

And yet nothing has come near touching me so much as the incident of to-day relating to the gift your little daughter sent to mine.

I do not know why you did not leave the doll with me. Nothing could have been more dear to the mother than the doll which a little girl, *and your daughter,* was willing to give up to our new baby.

I do not want your child to feel that her gift was not valued for what it was worth. It meant so much to her that it means a very great deal to us.

I wish we could have the doll and that its precious little donor could receive our heartfelt thanks, with the assurance that when our child first plays with a doll it shall be with the one she gave her.

Of course if we are to have it, it must be in the exact shape it was in when I saw it to-day.

Yours sincerely
Grover Cleveland.

The closing months of 1906 were uneventful, save for ceaseless pleas for speeches. But he was weary of speaking, and refused every call which did not lay a hand upon his conscience. He did, however, promise, at the urgent request of the Union League Club of Chicago, to deliver the Washington's Birthday address of 1907, under their auspices, although he shrank from the idea of the labor which such a promise entailed. Having completed it, he wrote to George F. Parker: "I have just finished a terrific and not a very victorious struggle in the preparation of something to say at Chicago on Washington's Birthday. I am consoled, however, by the reflection that it concludes probably my perplexities in that direction for the period of my natural life, and during the ensuing eternity, unless I fail to 'arrive,' as I hope to do."

Armed with his manuscript he reached Chicago, only to find that he could not escape with a single address. Indeed, he had made four before that strenuous twenty-second of February closed. His principal speech, a tribute to the memory of George Washington, was at once a eulogy and a warning. He read it from the manuscript with neither gesture nor sign of emotion, save when he turned from his praise of the first President to denounce the corruption, extravagance, and dishonesty of demagogues, or to attack a too slavish adherence to party and partisan interests.

"If your observance of this day," he said, "were intended to make more secure the immortal fame of Washington, or to add to the strength and beauty of his imperishable monument built upon a nation's affectionate remembrance, your purpose would be useless. Washington has no need of you. But in every moment from the time he drew his sword in the cause of American Independence to this hour, living or dead, the American people have needed him. It is not important now, nor will it be in all the coming years, to remind our countrymen that Washington has lived. . . . But it is important —and more important now than ever before—that they should clearly apprehend and adequately value the virtues and ideal of which he was the embodiment. . . . There should be no toleration of even the shade of a thought that what Washington did and said and wrote . . . has become in the least outworn, or that in these days of material advance and development they may be

merely pleasantly recalled with a sort of affectionate veneration, and with a kind of indulgent and loftily courteous concession of the value of Washington's example and precepts. These constitute the richest of our crown jewels."

In the evening he was introduced to the diners at the Union League Club by President Charles S. Cutting, who referred to the question: "What shall we do with our ex-Presidents?" Mr. Cleveland's reply was a genial comment upon the solution recently proposed by a prominent editor-enemy: "Take him out into a five-acre lot and shoot him." "That proposition," he said, "has never had my support. In the first place, a five-acre lot seems needlessly large, and in the second place an ex-President has already suffered enough. . . ."

Mr. Cleveland's delight at the attentions received on his sixty-ninth anniversary prompted his friends to undertake a larger celebration for the seventieth. In fact, they dared to plan a national observance of the birthday of the man who, ten years before, had left the White House a fallen leader, with few, even among his own party, prepared to do him reverence. Time, the revealer of all things, had dealt kindly with his fame, until now he who had never courted favor, even within his own party, found it in both parties.

John H. Finley, then President of the College of the City of New York, suggested that the day be kept as the nation's "out-of-doors day," and a flock of eager reporters arrived at Princeton to request Mr. Cleveland's reaction to the suggestion. They were received with cordiality, and retired primed with an interview upon the benefits of the simple life.

"I look with apprehension," he said, "upon the mad rush of American life, which is certain to impair the mental and physical vigor necessary to every human being. The wholesome sentiments which spring from country life are being overwhelmed by the ambitions and tendencies that flow out from our great cities. Few have the hardihood to withstand the swirl and rush of city life, or to remain indifferent to the promises of sudden wealth and the excitement of speculation in a metropolis, where immense fortunes are made and lost in a single day. . . .

"We are proud of our cities, of course. But we must not allow them wholly to shape our ideals and our ambitions. Nothing that the wealth of a city can buy will atone for the loss of that American sturdiness and independence which the farm and the small town have so frequently produced. . . . In my experience I have found that impressions which a man receives who walks by the brookside or in the forest or by the seashore make him a better man and a better citizen. They lift him above the worries of business and teach him of a power greater than human power."

Just before his birthday, he started south on a hunting trip, thus setting a good example to the millions who were asked to observe "out-of-doors day." Upon his seventieth birthday, therefore, only one letter reached him; but that one made all others unnecessary to his contentment:

> Princeton, N. J.
> *March 15, 1907.*

MY DEAREST:

I am so afraid that I will not get your birthday letter to you in time that I suppose it will be a day ahead! And maybe you will reach home anyway and so not get it, but in that case I think I might be able to express my birthday thoughts to you. I hope you will be well on Monday, just as well as you can be, then things will look bright to you and your new year will begin happily. Then I hope you will keep well, and it will go a long long way toward making your year happy. I hate to have you away on your birthday, but I realize that it will save you some strain—for many people seem to be thinking of you at this time. We all send much much love, and all the deepest best wishes of our hearts—and my heart is full of gratitude for what the years of your life have meant to me. You know how dearly I love you. You do not mind my saying it over, any day, and you won't mind it on this especial day—so I repeat it and repeat it, and I ask God's blessing on you for all the days.

Your loving wife<br>FRANK.

The oak box tells the tale of how many people were thinking of him on his seventieth birthday, and of how he cherished the records of their affection. It contains hundreds of letters and telegrams from men, women, and children in all walks of life, expressing pride, gratitude, and affection for this retired leader of men. One of the tributes which he most valued was an editorial in the New York *Sun,* so long his relentless persecutor and defamer. It declared: "As President, Mr. Cleveland enforced the laws and did not truckle to organized violence or crouch before public clamor. The man who taught the Chicago labor lords that there was a Government at Washington, the man who wrote the Venezuela message, is sure of an honorable place in history and of the final approval of his countrymen." In sending this editorial to Mr. Cleveland, Edwin Packard wrote: "If

Mr. Dana were living, I think that even he would make amends."

The day was celebrated at Caldwell, New Jersey, by the unveiling of a tablet in the room where he was born. Unsentimental though he appeared to the outsider, his heart was as responsive as that of a child, despite his long life of conflict; and this mark of affection touched the deepest emotions of his nature. To Richard Watson Gilder, one of the prime movers in the plan to make his birthplace also his memorial, he wrote:

Princeton, *March 25, 1907.*

MY DEAR MR. GILDER:

It was a complete misfit—a travesty on things as they should be—that I should be disporting in balmy air and all creature comforts, while you cold, hungry, and miserably forlorn, were finding your way to Caldwell, for the purpose of marking the time and place of my birth. You did what you ought not to have done. There is no process of calculation by which it can be made to appear a profitable investment for you. And yet when men reach the age of seventy, I believe their mental movements grow self-centered to such an extent, that consciously or unconsciously, they sort of believe their gratitude to be in some measure compensatory to those who honor them or suffer discomforts on their behalf.

I am so new to this venerable age of seventy, that I cannot tell at this moment how much I am under the influence of this idea. But my dear friend, one thing I know: Your kindnesses have been so many, and have extended through so many years, that the pages set apart for their record are full; and I long ago abandoned all hope of redeeming the one-sidedness of the account.

You must I think see how impossible it is for me to

do more than to say to you, that I am profoundly moved by the conception of the Caldwell incident and by the beauty of its completed manifestation. It stands for the thoughtfulness and affectionate remembrance of friends nearer my heart than all others.

Yours faithfully<br>GROVER CLEVELAND.

Richard W. Gilder
    Editor of The Century Magazine
    New York.

Among the many verses written in honor of the day, are the following by Eliza H. Morton:

> "Time's hand has lightly touched thy brow
> With lines of care.
> And as he touched, he whispered 'peace,'
> And stamped it there."

In general, his own reactions were less serious. To Commodore Benedict he wrote, when the day was over: "I am already regarding it as a small performance to do so easy a trick."

So successful had been the plan to encourage a nation-wide crop of birthday letters that he found it impossible to send personal acknowledgments. He therefore inserted in the New York *Times* the following grateful confession of helpless appreciation: "It seems to be impossible for me to acknowledge, except through the press of the country, the generosity and kindly consideration of my countrymen, which have been made manifest by congratulatory messages and newspaper comment on the occasion of my seventieth birthday. These have deeply touched me, and in the book of grateful recollection they are written where every remaining day of my life I can turn a page and read them."

The drift of politics during the next few months left him still uncertain which national organization was most entitled to be called by disciples of the "True Democracy" the common enemy. Eagerly he watched for signs of the long-hoped-for Democratic redemption, and found none. Bryanism was still Democracy, and Cleveland was as unwilling as ever to acknowledge the identity. Of Republican regeneration he had long since ceased even to dream, for the promises of McKinleyism, which his influence had done so much to enthrone, had bitterly disappointed him; while its successor, Rooseveltism, had never appealed to him as having even promise. "Concerning . . . political affairs," he wrote to Benedict, on August 17, 1907, "I feel like the farmer who started at the bottom of a hill with a wagon load of corn and discovered at the hill top that every grain of his load had slid out under the tail board. Though of a profane temperament, he stood mutely surveying his disaster until to a passing neighbor, who asked him why he didn't swear, he replied: 'Because by God I cannot do the subject justice.'"

For the Commodore's further delectation, he thus pictured his conception of the politics of the day, in which both parties looked strangely alike to him:

"I see our President has been making another 'Yes, I guess not' speech on business, corporations, etc., and has told the farmers how completely they should have the land and the fullness thereof; Gov. Hughes seems to be attempting neck-breaking acrobatics; Bryan smiles at both of them while performing his continuous tight-rope dance; and Hearst in his cage of wild beasts waits his turn to surprise and shock the multitude—'Open every hour of the day and night gentlemen; wonderful vaudeville performance—all seen under one tent.'"

He did not hesitate to declare, however, that if Bryan should be again nominated by the Democrats, he would vote for a Republican, should a satisfactory man be selected. When pressed for his opinion as to "a satisfactory man," he declared that he would consider Secretary Cortelyou such an one, and added: "I know of no one whom I could more heartily and conscientiously support." When Colonel John J. McCook asked him to name a Democrat whom he would be willing to support, he replied, "either Harmon or Gray."

As the spring approached, the political atmosphere took on the peculiar tenseness familiar to every man who has dreamed of national political power; and the hopefulness which had carried him through so many apparently desperate political battles began to return, despite his physical condition. On March 14th, he bared his heart to his old friend, E. Prentiss Bailey:

"I cannot rid myself of the idea that our party, which has withstood so many clashes with our political opponents, is not doomed at this time to sink to a condition of useless and lasting decadence. In my last letter to you I expressed myself as seeing some light ahead for Democracy. I cannot help feeling at this time that the light is still brighter. It does seem to me that movements have been set in motion which, though not at the present time of large dimensions, promise final relief from the burden which has so long weighed us down. I have lately come to the conclusion that our best hope rests upon the nomination of Johnson of Minnesota. The prospects to my mind appear as bright with him as our leader as with any other, and whether we meet with success or not, I believe with such a leader we shall take a long step in the way of returning to our old creed and the old policies and the old pians of organization which have heretofore led us to victory.

"I received a letter a few days ago from Judge Donahue of New York, an old war-horse of Democracy, now 84 years old, but still active in the practice of his profession. He said to me that, though he was by a number of years older than I, he not only hoped but expected to live to see a Democratic President in the White House. I often think that with my seventy-one years to be completed in four days now, such a hope and expectation on my part can hardly be reasonably entertained; but I confess that I am somewhat ashamed of such pessimistic feeling when I read the cheery and confident words contained in this old veteran's letter. I do not want you to suppose that a feeling of pessimism toward political affairs is habitual with me. On the contrary, such a condition of mind is quite infrequent and so temporary that it yields quickly to a better mood and a settled conviction that our party before many years will march from the darkness to the full light of glorious achievement. . . ."

His seventy-first birthday—and his last—found him with strength greatly depleted by the frequent gastro-intestinal attacks complicated by organic disease of the heart and kidneys from which he had suffered, with increasing violence, for many years. His loss of vitality alarmed his family and his physicians who, however, guarded the secret that his condition was serious. On April 14th, Mrs. Cleveland wrote, in strict confidence, to George F. Parker: "We have tried not to have it known, but he has had another attack within the last few days. While not so serious in itself, it came so soon after the one preceding that he was not so strong as usual, and it has left him in much weaker condition."

As the days passed it became more evident that he

could not rally the strength to resist this new attack, and he prepared to face the final battle of his strenuous life; but with little hope of earthly victory. His affairs were in order. He awaited his summons.

"During these last weeks," writes his sister, Mrs. Yeomans, "he sent to his old home for one of the worn hymn books that were used at family prayers in his boyhood." His mind instinctively reverted to the early lessons of hope which had been the inspiration of his life. "As weakness more encroached," wrote St. Clair McKelway, "he faced toward the inevitable with trust in the Almighty and with good will to mankind. The intent look which often came into his face was not due to apprehension."

On June 24, 1908, at 8.40 in the morning he died, as he had often expressed the wish to die, in his Princeton home, with his beloved wife beside him. His parting words are the key to his life: "I have tried so hard to do right."

His body was buried in the old Princeton Cemetery two days later, just as the setting sun touched the rim of the horizon. There, to-day, stands his simple gravestone, a shaft of granite on which is carved:

GROVER CLEVELAND
Born Caldwell, N. J.
March 18th, 1837
Died Princeton, N. J.
June 24th, 1908.

A mile away rises his national monument, the Cleveland Memorial Tower, erected by the contributions of men and women of varied races and political affiliations, many of whom had never seen his face, but all of whom wished thus to pay their homage to a great American.

Living, he dared to disregard party in the service of principle. Dying, he named no party as his heir. Dead, no party and no faction can fairly claim a monopoly of the glory with which the advancing years are steadily crowning his memory.

In the little oak box by his bedside was found a copy of Whittier's beautiful poem, "At Last":

> "When on my day of life the night is falling,
> And, in the winds from unsunned spaces blown,
> I hear far voices out of darkness calling
> My feet to paths unknown,
>
> Thou, who hast made my home of life so pleasant,
> Leave not its tenant when its walls decay;
> O Love Divine, O Helper ever present,
> Be Thou my strength and stay!"

# SOURCES

## A. PRIMARY SOURCES.

Partly in manuscript form; partly in the form of printed documents. The manuscripts consist chiefly of memoranda, diaries, letters written by Mr. Cleveland, and those written to him, speeches, etc., etc.

The printed primary sources are chiefly public documents, city, county, state or national, which have been published either as public archives or as private collections.

Mr. Cleveland, as have all our Presidents, left an enormous mass of manuscript material, but he left it in chaotic condition. The papers were packed into rough wooden boxes, without systematic arrangement, the important and the unimportant thrown together; and many of the most valuable manuscripts contain neither title, date, nor other indication of the purpose for which they were prepared. In most cases, except personal letters, the very authorship of the manuscript would be in doubt but for the fact that all are written in "copper plate," as he called his own neat but distressingly illegible handwriting. Practically every letter, message, proclamation, executive order, even the publicity notices and the successive copies of addresses often revised, are wholly in his own hand.

He apparently made no attempt to keep his files complete, and frequently the only copy of an important document was given to some friend who wished a specimen of his handwriting.

The forty or fifty thousand miscellaneous documents,

mostly letters to the President, but including the final copies of many of his presidential messages, which he brought from Washington at the end of his public life, he stored in a wing of Colonel Lamont's country house at Millbrook, New York, and apparently forgot. These, with a collection of thirty thousand manuscripts from the Library of Congress, and a smaller one from the attic of his Princeton home, constitute the bulk of the manuscript sources upon which his biography has been based.

I.   THE CLEVELAND MANUSCRIPTS

(1)  Memoranda from the following:

(a)  Mr. Cleveland's sisters, Mrs. Yeomans and Mrs. Bacon: sketches of his childhood days, giving glimpses such as only the members of his own family could give.

(b)  Richard Watson Gilder, one of Mr. Cleveland's most intimate friends: a collection of notes made immediately after important conversations with Mr. Cleveland. They are written upon the backs of envelopes, or stray scraps of paper of odd sizes and irregular shapes. Many of them are almost illegible, but all are worth the trouble of deciphering.

(c)  John G. Milburn, an eminent lawyer, whose friendship extended back into Mr. Cleveland's Buffalo days: a series of comments upon important incidents in Mr. Cleveland's public and private life.

(d)  Milburn and Locke: documents used by John G. Milburn and Franklin Day Locke in the trial of a suit brought by the Rev. George H. Ball against the Evening Post

Publishing Company, and involving the famous case of Maria Halpin.

(e) A committee of sixteen Republicans and Independents: a report upon the personal character of Grover Cleveland, made to the Mugwump National Committee during the presidential campaign of 1884.

(f) The Reverend Wilton Merle-Smith: bearing upon Mr. Cleveland's religious views.

(g) William B. Hornblower, with a supplementary memorandum prepared from Judge Hornblower's papers by his son, George Hornblower: especial reference to the circumstances connected with Judge Hornblower's appointment as an Associate Justice of the Supreme Court, and his rejection by the Senate.

(h) Otto Gresham, son of Secretary of State Gresham: relating to Mr. Cleveland's dealings with currency problems, and especially with the question of his influence upon the currency declarations of the Republican National Convention of 1896.

(i) Many of Mr. Cleveland's friends or close associates, including Elihu Root, Charles W. Eliot, Cardinal Gibbons, Edward W. Hatch, Thomas Cary, Chauncey M. Depew, Adlai E. Stevenson, etc., etc.: brief memoranda relating to particular incidents or impressions.

(2) Diaries:

A small pocket diary, in pencil, beginning August 27, 1898, and ending September 27, 1905. It contains 122 closely written pages.

Most of the entries relate to fishing. Diaries
for the years 1898, 1899, 1901, 1903, 1904, and
1905. Many of the pages are left blank, many
contain only a few lines of notes, but they are
of sufficient biographical value to cause regret
that the volumes for 1900 and 1902 are
missing.

(3)   Letters:

For the most part Grover Cleveland's letters were gathered from garrets and dusty private files all over the land. Their locations
were discovered by studying Mr. Cleveland's
own personal papers, noting the names of all
persons with whom he appeared to have been
upon terms making likely a personal correspondence, and writing to the persons in question, or to descendants or relatives. In this
way about 1500 manuscript letters were recovered:

(a)   Letters to Cabinet members:
102 to Wilson S. Bissell; 38 to Judson Harmon; 29 to Don M. Dickinson; 120 to Daniel
S. Lamont; 117 to Richard T. Olney; 90 all
told to the following: William C. Endicott,
Walter Q. Gresham, Charles S. Fairchild,
Thomas F. Bayard, William F. Vilas.

(b)   Letters to personal friends, acquaintances, etc.:

Louis L. Babcock                Thomas Cary
E. Prentiss Bailey              Mrs. Julius C. Chambers
Commodore E. C. Benedict        Mrs. Robert W. Chapin
Mrs. W. Cabell Bruce            Joseph H. Choate
Dr. Joseph B. Bryant            James Freeman Clarke
Andrew Carnegie                 William Clausen

George B. Cortelyou     George W. Hayward
Frederic R. Coudert     D-Cady Herrick
Paul D. Cravath     F. W. Hinrichs
Mrs. A. B. Creasey     William B. Hornblower
William J. Curtis     Joseph Jefferson
L. Clarke Davis     Daniel N. Lockwood
Bernard S. Deutsch     Dr. Wilton Merle-Smith
Mrs. Louis R. Ehrich     Alton B. Parker
Dr. Charles W. Eliot     George F. Parker
Admiral Robley D. Evans Theodore Roosevelt
A. B. Farquhar     Edward M. Shepard
Dr. John H. Finley     Oscar Straus
Mrs. Roderick E. Fletcher Henry T. Thurber
Colonel David M. Flynn   Mrs. Charles Tracy
Cardinal Gibbons     Lambert Tree
Richard Watson Gilder     Dr. Samuel B. Ward
A. C. Goodyear     Dean Andrew Fleming West
John Temple Graves     A. A. Wilson
John S. Green     Woodrow Wilson
M. D. Harter     Dr. Charles Wood

Of these, the letters to Commodore Benedict alone number 279, and all touch upon the lighter things of life: fishing, hunting, boating, cribbage, etc.

Mr. Julian B. Beaty, Mr. Cleveland's private secretary in 1904, kindly reproduced from his notebooks copies of 115 letters dictated by Mr. Cleveland during that year; Mr. George S. Bixby, the biographer of David B. Hill, sent a considerable collection which Mr. Cleveland wrote to Mr. Hill during the years of political association; and Mrs. H. F. Reid sent nineteen letters and one telegram to Ernest Gittings.

In these letters we see the man himself, simple, frank, and fearless, with the spirit of a crusader humanized by a sense of humor and a gift for friendship. Without them it would be difficult to picture him, for his formal papers are one and all wholly impersonal.

II.  PRINTED SOURCES.

(1)  State Collections

Public Papers of Grover Cleveland as Governor, one volume for 1883 and one volume for 1884. Argus Co., 1883 and 1884. There is a later edition in which the two years are bound together in one volume.

(2)  Federal Collections

The documents sent by President Cleveland to Congress, in connection with his various messages, are printed in the records of Congress, and are far too numerous for detailed discussion. The following are cited as having special reference to outstanding questions of foreign policy:

(a)  The Samoan Affair. The chief documents are in:

(1st)  House Exec. Doc., 164, 44th Congress, 1st Session, which gives the political history of Samoa. Foreign Relations, 1894, Appx. I, for Bates report.

(2d)  Foreign Relations, 1889, pp. 204-231, for texts of protocols on Samoan Conferences among European nations.

(3d)   House Exec. Doc., 238, 50th Congress, 1st Session.

(4th)   Senate Exec. Doc., 31, 50th Congress, 2d Session; Senate Exec. Doc., 68, 50th Congress, 2d Session.

(b)   The Hawaiian Affair:

(1st)   Foreign Relations, 1891.

(2d)   Foreign Relations, 1894, Appx. II.

(3d)   Foreign Relations, Volume VI.

(4th)   House Exec. Doc., 130, 49th Congress, 2d Session, Volume XXIII.

(5th)   House Exec. Doc., 48, 53rd Congress, 2d Session.

(c)   The Venezuelan Affair:

(1st)   The British Blue Book, 97, 1896.

(2d)   Senate Exec. Doc., 31, 54th Congress, 1st Session.

(3d)   Senate Exec. Doc., 226, 50th Congress, 1st Session.

(4th)   S e n a t e   Miscellaneous Docs., 54th Congress, 1st Session, Volume I.

(5th)   The British-Venezuelan Treaty, which ended the controversy, is in Foreign Relations, 1896, p. 254.

(3)   Miscellaneous Collections

(a)   *The Public Papers of Grover Cleveland, Twenty-Second President of the United States,* March 4, 1885, to March 4, 1889.

Washington Government Printing Office, 1889.

(b) *Writings and Speeches of Grover Cleveland,* edited by George F. Parker. Cassell Publishing Co., New York, 1892. 571 pages. A collection of Cleveland documents, 1881 to 1892, arranged according to topics.

(c) *Principles and Purposes of our Form of Government as Set Forth in the Public Papers of Grover Cleveland.* Compiled by Francis Gottsberger. George G. Peck, New York, 1892. 187 pages of extracts from Grover Cleveland's speeches, letters, and public papers from 1885 to 1892, without editorial comment.

(d) *Messages and Papers of the Presidents.* Edited by James D. Richardson. Government Printing Office, Washington, 1896 *et seq.* Volumes VIII and IX contain the official executive documents issued by Mr. Cleveland as President.

(e) *The Public Papers of Grover Cleveland, Twenty-Fourth President of the United States,* March 4, 1893, to March 4, 1897. Government Printing Office, Washington, 1897.

(f) *Letters and Addresses of Grover Cleveland.* Edited by Albert Ellery Bergh. The Unit Book Publishing Co., New York, 1909. One vol. 499 pages. The most complete general collection of Mr. Cleveland's papers.

**B** SECONDARY SOURCES

Mr. Cleveland's own books, pamphlets, and articles written for publication; scrapbooks of newspaper clippings; innumerable biographies, genealogical studies, magazine articles, and pamphlets, published during his life and since his death; and a vast mass of literature containing incidental reference to him. These are obviously too numerous to be catalogued exhaustively, but the following list will be found adequate to most demands:

I. WRITTEN FOR PUBLICATION BY GROVER CLEVELAND

(1)   Books, pamphlets, etc.

(a)   *What Shall We Do with It?* (meaning the surplus). Taxation and revenue discussed by President Cleveland, J. G. Blaine, H. Watterson, etc. Harper & Bros., New York, 1888.

(b)   *Thou Shalt Not Steal.* A few words on the tariff by Grover Cleveland, W. E. Russell, etc. A. J. Philpott & Co., Boston, 1892. 29 pages.

(c)   *Cleveland on the Money Question.* Washington, D. C., 1895.  4 pages.

(d)   *The Selfmade Man in American Life.* T. Y. Crowell & Co., New York, 1897.

(e)   *The Defense of Fishermen.* Privately printed, Princeton, N. J., 1902.  13 pages.

(f)   *Presidential Problems.* Century Co., New York, 1904. One vol. 281 pages. A painstaking description of the major conflicts of his second term. The chapters are in essence republications of his Stafford Little Lectures at Princeton University, which are available also in the form of booklets printed

by the Princeton University Press under the
following titles:

(1st)   The Venezuelan Boundary
Controversy, 1913, first printed as articles in the *Century Magazine,* June
and July, 1901, Vol. LXII.

(2d)   The Government in the Chicago Strike, 1913.

(3d)   The Independence of the
Executive, 1913.

(g)   *Fishing and Shooting Sketches.* Illustrated by Henry S. Watson.   The Outing
Publishing Co., New York, 1906.

(h)   *In the Matter of State Legislation
Limiting the Compensation of Officers of Insurance Companies.*   Brief in opposition
thereto.   New York, 1907.   11 pages.

(i)   *Compulsory Investment Legislation.*
Some considerations as to legislation requiring life insurance companies to make investments in certain states in which they are doing business.   The Association of Life Insurance Presidents, New York, 1907.   8 pages.

(2)   Magazine and Newspaper Articles

(a)   In the *Saturday Evening Post:*

"Does a College Education Pay?"
May 25, 1900.

"The Plight of the Democracy,"
December 22, 1900.

"The Young Man in Politics,"
January 26, 1901.

"The Uses of Adversity," March 9,
1901.

"Strength and Needs of Civil Service Reform," March 30, 1901.

"The Waste of Public Money," June 1, 1901.

"The Safety of the President," October 5, 1901.

"A Defense of Fishermen," October 19, 1901.

"The Serene Duck Hunter," April 26, 1902.

"The President and His Patronage," May 24, 1902.

"The Shadow of the City," September 19, 1903.

"The Mission of Fishing and Fishermen," December 5, 1903.

"The Democracy's Opportunity," February 20, 1904.

"The Cleveland Bond Issues," May 7, 1904.

"Some Fishing Pretenses and Affectations," September 24, 1904.

"Why a Young Man Should Vote the Democratic Ticket," October 8, 1904.

"Old-Fashioned Honesty and the Coming Man," August 5, 1905.

"Directors That Do Not Direct," December 1, 1906.

By far the most important of these articles is the one on the Cleveland Bond Issues. Its sub-title shows the character of the article: "A detailed history of the crime charged against an administration that issued bonds of the government in time of peace." It is about 10,000 words in length and gives Mr. Cleveland's interpretation of the circumstances which made the bond issues necessary. The original MS. is among the Cleveland papers.

In the New York *World* of May 15, 1904, appears a detailed reply to Mr. Cleveland's arguments.

(b)  In the *Youth's Companion:*
"The Civic Responsibility of Youth," July 2, 1903.
"The Country Lawyer in National Affairs," February 8, 1906.
"Our People and Their Ex-Presidents," January 2, 1908.

(c)  In the *Ladies' Home Journal:*
"Woman's Mission and Woman's Clubs," May, 1905.
"Would Woman's Suffrage Be Unwise?" October, 1905.
"The Honest American Marriage, A Plea for Home-Building," October, 1906.

(d)  In the *Independent:*
"Summer Shooting," June 2, 1904.
"A Word Concerning Rabbit Hunting," June 1, 1905.

(e)  In *Collier's:*
"Steady, Democrats, Steady," July 23, 1904.

(f)  In the *Pacific Monthly:*

"The Plight of Democracy and the Remedy," January, 1901.

(g)   In the New York *World,* Sunday Editorial Section, March 15, 1903: "Adversity as an Aid to Success."

II.   WRITTEN FOR PUBLICATION BY OTHERS

(1)   Scrapbooks:

(a)   The White House Scrapbooks, forty volumes, containing clippings from daily and weekly papers and magazines.   In general these clippings are grouped into volumes according to topics, four volumes dealing wholly with Civil Service Reforms, etc., etc.

(b)   Wedding Scrapbooks, three large volumes containing a varied assortment of clippings and pictures relating to Mr. Cleveland's wedding.   They were made by friends at the time of the wedding and subsequently presented to the President.

(c)   The Fairchild Scrapbooks, three volumes, containing newspaper clippings and press copies of letters relating chiefly to the history of the campaign of 1892.

(d)   The McKelway Scrapbooks, a set of about a dozen large folio volumes, containing chiefly articles and editorials written by Mr. McKelway, as editor of the Brooklyn *Eagle.* As Mr. McKelway was an intimate friend and a strong political supporter of Mr. Cleveland, these volumes are rich in biographical material.

(e)   George F. Parker Scrapbook of the Presidential Campaign of 1884, made up

chiefly of clippings from the New York
*World,* and containing many Cleveland car-
toons.

(f) 20th Century Press Clipping Bureau
of Chicago Scrapbook, covering the incidents
of Mr. Cleveland's visit to Chicago in October, 1903.

(g) New York Public Library Scrapbook of the death of Grover Cleveland. New
York, 1908.

(h) Princeton University Library Scrapbook, devoted wholly to clippings concerning
Mr. Cleveland's death.

(2)    Biographies:
(a)    *Life and Public Services of Grover
Cleveland.* By Pendleton King. G. P. Putnam's Sons, New York, 1884. 224 pages.

(b)    *Life and Public Services of Grover
Cleveland.* By Honorable William Dorsheimer. Hubbard Brothers, Philadelphia,
1884. A new and enlarged edition was prepared by W. U. Hensel, in preparation for the
Campaign of 1888. Hubbard Brothers,
Philadelphia. One vol. 588 pages.

(c)    *Life and Public Services of Grover
Cleveland and Thomas A. Hendricks.* By
Chauncey F. Black. Thayer, Merriam & Co.,
Philadelphia, 1884.

(d)    *Building and Ruling the Republic.*
By James P. Boyd. Garretson, Philadelphia,
1884. Part 4.

(e)    *Campaign of 1884. Biographies of
S. Grover Cleveland, and Thomas A. Hen-*

*dricks.* By Benjamin Le Fevre. Fireside Publishing Co., Philadelphia, 1884.

(f) *The Authorized Pictorial Lives of Stephen Grover Cleveland and Thomas Andrews Hendricks.* By Frank Triplett. N. D. Thompson & Co., Publishers, New York and St. Louis, 1884. One vol. 568 pages.

(g) *Stephen Grover Cleveland.* By Deshler Welch. J. W. Lovell Co., New York, 1884. 222 pages. Also published under the title *Life of Grover Cleveland,* Worthington, New York, 1884.

(h) *Early Life and Public Services of Hon. Grover Cleveland,* the fearless and independent Governor of the Empire State, and candidate for President. . . . Also the Life of Hon. Thomas A. Hendricks, candidate for Vice-President. By Thomas W. Handford. Caxton Publishing Co., Chicago and New York, 1884. 510 pages.

(i) *The Life of Honorable Grover Cleveland,* including his early days, District Attorneyship, Mayoralty of Buffalo, Governorship of New York, nomination at Chicago. Edited by J. B. McClure. Rhodes and McClure, Chicago, 1884. One vol. 218 pages.

(j) *Life and Public Services of Grover Cleveland,* with incidents of his early life, and an account of his rise to eminence in his profession; also containing his addresses and official documents as Mayor of the City of Buffalo, and Governor of the State of New York. By Frederick E. Goodrich. B. B. Russell, Boston, 1884. One vol. 504 pages.

A valuable campaign biography. Abundantly supplied with copies of documents accurately transcribed, many of which are not easily available elsewhere. As a campaign biography, however, it is history written with the intention of making the Democratic party appear spotless and the Republican party crooked and unreliable, a thesis scarcely consistent with fact in that period of the history of New York or of the United States.

(k) *A Man of Destiny*. Edited by W. P. Nixon. Belford, Clarke & Co., Chicago, 1885. 226 pages.

(l) *Life and Public Services of Grover Cleveland*. By William U. Hensel and George F. Parker. Guernsey Publishing Co., Philadelphia, 1888 and 1892.

(m) *Life and Public Services of Our Great Reform President, Grover Cleveland*. By Col. Herman Dieck. J. Dewing & Co., San Francisco, 1888. Also S. I. Bell & Co., Philadelphia. 554 pages.

(n) *Age of Cleveland*. By Harold Fulton Ralphdon. F. A. Stokes & Bros., New York, 1888. 135 pages. Compiled from contemporary journals. Copy in Library of Congress.

(o) *Grover Cleveland*. By Wm. O. Stoddard. Frederick A. Stokes Co., New York, 1888. One vol. 263 pages. The best campaign biography of Grover Cleveland, covering a much wider field than that of Frederick E. Goodrich, the only one comparable to it.

(p) *Distinguished American Lawyers*.

By Henry W. Scott. Webster, New York, 1891. "Grover Cleveland," pp. 161-172.

(q) *The History of the Democratic Party from Thomas Jefferson to Grover Cleveland.* . . . Lives of Cleveland and Stevenson. By Chandos Fulton. P. F. Collier, New York, 1892. 608 pages.

(r) *Life and Public Services of Grover Cleveland.* By William U. Hensel. Edgewood Publishing Co., Philadelphia, 1892. 556 pages.

(s) *A Life of Grover Cleveland,* with a sketch of Adlai E. Stevenson. By George Frederick Parker. Cassell Publishing Co., New York, 1892. 333 pages.

(t) *Cleveland and Stevenson, Their Lives and Record.* The Democratic campaign book for 1892, with a handbook of American politics up to date, and a cyclopedia of presidential biography. Compiled by Thos. Campbell-Copeland. C. L. Webster & Co., New York, 1892. One vol. 438 pages.

(u) *Grover Cleveland.* By James Lowry Whittle. Bliss, Sands & Co., London, 1896. F. Warne & Co., New York, 1896. One vol. 240 pages. In series, "Public Men of Today." A badly digested sketch of Mr. Cleveland's life. Its strong British point of view appears especially in Chapter XIV, "America and Great Britain," where the chief topic is the Venezuelan controversy. It is a volume of what is called popular history, showing little research and no special grace of style or conception.

(v) *Four Great American Presidents, Garfield, McKinley, Cleveland, Roosevelt.* J. M. Stradling & Co., New York, 1903. 309 pages.

(w) *Recollections of Grover Cleveland.* By George F. Parker. Century Co., New York, 1909. One vol. 427 pages. A book of considerable interest, containing the personal recollections of a man closely associated with Mr. Cleveland, especially during the latter years of his life. It contains many personal letters not elsewhere attainable. The same author has written many magazine articles about Mr. Cleveland, notably a series in the *Saturday Evening Post* ending in 1923, and an earlier series in *McClure's Magazine,* as follows:

(1st) "Cleveland the Man." The first administration and the second campaign. v. 32, pp. 337-346.

(2d) "Cleveland's Estimate of His Contemporaries." v. 33, pp. 24-34.

(3d) "Cleveland's Opinion of Men." v. 32, pp. 569-581.

(4th) "Cleveland's Venezuela Message." v. 33, pp. 314-323.

(x) *Mr. Cleveland, A Personal Impression.* By Jesse Lynch Williams. Dodd, Mead & Co., New York, 1909.

(y) *Grover Cleveland, A Record of Friendship.* By Richard Watson Gilder. Century Co., New York, 1910. First printed as articles in the *Century Magazine,* New

York, 1909, v. 78, pp. 483-503, 687-705, 846-860; v. 79, pp. 24-31. An artistic little volume, of much literary merit; depicting the human side of Grover Cleveland.

(z) *Grover Cleveland, A Study in Political Courage*. By Roland Hugins. The Anchor-Lee Publishing Co., Washington, D. C., 1922.

(3) Genealogical Works:

(a) *A Genealogy of Benjamin Cleveland, the Great-Grandson of Moses Cleveland of Woburn*. By Horace Gillette Cleveland. Rand McNally & Co., Chicago, 1879.

(b) *A Genealogical Register of the Descendants of Moses Cleveland of Woburn, Massachusetts*. Munsell, Albany, 1881.

(c) *An Account of the Lineage of Gen. Moses Cleveland of Canterbury, Conn., the Founder of the City of Cleveland, Ohio*. Also a sketch of his life. By H. Rice. W. W. Williams, Cleveland, Ohio, 1885.

(d) *The New England Ancestry of Grover Cleveland*. By W. K. Watkins and E. Putnam. The Salem Press, 1892. Privately printed. 35 copies made. Contains twenty-five pages, the first fifteen being taken up with charts by Walter K. Watkins and Eben Putnam. The rest is given up to notes presenting items of particular interest in connection with various members of the Cleveland family and collateral branches.

(e) *The Genealogy of the Cleveland and Cleaveland Families*. Compiled by Edmund James Cleveland and Horace Gillette Cleveland. Three vols. 3000 pages. The Case, Lockwood and Brainard Company, Hartford, Conn., 1899. An enormously detailed work, covering a vast range of genealogical records. By far the most valuable Cleveland genealogical work.

(4) Magazine Articles:

(a) "The President's Policy." By J. B. Eustis, Wm. R. Grace, and Theodore Roosevelt. *North American Review,* October, 1885, pp. 374-396. An attempt to combine in a single three-headed article a defense and a denunciation. The article by Mr. Roosevelt is the most interesting of the three, by virtue of its picturesque, violent language, and its frankly partisan criticisms.

(b) "Southern View of the Election of Cleveland." By A. G. Bradley. *Macmillan's Magazine,* 1885. Vol. 51, p. 372.

(c) "Possible Presidents: President Cleveland." By D. B. Eaton, *North American Review,* 1887. Vol. 145, p. 629, *et seq.*

(d) "Democracy Photographed. The Record of a Bogus Reformer. President Cleveland, a Wanton Pledge-breaker." New York *Tribune* Extra, No. 100. New York, 1888.

(e) "The Political Effect of the Message." By B. Smith. *North American Review,* 1888. Vol. V., p. 146, *et seq.*

(f) "La Lutte pour la Presidence aux Etats-Unis." By A. Moireau. *Rev. d. Deux Mondes,* 1889. Vol. 91, p. 642, *et seq.*

(g) "Regierung des Praesidenten Cleveland." *Unser Zeit,* 1889. Vol. 2, p. 208, *et seq.*

(h) "Defeat of President Cleveland." *Contemporary Review,* 1889. Vol. 55, p. 283, *et seq.*

(i) "Cleveland a Popular Leader." By Wilbur Larremore. *The Arena,* January, 1891. Vol. 3, pp. 147-156.

(j) "What Mr. Cleveland Stands For." By Charles Francis Adams. *Forum,* July, 1892. Vol. 13, pp. 662-670. A brilliant, characteristically frank defense of Mr. Cleveland's record on the tariff, civil service, the currency, and the pension question. It is also a promise that the Independents will support Mr. Cleveland in 1892.

(k) "Mr. Cleveland as President." By Woodrow Wilson. *Atlantic Monthly,* March, 1897. Vol. 79, pp. 289-300.

(l) "Second Administration of Grover Cleveland." By Carl Schurz. *McClure's Magazine,* May, 1897. Vol. 9, pp. 633-644. An article of great value by one of the recognized leaders of Civil Service Reform, and a Mugwump of great influence and ability.

(m) "Character Sketch of Grover Cleveland." By William Allen White. *McClure's Magazine,* February, 1902. Vol. 18, pp. 322-330.

(n) "Grover Cleveland." By Lyman Abbott. *New York Genealogical and Biological Record.* New York, 1908. Vol. 39, pp. 237-241.

(o) Tribute to the Memory of Grover Cleveland, June 26, 1908. New York Chamber of Commerce, 1908.

(p) "Grover Cleveland." By Henry Loomis Nelson. *North American Review,* New York, 1908. Vol. 188, pp. 161-187.

(q) "Grover Cleveland, a Princeton Memory." By Andrew Fleming West. *Century Magazine,* New York, 1908. Vol. 77, pp. 323-337.

(r) "Cleveland as a Teacher in the Institution for the Blind." By Fanny J. Crosby. *McClure's Magazine,* March, 1909, pp. 581-583. A series of recollections prepared for the Democratic Campaign Committee, and containing little of interest or value.

(s) "Cleveland as a Lawyer." By Wilson S. Bissell. *McClure's Magazine,* Vol. 32, pp. 583-585. New York, 1909.

(t) "Grover Cleveland Memorial Meetings in Brooklyn and Manhattan, 1909." Addresses by Dr. St. Clair McKelway, President William H. Taft, Senator Elihu Root, etc., Brooklyn *Daily Eagle,* 1909. Eagle Library No. 148.

(u) "Official Characteristics of President Cleveland." By Charles R. Lingley. *Political Science Quarterly,* Lancaster, 1918. Vol. 33, pp. 255-265.

(5) Pamphlets:

(a) Address by Henry Ward Beecher at the Brooklyn Rink, October 22, 1884. Circular No. 13 of National Committee of Republicans and Independents, New York, 1884. 8 pages.

(b) *Cleveland and the Irish,* true history of the great Irish Revolt of 1884. By John Devoy. Issued by the Irish-American Anti-Cleveland and Protective League, New York, 1888. 8 pages.

(c) *Tell the Truth,* an anonymous pamphlet dealing, in a manner most unfair to Mr. Cleveland, with the scandals of the presidential campaign of 1884.

(d) *The Democratic Party and Civil Service Reform.* By the Young Men's Democratic Club of Brooklyn. Issued on January 26, 1885, and containing a collection of extracts bearing upon the Civil Service Reform movement and Mr. Cleveland's relation thereto. 16 pages.

(e) *The Inauguration of Grover Cleveland, the President-elect,* March 4, 1885. A book for fifty million people. By Henry J. Kintz. W. F. Fell & Co., Philadelphia, 1885.

(f) *Defense of Grover Cleveland, in Regard to His Treatment of the United States Attorneys in Pennsylvania and Missouri.* By Edward M. Shepard. New York, 1887. Privately printed. 23 pages.

(g) *The Imaginary Conversations of "His Excellency" and Dan.* By C. W. Taylor with illustrations by F. H. Blair. Cupples and Hurd, Boston, 1888. A burlesque very popular in the days of Mr. Cleveland's second presidential campaign.

(h) Souvenir of the Reception and Dinner given by the Young Men's Democratic Club of the City of New York, to the Honorable Grover Cleveland, New York, May 27, 1889. Contains the addresses of Mr. Cleveland, W. C. P. Breckinridge, David B. Hill, Governor Hoadley of Ohio, Frederic R. Coudert and Ashbel P. Fitch.

(i)  Tammany Hall Souvenir of Inauguration of Cleveland and Stevenson. J. W. McDonald & Co., New York, 1893.  148 pages.

(j)  *King George. Chronicles of His Reign According to Simonides, the Scribe of the Tribe of Lechay.* First book. Published by the author, Allentown, Pa., 1894.  128 pages. Written in the style of the Scriptures.

(k)  Souvenir of the Annual Dinner of the Reform Club, held at the Waldorf Hotel, New York City, April 24, 1897. Martin B. Brown Company, New York, 1897. Contains Mr. Cleveland's address entitled "Present Problems," and addresses by John G. Carlisle, William L. Wilson, Edward M. Shepard, and others, all bearing more or less directly upon the history of Mr. Cleveland's fight for a sound currency.

(l)  *Cleveland's Last Message:* Life insurance and its relationship to our people. Spectator Publishing Co., New York, 1908.

(m)  *Good Citizenship.* Henry Altemus, Philadelphia, 1908.

(n)  *Tribute to Memory of Grover Cleveland,* June 26, 1908, by Chamber of Commerce of the State of New York. New York Chamber of Commerce, 1908.

(o) *Cleveland's Last Message, A Literary Forgery*. By Broughton Brandenburg. New York, 1908. 15 pages.

(p) *Proceedings of the Second Annual Meeting of the Association of Life Insurance Presidents,* including an account of the Cleveland Memorial Meeting. Printed by the Association of Life Insurance Presidents, New York, 1909.

(q) *Grover Cleveland Memorial,* the eighteenth of March, in the year one thousand, nine hundred and nine. DeVinne Press, New York, 1910.

(r) *Grover Cleveland:* Address delivered at the unveiling of the memorial tablet at the Buffalo Historical Society, May 20, 1912. By John G. Milburn. Buffalo Historical Society Publications, 1913, v. 17, pp. 121-126.

(s) *Proceedings at the Passing of Title to the "Old Manse," Grover Cleveland's Birthplace, Caldwell, N. J.* March 18, 1913. Grover Cleveland Memorial Association, 1913.

(t) *Was New York's Vote Stolen?* By Francis Lynde Stetson and William Gorham Rice. Reprint from *North American Review,* January, 1914. A critical examination of the contest over the election of 1884.

(u) *The Surgical Operation on President Cleveland in 1893.* By Wm. W. Keen. G. W. Jacobs & Co., Philadelphia, 1917. 52 pages.

(v) *Address on Grover Cleveland,*

March 18, 1919, Cleveland Memorial Service in New York City. By Leonard Wood. Published by the Cleveland Memorial Association, 1919.

(w) *Memorial Exercises of the Boston Bar Association before the Supreme Judicial Court in Memory of Richard Olney,* June 28, 1919. Geo. H. Ellis & Co., Boston, 1919. A pamphlet containing many items of interest with reference to the Chicago Strike, the Venezuelan Controversy, etc.

III. BOOKS CONTAINING IMPORTANT INCIDENTAL BIO-GRAPHICAL MATERIAL CONCERNING GROVER CLEVE-LAND

(1) *The President and His Cabinet,* indicating the progress of the Government of the United States under the administration of Grover Cleveland. By Charles B. Norton. Cupples & Hurd, Boston, 1888. 249 pages.

(2) *Biography of James G. Blaine.* By Gail Hamilton. Norwich, 1895.

(3) *History of Presidential Elections.* By Edward Stanwood. Houghton Mifflin Co., Boston, 4th ed., 1896.

(4) *The First Battle.* By William Jennings Bryan. A story of the campaign of 1896, together with a collection of his speeches and a biographical sketch by his wife. W. B. Conkey Co., 1897. 629 pages.

(5) *A History of the American People.* By Woodrow Wilson. Harper & Bros., New York, 1902. Five vols. See v. 5, pp. 170-253.

(6) *Our Presidents and How We Make Them.*

By A. K. McClure. Harper & Bros., New York, 1902. 481 pages.

(7) *American Tariff Controversies in the Nineteenth Century.* By Edward Stanwood. Houghton Mifflin Co., Boston, 1903. Two vols.

(8) *Autobiography of Seventy Years.* By George F. Hoar. Chas. Scribner's Sons, New York, 1903. Two vols. "President Cleveland's Judges," v. 2, pp. 172-181.

(9) *The Republican Party.* 1854-1904. By Francis Curtis. G. P. Putnam's Sons, New York, 1904. Two vols. "Convention of 1884—Nomination of Blaine—Moral Issue—Election of Cleveland," v. 2, pp. 116-162. "Administration of Cleveland," v. 2, pp. 163-179. "Conventions of 1892," v. 2, pp. 239-270. "Second Administration of Cleveland," v. 2, pp. 271-303.

(10) *Autobiography of Andrew D. White.* The Century Co., New York, 1905. Two vols. "Arthur, Cleveland, and Blaine," pp. 192-212.

(11) *The Democratic Party of the State of New York.* By James K. McGuire. 1905. Three vols. Grover Cleveland, v. 2, pp. 126-162.

(12) *James Gillespie Blaine.* By Edward Stanwood. Houghton Mifflin Co., Boston, 1905. 378 pages.

(13) *Recollections of Thirteen Presidents.* By John S. Wise. Doubleday, Page & Co., New York, 1906. Grover Cleveland, pp. 171-194.

(14) *A Political History of the State of New York.* By DeAlva Stanwood Alexander. Henry Holt & Co., New York, 1906-9. Three vols. "Cleveland's Enormous Majority," v. 3, pp. 483-499. A fourth volume has just appeared (1923), which covers

Mr. Cleveland's later political career in so far as it touched the field of New York politics.

(15) *Twenty Years of the Republic, 1885-1905.* By Harry T. Peck. Dodd, Mead & Co., New York, 1907. "The Return of the Democracy," pp. 1-48. "Two Years of President Cleveland," pp. 49-96. "President Cleveland Once More," pp. 306-349. In general, the best history of the Cleveland period, journalistic in style, but accurate in detail.

(16) *National Problems—1885-1897.* By Davis Rich Dewey. Harper & Bros., New York, 1907. The work of a well-known financial historian, and especially valuable upon the financial questions of Mr. Cleveland's administrations.

(17) *Speeches and Addresses, 1884-1909.* By Henry Cabot Lodge. Houghton Mifflin Co., Boston, 1909. 462 pages. Contains important incidental comment upon Mr. Cleveland's public actions, written by a leader of the opposition party.

(18) *The Autobiography of Thomas Collier Platt.* Compiled and edited by Louis J. Lang. B. W. Dodge & Co., New York, 1910. A frank discussion of American politics by a master politician. Of particular interest is the discussion in Chapter XVI, "The Gold Plank Controversy and How I Won It."

(19) *Random Recollections of an Old Political Reporter.* By William C. Hudson. Cupples & Leon, New York, 1911. Several chapters relate to Cleveland's administrations as Governor and President. Contains interesting material regarding Mr. Cleveland's personal characteristics, and is written in a light, journalistic style.

(20) *The United States in Our Own Time.* By E. Benjamin Andrews. Chas. Scribner's Sons, New

York, 1912. A rather forbidding volume, written from the point of view of a champion of Free Silver, and covering the period from Cleveland to Roosevelt.

(21) *Speeches, Correspondence and Political Papers of Carl Schurz.* Selected and edited by Frederic Bancroft. G. P. Putnam's Sons, New York, 1913. Data relating to the Mugwump campaign of 1884, Civil Service Reform, etc. Six vols.

(22) *Life of Thomas B. Reed.* By Samuel W. McCall, Houghton Mifflin Co., Boston, 1914. Contains an account of Cleveland's administration as viewed by the leader of the opposition.

(23) *American Diplomacy.* By Carl Russell Fish. Henry Holt & Co., New York, 1915. Third edition revised, 1919.

(24) *Sixty Years of American Life.* By Everett P. Wheeler. E. P. Dutton & Co., New York, 1917.

(25) *History of the United States from Hayes to McKinley, 1877-1896.* By James Ford Rhodes. The Macmillan Co., New York, 1919. One vol. 484 pages. The eighth volume of Dr. Rhodes' monumental history of the United States from the Compromise of 1850, includes the entire period of Mr. Cleveland's public life, and is invaluable as the interpretation of an historian of the first rank.

(26) *The Return of the Democratic Party to Power in 1884.* By Harrison Cook Thomas. Columbia University Press, New York, 1919. One vol. 225 pages.

(27) *Life of Walter Quintin Gresham, 1832-1895.* By Matilda Gresham. Rand, McNally & Co., Chicago, 1919. Contains many letters and other material bearing upon the public actions of Grover Cleveland. Two vols.

(28)  *Marcus Alonzo Hanna; His Life and Work.*
By Herbert Croly.  The Macmillan Co., New York,
1919.  Important with reference to the gold plank of
the Republican platform of 1896.  495 pages.

(29)  *Theodore Roosevelt and His Time, Shown
in His Own Letters.*  By Joseph Bucklin Bishop.
Charles Scribner's Sons, New York, 1920.  Two vols.

(30)  *Since the Civil War.*  By Charles Ramsdell
Lingley.  The Century Co., New York, 1920.
A volume of unusual interest, designed as a college
text.  Especially valuable in its treatment of financial
questions, and questions connected with the trust
problem.

(31)  *Recent History of the United States.*  By
Frederic L. Paxson.  Houghton Mifflin Co., New
York, 1921.  One vol.  602 pages.  A scholarly sketch
of the history of the United States from Hayes to
Harding, written from the point of view of a liberal.

(32)  *From McKinley to Harding; Personal Recollections of Our Presidents.*  By H. H. Kohlsaat.
Charles Scribner's Sons, New York and London,
1923.  Important with reference to the gold plank of
the Republican platform of 1896.

# INDEX

Abbett, Leon, I, 340
Aberdeen, Lord, II, 174
Adams, Charles Francis, I, 200, 319
Adams, Edward D., II, 97
Adams, Henry, I, 2
Adams, John, I, 168
Alaskan fisheries, I, 240
Alcred, King of Northumbria, I, 166
Aldrich, Senator, I, 274
Alger, Russell A., I, 296
Allen, John, I, 34
Allen, Lewis, I, 16
Allison, Senator, I, 274
Altgeld, John P., II, 148, 151-155, 156, 157, 158-162.
Alvensleben, von, I, 248, 249, 251
Alvey, Richard H., II, 198
American Railway Union, II, 143, 144, 149, 157, 169
American Tariff Reform League, I, 300
Ames, Governor, I, 311
Ames, Oakes, I, 75
Anderson, E. Ellery, I, 319, 327
Annual Register, II, 196
Anthracite Coal Strike, II, 303
Apaches, I, 229, 230
Apgar, Edgar P., I, 40, 81
Apia, I, 244, 245, 247, 248, 252, 255, 259, 260
Appointments and removals—relations between Executives and Senate, I, 168-183
Arbuckle Brothers, I, 152
Argus, Albany, I, 213
"Army of the Commonwealth of Christ," II, 142
Army of West Virginia, I, 214
Army Register, I, 203
Arnold, Benedict, I, 211
Arreas and Pensions Act, I, 190, 199
Arthur, Chester A., I, 38, 48, 201, 221, 222, 224, 269; II, 2
Articles of Confederation, I, 167
Assembly Bill No. 58, I, 52
Assembly of Wise Men. See Witenagemot
Association Hall, meeting at, I, 208
Athenians, I, 241
Atlantic Monthly, II, 43

Bache, Benjamin, II, 253
Bacon, Captain, I, 150, 151, 153
Bacon-Sterling Case, I, 149-154
Balfour, Hon. A. J., II, 200
Bancroft, George, II, 1
Barnum, William H., I, 98
Bass, Cleveland, and Bissell, I, 22
Bass, Lyman K., I, 19
Bates, G. M., I, 260
Battleship Maine wrecked, II, 271
Bayard, Thomas F., I, 80, 82, 84, 102, 145, 172, 241, 246, 247, 248-249, 250, 251, 296, 297, 302; II, 2, 7, 38, 48, 176, 177, 178, 179, 180, 187, 198, 199, 202
Bee, Omaha, II, 52, 77
Beecher, Henry Ward, I, 38, 150
Belknap, William W., I, 74, 76
Belmont, August, II, 21, 26
Belmont, August, & Co., II, 88
Benedict, Commodore, I, 308, 355; II, 27, 29, 260, 261, 267, 303, 316, 322, 323, 326, 365
Benton, M. E., I, 159, 160, 162, 163, 164
Berlin, Treaty of, I, 260, 262
Berliner Tageblatt, I, 249, 252
"Big Six." See Typographical Union No. 6
Bishop, Joseph Bucklin, I, 54; II, 302
Bishop, William, I, 193
Bismarck, I, 204, 250, 258, 260, 299
Bissell, Wilson S., I, 42, 98, 99, 113, 134, 136, 137, 149, 281, 293, 307, 315, 323, 324, 330; II, 5
Black, Chauncey F., I, 311
Blackburn, James, I, 133
"Black Eagle," I, 226
Blacklock (American Vice-Consul at Samoa), I, 256
Blaine, James G., I, 39, 48, 75, 76, 77, 79, 88, 89, 90, 91, 94, 95, 96, 98, 122, 146, 156, 260, 272, 274, 280, 290, 291, 292; II, 2, 49, 50, 177
Bland, Richard P., II, 35, 36, 79, 224
Bland-Allison Act, II, 16-18, 22, 218
Blatchford, Samuel, II, 130
Blount, James H., II, 55, 56, 57, 58, 61
Boies, Horace, I, 341

"Boss" system, I, 62, 78
Bradley, Sallie Ann, I, 194-197
Bragg, Edward S., I, 81, 332
Brandies, Mr., I, 248, 249, 255, 256, 257, 261
Brewer, David J., II, 198
Brinkerhoff, William, I, 356
Brinski, George, I, 191
British Guiana, II, 173, 177, 182, 198, 202
Britton, Charles P., I, 129, 130
Bryan, William Jennings, I, 333; II, 33-37, 77-78, 92-93, 203, 220, 223, 224, 227, 234, 236, 237, 238, 239, 276, 282, 286, 295, 296, 297, 298
Bryant, Dr. Joseph, I, 140; II, 27
Bryce, Mr., I, 255
Buchanan, James, I, 117, 189; II, 1
Buffalo, corruption in Board of Aldermen, I, 24
Burchard, Dr. Samuel, I, 95
Burnett, John D., I, 175, 183
Burr, Aaron, I, 90
Burt, Henry, I, 188
Bushy Head, I, 226
Butler, Benjamin F., I, 82, 89

Cabinet, Cleveland's first, I, 102-107
Cadwalader, John L., II, 131
Caffery, Senator, II, 102
Calhoun, John C., I, 121-122
Call, Senator, II, 250
Campaign of 1896, II, 203-237
Campbell, James E., I, 341
Campbell, Timothy J., I, 58, 63
Canal ring, I, 155
Cannon, Senator, II, 220
Carlisle, John G., I, 80, 82, 273, 341; II, 4, 5, 6, 22, 24, 78, 89, 104, 181
Carnegie, Andrew, I, 312; II, 24, 121-126, 139, 220, 242
Carter, Charles L., II, 52
Carter, James C., II, 131
Cary, C. S., I, 299, 326
Cass, Lewis, II, 1
Castle, William R., II, 52
Catchings, T. C., II, 115-119
Catiline, I, 211
"Cattle kings," I, 223, 224
Cederkrantz, Conrad, I, 261
Chamberlain, Joseph, I, 294
Chandler, Senator, II, 134
Charles I, I, 182
Chase, Secretary, I, 73; II, 1
Cherokees, I, 220, 226
Chickasaws, I, 220, 238, 239
China, I, 242
Choctaws, I, 220, 238, 239
Cicero, I, 211

Civic reform, I, 26
Civil Service Bill, I, 265
Civil Service Commission, first, I, 122
Civil Service Reform, I, 64, 88, 110, 122-165, 172, 205, 276, 277, 284, 313, 354; II, 11-12, 16.
Civil Service Reform Association, I, 123, 150
Civil Service Reform League, National, I, 123, 124
Civil War, I, 72, 73, 189, 192, 209, 265, 269, 272
Clay, Henry, I, 49, 90
Clayton, John M., II, 1
Clayton-Bulwer Treaty, II, 244
Cleveland, Aaron, I, 3
Cleveland, Anna, I, 4
Cleveland, L. F., I, 92
Cleveland, Mary Allen, I, 4, 15
Cleveland, Moses, I, 2, 3, 16
Cleveland, Richard Cecil, I, 4, 92
Cleveland, Richard Falley, I, 3, 4, 5
Cleveland, Stephen Grover, I, indifference to personal history, I, 2; lack of interest in family history, I, 2; English line traced back to Norman Conquest, I, 2; American line traced back to 1635, I, 2; origin of name, I, 2; variations in spelling of name, I, 2-3; father's and mother's early married life, I, 4-5; birth of, I, 5; at Fayetteville, I, 5-10, 13, 14; childhood, 1, 5-7; religious training, I, 6-7; boyhood, I, 8-16; essay written at age of nine, I, 9; letter received two years after entering White House, I, 9-10; at Clinton, N. Y., I, 10-13, 14; speech made on visit to old home at Fayetteville, N. Y., I, 10-11; his first job, I, 13-14; father's death, I, 15; in New York City, I, 15; letter to benefactor, I, 16; arrived at Buffalo, I, 16; studies law, I, 16-18; choses Democratic party, I, 18; admitted to the New York bar, I, 18; Assistant District Attorney, Erie County, N. Y., I, 18-19; war record, I, 19, 96-97; defeated in election for district attorney, 19; elected sheriff, I, 21; in the shrievalty, I, 21-22; declines attorneyship in New York Central R. R., I, 23; nominated for Mayor of Buffalo, I, 25; indorsed by Independents, I, 25; letter of acceptance, I, 25; elected, I, 26; in the mayoralty, 26-36; death of mother, I, 39; letter to Edward P. Apgar, I, 40-41; letter to Wilson S. Bissell, I, 42-43; nominated for Governor, I, 44;

letter to David B. Hill, I, 45; letter to Rev. William N. Cleveland, I, 47-48; elected Governor, I, 48; in the Governorship, I, 48-71; letter to John Kelly, I, 57; and Tammany Hall, I, 63; message of January 1, 1884, I, 64-66; and the Democratic National Convention, I, 76-84; nominated for President, I, 83; first speech of campaign, I, 85-86; letter to vice-commandant Koltes Post, G. A. R., I, 93-94; elected President, I, 97; alone in the White House, I, 100-116; "Henceforth I must have no friends," I, 100; his first Cabinet, I, 102-107; letter to Forty-eighth Congress, I, 107-109; letter from S. J. Tilden, I, 110; takes oath of office, I, 110; facing the political bread line, I, 117-165; letters from office seekers, I, 118-120; letter to George William Curtis, I, 124-126; and civil-service reform, I, 122; letter to the press on reappointment of Pearson postmaster of New York, I, 130-131; letter to Wilson S. Bissell, I, 134-136; letter to Charles W. Goodyear, I, 137-139; at play, I, 140-142; letter to King Leopold of Belgium, I, 144-145; letter to Joseph Keppler, I, 148; letter to Edward M. Shepard, I, 156; letter to Alton B. Parker, I, 160; executive order of July 14, 1886, I, 157-159; Benton and Stone case, I, 159-164; letter to A. H. Garland, I, 159-162; letters from Carl Schurz, I, 163, 164, 183; conflict with the Senate, I, 172-183; message to Forty-ninth Congress, I, 173; message of March 1, 1886, I, 179, 182; marriage, June 2, 1886, I, 186; letter from Joe James, 186; letter to New York *Evening Post,* I, 187; and the veterans of the Civil War, I, 189-217; letter from Horace White, I, 200; letter to John W. Frazier, I, 204-205; and the return of captured flags, I, 202-207; letter to Secretary Endicott, 207; "viper," "traitor," "unworthy to breathe the air of heaven," "skulker," "hater of Union soldiers," "oppressor of the widow and fatherless," I, 208; "sneaked like a whipped spaniel," I, 209; resolutions of Mitchell Post, G. A. R., I, 210-211; resolutions of Sam Rice Post, G. A. R., I, 211-214; letter from a veteran, 216; and the wards of the nation, the American Indians, I, 218-219; letter from Helen Hunt Jackson, I, 222-223; and the "cattle kings," I, 224-225; letter to General Sheridan, I, 228-229; letter to Hoke Smith, I, 237-238; Bismarck and Samoa, 1, 240-263; and foreign affairs, I, 240; undelivered message to Congress, I, 257-259; address before school in St. Paul, I, 267; and the tariff, I, 268-275, 289, 291, 294, 299, 301; message of December 6, 1887, I, 271-272; forged Albany *Times* letter, I, 275-278; letter to James Shanahan, I, 281-282; suggestions for platform, New York State Convention, 1887, I, 283; "the beast from Buffalo," I, 290; nominated for second term, I, 290; letter on New York gubernatorial nomination to William R. Grace, I, 292-293; letter to Bissell, I, 293; fisheries dispute, I, 294-296; Sackville-West incident, I, 296-297, 302-303; defeated for second term, I, 297; retires to New York, I, 302; resumes practice of law, 308; addresses Merchants Association, of Boston, I, 311; tribute of James Russell Lowell, I, 312; letter to John Temple Graves, 316-317; speech in Philadelphia on anniversary of the battle of New Orleans, I, 317-318; letter to E. Ellery Anderson on free coinage of silver, I, 319-320; address at Cooper Union, I, 322; first child born, I, 323; letter to Bissell, I, 323-324; address at Ann Arbor, 328-329; letter to Bissell, I, 330, 331; letter to Edward S. Bragg, I, 332, 333; letter to Justice Lamar, I, 334-336; letter to Bissell, I, 337-338; nominated third time, 341; letter to Bissell, I, 343-344; campaign of 1892, I, 343; notification of nomination at Madison Square Garden, I, 345-346; letter to Bissell, I, 347-348; letter to Bissell, I, 349; letter to Bissell, I, 350-351; dinner with Tammany men, I, 352-353; speech in Jersey City, I, 355-356; elected President, second time, I, 356; "greatest victory in history," I, 357; only President re-elected after defeat, II, 1; letter to L. Clarke Davis, II, 3; letter to Walter Q. Gresham, II, 4-5; second Cabinet, II, 1-6; and office-seekers, II, 6-8; takes second oath as President, II, 9; second inaugural address, II, 9-10; executive order, May 8, 1893, II, 15; and currency reform, II, 16; and Bland-

Allison Act, 16-18; financial situation, II, 16-25, 34-38, 75; letter from August Belmont, II, 21; declaration of April 2, 1893, II, 25; operation on mouth, II, 27-30; special message to Congress, August 8, 1893, II, 32-33; and Bryan, II, 33-37; letter to Ambassador Bayard, II, 39-41; and Hawaii, II, 45-73; and the four bond issues, II, 74-106; vetoes the Seignorage Bill, II, 81; annual message December 3, 1894, II, 84; letter to Ambassador Bayard, II, 89-92; annual message, December 21, 1895, II, 95; letter from J. P. Morgan, II, 99-101; letter to Senator Caffery, II, 102; letter from Don Dickinson, II, 113-114; letter from Senator Palmer, II, 114-115; letter to Hon. T. C. Catchings, II, 115-119; letter from Wayne Mac Veagh, II, 119-121; letter from Andrew Carnegie, II, 121-126; letter to Attorney-General Harmon, II, 128-130; Senator Hill and nominations to Supreme Court, 130-137; letter to Joseph H. Choate, II, 133; letter from William B. Hornblower, II, 135-136; letter to Senator Hill, 136-137; and the Pullman strike of 1894, II, 138-172; letter to Andrew Carnegie, II, 139-140; special message April 22, 1886, II, 140; letter from Governor Altgeld, II, 151-155; reply to Altgeld, II, 156; telegram from Altgeld, II, 158-162; dispatch to Altgeld, II, 163; proclamation of July 8, 1894, II, 164-165; second proclamation, II, 166; telegram from Debs and associates, II, 167-169; and Venezuelan affair, II, 173-202; letters to Olney, II, 180-181, 183; message to Congress, December 17, 1895, II, 188; letter from Bayard, II, 190-191; reply to Bayard, II, 192-196; letter to Chicago business men, II, 204-206; letter to Governor Stone, II, 206-207; letter from Don M. Dickinson, II, 208-210; letter to Democratic newspaper editors, II, 210-211; letters to Dickinson, II, 213-217, 221-223; letter to Colonel Lamont, II, 225-226; letter to Hoke Smith, II, 227-229; replies of Smith, 230-231; telegram from D. C. Griffin, II, 232; reply to Griffin, II, 232; letter to Colonel Lamont, II, 233-234; speech before the College of New Jersey, 234-235; letters to R. W. Gilder, II, 239-242; and the Cuban revolution,

II, 245-252, 271-276; last annual message, December 7, 1896, II, 248-249; letter to F. Coudert, II, 251; letter to A. B. Farquhar, II, 252; denunciations by extreme press, II, 253; life at Princeton, II, 256-270, 285-286; letter to Charles S. Fairchild, II, 262-263; speech before Reform Club, II, 263; receives degree at Princeton, II, 265; letter to Gilder, 265-266; letter to Olney, II, 266; letter to President Patton, 266-267; appointed Stafford Little Lecturer on Public Affairs, 11, 269; elected trustee Princeton University, II, 270; letter to W. R. Hearst, II, 272; Commencement address at Lawrenceville, II, 274-275; letter to Edward M. Shepard, II, 277; letter to Judson Harmon, II, 277-278; letter to Olney, II, 278-279; Olney's reply, II, 279-281; letter to Edward M. Shepard, II, 282-283; letter to Harmon, II, 287-290; letter to A. S. Abeel Co., II, 291-292; letter to Bissell, II, 292-294; letter to John S. Green, II, 295; letter to Don M. Dickinson, II, 296-297; false report of interview with, II, 298-299; letter from Theodore Roosevelt, II, 299-300; trepidation regarding Roosevelt's administration, II, 302-303; and the anthracite coal strike of 1902, II, 303-314; letter to Roosevelt, 305-306; views on labor and capital, 306-310; letter to Carnegie, II, 311-312; letters from Roosevelt, II, 313-314; letter to Joseph Garretson, II, 315; and third term, II, 315-322, 329-332; greeting at the Louisiana Purchase Exposition, April 30, 1903, II, 317-321; letter to Commodore Benedict, II, 323; birth of second son, II, 324; letter to John G. Hibben, II, 324; announcement to neighbors, II, 325-326; letter to St. Clair McKelway, II, 327; death of daughter Ruth, II, 327-329; letter from Colonel Lamont, II, 329-330; letters to Lamont, II, 333-334; letter to Hornblower, II, 335-336; letter to Olney, II, 336; letter from Alton B. Parker, II, 337; letter to Olney, II, 338; letter to James Smith, Jr., II, 338-339; Smith's reply, II, 339-340; telegram from A. B. Parker, II, 342; letter to Parker, II, 342-343; letter to Farquhar, II, 346-347; disappointment at Roosevelt's election, II, 346; letter to Gilder, II, 348-349; and the reorganization of the Equitable Life Assurance Association, II, 350-364; letter from Thomas F. Ryan, II, 351-353; reply to Ryan, II, 353-355; appointed trustee of the Equitable, II, 355; letter from Paul Morton, II, 358-359; reply to Morton, II, 359-360; head of Presidents' Association of Life Insurance Companies, II, 360; letter to Morton, II, 361-362; letter from Benedict, II, 365-368; letter from Mark Twain, II, 368-369; letter from Woodrow Wilson, II, 369-370; letter to Gilder, II, 370; letter to Carnegie, II, 371; letter to Wilton Merle Smith, II, 372; letter to William F. Vilas, II, 372-373; letter to George Allen Bennett, aged nine, II, 373-374; letter to Hornblower, II, 375-376; address before Union League Club, Chicago, II, 375-378; letter from Mrs. Cleveland, II, 378-379; tribute by the New York *Sun*, II, 379-380; his seventieth birthday, II, 378-381; letter to Gilder, 380-381; letter to E. Prentiss Bailey, II, 383-384; death, II, 385; memorial tower, II, 385

Cleveland, William, I, 3
Cleveland, William Neal, I, 4, 13, 47
Cleveland and Bissell, I, 24
"Cleveland and the Irish," I, 95
Clews, Henry, II, 22
Cochran, Bourke, I, 154-340
Colfax, Schuyler, I, 76
Columbian Exposition, II, 141
*Commercial Gazette*, I, 146, 272
Confederate flags, I, 202-207
Congo, the, I, 144-145
"Congress, Berlin," I, 260
Conkling, Roscoe, I, 96
*Constitution*, Atlanta, II, 253, 300
Constitutional Convention of 1787, **I**, 167, 170
"Contemptible politician," I, 208
Contract, obligation of, I, 52
Cooper-Hewitt, I, 98
Cooper Union, New York, Democratic mass meeting at, I, 322
Cornell, Alonzo B., I, 26, 34, 35, 36, **38**
Coudert, Frederick R., I, 292, 327; **II,** 131, 134, 136, 250-251
County Democracy, I, 60
*Courier-Journal*, I, 265
Crédit Mobilier, I, 73
Creeks, I, 220, 221, 237
"Crime of 1873," II, 37
Croker, Richard, I, 292, 326, 327, **348,** 352, 353

Cromwell, I, 37
Crook, General, I, 229, 230
Crow Creek, I, 221
"Crown of thorns and cross of gold," II, 224
Cuba, I, 242; II, 245-252, 271-275. *See* also Spanish-American War.
Currency bill, II, 284
Currency reform, II, 16
Curtis, George William, I, 76, 90, 123, 124, 147
Curtis, William Elroy, II, 80, 212, 285
Cushing, Caleb, II, 1
Cuyler, Theodore L., I, 147

*Daily Evening Telegram,* Philadelphia, I, 320
Daniel, Hon. John W., II, 223, 224
Davenport, Charles, I, 155
Davis, L. Clarke, I, 310; II, 3, 23, 42, 112, 217, 257
Dawes Commission, I, 236-238
Dawes, Henry L., I, 231, 232, 236
Debs, Eugene V., II, 144-145, 146, 149, 157, 158, 166, 169, 170, 171
*Democrat,* Wilmington, O., I, 195
Democratic Conventions, National, I, 68, 69, 70, 71, 77-84, 102, (1884) 283, (1888) 289, (1892) 326, 328, 330, 338-342, 352; II, (1896) 203, 217, 223, (1900) 286, (1904) 331, 338, 340-344
Democratic Society of Pennsylvania, I, 311
Dependent pension bill, I, 199, 200
Depew, Chauncey M., I, 23, 188, 292
Deutsch Bank, II, 97
Devoy, John, I, 95
Dewey, Admiral George, I, 242; II, 72
Dickens, Charles, I, 268
Dickinson, Don M., II, 113, 208, 212, 213, 268, 296-297, 301
Dingley Bill, II, 262
"Dishonor, a century of," I, 222
*Dispatch,* I, 113
Doge, George F., I, 93
Dole, President, II, 51, 67, 68
Dorsheimer, William, I, 20-21, 69
Downing Street, I, 240
Drum, Adjutant-General, I, 202, 203, 204, 205
DuBois, Senator, II, 220
Duskin, George M., I, 175, 183

*Eagle,* Brooklyn, I, 298
Eardwulf, Bishop, I, 166
Eaton, Commissioner, I, 154
Eaton letter, I, 157
Edmunds, Senator, I, 175, 176
Edwards, Jonathan, I, 2

Elections, (1800) I, 90; (1824) I, 90; (1876) I, 90, 97; (1892) II, 1; (1896) II, 236; (1900) II, 345

Elkins, Senator, II, 101

Emory, Frederic, II, 43

Endicott, William C., I, 103, 202, 203, 206, 303

England, I, 240-257, 262, 272, 302-303

Enrollment Act, I, 93

"Entangling alliances," I, 262

Environment, heredity and, I, 1-23

Equitable Life Assurance Association, reorganization of, II, 350

Erdmann, Dr. John F., II, 28

Evans, Admiral, II, 255, 257

Evarts, William M., I, 168, 243; II, 1, 177

*Evening Bulletin,* San Francisco, II, 67-68

*Evening News,* Baltimore, II, 237

*Evening Post,* New York, I, 150, 187, 272

Ewing, Thomas, II, 1

Executive, independence of, I, 166-188

*Express,* Buffalo, I, 37

Fairbanks, Charles W., II, 218, 219

Fairchild, Charles S., I, 327, 328

Fairchild, General, I, 68, 208, 209, 216

Farmers' Alliance, I, 314

Farnsworth, General, I, 84

Farquhar, A. B., II, 249, 252; II, 294

Faulkner, Senator, I, 291

First Congregational Church at Windham, Connecticut, I, 3

First National Bank of Buffalo, failure of, I, 51

Fish, Hamilton, II, 1, 177

Fisheries disputes, I, 294-296

Fisk, Pliny, II, 98

Five-cent-fare bill, I, 51, 321

Five Civilized Tribes, I, 220, 235, 236, 237

Flanagan murder case, I, 33

Flower, Roswell, P., I, 43, 44, 82, 98, 103, 351

Folger, Charles J., I, 38, 39

Folsom, Frances, I, 184-186

Folsom, Oscar, I, 184

Foraker, Governor, I, 206; II, 221

Forest Assize of 1184, I, 166

Foster, John W., II, 52

Four bond issues, II, 74

"Four lean months," II, 238-255

Francis, David R., II, 80

Francis, Mayor of St. Louis, I, 217

Franklin, Benjamin, II, 151

Frazier, John W., I, 204

Free Silver Democrats, II, 208, 217

Frelinghuysen, Secretary of State, II, 177

Fritze, Captain, I, 256

"From Greenland's Icy Mountains," I, 6

Fuller, Chief-Justice, I, 105

Garfield, James A., I, 117, 123, 171, 201, 305; II, 2

Garland, Augustus H., I, 105

Gassman, Mayor, I, 221

*Gazette,* Elmira, I, 188

General Managers' Association, II, 143, 149

George III, II, 151

German Emperor, I, 244-245, 253, 255

Germany, I, 240-262

Geronimo, I, 230

Gettysburg, I, 204

Gibson, Dr. Kasson C., II, 29

Gilder, Richard Watson, I, 54, 201, 321, 354, 357; II, 6, 8, 30, 42, 239-242, 252, 284

Gilman, Daniel C., II, 198

Gladstone, William E., I, 147; 197

Glaman, Charles, I, 193

Gold standard, I, 106, 107

Goodyear, Charles W., I, 91, 136, 137, 143, 149

Gorman, Senator, I, 98, 290, 291, 326, 337, 341; II, 113

*Gospel of Wealth,* II, 139

Gould, Jay, I, 38, 97

Grace, William R., I, 282, 289, 290, 292, 327

Grady, Thomas F., I, 56, 57, 58, 59, 60, 61, 62, 63, 77, 81, 129

Grand Army of the Republic, I, 199, 201, 203, 208, 209, 210, 211, 212, 213, 214, 215, 216, 265

"Grandiloquent swell, a." *See* Conkling, Roscoe

Grant, Ulysses S., I, 2, 122, 123, 171, 201

Granville, Lord, II, 175, 176

Graves, John Temple, I, 316

Gray, George, II, 5

Great Council of the Realm, Norman, I, 166

"Greatest victory in history," I, 357

Green, John S., II, 295

Greenebaum (American Consul at Samoa), I, 245, 246

Gresham, Otto, II, 219

Gresham, Walter Q., I, 292; II, 3-5, 59, 60, 61, 80, 147, 178, 179, 180, 218, 220

Grosscup, P. S., II, 150

"Grover and John Bull," II, 38
Guiteau, I, 38
Guthrie, Mr., II, 1

Half-Breeds, I, 59
Hamilton, Alexander, I, 111; II, 94
Hamilton College, I, 11
Hand, Clifford A., II, 131
Hanna, Mark, II, 220
Harmon, John, I, 188
Harmon, Judson, II, 128-130, 225, 267, 277, 287
Harrison, Benjamin, I, 2, 234, 235, 259, 262, 292, 298, 299, 346, 354; II, 12, 20
Harrison, William Henry, II, 1, 2
Harrity, William F., I, 356
Hart, Alphonso, I, 196
Harter, Congressman, I, 346
Harvey Fisk & Sons, II, 98
Hatch, Edward W., I, 35
Hatch, General, I, 221
"Hater of Union soldiers," I, 208
Hawaii, I, 240, 241; II, 45-73, 177, 182
Hay, John, I, 242
Hayes, Rutherford B., I, 90, 123, 171, 201
Hendricks, Thomas A., I, 80, 82, 83, 84, 89
Henry II, I, 166
Henry III, I, 166
Henry V, king of England, I, 2
Henry, Patrick, I, 2, 49
Herald, Chicago, II, 58
Herald, Newport, R. I., II, 61
Herald, New York, I, 59, 78, 306; II, 57, 92, 190, 284, 304
Herbert, Hilary A., II, 6
Herbert, Michael H., I, 302; II, 181
Heredity and environment, I, 1-23
Herrick, D. Cady, I, 70, 292, 293, 337
Heusner, Commodore, I, 252
Hill, David B., I, 45, 149, 155, 157-158, 279, 281, 282, 289, 290, 294, 298, 304-307, 310, 314, 315, 320, 321, 322, 324, 325, 326, 327, 328, 329, 336, 337, 340, 341, 342, 344, 348; II, 83, 126, 131, 132, 223, 224, 225
Hill-Murphy machine, I, 336
Hoadley, Governor, I, 82
Hoar, Senator, I, 74, 183
Hohenzollerns, I, 250, 262
Holy Writ, I, 77
Home Missionary Society, American, I, 10
Hornblower, William B., I, 300; II, 130-132, 135-136
House Bill No. 155, I, 197
How, James, I, 152
Hoyt, M. E., I, 15

Hudson, William C., I, 26, 68, 76, 77, 78, 86, 87, 88

"I am a Democrat," I, 330. See also Hill, David B.
Ifu, I, 253
"Inbred Descendants of Charlemagne," etc., I, 2 n;
Indian Emancipation Act, I, 231
Indian lands, opening of, I, 221-227
Indian, North American, I, 218-239
Indian Territory, I, 220, 223, 228, 235, 239
Ingalls, Senator, I, 288
Injunction against railway strikers, II, 146-150, 171-172
Inter-Ocean, Chicago, II, 13
Interstate Commerce bill, I, 265
Irish, John P., II, 290
"Iron Chancellor," I, 260. See also Bismarck
Irving Hall Democrats, I, 57

Jackson, Andrew, I, 78, 90, 121, 169, 170, 277, 325
Jackson, Helen Hunt, I, 222
Jacobs, John C., I, 62
James, D. Willis, I, 98
James, Joe, I, 186
Janeway, Dr. E. G., II, 28
Jefferson, Thomas, I, 2, 45, 90, 111, 168, 339, 340
Jenckes, T. A., I, 126
Johnson, Andrew, I, 180, 181; II, 1
Johnson, Reverdy, II, 1
Johnston, Gabriel, I, 167
Johnston, George D., II, 12
Jones, Senator, II, 113
Jordan, David Starr, I, 2
Journal, Atlanta, II, 227
Journal, Chicago, I, 272

Kalakaua, King, II, 49
Kamehameha III, II, 46
Kane, Captain, I, 259
Kasson, J. A., I, 260
Keegan, Vicar-General, I, 152
Keen, Dr. W. W., II, 27
Kelly, John, I, 43, 44, 45, 55, 56, 58, 59, 60, 61, 62, 63, 70, 77, 79, 82, 89, 95, 129, 130, 290, 321
Kempff, Commander, I, 255
Keppler, Joseph, I, 148
Kernan, John D., II, 170
Kidd, M. H., I, 236
Kiernan, John J., I, 62
Kimberley, Lord, II, 177, 179
Kimberley, Rear-Admiral, I, 254, 257, 259

King John, the wicked, I, 166
Kip, William F., I, 95
Koltes Post, G. A. R., 97-98

Lacedæmonians, I, 241
Lamar, Q. C., I, 104, 105, 338
Lamberton, Captain, II, 255
Lamont, Daniel, I, 55, 76, 84, 85, 86, 89, 90, 97, 110, 113, 114, 128, 129, 134, 140, 188, 216, 275; II, 5, 6, 181, 218, 225, 233, 253, 257, 267
Lanning, Cleveland, and Folsom, I, 19
Lawton, Henry W., I, 230
Leader, Pittsburgh, II, 268
Leary, R. P., I, 256
Lee, Charles E., I, 269
Lee, Gen. Fitzhugh, II, 271
Lee, Robert E., I, 2
Leopold of Belgium, King, I, 144
Liliuokalani, Queen, II, 49-50, 54-55, 61, 66
Lincoln, Abraham, I, 49, 73, 102, 111, 117, 118, 147, 211, 278; II, 1
Locke, Judge, I, 34
Lockwood, Daniel, I, 80
Lodge, Henry Cabot, II, 102
Lodi, bridge of, I, 33, 36
"Lost Cause," I, 206
Louis XIV, I, 117; II, 186
Lowell, James Russell, I, 311, 312; II, 43
Lyman, Charles, II, 12

Mack, Frank W., I, 69
Mackin, James, I, 62
Mac Veagh, Wayne, II, 119
"Made in Germany," I, 261
Madison Square Garden, I, 345
Malietoa, I, 244, 245, 246, 248, 251, 252, 253, 254, 255, 260, 261
Manhattan Railway Company, I, 52
"Manifest destiny," II, 45-73
Manning, Daniel, I, 40, 42, 43, 44, 45, 70, 71, 76, 78, 79, 83, 98, 103, 105; II, 16
Manning, John B., I, 42
Manton, Marble, I, 107
Marcy, William L., II, 1, 46
Marsden, Joseph, II, 52
Massachusetts Tariff Reform Association, I, 300
Mataafa, I, 254, 257, 258, 259, 261
Maynard, Isaac H., II, 131
McClellan, General, I, 73
McClure, A. K., II, 298
McDonald, Joseph E., I, 80, 82, 83, 84
McKelway, St. Clair, I, 102, 106, 298, 326-327
McKenon, Archibald S., I, 236

McKinley bill, II, 107, 109, 115
McKinley, William, I, 242, 273; II, 19, 71, 217, 220, 231, 234, 236, 251, 253, 261, 273, 276, 284, 296, 297, 300
McLaughlin, "Boss," I, 149
McPherson, Senator, I, 355
McVicar, John, I, 14
Meade, General, I, 73
Mexican War, I, 201
"Miantinoma," I, 226
Milburn, John G., I, 22; II, 88
Milchrist, Thomas E., II, 150
Miles, General, I, 230; II, 150, 151, 162
Miller, Warner, I, 298
Mills bill, I, 273, 274, 290
Mills, Roger Q., I, 273
Mitchell, John, II, 303, 304, 305, 313
Mitchell Post No. 45, G. A. R., I, 210-211
Mohawk Conference, I, 224, 227, 231
Monroe Doctrine, II, 75, 177, 178, 182, 186, 199, 200
Monroe, R. G., I, 327
Moore, John Bassett, I, 263; 183-186
Morgan, J. Pierpont, I, 2; II, 85-89, 96-101
Morgan, J. P., & Co., II, 88, 96
Morgan, J. S., & Co., II, 88
Morgan, Senator, II, 132
Morning Herald, Sydney, I, 249
Morning News, Savannah, II, 58
Morning Post, London, I, 273
Morrison, William R., I, 341
Morton, Julius Sterling, II, 6, 77
Morton, Levi P., II, 83
Murphy, Charles, I, 280, 289, 324, 325, 326, 327, 328, 336, 343, 349, 350, 352; II, 83
Murphy, Col. M. C., I, 58, 61
Mugwump campaign of 1884, I, 68-99
"Mugwumps," I, 71, 79, 88, 90, 92, 121, 126, 150, 163, 336, 350; II, 14
Mutual Life Insurance Company, II, 359

Napoleon, I, 33
Nation, the, I, 208, 272
National City Bank, II, 97
National Democratic party, II, 231-234
Neal, Ann, I, 3
Nelson, Henry C., I, 61
News, Galveston, I, 264
New York Institute for the Blind, I, 15
New York Life Insurance Company, II, 358
Noble, John W., I, 235
Nordhoff, Charles, II, 57, 58

*North American Review*, I, 88
*North Missourian*, I, 162

O'Brien, John W., I, 153
Oklahoma, I, 234
Olney, Richard B., II, 5, 59, 60, 72, 73, 89, 146, 163, 180, 182, 186, 188, 190, 198, 201, 242, 244, 246, 247, 261, 268, 278
"Oppressor of the widows and fatherless," I, 208
O'Reilly, Dr. R. M., II, 27
Ottendorfer, Oswald, I, 94

Pago-Pago, I, 242, 244, 262
Palmer, John, II, 233, 234
Palmer, Senator, I, 326, 337; II, 114-115
Parker, Alton B., I, 155
Parker, George F., I, 92, 106, 152
Parliament, British, I, 166, 182
Parsons, John E., II, 131
Pattison, Robert E., I, 341
Patton, President, II, 266, 267
Pauncefote, Sir Julian, II, 179, 186, 242
Pauper Pension bill, I, 200
Payne, Colony, I, 221
Payne, Henry B., I, 104
Pearson, Mr., I, 128-131
Peckham, Wheeler H., II, 132-133, 136, 137
Pendleton Act, I, 123
Pension Bureau, I, 104, 193, 201
Pensions, I, 189-201, 350
Pettigrew, Senator, II, 220
Phelps, E. J., I, 302, 303
Phelps, William Walter, I, 260
Philippine Islands, I, 242
Pickett's Division, I, 204
Pierce, Franklin, II, I, 46
Pilsach, Baron Senfft von, I, 261
Plasson, H., II, 250
Platt, Thomas C., II, 221
Polk, James K., II, 1
Populists, I, 354
*Post*, Washington, II, 163
Postal Rule No. 1, II, 12
Presidency, throwing away the, I, 264-301
Presidential election of 1876, I, 25
Presidents' Association of Life Insurance Companies, II, 360
Princeton Theological Seminary, I, 3
Proclamation of July 8, 1894, against Railway strikers, II, 164, 165
"Public office is a public trust," I, 88
"Public officials are the trustees of the people," I, 25

*Public Opinion*, I, 265
Pullman Palace Car Company, II, 143, 171

Quay, Senator, II, 128
Quincy, Josiah, I, 312

Randall, Mr., I, 82, 83, 84, 273, 291
*Random Recollections of an Old Political Reporter*, I, 68
Rebellion, war of, I, 211
"Rebel Yell," I, 212
*Record*, Chicago, II, 80, 285
Redmond, John, II, 197
Reed, Thomas B., I, 273, 274
Rees, W. L., I, 253
Reform Governor, the, I, 37-71
Reid, Whitelaw, I, 354
*Republican*, Springfield, I, 188
Republican conventions, National I, 74-76, 90-96, 292; II, 221
Revolution, American, I, 167
Revolution of 1688, I, 167
"Revolution of 1800," I, 169
Richardson, William A., I, 76
Robinson, Edmund Randolph, II, 131
Rockefeller, John D., I, 2
*Rocky Mountain News*, II, 38
Rogers, Bowen, and Rogers, I, 16, 18
Rome, Church of, I, 77, 95
Roosevelt, Theodore, I, 2, 53, 59, 65, 88, 111, 123, 181, 217, 242; II, 12, 13, 299, 300, 301-312
"Roosevelt luck," II, 301
Root, Elihu, I, 246; II, 131
Rothschild, N. M., & Sons, II, 88, 94
"Rum, Romanism, and Rebellion," I, 95
Russell, William E., I, 339, 341; II, 224

Sackville-West, Sir Lionel, I, 240, 296, 297, 302-303
Salisbury, Lord, I, 297, 303; II, 176, 183, 186, 187, 188, 200, 201, 202
Samoa, I, 240-263, 295; II, 45, 53, 177, 182
Sam Rice Post, G. A. R., I, 211
Sanborn, John D., I, 76
"Scarlet woman," I, 77
Schiff, Jacob H., II, 37
Schomburgk, Sir Robert, II, 173, 174
Schouler, James, I, 178
*Schrechlichkeit*, I, 256
Schurz, Carl, I, 76, 88, 90, 127, 128, 132, 155, 163, 179, 268; II, 1, 12, 24, 74, 80
*Scientific Monthly*, I, 2
Scott, William L., I, 98
Secession, Mississippi Ordnance of, I, 104
Seignorage bill, II, 79-82

Seminoles, I, 220, 234, 236, 239
Severance, Mr., II, 46
Sewall (American Consul at Samoa), I, 255
Seward, W. H., II, 1
Shanahan, James, I, 281
Sheehan, John C., I, 25, 231, 343, 348, 349, 350, 351, 352, 353; II, 83
Shepard, Edward M., I, 150, 152, 153
Shepard, Henry M., II, 147
Sheridan, General, I, 73, 223, 224, 228
Sherman, General, I, 73, 206
Sherman, John, I, 292; II, 1, 44, 243, 244
Sherman law, II, 20, 22, 23, 25, 28, 31, 35, 37, 42, 75, 76, 95, 107, 109, 171
Sigiraed, King, I, 166
Silver, free coinage of, I, 315, 316, 324, 329, 330, 332, 342, 343; II, 16-27
Sioux, I, 235
Sir John Franklin Expedition, I, 111
"Skulker," I, 208
Slocum, Gen. Henry W., I, 43, 44
Smalley, E. V., I, 290
Smith, Hoke, I, 237; II, 5, 227
Smith, Dr. Wilton Merle, I, 355; II, 8
"Snap convention," I, 326, 327, 328, 329, 330, 337, 342
"Snivil Service Reform Act," I, 154
Sound-money standard, I, 346, 354
Southwest Sentinel, I, 229
Spanish-American War, I, 242. See also Cuba
Spinney, George F., I, 278, 280
Spoils system, I, 170, 176; II, 15
Springer bill, II, 141
Stalwarts, I, 59
Standard, London, II, 243
Standard Oil, I, 104
Stanton, Secretary, I, 73
"Stars and Bars," I, 213
"Stars and Stripes," I, 213, 253
Steinberger, A. B., I, 242, 243
Sterling, George H., I, 149, 150, 151, 152, 153
Stetson, Francis Lynde, I, 86, 126, 337; II, 96
Stetson, William L., II, 204
Stevens, John S., II, 49, 55, 56, 57, 58, 59
Stevenson, Adlai, I, 341
Stevenson, Robert Louis, I, 259, 261
Stewart, John A., II, 97
Stewart, Senator, II, 105
Stickney, Albert, II, 131
Stillman, James, II, 97
Stone, Cuthbert, I, 192-193
Stone, William A., I, 159, 160, 161, 162, 163, 164

Straus, Isadore, II, 181
Strong, William L., II, 83
Sumner, Charles, I, 203
Sun, Baltimore, I, 113; II, 290
Sun, New York, I, 97, 164, 186, 265, 296, 307
Sunderland, Rev. Dr., I, 186
Supreme Court, U. S., I, 218, 226
Tamasese, I, 245, 253, 254, 255, 256, 257, 260
Tammany Hall, I, 43, 44, 45, 55, 56, 57, 58, 59, 63, 70, 77, 78, 79, 81, 82, 83, 88, 89, 129, 130, 155, 265, 278, 290, 321, 326, 330, 340, 344, 347, 348, 349, 351, 352, 354; II, 224
Tariff, I, 268-275, 290-291, 294, 299-301, 341, 342, 347, 356; II, 11, 19, 75
Taylor, Zachary, II, 1
"Tecumseh," I, 226
Teller, Senator, II, 220
Tenure of Office Act, I, 170, 171, 172, 176, 180
Thurber, Henry T., II, 77
Thurman, Allen G., I, 80, 82, 84, 266
Thurston, J. B., I, 248
Thurston, Lorin A., II, 52, 58
Tibbitts, F. G., I, 14
Tilden, Samuel J., I, 25, 43, 79, 81, 82, 97, 103, 105, 277; II, 2
Times, Albany, I, 275
Times, Chicago, II, 156
Times, Kansas City, II, 253
Times, London, I, 251; II, 243, 299
Times, New York, I, 150, 297; II, 57, 299, 315
Times, Philadelphia, I, 209; II, 297
Tonga Islands, I, 252
Torrance, C. C., I, 18
Tracy, Benjamin F., I, 337
"Traitor," I, 208
Tree, Lambert, II, 7
Tribune, Chicago, I, 140
Tribune, New York, I, 96, 97, 174, 273, 297; II, 58, 83, 243
Tuttle, General, I, 210
Tutuila, I, 242, 262
Twain, Mark, I, 229, 230; II, 13-14
Tweed Ring, I, 103
Tyler, President, II, 1
Typographical Union No. 6, I, 96

Union flags, I, 202, 207
Union Veterans' Legion, I, 215
Union White Lead Manufacturing Company, I, 152
United Mine Workers of America, II, 303
United States Trust Company, II, 84, 98

Unprecedented restoration, an, I, 324-357
"Unworthy to breathe the air of heaven," I, 208
Urban, George, I, 41

Van Buren, Martin, I, 78, 277
Vanderpoel, Major Isaac K., I, 19
Van Etten, Mary A., I, 194
Van Sinderen, Howard, II, 82
Venezuela, I, 240, 241, 257; II, 65, 96, 173-202, 243
Vermandois, Isabel de, I, 2
Vest, Senator, I, 175; II, 113, 224
Veto Mayor, the, I, 24-36
Vilas, William F., I, 102
"Viper," I, 209
Vorhees, Senator, I, 326, 337

Waite, Chief Justice, I, 110
Wales, Prince of, II, 197
Walker, Edwin, II, 146
Walker, Robert J., II, 1
Wallenstein, Mr., II, 4
Wall Street, I, 163; II, 34, 36, 96
Washburn, Elihu, II, 1
Washington, George, I, 2, 111, 168, 211, 218, 261, 277, 278, 328
Watterson, Henry, I, 106
Webster, Daniel, I, 346; II, 46
Weed. Thurlow, I, 315
"We love him for the enemies he has made," I, 82, 83, 332
West, Dean, II, 259, 267, 287
West, William H., I, 75, 76
Weyler, Valeriano, II, 247
Wheeler, Everett P., II, 83
White, Andrew, I, 53, 90; II, 198

White, Edward Douglas, II, 134
White, Horace, I, 200
White, Senator, II, 130, 223
"White-plumed knight," I, 75. See also Blaine, James G.
Whisky Ring, I, 73
Whitney, William C., I, 98, 103, 104, 216, 255, 289, 290, 297, 327, 336, 337, 341, 342, 343, 347, 348, 349, 350, 351, 352, 354; II, 4, 224
Wilder, William C., II, 52
Williams, Jesse Lynch, II, 259
Willis, Albert S., II, 60, 61, 62, 63, 66
Wilmot proviso, I, 347
Wilson bill, II, 108-114, 127, 128, 134
Wilson-Gorman tariff, II, 107-137
Wilson, James, I, 170
Wilson, William L., II, 109
Wilson, Woodrow, II, 43-44
Winnebagos, I, 221
Wintenagemot, Anglo-Saxon, I, 166
"With the advice and consent," I, 166
Woman's National Indian Association, I, 246
Wood, Dr. Charles, II, 270
Wood, Leonard, I, 230; II, 225
Woodworth, Alvah, I, 8
World, New York, I, 58, 59, 61, 84, 95, 150, 156, 216, 265; II, 89, 98-99, 101, 102, 104, 197
World's Fair. See Columbian Exposition
Worthington, Nicholas E., II, 170
Wright, Carroll D., II, 170

Yale College, I, 3
Yeomans, E. B., I, 151
York, Duke of, II, 197

THE END

Unprecedented restoration, and I., 322, 327

Unworthy to breathe the air of heaven, I., 208

Urban Crozier I., 41

Van Buren, Martin, I., 76, 277
Vanderpoel, Major Isaac K., I., 19
Van Ename, Mary A., I., 191
Van Sinderen, Howard, II., 82
Venezuela, I., 210, 212, 333; II., 66, 96, 132, 200, 343
Veramendi, Isabel de, I., 2
Vera, Samana, I., 173; II., 123, 224
Vera, Maxey the, I., 41, 50
Vesta, William F., I., 202
"Viper," I., 200
Vorhees, Senator, I., 322, 337

Waite, Chief Justice, I., 110
Wales, Prince of, II., 397
Walker, Edwin, II., 146
Walker, Robert J., II., 1
Waldauer, Mr., II., 4
Wall street, I., 101; II., 12, 36, 96
Washburn, Elihu, II., 1
Washington, George, I., 171, 105, 217, 110, 202, 277, 208, 339
Waterson, Henry, I., 208
Webster, Daniel, I., 262; II., 38
Weed, Thurlow, I., 315
"We love him for the enemies he has made," I., 82, 83, 317
Wen, Dean, II., 379, 380, 382
Wen, William, II., I., 51, 79
Weyler, Valeriano, II., 230
Wheeler, Everett P., II., 81
White, Andrew, I., 33, 90; II., 198

White, Edward Douglas, II., 134
White, Horace, I., 200
White, Reginald, II., 170, 223
White-plumed Knight, I., 79. See also Blaine, James
Whitney-Ring, I., 83
Whitney, William C., I., 98, 101, 103, 210, 225, 226, 200, 202, 322, 330, 337, 341, 332, 343, II., 329, 350, 351, 352, 356; II., 44
Wilder, William C., II., 41
Williams, Jesse L. and II., 239
Willis, Albert S., II., 60, 61, 62, 63, 64
"Illinois provision," I., 317
Wilson bill, I., 262; I., 137, 162, 334
Wilson seaman (not), II., 163, 337
Wilson, James I., 170
Wilson, William L., II., 169
Windsor, Woodrow, II., 88-91
Windebago, I., 322
International, Anglo-Saxon, I., 286
"With that love and contract," I., 106
Women's National Indian Association, I., 231
Wood, Dr. Charles, II., 370
Wood, Leonard, I., 290; II., 225
Wooldridge, Aleph, I., 8
World, New York, I., 58, 60, 82, 93, 180, 182, 210, 292; II., 89, 95, 96, 101, 102, 337
World's Fair, I. See Columbian Exposition
Worthington, Nicholas E., II., 170
Wright, Carroll D., II., 170

X of a Culture, I.
Yeomans, I., II., 191
York, Duke of, II., 197

# DATE DUE

| | | | |
|---|---|---|---|
| | | | |
| | | | |
| | | | |
| | | | |
| | | | |
| | | | |
| | | | |
| | | | |
| | | | |
| | | | |
| | | | |
| | | | |
| | | | |
| | | | |
| | | | |
| | | | |
| | | | |